FINANCIAL STABILITY IN A CHANGING ENVIRONMENT

Financial Stability in a Changing Environment

Edited by

Kuniho Sawamoto
Director of the Institute for Monetary and Economic Studies
Bank of Japan

Zenta Nakajima
Deputy Director of the Institute for Monetary and Economic Studies
Bank of Japan

and

Hiroo Taguchi
General Manager
Matsuyama branch of the Bank of Japan

M

St. Martin's Press

First published in Great Britain 1995 by
MACMILLAN PRESS LTD
Houndmills, Basingstoke, Hampshire RG21 2XS
and London
Companies and representatives
throughout the world

A catalogue record for this book is available from the British Library.

ISBN 0–333–60641–8

10 9 8 7 6 5 4 3 2 1
04 03 02 01 00 99 98 97 96 95

Printed and bound in Great Britain by
Antony Rowe Ltd
Chippenham, Wiltshire

First published in the United States of America 1995 by
Scholarly and Reference Division,
ST. MARTIN'S PRESS, INC.,
175 Fifth Avenue,
New York, N.Y. 10010

ISBN 0–312–12474–0

Library of Congress Cataloging-in-Publication Data
Financial stability in a changing environment / edited by Kuniho Sawamoto, Zenta Nakajima, and Hiroo Taguchi.
p. cm.
Includes index.
ISBN 0–312–12474–0
1. Monetary policy—Congresses. 2. Foreign exchange administration—Congresses. 3. International finance—Congresses.
I. Sawamoto, Kuniho. II. Nakajima, Zenta. III. Taguchi, Hiroo.
HG230.3.F556 1995
332.4'6—dc20

94–31338
CIP

Contents

Editors' Preface

This book is a record of the proceedings of the Sixth International Conference organized and sponsored by the Institute for Monetary and Economic Studies of the Bank of Japan and held in Tokyo on 28–29 October 1993. The conference was devoted to 'Financial Stability in a Changing Environment'. Many countries, including those of the conference participants, have been experiencing significant changes in banking that have had a profound impact on financial stability. The organizers considered it imperative to invite prominent policy-makers and economists from central banks in Asia, Oceania, North America, and Europe, as well as from international organizations and academic institutions to discuss this important topic.

The conference consisted of five sessions, including the opening and concluding ones. The opening session commenced with opening remarks by Governor Yasushi Mieno of the Bank of Japan and was followed by two keynote speeches by Allan H. Meltzer and Stanley Fischer, both Honorary Advisers of the Institute.

The first session, entitled 'Recent Changes in the Financial System – Background and Consequences', reviewed recent changes in the financial system worldwide – with particular emphasis on financial innovation, deregulation and internationalization – and their implications for financial stability. Four papers presented by Zenta Nakajima and Hiroo Taguchi, William Poole, Jeffrey A. Frankel, and Naoyuki Yoshino, aimed at comparing across regions the process of the changes in the financial system and extracting the common background and consequences.

The second session was devoted to 'Prudential Policy and Financial Stability', where the following two main points were addressed: (i) the rationale for, and (ii) an optimal design of, prudential policy. Two papers, prepared by Mark J. Flannery and George J. Benston, argued for two different prudential policy frameworks.

The third session, 'Role of Central Banks in Maintaining Financial Stability', primarily focused on the relationship between the two ultimate goals of central banks – price stability and financial stability. The paper by Bennett T. McCallum discussed central banks' role as lender of last resort and its implication for stabilization policy, while Charles A. E. Goodhart prepared a paper discussing the importance of asset prices as an indicator for monetary policy.

In the concluding session, an overview of the discussions, which appears in this volume as a conference summary, was presented orally by Edward J. Kane.

In planning and organizing the conference, We received invaluable advice from many individuals, particularly Allan H. Meltzer and Stanley Fischer. We would also like to extend our appreciation to all conference participants, who either prepared such high quality papers, acted as preassigned discussants, or actively participated in general discussions. We are also greatly indebted to the staff of the Institute, in particular Wataru Takahashi, Tetsufumi Yamakawa and Makoto Ohsawa, for making the conference so successful.

It is our hope that publication of this book will help the understanding of the complex problems various countries are facing and encourage further research to seek solutions.

KUNIHO SAWAMOTO
ZENTA NAKAJIMA
HIROO TAGUCHI

Notes on the Contributors

George J. Benston is Harland Professor of Finance, Accounting and Economics, at the Business School and Department of Economics at Emory University. His area of research is in financial economic accounting.

Stanley Fischer is Professor of Economics at the Massachusetts Institute of Technology, and Honorary Adviser, Institute for Monetary and Economic Studies, Bank of Japan. His main areas of research are in macro-economic policy and inflation, develop.

Mark J. Flannery is Professor of Department of Finance at the Graduate School of Business Administration, University of Florida. His main areas of research are in corporate finance and information economic.

Jeffrey A. Frankel is Professor of Department of Economics at University of California, Berkeley. His main areas of research are in international financial market, trade blocs, Pacific Rim, yen.

Edward Frydl is Vice President and Assistant Director of Research, Research Administration Division, Federal Reserve Bank of New York.

Marvin Goodfriend is Senior Vice President and Director of Research, Research Department, Federal Reserve Bank of Richmond.

C. A. E. Goodhart is Professor at London School of Economics and Political Science. His main areas of research are in monetary economics and central banking.

Akiyoshi Horiuchi is Professor, University of Tokyo.

Jerry L. Jordan is President and Chief Executive Officer, Federal Reserve Bank of Cleveland.

Edward J. Kane is James F. Cleary Professor in Finance at Boston College.

Mervyn King is Chief Economist and Executive Director, Bank of England.

Göran Lind is Senior Manager of Supervisory and Structural Issues, Sveriges Riksbank.

Bennett T. McCallum is Professor at Graduate School of Industrial Administration, Carnegie-Mellon University. His main areas of research are in macro and monetary economics.

Allan H. Meltzer is University Professor of Political Economy and Public Policy at Carnegie-Mellon University and Visiting Scholar at the American Enterprise Institute and Honorary Adviser, Institute for Monetary and Economic Studies, Bank of Japan. His areas of research are in monetary theory and the growth of government.

Thomas C. Melzer is President, Federal Reserve Bank of St Louis.

Yasushi Mieno is Governor, Bank of Japan.

Zenta Nakajima is Deputy Director, Institute for Monetary and Economic Studies, Bank of Japan.

Robert T. Parry is President and Chief Executive Officer, Federal Reserve Bank of San Francisco.

Franco Passacantando is Director, Monetary and Financial Sector, Research Department, Banca d'Italia.

Jean-Pierre Patat is Deputy General Manager, Research Department, Banque de France.

William Poole is Professor of Department of Economics at Brown University. His main areas of research are in monetary theory and policy and macroeconomics.

Kuniho Sawamoto is Director of the Institute for Monetary and Economic Studies, Bank of Japan.

Richard F. Syron is President and Chief Executive Officer, Federal Reserve Bank of Boston.

Hiroo Taguchi is General Manager of the Matsuyama branch of the Bank of Japan.

Graeme J. Thompson is Deputy Governer, Reserve Bank of Australia.

William Witherell is Director, Financial, Fiscal and Enterprise Affairs, Organization for Economic Cooperation and Development.

Naoyuki Yoshino is Professor of Department of Economics at Keio University. His main areas of research are in monetary theory and policy and macroeconomics.

Opening Remarks

Yasushi Mieno
Governor, Bank of Japan

I would like to welcome you to the Sixth International Conference organized by the Institute for Monetary and Economic Studies. It is a great honor for the Institute, and also for the Bank of Japan, that so many distinguished experts from fellow central banks, international organizations, and academic institutions have gathered here to participate in this meeting.

The organizers of the conference have chosen as its theme 'Financial Stability in a Changing Environment'. I am sure that there is no need to explain to you why they have done so. The very essence of a central bank's mission lies in maintaining price stability and securing the soundness of the financial system. In my almost fifty-year long career with the Bank of Japan, never here I found this dual task as challenging as it is now.

In Japan, both the real sector and the financial system are faced with various problems which are the result of the excessive economic boom of the late 1980s, often termed the 'bubble economy', and the subsequent sharp decline of asset prices. Similar volatile movements in asset prices accompanied by some financial system friction have been observed in many other parts of the world as well, although the magnitude and kind of friction have varied from country to country.

The problems we are faced with are not new; there is no lack of episodes in monetary history where financial stability was at stake. It is also true, however, that the recent problems are not a mere repetition of previous similar episodes. The advance of telecommunications and data-processing technology has dramatically increased the speed at which problems in one part of the financial system can spread to other parts and even beyond to different economies. Moreover, bank behavior during the last decade is certainly not unrelated to dramatic changes in the financial environment, such as the tide of financial innovation and deregulation, as well as the increased international linkage of financial markets.

It is obvious that we cannot, and should not try to, stem this tide of financial innovation, deregulation, and expanded international capital flows. Instead, our task is to design a solid framework for securing financial stability in the new environment. While the nature of prudential problems requires pragmatism and flexibility in handling individual cases, we need to establish a set of policy principles to cope with them. In this context, I wish to stress a few tasks which I consider essential for achieving financial stability.

First, economic performance in the 1980s once again taught us the plain, sobering fact that an inflationary environment is a threat to financial stability and must therefore be contained. An important issues that has re-emerged for policymakers is how to deal with *asset price inflation*. While some further theoretical breakthrough regarding the mechanism of asset price fluctuation is greatly desired, we at the Bank of Japan are firmly determined not to allow its resurgence.

Second, significant progress has been made in strengthening the capital position of banks in many countries. Japanese banks also are largely liberated from capital constraints, even under today's depressed stock prices. As we move toward further improvement, which is clearly desirable, I would stress the importance of establishing a financial infrastructure which will enable market participants to evaluate and properly assess banks' capital position and other balance sheet items. This will naturally have to cover a wide range of complex topics including tax and accounting systems.

Third, supervision must remain an important safeguard for stability as, in my view, capital alone cannot be a panacea. The challenge to supervisors is ever growing amid today's immensely complex market forces. Being closely in touch with banks both in the payments system and in the money market, central banks can make significant contributions in enhancing financial integrity through stronger but flexible supervision.

Fourth, the ultimate cornerstone for a sound financial system rests with the profit generating strength of financial institutions. Commercial banks' profit performance varies sharply across countries. However, given the underlying trend of the weakening franchise value of banks, they should be given more room to diversify activities while minimizing the risks, in a manner that best suits each country's reality.

Finally, I wish to underline the importance of providing a safe and efficient payments system as a vital part of the financial infrastructure.

These tasks are all easier said than done, and efforts to achieve them may not always enjoy general support. There may arise circumstances which will make it difficult, but also imperative, that the central bank adhere to its principles. For central banks to overcome these difficult situations, advice from, and close co-operation with fellow central bankers is essential. To be able to cope with all kinds of problems and obtain public support for our policy, we need the help of economic theory.

Admittedly, financial systems differ considerably among countries with regard to regulatory and market structure, reflecting differences in history, political system, and preferences of the people; there are also significant differences as to how and to what extent central banks are involved in prudential policy and operation. Thus, no one would be so naive as to believe that lessons obtained in one country can be directly applied elsewhere.

Nevertheless, the fact that many countries have been experiencing similar problems suggests that we should be able to learn from each other's success or failure. I sincerely hope that this conference will contribute toward that end.

Part I
Keynote Speeches

1 Regulatory Arrangements, Financial Stability and Regulatory Reform

Allan H. Meltzer*

What can be learned from the experience of the past decade or two about financial regulation, supervision and deposit insurance or a financial safety net? Is there a better way to provide safety and soundness in the future than in the recent past? Does financial regulatory policy conflict with monetary policy?

Commercial banks, building societies, investment banks, and insurance companies in many countries have been under stress. The precise problems, patterns and outcomes differ across countries, but in several countries many financial firms failed, merged, or restructured. Many received an infusion of government capital. Some examples are the thrift bailout in the United States, the Japanese pension funds' purchases of common stock, and the Swedish government's investment in bank equity to prevent insolvency. Others could be added.

The form and extent of regulation and supervision differ across countries as do the lending and investment powers of banks and financial institutions. Hence any lessons to be drawn are general not specific. One general lesson stands out: in many countries regulation and supervision did not prevent sizeable losses by the banks and the public. Although quantitative losses differed from country to country, Nakajima and Taguchi (1993) report that the effects on banks of the decline of real estate prices was qualitatively similar in the US, Japan, United Kingdom, Norway, Sweden and Australia. Other countries could be added. The experience in the US of more heavily regulated sectors, such as savings and loans or banks, was worse than in less regulated financial institutions such as insurance companies.

* I thank my colleague Bennett McCallum for several useful discussions and George Benston for comments on an earlier draft.

Money market mutual funds (or other open-end mutual funds), all of which are exempt from deposit insurance and not subject to banking regulation and supervision, neither failed nor were forced to merge. Most of these funds mark assets to market or severely limit differences between book and market values.

One of the main lessons to be drawn from recent experience is that banking regulation and supervision were neither necessary nor sufficient to prevent failures and, in many cases, to avoid relatively large social costs. Many of these costs resulted from the waste of resources in projects that failed. Public policies added to the problem by requiring or permitting taxpayers to share in the losses. Although fraud and chicanery were present also, they were not the leading cause of failure in most countries.

The second main lesson is that a financial crisis was avoided. Few depositors in failed or weak banks ran to gold or currency as they had in the US in the 1930s. Open market gold prices fell during the period of stress. Mainly, depositors moved from weaker to stronger banks, so there was no forced contraction of the system. Particularly in the United States, the financial system proved more durable than it had in the early 1930s or on several earlier occasions. In Anna Schwartz's (1987) characterization, this was a pseudo-financial crisis; there was no systemic failure of the payments system. There were, however, substantial costs, so it is useful to consider alternative arrangements that may lower the costs.

The third main lesson concerns the role and responsibility of regulators. Regulatory and supervisory arrangements have changed in several ways. Following the 1988 Basle agreement uniform risk-adjusted capital standards became the norm for banks in major countries. In the United States, the Federal Deposit Insurance Corporation Improvement Act (FDICIA) of 1991 placed greater weight on bank capital and less weight on government deposit insurance to safeguard bank depositors from loss of nominal deposits and real wealth. The Reserve Bank of New Zealand has proposed greater reliance on markets and less direct supervision and regulation. Nakajima and Taguchi (1993) discuss this issue as a problem of dealing with moral hazard. Others have proposed institutional changes to reduce the costs of regulations and moral hazard.

The chapter discusses each of these issues. Although most of my examples are drawn from US experience, many of the problems are general and, I believe, some general conclusions can be drawn.

I REGULATION AND SUPERVISION

In the modern theory of finance, risk arises from unforseen events. Efficient firms and markets eliminate systematic risk. The risk that remains is non-systematic – the result of unforseen and uninsurable events.

The problems that most concern financial supervisors and regulators are not mainly systematic risks arising in markets where information is used efficiently and risks are correctly priced. Banks and other financial institutions acquire assets that trade infrequently or not at all. The pricing of bank loans involves credit evaluation, including subjective estimates of future cash flow, risk, the quality of management and other factors specific to a particular loan.

Much bank supervision and regulation attempts to limit bank risk by constraining bankers' choices or substituting regulators decisions for those of bankers. Since the interest of the two groups differ, perceptions of risk differ at times.[1] These differences aside, there are four distinct problems in using bank regulation and supervision to control risk or protect the payments system or depositors.

First is uncertainty in the Keynes–Knight sense. An unanticipated event shifts the distribution of actual or anticipated returns. If the change is relatively large, losses, bankruptcy, or illiquidity at financial institutions become a problem.

The oil shock of 1973–74 is an event of this kind. Prices of existing capital assets declined, and the risk of bankruptcy and default rose. There were losses but no financial crisis. Bagehot (1873) and Schwartz (1987) give examples of earlier events that caused panics – large, sudden changes in anticipations of returns and risks. More recent events are the 1982 default by the Mexican government followed by other governments, the October 1987 decline in stock prices on markets in twenty countries (or more), and the decline in real estate prices in New York, London, Tokyo, Sydney, and other cities at the end of the 1980s.

In Bagehot's or Schwartz's account of earlier periods, examination and supervision play no role. This is not surprising, if the events triggering financial problems are not forecastable events. The distinguishing difference they find between problems at an individual bank and systemic problems – between real and pseudo financial crises – resulted from the action or inaction of the central bank as lender of last resort. Schwartz's account shows that, once the triggering event occurred, depositors acted on knowledge or presumptions about the vulnerability of particular banks conditional on the triggering event. Nevertheless, absent the unanticipated triggering event, there was no reason for a run and no information that a supervisor or regulator could be expected to find.[2]

Benston (1973) examined cases of fraud. He found that examiners rarely detect fraud or misuse of assets in a timely way. Often, differences in asset valuations by examiners or supervisors and bankers reflect differences in evaluation. Fraud is rare, and rarer still are cases of fraud found by financial regulators or banking supervisors before the bank's capital is impaired.

The second class of problems arises as a consequence of regulations or laws that distort incentives or opportunities. Fractional reserve banking increases opportunity for bank runs. Deposit insurance or a public safety net creates conditions under which moral hazard becomes a problem particularly when bank capital is low. The safety net may be an implicit rather than explicit guarantee, but if it is generally believed that governments guarantee deposits and at times even equity against loss, financial institutions have an incentive to make high risk loans when the value of equity falls below some minimum. Policies that encourage the belief that some banks or financial institutions are too big to fail have similar effect.

Peltzman (1970) investigated the response of bank capital to regulations affecting capital adequacy. He found no evidence that the regulations had any effect. The principal policy effect on capital came from the availability of deposit insurance. Peltzman found that deposit insurance substituted for private capital. The availability of deposit insurance and the increased real value of insurance coverage in recent years increased moral hazard.

One hundred percent reserve requirements held in Treasury bills or equivalent would eliminate bank runs. Marked to market accounting, where it is feasible, could provide timely information to depositors and the public about risks in particular banks or financial institutions. Marked to market accounting provides information about portfolio losses. It has the defect that many bank assets cannot be priced accurately.

The experience of money market funds provides a useful benchmark. None of these funds failed during the period of recent weakness. The funds are subject to less direct regulation than banks and thrift institutions. They do not have deposit insurance. Instead, most restrict their portfolios to short-term assets and try to manage their assets so that the current market value of the asset portfolio remains consistent with a fixed par value.

The third type of problem arises when there are known risks but regulators do not act. The costs to taxpayers of US thrift industry failures were increased by delays in closing institutions with negative net worth. Some of these delays were the result of political interference. But a supervisory process that is open to substantial interference and forbearance is a faulty process.

The thrift failures in the US were anticipated, not unanticipated. Two economists at the supervisory agency, James Barth and Dan Brumbaugh, circulated estimates of the number and net liabilities of insolvent thrift institutions for several years before many of the insolvent institutions closed. Regulators responded by reducing capital requirements. They also lowered accounting standards by introducing regulatory accounting principles (RAP) in place of generally accepted accounting principles (GAAP). GAAP accounting would have required recognition of failures earlier. The shift to RAP and the lowering of capital requirements can be explained as an attempt to hide or obscure the growing problem rather than insist upon closures and appropriations sufficient to cover losses.

US regulators in the 1980s were unwilling also to require commercial banks to recognize losses on loans to developing countries. Regulators encouraged banks to book additional loans so that interest payments could be recorded as paid. This continued subterfuge added to the developing country debt and delayed resolution of the debt problem; most of the banks preferred to postpone recognition of losses on their balance sheets. Many succeeded in doing so for most of the 1980s.[3]

Russell (1993) studied failures of New England banks in the 1980s. The failures cost the bank insurance fund more than $6 billion. Most of the failures involved banks that had a relatively large proportion of assets in commercial real estate. When real estate prices fell, many of the loans became non-performing. Bank managements typically stopped making new commercial real estate loans as problems emerged, but they did not sell off old loans. Regulators did not foresee the problem. They allowed the banks to keep their real estate portfolios, and they acted too late to prevent the failures.

Horvitz (1992) finds very different responses by Texas banks and savings and loans, particularly the latter, to developing problems. Again, the problems were not suddenly thrust on the financial institutions. Some banks and thrifts increased lending on risky assets.

Many were unit banks with heavy concentration of loans in their region. Regulators were slow to respond, in part because the Federal Savings and Loan Insurance Corporation did not have the resources to pay out deposits if they closed an association. Political intervention also played a role.

Regulators and supervisors in several countries were slow to recognize and respond to the, at times, illegal practices at the Bank of Credit and Commerce International (BCCI). Fraud and mismanagement continued and losses to depositors increased.

Regulation and supervision were inadequate in these and other cases. Regulatory inaction or delay may reflect pressures from within government. Whatever the motivation, it seems clear that reducing or avoiding political pressure for forbearance must be part of the redesign of regulatory and supervisory arrangements.

The fourth type of problem is inappropriate or incorrect regulation. One recent example was the legal requirement that US savings and loans divest so-called junk bonds by a fixed date. Forced sales lowered the price and increased the losses of thrift institutions, insurance companies and other bond holders. Once the forced sales were completed, prices of junk bonds rose.

The law increased losses to owners of thrifts, insurance companies, and to the deposit insurance fund and taxpayers. The proximate reasons for the law appear to be that the press, including much of the quality press, were critical of the junk bond market. They tied thrift industry failures to defaults on junk bonds, although these would have had a relatively small role if forced sales had been avoided.

The Basle agreement set risk-based capital standards. The hypothesis is that risk of failure can be reduced by requiring capital to increase as the share of risky assets in the portfolio rises. Peltzman's (1970) findings raise a cautionary note about the effectiveness of this type of regulation. Also, it has proved difficult in practice to set risk based capital standards to take account of both interest rate risk and credit risk and to keep up with significant innovations in financial practice.

Other examples of unforseen effects of regulation include the interest rate ceilings on thrift and bank deposits and the design of the deposit insurance system. These regulations encouraged innovation to avoid the regulations and delayed reform of the thrift industry (Kane, 1989). Interest rate regulations were destructive of bank capital during the period of rising average inflation. Ceilings on interest rates, and prohibition of interest payments on demand deposits, prevented price competition. Financial institutions built branches and engaged in other costly forms of competition. Rules that prohibited branching discouraged portfolio diversification thereby increasing risk and bank failure rates.

Some regulations may serve a social purpose when they are introduced. The lesson, repeated many times, is that once introduced they are slow to change. Those who benefit opposed change; inertia sustains other regulations. Regulators and legislators often delay changes until the social cost is high. Prohibition of interstate banking and Glass-Steagall in the United States, or rule 65 in Japan, are well-known examples of regulations that have lost any rational basis they may have had.

The aim of this section is not to suggest that all financial regulation is misguided or that banking and financial firms should be unregulated. Evidence that auditors are slow to detect fraud and failure does not mean that audits are useless. Anticipation of audits probably deters some wrongdoing or excessive risk taking. However, an improved system of regulation and supervision cannot be constructed without recognizing that regulators and supervisors in many countries and many time periods have failed to prevent costly financial problems.[4] Some of the regulatory failures arose because regulators could not anticipate structural changes and, like everyone else, remained uncertain after the event about whether the changes were permanent or transitory. In such cases, bankers and markets can misprice (with hindsight) risky assets. Some of the regulatory mistakes are based on inappropriate rules, laws and regulations. And some result from political pressures that are unavoidable when regulators and supervisors have discretionary judgment.

The main economic rationale for financial regulation and supervision is to prevent failure of the payments system. Some would broaden the statement of purpose to include the entire financial system. The emphasis in either case is on the system, not individual firms or institutions. The reason for this emphasis is that, in principle, well designed regulation can reduce the risks that society must bear.

Two issues arise. First is the relation between safeguarding the payments system and monetary control to achieve general macroeconomic goals, such as maintaining the internal or external value of money. The issue here is whether society must grant authority to a central bank that, once granted, can be used to inflate or deflate money values. Second is the type of regulatory and supervisory framework that minimizes the risks from deposit insurance or some other explicit or implicit guarantee of the nominal value of deposits. The risks and costs here include political intervention to prevent closure, rules that restrict financial innovation and risk taking, and the shift of losses to taxpayers. A promising approach in recent literature substitutes market discipline for regulation and supervision while retaining some regulatory oversight. I discuss these issues in turn.

II BANK RUNS AND SYSTEM FAILURES

Recent experience, and experience in the 1930s, differs in important respects from the late nineteenth-century experiences described by Bagehot (1873) and Schwartz (1987). After 1866, English financial stress did not result in a collapse of the payments system. The Bank of England acted promptly as lender of last resort.

In the 1980s, although there were substantial financial problems, bank failures and liquidations, the payment system did not fail anywhere. There were no runs on banking systems, although there were runs on currencies that, in part, may have reflected concerns about bank safety. But public funds were used to save individual banks. Banking regulators or legislatures in many countries prevented individual failures at substantial cost or risk to taxpayers.

More than a century ago Walter Bagehot proposed a rule that avoids crises affecting the payments system (Bagehot, 1873). I have summarized Bagehot's rule elsewhere. Meltzer (1986, pp. 82–3).

> 'First. That these loans should only be made at a very high rate of interest. This . . . will prevent the greatest number of applications by persons who do not require it [assistance.] The rate should be raised early in the panic, so that the fine may be paid early; that no one may borrow out of idle precaution without paying well for it. . . .
>
> 'Secondly. That at this rate these advances should be made on all good banking securities, and as largely as the public asks for them. The reason is plain. The object is to stay alarm, and nothing therefore should be done to cause alarm. But the way to cause alarm is *to refuse some one who has good security to offer*. . . . If it is known that the Bank of England is freely advancing on what in ordinary times is reckoned a good security – on what is then commonly pledged and easily convertible – the alarm of the solvent

merchants and bankers will be stayed. But if securities, really good and usually convertible are refused by the Bank, the alarm will not abate, the other loans made will fail in obtaining their end and the panic will become worse and worse. . . . The only safe plan for the Bank is the brave plan, to lend in a panic on every kind of current security, of every sort on which money is ordinarily and usually lent.'

Bagehot (1962, p. 97 emphasis added)

I summarized Bagehot's rule in four points.

(1) The central bank is the only lender of last resort in the monetary system.
(2) To prevent illiquid banks from closing, the central bank should lend on any collateral that is marketable in the ordinary course of business. It should not restrict lending to paper eligible for discount at the central bank in normal periods.
(3) Central bank loans, or advances, should be made on demand at a rate of interest above the market rate. This discourages borrowing by those who can obtain accommodation in the market.
(4) The above three principles of central bank behavior should be stated in advance and followed in a crisis.

Bagehot placed great stress on what we would now call credible commitment to a rule for crisis management. His book, *Lombard Street*, does not criticize the Bank of England for failing to lend in a crisis. The principal criticism, repeated several times, is that the Bank hesitated before acting. Hesitation allowed distress and panic to spread.

Bagehot's rule would leave no scope for central bank discounting in the ordinary course of business. The quantity of base money would be determined by open market operations. Demand for discounts at a penalty rate would signal that credit markets were not operating properly – that there was a market failure and an actual or incipient crisis. The central bank would meet the crisis by providing reserves on demand at a penalty rate through the discount window. When the crisis passed, discounts would be repaid and growth of base money would again be controlled entirely by open market operations. If the central bank followed a monetary rule, Bagehot's rule for discounting would be part of the monetary rule.

Neither Bagehot nor his contemporaries saw any conflict between the role of a central bank as lender of last resort and its role as supplier of base money under a rule for monetary policy. The gold standard was the operating rule in England at the time and, I suspect, it never occurred to Bagehot or to the directors of the Bank of England that the gold standard was inconsistent with the rule for crisis management, although they knew that it would be necessary on some occasions to suspend convertibility temporarily. The reason is that currency issue was subject to a 100 percent gold reserve under the 1844 Act, so the Bank of England could not always satisfy the demand for Bank of England notes during a crisis unless the government suspended convertibility. With that proviso, the rule and the gold standard were compatible.

The issue of compatibility was raised later by critics of rules for monetary policy. The critics pointed out that if the central bank followed a monetary rule instead of responding to a crisis, the payments system would be at risk. To safeguard the financial system, the rule would have to be suspended. This claim is false.

Bagehot's rule is consistent with rules for price stability such as those proposed by Friedman (1959), McCallum (1988) and Meltzer (1987). During a crisis, growth of the monetary base would respond to the demand for base money at the discount window. The supply of base money would increase relative to the normal operation of the rule. There would be no need for discretionary judgment by the central bank. Market responses would replace discretion. The penalty rate assures that discounting would be limited to times of market failure. When the increased demand for base money ended, growth of the base would again be given by the rule for price stability.

Goodfriend and King (1988) suggest that the discount window be permanently closed. In their scheme, base money would be supplied only through open market operations. Their proposal has the advantage of eliminating the subsidies to discounting and the complex administrative arrangements introduced in many countries to limit discounting.

In commenting on their paper (Meltzer, 1988), I pointed out that, if the discount window operated according to Bagehot's rule, banks or financial institutions would have access to base money even if the central bank failed to act. In the depression of the 1930s, and in many of the panics discussed by Bagehot, access to base money at a penalty rate would have eliminated the threat to the payment system. Discounting is socially valuable if it can be done at a penalty rate. Their proposal removed this safety net.

In his paper for this conference, McCallum (Chapter 9) blunts this criticism by combining a rule for base growth with a rule for smoothing interest rates. Instead of having the banks borrow at a penalty rate, McCallum's rule requires the central bank to respond to the sudden increase in market interest rates, as in a crisis, by increasing the stock of base money. His simulations use the weekly average Federal funds rate, not the daily rate that would rise suddenly in a financial crisis. It is not clear how fast his proposal would work in an incipient crisis, but if it supplied the desired amount of base money on demand, the two procedures would be similar. Differences might arise because of timing of reserve supply or uncertainty of response. These issues cannot be settled here.

This discussion presumes that the banking system remains subject to runs and potential crises. Recent work questions whether reform should seek a more efficient way to supervise and regulate banks and other intermediaries that reduces regulatory burden and the risk of bank runs.

III REPAIRING REGULATORY SYSTEMS

The recent problems of banking systems in many countries and heightened understanding of principles of insurance and risk have produced new proposals for reform of regulation and supervision. Several proposals recognize that regulatory arrangements and regulations change the incentives faced by participants and the riskiness of the system. The best parts of this new literature also recognize that forbearance and political intervention are present and not likely to disappear if there is scope for their operation. An efficient system of regulation must seek to minimize regulatory burden and the costs of the safety net while recognizing that political intervention to prevent failure or to shift the costs of failure can raise social cost.

The distinguishing feature of the new approach to regulation is increased reliance on market forces. The new proposals do not eliminate supervision and regulatory oversight; they supplement and, to a degree substitute, market forces for more traditional methods of regulation. Two of the proposals I discuss have been made by central bankers and two by academic economists. One of the academic proposals was the intellectual foundation for the recent legislation in the United States known as FDICIA – the Federal Deposit Insurance Corporation Improvement Act.

Both the Reserve Bank of New Zealand (1993) and the President of the Federal Reserve Bank of Cleveland (Jordan, 1993), propose to expand the amount of publicly available information about the quality of bank portfolios. Banks would publicly release information that has been available to regulators but withheld from the public. Depositors are expected to respond to information on the quality of a bank's portfolio by withdrawing deposits from riskier banks. This response is expected to alter banks' practices. Knowing that their position would become public, banks would be quicker to respond to potential losses and more careful about making marginal loans.

The Reserve Bank proposal is preliminary. If adopted, it would require banks to post a credit quality rating at each branch.[5] Minimum capital requirements and publicly available information on asset quality would substitute for direct examination. The Reserve Bank would monitor published reports, license banks, and enforce capital standards along lines similar to those proposed by Benston and Kaufman (1988). Troubled banks would be required to stop lending if capital fell below 6 percent of assets and management would be replaced at a 3 percent ratio. Banks would disclose credit quality quarterly and would be audited semi-annually. The Reserve Bank would retain the right to ask for additional information and would continue to serve as lender of last resort. The lender of last resort function would be executed in the open market. There is no explicit deposit insurance.

Jordan's proposals for changes in regulation and supervision are broadly similar to the Reserve Bank proposals. Capital value and published information on portfolio valuations and losses replace the judgment of regulators. This information about management and performance signals to depositors, lenders and equity owners. Regulation and supervisory mandates come to the fore when losses reduce capital below a fixed threshold. Jordan does not discuss deposit insurance or the lender of last resort function.

Proponents believe that the new system will be less costly and more effective. The scope for cost reduction is large. Jordan reports that out-of-pocket costs of the present system of regulation were between 25 and 50 percent of industry profits in 1992.

Benston and Kaufman (1988, 1993) would retain deposit insurance but reduce its role. Banks would issue uninsured subordinated debentures and equity. Benston and Kaufman somewhat arbitrarily set 'adequate' total capital at 10 percent of assets and measure assets at market value to the extent possible. The role of regulators increases as capital falls relative to assets. For example, when capital falls below

6 percent of assets, the regulator would be required to suspend payment of dividends, interest on subordinated debt, and net payments to parents or affiliates. This would put the bank in default and invoke action by creditors. Below 3 percent, supervisors would be required to take control of the bank, recapitalize it, or liquidate it.

A main aim of the Benston–Kaufman proposal is to increase the incentives of the creditors and owners to monitor the banks' performance and protect their interest. If the proposal had been in place in the 1980s, there would have been less forbearance, less delay in response, and smaller losses borne by taxpayers to pay for the losses at US thrift institutions.

Some of the features of the Benston–Kaufman proposal have been enacted as part of the FDICIA. As the authors note, the law 'imposes less severe, less mandatory, and less rapid regulatory responses' than they proposed. Benston and Kaufman (1993, p. 47). In fact, FDICIA leaves much room for discretion and, therefore, forbearance. This weakens the protection of the deposit insurance fund and taxpayers.

Merton and Bodie (1993a) raise four objections to reliance on capital requirements, particularly subordinated debentures. First they note (p. 17) that the protection furnished by capital requirements is effective only if regulators promptly close failing banks. This is correct but partial. Many banks and thrifts that would have been forced to close in 1981 had become viable again a few years later. There are costs of early closing, when declines are transitory, as well as costs of delay (see Kane and Yu, 1993). This is not an argument for forbearance; it recognizes that there are deadweight costs of closing banks, so there are costs of acting early as well as late.

A second problem is the appropriate size of the required ratio of capital to assets. The amount of capital deemed to be adequate depends on the volatility of asset prices, the mix of assets that a bank holds, and the covariance of asset prices. If banks respond to higher capital requirements (or falling asset prices) by increasing risk, norms based on past experience will be poor guides to future risk. The problem for regulators is to set standards for capital adequacy and intervention knowing that banks will react to the standards by choosing a different risk position. The Basle riskbased capital requirements are an effort to assess the risk in bank assets and relate bank capital to asset risk. The Basle procedure seems a blunt instrument, however, for dealing with a complex and changing problem, and it neglects the effect of covariance when assessing risk.

A third problem is pricing the risk assumed by the debenture holders. If the debenture holders are subordinated to the bank insurance fund, they share the residual risk with the equity owners. This would heighten their interest in monitoring the bank, but also raises the risk premium on subordinated debentures. Benston and Kaufman clearly intend the debentures to be subordinate to the insurance fund to prevent holders from selling the best assets and leaving defaulted securities to the insurance fund. However, the symmetric risk is also present and must be reflected in the yield on the debentures. The authors do not consider whether the system they propose would permit banks to earn a competitive return. Nor do they allow for the risk of political interference that would delay regulatory enforcement of the capital requirements.

Fourth is the problem of monitoring banks' assets to establish value. Many of the problems of supervision and regulation return. Marking bank loans and non-marketable securities to market requires considerable judgment whether it is done by the bank, its auditors, or regulators. The specialized skills and specific information needed to make these judgments are the banker's stock-in-trade. Others can acquire these skills, but they cannot readily do so without learning the techniques that prudent bankers have mastered. There is bound to be a relation between the risks borne by providers of capital and the returns to capital. It is not sufficient to point out that non-banks are able to borrow and sell equity. The issue is whether banks that are subject to audits and regulation, reserve requirements and deposit insurance premiums can compete effectively against less regulated competitors.

Despite these unresolved problems, the Benston–Kaufman proposal is a useful step towards great reliance on market information and private incentives. A remaining issue is whether there is a less regulated alternative that allows banks to meet growing competition from non-bank intermediaries.

A more radical alternative would separate deposit taking from lending. Friedman (1959) proposed 100 percent reserves against demand and time deposits with interest paid on reserves. Lending and security acquisition would be financed by issuing securities and equity as is done by finance companies, real estate trusts, and many other lenders.

Several proposals of this kind have been made in recent years. Banks subject to 100 percent reserve requirement are now called 'narrow' banks. Although Merton and Bodie (1993a, b) deny that theirs is a narrow bank, the only difference is that their bank would be part of an institution that makes loans and acquires securities. Deposits would be subject to a 100 percent reserve of Treasury bills, as in a narrow bank, and the Treasury bills would be held in custody at a Federal Reserve Bank. Loans and securities would be financed by issuing debt and equity, Government would offer deposit insurance. It is not clear what risk the insurance would absorb.

The Merton–Bodie proposal removes the distinction between banks and non-banks in lending and investing. All financial institutions would be subject to the same rules. Losses on loans would be borne by lenders and investors as in non-bank financial markets.

Merton and Bodie argue that banks are relatively expensive providers of deposit services. They note that money market mutual funds provide similar services at 10 percent of the non-interest cost of banks. Some money market funds have 100 percent of their assets in short-term Treasury securities, so they resemble the proposed system. However, currently there are limits on the number of checks per month that can be drawn on a money market fund. And part of the cost difference is locational, so there may be offsetting benefits to the bank. The evidence shows, however, that money market funds have taken and held a significant share of the deposit business.

Benston and Kaufman (1993) argue that separation of lending and deposit taking removes economies of scope or synergies. They note that the two functions have been provided jointly for centuries under very different regulatory and monetary conditions. They suggest that removal of the opportunity to combine these functions in a single firm is socially costly. This cost may offset part of the gain from reducing risk and regulation.

Which type of bank would be more likely to survive in a competitive market? The answer depends on the costs of attracting capital and providing services in alternative ways, on possible economies of scope, on the likelihood of greater political intervention under one proposal or the other. I do not believe we can decide a priori.

There is no reason to choose one or the other. Banks and the public could be offered a choice. Banks could either hold more capital, as in FDICIA or Benston–Kaufman, or they could choose to avoid banking regulations and their costs by separating deposit taking into a narrow bank. A similar proposal is made in Brookings Task Force (1989). The latter would require minimal capital for the banking function. Perhaps there could be mixtures of the two, a trade-off between the size of the ratio of capital to assets and the percentage of short-dated government securities held as collateral for deposits. Banks would use market information to decide how to operate, much as they now choose state or federal charters in the United States.

A simple experiment could be run in the US. Remove restrictions on checking accounts, such as the number of checks that can be written, from money market funds that hold only Treasury bills. The resulting narrow bank would then compete with other banks, and the public would decide where they wish to hold deposits.

IV CONCLUSION

Deposit banking has social benefits, but most depositors lack the skill, knowledge, incentives, or opportunity to monitor their bank's position. A central issue at this conference is how to organize or change the regulatory and supervisory system to achieve the benefit of deposit banking at lowest (or lower) cost.

Experience in several countries during the last decade suggests that traditional methods of bank insurance regulation and supervision worked poorly in the past decade. Moral hazard, errors of judgment, political intervention, and fraud had a part in the failures and losses. Regulatory and supervisory systems could not or did not prevent these problems. In some cases, the explicit deposit insurance system or implicit safety net contributed to the size and scope of the problem. The chapter discusses some principal reasons for failure.

Several proposals for reform of the regulatory system call for reliance on market discipline as a supplement or substitute for traditional regulation. One type of proposal would increase the amount of capital and impose rules for capital maintenance. A second type would separate deposit taking and lending activities. So-called narrow banks would offer deposits backed entirely by Treasury bills or other riskless assets. Lending would be separated and financed by issuing debt and equity. Lenders' liabilities would be uninsured. Regulations would be reduced.

The two proposals have different costs and benefits. It is not clear whether the loss of economies of scope under the narrow bank is large enough to offset the increased capital costs and regulatory costs of the alternative. Experiments in several countries would be useful.

Both proposals, particularly the narrow bank, differ from the Basle proposals for risk-based capital. The Basle rules assign financial assets to arbitrary risk groups. A bank chooses its asset position, on the margin, taking account of the cost of increasing capital. Regulators decisions, not market forces, determine the portfolios that banks hold. It is hard to see how banks would flourish in competition with less regulated financial institutions.

A related issue is the role of the lender of last resort. A narrow bank eliminates the need for a lender of last resort for the banking system, but there are advantages to having a lender for the financial system to prevent spread of default. The design of a lender to avoid both subsidies and interference with goals of monetary policy such as price stability has long been possible. Rules for the lender devised by Bagehot a century ago remain appropriate.

Reform of regulation and supervision can reduce risk. But it does not require much vision to see that many of the problems of banking and financial markets in recent decades have been either caused or worsened by unstable monetary and fiscal policies. Relatively safe and sound banking and financial systems cannot be produced solely by reform of regulation. Economic policy, too, should change. More stable, more predictable, less inflationary policies are the senior partner in the effort to maintain financial stability.

Notes

1. Differences about the valuation of particular assets may have very little relation to portfolio risk and even less to systemic risk to the payments system.
2. Not all events are of this kind. Below, I consider cases where information was available but not used.
3. Equity markets estimated the value of the losses at publicly traded banks. Meltzer (1986) shows that the shares of banks with developing country debt declined absolutely and relative to other bank shares.
4. Not all failures are undesirable. Failure eliminates unprofitable firms.
5. This is similar to the proposal in Meltzer (1967), but I accompanied the proposal with a recommendation that deposit insurance be privatized and related to risk. My views on insurance have changed, as noted below.

References

Bagehot, W. (1873) *Lombard Street* (London: Scribners, Armstrong). Reprinted 1962 (Homewood R. D. Irwin).

Benston, G. J. (1973) 'Bank Examination', *Bulletin of the Institute of*

Finance, Graduate School of Business Administration, New York University (May) entire issue.

Benston, G. J. and G. G. Kaufman (1988) 'Regulating Bank Safety and Performance', in W. S. Haraf and R. M. Kushmeider (eds), *Restructuring Banking and Financial Services in America* (Washington: American Enterprise Institute) pp. 63–99.

Benston, G. J. and G. G. Kaufman (1993) 'Deposit Insurance Reform: A Functional Approach-Comment', *Carnegie Rochester Conference Series on Public Policy*, vol. 38 (June) pp. 41–9.

Brookings Task Force (1989) *Restructuring America's Financial Institutions* (Washington: The Brookings Institution).

Friedman, M. (1959) *A Program for Monetary Stability* (Fordham).

Goodfriend, M. and R. G. King (1988) 'Financial Deregulation, Monetary Policy, and Central Banking', *Economic Review*, Federal Reserve Bank of Richmond, vol. 74: (May–June) pp. 3–22.

Horvitz, P. (1992) 'The Causes of Texas Bank and Thrift Failures', in P. E. Brock, (ed.), *If Texas Were Chile* (San Francisco: Institute for Contemporary Studies) pp. 131–160.

Jordan, J. L. (1993) 'A Market Approach to Banking Regulation' Federal Reserve Bank of Cleveland (multilithed), March.

Kane, E. J. (1989) *The S&L Insurance Mess: How Did It Happen?* (Washington: The Urban Institute Press).

Kane, E. J. and M. T. Yu (1993) 'How Much Did Capital Forbearance Add to the Tab for the FSLIC Mess?' Boston College (August).

McCallum, B. T. (1988) 'Robustness Properties of a Rule for Monetary Policy', *Carnegie Rochester Conference Series on Public Policy*, vol. 29 (Autumn) pp. 173–203.

Meltzer, A. H. (1967) 'Major Issues in the Regulation of Financial Institutions', *Journal of Political Economy*, vol. 75: suppl. (July–Aug.) pp. 482–501.

Meltzer, A. H. (1986) 'Financial Failures and Financial Policies', in G. Kaufman and R. Kormendi (eds), *Deregulating Financial Services* (Cambridge: Ballinger) pp. 79–96.

Meltzer, A. H. (1987) 'Limits of Short-Run Stabilization Policy', *Economic Inquiry*, 25 (Feb.) pp. 1–14.

Meltzer, A. H. (1988) 'The Policy Proposals in the AEI Studies', in W. S. Haraf and R. M. Kushmeider (eds), *Restructuring Banking and Financial Services in America* (Washington: American Enterprise Institute).

Merton, R. C. and Z. Bodie (1993a) 'Deposit Insurance Reform: A Functional Approach', *Carnegie Rochester Conference Series on Public Policy*, pp. 1–34.

Merton, R. C. and Z. Bodie (1993b) 'Reply to Benston and Kaufman', *Carnegie Rochester Conference Series on Public Policy*, vol. 38 (June) pp. 51–55.

Nakajima, Z. and H. Taguchi (1993) 'Toward a More Stable Financial Framework: Long-term Alternatives', Institute for Monetary and Economic Studies, Bank of Japan (July).

Peltzman, S. (1970) 'Capital Investment in Commercial Banking and Its Relationship to Portfolio Regulation', *Journal of Political Economy*, vol. 78 (Jan.–Feb.), pp. 1–26.

Reserve Bank of New Zealand (1993) *Proposed Revisions to Banking Supervision Arrangements* (Willington: Reserve Bank of New Zealand).
Russell, R. E. (1993) 'Lessons from New England Bank Failures', *New England Economic Review* (May–June) pp. 13–35.
Schwartz, A. J. (1987) 'Real and Pseudo Financial Crises', in Anna J. Schwartz (ed.), *Money in Historical Perspective* (Chicago: University of Chicago Press) pp. 271–88.

2 International Capital Flows, the International Agencies and Financial Stability

Stanley Fischer

The 1987 stock market crash moved around the world within a day, a reflection of the integration of the international capital markets that by now has erased most of the obstacles to capital flows erected during the Great Depression and World War II. Today capital flows freely among the major industrialized countries, and even though policymakers occasionally express their exasperation over the consequences, no one seriously believes that it is possible to stop it.[1] Many middle income countries are returning to the global capital markets as industrialized country investors search out emerging markets, and as the international bond markets welcome issues by countries that only a short while ago were regarded as hopelessly mired in debt. In brief, international capital markets are as linked today as they were in the heyday of the international gold standard a century ago.

Globalization of finance is one important aspect of the growing sophistication of the capital markets that has created concern about potential financial instability. The international context features prominently in several of the papers for this conference: most extensively, in Chapter 3, Nakajima and Taguchi ascribe the asset price inflation of the late 1980s in part to the co-ordinated response to the stock market crash; in Chapter 4 Poole concludes that while increased capital mobility has reduced the independence of monetary policy, it has not fundamentally affected its potency; and in Chapter 5 Frankel worries about the sustainability of the increased capital flows to developing countries and the possibility of a replay of 1982. Chapters 7 and 8 on bank regulation and safety nets by Benston and by Flannery pay little attention to the international context beyond their discussion of the Basle capital adequacy standards for banks.[2]

The Basle capital standards embody two principles that are likely to become increasingly common as financial integration forces greater uniformity of regulations. First, the regulations are uniform across countries; and second, the responsibility for enforcing them rests firmly with national authorities. It is remarkable that the negotiators in the Basle group reached a strong and reasonably simple international agreement on an issue of great concern to a major domestic interest group – the banks. It is hard to believe that a similar agreement would have been achieved in the United States had the negotiations taken place in the domestic political arena. The Basle Committee along with other agencies is now attempting to expand the capital adequacy standards to cover market risk from traded securities held by banks. In time, they will probably turn to off-balance sheet items and derivative securities.

Because of the overlap between the activities of banks and securities firms in holding and trading marketable securities, there is also a need to co-ordinate regulation of the banks and of securities firms. The Basle Committee along with IOSCO (the International Organization of Securities Commissions) is working on changing regulations to bring both types of firm under a common regulatory framework, and to harmonize their minimum capital standards.[3] However, these very complicated negotiations are not making much progress.

As the international capital markets become increasingly interdependent,[4] the pressure for uniformity in regulations is bound to grow. But as both the Uruguay Round and the negotiations over the regulation of banks and securities firms show, agreements may be very difficult to reach. No doubt it was easier to agree on the Basle bank capital adequacy standards because those negotiations involved only the central banks. But even without formal agreements, the mobility of international capital forces some convergence in regulations, including taxation. For instance, implementation by any one country of the Tobin short-term financial transactions tax proposal, which has the goal of reducing speculation, would fail unless all financial centers agreed. This market-driven convergence of regulations would tend to converge on the least onerous regulatory conditions.

The focus of this conference is very much on the domestic policy and regulatory changes needed to deal with growing financial sophistication and the possibilities of financial instability. But growing cross-border capital flows, in particular, flows to developing countries, open up many other potential instabilities. Further, international agencies have played and will in future play a role in dealing with these problems.

The international debt crisis of the 1980s is of course the most spectacular recent example of a deep financial crisis associated with international capital flows to developing countries. The revival of capital flows to many of the same countries, albeit not flowing in the same forms, reopens the questions I now take up. What were the causes of the debt crisis? What role did the international agencies, the IMF and the World Bank, play in creating and dealing with the crisis? What mistakes were made, and what can be done to prevent mistakes in future? Should we worry that another debt crisis is in the making?[5]

In the second part of this chapter, I turn to the more general question of the potential role in support of domestic and international financial stability of the Bretton Woods twins in the international financial system. The question is particularly appropriate in the year before the fiftieth anniversary of the IMF and the World Bank, a year during which their purpose and functions will be subjected to renewed scrutiny.

I THE INTERNATIONAL DEBT CRISIS

The international debt crisis developed slowly in the 1970s after the first oil shock, matured with extraordinary speed during the second oil shock from 1980 to 1982, and was painfully resolved over the next decade.[6]

The source of the international debt crisis was the notion that the balance-of-payments surpluses of the oil-exporting countries should be recycled to the developing countries, to enable them to continue growing in the new high-price energy environment. Because the oil-surplus countries preferred to invest in industrialized countries, the recycling was undertaken through the intermediation of industrialized country banks, rather than by direct lending from the surplus countries to the borrowers.

Recycling created no special problems during the second half of the 1970s when the world economy was growing, inflation was high, and real interest rates were low. Table 2.1 presents debt data for the 1980s and early 1990s. Debt indicators in 1980 were high but not extraordinary by historical standards. The second oil-shock hit in 1979. In the next two years, the external debts of the large Latin American debtors to commercial banks doubled in nominal terms.[7] The debt–export ratio for Latin American debtors increased from

Table 2.1 Debt indicators, 1980–92

	1980	*1985*	*1987*	*1990*	*1992*
Debt/Exports (%)					
Debt-reporting countries	127.6	182.7	203.6	166.7	178.4
Latin America and Caribbean	195.5	312.9	366.4	254.2	248.4
Interest/GNP (%)					
Debt reporting countries	2.2	2.6	2.2	1.8	1.6
Latin America and Caribbean	3.5	5.5	4.1	2.1	1.8

Source: *World Debt Tables*, 1992–93 (World Bank), Vol. 1.

200 to 300 within three years, with the changes coming from both the numerator and the denominator. Of course, much of the debt flowed out immediately in the form of capital flight, but the official borrowers were left with the liabilities.

The debt crisis would be resolved over the next decade by the developing countries themselves, the creditor country governments, and the commercial banks. All three parties had contributed to creating the crisis. The debtors were for the most part pursuing highly expansionary fiscal policies, funded by external borrowing. Many of the debtors experienced a sharp worsening of the terms of trade, but the terms of trade cannot have been the whole story, for the country where the crisis was first recognized, Mexico, had *benefitted* from the oil price increase.[8] The creditor countries, notably the United States, tightened monetary policy at the end of the 1970s; the fiscal-monetary mix in the United States produced extremely high real interest rates by 1982. The increase in real interest rates from negative to high positive levels increased the debt-servicing burden virtually overnight. The worldwide recession that accompanied the (needed) tightening of monetary policy reduced developing country exports. The public sector contributed also because bank supervisors had failed to warn banks of the dangers of their growing exposure to the developing countries. The banks in turn contributed to the crisis by overlending, by not exercising caution in their loans, and by their herd behavior.

The much-quoted statement by Walter Wriston that sovereign borrowers do not go bankrupt must have encouraged the banks to keep lending well beyond the point of prudence. It may just be though that Wriston was right – and that the outcome of the debt crisis a decade later shows that the authorities will not permit a sufficiently general mistake to do major damage to the banks.

The debt strategy began to take shape once it became clear that the debtors could not service their debts without continuing infusions of money, which the private sector would not willingly provide. From 1982 to 1985 the strategy was one of concerted lending, with the official sector and the banks combining to provide the financing needed to meet adjustment plans approved by the IMF. At this point, the IMF was playing an essential role in preventing the failure of major United States banks and other banks. At the end of 1982, the exposure of the nine largest US banks to the debtor countries was nearly three times their capital: any realistic writedown of these assets would have put several of the banks into bankruptcy. That did not happen.

What would have happened had the international agencies not been involved? In the face of a major threat to their largest banks, national banking authorities would have found a way of avoiding widespread formal bankruptcies. The burden of the resolution of the crisis would probably have been different. In the event, the crisis was solved by increasing lending to the debtors, to enable them to service the debt. The alternative would have been to recognize early that the debtors could not pay, to write down their debts and thereby remove the uncertainty that dogged the debtors through the 1980s, and for the creditor governments to lend to their banks to enable them to restructure and survive the crisis. Perhaps in the process the creditor governments would have forced the worst-affected banks to go out of business.

Which would have been the better outcome? From the viewpoint of the industrialized countries, it would have been better in the long run had at least one major bank been required to pay the price of its bad loans by going out of business. Such an example would have helped discourage the herd behavior of banks. The developing country debtors would have preferred an outcome that wrote down their debts sooner rather than later. It has to be recognized though that the debt strategy of the 1980s resulted in the worldwide structural adjustment strategy, which has brought many of the previous debtors into the modern world. I believe that this outcome was attained earlier than it would otherwise have been because of the continual pressure from the external debt negotiations.

It is clear that the debt reduction phase of the strategy was delayed too long. By 1986, most academics were convinced that the indebted countries would not start growing again without debt reduction. They argued for debt reduction *in the context of tough adjustment programs.*

By that stage, phased debt reduction could have taken place without endangering the international banking system. None the less, the Baker strategy prolonged the period without officially-sanctioned debt reduction by another three years.

Opponents of debt reduction argued at the time that it would not be in the interests of the debtors, for it would keep them out of the international capital markets for at least forty years, as long as they were kept out after the debt crisis of the 1930s. In the event, the large-scale flow of capital to former debtors has resumed within a few years of their debt-reduction operations, and in some cases, notably Brazil, even before the Brady deal has been done. The late great Italian Finance Minister and economist, Luigi Einaudi, is often quoted as saying 'The capital markets have the memory of an elephant, the heart of a lamb, and the legs of a hare'. More likely, they have the memory of a crocodile, which is supposed to be 24 hours.

What lessons should we draw from the debt crisis? First, we should expect similar episodes in future. It was after the debt crisis that the real estate crisis hit United States banks, and similar difficulties around the world are detailed in Chapter 3 by Nakajima and Taguchi. It is unlikely that capital adequacy standards will prevent similar crises in future – crises on a scale that will lead to large-scale official intervention. The banks knowingly lend in herds, because safety in the form of government protection lies that way.

Second, recent lending patterns are not reassuring about the ability of the private sector to monitor and draw the correct conclusions from the behavior of governments. Governments that are very far from stability are able to raise large sums in the international capital markets. To be sure, they pay a sizeable premium, but as the credit rationing literature teaches us, that raises the likelihood of default.

Third, the international agencies, both the IMF and the World Bank, played an important part in financing and encouraging good economic policies, structural adjustment, that were pursued by many debtors during the 1980s, and that many of them continue to pursue in the 1990s.

Fourth, the international agencies provided a convenient coordinating mechanism through which the creditors were able to collaborate on the debt strategy, and in which creditors and debtors could in effect negotiate with each other over the strategy.

Without the international agencies, the debt crisis would likely have been over sooner. But it is also likely that the output decline in

Table 2.2 Aggregate net long-term resource flows to developing countries, 1985–92 ($ billion)

	1985	*1988*	*1990*	*1992*
Aggregate net flows	73.4	76.1	98.0	134.3
Private loans	21.8	14.5	11.4	25.9
Commercial banks	8.5	9.4	−4.1	
Bonds	6.0	3.9	3.2	
Other	7.3	1.3	12.4	
Foreign direct investment	11.0	19.7	24.0	38.3
Portfolio equity investment	0.0	0.0	3.8	8.1 (27.2)

Note: The figure in parentheses in the last column, last row is aggregate portfolio investment, presumably including bonds and short-term instruments.
Source: *World Debt Tables*, 1992–93 (World Bank), Vol. 1.

the indebted countries would have been greater, since they would have had to adjust more drastically to the cutoff of funding.

The next question is whether we should be worried about the potential for another debt crisis. Table 2.2 presents data on recent flows to developing countries. These have increased markedly since 1990, and appear to have increased further since 1992 (not shown in the table). In particular, there appear to be large amounts of foreign funds in short-term markets in Mexico and other Latin American countries.

The most noteworthy aspect of the recent capital flows is that they predominantly take the form of foreign direct and portfolio investment. Capital inflows of this form present far less difficulties for the host countries than floating interest rate loans from commercial banks, particularly in the cases of foreign direct investment (FDI) and equity investment, because the risks are better shared with the host country. The potential instability in the current situation arises from the short-term investments that would flee rapidly in the event of a shock, for example a rejection of NAFTA, thereby putting severe strain on the exchange rate. It may also be that the current flows of equity into emerging markets are being made on a herd basis, and that many investors will later be disappointed. If foreign investors decide to withdraw in a hurry, the emerging stock markets could be badly hit. However, there seems to be little systemic risk from such an event. The conclusion is that we do not yet have to worry about a repetition of the debt crisis.

The international agencies can help mitigate and delay future debt crises by improving information about international capital flows. The IMF prepares regular reports on the global capital markets. So does the World Bank, through its quarterly report on international capital flows to developing countries, and the *World Debt Tables*. These publications, as well as those of the BIS, should help international investors as well as governments make better-informed decisions.

Beyond their reports on the capital markets, both agencies can help inform international investors about the prospects in individual economies. The agencies have extraordinary access to information about the developing countries, but that information is not generally made public. There are good reasons that much information is kept confidential: confidentiality makes it easier for governments to discuss their situation freely with the agencies; it is easier for the staff to express strong judgments if they will not be made public; certain subjects – such as a possible need for devaluation, or a potential financial crisis – could become self-fulfilling prophecies if made public. None the less, there is a vast amount of useful information, and especially data, that the agencies could make public very quickly, and that would help international investors. For instance, the Fund's *Recent Economic Developments* publication, which provides the economic data and background on each country for an Article IV consultation, could generally be made available within a few weeks of the Board discussion.[9]

II THE IFIS AND INTERNATIONAL STABILITY

Aside from improving the flow of information, what else can the Bank and the Fund do to increase the stability of the international financial system? We start by discussing what they do now, and then turn to changes that could be made as they enter their second half-century – recognizing of course that both agencies have been evolving during their first half century.

The Bretton Woods twins were set up after World War II to help prevent a repetition of the breakdown of the international economy and to help restore a functioning international economy. Together with the GATT, they have contributed to the extraordinary success of the post-war international economy.

They have contributed in several ways. First, the World Bank through its project lending and later through its adjustment loans has helped increase the flow of resources to the developing countries. Equally important, the expertise that comes with the projects, and the generally good economic policies that come with the adjustment lending, make an important contribution to raising the implementation capacity of the borrowing country. Similarly, IMF expertise, and the need for countries to be able to deal with the IMF, helps developing countries improve the standards of their own policy making.

Second, conditionality has played an important role in helping developing countries carry out politically difficult but economically useful policies. This point needs to be made carefully: policies undertaken only to obtain Fund or Bank financing are unlikely to be successful; but a government that needs external support and funding to undertake policies it owns[10] will benefit from conditional support from the international agencies.

Third, the international agencies have consistently pushed for sound macroeconomic policies and for market-oriented policies. The World Bank's emphasis on trade liberalization has been particularly important in this regard. The pressures from the Bank and the Fund to pursue market-oriented policies have helped create the drive to integration with the world economy that is increasingly evident in developing countries – especially because these pressures have been accompanied by loans.

These contributions of the Bretton Woods twins have mostly affected the developing countries. In strengthening their economies, the international agencies have contributed in an important way to international economic and financial stability. The agencies will doubtless continue to do so in their second half-century.

What more could the agencies do? They are under pressure to change the emphasis of their lending, to support the private sector, to deal with gender issues in development, to condition loans on environmental policies, and so on. Important as these issues are, I will not deal with them in any detail here. There are some common elements though: these pressures often come from industrialized countries, sometimes from non-governmental organizations, and they are generally resented and resisted by both the developing countries and the agencies. Then as time goes by, it begins to be understood that the pressure groups have a point, and some of what they suggest becomes embodied in the conventional wisdom of development. Of course, it would be silly to accept every fashionable suggestion that comes along, but the record shows that more open-mindedness would not hurt.

I will conclude with two more points, one about the Bank, one about the Fund. The World Bank was originally expected to act more as a guarantor of private investments than as a direct lender. By acting as a guarantor, the Bank would encourage the flow of private investment directly, by reducing the risk of international investments, and also indirectly, by having to work more closely with the private sector. The Bank has occasionally revisited the possibility of acting as a guarantor of private investments, but has never been able to find an effective way of doing so. Its newest subsidiary, MIGA, the Multilateral Investment Guarantee Agency, has been set up to guarantee against political risk, and is beginning to get off the ground. But MIGA does not cover economic risks.

Potential private investors frequently ask the Bank to take a more active guarantee role. Whether they would still want the Bank to participate if it charged market prices for the guarantees could only be discovered if the Bank were to undertake this task. It is a possibility that bears re-examination as private sector flows to developing countries increase.

The IMF's articles of agreement require it to 'promote international monetary cooperation . . . [by providing] . . . the machinery for consultation and collaboration on international monetary problems'. The Fund is also required to 'promote exchange stability, to maintain orderly exchange arrangements among members, and to avoid competitive exchange depreciation' (Article I).

The Fund does provide the machinery for consultation and collaboration on international monetary problems. There is probably no forum in which more serious regular discussion of international financial issues takes place than in the Fund's Executive Board. Further the Fund Board has on occasion served as the locus in which decisions on international monetary issues are ratified. However, the decisions are made elsewhere, generally by the G-7. This is no surprise, for the Fund Board is an unwieldy group in which to negotiate.[11]

The real challenge for the IMF is whether it will ever be able to resume its role as the guardian of the international monetary system, promoting exchange stability and orderly exchange arrangements, elements that would increase global financial stability. It lost that task when the world moved to flexible exchange rates in 1973, and it has yet to find another central monetary task. To be sure, it takes part in G-7 discussions, and has been charged with the task of developing indicators of world economic conditions, but its G-7 role seems to be limited.

So long as exchange rates among the major currencies continue to float, the Fund is unlikely to regain its role as the guardian of the international system. And at least in the next decade, there seems to be little prospect of a return to fixed rates among Japan, the United States, and Europe. To be sure the Fund can help promote fixed rates between developing countries and trading partners, a trend that is likely to accelerate if the Argentine fixed exchange rate policy succeeds, and as the attraction of currency board solutions for high inflation countries increases.

In the meantime, the Fund will have to earn its way into being heard on international monetary issues through the quality of its analysis of economic issues, and in particular by suggesting improvements in the current system. It already contributes internally through Article IV consultations and Board papers on major issues, and in public through the *World Economic Outlook*, and these analyses are usually of high equality. If the Fund comes to be seen by both governments and the public as the premier applied macroeconomic policy analysis institution, it can gradually regain its role in the international system. That could happen in two ways: either the Fund itself could become the central organization in the international system, or the G-7 will find it useful to give the Fund a more active and important role in its deliberations.

But for the foreseeable future, it seems that the Fund, like the Bank, will continue to contribute to global financial stability mainly through its operations in the developing countries.

Notes

1. However, Eichengreen and Wyplosz (1993) propose slowing international capital flows by imposing margin requirements on foreign exchange borrowings.
2. See Goldstein *et al.* (1992, Ch. IV). Goodhart also discusses the Basle standards in Chapter 10.
3. See Goldstein *et al.* (1993, Ch. IV), for details.
4. It is common to attribute the growing integration of international capital markets to financial innovations (many of them associated with the spread of derivatives) and to technological improvements that have reduced the costs of communication. However, judging by economic criteria such as the correlation of short-term securities returns across international markets, the international capital markets were as closely

integrated in the gold standard period as they are now. The telegraph was the key invention in linking capital markets.

5. Jeffrey Frankel raises several of these issues Chapter 5 of this volume.
6. The African debt crisis has not yet been resolved and heavy external indebtedness to the official sector places a significant burden on the African countries. However, grants far outweigh the servicing costs of the debt.
7. Sachs (1989, Table 1.3, p. 9), shows the net liabilities of Argentina, Brazil and Mexico to BIS banks rising from $56.6 to $104.5 billion from December 1979 to December 1981.
8. Warner (1992) argues that it was the oil price decline in 1982, rather than the debt, that caused Mexico's difficulties.
9. These issues are discussed at greater length in Fischer (1993). Some critics are concerned that by making such information public, the international agencies would be trespassing on the territory of private sector consulting firms. Perhaps so, but the market for information is generally one with externalities; in this case, the externality arises because the agencies need to collect the information for their own purposes, and once they have done so, the marginal cost of making it available is very low. The Fund would of course charge for the publications.
10. The first World Bank study on adjustment lending (1989) identified a country's 'ownership' of its program as a key determinant of the success of the program.
11. It is probably also true that improvements in communications since 1945 have made for greater centralization of authority in all international organizations, private and public. Headquarters must have more control now than it did then, with the result that principals make more decisions and representatives fewer.

References

Eichengreen, B. and Wyplosz, C. (1993) 'The Unstable EMS' (London: Centre for Economic Policy Research), Discussion Paper 817 (May).

Fischer, S. (1993) 'The IMF and World Bank at Fifty', mimeo, MIT.

Goldstein, M. *et al.* (1992) *International Capital Markets* (Washington, DC: IMF) (September).

Goldstein, M. *et al.* (1993) *International Capital Markets*, Part II (Washington, DC: IMF) (August).

Sachs, J. D. (1989) *Developing Country Debt and Economic Performance*, volume 1 (Chicago: University of Chicago Press).

Warner, A. M. (1992) 'Did the Debt Crisis Cause the Investment Crisis?', *Quarterly Journal of Economics*, vol. 107, no. 4 (November) pp. 1161–86.

Part II
Recent Changes in the Financial System – Background and Consequences

3 Toward a More Stable Financial Framework: Long-term Alternatives – an Overview of Recent Bank Disruption Worldwide*

Zenta Nakajima and Hiroo Taguchi

I INTRODUCTION

The period during the late 1980s through to the early 1990s may well come to be known as 'the era of global financial turmoil', unequalled in magnitude of shock and geographical scale since the early 1930s. Successive waves of asset inflation and deflation have swallowed up various financial institutions – banks, securities houses, insurance companies and non-banks – all at once. Despite considerable government intervention in terms of crisis management, financial stability remains at stake across the world.

This chapter is an attempt to present an overview of recent global financial distress. Many researchers, government agencies, central banks, and international organizations have already published surveys that deal with various aspects of current financial disruption. Like these previous works, this chapter tries to put into perspective

* Part of this chapter represents joint work with Wataru Takahashi, Tetsufumi Yamakawa and Kazuhiko Ishida. The views expressed in the chapter are those of the authors and do not represent those of the Bank of Japan or the Institute for Monetary and Economic Studies. We thank participants of the Sixth International Conference of the Institute for Monetary and Economic Studies, Bank of Japan, and the Conference on Financial Stability organized by Macquarie University's Centre for Studies in Money, Banking and Finance, particularly to Messrs Mark Flannery, Edward Frydl, Keimei Kaizuka, Ian Macfarlane, Allan Meltzer and William Witherell for their helpful comments. The discussions we had with our colleagues at the Bank of Japan were also indispensable for preparing this chapter. However, the authors are solely responsible for possible errors.

the financial problems by bringing together the recent experiences of the major industrialized countries. What differentiates this chapter from the other surveys is probably its exclusive concern with learning lessons from the current state of affairs in search of a new hazard-proof system. In dealing with financial problems, the chapter focuses on banks, which lie at the core of any financial system. To capture lessons, the chapter simplifies reality. In stressing some points and ignoring others, it may even border on doing injustice to the actual sequence of events in some countries. In particular, we underline the importance of the moral hazard problem. We realize that financial distress is manifold in nature and can only be accounted for by a combination of many diverse factors. In considering the relationship of financial stability with public safety nets, however, we consider it strategically important to focus on moral hazard.

The chapter is organized as follows. Section II summarizes the recent bank disruption experience of the major industrialized countries. It focuses on factors commonly observed across the world. Section III elaborates on a number of selected countries with more emphasis on individual circumstances, thereby supplementing Section II. Based on Sections II and III, Section IV explores an optimal regulatory system logically tenable from a long-term perspective.

II FINANCIAL INSTABILITY WORLDWIDE

In the 1980s and early 1990s, many industrialized countries have seen their financial systems undergo the most serious test since the late 1920s and early 1930s. Difficulty came in ways that varied from country to country, reflecting differences in financial structure and regulatory system. There was, however, a phenomenon common to all the countries experiencing financial disruption. That is, banks suffered a rapid deterioration in the quality of their assets – particularly loans to real-estate related projects – and in profitability. Many became insolvent or nearly so.

This section briefly reviews the process of bank disruption and examines the causes. Focus will be on identifying factors commonly observed across the board.[1]

Bank Disruption Worldwide[2]

In the United States, hundreds of S&Ls and commercial banks, including some large ones, failed in the late 1970s and 1980s (Figure

3.1a). In Japan, although there have been no major bank bankruptcies since the war, numerous banks now find themselves left with problem loans; several institutions have been in effect dissolved through merger (Figure 3.1b). Several European countries have also suffered financial turmoil. Difficulty was most pronounced in the Nordic countries (Figure 3.2), and was also severe in the United Kingdom and some others. In Australia and New Zealand too, banks fell into serious trouble. Besides Japan, a few countries in Asia have suffered bank disruption, albeit to a lesser degree.

While many industrialized countries have faced financial turmoil, some countries have been exempt, the most notable one being Germany. This chapter focuses on a number of selected countries where bank disruption was most acutely felt. We will leave unanswered for future research the question why Germany and some others have not experienced the same financial stress.

Background

The background against which many industrialized countries experienced severe bank disruption can be classified into (i) the cyclical factor, and (ii) the structural factor. These two factors combined to generate successive waves of global asset inflation and deflation, creating turmoil for banks.

First, the cyclical factor. It was well into the second half of the 1980s that stimulative macroeconomic policy continued to prevail globally. Monetary policy, in particular, remained relaxed. After a large swing in interest rates in the early 1980s, the United States experienced a long phase of monetary expansion into mid-1988. Germany and the United Kingdom also saw their monetary relaxation continue until mid-1988. Japan's monetary policy eased significantly during 1986–7, with the discount rate lowered to a record 2.5 percent; this monetary easing continued until mid-1989. The stock market crash in the autumn of 1987 is likely to have prolonged monetary relaxation worldwide than otherwise would have been the case.

Such macroeconomic policy is said to have contributed, directly and through a cyclical upswing in economic activity, to a sharp rise in asset prices, which then created an atmosphere in which banks lost sight of what they were doing. Many economists and bankers have put forward the argument that, had macroeconomic policy been better conducted, the subsequent problems banks had to face would have been much more moderate.

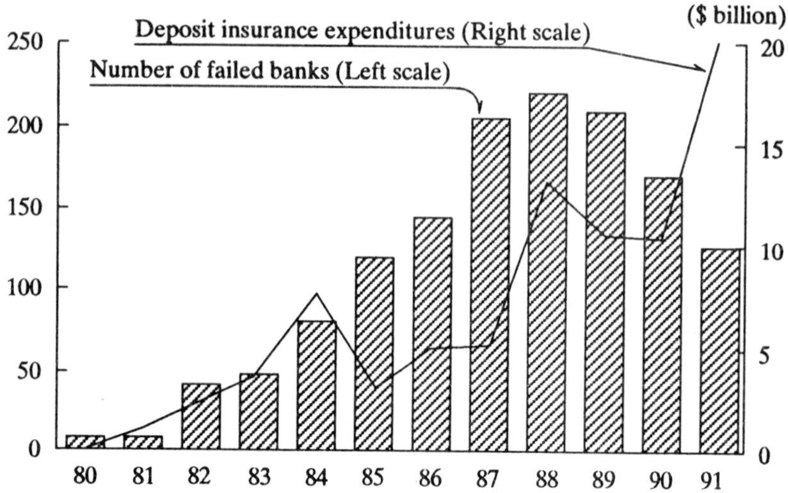

(a)

Source: FDIC (1991).

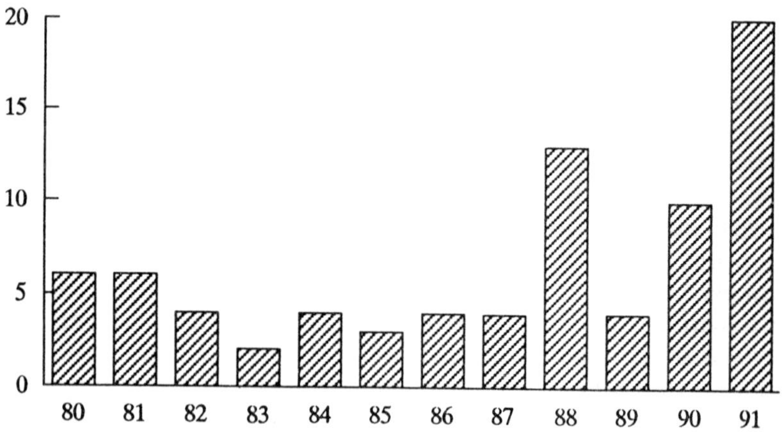

(b)

Source: Ministry of Finance (1992).

Figure 3.1 (a) Number of failed banks in the United States. (b) Number of bank mergers in Japan

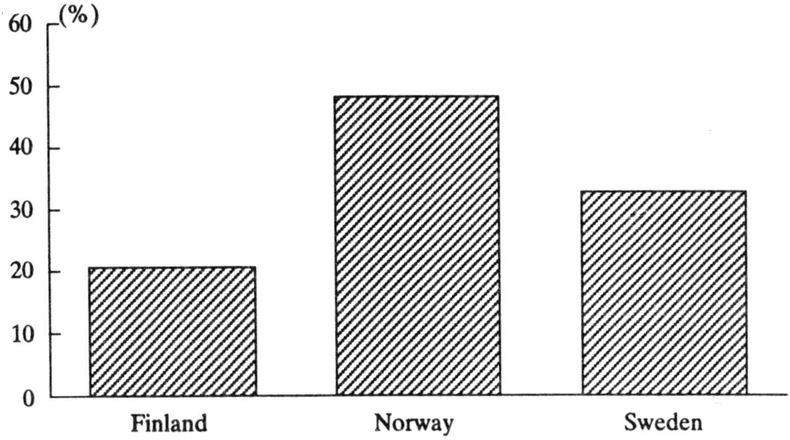

Figure 3.2 Total assets of the three largest problem banks in the Nordic countries (end 1992). (% of total assets of the industry). *Source*: Berg (1993).

This argument, however, is hardly convincing. True, economic fluctuations in the 1980s were large. But those in the 1970s were even larger. True, macroeconomic management in the 1980s may have been excessively stimulative. But that in the 1970s was not flawless, either. The banking industry withstood the testing of the two oil crises in the 1970s. Obviously, the main cause of bank disruption in the 1980s cannot be fully attributed to the cyclical factor; it must be sought somewhere else.

In this regard, what attracts our attention most as a commonly observed phenomenon over a wide range of areas across the world is a sharp increase in bank loans on real estate, closely followed by a rapid rise in property prices (Figure 3.3). We consider it well accepted that asset inflation in the late 1980s, as typically represented by the property boom, was largely credit-induced (Corrigan, 1992; Noguchi, 1992; BIS, 1993, especially pp. 163–4). Banks had traditionally exercised caution in extending loans to real estate, especially to commercial real-estate projects, which had been seen as a profitable area but too risky for bankers to enter. What triggered a global turnaround in bank behavior in the 1980s? We must now examine the structural factor.

In the late 1970s and 1980s, government regulation of the banking sector shifted worldwide from the restriction of market forces to

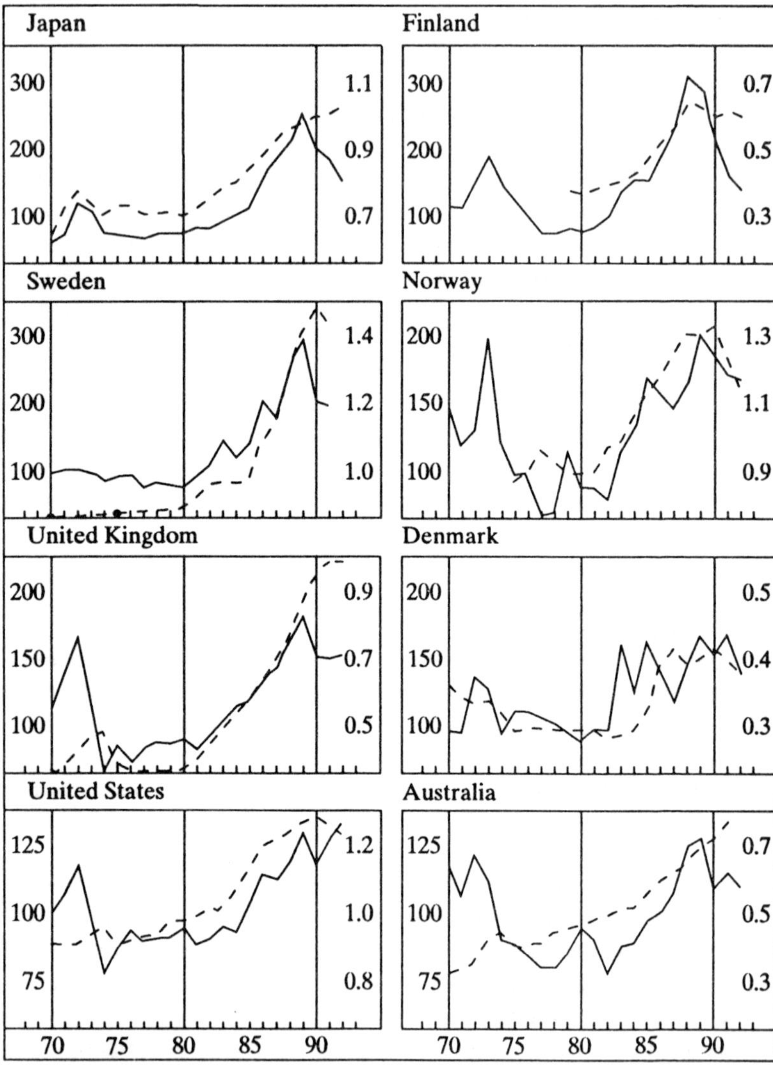

Figure 3.3 Real aggregate asset prices and credit. —— Real aggregate asset prices (1980 = 100; left scale), - - - Total private credit/GDP ratio (right scale). For Denmark, bank credit only; for Sweden, data shown for 1970, 1975, and 1980 onwards. (*Source*: BIS (1993).)

more market-oriented systems. Interest rate controls were progressively disbanded (Table 3.1). The main driving force was the fact that the regulated banking sector was increasingly exposed to competition from uncontrolled financial sectors, securities houses in particular. We do not intend to discuss the deregulation process itself in detail; it suffices here just to mention that financial innovation based on the rapid progress of telecommunications and data processing technology was a major factor that forced the unravelling of regulation.

In any case, increased competition triggered deregulation, which in turn intensified competition among banks themselves as well as with other financial institutions, including securities houses, insurance companies, pension funds, etc. The process occasioned a sharp squeeze on banks' profit margins. On the liability side, the deregulation of deposit rates and competition for funds with other financial institutions brought about a visible increase in funding costs. On the asset side, securitization, for example, eroded banks' relative position as lenders.

In the old less competitive framework, banks used to enjoy sizable economic rents, or franchise values, thanks to regulation on pricing, type of service, entry, etc. In the late 1970s and 1980s, competition intensified and successive deregulation and financial innovation proceeded, both eroding banks' profit margins. In the process, the franchise value of banks declined. Deregulation made itself felt, first in urban areas and then in the provinces, gradually but steadily.

In response to downward pressure on profit margins, banks rapidly increased the provision of credit to profitable but riskier projects, that is, real estate projects. In Japan, the ratio of bank lending to real estate firms and non-bank financial institutions[3] to total bank lending rose from 17.9 percent in 1985 to 26.7 percent in 1992, and in the United States from 28.7 percent in 1980 to 42.2 percent in 1992. A sharp increase in real estate loans also occurred in the Nordic countries, the United Kingdom, and some Oceanian and Asian countries.

In addition to increasing loans to real estate firms, Japanese banks extended considerable credit to business firms for investment in stocks and other financial assets. US banks and S&Ls increased lending for LBOs and investment in junk bonds, thereby considerably increasing their exposure to highly leveraged trading (HLT).

Such aggressive lending by banks for projects related to real estate and investments in financial assets obviously contributed to a sharp rise in the prices of property and other assets (Table 3.2 and Figure 3.3). In addition to increasing the value of assets held as collateral,

Table 3.1 Chronology of financial deregulation in major countries

Year	*Japan*	*United States*	*United Kingdom*
1977		In 1970, rates on CDs with maturity of 30–89 days deregulated. In 1972, saving banks began offering NOW accounts. In 1973, rates on CDs with maturity of 90 days or over deregulated.	Following the package of reforms known as 'Competition and Credit Control' introduced in 1971, bank interest rates were largely determined by market forces. In 1973, the Supplementary Special Deposits Scheme (Corset) was introduced. In 1977–8, building societies began offering high-yielding time deposits.
1978		*May* Commercial banks and thrift institutions authorized to issue money market certificates (MMCs) (26-week maturity; minimum denomination: $10 000).	
1979	*May* Introduction of CDs of minimum ¥500 million with 3–6 months maturity. • Minimum CD amount gradually lowered to ¥50 million, and maturities diversified.	*December* Commercial banks and thrift institutions authorized to issue small saver certificates (SSCs) (30–48 month maturity; no minimum denomination).	*October* Banking Act 1979 enacted. • Within the monetary sector a distinction is drawn between recognized banks and other (licensed deposit-taking) institutions. • Establishment of Deposit Protection Fund.
1980	*December* Foreign Exchange and Foreign Trade Control Law revised.	*March* The Depository Institutions Deregulation and Monetary Control Act (DIDMCA) enacted; • This legislation authorized NOW accounts nationwide. • Phase out and ultimate elimination of deposit rate ceilings over 6 years.	*June* Abolition of the Corset. *September* Lloyds Bank started to offer interest-bearing current accounts with some restrictions.
1981		*June* The Depository Institutions Deregulation Committee (DIDC) adopted a schedule for gradual elimination of Regulation Q.	*August* Suspension of minimum lending rate (MLR).
1982		*March* The DIDC adopted a new schedule for gradual phase-out of interest ceilings. *September* Introduction of 7 day-1 month MMCs.	

		October Garn-St Germain Depository Institutions Act enacted. • Authorization of MMDAs, Super NOWs, etc. *December* Introduction of money-market deposit accounts (MMDA) (minimum denomination: $2500).	
1983		*January* Introduction of the Super NOW accounts (minimum deposit: $2500). *April* Liberalization of interest rates on time deposits over 2½ years. *October* Liberalization of interest rates on time deposits from 32 days to 2½ years.	
1984			*February* Midland Bank introduced High Interest Cheque Account (linked with market rates).
1985	*March* Introduction of MMCs (minimum: ¥50 million; maturity: 1–6 months) • Minimum MMC amount gradually lowered to ¥10 million, and maturities diversified. *October* Introduction of large-denomination time deposits of minimum ¥1 billion, with maturity 3 months to 2 years.		
1986	*December* Establishment of Japan Offshore Market.	*January* Abolition of minimum time deposit amount. Abolition of minimum MMDA and Super NOW account amounts. Abolition of interest rate ceiling on NOW accounts.	*July* Building Societies Act 1986 enacted. *November* Financial Services Act 1986 enacted.
1987	*November* Establishment of commercial paper (CP) market.		*May* Building societies started to pay interest on cheque accounts. *October* Banking Act of 1987 enacted.

Table 3.1 (Con't)

Year	*Japan*	*United States*	*United Kingdom*
1988			*October* Midland Bank introduced interest-bearing current accounts with no restrictive features.
1989	*June* Introduction of small-denomination MMCs of minimum ¥3 million, with maturity 6 months or 1 year. *October* The minimum amount for large-denomination time deposit was finally lowered to ¥10 million. Following this, MMCs were abolished.	*August* The Financial Institutions Reform, Recovery and Enforcement Act (FIRREA) effected: • Abolition of Federal Sayings and Loan Insurance Corporations (FSLIC). • Establishment of the Resolution Trust Corporation (RTC). • About $100 billion in new government funds to recapitalize insolvent S&Ls.	
1991	*October* The deposit Insurance Corporation approved financial assistance (for the first time) for the Iyo bank in its bail-out merger with the Toho Sogo Bank.	*December* Federal Deposit Insurance Corporation Improvement Act (FDICIA) effected: • Prompt corrective action by regulators tied to bank capital ratios. • Introduction of risk-based deposit insurance premiums. • Timely recapitalization or liquidation of a bank when its capital asset ratio declines below 2%.	
1992	*June* Financial System Reform Law enacted. Introduction of money market instalment savings. Abolition of the minimum amount for small-denomination MMCs.		
1993	*January* Establishment of the Cooperative Credit Purchasing Company. *June* Liberalization of interest rates on time deposits with specified periods. • Liberalization of interest rates on time deposits completed.		

Table 3.2 Property prices in major countries (% change from a year earlier)

	Country/city	*1980–85 average*	*1985–90 average*	*1985*	*1986*	*1987*	*1988*	*1989*	*1990*	*1991*
Commercial	United States	8	1	5	4	5	2	0	–7	–18
	Japan	7	22	13	48	61	3	5	4	–7
	United Kingdom	2	5	–1	6	16	35	1	–24	–20
	Canada	NA	5	3	4	6	8	9	–3	–6
	Australia	18	11	11	17	40	30	6	–24	–21
	Sweden	6	21	12	27	–8	49	–2	51	–1
Residential	New York	16	5	27	20	14	0	0	–5	–2
	Tokyo	4	19	3	22	69	0	7	7	–9
	London	14	13	16	23	24	24	2	–7	–5
	Toronto	7	14	16	38	25	26	3	–15	–4
	Stockholm	2	17	6	10	21	28	19	11	3
	Sydney	5	11	11	14	25	53	–13	–10	8

Source: BIS (1992).

the surge in asset prices improved actual and prospective profitability, thus prompting bankers to finance even more asset purchases. This process of bank lending and asset inflation feeding on each other pushed up asset prices to levels unjustifiable by economic fundamentals. This is none other than the formation of a speculative bubble, a phenomenon commonly observed in many areas of the world, particularly in the late 1980s.

In the meantime, monetary policy had turned tight in various countries toward the end of the decade. The bubble by its very nature was destined to burst, though the actual timing varied from country to country. In the United States, real estate prices were seen to be falling across the country by 1989, but in Japan asset inflation did not come to a halt until 1990. One may identify 1988–90 as when the bubble collapsed completely worldwide.

The fall in property prices and defaults on property loans caused a serious deterioration in the asset quality and profitability of banks (Danton, 1992). Loan loss provisions increased tremendously. The movement of share prices was of relatively less importance to banks in many countries, except in Japan and Finland. Japanese banks, in particular, suffered from a substantial decline in unrealized profits on equity holdings due to the collapse of share prices.

In the Nordic countries, banks incurred huge losses. In most other countries, profit margins declined steeply (Table 3.3). Occasionally, governments and central banks were called upon to effect crisis management. With banks thus under such severe strain, financial systems became destabilized worldwide on a scale unequalled since 1929–33. We may note in passing that, while banks in most major industrialized countries have experienced turmoil in just the recent few years and have hardly recovered, US banks experienced a similar phase, mostly in the 1980s, and have now possibly overcome the worst.

Expansive Banking and Moral Hazard

The question now arises as to why banks in so many countries adopted expansive strategies in response to downward pressure on profit margins and franchise values. In particular, why did they extend so much credit for real estate projects and equity investments, both more or less speculative areas from which bankers had traditionally shied away?[4]

It is clear that this expansive strategy was not the only option

Table 3.3 Pre-tax profit of major banks in 1991 and 1992 (%)

Countries	*Number of banks*	*Return on assets*		*Loan loss provisions*		*Net interest margin*	
		1991	*1992*	*1991*	*1992*	*1991*	*1992*
		% of total assets					
United States	15	0.60	1.12	1.13	0.97	3.19	3.45
Japan[(1)] [(2)]	21	0.31	0.22	0.09	0.14	0.81	0.97
Germany[(3)]	3	0.63	0.67	NA	NA	2.15	2.11
France	6	0.39	0.29	0.67	0.73	2.13	2.20
United Kingdom	4	0.35	0.29	1.41	1.50	3.08	2.99
Canada[(2)]	6	1.26	0.60	0.54	1.11	3.24	3.12
Australia[(2)]	4	1.07	−0.25	1.27	1.88	3.66	3.43
Denmark[(4)]	2	0.01	−1.03	1.26	1.56	2.72	2.78
Finland	3	−0.49	−1.67	0.90	2.23	1.70	1.47
Netherlands	3	0.59	0.61	NA	NA	2.14	2.20
Norway	4	−3.77	−1.22	3.68	2.34	2.52	2.69
Spain	6	1.24	0.94	0.55	0.60	3.35	3.00
Sweden	6	−0.41	−1.99	1.82	3.20	2.37	2.28
Switzerland	3	0.74	0.73	0.48	0.57	1.45	1.40

Notes: Data not fully comparable from country to country. (1) For 1992, half-year results at an annual rate. (2) Fiscal years. (3) Partial net operating profit, which excludes loan loss provisions, gains/losses on own trading and extraordinary items. (4) Securities portfolio marked to market.
Source: BIS (1993).

available. Banks, when faced with profit squeezing pressure, could have focused more on higher-quality loans and investments (i.e. more profitability and less risk), thereby maintaining profit margins. Of course, better investments and loans are more limited in availability, necessitating a more selective and self-disciplined strategy. In fact, even in countries where serious bank disruption occurred, we find many instances of banks which adopted selective strategies and managed to minimize problems and remain sound. Thus, banks that adopted expansive strategies and ran into difficulties committed mismanagement. The background against which many banks adopted expansive, rather than selective, strategies is complicated and manifold, but we point out the following three factors.

First, the growth inertia factor. During the several decades preceding the 1970s and 1980s, the banking industry flourished and grew in a relatively well-protected environment. Having been used to growth for so long, banks tended to take it for granted. Then competition increased, deregulation proceeded, and the franchise value of banks was eroded. Completely used to growth inertia, many banks, however, were obviously slow to adapt themselves to the new situation. Moreover, banking happens to be an industry with large sunk costs not only in tangible assets like buildings and computer systems but also in intangible assets like reputation, long-term customer relationships, and human capital. This made it all the more difficult for banks to reduce involvement.

Second, the bandwagon effect. People tend to join others in doing something fashionable because they are afraid of being left behind alone. Bank after bank ventured into real estate-related loans because they thought managerial risk would be minimized if they undertook action similar to those of their competitors.[5] The average degree of relative risk tolerance increased.

Third, the moral hazard problem. Most industrialized countries have some kind of a public safety net in place. Public safety nets, consisting of deposit insurance, lender of last resort, etc., are often indispensable in preventing, for example, a local disruption from developing into a system-wide crisis. It is well known, however, that they have a serious side-effect in terms of moral hazard, unless employed in an appropriate manner.

In the United States, for example, the sharp rise in interest rates in the early 1980s undermined the solvency of many S&Ls. The difficulties, however, were considered temporary and, if allowed enough time, manageable by the institutions impaired. Based on this forbearance policy, they were allowed to continue in operation. S&L managers ran around, collecting deposits by offering premium rates and investing funds collected in very profitable but also very risky assets. Depositors kept their money with the insolvent S&Ls because their deposits were well protected by the FSLIC (Federal Savings and Loan Insurance Corporation). Both depositors and S&L management considered this a 'Heads I win, tails the FSLIC loses' situation. The FSLIC was thus destined to run out of funds sooner or later. This is an outright case of moral hazard.

In Japan, things were less straightforward. In the last few decades, up until very recently, there was no single incident of bank closure in a strictly legal sense. Very few simply believed this was because bank managers had been sufficiently astute; rather, many believed it was more due to government policy allowing no dropouts. Whether there had been a consistent government policy on bank protection – often referred to as the 'convoy scheme' – is unclear. But this no-bank-failure myth is likely to have provided the background against which many banks continued for years to extend massive credit to speculative projects related to real estate and equity investments. Bank managers may have indeed recognized the risks they were taking, at least when they were gone halfway through, but they kept taking it. They may have thought that, because they were all travelling the same perilous path, a government bailout was inevitable should any of the disaster scenarios materialize. If this was the case, then we may call it moral hazard, because bankers' behavior was based on the recognition of implicit government protection.

The moral hazard problem may take various forms, depending upon type of public safety net, regulatory system, financial system, ways in which governments intervene, etc. Moreover, as we pointed out earlier, the background against which many banks adopted expansive strategies is complicated and manifold in nature. In considering the relationship of financial stability with public safety nets, however, we consider it of strategic importance to focus on the moral hazard factor.

Government Responses

In contrast to remarkable similarities across the board in terms of the mechanism by which bank disruptions occurred, government action in response varied from country to country (Table 3.4). Formal government intervention appeared most sweeping in the United States and the Nordic countries, albeit in quite different fashions. This time around, US bank supervisors ordered the closure of commercial banks and S&Ls; they also activated deposit insurance on a large scale through either direct payoffs or purchases and assumptions (P&As). In the meantime, a huge amount of public money was injected to replenish insurance funds. In the Nordic countries, governments bailed out some major troubled banks by nationalizing them. In Australia, a troubled state bank was absorbed by a federally owned bank with the financial assistance of the state.

In Japan, official involvement has been more limited and indirect. There have been a few cases of the deposit insurance system providing grants and other forms of financial assistance to a bank merging a problem bank, but with virtually no direct use of government money. More typically, banks have solved problems among themselves,

Table 3.4 Bank support operations in selected countries

Institutions	*Recipients*			*Total support*[1]			*Government support*	
	Number		*Assets as % of industry*	*% of recipients' assets*	*% of GDP*	*Billions of local currency units*	*% of total support*	*% of government deficit*
	Absolute	*% of industry*						
United States								
1980–87 average	118	0.7	0.6	59.6	0.3	12.5	—	—
1989–91 average	378	2.4	2.3	70.3	1.5	81.3	54.6	25.5
1992	191	1.4	1.7	49.7	0.7	39.5	68.4	9.2
Peak (1988)[2]	426	2.6	3.2	73.9	2.3	113.7	—	—
Norway								
1988	2	1.0	2.5	5.4	0.1	0.8	25.0	1.3[7]
1989	7	3.8	3.9	16.5	0.6	3.9	14.6	6.5[7]
1990	9	5.3	4.5	6.8	0.3	1.9	—	—
1991	17	10.5	59.4	4.1	2.0	14.0	59.8	298.9
1992	11	7.4	69.8	2.8	1.7	12.0	100.0	50.6
Finland								
1991 (individual)	28	6.3	15.7	3.7	0.9	4.6	84.5	13.2
1992 (individual)[3]	22	6.0	23.8	15.1	5.7	28.2	86.2	58.9
1992 (general)[4]	135	33.0	92.4	1.1	1.6	7.9	100.0	19.2
Sweden								
1991	1	0.8	18.2	1.5	0.3	4.2	100.0	19.8
1992	3	2.7	26.9	7.1	2.0	19.3	100.0	26.0
1993[5]	1	0.9	4.4	50.7	2.4	34.0	100.0	24.1
Japan								
1991–92[6]	2	0.3	0.1	3.3	0.0	28.0	—	—

Notes: (1) Total support provided to institutions in distress by private guarantee/insurance funds or by governments. (2) Peak measured in terms of percentage of assets of all institutions supported. (3) A single joint stock company was formed through a merger of 41 savings banks, some of which were in distress. (4) General capital injection. (5) Industry assets, total number of banks, GDP and government deficit in 1992. (6) Only mergers assisted by the bank deposit insurance fund. (7) Surplus.
Source: BIS (1993).

under the leadership of the government and/or the central bank. In the United Kingdom, banks solved most of the problems themselves. Indonesia ordered the central bank to initiate liquidation of a failed bank.

While differences with regard to losses eventually shouldered by depositors were small (both insured and non-insured deposits were practically all honored, except those held by a number of very small banks in the United States), there were marked differences in the burden on shareholders: in the United States and Australia, bank failures caused, in many instances, the loss of shareholder equity; while shareholders of troubled banks in Japan and Europe were able to maintain their stakes.

III EXPERIENCE OF BANK PROBLEMS IN SELECTED COUNTRIES

This section summarizes the experience of banking problems in some selected countries (Japan, the United States, the United Kingdom, Nordic countries, Australia, and Indonesia) in somewhat more detail.[6] As with the previous section, readers are reminded of some possible over-simplifications.

Japan

Change in the banking environment

In the second half of the 1980s, there were significant changes in the environment in which Japanese banks operated.[7]

Deposit rates were gradually liberalized from 1985 (Table 3.1). Large-denomination time deposits bearing market rates and money market certificates (MMCs) were introduced in 1985, small-denomination MMCs in 1989, and restrictions on minimum amount and maturity of such deposits were gradually relaxed thereafter. In June 1993, interest rates on time deposits became virtually free of any regulation. As a result of such gradual deregulation, deposits at city banks bearing market-determined rates as a percentage of total deposits were well over 70 percent in 1990, compared with only 22 percent in 1985 (Figure 3.4(a), 3.4(b)).

The issuance of CP has been permitted since 1987 for a limited number of firms. More importantly, large companies turned to the capital markets (both domestic and overseas) for funds. Although

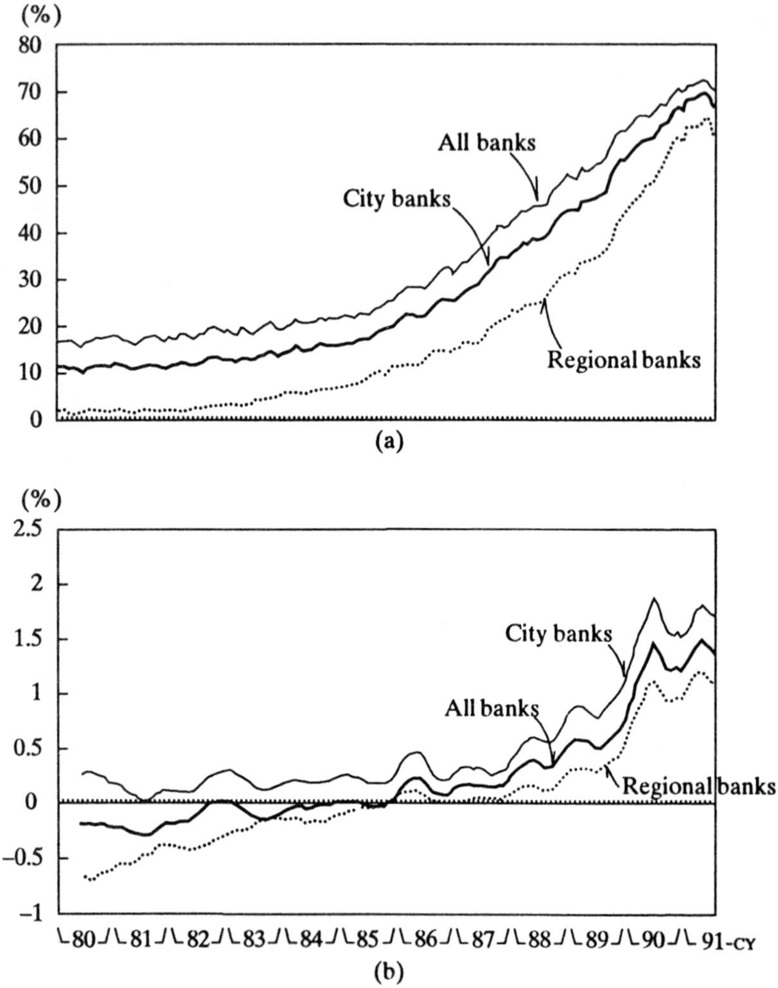

Figure 3.4 Development of deposit rate liberalization and effect on funding costs of banks. (a) Ratio of funds procured at market rates. (b) Average funding cost minus regulated deposit rate. *Notes*: (1) Ratio of funds procured at market rates = (call money + bills sold + borrowings excluding Bank of Japan loans + foreign currency deposits + non-resident yen deposits + MMCs + small-denomination MMCs + large time deposits + CDs)/total funds. (2) Average funding costs = weighted average of cost of liabilities except for derivative deposits. (3) Regulated deposit rate = 3-month time deposit rate. (*Source*: Bank of Japan, *Economic Statistics Monthly* (various issues).)

banks purchased the bulk of paper (including CP) issued in the capital markets and thus remained the most important financing source for the corporate sector, their influence on that sector has gradually waned.

Aggressive lending to real estate and non-bank firms

The most conspicuous response of Japanese banks to the actual and potential loss of their franchise value was to expand lending to less traditional areas, in particular to real estate and non-bank financial institutions ('non-banks').[8]

Between 1985 and 1992, bank loans to the real estate industry grew 13.7 percent annually, compared with 6.6 percent for total bank lending, and the share of such loans to total bank lending rose from 7.5 percent in 1985 to 12.1 percent in 1992 (Table 3.5). Lending to 'non-banks' also grew rapidly, from 10.4 percent to 14.0 percent of total bank lending. Many of these 'non-banks' were bank affiliates whose purpose was to lend to real estate firms and effect equity investments. Banks also expanded their equity portfolios, directly, or indirectly through special trust funds (*tokkin* funds etc.). Similar behavior was observed on the part of many agricultural cooperatives.

One may argue that the fact that increased lending to the real estate industry as well as increased equity investments (followed by a deterioration in the quality of such assets when asset prices fell) is not sufficient to show that financial institutions had become more willing to take greater risks since poor *ex post* performance may not reflect *ex ante* risk assessment. But, in the early 1980s many banks reorganized their corporate structure to reduce the discretionary authority of sections which screened and authorized new lending. One may also argue that the so-called life employment system made it difficult for Japanese banks to trim activities even if they saw franchise value declining. The fact is that many banks increased staff in the late 1980s in the midst of a serious shortage of white-collar workers.

In short, while it cannot be totally denied that the macroeconomic policy setting (reviewed briefly below) contributed to some extent to the wide swing of asset prices and the serious situation of banks, it is obvious that the main reason for bank problems was their mismanagement in responding to intensified competition. An important background factor to this mismanagement is likely to have been, in turn, their tacit expectation of assistance from peer banks and the authorities in case of difficulty, which was supported by the fact

Table 3.5 Real estate-related loans in Japan (¥ trillion)

	Outstanding loans and discounts[1] *(end year)*								*Average growth rate*
	1985	*1986*	*1987*	*1988*	*1989*	*1990*	*1991*	*1992*	*1985–92*
Total outstanding loans and discounts	222.8	244.4	265.9	288.2	315.7	333.3	341.3	348.1	6.6
Real estate	17.2	23.5	27.5	31.4	35.9	37.1	39.5	42.2	13.7
	(7.5)[2]	(9.6)	(10.3)	(10.9)	(11.4)	(11.1)	(11.6)	(12.1)	
Non-banks	23.2	29.7	36.9	41.8	47.4	48.7	47.2	47.8	10.9
	(10.4)	(12.2)	(13.9)	(14.5)	(15.0)	(14.6)	(13.8)	(14.0)	

Notes: (1) Loans and discounts of all banks excluding Regional Banks II. (2) Figures in parentheses indicate percentage share of total outstanding balance of loans and discounts.

Source: Bank of Jpana, *Economic Statistics Monthly* (various issues).

that no bank had been allowed to go bankrupt in the previous few decades.[9]

Macroeconomic policy setting

The increase in real estate prices in central Tokyo had already started in the early 1980s, but accelerated sharply around 1986–7 (Table 3.2). The rapid increase gradually spread to the suburbs of Tokyo and to other major cities. The increase in stock prices accelerated virtually hand in hand with the rise in land prices.

Several non-monetary factors are cited as background to the rise in land prices, among others: (i) the increased importance of Tokyo as a major world financial and trade center, and (ii) the favorable tax treatment of investments in land – the effective inheritance tax on real estate was much lower than on other assets; the capital gains tax could be avoided if income from the sale of real estate was reinvested in other real estate.

It is also true that the economic environment and macroeconomic policy contributed to some extent to the increase in asset prices. Monetary ease continued: the official discount rate, which had already been lowered four times in a short period, was lowered again to a historical low of 2.5 percent in February 1987 and remained there until mid-1989.

The economy, which had been in recession due mainly to the deflationary impact of the substantial appreciation of the yen, exhibited signs of recovery around the end of 1986 and then showed brisk growth in 1987 and 1988. However, monetary policy was not changed as prices of goods and services remained stable due to the appreciation of the yen, in stark contrast to the sharp rise in land and stock prices.

While the non-monetary factors and macroeconomic policy settings contributed to the hike in asset prices, the main reason was obviously the aggressive lending behavior of banks. Their massive increase in lending for real estate and stock purposes nurtured the boom in these markets and higher asset prices, which, in turn, enabled further lending to these businesses by increasing the collateral value of assets.

Decline in asset prices

By early 1989, however, it became evident that inflationary pressures were mounting, and monetary policy was tightened in May 1989. The Ministry of Finance, for its part, asked the banks in 1990 to contain

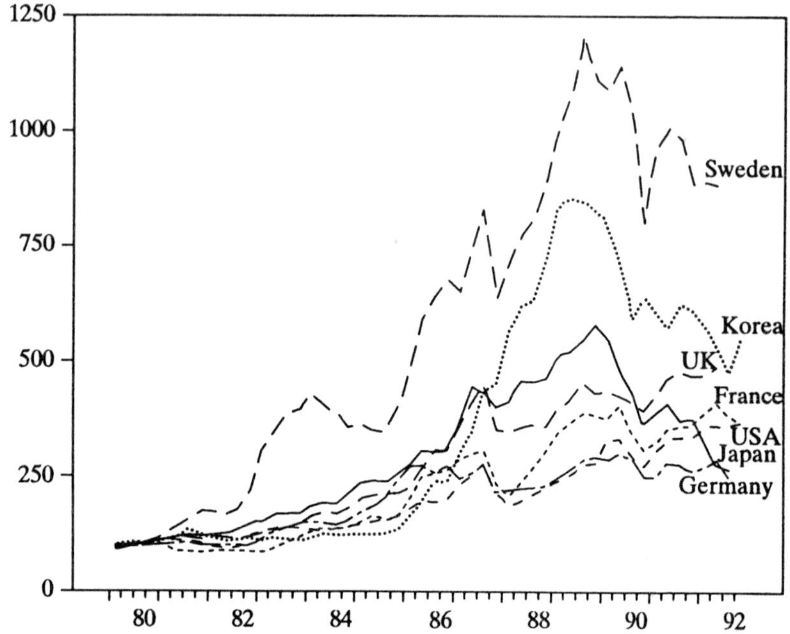

Figure 3.5 Recent stock price developments in major countries (1980 average = 100). (*Source*: IMF, *International Financial Statistics* (various issues))

Table 3.6 Non-performing assets and banks' capital positions in Japan[1]

	Non-performing assets – 6 months or more (¥ billion)		*Total loans outstanding (¥ trillion)*
		Uncovered by collateral or guarantee	
1992 March[2]	7,992.7	2,561.9	398
1992 September	Around 12,300.0	Around 4,000.0	396
1993 March	12,774.6	NA	395

Notes: (1) Based on interviews with city banks, long-term credit banks and trust banks. (2) Balance at period end.
Sources: Ministry of Finance; Bank of Japan.

the growth rate of their real estate-related lending to less than that of total lending. Asset prices continued to rise for a while thereafter, but stopped rising or started to decline around the end of 1989. The Nikkei Stock Average peaked in December 1989 at 38,917 and fell rapidly to record a low of 14,309 in August 1992 (Figure 3.5). The movement of land prices varied considerably from region to region, but clearly changed to a downturn in 1990.

The quality of bank loans deteriorated significantly as a consequence of the fall in land and stock prices: total non-performing assets held by city banks, the bulk of which consisted of loans to real estate and non-bank firms, stood at ¥12.8 trillion at the end March 1993, or 3.2 percent of total outstanding loans, and thus recorded a 60 percent increase in only one year (Table 3.6).

Policy reaction

Banks and financial institutions encountering difficulties have received support from others in the sector, either by merger or substantial financial assistance. An example of the former was the merger of the Toho Sogo Bank, a small regional bank which became insolvent, with the Iyo Bank, a larger and sound bank in the same region; and a typical example of the latter was the assistance provided by banks to Nippon Housing Loan, a non-bank financial firm specializing in mortgages and which held a vast amount of non-performing assets, the failure of which would have caused serious problems for agricultural co-operatives. Another joint effort of the banking sector to overcome current difficulties was the establishment of the Corporative Credit Purchasing Cooperation (CCPC), an institution designed to facilitate the liquidation of the real estate assets of banks.[10]

Though some assistance was provided by the Deposit Insurance Corporation in cases such as the Toho Sogo/Iyo merger, and the CCPC opened the way to some considerable tax relief, explicit financial support from the public sector has so far been kept to a minimum.

United States[11]

Change in the banking environment

The environment surrounding US banks changed considerably in the 1980s, and competition increased both within the sector and also with non-bank financial institutions.[12]

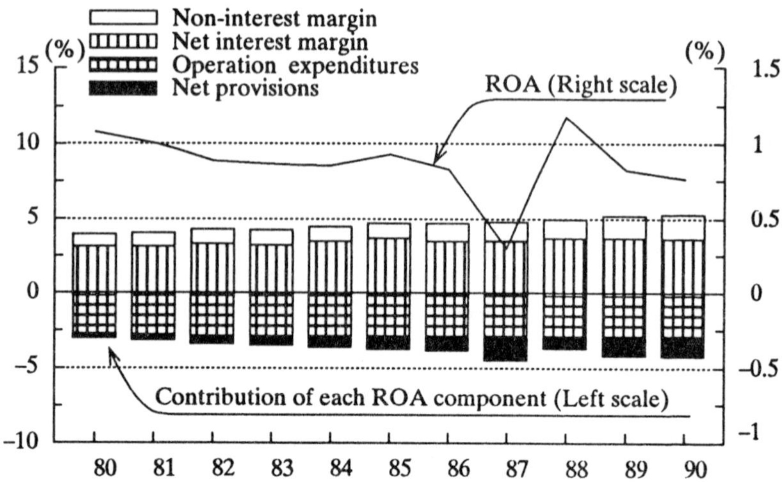

Figure 3.6 ROA of US commercial banks. (*Source*: OECD, *Bank Profitability: Statistical Supplement: Financial Statements of Banks* (various issues))

With regard to deregulation which affected bank liabilities, MMCs and MMDAs were introduced in 1978 and 1982, respectively (Table 3.1). Interest rates on these instruments were set competitively; they also had to compete with MMMFs offered by investment banks. In the case of S&Ls, funding cost also rose due to increased recourse to broker deposits.

On the asset side, the increased use of CP by large companies meant banks lost some of their traditional prime-quality borrowers. Competition was further strengthened by the increased activities of various types of non-bank banks: credit card companies and finance companies owned by large enterprises, for example.

Increase in riskier assets

In spite of these developments which should have caused a decline in bank profitability, the net interest margin of US commercial banks actually remained stable until the late 1980s (Figure 3.6). This was enabled mainly by increased lending to more risky areas. In the early 1980s, large money-center banks increased sovereign loans to 'middle income' debt countries; as problems with these loans became evident in the mid-1980s, they changed their strategy to emphasize

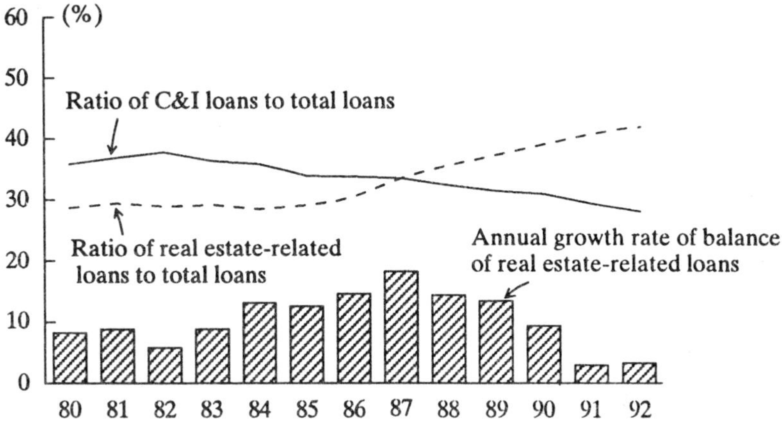

Figure 3.7 Real estate-related* loans (revolving home equity and other real estate-related loans) in the United States. (*Source*: *Federal Reserve Bulletin* (various issues))

lending related to highly leveraged trading (HLT) and real estate-related projects. Although no data is available for HLT-related lending, the share of real estate-related lending to the total lending of US commercial banks rose from 28.7 percent at the end of 1980 to 42.2 percent at the end of 1992 (Figure 3.7).

The composition of S&L assets also changed significantly: the share of their traditional asset, mortgage loans, declined, giving way to riskier assets, in particular lending to non-residential property projects and investments in junk bonds.

There are several reasons why banks and S&Ls responded to the loss in their franchise value by increasing holdings of these riskier assets.[13] The boom in real estate markets towards the mid-1980s made investments in such assets attractive. In the case of S&Ls, regulation on the range of assets they were allowed to hold was relaxed considerably in 1980 and 1982, and thus paved the way for an increase in riskier assets. With regard to HLT, the development of financial techniques such as LBO financing was certainly an important factor. It should also be pointed out that the existence of the Glass–Steagall and McFadden Acts has limited efforts to diversify their scope of business to promising new areas.

However, perhaps the single most important factor behind the mismanagement of banks and S&Ls was moral hazard caused by the

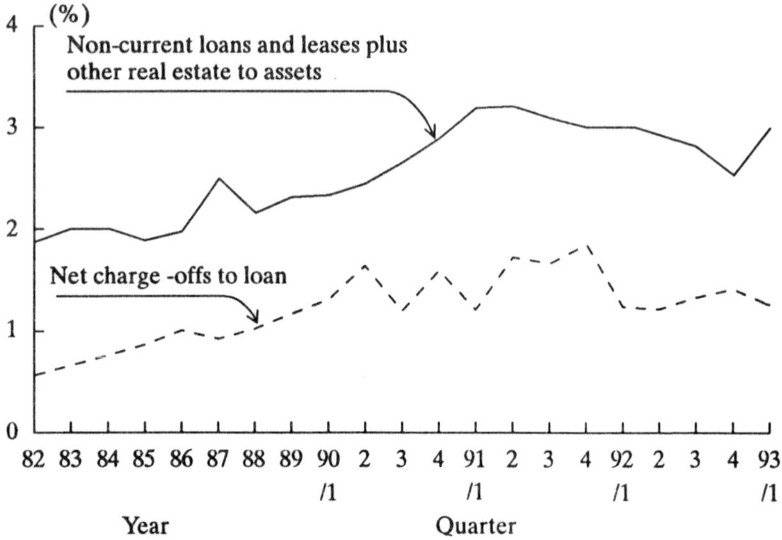

Figure 3.8 Bad loans of US banks. (*Source*: FDIC, *Quarterly Banking Profile* (various issues))

active utilization of deposit insurance schemes, the application of which in many cases was generous, as will be discussed later.

Decline in asset quality

The timing at which the real estate market turned to decline varied considerably from region to region. But, by the late 1980s, real estate prices were tumbling in most parts of the country, reflecting, among other factors: (i) the overhang of commercial real estate as a result of previous heavy investments; (ii) less favorable tax treatment; (iii) decrease in direct investment from abroad; and (iv) the re-regulation of S&L lending in real estate projects.

HLT also came into trouble, and prices of junk bonds dropped sharply. As a reflection, the quality of bank assets deteriorated significantly. The proportion of bad assets, i.e. non-performing loans plus 'other real estate owned' (OREO) to total assets of US commercial banks, which was around 2 percent in the early 1980s, rose throughout the 1980s and reached 2.9 percent at the end of 1990 (Figure 3.8). In particular, the same ratio for real estate-related lending alone was as high as 5.4 percent at the end of 1990. The same tendency was observed among S&Ls on a more serious scale.

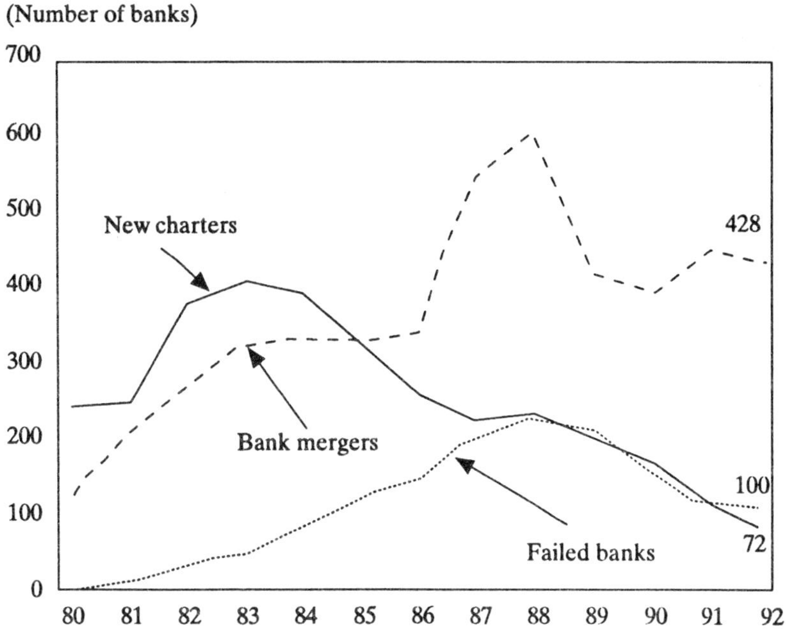

Figure 3.9 Structural changes among FDIC-insured commercial banks, 1980–92. (*Source*: FDIC, *Quarterly Banking Profile* (4th quarter, 1992))

As a result of the deterioration in assets, bank failures increased consistently in the 1980s to reach a peak in 1988 when 221 FDIC insured banks failed. Although the number of failures declined somewhat thereafter, a relatively large bank, The Bank of New England, failed in 1991 (Figure 3.9).

Use of deposit insurance funds and reform

The US case stands out clearly from that in other countries in that many banks and S&Ls were virtually closed in activating deposit insurance systems, either through being liquidated and making direct payoffs (applied mainly to very small banks) or through the provision of financial assistance via their purchase and acquisition by other banks (applied to larger banks). As a result, the balance of deposit insurance funds deteriorated significantly; in fact, in order to prevent deposit insurance funds becoming insolvent, a large amount of public money had to be injected (Figure 3.10).

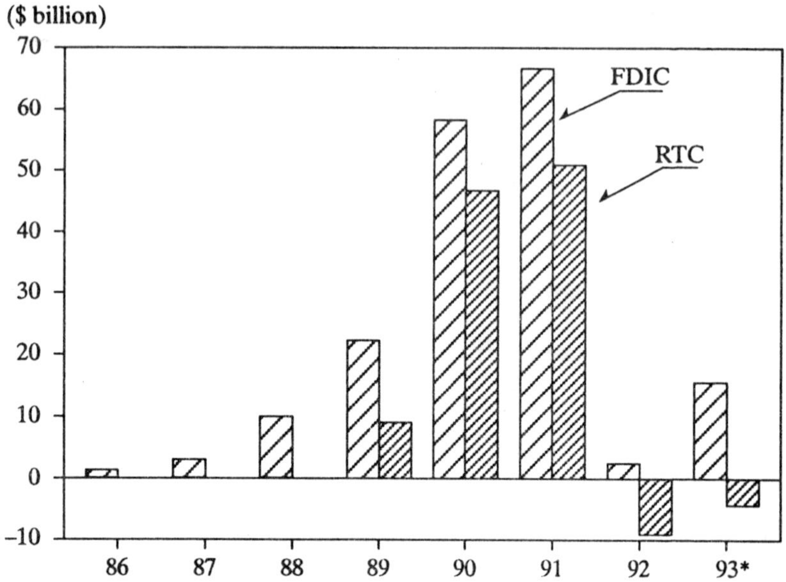

Figure 3.10 FDIC and RTC-related expenditures. *, Estimated. (*Sources*: US Department of the Treasury, *Monthly Treasury Statement* (various issues); US Government, *Economic Report of the President* (various issues))

The fact that a vast amount of taxpayers' money had to be used to keep the financial system afloat triggered major reforms in bank regulation and deposit insurance schemes. The focal measures were the Prompt Corrective Action rule introduced in the FDICIA (Federal Deposit Insurance Company Improvement Act) which came into effect in 1993, under which the level of supervision varies according to the strength of a bank's capital base, and obligatory closure is applied when a bank cannot maintain its capital/asset ratio above a certain level (Table 3.7). With regard to S&Ls, the FIRREA (Financial Institutions Reform, Recovery and Enforcement Act) of 1989 introduced re-regulation with regard to the type of asset they could invest in, and broker deposits were prohibited.

Banks, for their part, have changed their management strategy: lending has become more prudent, and many commercial banks have streamlined their organization and reduced the number of employees. As a combined effect of these efforts and widening lending

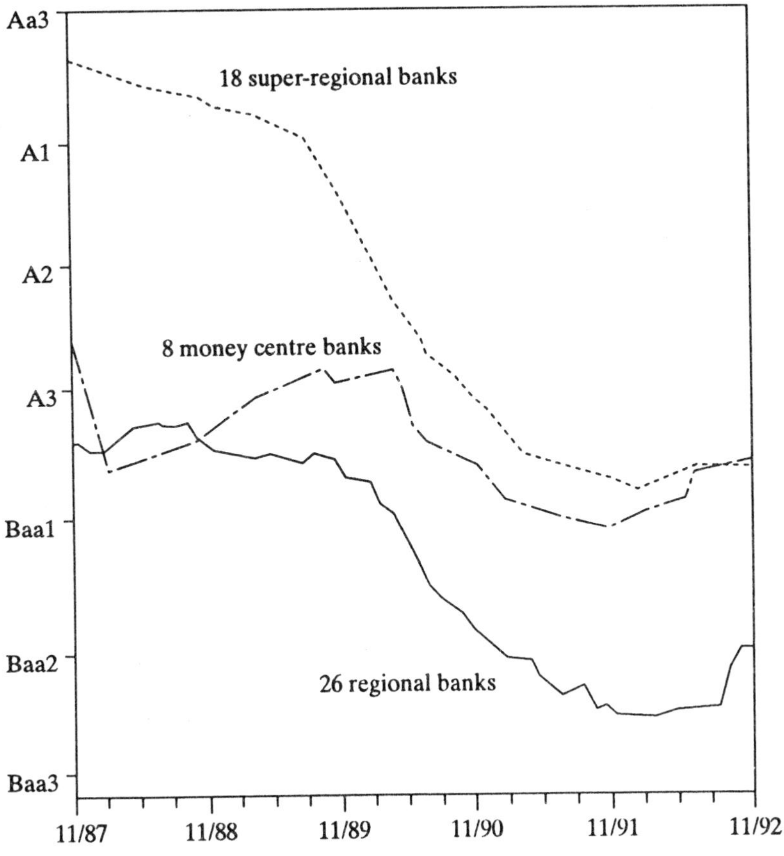

Figure 3.11 Average ratings for major US banks. (*Note*: Ratings are for long-term debt.) *Source*: *Moody's Corporate Credit Report* (various issues), *et al.*

margins due to an accommodative monetary policy, profitability is showing signs of recovery. In addition, banks, the large money center banks in particular, have reinforced their capital base considerably by issuing common stock, preferred stock, and subordinated debt, partly in response to the above-mentioned re-regulation, but also partly due to their changing conception of the importance of capital as a buffer. Upgrading by the rating agencies illustrates that these efforts are highly evaluated by market participants (Figure 3.11).

Table 3.7 Supervisory action *vis-à-vis* depository institutions under provisions of the FDICIA for prompt corrective action

Capital zones	*Capital measures (%)* Total risk-based capital ratio	Tier 1 risk-based capital ratio	Tier 1 leverage ratio	*Mandatory and discretionary actions*
Well capitalized	10 or above &	6 or above &	5 or above	— May not make any capital distribution or pay a management fee to a controlling person that would leave the institution undercapitalized.
Adequately capitalized	8 or above &	4 or above &	4 or above(1)	
Undercapitalized	Under 8 or	Under 4 or	Under 4(2)	— Subject to increased monitoring. — Must submit a capital restoration plan. — Restriction on growth of the institution's total assets. — Prior approval of the appropriate agency is required prior to acquisitions, branching, and new lines of business.
Significantly undercapitalized	Under 6 or	Under 3 or	Under 3	— Must sell enough additional capital. — Interest rates paid on deposits must be restricted to the prevailing rates in the region. — Restriction on asset growth or reduction of total assets may be required. — May be required to hold a new election of its board of directors.

Critically undercapitalized	2 or under[3]	— Must be placed in conservatorship or receivership within 90 days. — Must be prohibited from doing any of the following without the prior approval of the FDIC: • Enter into any material transaction other than in the usual course of business. • Extend credit for any highly leveraged transaction (HLT). • Make any material change in its accounting methods. • Pay excessive compensation or bonuses.

Notes: (1) Above 3% for composite 1-rated banks and savings associations, subject to appropriate federal banking agency guidelines. (2) Under 3% for composite 1-rated banks and savings associations, subject to appropriate federal banking agency guidelines. (3) Ratio of tangible equity to total assets.
Source: Federal Reserve Board, Press Release (18 September 1992).

Table 3.8 Real estate-related loans in the United Kingdom

	Outstanding amount at year-end								Average growth rate
	1985	*1986*	*1987*	*1988*	*1989*	*1990*	*1991*	*1992/3Q*	*1985–92*
Total lending balance[1]	264.8	323.3	382.9	473.7	587.5	650.5	668.7	688.9	14.6
[2]	(13.7)	(22.1)	(18.4)	(23.7)	(24.0)	(10.7)	(2.8)	(3.0)	
House purchase	117.9	142.5	167.5	200.6	231.7	262.4	288.0	304.6	14.5
	(19.0)	(20.9)	(17.5)	(19.8)	(15.5)	(13.2)	(9.8)	(5.8)	
Building societies[3]	97.2	116.6	131.6	155.3	152.5	176.7	197.6	209.2	11.6
	<82.4>	<81.8>	<78.6>	<77.4>	<65.8>	<67.3>	<68.6>	<68.7>	
Banks	20.7	25.9	35.9	45.3	79.2	85.7	90.4	95.4	24.4
	<17.6>	<18.2>	<21.4>	<22.6>	<34.2>	<32.7>	<31.4>	<31.3>	

Notes: (1) Bank lending to private sector (excluding overseas sector) + building society lending. (2) Growth rate per year in parentheses. (3) Share of house purchases in angular brackets.
Source: Central Statistical Office, *Financial Statistics* (various issues).

United Kingdom

Deregulation in the scope of activities

In the United Kingdom too, the deregulation of deposit rates made progress toward the end of the 1970s, and a great variety of new financial instruments, in particular interest-bearing deposits with facilities, were introduced in the 1980s.[14] However, the impact on banks' funding costs was relatively limited.

Perhaps more important was increased competition on the lending side. The abolition of the 'corset' in 1980 lowered the marginal cost of lending for clearing banks. A major target area they chose to take advantage of with this new competitive edge was real estate lending. Then, the Building Society Act of 1986 enabled building societies to offer checking accounts and to engage widely in real estate intermediation – the building societies responded to this deregulation by increasing their activity in the real estate loan market (Table 3.8).

These strategies on the part of clearing banks and building societies naturally resulted in a relaxation of lending conditions and the rapid growth of real estate lending, especially in the second half of the 1980s, which went in tandem with the boom in real estate investment. The share of real estate-related loans (construction and house purchase) to total domestic loans, which was 15 percent at the end of 1985, rose to 23 percent at the end of 1990.

Decline in the real estate market

The UK economy expanded continuously until 1988.[13] However, as overheating and a pick-up in inflation became evident, partly due to prolonged monetary ease in response to the stock market crash of October 1987, the UK authorities tightened monetary policy in mid-1988. The subsequent rise in interest rates caused a sharp decline in new mortgage loans, which, in turn, triggered a fall in real estate prices, particularly in South East England.[16]

Rising mortgage rates and decline in property prices caused great difficulties for borrowers; for banks and building societies, it meant increased bad assets such as non-performing loans and illiquid real estate. Thus, clearing banks and building societies had to increase considerably provisions for bad debts in 1989 and 1990 (Figure 3.12) – a number of these financial institutions recorded sizable overall losses. However, the problems have been dealt with by the banks concerned, and bank closure was limited only to a very special case – the BCCI.

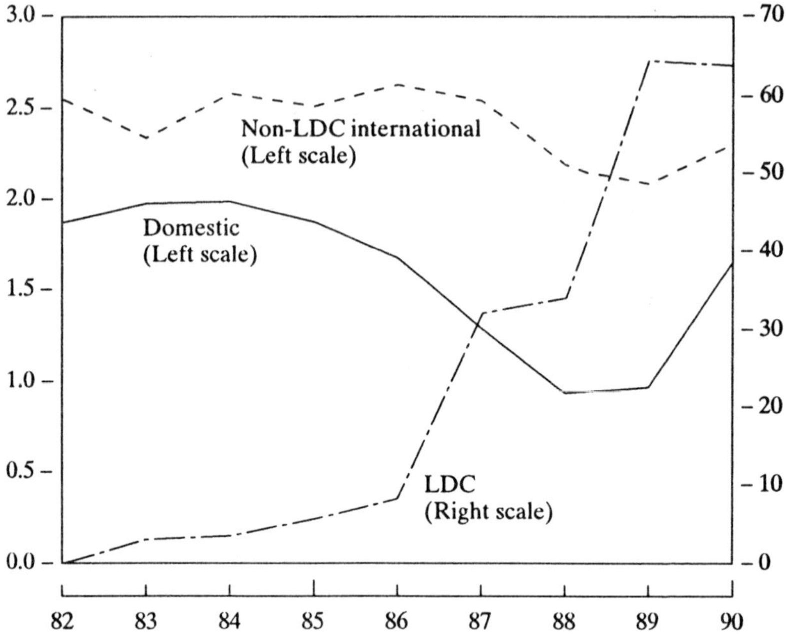

Figure 3.12 Bad debt provisions outstanding as a percentage of lending in the United Kingdom. (*Source*: Colwell (1991))

The Nordic Countries[17]

Deregulation of lending activities

The gradual deregulation of deposit rates, which started in the 1980s, tended to raise funding costs. However, a more important change was the increase in lending competition, triggered by the abolition of quantitative controls on bank lending.

Norway started to lift tight controls on the amount of domestic credit in 1984 and, by 1988, all quantitative controls had been removed. In Sweden, quantitative control by the Riksbank on bank lending had been totally abolished by 1985.

As these liberalization measures coincided with economic expansion and a booming real estate market, competition among banks in real estate lending increased considerably. In Sweden, competition was further intensified by finance companies. Finance companies had expanded their activities in the 1980s, when they were used to circumvent the quantitative controls on bank lending; but as these controls were lifted, they concentrated on financing the high-risk real-asset investments of the household sector.

The banks thus considerably increased their real estate-related exposure, both directly by their own lending to the real estate industry and also indirectly through lending to finance companies. Many observers point out that expectations of generous official support, actually obtained as will be explained later, was an important background factor behind this careless management on the part of financial institutions – the moral hazard problem. Needless to say, the injection of money into real estate further fed expansion of the sector. That interest payments were tax deductible in the Nordic countries, in combination with high income tax rates, gave another impetus to the household sector for financing investments in real estate and stocks.

Real estate and stock markets collapsed in the late 1980s as monetary policy was tightened to cope with the increase in inflationary pressure and the economies went into recession. In Norway, the softness of the crude oil market added to the decline in business activity.

The decline in real estate prices caused significant losses on bank loans to real estate developers and an increase in non-performing mortgage loans to households. This is clearly illustrated in the sharp increases in the percentage of loss provisions to total bank loans (Figure 3.13). Many banks had to report sizable losses as a consequence of this deterioration in the quality of their assets.

Official bailout

The outstanding feature of banking turmoil in the Nordic countries was the substantial, in many cases generous, involvement of the official sector.

In Norway, virtually all major banks are reporting losses. To keep them afloat, financial assistance was provided during 1988–90 from deposit insurance funds. But as these funds themselves became short of capital, the government founded (March 1991) the Norwegian Bank Guarantee Fund (NBGF) to assist in the bail-out operations of such deposit insurance funds. In December 1991, NBGF funds were increased; in addition, a reduction in interest payments due on borrowing from the central bank was extended.

In Sweden, as most of the larger banks ran losses, the government provided direct support in various forms: it nationalized one of the largest commercial banks, and bailed out another large bank by providing government guarantee; some large savings banks were

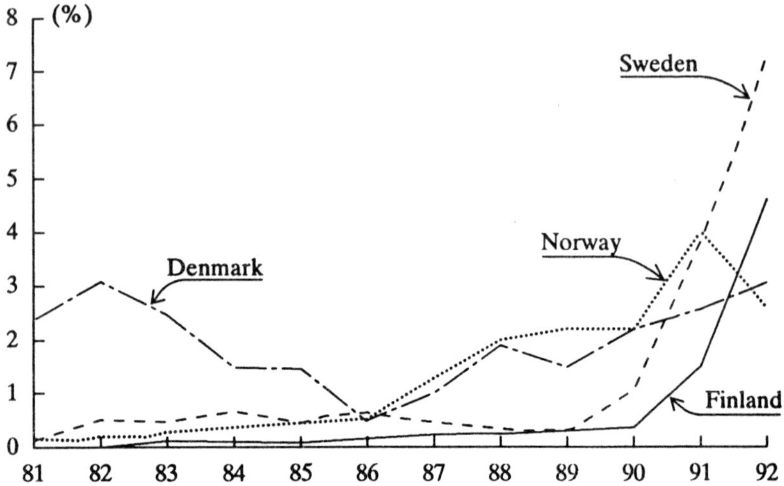

Figure 3.13 Loss provisions as a percentage of loans in Nordic countries. (*Source*: Berg (1993))

granted government guarantee and financial assistance. An important factor which is pointed out as a background to this government support was the concern that banks' problems may spur speculative capital outflow and further weaken the Swedish Krona.

Oceania and Asia

Banks in Australia and New Zealand[18] experienced quite serious problems in the late 1980s. Problems were not as serious in most Asian countries outside Japan, partly because deregulation and financial innovation had not made as much progress as in Europe and North America. However, problems were not absent either, particularly in Indonesia, Korea, and Malaysia. We will briefly review the cases of Australia and Indonesia.

Australia[19]

In Australia, banks responded to the increased competition triggered by deregulation and resultant penetration of foreign banks by expanding their balance sheets, especially during the economic expansionary period and real estate boom after monetary ease in 1987.

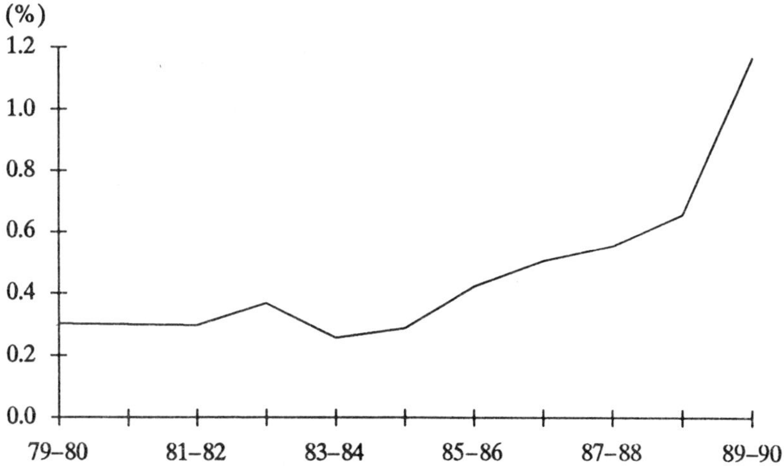

Figure 3.14 Charge to profit for bad and doubtful debts of major Australian banks (percentage of loans and acceptances.) (*Source*: Grenville (1991))

The quality of bank assets, which had been quite stable in the first half of the 1980s, gradually deteriorated from the mid-1980s, as can be seen from Figure 3.14. The problems came quickly to the fore as the economy went into recession in 1989 and the real estate market collapsed: banks' non-performing loans nearly doubled between June 1990 and June 1991 (Figure 3.15). Such deterioration in asset quality had a severe impact on profitability. Although there has been no formal bank failure, a few banks had to be absorbed by healthier banks; a state bank had to be bailed out by financial assistance from a state government through merger with a federally-owned bank.

Indonesia

Indonesia deregulated its banking system in 1983 and 1988, which included the complete abolition of the regulation of deposit rates and quantitative controls on bank lending, and effected liberalization with respect to opening new banks and branches. As a result of these measures, the number of banks and branches expanded remarkably. These measures have succeeded in fostering competition in, and increasing the efficiency of, the banking industry, and in mobilizing domestic savings the country needed for growth. However, many newly established banks (which had only a weak customer base)

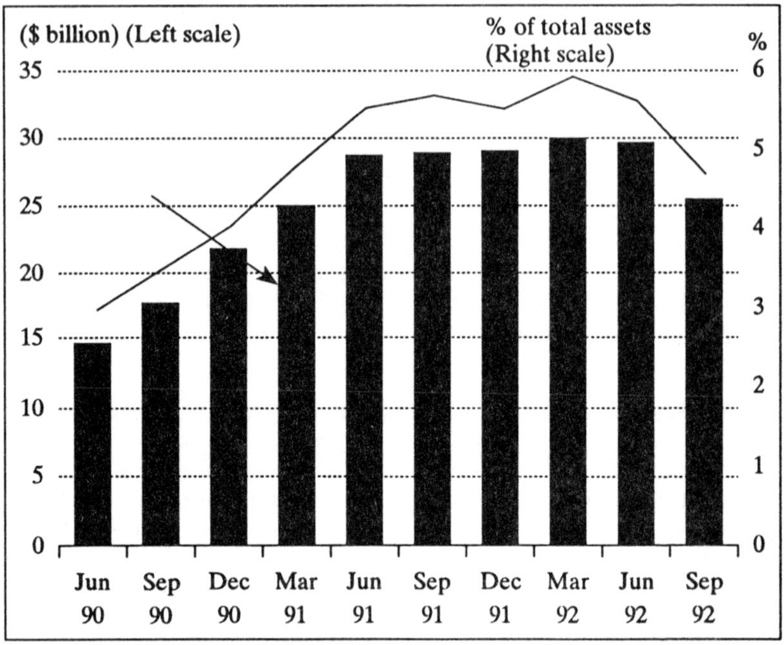

Figure 3.15 Total non-performing loans of Australian banks. (*Source*: Reserve Bank of Australia (1993))

tried to expand by concentrating their lending to the real estate area, such as office buildings and housing for foreigners. These businesses boomed mainly due to increased demand caused by the growth of inward direct investment. In some cases, banks not only lent to these projects but even purchased real estate themselves.

However, as the Bank of Indonesia tightened monetary policy in 1990 and real estate prices turned downward, many banks came under severe pressure. The most drastic case was the liquidation in 1992 of Bank Summa, a medium-sized bank owned by a rich family. The fact that a considerable part of that bank's deposits were lost has impaired confidence in the banking system as a whole.

IV PROSPECTIVE CONFIGURATION OF BANK REGULATION AND PUBLIC SAFETY NETS

The purpose of this last section is to consider, based on discussions in Sections II and III, what an ideal regulatory system should look like to prevent a repeat of the violent financial disturbances. It should be emphasized that our concern is to explore a regulatory system logically tenable from a long-term perspective. Our focus is not on crisis management or short-run prescriptions. The outline is as follows. We first summarize the lessons to be drawn from recent worldwide bank disruption. The moral hazard aspect is stressed. Then, we develop a conceptual framework as a yardstick by which to measure the degree of bank protection embodied in the existing banking system. We then discuss what the banking system should be in the long run, and what should be done in the interim. Finally, the role of central banks is explored.

Mismanagement

It has been argued in Sections II and III that the financial fragility phenomenon observed in many industrialized countries in the late 1980s and in the early 1990s, while possibly exacerbated by misguided macroeconomic policy and cyclical swings in economic activity, was essentially due to banking mismanagement. That is, increased competition exerted downward pressure on banks' profit margins, driving banks to run after assets with higher returns, presumably to maintain profit margins. Assets with higher returns, other things remaining equal, ordinarily come with greater risks. Banks thus became deeply involved in high-return, high-risk loans for real estate and equity investments, many of which subsequently proved to be problem loans. With a huge amount of bad loans, many banks now find themselves forced into intensive restructuring and balance sheet adjustment. Some banks that became insolvent have been merged or purchased by healthier institutions, occasionally with government or central bank assistance. Put differently, when faced with the overbanking situation generated by heightened competition, banks should have shrunk, as any economic textbook tells them to. But this they did not; in fact, they tried to grow out of their difficulties. They ran afoul of basic economic rules; this is nothing but mismanagement.

The question is, what caused banking mismanagement worldwide? Many complex factors were involved, and to answer the question in a logically straightforward manner is hard. It all took place in a strange atmosphere often epitomized as the bubble build-up. Drawing upon the recent experience of the industrialized countries, in Section II we pointed out three factors: (i) the growth inertia factor; (ii) the bandwagon effect; and (iii) the moral hazard problem.

The growth inertia factor is now behind us and is of little importance when considering the future. Of the remaining two factors, we consider the moral hazard problem to be more essential than the bandwagon effect, because the latter amplifies the problem, but cannot trigger it. It needs something else to trigger the process, which is what moral hazard did. These are the lessons from the recent bank disruptions experienced worldwide.

Outlook for the Banking Environment

Bank disruption is likely to be with us for a while longer. The streamlining of the banking industry, consisting of both restructuring efforts by individual banks and industrywide consolidation through mergers and acquisitions, must continue. In fact, rescue plans of various kinds have been disclosed and implemented, with due regard being paid to individual circumstances. Solution to specific individual cases often requires pragmatic wisdom and had better be left to those directly involved.

The question we would like to address here is one from a longer perspective, i.e.: 'What should be done after the dust has settled?' Put more specifically, when asset deflation is behind us and the economy has returned to normal, what actions or measures should be taken to prevent banks from repeating mismanagement? To know this, we must first verify whether the increased competitive forces, which drove banks into mismanagement in the 1980s, will still exist. In what follows, we shall briefly examine the outlook for these forces.

Deregulation of interest rate controls

Interest rate regulation had virtually disappeared in the major industrialized countries by the end of 1990. The increase in funding costs experienced by banks in the late 1980s will disappear.[20] In a fully deregulated market, however, pricing competition is likely to be intense for banks, both among themselves and with other financial institutions and non-banks. Pressure to increase costs on the liability side and to reduce earnings on the asset side will remain enormous.

External competition

Attempts by foreign banks to make inroads into the domestic markets of host countries became popular in the late 1980s. They, however, have proven to be not as profitable as originally expected. The problem with this approach to develop loan business with local firms lies primarily in the fact that access by foreign banks to stable and inexpensive funding sources on a retail-deposit basis is quite limited. Moreover, exhaustion from involvement in domestic financial turmoil has made major international banks cautious about further expansion abroad. As part of cost-cutting efforts, some banks have even reduced international operations. Thus, external pressure in terms of competition may have diminished.

This may, however, be a temporary phenomenon. Many major international banks keep trying to acquire existing local banks with a solid retail base in target countries or to conclude cross-shareholding arrangements with them, thereby still following their retail-oriented strategy.

Market desegregation or decompartmentalization

The breakdown of barriers between banking and other financial institutions (securities houses and insurance companies, in particular) had become notable by the end of the last decade. The trend for market desegregation or decompartmentalization, reflecting the general desire of financial institutions to expand their range of activities (consequent upon the increase in competition from non-banks and the removal of legal impediments), will probably continue or even intensify during the current decade.

Japan formally took action in April 1992 to launch a revised legal system, whereby commercial banks, long-term credit banks, trust banks, and securities houses are allowed mutual entry into one another's business area via separate subsidiaries under one holding.[21] Because of the firewall clauses and other conditions attached, it does not necessarily follow that market segregation, particularly the separation between banking and securities, will disappear. Nevertheless, the move will definitely promote and enhance bank activities relating to securities and trusts. In the United States, while the Glass–Steagall Act will formally stay in place, market segregation between the banking and securities sectors has been relaxed by a series of permissive interpretations of the law by the Federal Reserve Board, allowing bank affiliates to underwrite and deal in a fairly wide range of securities, including municipal bonds, CP, mortgage-related securities, consumer receivables-related securities, etc. The Supreme Court's decision in February 1990 in favor of the Federal Reserve Board's approval of bank securitization activities will accelerate market desegregation further.

Progress of information technology
Progress in electronic information technology will continue to intensify competition among banks, and between banks and other financial institutions and non-banks. Future developments in information technology, such as electronic data interchange (EDI), may in fact pose a considerable threat to the competitiveness of banks. Specifically, computer firms, software firms, value-added networkers (VAN), capable of setting up advanced communication networks, have shown great interest in venturing into areas hitherto considered the preserve of banks – like inter-company payment channels, management of receivables and payables, order routing and matching, trading of money market instruments, foreign exchange broking, clearing, settlement, book entry systems, etc.

The four factors just considered are naturally not exhaustive, but are sufficient to suggest that banking will remain exposed to competitive pressure as strong as or even stronger than ever. What then ought to be done to discourage banks from mismanagement?

Most of the deregulatory efforts undertaken in the late 1970s and 1980s in the major industrialized countries were considered to be wholly justifiable on welfare economic grounds. In retrospect, however, they may have tipped the balance between the moral hazard risk inherently attached to any public safety net and the set of obligations that the beneficiaries should obey. For example, any private insurance company would attempt to regulate those they insure in order to reduce the insured's risk. Analogously, any government or central bank should regulate (or supervise) the banks covered by public safety nets, thereby mitigating the moral hazard problem. The removal of regulations on banks in the 1970s and 1980s may have had the effect of eliminating the deterrent that held moral hazard in check for the preceding 30 to 40 years. It follows then that in order to avoid a recurrence of mismanagement based largely on moral hazard, some form of re-regulation is inevitable. Is this reasoning correct?

In a progressive capitalist society, competition is what makes every industry tick. We can easily cite many instances of an industry, which used to enjoy a huge rent or excess profit under little competition, suddenly finding itself exposed to increased competition and reduced rent. Banks are no exception; they may have simply reached the phase where banking needs have come to be partially provided by non-banks. Economic efficiency for society as a whole may not have diminished; it may, in fact, have increased. Re-regulation then is not desirable.

Moreover, to attempt to return financial systems to what they were in previous decades is equivalent to trying to return the exchange rate system to the Bretton Woods regime; it is infeasible. Governments did not deregulate willingly or voluntarily; they were forced into deregulation. The widespread dispersion of financial innovation, aided by the progress of computer information technology, made it impossible for banks and their supervisors to maintain the regulatory environment that protected the domestic banking industry from competition with securities houses, non-banks, foreign banks, etc. It was banks themselves that, faced with the emergence of MMMFs, cried out for the removal of ceilings on deposit rates. To re-regulate with direct controls similar to the ones formerly in place is, therefore, out of the question.

We consider it safe to assume that banks will continue to play a substantial role in society for the next decade or two at least. What kind of a regulatory response is then relevant to keep moral hazard in check, while maintaining safety nets, thereby preventing a recurrence of a banking crisis? To this question we now turn.

Toward an Optimal Configuration of Bank Regulation and Safety Nets

In what follows, we will first develop a conceptual framework, consisting of three ideal types of banking regimes. Comparing these with the existing banking system helps us to understand where we stand and where we should go. Of course, this sort of analysis carries with it a limitation, as most comparative analysis does. It ignores not only economic costs to be incurred but also numerous political and institutional difficulties that will arise in the transition from one regime to another. Nevertheless, we consider it vitally important to know logically whether one should stay where one is, with various practical safeguards added, or whether one should aim for another regime as an ultimate target.

First, let us consider what makes the banking industry so special and distinct from other industries. Banks provide both payment and intermediation services. The provision of payment services by a group of many individual banks constitutes a payment system, which is a vast and delicately intertwined network, operated with the aid of advanced computer technology. Even default by a single bank on a payment obligation in the long chain of clearing and settlement could wreak havoc with the entire system. The essence of bank intermediation, on the other hand, primarily lies in purchasing illiquid assets with liquid liabilities.[22]

Thus, banking centers on risk management. Whether or not banks are so unstable as to require special public policy concern is, however, another matter. Many scholars have tried to establish theoretically that banks are special, using the market failure argument that focuses on the cost of monitoring information, the huge external costs of bank failure, etc. We do not consider the matter determined conclusively yet. It may not be possible to determine whether banks are special or not on purely a priori grounds. The importance of banks in a society appears to depend largely upon various factors, including socio-economic structure, history, political system, etc. After all, it is society which must determine whether banks are special or not, with due regard to both economic efficiency and reality.[23] Depending upon how important or special society considers banks are, we can conceive of the following three regimes:

Regime I (the laissez-faire, no public safety-net regime)[24]
If the banking sector is considered to be not so different from any other industry, then the maintenance-of-the-financial-stability argument loses much of its meaning. Market forces would determine the appropriate structure and activities for banks, which would be free to pursue activities that management believes to be profit-maximizing. If a bank failed, it would simply exit from the market. If customers wanted deposits insured, then private insurance companies would accommodate them.[25] There would be no need for public safety nets such as prudential regulation and supervision, deposit insurance, and lender of last resort.

So much for Regime I. Next, let us consider the case where society has determined that banks are special. Wherever banks are considered special and a public safety net of some kind is introduced to bail out banks or to protect depositors from bank failure, there arises a need for bank regulation to avoid moral hazard. For, when a bank recognizes that the government or central bank would unconditionally bail it out in the event of a crisis, there would be nothing preventing it from offering a premium on deposits and using funds thus collected to purchase riskier but more profitable assets. As private insurers regulate those they insure, governments or central banks, when involved in risk bearing or liquidity support, should regulate the beneficiaries. The view that a public safety net creates a need for bank regulation and supervison seems widely accepted among scholars (Flannery, 1982, 1993).

Of those who consider banks to be special, there are two kinds depending upon whether one views that their special nature derives from (i) the provision of payment services only, or (ii) the synergetic provision of payment services and intermediation. The former view considers payment services to be special and, therefore, to be insulated for special protection.[26] We shall call it Regime II. The latter represents a more orthodox, traditional view of banking. It emphasizes the economies of scope aspect and maintains that the industry would become too inefficient if payment services and the intermediation function were separated. It considers a bank in its entirety to be special and, therefore, to be protected. We shall call it Regime III. A more precise elaboration of the two regimes is in order.

Regime II (the partial public safety net regime)

This regime starts by bifurcating bank deposits into transaction account and investment account balances. While the weight of banks in total lending has been declining in recent decades, their role in clearing and settlement has become increasingly more important.[27] As mentioned earlier in this section, with the advance of telecommunications and data-processing technology, national and international payment systems have developed into a closely interwoven network of each individual bank's transaction balances. The recent trend is toward the belief that payment systems are the life-blood of the national or international economy and that their security is of greater value to society than to an individual bank, thus meriting protection by a public safety net. The government or central bank should stand ready to assist if a bank defaults on its payment obligations, provided that transaction account funds be invested only in short-term government bills or equally safe securities. Put differently, banks would have to collateralize their publicly protected deposits with fail-safe investments. Lending or investment activities by banks must be funded with investment account balances uncovered by any public safety net.[28]

The idea of Regime II is to bring only bank payment services under the public policy umbrella, with all other activities relating to the intermediation function being taken care of by the market mechanism, thereby minimizing the moral hazard risk. Some caveats are in order. In some economies, there may not be enough short-term government paper to back the protected transaction accounts. Moreover, as long as interest rate control on transaction deposits is binding, there may exist an incentive to minimize the holding of these deposits and to transfer funds from investment accounts only shortly before the money is needed for settlement. A failure in the transfer of funds could have an adverse effect on the smooth functioning of the payment system.

Regime II is not as far-fetched as it may sound. Money market funds with checking account privileges that invest in T-bills or other short-term government notes are now extensively provided by securities houses.

Regime III (the complete public safety net regime)

This regime regards both payment services and intermediation as synergetically constituting the special nature of banks.[29] Practitioners, including central bankers, tend to have sympathy with this view. Some scholars have applied the asymmetric information hypothesis in an attempt to show the importance of intermediation (e.g., Diamond, 1984).

In contrast to Regime II, this regime does not attempt the bifurcation of bank deposits; instead, it brings all kinds of deposits under the umbrella of public protection, irrespective of whether they are on transaction account or investment account. In this regime, bank bankruptcies would not, in principle, be allowed.

To avoid moral hazard inherent in this regime, banks must be required to comply with a considerably more comprehensive and probably harsher set of regulations and prudential measures. An illustrative example may be a combination of the following:

(i) Capital adequacy standards
- Capital measurements and standards are based on a market value framework for assets, liabilities, and off-balance sheet items.
- Capital ratios must be set at a level high enough to cover interest risk as well as credit risk, and, therefore, will probably be higher than is currently required, say, under the Basle Accord.

(ii) Premiums on deposit insurance
- Basically, all deposits are to be insured. This requires banks to pay premiums on all deposits. This is because, when rescuing a small bank, the least expensive way often entails

that bank's being taken over by another healthier bank, in the process of which all liabilities, both insured or uninsured, are protected. Moreover, large banks in trouble are more often than not allowed to be bailed out, based on the 'too large to fail' doctrine or whatever, and in the bail-out process all liabilities are equally protected. In other words, the distinction between insured and uninsured is hard to enforce in practice.
- Premiums must be determined actuarially, based on risk. This implies that premiums can be different from bank to bank.

(iii) Regulation of interest rates on deposits
- Interest rates on insured deposits will be restricted, say, to T-bill rates. In principle, since all deposits, large or small, are to be insured in this regime, all interest rates on deposits will be regulated.

(iv) Monitoring of bank management, loan, and investment policies
- Regular and frequent on- and off-sight inspection of balance sheets and management must be conducted by bank supervisors.
- Monitoring must be accompanied by the right to seize collateral, if the assets seem likely to dip below a certain value.

Any other requirement that is more effective and inexpensive can be added to the list. In addition to these, entry into banking as well as exit out of it are severely restricted.

Now that we have developed a conceptual framework, let us see which of the three regimes fits the actual world the closest. We observe that many industrialized countries are equipped with some kind of a safety net for banks and an accompanying set of regulations and supervisions. Moreover, in most cases of banks failures, both insured and non-insured deposits were protected *ex post*. Thus, obviously Regime III (the complete public safety net regime) comes closer to the actual picture than the other two alternative regimes. We may roughly describe the current regulatory system as one that used to be more similar to Regime III, but which has started diverging from it in recent years.[30] The question is: should we allow the actual system to move toward something similar to Regime III, with a regulatory system sufficiently reinforced to prevent moral hazard? Or, should we envisage Regime II or even Regime I as an ultimate target system?

Recent experience in many industrialized countries indicates that the regulatory system, as envisioned in Regime III, may have only a limited possibility to be a model for the future course of bank regulation. The set of regulations required includes those that are no longer possible of implementation. First, re-regulation of interest rates on deposits will be hard for banks to comply with, both politically and in view of the circumstances in which interest rates were deregulated.[31] Also, to assess each bank's risk is a formidable task for the government. Even if risk assessment is effected, the government might find it politically difficult to reflect it in premiums; uniform treatment is a basic public policy rule.[32] In addition, clerical costs for complying with various requirements – often referred to as 'regulatory burden' – may surge considerably.

The second difficulty with it is that it assumes that bank supervisors can monitor bank management and investment policies well, at least better than depositors. Are regulators and supervisors that competent? We have evidence that bank supervisors have just failed to persuade bank managers from making risky investments. Increasing the number of supervisors (ignoring the costs incurred) may eventually overwhelm the argument that 'anything the government can do, the private sector can do equally well or better'. But then it must be well justified by the analysis of costs and benefits.

Third, with regard to capital requirements and deposit insurance premiums, it is very difficult for regulators to determine appropriate levels.[33] And, even if an optimal level is somehow calculated, there is no logical guarantee that it will be politically feasible. As soon as the government announced a program or scheme to move the system toward certain target levels, all kinds of politically-motivated lobbying activities against it would be seen. This is probably the most fundamental difficulty with the total public safety net regime. One has only to remember the recent episodes of various pressures being applied to regulators an supervisors, using the credit crunch type of argument to make more loans available.[34]

One cannot thus be very optimistic about moving toward a Regime III-like system. In countries where a set of regulations and prudential measures sufficiently comprehensive to deter moral hazard can be installed, a Regime III-like system remains an available option. Some European countries and possibly Japan might prefer to stay in this regime. In countries where the situation is otherwise, care must be taken to strike a balance between re-regulation and more reliance on market discipline. The United States may be an example of a country that has taken a step forward in this direction. Experience seems to suggest that, in the banking industry as well as elsewhere,[35] one may think of tilting toward relying more on market discipline and less on regulation.

No matter how long it might take to attain, any system should be designed to aim for something logically tenable. From this perspective, where should the banking system go from here? In view of the increased importance and complexity of payment systems, bank provision of such services is likely to be an area that merits protection by a public safety net. Then, an optimal configuration of bank regulation and public safety nets may be something similar to Regime II. In this regard, we must emphasize that payment systems are subject to constant change and that we must constantly monitor developments in information technology and network theory. Technological progress may enable non-banks (computer makers, software houses, value-added networkers) to offer competitive clearing and settlement services, currently considered the exclusive preserve of banks.

We may also note that Regime II does not have any device to protect small savers with investment account balances. With richer investment menus, including short- to medium-term government notes, now available for small savers, we consider it fairly safe to assume that small-saver protection is not as necessary as it used to be. There may, however, arise a situation, where a Regime II-like system is introduced, with investment markets for small savers remaining very limited. In cases like this, some protection for them may have to be incorporated.

What care should be taken in the interim until an ultimate target regime (either a Regime III-like or Regime II-like system) is attained? There exists at present an overbanking situation, with many banks remaining exhausted. While the recent favorable interest rate environment has allowed them some respite, the normal yield curve relationship that now prevails cannot be expected to last forever. As long as there remains overbanking, we cannot risk experimenting with dramatic change. Particularly when the long-term target is a Regime II-like system, we are well advised to adopt a moderate, pragmatic approach in the transitory phase.

As we argued earlier in this section, competition for banks will probably continue to intensify, and the overbanking situation will persist. Thus, the regulatory system must be vigilant enough not to allow banks to seek high-return, high-risk assets any more. Bank supervisors must see to it that they will never again try to grow their way out of difficulty. To restrain effectively any undue growth in risky assets, various prudential measures, including capital adequacy ratios, may have to be intensified and made more comprehensive than hitherto. Re-regulation, wherever feasible and not inimical to the competitiveness of banks, must be implemented in order to mitigate moral hazard.

On the other hand, deregulatory efforts must be continued. The recent squeeze on banks' profit margins, which we have assumed to be a reflection of increased competition, may have been partly due to various restrictions on bank activities. To the extent that this is true, the proper response is not the shrinkage of banks, but the removal of restrictions. What occurs to mind are the restrictions in the United States and Japan preventing commercial banks from engaging in investment banking. As mentioned earlier, Japan has just allowed commercial banks and securities houses limited entry into each other's markets, with many of the restrictions remaining in place. The same can be said of the US system. Much more remains to be done in this area. Regulating investment banking may be utterly incompatible with deregulating commercial banking.

Thirdly, the correction of overbanking must proceed in an orderly fashion. This involves depositor protection and bank exit problem rules schemes. To avoid moral hazard, risk-based premiums, ceilings on deposits to be protected, early closure, etc. could be introduced. In this regard, the FDICIA of the United States may be a model example; it merits close scrutiny by other countries. By all means, the degree of generosity in protection schemes must be phased down.

The Dual Responsibility of a Central Bank

In point of fact, central banks play a vital role in maintaining financial stability. Historically, many central banks, *inter alia* the US Federal Reserve System, were founded primarily to cope with bank disruption (Meulendyke, 1989). This role of the central bank represents its function as lender of last resort. More recently, on the other hand, central banks have come to play a major role, via monetary control, in macroeconomic management – price stability, in particular. This role is now widely considered the central bank's monetary policy proper. In brief, central banks are responsible, either *de jure* or *de facto* or both, for maintaining: (i) monetary stability and (ii) financial stability. In what follows, we discuss how this dual responsibility would be met in each of the above three regimes.

In actual practice, central banks are called upon to intervene as lender of last resort in all kinds of diverse ways imaginable. For simplicity, therefore, we group them into two prototype cases, which we hope capture the essential features of occasions when the central bank is called upon to intervene:

(i) when a bank is likely to default on settlement obligations, which in turn could generate a systemic crisis; and
(ii) when a bank's failure is likely to spread system-wide through contagious runs, causing numerous other solvent banks to fail.

We will refer to case (i) as *settlement risk* and case (ii) as *contagion risk*.

Settlement risk is inherent in payment systems; nowadays it is aggravated by massive intra-day credit exposure. The central bank is closely and constantly involved in bank clearing and settlement and is naturally concerned with the safety and soundness of the payment system.[36] For example, when the Bank of New York became illiquid back in 1986 due to computer trouble, the New York Fed stepped in and provided enormous liquidity support. That was quintessentially a case of settlement risk. The central bank's involvement in assuming the risk of failing participants constitutes one of the major background for its bank monitoring, regulation, and supervision activities.

Case (i) and (ii) both refer to systemic risk, and are not necessarily mutually exclusive. With settlement risk, what is really needed is liquidity support. It tends to be associated with a situation where a solvent bank faces liquidity problems for some technical reasons, such as computer trouble. Liquidity support by the central bank is certain to be repaid as soon as the technical trouble has been overcome. What if an insolvent bank faces liquidity problems? Take the BCCI case for example. Suppose some healthy banks had fallen into liquidity difficulties due to BCCI's default on its payment obligations. The central bank would have had to step in and provide liquidity assistance (*not* to BCCI), with BCCI being immediately removed from the payment systems in which it had been participating. Normal operation of the payment systems would thus be maintained. When the situation returns to normal, liquidity assistance by the central bank would be repaid in full. In other words, with regard to settlement risk, liquidity support by the central bank would not likely disturb monetary control; the total amount of liquidity would remain stable over time.

Contagion risk represents a broader concept, occasionally including settlement risk. Suppose there is a run on deposits at some regional bank. Deposit withdrawals may contagiously spread to other banks in the same region, then to banks in neighboring regions, etc. The process may or may not deter the smooth functioning of the payment system. Contagion risk could involve liquidity assistance by the central bank, even where the solvency of the bank in question is not transparent. In this case, there is no guarantee that liquidity support by the central bank would be repaid in full. In addition to keeping supervisory eyes vigilant and securing sufficient collateral, central bank assistance might as well be limited to a bridge-loan type to buy time until other private or government rescue efforts are organized, thus securing compatibility with the monetary stability target. Another more delicate situation is where a group of banks on the verge of insolvency is deemed likely to have a systemic knock-on effect. The central bank might then be placed under enormous pressure to lower interest rates, at a potential cost of sacrificing monetary stability, to prevent them from actually becoming insolvent.[37]

We are now ready to put the central bank's role in perspective in terms of the conceptual framework previously developed. In a Regime I-like system, there exists no room for a public safety net for banks. It follows then that the central bank has little role to play, either.[38] In a Regime II-like system, the central bank focuses on settlement risk only. Contagion risk would not be its concern. Dual responsibility would be easily fulfilled. In a Regime III-like system, the central bank is concerned with both risks. The central bank may often be required to neutralize the effect of its liquidity support on the total volume of monetary reserves by absorbing an equivalent amount of liquidity in the money market.[39] Limiting liquidity support to a short-term bridge-loan type would facilitate the job. Moreover, the central bank might be required in this regime, with an eye to preventing a group of banks from becoming insolvent, to induce overall interest rates to turn downward as long as there appears to be the risk of a systemic knock-on effect.

It must have become clear by now that the central bank's dual responsibility would be met more easily in Regime II than in Regime III. In Regime III, the central bank may often be required to reorder policy priorities.

In considering the dual responsibility of the central bank, another issue of somewhat different nature may as well be tackled. Some economists and central bankers think that bank problems would have non-negligible effects upon real economic activity, even when conditioned on the same degree of monetary control.[40] According to this view, it is conceivable that the central bank may relax monetary control more than otherwise to improve banking conditions first, thereby ameliorating the adverse effects upon the real sector. And, as soon as banking has returned to normal, the central bank would then concentrate on adjusting monetary control to be consistent with the real sector. We must wait for further empirical research to be done in this area.

Notes

1. In this chapter, we use the word 'banks' in a broad sense which includes a variety of institutions that accept deposits from the public at large. For example, S&Ls in the United States, and *shinkin* banks and agricultural co-operatives in Japan are regarded as 'banks'.
2. A host of surveys on this subject have been published. For example, see OECD (1992) and BIS (1993).
3. Japanese non-banks mostly specialize in real estate financing. Loans to non-banks can, therefore, be regarded as being channelled through to real estate firms.
4. See Keeley (1990) for discussion on the relationship between competition, franchise value, and risky investment.
5. This proposition has some theoretical underpinning (e.g. Nalebuff and Stiglitz, 1983a, b).
6. Several papers provide summaries of banking problems in various countries, e.g. OECD (1992) and Goodhart and Schoenmaker (1993).
7. For a detailed description of the process of deregulation and financial innovation in Japan, see Takeda and Turner (1992).
8. See Bank of Japan (1991).
9. It is also pointed out that imperfections in bank accounting and disclosure rules prevented the market from exerting a disciplinary influence.
10. Banks can sell assets backed by real estate to the CCPC at fairly assessed prices. The necessary funds are loaned to the CCPC by banks selling such assets. As a result, banks can realize potential losses when they cannot liquidate assets immediately in the market, and thus become able to obtain tax relief. When the real estate is actually thereafter liquidated, the profit/loss is attributed to the bank which sold the asset.
11. Although mismanagement due to moral hazard was much more severe for S&Ls than commercial banks, we do not make any significant distinction in this chapter, since we believe that the basic nature of the problem was common to both.

12. See, for example, Brunner *et al.* (1991), and Duca and McLaughlin (1990).
13. See, for example, Congressional Budget Office (1993), Simons (1990), and Borio (1990).
14. For a description of the process of deregulation and financial innovation in the United Kingdom, see, for example, Danton (1992) and Colwell (1991).
15. For the development of the UK economy, see Bank of England (1993).
16. King (1993) discusses the real impacts on UK household behavior of decline in asset prices.
17. As for the experience in Nordic countries, the authors benefited greatly from Berg (1993).
18. Sherwin (1993) and Reserve Bank of New Zealand (1993) provides detailed discussion on the development of bank problems in New Zealand and the recent moves on the part of supervisors to take lessons from that experience.
19. Detailed discussion of bank difficulties in Australia are provided in Grenville (1991) and Reserve Bank of Australia (1993).
20. In some countries, however, the actual impact of deregulation has not fully worked itself out yet. In Japan, for example, official deregulation was completed in June 1993 (with interest rates on demand deposits remaining regulated as the sole exception) but it will be some time before it pervades the whole banking community, including remote regional banks.
21. Some regional banks are allowed direct entry into trust activities as well as via separate subsidiaries.
22. For discussion of the role of banks in intermediation, see Diamond (1984), Fama (1985) and James (1987).
23. This does not rule out the possibility that society could be wrong in terms of choice.
24. This regime finds some advocates among scholars (e.g. Dowd, 1992, 1993).
25. Some authors attempt to show, by citing historical examples, that private insurance could work, if the system is well designed (e.g. English, 1993).
26. Various 'narrow bank' proposals are an attempt to incorporate this idea.
27. Pierce (1991) provides an elaborate account of this process.
28. This idea differs from a narrow bank in that it requires no formal firewall between the bifurcated activities; only the assets held against protected transaction accounts are somehow earmarked. Thus, synergy between payment and intermediation functions is affected only very marginally, if at all. For a more formal discussion of a system of this type, see Merton and Bodie (1993).
29. Goodhart (1987) views the intermediation function, not necessarily the payment service function, as fundamental. However, his case could be incorporated in Regime III.
30. This description is very rough, because it ignores many visible differences that exist across countries. Japan, for example, with a set of quite tough restrictions imposed on the banking sector, still fits in well

with Regime III in the sense that it has allowed no major bank closure in the post-war period. In contrast, the United States seems, with the FDICIA and other new regulatory measures in place, to have substantially deviated from Regime III. The nationalization of banks, as in the Nordic countries, can be seen as an extreme form of Regime III.

31. Stiglitz, for example, insists on regulating deposit interest rates (Stiglitz, 1993).
32. Risk-based premiums have been introduced by FDICIA in the United States. If other countries follow suit, it may not represent as big an obstacle as it tends to be considered.
33. The costs of setting capital requirements at the wrong level can be substantial. Merton and Bodie (1993) point out that 'in the case of thrift, we have seen the results of setting them too low. But there is also a cost of setting them too high'.
34. Pressure on regulators has been more or less visible in many countries, but most typically in the United States under the Bush Administration in 1991–92.
35. Airlines, railroads, etc. are a case in point. They deal in human lives; banks do not.
36. Goodhart and Schoenmaker (1993) say something to the effect that through its support of a participant likely to fail on its obligations, the central bank is in effect the implicit guarantor of the system.
37. If contagious runs develop into a situation where the public's demand for money shifts from bank deposits to currency, then the central bank would have no choice but to concentrate on satiating increased demand for currency, for the moment at least. But this cash-drain scenario is not likely to jeopardize overall monetary stability, because a cash drain is ordinarily accompanied by an offsetting decline in the credit multiplier.
38. In Regime I, whether a central bank even exists or is needed is not clear, but it is a topic beyond the scope of this chapter.
39. This is what Goodfriend and King call banking policy (Goodfriend and King, 1988).
40. Some argue that bank disruption may exert adverse effects upon the real economy through a deterioration in intermediation. See Bernanke (1983).

References

Bank of England (1993) 'Financial Market Developments', *Bank of England Quarterly Bulletin* (May) pp. 213–21.

Bank of Japan (1991) 'Recent Developments in Lending Rates – Changing Behavior of Banks under Interest Rate Liberalization', Research and Statistics Department. *Special Paper*, 206.

Bank of Japan (various issues) *Economic Statistics Monthly*, Research and Statistics Department.

Berg. S. A. (1993) 'The Banking Crises in the Scandinavian Countries.' Prepared for the 29th Annual Conference on Bank Structure and Competition, Federal Reserve Bank of Chicago, 5–7 May 1993.

Bernanke, B. S. (1983) 'Nonmonetary Effects of the Financial Crisis in the Propagation of the Great Depression', *American Economic Review*, vol. 73 (2) pp. 257–76.
BIS [Bank for International Settlements] (1992) *62nd Annual Report.*
BIS [Bank for International Settlements] (1993) *63rd Annual Report.*
Board of Governors of the Federal Reserve System (various issues) *Federal Reserve Bulletin.*
Borio, C. E. V. (1990) 'Banks' Involvement in Highly Leveraged Transactions', *BIS Economic Papers*, 28.
Brunner, A. D., J. V. Duca and M. M. McLaughlin (1991) 'Recent Developments Affecting the Profitability and Practices of Commercial Banks', *Federal Reserve Bulletin. Board of Governors of the Federal Reserve System*, vol. 77 (7) pp. 505–27.
Central Statistical Office (various issues) *Financial Statistics.*
Colwell, R. (1991) 'The Performance of Major British Banks, 1970–90', *Bank of England Quarterly Bulletin* (November) pp. 508–515.
Congressional Budget Office (1993) *Resolving the Thrift Crisis.*
Corrigan, E. G. (1992) 'Challenges Facing the International Community of Bank Supervisors', *Quarterly Review. Federal Reserve Bank of New York* (Autumn) pp. 1–9.
Danton, G. (1992) 'Major International Banks' Performance: 1980–91', *Bank of England Quarterly Bulletin* (August) pp. 288–97.
Diamond, D. W. (1984) 'Financial Intermediation and Delegated Monitoring', *Review of Economic Studies*, vol. 51, pp. 393–414.
Dowd, K. (ed.) (1992) *The Experience of Free Banking* (London: Routledge).
Dowd, K. (ed.) (1993) 'Deposit Insurance: A Skeptical View', *Review. Federal Reserve Bank of St. Louis* (January/February) pp. 14–17.
Duca, J. V., and M. M. McLaughlin (1990) 'Developments Affecting the Profitability of Commercial Banks', *Federal Reserve Bulletin. Board of Governors of the Federal Reserve System*, vol. 76 (7) pp. 477–99.
English, W. B. (1993) 'The Decline of Private Deposit Insurance in the United States', *Carnegie-Rochester Conference Series on Public Policy*, vol. 38, pp. 57–128.
Fama, E. (1985) 'What Different About Banks?' *Journal of Monetary Economics*, vol. 15, pp. 29–39.
FDIC [Federal Deposit Insurance Corporation] (1991) *Annual Report.*
FDIC [Federal Deposit Insurance Corporation] (various issues) *Quarterly Banking Profile.*
Flannery, M. J. (1982) 'Deposit Insurance Creates a Need for Bank Regulation', *Business Review. Federal Reserve Bank of Philadelphia* (January/February) pp. 17–27.
Flannery, M. J. (1993) 'Government Risk-Bearing in the Financial Sector of a Capitalist Economy', in M. S. Sniderman (ed.), *Government Risk-Bearing*, Proceedings of a Conference held at the Federal Reserve Bank of Cleveland (Kluwer Academic Publishers) pp. 71–107.
Goodfriend, M. and R. G. King (1988) 'Financial Deregulation, Monetary Policy, and Central Banking', *Economic Review. Federal Reserve Bank of Richmond* (May/June) pp. 3–22.

Goodhart, C. (1987) 'Why do Banks Need a Central Bank?', *Oxford Economic Papers*, vol. 39, pp. 75–89.

Goodhart, C. and D. Schoenmaker (1993) 'Institutional Separation between Supervisory and Monetary Agencies.' Paper presented at Bocconi University Conference on Monetary Policy and Bank Supervision held in Milan, Italy, April 1993.

Grenville, S. (1991) 'The Evolution of Financial Deregulation', *The Deregulation of Financial Intermediaries* (Reserve Bank of Australia) pp. 3–35.

IMF [International Monetary Fund] (various issues) *International Financial Statistics*.

James, C. (1987) 'Some Evidence on the Uniqueness of Bank Loans', *Journal of Financial Economics*, vol. 19, pp. 217–235.

Keeley, M. C. (1990) 'Deposit Insurance, Risk and Market Power in Banking', *American Economic Review*, vol. 80 (5), pp. 1183–1200.

King, M. (1993) 'Debt Deflation: Theory and Evidence.' Presidential Lecture delivered to the European Economic Association in Helsinki, 27 August 1993.

Meulendyke, A.-M. (1989) *U.S. Monetary Policy and Financial Markets*, Federal Reserve Bank of New York.

Merton, R. C. and Z. Bodie (1993) 'Deposit Insurance Reform: A Functional Approach', *Carnegie-Rochester Conference Series on Public Policy*, vol. 38, pp. 1–34.

Ministry of Finance, Japan (1992) *41st Banking Bureau Annual Report* (in Japanese).

Nalebuff, B. and J. E. Stiglitz (1983a) 'Prizes and Incentives: Toward a General Theory of Compensation and Competition', *Bell Journal of Economics and Management Science*, vol. 14 (Spring) pp. 21–43.

Nalebuff, B. and J. E. Stiglitz (1983b) 'Information, Competition and Markets', *American Economic Review*, vol. 72 (2) pp. 278–84.

Noguchi, Y. (1992) *Bubble no Keizaigaku (Economics of Bubbles)* (in Japanese), (Tokyo: Nihon Keizai Shinbun).

OECD (1992) *Banks Under Stress*.

OECD (various issues) *Bank Profitability: Statistical Supplement: Financial Statements of Banks*.

Pierce, J. L. (1991) *The Future of Banking* (New Haven & London: Yale University Press).

Reserve Bank of Australia (1993) 'Recent Developments in the Profitability and Capital Positions of Banks', *Reserve Bank of Australia Bulletin* (January) pp. 10–13.

Reserve Bank of New Zealand (1993) 'Proposed Revisions to Banking Supervision Arrangements', June, 1993.

Sherwin, M. (1993) 'Efficiency, Stability and Regulation in the Financial Sector: the New Zealand Experience.' Paper presented at the Conference on Financial Stability organized by Macquarie University and Reserve Bank of Australia, Sydney, Australia, 31 October–1 November 1993.

Simons, K. (1990) 'New England Banks and the Texas Experience', *New England Economic Review. Federal Reserve Bank of Boston* (September/October) pp. 55–62.

Stiglitz, J. E. (1993) 'Perspectives on the Role of Government Risk-Bearing within the Financial Sector', in M. S. Sniderman (ed.), *Government Risk-Bearing*, Proceedings of a Conference held at the Federal Reserve Bank of Cleveland (Kluwer Academic Publishers) pp. 109–130.

Takeda, M. and P. Turner (1992) 'The Liberalization of Japan's Financial Markets: Some Major Themes', *BIS Economic Papers*, 34.

US Department of the Treasury (various issues) *Monthly Treasury Statement.*

US Government (various issues) *Economic Report of the President.*

Comments

Edward J. Frydl*

In their chapter, Nakajima and Taguchi formulate and address a critical issue facing financial regulators today: do the problems of widespread financial excess that emerged in the 1980s reflect a fundamental flaw in financial structures rather than particular historical circumstances? In short, the authors answer yes and place the blame on the high degree of moral hazard introduced into contemporary banking by the extensive official safety nets provided by modern governments. The starting point is the erosion of the traditional banking franchise – the inermediation role of taking deposits and making commercial loans – under the forces of increased external and internal competition and technical change. Banks responded to the challenge of an eroding franchise by taking on more lending risk to achieve higher returns. Banks took this risk with impunity because of the safety net supporting them. Not only are bank deposits fully guaranteed in practice but in many countries lender of last resort credit and official forbearance will seek to prevent any bank failure. And countries that embraced deregulation as a policy gave their banks a green light to exploit this moral hazard aggressively.

The authors believe that deregulation is an irreversible change in the character of the financial system and that the basic forces of competition and technological innovation are long-lasting. In consequence, the tendency to financial excess will remain unless financial structures are reformed to reduce moral hazard. To achieve this result, they argue in favour of a kind of narrow banking system, with deposit instruments, that is, money, supported not by government-provided insurance but by earmarked safe assets. The official safety net would backstop only the payments system proper, not the credit supply.

Is this the right way for policy to go? My first comments will basically emphasize the complexity of the issues and the difficulty in diagnosing the problem of financial excess. Of course, safety net support of bank deposits has given depositors less incentive for vigilance

* These comments are the author's views and do not necessarily represent the views of the Federal Reserve Bank of New York.

compared to less secured creditors and investors in banks. But I do not think this kind of moral hazard was key in causing the excesses. Extending that safety net to protect the interests of shareholders and even management is a much more serious problem of moral hazard, but not really the one Nakajima and Taguchi concentrate on in their prescriptions.

Can we be very sure that the observed pattern of global financial excesses arose from enduring structural flaws rather than particular historical circumstances? The case for a negative answer notes that the most serious banking system disruptions resulted from lending to commercial real estate. Over-extension in real estate, however, can be explained without reliance on moral hazard, as a likely consequence of the global inflation cycle. Around the world real estate had proven itself the premier asset in inflationary times. If investors and lenders were generally skeptical about governments' resolve to end inflation, they could have become heavily exposed in real estate and unpleasantly surprised when inflation actually did fall, regardless of moral hazard. From tulipmania in seventeenth-century Holland to the latest Ponzi scheme that just swept through Romania, history is filled with examples of bubbles financed by people's own money. In the United States, not just banks but also non-bank lenders removed from the safety net – insurance companies and finance companies – were caught up badly in commercial real estate as well.

No simple theory convincingly explains the global pattern of financial excess, however. As a rough stylized fact, the worst excesses hitting the banking system occurred in Japan, Scandinavia, and the United States, with lesser excesses in nations such as the UK, Australia, possibly Canada and Spain. Other countries in Continental Europe avoided the worst. Now this pattern does not fit so neatly with the inflation cycle theory: one would expect the worst disruptions in countries where the disinflationary surprise was greatest and that did not apparently happen. But neither does the pattern clearly fit the Nakajima–Taguchi moral hazard view. In fact, there is no obvious way to rank the degree of moral hazard across countries and the authors do not provide a scheme to do so.

Another qualification I would make is to contest the usefulness of depositor discipline on bank behavior. Loss to depositors becomes a non-negligible probability only when asset deterioration has eaten well into a bank's capital buffer. If the bank had been following a misguided lending policy, rather than being just unlucky in some outcome, the depositors may by then well feel that there are more losses in the pipeline and they will 'discipline' the bank by shutting off funding and running. Compared to shareholders, even uninsured depositors have little incentive to get into the decision-making process early. Reform efforts directed at stabilizing the banking system should seek to strengthen the active involvement and sense of responsibility of shareholders rather than relying on depositor discipline.

The authors conceive deregulation as an irreversible structural fracture – the breaking of an egg – and think that it is not possible to reconstitute the set of regulations that kept moral hazard in check. But the principal effect of deregulation on bank behavior may have been as a signal of a relaxed official attitude to risk-taking in finance. If so, this signal is certainly reversible through imposition of new requirements – e.g., the extension of Basel capital rules to market risk and FDICIA-style regulation – rather than through the restoration of the old system.

Finally, I want to comment on the social value of the narrow bank proposal. This idea has unusually eclectic support. For example, if the low risk assets used to back the liabilities of the narrow bank are deposits at the central bank, we have something akin to Milton Friedman's 100 percent reserve requirement from his early proposal for monetary stability. In recent years, James Tobin has signed on to a more contemporary version that uses T-bill backing. This illustrates what I consider to be a universal psychological law: no two individuals can disagree on everything. What can be said against a proposal that has such an illustriously wide swath of support? If banks have to earmark low-yielding assets against deposits (which will presumably continue to require reserve backing), a high-debit-volume deposits business may no longer be profitable; even a low-debit-volume savings deposit business may be at too great a competitive disadvantage relative to money market mutual funds that hold no reserves. A narrow banking system will be a narrow, possibly less efficient, channel for central bank monetary policy operations. I do not mean that in a narrow banking system open market operations cannot affect the portfolio equilibrium of the economy, but rather that the constraints set up by earmarking assets may change the dynamics of open market operations in unclear ways.

Furthermore, the banking system now acts as a kind of amplifier of lender of last resort efforts in instances of market disruption. In a narrow banking system this role would be lost. Central banks would have to refrain from assistance in market crises or lend directly to final borrowers. Both alternatives are inferior to the status quo.

It is not reasonable to believe that society will tolerate no interventions to manage shocks to credit markets if only money supply is stabilized. This is so even if we grant that the private sector would innovate effective mechanisms to stabilize markets after financial shocks (which is questionable since investments made to secure financial systemic stability have strong public good elements). A question of justice is involved. Such mechanisms may well require unacceptable concentrations of market power. Take an example from US history. The Federal Reserve was established not because J. P. Morgan failed to act as an effective lender of last resort in the 1907 banking crisis, but because he did act so. The country made a political decision that such responsibility should not be concentrated in private hands.

What is more, putting the focus only on the moral hazard arising from safety nets gives a distorted view of social costs and benefits. As Larry Summers noted, if the safety net prevented one moderate recession, it has probably more than covered all the moral hazard costs from the thrift and bank crises. Has the safety net prevented a recession? To know for sure we would have to get Professor Fogel and that wonderful machine he has that sees into parallel universes. But consider one suggestive bit of evidence. After the 1987 stock market crash, central banks pushed all their safety net buttons hard. The consensus forecast on the economy deteriorated substantially with many predicting recession in 1988. Recession did not happen. What do we think would have happened if current safety net interventions had not been in place?

How would the lender of last resort mechanism work in a narrow banking world? The narrow bank is, after all, disconnected from the credit supply process by design. And if there were a special class of non-bank institutions connected by their charters to the central bank discount window they almost certainly would be subject to some prudential regulation and we might as well call them banks; such an arrangement would make the narrow banking regime something of a charade. So, lender of last resort aid would have to go directly to non-banks. This is something the Federal Reserve, for one, has scrupulously avoided, turning down over the years inquiries for assistance from various non-bank borrowers because that type of lending inevitably politicizes the discount window and in the end, paralyzes it.

Is this really a better set-up? Cutting down the Appalachian forests will reduce Lyme disease; and cutting down the banking system will reduce moral hazard. But the narrow banking regime prescription is out of proportion to the diagnosis of moral hazard. We need a second opinion before we do this operation.

Comments

William Witherell*

1. During the last decade, and especially in the last four years, banks and other financial institutions in many industrialized countries have been faced with large losses; and, in several instances, rapidly eroding capital bases have required large-scale injections of public funds. The fact that OECD's Committee on Financial Markets will be devoting an important part of its next meeting to considering many of the same issues that we will be discussing at this conference is not a coincidence; policy makers in most of our countries are actively reviewing their strategies for preventing severe banking problems and addressing banking problems that do arise (see, for example, the recent OECD study *Banks Under Stress*, OECD, 1992). The Nakajima–Taguchi chapter provides a valuable overview of the recent bank crises, seeking to identify some common elements or thread. Then, using a conceptual framework based on three idealized types of banking regimes, it explores from a long-term perspective the possible outlines of an optimal regulatory system. The chapter raises in a coherent fashion many of the issues that are addressed at greater length in other papers for this conference and provides a framework for considering them. My comments are concerned mainly with questions of emphasis, both in the analysis of recent events and in the drawing of lessons for financial supervisory and regulatory policies.

2. The review of the recent serious banking problems and banking crises in Sections II and III of the chapter reveals many factors uniquely related to particular episodes and local circumstances and to cyclical factors. There are, however, also a number of common, structural factors or determinants of banking troubles. In each case, banks have been beset by a surge in credit losses largely, but not exclusively, related to real estate loans, loans to firms for investment in financial assets and participation in the derivatives markets. These losses elicited a policy response by the government aimed at maintaining financial stability. In the run-up to these large banking losses, each country witnessed a significant change in the pattern of bank

* The views expressed in this comment in no way commit the OECD or its Member governments.

lending following an episode of financial innovation and liberalization. These changes included a growing concentration of loans to particular economic sectors or a sharp expansion in bank lending relative to nominal GDP or both. Although both of these developments point to increased risk-taking by banks, their net operating profits remained broadly stable as the lending pattern changed. That is, additional earnings from operations were generated to cover the potential increase in loan losses from the riskier portfolios. Eventually, the riskier lending activities of the banks were exposed by an adverse shock, such as an unanticipated tightening of monetary policy, recession or a sectoral disturbance.

3. The Nakajima–Taguchi chapter underlines the role that moral hazard may have played in contributing to the increased risk taking by banks in these cases of banking troubles and states their objective as searching for a 'new hazard-proof system'. Looking at the cases described in the chapter, I do question the primacy given to this objective. Seeking a hazard-proof system can lead to proposals which are either politically infeasible or sub-optimal from an economic welfare point of view. Moral hazard certainly appears to have been an important factor in Japan and in the US savings and loan sector but this is less evident for the other cases. Looking at the US commercial banking sector, for example, I think that the explanation lies more in the mismanagement by banks of the risks related to the sharp increase in competitive pressures that resulted from financial liberalization and innovation. 'Herding' or the 'bandwagon effect' was probably a contributing factor behind the building-up of banking problems; lenders (or intermediaries) felt secure in the knowledge that their competitors were making the same judgements regarding the consequences of uncertainty. In retrospect, risk premiums proved too low and assumptions regarding the diversifiability of risk were wrong.

4. In considering the structural factors underlying the episodes of bank disruption, the chapter correctly emphasizes the worldwide shift of government regulation of the banking sector to more market-oriented systems, in other words, to financial liberalization. Reductions in entry barriers, deregulation of interest rates, liberalization of international capital flows, desegmentation, relaxation of legal restrictions to form financial conglomerates have all contributed to dramatic changes in competitive conditions among financial intermediaries. No longer could banks rely on the cushion of excess profits or rents due to cartelized and protected markets. On both the liabilities

side and the assets side banks were (and are) confronted with intense competition from non-banks. Funding became more expensive for banks, while many banking institutions became more active in the riskier segments of the credit market. The combination of these developments led to a pronounced deterioration in the profitability and asset quality of banks in many OECD countries. Lower profits entailed reduced ability to maintain capitalization, while lower prices and the pressure to increase quantities in many cases meant that too low risk premiums were charged. In addition, financial innovations instilled new forms of uncertainty in the market place. Complex new instruments, methods and technologies have raised significant challenges for both bank managers and supervisors.

5. It is during the period of financial liberalization when such problems are most likely to arise as bank managers have to learn how to operate in a new setting, as the distortions created during the previous period of excessive regulation have to be unwound and as bank supervisors find that their guidelines and standards are inappropriate for a more competitive and 'modern' financial market. Bank managers needed to develop appropriate risk management procedures and guidelines. In the cases under consideration there appear also to have been significant instances of financial market failure to correct promptly market expectations with respect to asset prices that did not conform to economic realities, in particular, the consequences of general deflation. It is not surprising that in such a period management mistakes and regulatory shortcomings occurred. Moral hazard in varying degrees aggravated these problems; but even in the case of Japan, I would hesitate to claim that moral hazard 'triggered the process'.

6. One should expect and, I think, accept, that there will be more bank problems and failures in a more deregulated environment, *especially during the transition period.* The issue is whether, even with a larger number of distress cases, the system has enough safeguards to contain systemic risk and minimize the need for bail-outs at the expense of the taxpayer. There is no reason to think that the bank mismanagement we have witnessed is a long-term characteristic of the more competitive financial landscape. Recently, there has, in fact, been a significant easing of strains in the banking sectors of most OECD countries as evidenced by lower loan losses, a return to profitability in some countries and a rise in bank share prices. Banks in a number of OECD countries have been in a position to raise large volumes of equity capital through recourse to the share market.

These developments are, at least in part, the fruits of profound changes in banking in recent years. Asset growth has been de-emphasized, while efficient use of capital is now a much greater concern for bankers. Indeed, it has become a key parameter for banking strategies. Banks are now stressing product lines that are profitable while devoting far more resources to the risk management function and have instituted more rigorous tests to determine whether assets are properly priced. Capital ratios are being strengthened not only by raising new capital but also through the sale of assets, especially via securitization.

7. An optimal system for the modernized financial markets of the present and the future should be based on the development of effective *prudential supervision* tied to capital adequacy provisions, which is distinctly different from the excessive *regulation* of the markets which characterized the past. Government authorities should not attempt to remove risk from financial markets but, rather, should recognize that the rational analysis, management and pricing of risk is a basic function of financial markets and financial institutions. Supervisory and regulatory authorities have been stepping up their efforts to lead bank management to adopt suitable risk evaluation and control procedures. Considerable progress has been made in putting into place more stringent risk-based capital requirements to induce more prudent behavior and to provide a financial buffer against losses. Improvements in consolidated supervision and in financial disclosure requirements also should help to minimize the probability of reoccurrences of serious banking disturbances in the future.

8. The conceptual framework presented in Section IV of the chapter is intended to assist a search for an optimal configuration of bank regulation and safety nets, with the stress being on moral hazard considerations. Moral hazard is connected to safety nets or insurance schemes to the extent that the existence of such insurance provides increased incentives for risk-taking that, in turn, increase the likelihood of an insurance pay-off. The result of moral hazard incentives in the banking system is that management may be less vigilant about the risk of the bank's activities or, indeed, turn the resources of the bank to its own advantage without the knowledge of the bank's creditors and/or shareholders. *Effective bank supervision tied directly to the amount of bank capital together with greater accountability of management is probably the best approach to reduce moral hazard incentives.* The chapter suggests three-way breakdown of regulatory systems and the associated perceptions of the public responsibility of a central bank. In addition to considering these as three alternative

systems, one can imagine a non-exclusive system in which the financial institution can opt for one of three statuses: (a) investment/finance company with no officially insured deposits or access to central bank credit, (b) narrow bank with insured deposits and only low risk money market assets, and (c) a broad bank. Each institution would be subject to progressively stricter supervisory regimes. A variation of this would be to permit financial services conglomerates where only a core narrow bank has access to the safety net and the remainder of the conglomerate is free to engage in more risky activities under less stringent supervision.

9. I do think that the formulation of Regime III is too narrow, particularly as it is the regime found in nearly all OECD countries. In effect, if one proposes Regime I or II, one is seeking to redefine the system whereas to accept Regime III is to accept the current system and try to improve it. The chapter asserts that once one accepts the principle that the central bank is responsible for payments and for solvency, one must logically have a rigid system with all of the restrictions mentioned. However, Regime III is compatible with no deposit insurance (or very low insurance) or premia based upon the quality of the bank's balance sheet. The reform proposed in the US would have geared premia and permissible activities to the strength of banks. In fact, a reduction of deposit insurance to only that which is necessary to protect narrowly-defined 'small savers' may be desirable. Most would agree that the protection in the US system had expanded to excessive proportions and that the official commitment should be reduced. It might also be desirable to develop systems for private deposit insurance.

10. As indicated in the chapter, the effective 'safety net' in most countries appears to be much broader than the legal one. Even in countries with no formal deposit insurance system most authorities (according to the text, including those of Japan) will not allow bank depositors to lose money – even if depositors are not insured. Moral hazard considerations have led authorities to allow considerable ambiguity concerning commitments to rescue banks and their depositors. In view of the deregulation that has occurred, one might ask whether there should be a concurrent greater willingness to accept bank failures and, in that case, specification by officials of the risks depositors must bear. Private deposit insurance might then develop.

11. I would have liked to see some discussion in the chapter of bank exit problems and how these would be handled under an optimal system. Arguably the advance of technology and innovation along

with competition from other financial institutions may have created over-capacity in the banking sector. I question whether it is possible for all banks in a market to resolve the problem by emphasizing higher quality credits. The result of excess capacity is that returns on normal business are driven to uneconomic levels, and without the possibility of orderly exit, banks are led to ignore risk while seeking high rates of asset growth.

12. *In conclusion*, in seeking to identify long-term alternatives for a more stable financial framework, I believe it is necessary to begin with the recognition that it is *neither feasible nor desirable to turn back the clock* on financial liberalization or modernization. The authors reach a similar conclusion, but it appears, with some regret. The structural changes since the early 1980s followed a period of some 20–30 years during which most domestic financial markets had barely changed in terms of their functional structure, operative capacity and overall efficiency. The forces that led to these changes are not diminishing. The overall result of these changes has been an evident increase in the efficiency of our financial markets; both the attractiveness of saving and the flexibility of investment have been enhanced. Savers have more choices and can earn higher returns. Investors have greater access to finance at market rates without rationing. The combination of deregulation measures and technological advances have contributed to a growing institutionalization of savings and increased globalization of investors' portfolios. Also, financial market innovations have provided greater scope for managing risks. Finally, liberalized and globalized financial markets can impose helpful discipline on governments' conduct of macroeconomic policies. In short, it is undeniable that today's 'modernized' finanial markets are better suited to the requirements of a more market-oriented overall economic setting. The 'optimal' system must be similarly market-oriented, stressing effective prudential supervision.

4 Monetary Policy Implications of Recent Changes in the Financial Systems in the United States and Europe

William Poole[1]

Financial markets have evolved significantly in recent years in the United States and Europe. Although economic growth has slowed almost everywhere among high-income countries, growth would have slowed even more without improvements in economic efficiency arising from the growth of world trade and accompanying developments in international finance. The differential attitude toward freedom of trade and international capital flows – the attitude that free trade was to be encouraged but international capital flows were to be controlled – has broken down to a considerable extent. In part this change reflects the profitability of trade in financial services, which cannot occur without the capital flows to be serviced. The change in attitude also reflects recognition of the intimate relationship between trade in goods and services and the financing mechanisms including long-term capital flows, short-term trade finance, and foreign exchange dealing that accompany trade.

My emphasis in this chapter will be on the United States and the major European countries – France, Germany, Italy, Netherlands, and the United Kingdom. Even though Netherlands is considerably smaller than the larger European economies, I include it for detailed examination in this study because of its importance in the capital markets and because its close integration with Germany provides useful lessons in understanding behavior in the capital and foreign exchange markets. Although I occasionally provide data for other European economies and for Canada, my comments will refer to the first list of countries unless indicated otherwise.

I BACKGROUND

It is hard to exaggerate how different US and Western European economies appear today compared to fifteen years ago. In most countries, inflation is much lower and unemployment much higher. In most countries, interest rates are much lower and share prices much higher. Capital markets are much more competitive and more tightly integrated than before. In this section, I will review these basic background facts before moving to an evaluation of their significance for monetary policy.

Inflation, Economic Growth, and Unemployment

Figure 4.1 shows that inflation has fallen in almost all the countries of Western Europe and North America.[2] Inflation rates have not only declined but also for major countries have tended to converge, as shown in Figure 4.2. Inflation in the neighborhood of about 3 percent is coming to be considered 'normal', whereas ten years ago the declines in inflation in the early 1980s were feared by many to be temporary. Experience has, of course, differed in detail from one country to another, but Figure 4.2 suggests that the common experience of falling inflation is the real story rather than the differences in experience across countries.[3]

Unfortunately, declining inflation has been accompanied by declining growth in most countries, as shown in Figure 4.3. The United Kingdom is perhaps the most interesting exception to the overall pattern of declining growth. The pro-growth reforms of the Thatcher Government appear to have worked. Along with slower growth has come rising secular unemployment in all major countries, with the possible exception of the United States. Figure 4.4 shows that US unemployment has fluctuated around a roughly unchanged trend whereas European unemployment has risen substantially. Indeed, for the major European countries the unemployment rate in 1993 is back to the peaks of the early 1980s when inflation was being brought down by restrictive monetary policies.

Interest Rates and Share Prices

Figure 4.5 shows government bond yields. The US bond yield declined almost continuously after 1981 as inflation and inflation expectations fell. European rates also declined significantly after 1981, but

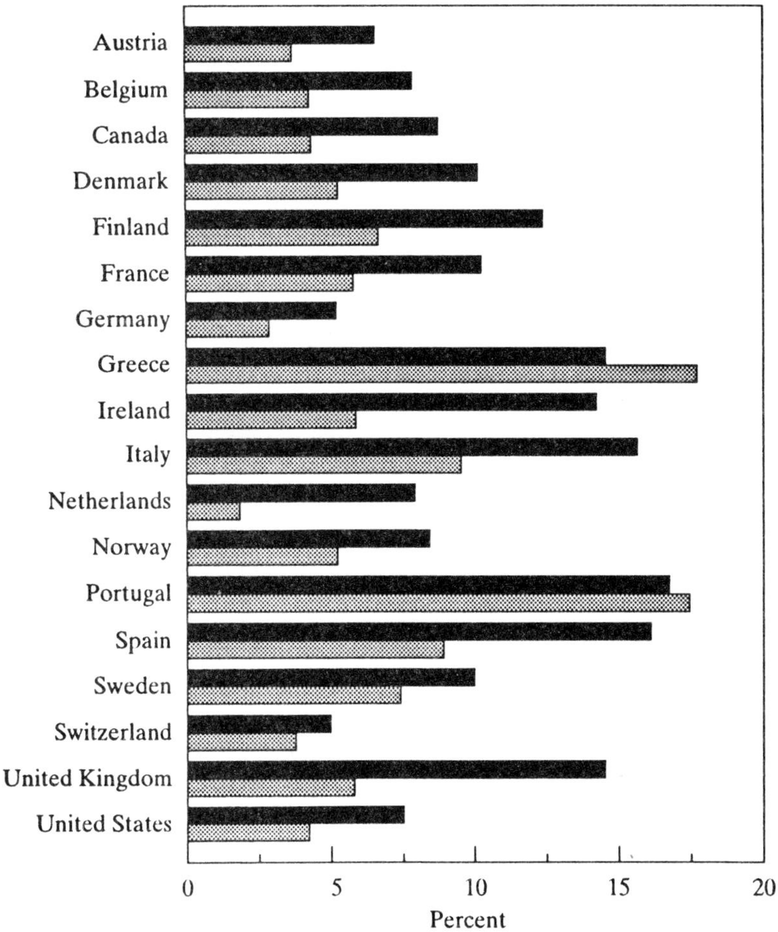

Figure 4.1 Inflation in Europe, United States and Canada. Average annual rate, 1970–80 (black bar) and 1980–91 (gray bar). (*Source*: World Bank, *World Development Report*, Table 1)

backed up in the late 1980s as inflation rose somewhat in some countries – especially in Germany. The figure suggests that the German and Dutch capital markets became increasingly integrated over the course of the 1980s; after 1987, the bond yields in the two countries are almost identical.

Figure 4.6 shows money market rates which, depending on the country, are either call money rates or interbank rates. These rates,

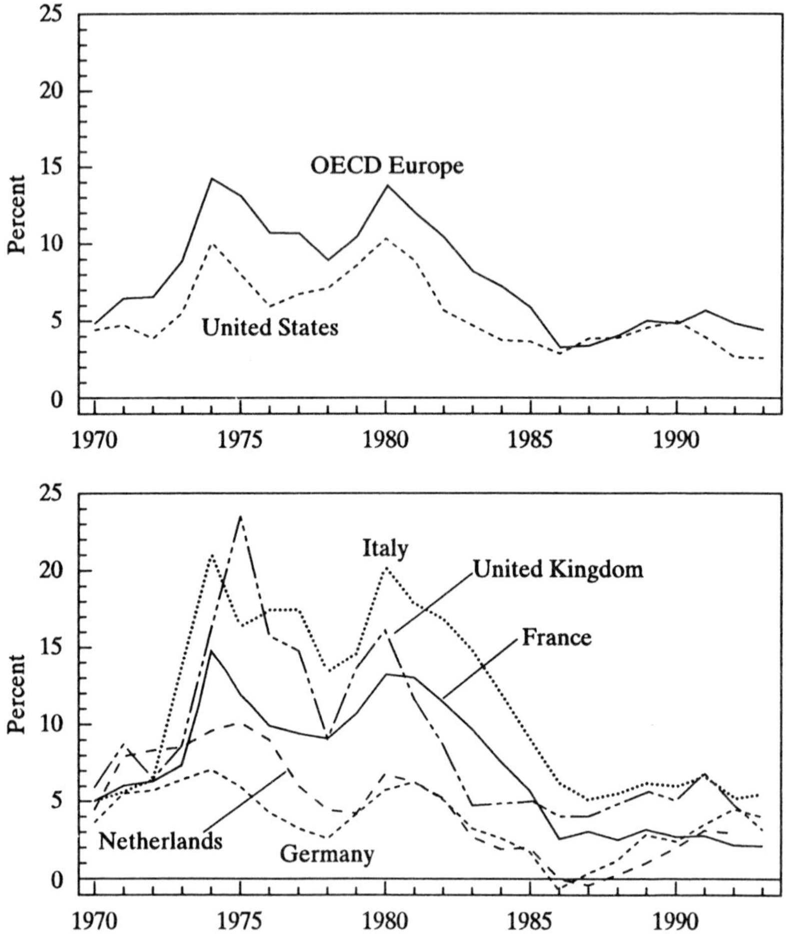

Figure 4.2 Inflation rate, major European countries and United States, 1970–93. (*Source*: OECD; 1993 is OECD estimate)

of course, are much more volatile than bond yields. Although short rates peaked in 1981 for most countries, the increase in rates in Germany from 1988 to 1992 was substantial, and influenced rates in many other countries. As with the previous figure, Figure 4.6 suggests a tight integration of the German and Dutch money markets but less close integration of other money markets.

Figure 4.7 shows industrial share prices. Share prices ended the 1970s at or below their levels at the beginning of the decade; given

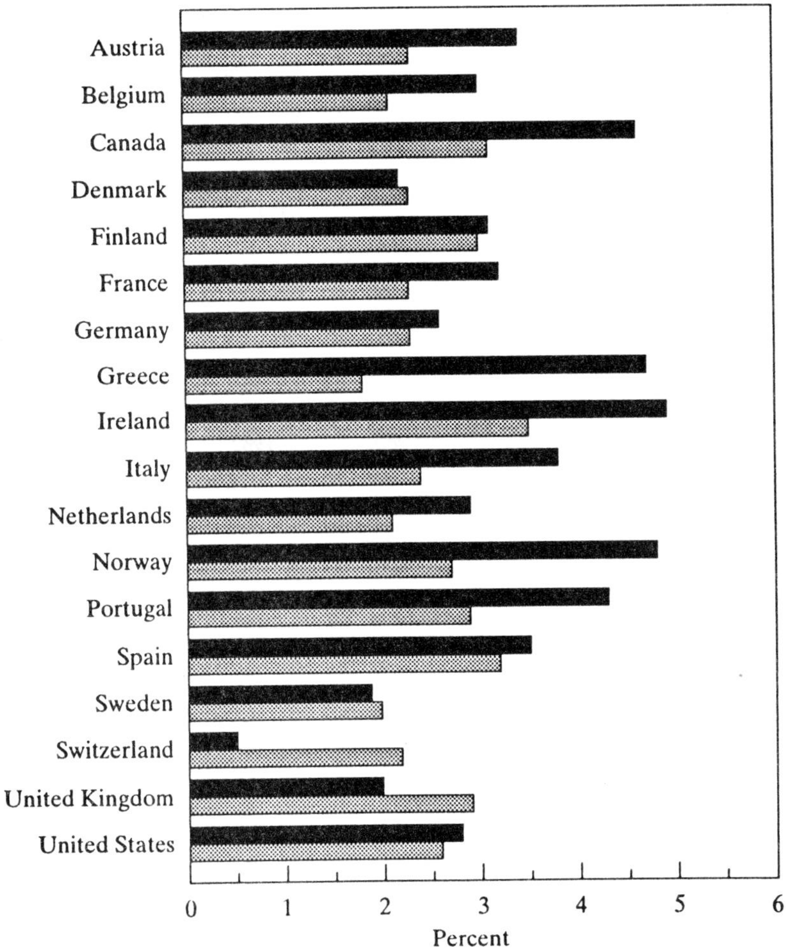

Figure 4.3 Real GDP growth in Europe, United States, and Canada. Average annual rate, 1970–80 (black bar) and 1980–91 (gray bar). (*Source*: World Bank, *World Development Report*, Table 2)

the inflation of the 1970s, the real value of share prices suffered a remarkable decline. After 1980, share prices rose substantially in all countries. Given that real growth was lower in most countries in the 1980s than in the 1970s, we might have expected poorer performance of corporate profits and of share prices. Instead, share prices rose substantially in the 1980s, especially over the 1981–86 period, suggesting the importance of the greater stability and confidence

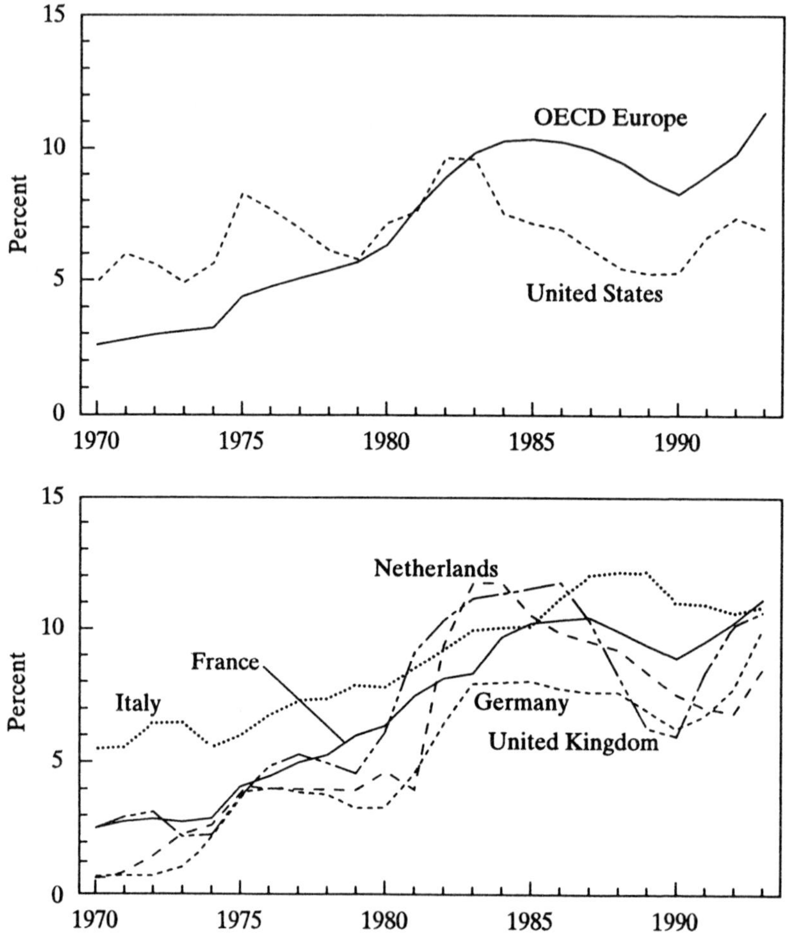

Figure 4.4 Unemployment rate, major European countries and United States, 1970–93. (*Source*: OECD; 1993 is OECD estimate)

associated with lower inflation, and of lower inflation itself through a variety of mechanisms.

Financial Market Integration

The Bretton Woods system was based on the premise that fixed exchange rates and liberal trading policies would increase world output and welfare, but that capital controls were a legitimate and even

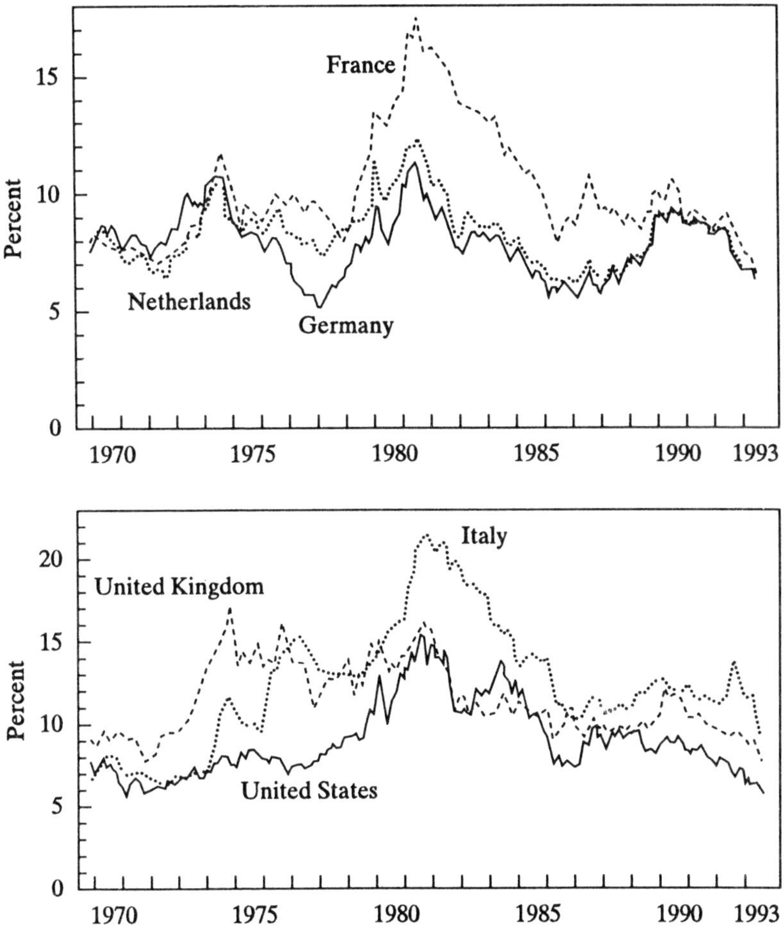

Figure 4.5 Government bond yields, selected countries. Monthly, 1970:1–1993:9. (*Source*: IMF, *International Financial Statistics*)

desirable way to assist in the maintenance of exchange rate stability. The international financial system lived with that legacy until the late 1970s and early 1980s, when most countries abandoned or began to abandon capital and exchange controls.[4] The gains from financial market integration, improved efficiency in allocation of capital, and trade in financial services became as important to countries as the gains from integrating goods markets through policies of reduced trade restriction.

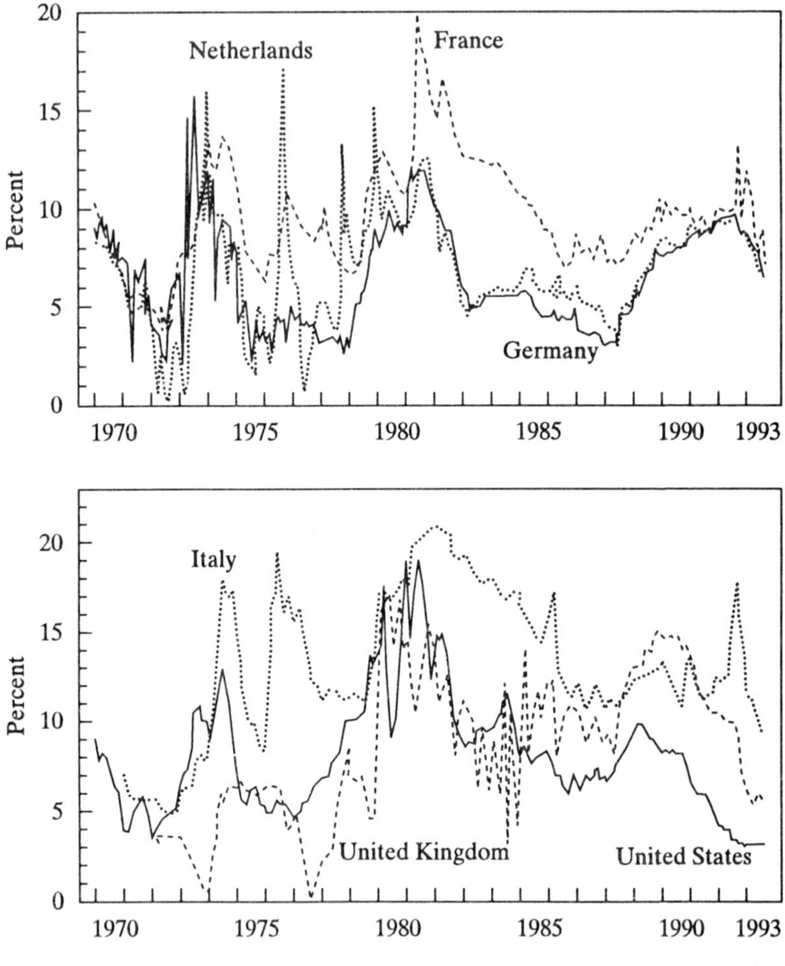

Figure 4.6 Money market rates, selected countries. Monthly, 1970:1–1993:9. (*Source*: IMF, *International Financial Statistics*)

Richard Marston studied the effects of capital controls during and after the Bretton Woods period. He concluded that 'in three major national markets [Germany, United Kingdom, and United States] capital controls imposed during the Bretton Woods period led to large covered interest differentials that distorted investment and borrowing decisions' (Marston, 1993, p. 537). Marston presents a figure showing striking evidence of large differentials between Euro-sterling and British interest rates during the controls period and near

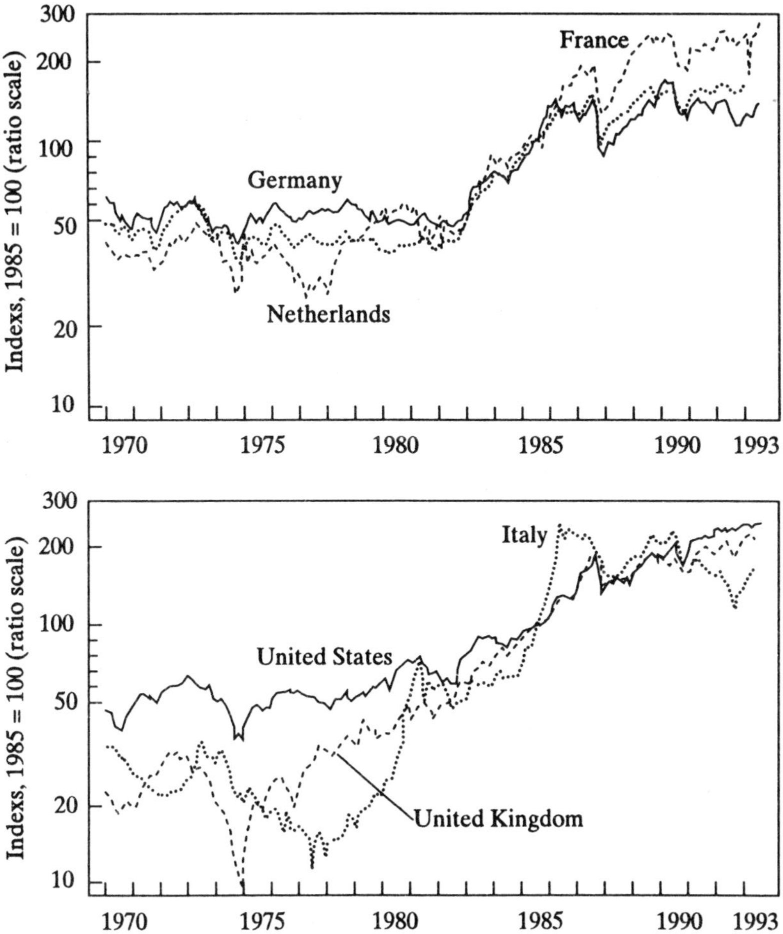

Figure 4.7 Industrial share prices, selected countries. Monthly, 1970:1–1993:9. (*Source*: IMF, *International Financial Statistics*)

zero differentials when British controls ended in 1979 (Marston, 1993, p. 524), and a similar figure with similar findings for Euromark and German interest rate differentials (Marston, 1993, p. 526).

Morris Goldstein and Michael Mussa (1993) have written a thorough survey of the massive literature on international capital market integration. One of their basic conclusions supports the work of Marston just discussed; interest differentials between offshore and domestic markets for the same instrument have largely disappeared, except in periods of currency distress when investors come to fear reimposition of controls. The same conclusion applies to covered interest parity for instruments of comparable maturity and risk denominated in different currencies. In the absence of controls, or threat of controls, we may conclude that markets in short-term liquid assets of major countries are so thoroughly integrated that for all practical purposes national money markets function as parts of a single world money market. A country can maintain a short-term interest differential with another country only if it is willing to accept an offsetting forward exchange rate differential. If a country is not willing to accept a forward exchange rate differential because of a policy of fixing exchange rates, then it cannot maintain an interest rate differential. This situation is quite different from the one prevailing during the Bretton Woods period of fixed exchange rates when many countries maintained capital controls and capital markets were much less well integrated than they are today.

Capital market integration cannot, however, be altogether complete for countries with floating exchange rates or fixed rates subject to change. Covered interest arbitrage maintains a tight relationship between the interest differential between two countries and the forward premium or discount on the exchange rate, but does not yield the net capital flow from one country to another that may be required to bring uncovered interest rates together. Although Treasury bills in two countries may have, and typically do have, zero default risk, uncovered investment positions across national borders carry exchange-rate risk that prevents investment in Treasury bills in two different countries from having identical risk characteristics. Depending on the characteristics of the lender – which country is the lender's home country, the location of the lender's business assets, and so forth – an uncovered investment in Treasury bills in one country will generally carry either more or less risk than investment in Treasury bills in the other country. However, the fact that risk of exchange rate changes prevents complete integration of capital markets does not necessarily argue for currency union (or irrevocably fixed exchange rates) because a currency union may create other risks.

Once past liquid money-market instruments, Goldstein and Mussa conclude that capital market integration is decidedly incomplete, although much greater today than a decade or so ago. Expected real returns probably differ substantially across major countries (French and Poterba, 1991), and portfolios are far short of being optimally diversified internationally. Investors display a 'home bias' that is not fully understood. The bias may reflect risk aversion and/or lack of knowledge about foreign investing.

If international capital markets are not yet fully integrated, their current scale after especially rapid growth in the 1980s is enormous. The Bank for International Settlements reports that total cross-border claims of reporting banks amounted to over $6 trillion at the end of 1992 (BIS, 1993, p. 99). International bond issues outstanding at the end of 1992 amounted to $1211 billion in straight fixed-rate issues, $211 billion in floating rate issues, and $254 billion in equity-related issues (BIS, 1993, p. 115). In a table reporting issuing activity in domestic and international bond markets for OECD countries, the BIS reports outstanding at the end of 1992 domestic issues of $14,070 billion and international issues of $1687 billion (BIS, 1993, p. 117).

If risk and unfamiliarity are major reasons why portfolios are not more diversified internationally, as Goldstein and Mussa argue, then the growth of the derivatives markets (futures, options, swaps) suggests that the trend toward more international diversification is likely to continue. Derivatives permit more expert risk management because professional investors can assume risk profitably through derivatives while selling less risky positions to risk-averse investors.

There are many other dimensions of change in the financial markets in recent years. Particularly noteworthy are the recovery from the LDC debt crisis of the early 1980s, the stock market crashes in 1987, and the banking difficulties experienced in some countries. These are beyond the scope of this chapter.

II IMPLICATIONS FOR MONETARY POLICY

The changing macroeconomic environment and tighter integration of international capital markets creates changed conditions in some respects for macroeconomic policy, and especially for monetary policy. The most obvious implications relate to exchange rate policy, which subject I take up first.

EMS – RIP?

The exchange rate mechanism of the European Monetary System suffered two crises within a year, in September 1992 and July 1993. The second crisis was especially important, as France gave up its effort to maintain a tight peg to the DM. Should Europe now find a way to say that the EMS should rest in peace, and that a more orderly system of floating rates be accepted?

Pressure to limit exchange rate fluctuations, and if possible peg rates in narrow bands, arises for two main reasons. First, fluctuations in nominal exchange rates during the floating rate period have been highly correlated with fluctuations in real exchange rates (Mussa, 1986; Frankel and Meese, 1987; Grilli, and Kaminsky, 1991; Obstfeld, 1993, figures 4.2 and 4.3). Changes in real exchange rates change international competitive positions, to the perceived disadvantage of exporting firms and import-competing firms in countries with appreciating currencies. Reducing trade barriers, or preventing creation of new barriers, is a difficult and delicate political problem for all governments. Government officials, even when inclined toward freer trade as individuals (as many are), believe themselves constrained by democratic political forces which are often inclined toward trade restriction. Thus, officials have an incentive to avoid conditions that give greater force to protectionists, and currency instability seems to be one of those conditions. An extreme version of this view of exchange rates is that 'floating rates are not feasible in Europe in practice' (Eichengreen and Wyplosz, 1993, p. 120). Whatever difficulties floating rates may cause, this extreme position is surely wrong given that Europe has in fact lived with exchange rate fluctuations for more years than not since the EC was created.

Economists sometimes inadvertently contribute to protectionist pressures by arguing a misleading view of the significance of current account balances. A striking feature of much of the recent analysis of international finance is that it assumes that international capital flows 'finance' current account 'imbalances'.[5] This view encourages governments to think of current account balances, positive or negative but especially negative, as a problem to be corrected. In fact, there need be nothing abnormal about a country experiencing a capital flow in or out and an accompanying current account balance of the opposite sign. Current and capital account balances are simultaneously determined. Indeed, in the short run it is probably more accurate to think of the current account 'financing' the capital account than the other way around; asset demand and supply considerations determine the exchange rate in the short run and the current account responds to exchange-rate changes.

Richard Cooper, recognizing the damage that can be caused by misinterpretation of balance-of-payments data, has recommended that,

> the European Community should abandon its effort to continue to collect current account data on member countries with respect to intra-Community trade after the abolition of border controls in 1992. . . . Indeed, the continued publication of current account imbalances may give rise to anxieties where none are warranted. We do not have current account figures for the states within the United States, and although such data would be useful for some analytical purposes, on the whole I believe it is beneficial not to have such figures.
>
> (Cooper, 1991, p. 180)

Reinforcing this position is the fact that world trade data are error prone. The IMF reports in *International Financial Statistics* that world exports in 1992 were $3644.9 billion whereas world imports that same year were $3768.6 billion. Thus, in 1992 statistical agencies in countries around the world managed to lose $124 billion of exports, or to find $124 billion of imports that did not exist, or some combination. Policies chasing after poor data are pure folly.

The second main reason for an effort to peg exchange rates is that the EMS has been viewed as a transitional step on the way to full currency union – a single common currency. The case for currency union is partly the same as the case for fixed rates outlined above and partly political. A single currency would certainly reflect a higher degree of political unification of the member states of the EC than now exists. With the collapse of the fixed parities system – only the guilder–DM peg remains – some have become more pessimistic about the prospects for eventual currency union.

Lessons from the Classical Gold Standard[6]

We can deepen our understanding of the issues facing exchange-rate policy today by reviewing experience under the gold standard before World War I. We know first of all that a system of fixed exchange rates can survive in stable form for many years, as experience during the classical gold standard demonstrates.

> In the core period and area of the gold standard, [exchange] rates were truly fixed and not just pegged, subject to change, as under the Bretton Woods system. They were so much fixed that the maintenance of gold parity between currencies came to be taken for granted. It is quite remarkable that from 1879 to 1914 . . . there were no changes in parities between the United States, Britain,

> France, and Germany – not to speak of a number of smaller European countries.
>
> (Dam, 1982, p. 38)

Economists have tended to concentrate on the properties of the fixed-exchange rate system without giving sufficient attention to its prerequisites. However, those who have studied the gold standard from legal and/or historical perspectives have always emphasized that contemporaries viewed the gold standard above all as in the *domestic* interest of the country adopting or maintaining it. Anna Schwartz has studied international currency agreements that were and were not implemented. In a 1987 paper, in a section entitled, 'Why Were Certain International Monetary Proposals Implemented?' Schwartz concludes that, 'international monetary arrangements are implemented, the preceding global examples suggest, only when national economic interests are not subordinated' (Schwartz, 1987, p. 397). In the same paper, in a section entitled, 'Why Were Selected International Monetary Proposals Not Implemented?' Schwartz says that 'one conclusion that emerges from investigation the fate of defeated international monetary proposals is that they were judged not to serve national interests' (Schwartz, 1987, p. 398).

The national interest in adhering to the gold standard was very strongly felt:

> In addition to the objective factors, mention must also be made of the weight of the psychological belief in the unquestioned and unquestionable obligation to adhere to the gold standard and to the specific fixed price of gold. Flouting the gold standard risked the opprobrium of one's own countrymen and of the rest of the world. Political leaders did not regard the gold standard as a policy instrument subject to manipulation in the pursuit of other goals. The hold of the gold standard as the guarantor of the domestic value of a currency and of stable international financial dealings was sacrosanct.
>
> (Schwartz, 1984, pp. 16–17)

What were the national interests people believed were served by the gold standard?

> The chief benefit for countries that adopted the gold standard at the close of the nineteenth century was access to capital markets,

centered in London, Paris, or Berlin. That benefit was invaluable for developing countries, which was the stage of economic maturity of most countries at the time. The chief cost, as viewed at the time, was the need to acquire a gold reserve. Except for Germany, which obtained its as the war indemnity from France in 1870–71, countries borrowed at home and abroad to get the funds with which to buy gold. The standing as a debtor the country achieved by embracing the gold standard far outweighed the interest cost of such borrowing.

With that choice made, governments did not have to coordinate policies they adopted explicitly, in pursuit of their national economic interest. Coordination was achieved by the maintenance of convertibility, which fixed exchange rates between national monetary units within narrow limits, with no external agency guiding the result. National price levels moved in close harmony. It was no myth of the gold standard world, as some latter-day critics describe it, that people, goods, capital, and money moved with reasonable freedom across national boundaries. International monetary arrangements reflected the independent choices of countries linked by market forces.

(Schwartz, 1987, p. 393)

Kenneth Dam has a similar view:

The rise of the gold standard to international dominance thus owed little or nothing to diplomacy. On the contrary, it was the product of a series of national decisions, each taken primarily for reasons of national interest, without extensive regard to the needs of the international community.

(Dam, 1982, p. 23)

Contemporary observers saw the issue the same way. John Stuart Mill, in his *Principles of Political Economy* (7th and last edition, first printed 1871), says that,

such a power [to issue inconvertible paper money], in whomsoever vested, is an intolerable evil. All variations in the value of the circulating medium are mischievous; they disturb existing contracts and expectations, and the liability to such changes renders every pecuniary engagement of long date entirely precarious. The person who buys for himself, or gives to another, an annuity of 100*l*.,

> does not know whether it will be equivalent to 200*l*. or to 50*l*. a few years hence. Great as this evil would be if it depended only on accident, it is still greater when placed at the arbitrary disposal of an individual or a body of individuals; who may have any kind or degree of interest to be served by an artificial fluctuation in fortunes; and who have at any rate strong interest in issuing as much as possible, each issue being in itself a source of profit. Not to add, that the issuers may have, and in the case of a government paper, always have, a direct interest in lowering the value of the currency, because it is the medium in which their own debts are computed. (Mill, 1936, p. 544)

A fixed exchange rate system can work when countries subordinate their short-run interests, or what may appear to be their short-run interests, to doing whatever is necessary to maintain the exchange-rate peg. The Netherlands shows that exchange-rate stability is not a gold-standard anachronism. The Dutch believe that it is in their national interest to peg tightly to the DM, and they have done so. No one today questions the commitment because the peg does seem to be in the Dutch interest. If Germany came to have a sufficiently screwed-up monetary policy, the Dutch would presumably find it in their interest to unpeg, and speculation would arise to that effect.

The national interest of other countries in pegging to the DM is not so clear. Was it really in the interest of France to raise interest rates to maintain the tight peg to the DM in 1993 when its unemployment rate had been continuously above 8 percent since 1982, and was expected to average above 11 percent in 1993? (see Figure 4.4). Whatever the correct answer to this question, it is not difficult to understand that many people would have doubts about the wisdom of maintaining high interest rates to support the exchange rate peg. Moreover, doubts about the French commitment meant that it had to maintain interest rates *above* those in Germany to support the franc. The weaker the French economy, in part because of the high interest rates, the less likely it appeared that France would maintain the exchange-rate peg, and so the higher interest rates had to go to support the exchange rate. The only way France could support the exchange-rate peg was to bear whatever pain was necessary to convince currency traders that the peg would survive. How long that would take no one knew.

A serious problem with the EMS is that a country's peg to the DM is a peg to a particular currency. The gold standard, in contrast, was an external standard not tied to any particular country. Although the gold standard in fact depended importantly on the skill and wisdom of the Bank of England, as analyzed so brilliantly in 1873 by Walter Bagehot in his *Lombard Street*, that Bank was itself subject to the external discipline of the gold standard and not free to set its own policy independent of that discipline. The EMS, however, has been a DM standard; when German reunification created a large domestic disturbance yielding higher inflation and higher interest rates, that disturbance was spread throughout the area pegged to the DM. The same would have happened under the gold standard, but with this important difference: no country that perceived the gold standard as being in its own national interest would have been forced to maintain much higher interest rates than the average across all countries because of devaluation fears. The difference in recent experience between Netherlands and France is instructive; as can be readily seen in Figure 4.6, Dutch interest rates have tracked German rates closely whereas French rates jumped considerably above German rates.

There is an enormous literature, and considerable controversy, on how well the gold standard worked to stabilize the price level and interest rates, and on how costly the system was to output stability. But the effectiveness of the system in stabilizing exchange rates and expectations concerning exchange rate changes is not in doubt. This stability, however, required an unbending commitment to the gold standard system. Fixed exchange rate systems do not provide stability without comparable commitment. With the recent collapse of fixed rates within the EMS, with the guilder–DM exception proving the point, we should now regard the case as settled that fixed exchange rate systems do not provide stability unless countries are willing to devote monetary policy to the single goal of fixing the exchange rate.

Is the Prospect of European Currency Union Dead?

Before the currency crisis of September 1992, many economists were optimistic about the prospects for a European currency union. For example, C. Fred Bergsten at a conference in the fall of 1991 said that, 'after numerous initial doubts, the EMS is now widely viewed as a resounding success. Indeed, it has been so successful that it will probably evolve into a full Economic and Monetary Union (EMU) within this decade' (Bergsten, 1993, p. 588). Others at the same conference were more cautious. 'Historians following too close on the heels of events, it is said, risk getting kicked in the teeth' (Eichengreen,

1993, p. 621). Does the currency turmoil of September 1992 and July 1993 doom the EMU?

France and other countries had, of course, hoped that Germany would take some of the pressure off by lowering German domestic interest rates, and as of this writing they continue to hope that depreciation of their currencies against the DM will be limited by German rate cuts. Germany, on the other hand, has viewed its inflation problem as a serious one requiring tight monetary policy. No political mechanism exists within the EC to reconcile differing views on what monetary policy is appropriate. A currency union would not eliminate such problems, as regional differences in appropriate monetary policy would still exist. In the United States, for example, the recession of 1990–91 and subsequent slow recovery was especially painful for the two coasts, with the Midwest doing comparatively better. Monetary policy is set in the United States in a unified fashion, primarily on the basis of feedback from national average statistics on inflation, unemployment, and so forth. A common EC currency would also require an EC monetary policy that somehow reconciled, or cut through the middle of, divergent regional interests.

A common EC currency may or may not be desirable, but judging its desirability by experience under the EMS is a mistake. A fixed exchange rate system has severe deficiencies compared with a common currency. As discussed in the previous section, experience demonstrates that a fixed rate system can be stable only for countries willing to subordinate their monetary policies to a center currency, as the Netherlands has with respect to the DM. Otherwise, countries will negotiate with each other about monetary policy, but in the end some country or the other will go its own way and the system will collapse, as is assured with the integration of financial markets in today's world. If there is enough political agreement to settle on a common monetary policy, then countries might as well have a common currency and avoid the instabilities and extra costs of separate currencies.

Another way to put this point is that the only reason to maintain separate currencies is to the retain the option of changing the exchange rate; that option is exactly what makes the system unstable. If countries really want to forego that option because they really want fixed exchange rates, then they should negotiate the terms of a currency union. Until they can negotiate a currency union, a stable currency system requires that they either subordinate monetary policy to a center currency or accept the reality of floating exchange rates.

A common fiat currency system requires negotiation; it cannot be simply adopted by individual countries the way the gold standard was. The essential lesson from the gold standard, which was a durable system, and from fixed-exchange rate systems that have all lasted at most a few years at a time, is that individual countries must see currency union as in their national interest and not just as international obligations for vaguely understood international purposes.

What advantages and disadvantages might countries see to belonging to a European Monetary Union? For a country such as Italy, the advantages would certainly include lower average inflation, improved and lower-cost access to world capital markets, and reduction of disturbances to trade arising from changes in exchange rates. These are the same advantages that attracted countries to the international gold standard in the late nineteenth century. The disadvantages would be the elimination of local autonomy over monetary policy and the loss of a national currency as a symbol of national identity. For Italy, monetary policy is probably less important as a stabilization tool than as a revenue source through inflation that eases fiscal constraints. For France and the United Kingdom, the use of monetary policy for domestic stabilization probably has some value; they will have to see the loss of the monetary-policy instrument and the symbolic value of a separate national currency as worth the gains in other areas before they will want to proceed to monetary union. Germany will have to be convinced that the political mechanisms controlling a common monetary policy will yield low inflation, and that the political gains from tighter union, especially with France, are worth the risks of higher inflation.

Monetary Targeting

Many central banks have announced monetary targets since the mid 1970s, and these targets played a role in the more disciplined monetary policies that brought down inflation in the early 1980s.[7] Table 4.1 provides an indication of the richness, if that is the right word, of targets since 1980.[8] Blank cells in the table indicate the absence of announced targets for the year in question. The table understates the uneven influence of announced targets; some countries have sometimes called the targets 'monitoring ranges', and all countries have often or even typically failed to reach the announced target ranges. Moreover, statistical definitions of the various monetary concepts have changed from time to time.

Table 4.1 Published objectives of monetary policy

	1980	*1981*	*1982*	*1983*	*1984*	*1985*	*1986*	*1987*	*1988*	*1989*	*1990*	*1991*	*1992*	*1993*
Canada	M_1	M_1	M_1									CP	CP	CP
France	M_2	M_2	M_2	M_2R	M_2R	M_2R	M_2R	M_2	M_2	M_2	M_2	M_3	M_3	M_3
							M_3	M_3						
Germany	CBM	CBM	CBM	CBM	CBM	CBM	CBM	CBM	M_3	M_3	M_3	M_3	M_3	M_3
Italy	TDC	TDC	TDC	TDC	TDC	TDC	CPS	CPS	M_2	M_2	M_2	M_2	M_2	M_2
						M_2	M_2	M_2	CPS	CPS	CPS	CPS		
Netherlands	M_2	M_2					DM_2	DM_2			DM_2			
Switzerland	CBMA	CBMA	CBMA	CBMA	CBMA	CBMA	CBMA	CBMA	CBMA	CBMA	CBM	CBM	CBM	CBM
United Kingdom	£M_3	£M_3	M_1	M_1	M0	M0	M0	M0	M0	M0	M0	M0	M0	M0
			£M_3	£M_3	£M_3	£M_3	£M_3	£M_3					M_4	M_4
			PSL	PSL									RPIX	RPIX
United States	M_1	M_1	M_1	M_1	M_1	M_1	M_1	M_2	M_2	M_2	M_2	M_2	M_2	M_2
	M_2	M_2	M_2	M_2	M_2	M_2	M_2	M_3	M_3	M_3	M_3	M_3	M_3	M_3
	M_3	M_3	M_3	M_3	M_3	M_3	M_3	TDNS	TDNS	TDNS	TDNS	TDNS	TDNS	TDNS
	CR	CR	CR	TDNS	TDNS	TDNS	TDNS							

Note: CBM = central bank money; CBMA = adjusted monetary base; CP = consumer prices; CPS = credit to the non-state sector; CR = credit proxy, bank credit; DM_2 = contribution of the banking system to M_2 creation; M0 = wide monetary base; M_2R = M_2 holdings of residents; PSL = private-sector liquidity; RPIX = retail prices excluding mortgage interest payments; TDC = total domestic credit; TDNS = total domestic debt of non-financial sectors;
Source: Bank for International Settlements, *Annual Report*, 1980 to 1993.

Although monetary targets seemed to have operational significance for monetary policy in the late 1970s and early 1980s, by 1993 little significance remained except, perhaps, in Germany. Central banks abandoned monetary targeting as the income velocity of money seemed to become unstable and unpredictable. The appropriate role of monetary targeting is an extremely important issue; I will look first at the instability of velocity in the 1980s and then discuss what conclusions ought to be drawn from this experience.

The Problem of Unstable Velocity

Figure 4.8 documents what happened to velocity in six countries using the IMF's definition of 'money', here called 'narrow money'. The figure shows clearly the relatively smooth upward trend to narrow money velocity in the United States, and subsequent reversal of trend and increased variability that led the Federal Reserve to abandon its M1 targets in 1987. (M1 was the most important of the Fed's announced targets until the Fed relaxed its efforts to achieve a money growth target in the fall of 1982.) Figure 4.9 repeats the exercise for the IMF's definition of money plus 'quasi-money', here called 'broad money'.

For both narrow and broad definitions of money, velocity was more stable year to year and its trend growth more stable before 1980 than after 1980. In fact, Benjamin Friedman and Kenneth Kuttner (1992) conclude that in the United States the relationship between nominal income and money entirely disappeared after 1980. Breaks in the money series explain part of the variability of velocity in Figures 4.8 and 4.9, but this fact obviously does not strengthen the case for monetary targeting.

The perception of unstable velocity was the most important single factor leading central banks to abandon monetary targeting, but this perception has been supported by the logic of financial innovation and deregulation as the source of the instability. The obvious changes in financial markets in recent years have provided new raw material for the intellectual case against monetary targeting. If this case is wrong, or incomplete, then the argument against monetary targeting is weaker than it appears.

Although central banks have largely abandoned monetary targeting, monetary policymakers who ignore money growth altogether do so at their peril. The UK's problem of a sharp acceleration of inflation in the late 1980s, followed by severe recession, was largely a consequence of ignoring money growth. As documented in Poole (1992),

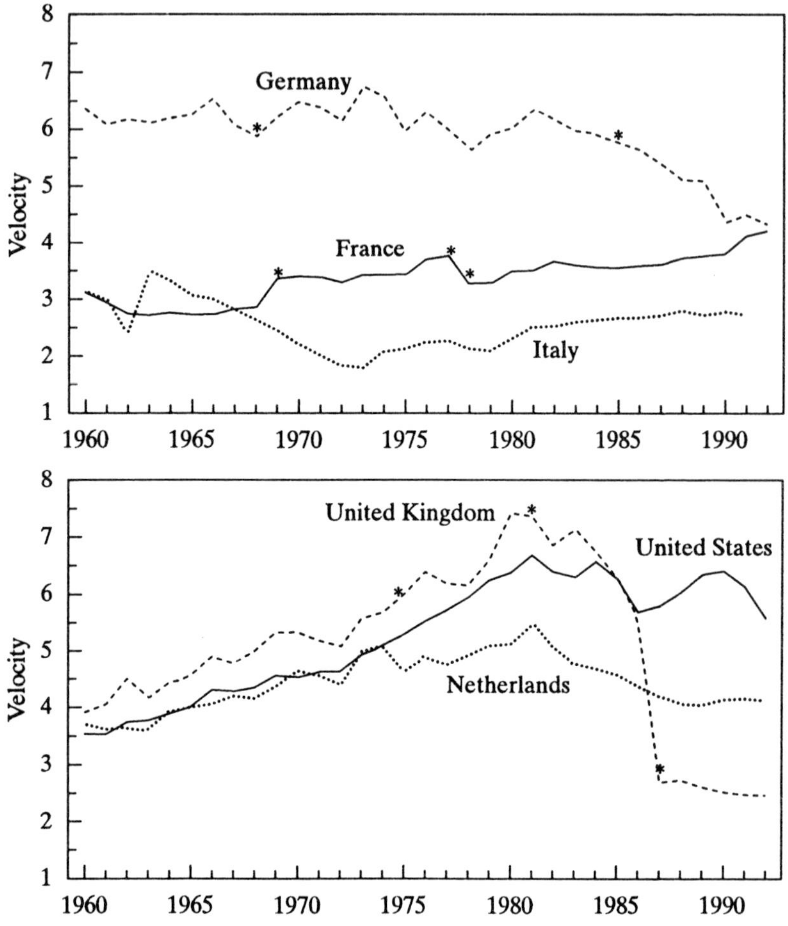

* indicates break in money series

Figure 4.8 Narrow money velocity, selected countries, 1960–92. (*Source*: IMF, *International Financial Statistics*)

the UK's M1 (national definition) 12-month growth peaked at about 25 percent in early 1986 and remained above 15 percent until late 1988. Growth in M2 (national definition) peaked at about 15 percent in mid 1986 and remained above 10 percent until 1989.

Many observers have argued that recent behavior of velocity shows that monetary policy *should* ignore money growth. Friedman and Kuttner put the point this way:

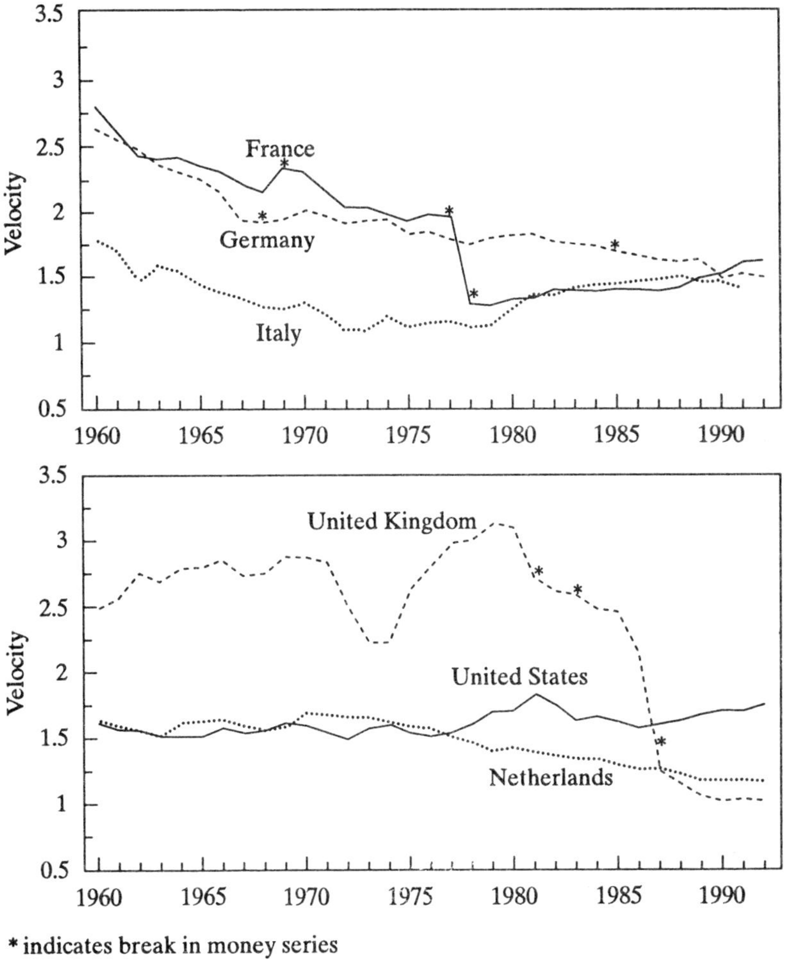

Figure 4.9 Broad money velocity, selected countries, 1960–92. (*Source*: IMF, *International Financial Statistics*)

The deterioration of the evidence supporting a relationship to either real or nominal income, or to prices, appears not just for M1 but for other monetary aggregates and for credit as well. Evidence from earlier samples indicating cointegration of real income and real money balances (with due allowance for the effect of interest rates) also disintegrates when the sample extends into the 1980's.

These changes over time in observable empirical relationships

> bear strongly negative implications for many familiar monetary-policy frameworks that center the design and implementation of policy on money (or credit). The point is not just that the money-income relationship does not satisfy the stringent conditions that would be required to render optimal the strict use of money as an intermediate target. More importantly, there is no evidence to show that fluctuations in money contain any information about subsequent movements in income or prices.
>
> (Friedman and Kuttner, 1992, pp. 490–91)

Evidence of the relationship between money growth and inflation over long time series and evidence from a cross-section of countries with widely differing inflation rates is simply too extensive to be dismissed. Consider Figure 4.10, which provides cross-section views of the stability of velocity for 1970–80 and 1980–91 for the countries listed as 'high-income economies' in the tables in the back of the World Bank's *World Development Report 1993*.[9] For both panels in the figure, the horizontal axis measures the average annual increase of broad money less the average annual increase in real GDP (equivalent to the growth rate of the ratio of money to real GDP) and the vertical axis the average annual change in the GDP deflator. If velocity were constant over time for each country individually, each point would lie on the diagonal. The points do stretch pretty much along the diagonal for the 1970–80 period, but are scattered to a considerably greater extent for the 1980–91 period. Some of the individual observations are identified in the figures so we can see which countries are farthest from the diagonal. Given the extensive discussion of the 'breakdown' of the velocity relationship for the United States, observations in the figure for the United States are also identified.

Figure 4.10 does suggest greater variability of inflation after 1980 than before. However, note that, putting Israel aside, inflation ranged from 5 percent to 16 percent per year for the 1970–80 period but only from about 1.5 percent to 9.5 percent for the 1980–91 period. The countries with the lowest inflation – Japan, Netherlands, Singapore, and Germany – experienced the largest proportional deviations of actual inflation from predicted inflation based on money growth and the assumption of stable velocity.

The issue is how we can reconcile the following facts: (1) Using quarterly data for the United States, and probably for many other countries with relatively low rates of inflation as well, the relation-

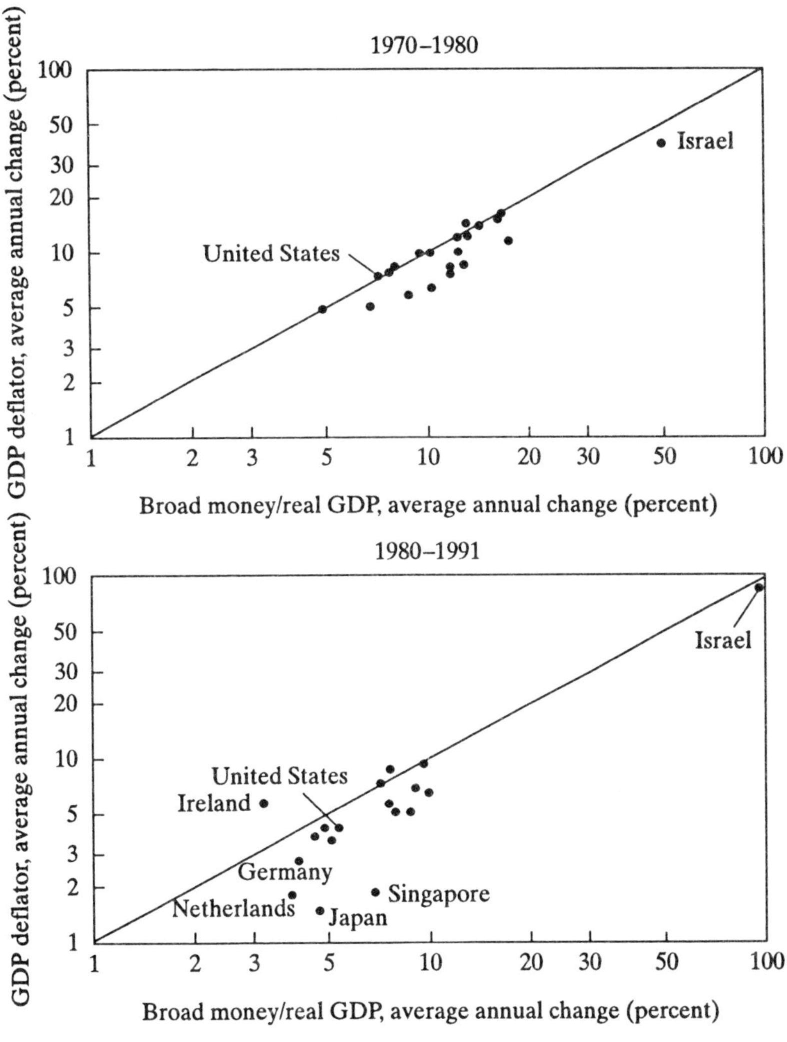

Figure 4.10 Money growth and inflation, high-income countries. (*Source*: World Bank, *World Development Report 1993*, Tables 1, 2, 13)

ship between money and prices is non-existent or very weak; (2) Using long time series for individual countries encompassing varying inflation, the relationship between money and prices fits the quantity theory model reasonably well; (3) Using cross-section data covering countries with differing inflation rates, the relationship between money and prices fits the quantity theory model reasonably well.

Unstable Velocity as a Consequence of Optimal Monetary Policy
Most observers have interpreted the increased variability of velocity as reflecting behavioral change in the private economy, including that related to financial innovation and deregulation. However, Tanner (1993) argues that 'from a fundamental point of view, [the weak relationship between money and income] just may mean that contracyclical monetary policy was being more effectively followed in the 1980s.' I believe that Tanner's explanation is substantially correct; the variability of velocity is actually a symptom of central bank success in reducing inflation rather than evidence that the functional relationship between money growth and inflation has broken down.

Consider the following simple model:

$$Y = \alpha_0 + \alpha_1 X + \beta M + \varepsilon \tag{4.1}$$

with means $\mu_\varepsilon = \mu_X = 0$, variances σ_ε^2, σ_X^2, and covariance $\sigma_{\varepsilon X} = 0$. The central bank observes the vector X, and adjusts M to offset the effects of X on Y (GDP).

The optimal M is

$$M^* = \frac{Y_f - \alpha_0 - \alpha_1 X}{\beta} \tag{4.2}$$

where Y_f is the target level of GDP.

We can show that

$$\sigma_{YM} = 0 \tag{4.3}$$

Now suppose M is not set at M^* but instead at

$$M = \lambda M^*, \quad \lambda > 1, = 1, \textit{or} < 1 \tag{4.4}$$

Then,

$$\begin{aligned} \sigma_{YM} &= [\alpha_1 X(1-\lambda)+\varepsilon]\left[-\frac{\lambda}{\beta}(\alpha_1 X)\right] \\ &= -\alpha_1^2\left(\frac{\lambda}{\beta}\right)(1-\lambda)\sigma_X^2 \end{aligned} \tag{4.5}$$

$$\begin{aligned} \text{If } \lambda &= 1.0, \text{ then } \sigma_{YM} = 0 \\ &< 1.0, \text{ then } \sigma_{YM} < 0 \\ &> 1.0, \text{ then } \sigma_{YM} > 0 \end{aligned} \tag{4.6}$$

If monetary policy is optimal ($\lambda = 1.0$), then M and Y are uncorrelated. If monetary policy under-reacts to information in X (λ

< 1.0), then money and GDP are *negatively* correlated. The intuition of this apparently strange result is straightforward. Suppose that X rises, which tends to push Y up, and that policymakers respond by reducing M. However, when policy under-reacts, M does not decline by enough to offset the full effects of X and so what we observe is a negative correlation between M and Y. If policy overreacts ($\lambda > 1.0$), then monetary disturbances dominate the outcome, yielding a positive correlation between M and Y.

We can also examine this issue in an econometrics setting. Estimation of private sector monetary relationships – β in the simple model above – may yield biased coefficients if policymakers respond to information in X. If X (or some part of it) is not observed by the econometrician, then the unobserved variable is part of a regression's error term. Policy makes M correlated with the true error term, introducing bias in coefficient estimates. If we think of the systematic part of the velocity relationship as measuring the demand for money, then optimal policy may make the demand for money appear highly unstable.

This is a very old point, long a part of the optimal control and econometrics literatures.[10] To summarize, optimal policy destroys the simple correlation between policy instruments and policy targets (goals), or the level of utility from a utility function combining multiple targets into one objective function.

Tanner (1993) argues that a model including interest rates, stock prices, and other variables can explain observed fluctuations in M2 velocity in the United States – that is, that the structural relationship between money and other economic variables has not fallen apart. His model of the structural relationship may or may not be satisfactory but, even if it is, putting substantial weight on unpredictable variables such as interest rates and stock prices does not rescue the case for fixed money-growth targets. If, for example, the money-demand function has a relatively high interest elasticity, then real disturbances will cause changes in nominal income unless the central bank is successful in offsetting the disturbances by changing money growth. Of course, the *theoretical* possibility that the central bank can offset disturbances does not mean that it *in fact* can or will do so, or do so more successfully than the private sector would under a policy of steady money growth. The minimal conclusion from experience after 1980 is that central banks can permit wide fluctuations in money growth without destabilizing nominal GDP; I think it reasonable to accept the stronger conclusion that many central banks have made nominal GDP growth more stable than it would have been if money growth had been stable.

Monetary policymakers in most countries have operated by controlling short-term interest rates on a day-to-day basis. The financial environment has changed significantly as policy has been effective in reducing inflation and establishing greater credibility. Monetary policy, at least as I have followed it in the United States, seems fairly straightforward in conception. Pursuing the key objective of low, or lower, inflation over the medium term, the authorities track numerous measures of the state of the economy, and then press interest rates up or down bit by bit until the balance of real growth and inflation seems about right. Provided the central bank moves interest rates soon enough, the procedure works because the response of the economy to interest-rate changes is rapid enough that policymakers can readjust rates if necessary before the economy goes too far off track. Money growth is important in the information set, but central banks do not adjust interest rates in pursuit of a money-growth target *per se*. Central banks breach announced money-growth ranges when various measures of money are going off in different directions, and when other information seems to disconfirm the message from money growth. Policymakers seem less impatient with respect to unemployment and real growth than they used to be; they are more willing than before to let the real economy evolve by itself against the backdrop of low and stable inflation.

Political objectives other than low inflation naturally intrude into the monetary policy process. German unification obviously affected monetary policy in Germany. France's objective of a tighter EC relationship with Germany led it to hold on to its exchange-rate objective longer than its macroeconomic situation in isolation might have warranted. But the most important common feature of monetary policy among the countries studied in this chapter is the commitment to lowering inflation from the high rates of the 1970s. On the whole, central banks have been highly successful in offsetting disturbances, such as the sharp decline in oil prices in 1986. Given this success, markets have displayed reduced sensitivity to reported fluctuations in money growth; that is, markets have been willing to hold excess money balances temporarily without developing fears that rising inflation was just around the corner. The net result has been less stable velocity than before.

What is not understood, certainly not at a quantitative level, is exactly how central banks have achieved their success in reducing inflation while often breaching money growth targets. Discretionary policy is certainly not random policy; it seems to involve interest-rate feedback control based on a high weight on the policy objective of holding down inflation and an ability to distinguish transitory from longer-lasting economic developments. Central banks evaluate financial conditions, including certainly money growth, in sorting out when interest rate adjustments are appropriate. I wish I had a better understanding of how this process works, but I do not.

The Appropriate Role for Monetary Targets

The appropriate lesson from experience after 1980 is not that financial changes have made money growth irrelevant but that central banks can indeed produce better outcomes through what is usually called 'discretionary' monetary policy than by adhering to money growth targets. Acceptance of the argument that an astute central bank can indeed produce better outcomes for the economy through discretionary policy than by adhering strictly to monetary targets does not lead to the conclusion that monetary aggregates targets have no role. In fact, the traditional arguments for aggregates targets remain largely unaffected.

Most advocates of money growth targets have been willing to accept the idea that target ranges rather than single-valued targets are appropriate. Experience after 1980 reinforces the case for ranges; central banks can adjust policy within the ranges to offset disturbances. However, in recent years central banks have often breached even relatively wide ranges without unfortunate effect, and indeed with stabilizing effect. Nevertheless, announced ranges are still useful because they force, or should force, central banks to face up to the risks they are running by permitting money growth above or below rates expected to be consistent with inflation and other ultimate goals of policy. If investigation convinces a central bank that there is a compelling case for breaching an announced target range, then such a policy is appropriate. However, even a range that is breached can play a useful role because announcing ranges keeps money in the forefront of policy debate and helps to avoid a situation in which money growth is considered just another of scores of relevant variables.

Announced target ranges also provide guidance about monetary policy to the markets. A central bank may find it awkward to explain why it believes breaching a target range is appropriate, but the dialog about policy forced by announced ranges helps to inform markets about policy. An important feature of policy dialog in recent years has been central bank analysis of the goal of reduced inflation and maintenance of low inflation once achieved. Money growth targets should be viewed as instrumental in achieving the goal and not as ends in and of themselves. Given that high money growth so often leads to inflation, announced targets serve the valuable function of requiring central banks to explain why conditions require money growth outside the announced range if monetary policy is to achieve its announced goals.

Announced target ranges can be valuable in helping central banks avoid policy mistakes due to political pressure. In 1992–3, for example, monetary policymakers in Germany could appeal to money growth targets as part of their public case for staying with policies to resist inflation. British policymakers should have appealed to money growth targets in 1987 to break off earlier from the policy of stabilizing and then pegging sterling to the DM.

Prudential Policy

Prudential aspects of monetary policy are concerned with safeguarding the stability of the financial system, and especially the banking system. Prudential policy usually concentrates on matters of regulation, supervision and examination.

There are four basic ways for banks and other financial institutions to get into trouble: fraud, high costs and poor management, assumption of excessive interest-rate risk and assumption of excessive default risk. The changing financial environment has implications for all but the first of these ways for banks to get into trouble.

Without question, financial markets have become more competitive in recent years as regulations have broken down and/or been dismantled. Banks face increased competition from non-bank financial intermediaries, from securities markets, and from competitors in other countries. Inefficient banks will lose market share, and in extremis be driven into bankruptcy. Given the commitment to greater international integration of financial markets, central banks cannot protect their commercial banks from inefficiency; inefficient banks must either become efficient or be eased gracefully from the scene.

With regard to default risk and interest-rate risk, the starting point for analysis must be recognition that banks are in the business of managing and bearing risk. It is always possible that sufficiently adverse outcomes will bankrupt even banks that manage risks well.

Occasional bank failures have no implications for systemic financial stability; only when the risk of failure is widespread should central banks be concerned.

Widespread failures are almost invariably a consequence of major changes in the macroeconomic environment that place many banks at once out in the tails of the probability distributions of the risks they assume. Thus, by far the most important feature of sound prudential policy is sound macroeconomic management. For example, the widespread failure of agricultural banks in the United States in the mid 1980s was less a consequence of these banks making unsound loans in the late 1970s than of an enormous economic cycle in inflation and disinflation, with an accompanying cycle in the foreign exchange value of the US dollar. No reasonable person could have predicted the swings in real interest rates and prices of agricultural commodities experienced over the 1978–84 period.

It is because macro stability is central to financial stability that I have concentrated in this chapter on issues of exchange-rate management and the variability of velocity. Drawing the right lessons from recent experience should assist central banks in maintaining macroeconomic stability.

III CONCLUSIONS

Integration of the financial markets of high-income countries has changed the macro policy environment in an important way. Countries have much less freedom than a decade ago to pursue independently determined exchange rate and domestic policies. The United States and the countries of Western Europe have returned much of the way to the degree of capital market integration that characterized the classic gold standard era.

Financial markets have changed in many other ways that I have not discussed because the topics are taken up elsewhere in this volume or are well-known. These include problems in banking, growth of securitization, and so forth. These developments are highly important in a number of respects, including especially their microeconomic efficiency aspects. We should, however, not underestimate the importance of lower inflation for many of the changes we observe. Inflation, on both the way up and the way down, creates many deep-seated changes in an economy that are too readily attributed to 'institutional' change. An easy example is that recent issuance of

50-year and 100-year corporate bonds in the United States is a consequence of low inflation and not of institutional change.

Some have argued that changes in financial markets have created a new world for monetary policymakers by creating instability in the income velocity of money. My thesis, though, is that the recent behavior of velocity has more to do with the success of monetary policy in bringing down inflation and in responding to economic disturbances than to institutional change in the financial markets. Unstable velocity is exactly what we should observe from optimal monetary policy. Many policymakers treat the instability of velocity as a problem; they should instead treat it as evidence of their own competence.

Notes

1. I thank Data Resources, Inc. for providing access to its data bank, from which I drew the data for many of the figures in this chapter.
2. Note that the World Bank – the source of the data for Figure 4.1 – measures a rate of change by a least-squares regression rather than a compound rate calculated from the initial year to the terminal year. This procedure prevents the initial or terminal year from having an undue influence on the estimate.
3. The dates in the titles of the figures, including this one, are not entirely accurate due to data reporting lags that differ from one country to another.
4. See Goldstein and Mussa (1993), Table 1, for a list of liberalizing steps and their dates among the major industrial countries.
5. An excellent illustration of this proposition is the recent conference volume, *International Adjustment and Financing: The Lessons of 1985–1991* (Bergsten, 1991). In the abstract, the authors of papers in this volume comment from time to time that the current account, the capital account, exchange rates, and other macroeconomic variables are simultaneously determined, but the detailed analysis almost always treats the exchange rate as a more or less exogenous, or at least policy-influenced, variable and the capital account as passively financing the current account.
6. The references at the end of the chapter contain a number of items beyond those mentioned specifically in this section that help to provide a perspective on insights from the gold standard period relevant to understanding current conditions.
7. Bernanke and Mishkin (1992) provide a useful overview of experience with monetary targeting in Canada, Germany, Japan, Switzerland, United Kingdom and United States.

8. I have constructed the table from tables in the annual reports of the BIS. The BIS tables are not perfectly consistent from one year to the next, and so my table may contain minor errors.
9. A number of high-income countries are not included in the figure because discontinuities in their monetary data make inclusion impossible.
10. See, for example, Theil's proof that under optimal policy in a certainty-equivalence model with a quadratic loss function the loss is independent of the controlled variables (policy instruments), which implies that target variables and controlled variables are uncorrelated (Theil, 1964, pp. 54–6). To my knowledge, Teigen (1964) was the first to provide estimates of the demand for money in a simultaneous equations framework.

References

Bagehot, W. (1910) *Lombard Street* (New York: E.P. Dutton & Co.) (first edition 1873).

Bagehot, W. (ed) (1991) *International Adjustment and Financing: Lessons of 1985–1991* (Washington, DC: Institute for International Economics).

Bergsten, C. F. (1993) 'The Collapse of Bretton Woods: Implications for International Monetary Reform', in M. D. Bordo and B. Eichengreen, *A Retrospective on the Bretton Woods System: Lessons for International Monetary Reform* (Chicago: University of Chicago Press) pp. 587–93.

Bernanke, B. S. (1993) 'The World on a Cross of Gold', *Journal of Monetary Economics* 31 (April), pp. 251–67.

Bernanke, B. S. and F. Mishkin (1992) 'Central Bank Behavior and the Strategy of Monetary Policy: Observations from Six Industrialized Countries', *NBER Macroeconomics Annual* (Cambridge, Mass.: MIT Press) pp. 183–228.

Bernstein, E. M. (1993) 'How the International Monetary Fund Saw Postwar Payments Problems', in Bordo, M. D. and B. Eichengreen, *A Retrospective on the Bretton Woods System: Lessons for International Monetary Reform* (Chicago: University of Chicago Press) pp. 495–504.

Bernstein, E. M. (BIS, 1993) Bank for International Settlements *63rd Annual Report.*

Bloomfield, A. (1959) *Monetary Policy Under the International Gold Standard, 1880–1914* (New York: Federal Reserve Bank of New York).

Bordo, M. D. (1981) 'The Classical Gold Standard', *Federal Reserve Bank of St. Louis Review* (May) pp. 2–17.

Bordo, M. D. (1984) 'The Gold Standard: The Traditional Approach', in M. D. Bordo and A. J. Schwartz (eds), *A Retrospective on the Classical Gold Standard* (Chicago: University of Chicago Press) pp. 23–113.

Bordo, M. D. and A. J. Schwartz (eds) (1984) *A Retrospective on the Classical Gold Standard* (Chicago: University of Chicago Press).

Bordo, M. D. and B. Eichengreen (eds) (1993) *A Retrospective on the Bretton Woods System: Lessons for International Monetary Reform* (Chicago: University of Chicago Press).

Cooper, R. (1991) 'Comment', in C. F. Bergsten (ed.), *International*

Adjustment and Financing: Lessons of 1985–1991 (Washington, DC: Institute for International Economics) pp. 178–81.

Dam, K. (1982) *The Rules of the Game: Reform and Evolution in the International Monetary System* (Chicago: University of Chicago Press).

Dornbusch, R. (1993) 'Comment', in M. D. Bordo and B. Eichengreen, *A Retrospective on the Bretton Woods System: Lessons for International Monetary Reform* (Chicago: University of Chicago Press) pp. 99–104.

Eichengreen, B. (1993) 'Epilogue: Three Perspectives on the Bretton Woods System', in M. D. Bordo and B. Eichengreen, *A Retrospective on the Bretton Woods System: Lessons for International Monetary Reform* (Chicago: University of Chicago Press) pp. 621–57.

Eichengreen, B. and C. Wyplosz (1993) 'The Unstable EMS', *Brookings Papers on Economic Activity 1993*:1, pp. 51–124.

Frankel, J. A. and R. Meese (1987) 'Are Exchange Rates Excessively Variable?' *NBER Macroeconomics Annual* (Cambridge, MA: MIT Press) pp. 117–52.

French, K. R. and J. M. Poterba (1991) 'Investor Diversification and International Equity Markets', *American Economic Review*, vol. 81 (May) pp. 222–6.

Friedman, B. M. and K. N. Kuttner (1992) 'Money, Income, Prices, and Interest Rates', *American Economic Review*, 82 (June) pp. 472–92.

Giovannini, A. (1989) 'How Do Fixed Exchange Rate Systems Work? Evidence From the Gold Standard, Bretton Woods and the EMS', in M. Miller, B. Eichengreen, and R. Portes, *Blueprints for Exchange Rate Management* (London: Academic Press) pp. 13–41.

Giovannini, A. (1993) 'Bretton Woods and Its Precursors: Rules versus Discretion in the History of International Monetary Regimes', in M. D. Bordo and B. Eichengreen (eds), *A Retrospective on the Bretton Woods System: Lessons for International Monetary Reform* (Chicago: University of Chicago Press) pp. 109–47.

Goldstein, M. and M. Mussa (1993) 'The Integration of World Capital Markets', in Federal Reserve Bank of Kansas City, *Changing Capital Markets: Implications for Monetary Policy* (conference volume forthcoming)

Grilli, V. and G. Kaminsky (1991) 'Nominal Exchange Rate Regimes and the Real Exchange Rate: Evidence from the United States and Great Britain, 1885–1986', *Journal of Monetary Economics*, vol. 29 (April) pp. 191–212.

Ikenberry, G. J. (1993) 'The Political Origins of Bretton Woods', in M. D. Bordo and B. Eichengreen (eds), *A Retrospective on the Bretton Woods System: Lessons for International Monetary Reform* (Chicago: University of Chicago Press) pp. 155–82.

Marston, R. C. (1993) 'Interest Differentials under Bretton Woods and the Post-Bretton Woods Float: The Effects of Capital Controls and Exchange Risk', in M. D. Bordo and B. Eichengreen (eds), *A Retrospective on the Bretton Woods System: Lessons for International Monetary Reform* (Chicago: University of Chicago Press) pp. 515–40.

McKinnon, R. I. (1993) 'The Rules of the Game: International Money in Historical Perspective', *Journal of Economic Literature* 31 (March) pp. 1–44.

Mill, J. S. (1936) *Principles of Political Economy*, 7th edn (London: Longmans, Green and Co. [7th edn first printed 1871]).

Mussa, M. (1986) 'Nominal Exchange Rates and the Behavior of Real Exchange Rates: Evidence and Implications', *Carnegie-Rochester Conference Series on Public Policy*, vol. 25, pp. 117–214.

Obstfeld, M. (1993) 'The Adjustment Mechanism', in M. D. Bordo and B. Eichengreen (eds), *A Retrospective on the Bretton Woods System: Lessons for International Monetary Reform* (Chicago: University of Chicago Press) pp. 201–56.

Poole, W. (1992) 'Exchange-Rate Management and Monetary-Policy Mismanagement: A Study of Germany, Japan, United Kingdom, and United States After Plaza', *Carnegie-Rochester Conference Series on Public Policy*, vol. 36, pp. 57–92.

Schwartz, A. J. (1973) 'Secular Price Change in Historical Perspective', *Journal of Money, Credit and Banking* (February), part II, pp. 243–69.

Schwartz, A. J. (1984) 'Introduction', in M. D. Bordo and A. J. Schwartz (eds), *A Retrospective on the Classical Gold Standard* (Chicago: University of Chicago Press), pp. 1–20.

Schwartz, A. J. (1986) 'Alternative Monetary Regimes: The Gold Standard', in C. D. Campbell and W. R. Dougan (eds), *Alternative Monetary Regimes* (Baltimore: The Johns Hopkins University Press), pp. 44–72.

Schwartz, A. J. (1987) *Money in Historical Perspective* (Chicago: University of Chicago Press).

Tanner, J. E. (1993) 'Did Monetarism Die in the 1980s?', *Journal of Economics and Business*, vol. 45 (August, October), pp. 213–29.

Teigen, R. L. (1964) 'Demand and Supply Functions for Money in the United States: Some Structural Estimates', *Econometrica*, vol. 32 (October), pp. 476–509.

Theil, H. (1964) *Optimal Decision Rules for Government and Industry* (Amsterdam: North-Holland).

Yeager, L. B. (1984) 'The Image of the Gold Standard', in Bordo, M. D. and A. J. Schwartz (eds), *A Retrospective on the Classical Gold Standard* (Chicago: University of Chicago Press), pp. 651–69.

Comments

Göran Lind

Since I am no academician but a central banker, I will not attempt to discuss this chapter from an academic perspective. Rather, I will look more to the aspects of the central banker and try to see how the theories presented by Professor Poole relate to my own experiences.

The chapter discusses primarily three topics:

- The problems surrounding the European Monetary system, EMS.
- The arguments for and against creating a European Monetary Union, EMU.
- Why the velocity of money has gradually become more unstable.

I will discuss these topics one by one. First, however, I wish to make a few comments on the general background outlined in the chapter.

Comments on the General Background

My first comment regards the trends of unemployment. It is apparent that unemployment rates in the US are much more stable over the economic cycle than those of most European countries. Particularly in recent years, when we have witnessed an increase in structural unemployment in Europe, US rates have continued to oscillate around 7 percent. This is an issue that has been discussed elsewhere. Is there something we as Europeans could learn from Americans or is the major and simple explanation that the number of job-seekers increase in the US in good times and drop when employment is scarce? The explanation for this might be the less generous financial benefits for unemployed persons in the US compared with those in Europe. In Europe, the benefits are often conditioned by the fact that you are still actively looking for a job, which gives you an inducement to stay in the job-seeking category also in a statistical sense.

My second comment relates to the statement that 'capital controls were a legitimate and even desirable way to assist in the maintenance of exchange rate stability' in the Bretton Woods system. I do not think this statement gives the complete picture. The IMF Charter (Article VIII) includes explicit stipulations against any restrictions on current payments. Furthermore, while restrictions on long-term capital flows are accepted by the IMF as a method to counteract sharp capital flows, they are only encouraged in one specific situation. That situation occurs when borrowed funds from the IMF cannot be used for the purposes intended but rapidly flow out of the country. However, I think that the attitude of the IMF towards exchange controls is not totally clear.

My third comment. Professor Poole mentions the 'home bias' which implies that investors tend to have a larger share of their investments in securities issued in the home country than is financially optimal and therefore rational. I think, however, that some home bias will always remain also on rational grounds. The domestic investor is always in a better position than the foreign investor to interpret what is actually going on in the domestic political process. We all know that politicians sometimes are saying things while meaning something different. It is therefore insufficient just to read his statement but you must also know who he is and in what circumstances he acted. It would be almost impossible for an outsider to get this kind of knowledge. At least it would cost large amounts, for instance to set up an office in the country concerned to gather information.

What I have said about politics also applies to information about the general economy and about corporations. Interpretation of such information is always easier if you know the local circumstances.

Now I will turn to the specific topics of the chapter, starting with the problems and lessons of the EMS.

Problems and Lessons of the EMS

Professor Poole discusses the EMS against the functioning of the gold standard. I agree that the gold standard had many attractive features from a monetary policy perspective. However, I think that comparisons should not be drawn too far. An important difference of surrounding circumstances is of course the relatively recent occurrence of large and swiftly moving capital flows. How would the gold standard have stood up against capital movements of the magnitude recently recorded? The crucial factor in any monetary system, as Professor Poole in my view rightly stresses, is the political commitment from the countries attached to the system. I also agree that the EMS contains a specific problem following from the fact that all currencies are in practice tied to other specific currencies, and in particular to the DM. But I disagree on the emphasis put on the so called national interest to stay in the EMS. The real issue is not whether it is in the French national interest to hike its interest rate levels in order to stay pegged to the DM, but if it is in the French interest to underline and increase confidence in the political commitment to maintain low inflation. An interest rate hike would act as a strong signal that this is the case.

Another comment. Professor Poole states that 'fixed exchange systems do not provide stability unless countries are willing to devote monetary policy to the single goal of fixing the exchange rate'. In my opinion there has been no lack of willingness to fully use the monetary policy to defend exchange rates during the turbulence in 1992 and in 1993. Coming from Sweden, I remember well the Riksbank's decision in the autumn of 1992 to increase interest rates to 500 percent to defend the Krona even during a deep recession and risking to further undermine an already fragile financial system. As I see it, the major problem is rather the large budget deficits in many countries which restrict the conduct of an active fiscal policy. This fact leads to speculation about a further need for monetary adjustments, i.e. to an unbalanced policy mix, which then destabilizes the exchange markets.

In the chapter, one of the main factors behind the EMS problems in the summer of 1993 is discussed. This relates to the diverging policy views between Germany on the one hand and other EMS participants on the other. The conclusion is then drawn that 'No political mechanism exists within the EC to reconcile differing views on what monetary policy is appropriate. A currency union would not eliminate such problems, as regional differences in appropriate monetary policy would still exist.' Yes, that may be the case. But there would still be a major improvement from today's situation. Since the monetary policy in a monetary union is to be decided on the basis of the situation in the whole union a country with higher than average inflation must make use of fiscal policy to combat inflation. In the case of the reunification of Germany, this would have implied a more balanced policy-mix than the one we have actually seen.

Professor Poole puts the question if we should let the EMS rest in peace. This is, of course, one of the most hotly debated financial topics at present among many groups of people. My view is the following: an EMS which – for example for reasons of politics – tries to be too rigid, i.e. not taking into account a pent-up need for exchange rate adjustments will in the end always be forced to make realignments. In this way, the loss of credibility and prestige becomes even worse. A more flexible EMS may, in fact, be a better stabilizer for the exchange markets provided that there is agreement on economic policy convergence and monetary co-operation between the countries involved. But then it is rather the policy commitment than the EMS as such which will accomplish the goal. And given such a commitment countries may as well go all the way and have a common currency. The primary use of the EMS would thus be as a transitional vehicle leading to the EMU. Maybe, a swift creation of a mini-EMU consisting of, say, Germany, France and the Netherlands would have favourable effects. Such a group of countries with similar views on important policy issues, not least on fighting inflation, and with rather similar economic structures, could turn into quite a successful monetary union. This might then induce other countries to make the economic-policy commitments necessary to join the group.

Suggestions have lately been put forward, e.g. by M. Delors, to restrict large, so called speculative, movements in the international financial markets. The underlying motive is said to be that some large transactions are being made solely for the purpose of manipulating the markets to create gains for the speculators. The ensuing turbulence of interest rates and exchange rates could have harmful effects on the real economy in the countries affected. I do not question this description, although I think that the actual volume of such purely speculative transactions should not be exaggerated. However, I have difficulty in finding appropriate measures against this problem. Outright exchange regulations would certainly not work in today's highly integrated international environment. Maybe a so-called Tobin turn-over tax on, especially, very short-term transactions would throw some sand in the wheels. But this would also hit the legitimate international financial transactions and increase costs for trade financing etc. Also, since the financial markets are highly innovative they would surely find ways to circumvent the tax; ways which make these markets more opaque. In addition to other disadvantages, such a development is not in the interest of the supervisory authorities.

Pros and Cons of a EMU

On this issue I have a problem to become a constructive discussant since I agree with Professor Poole's most important statement. He says that 'the only reason to maintain separate currencies is to retain the option of changing the exchange rate. . . . If countries really want to forego that option because they really want fixed exchange rates, then they should negotiate the terms of a currency union'. I agree with Professor Poole that the very option of being able to change exchange rates makes any pegged system potentially unstable, either because economic fundamentals change or because financial market participants do not believe in the official commitments and wish to put them to the test.

So the logic is that if a country is prepared to make the policy sacrifices needed to achieve the required economic convergence with other countries there is no need to retain the option to change the exchange rate. This could only be harmful to the credibility of the commitment. Instead, the country should opt directly for a monetary union with a single currency. If there is firm commitment from all the countries involved, the criterion presented by Professor Poole in relation to the gold standard, i.e. that participation must be voluntary and based upon the self-interest of each country, is fulfilled. No country would make such an extensive commitment without being certain that the net effect for the country is positive.

I may also note that Professor Poole does not seem fully consistent as to the motives for a currency union. He says that 'The case for a currency union is partly the same as the case for fixed rates . . . and partly political'. This implies that, in his opinion, there are no extra economic benefits specifically to be derived from establishing a currency union. But elsewhere he states that '. . . countries might as well have a common currency and avoid the instabilities and extra costs of separate currencies' thus implying that there indeed are economic gains to be made. A constructive interpretation, and one to which I would agree, is that the political commitment comes first and once there is political commitment the economic benefits will be windfall gains.

The Velocity of Money

Let me start with the thesis put forward by Professor Poole:

> The recent behaviour of velocity has more to do with the success of monetary policy than to institutional change in the financial markets. Unstable velocity is exactly what we should observe from optimal monetary policy. Many policymakers treat the instability of velocity as a problem; they should instead treat it as evidence of their own competence.

This is of course music to the ears of a central banker, but is it correct? I am not in a position to dispute nor to confirm this. However, the model presented does not, in my view, really prove the thesis just quoted. In the model, M (money) is adjusted to offset the effects of the vector X (which is undefined in the model) on Y (GDP). But the thesis is rather that monetary policy measures have affected inflation, which is not explicitly mentioned in the model. I believe, however, that the model could be easily changed to take account of these formal criticisms.

In Sweden, the Riksbank has never used monetary aggregates as intermediary targets but only as indicators seen together with a number of other indicators. One limitation of leaning too much on developments in monetary aggregates is the following: If the authorities use a narrow monetary aggregate target this is relatively easy to monitor and steer but it may be difficult to get the results desired from monetary policy solely by manipulating this narrow aggregate, since the aggregate is really too narrow – for example: notes and coins – to have a broad impact on the parameter you actually want to affect, such as inflation. Today, one might even question the usability of such monetary aggregates only comprising domestic components since the internationalisation of financial markets makes it increasingly easy to shift between liquidity expressed in different currencies. On the other hand, a broad monetary aggregate is a better indicator of developments but is difficult to steer through monetary policy.

Professor Poole's conclusion is that the discretionary monetary policy by central banks has proven more successful against inflation than a monetary policy simply adhering to monetary growth targets. I agree with this description and my conclusion is then that the central banks should look to a number of indicators, not merely monetary aggregates, before deciding on monetary policy. This will provide a broader picture of the state of the economy and of inflationary developments and expectations. Ever since the decision to float the Swedish krona in November 1992, the Riksbank has been busily working on identifying and analysing which indicators provide the best information. The same task has been performed in other central banks. In my view, discussing these issues among central banks and other interested parties is one of the most constructive things we can do at this juncture. One of the things that should be addressed is the degree of openness towards the public. I have, however, heard Mr King's views on this and I agree with him that publication of indicators and targets may be useful because they necessitate an open discussion when the central bank or, indeed, the Ministry of Finance, wants to change the parameters.

Professor Goodhart and others advocate a broader definition of the concept of inflation, one, for example, including asset price developments. I have no firm opinion on this issue and even if such a broad definition may be correct for theoretical reasons, it may be impossible to implement practically. However, this question should also be thoroughly discussed among the policy-makers since the outcome of such a debate might drastically affect the conduct of monetary policy.

Summary

The future of the EMS and the creation of an EMU is to a large extent a matter of political commitment to international economic integration, convergence and co-operation. If such commitment is forthcoming it is better to have a common currency and thus to discard the option of being able to change exchange rate relations, since the markets will always distrust any statement that a country will never use this option. The emphasis on political commitment does not imply that EMS or EMU will not provide economic gains – on the contrary. But you can never achieve these gains without the commitment.

As to monetary policy, I note that many countries are changing into a broader perspective, for instance using a number of indicators, than merely trying to monitor or steer some monetary aggregate. The most fruitful discussion today would probably be around the pros and cons of such a broad approach to monetary policy, including the definition of inflation.

Comments

Richard F. Syron

Upon my leaving graduate school in the late 1960s, one of my professors – very much in the American Cambridge tradition – questioned the logic of why I would go to work at the Federal Reserve. 'We all know money doesn't matter much, if at all', he stated, 'there is nothing the Fed can do to affect the economy'.

It is more than a little encouraging to have gotten to the point where we know that institutional mechanisms through which money matters are also important, and not merely a veil for macroeconomic growth and stability. On that score, I would note that institutional change had been a very consistent element in monetary policy deliberations over the last few years.

I would like first to comment on Professor Poole's chapter and then the Nakajima and Taguchi chapter.

Let me start by noting that I found myself in great agreement with Professor Poole. Thus, my observations are in the way of a different perspective, rather than a difference in interpretation of the facts.

On the issue of the undesirability and unworkability of capital controls, I would only add to Poole's observations that this is an area where the policy prescriptions consistent with the preference of most economists are completely consistent with institutional reality.

As anyone who has dealt with this in a reasonably open economy knows, the enabling advances in the technology of payments, information, and financial instrument development have made it extraordinarily difficult to constrain activity within any set of boundaries.

All of this has happened in a world in which the value of financial transactions relative to the real economy have grown dramatically; thus, it would be foolhardy to ignore these developments and not focus adequately on supervisory and payments risk concerns.

However, in a more fundamental sense, it seems fairly clear that the development of most new financial instruments has added markedly to financial and economic efficiency. While we can find exception to this generality, the ratio of gain to risk has been high thus far. It follows that the appropriate approach would be to develop sufficient supervisory familiarity with these new instruments and to ensure that institutions are prudent and well-capitalized.

While I share Poole's views on the efficiency of currency unions versus common currencies, I am less optimistic than he regarding a common European currency.

In the US we are emerging from a recession in which there has been an enormous variance in the experience of different parts of the nation. New England and the mid-Atlantic states are only now beginning to recover from what was for those regions an extremely deep downturn. While California may not yet have reached a similar point, in some other parts of the nation it would be difficult to find evidence of a recession.

This is not a new phenomenon. Some time ago I did some research examining the relative response of regions in the US to the business cycle. I expected, given advances in transportation and communications, greater convergence. I was completely wrong. If anything, the experience of the US is that regions are becoming less rather than more alike in economic performance. (Why is another matter.) This, of course, leads to any number of inquiries in the US of why economic policy has to be the same for all regions of the United States.

The advantages of a common currency for the US are beyond question; however, I wonder if the same applies for Europe at this time. After all, the US does have a common language and a culture in which people consider themselves primarily Americans and not New Englanders or Midwesterners. However, even in the US, labor mobility is much less than desirable, and is particularly poor during periods of structural disturbances, an example being our current experience with defense conversion.

The US, through unemployment compensation and other automatic stabilizers, does have a system where at least to some extent regional differences are muted by a common fiscal system. How would Europe deal with similar disruptions?

Economic preference also seems to vary more significantly within Europe than the US. The obvious example is recent German concerns about inflation and its impact across Europe. For these and other reasons, I wonder – in a world where fiscal policy is less and less an option – why the different nations of Europe would give up monetary policy flexibility anytime soon. I think it is worthwhile to consider some ways of maintaining the gains monetary policy has brought against inflation short of a common currency. At the very least, it seems to me that fairly strong convergence criteria should be satisfied first.

Monetary Policy and Money Velocity

Of course, as someone from the Fed, I feel compelled to discuss Poole's comments about money velocity, and monetary policy in general.

Let me first note where I agree, and then share some questions I might raise.

I share the view that recent breakdowns of traditional relationships do not mean that monetary aggregates have no role in monetary policy. I believe most of my Fed colleagues would agree with me on this.

However, that is entirely different from believing, given the change in velocity, that a strict aggregates approach can be followed with any precision for intermediate term stabilization policy, or that stabilization policy has no value.

Poole's data, and particularly his Figures 4.8, 4.9 and 4.10, tell me that at lower levels of inflation, the tie between money and prices is much more tenuous, at least in the short to intermediate run. Unfortunately, I am not sure I draw as much comfort as he does about the success of monetary policy from the breakdown of the money/price relationship at lower levels of inflation, shown in his Figure 4.10.

I would like to believe that the breakdown in velocity in the last few years is primarily the result of increased competence by us, but I'm skeptical. I understand, or at least I think I understand, control theory, but I think that is only part of the story. Most people agree that money has changed a great deal over the last three decades. As will be noted several times in this volume, depository institutions were a much larger part of the financial system in the 1960s and were virtually the only institutions with transaction accounts.

I will not bore you with the overly familiar story of the ease with which one can transfer between narrow and broader definitions of money and financial assets. Similarly, the development of check accessible home equity lines of credit and brokerage accounts with mutual funds have severely changed how individuals regard their demand balances. If all of these changes were well understood or if we had reached a new equilibria, things might be different, but I do not believe that is the case. Personally, I find it hard to believe that continued technical changes have not contributed greatly to instability in the demand for traditionally defined money.

Moreover, even if velocity is changing for the right reasons, it is still changing. The lesson I draw from all this is not that monetary aggregates do not matter. On the contrary – they matter a great deal. It is just that the time period in which they provide an adequate gauge for policy is longer, not shorter.

I am also in agreement with Poole concerning the usefulness of target ranges for the aggregates in current circumstances. I believe they provide a useful discipline for monetary policy, even if they may have to be violated at times.

Beyond that, the aggregates seem to me an indispensable guide in periods of higher inflation. Having worked as the Fed Chairman's assistant in 1980 and 1981, I am convinced that we could not have controlled inflation without strong adherence to an aggregates policy, for a wide range of economic and political reasons known to all of us.

Nakajima and Taguchi Paper

I found this chapter to be a particularly valuable review of developments in the banking industry around the globe. One thing that strikes me is that despite vast differences in legal structure, regulations, tax laws, macropolicy, and culture, the recent experience of banks has been similar.

There is value in looking for causes of problems that cross national boundaries. It would be too much of a coincidence for banks to have similar experiences in so many places for entirely different reasons. Thus, I do not think you can completely absolve macropolicy from any blame in banking problems. While some of my colleagues might disagree, I particularly think price volatility in the 1970s and 1980s was a real factor in the S&L problem in the US.

The S&L débâcle is an example of everything that went wrong in US financial regulation. While the S&L problem may well have occurred anyway, S&Ls were clearly very damaged by fluctuations in the price level.

The rate risk embedded in S&Ls portfolios made the industry functionally insolvent in the early 1980s, as a result of the rise in nominal rates accompanying inflation. Many of those that survived that insolvency believed that inflation was here to stay, and took a large credit risk on continued price appreciation in real estate. As long as prices were rising steadily and monotonically, there was no need to be concerned about collateral.

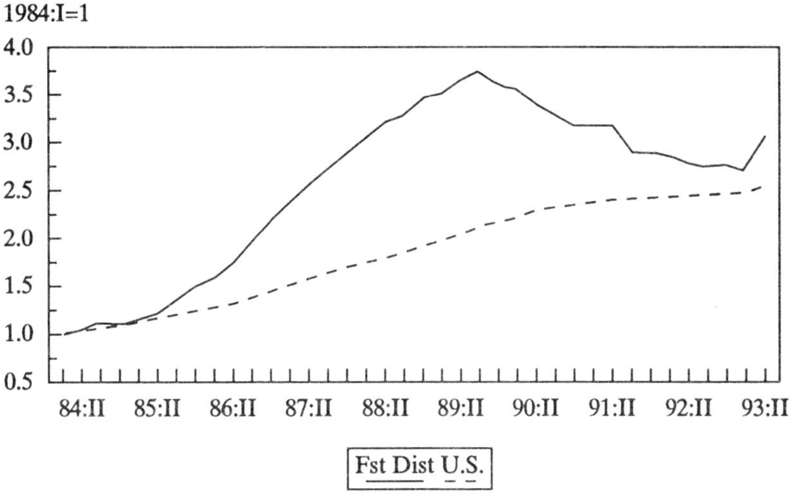

Figure 1 Domestic real estate loans. First District and US Commercial Banks. (*Source*: Board of Governors of the Federal Reserve System)

Even more fundamentally, while the industry did play a useful role in the United States in the 1930s to the 1960s because of inefficiencies in mortgage markets, by the 1970s these inefficiencies were disappearing and so was the need for a specialzied housing lender.

The S&L industry's ultimate franchise, however, was not their economic, but rather their political base. Their extraordinarily strong lobby combined with homebuilders and real estate agents meant they were not going to go without some substantial pain. And that is what happened. There was no real constraint on capacity, given deposit insurance. As in many other sectors, excess capacity went into real estate.

While most of the problems in commercial banks stemmed from real estate as well, the dynamic was somewhat different. First, commercial banks did not have the same problem with interest rate risk. However, they also took too much credit risk in one area, and the supervisory process did not adequately focus on concentration. Banks' unwillingness to downsize and regulatory constraints on diversifying contributed to the problems of the commercial banking industry.

The results of this are reflected in Figures 1–4. They portray the experience of New England not only because I am most familiar with it, but also because it is a particularly egregious case.

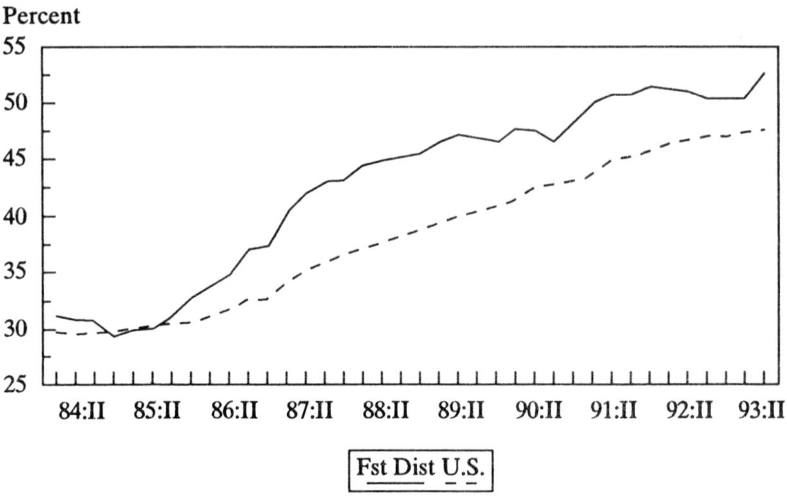

Figure 2 Domestic real estate loans to total domestic loans. First District and US Commercial Banks. (*Source*: Board of Governors of the Federal Reserve System)

Thus, drawing on the US experience, I would suggest that some of the factors occurring over the last decade that may cross national boundaries are:

(1) *Overcapacity in traditional financial institutions.* It seems apparent that enormous strides in technology and the development of non-bank sources of funds and services have resulted in over-capacity. While there may not be formal barriers to exit, no one wants to eliminate their own job. In many cases financial intermediaries have been franchises seeking business. Combined with deposit insurance, this becomes a recipe for an expensive disaster.

(2) *Across the globe, banks may well have been over-regulated, but undersupervised at the same time.* My own view is that this was certainly true in the US.

(3) *Compared with other institutions with similar risk characteristics, banks may well have been undercapitalized.*

(4) *Bank supervisory policy may have been procyclical*, at least in the up part of the cycle, and I suspect in the down part as well.

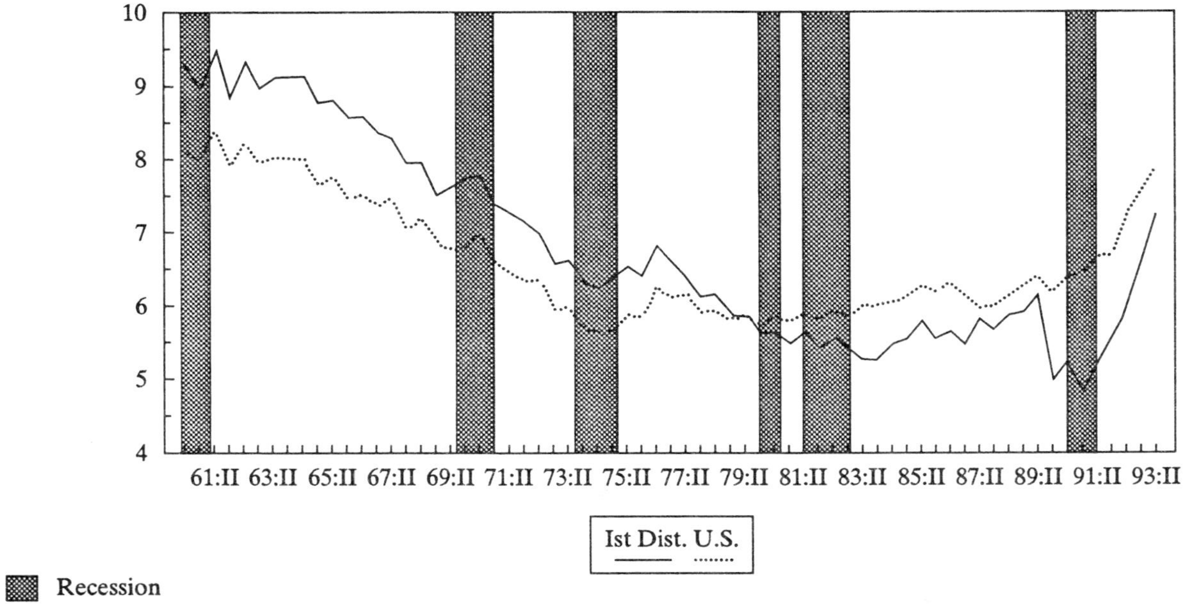

Figure 3 Equity capital as a percentage of total assets. US and First District Commercial Banks. *Note*: Equity capital consists of common stock, surplus, undivided profits and capital reserves (less net unrealized losses on marketable securities), perpetual preferred stock and related surplus, and cumulative foreign currency translation adjustments. (*Source*: Board of Governors of the Federal Reserve System)

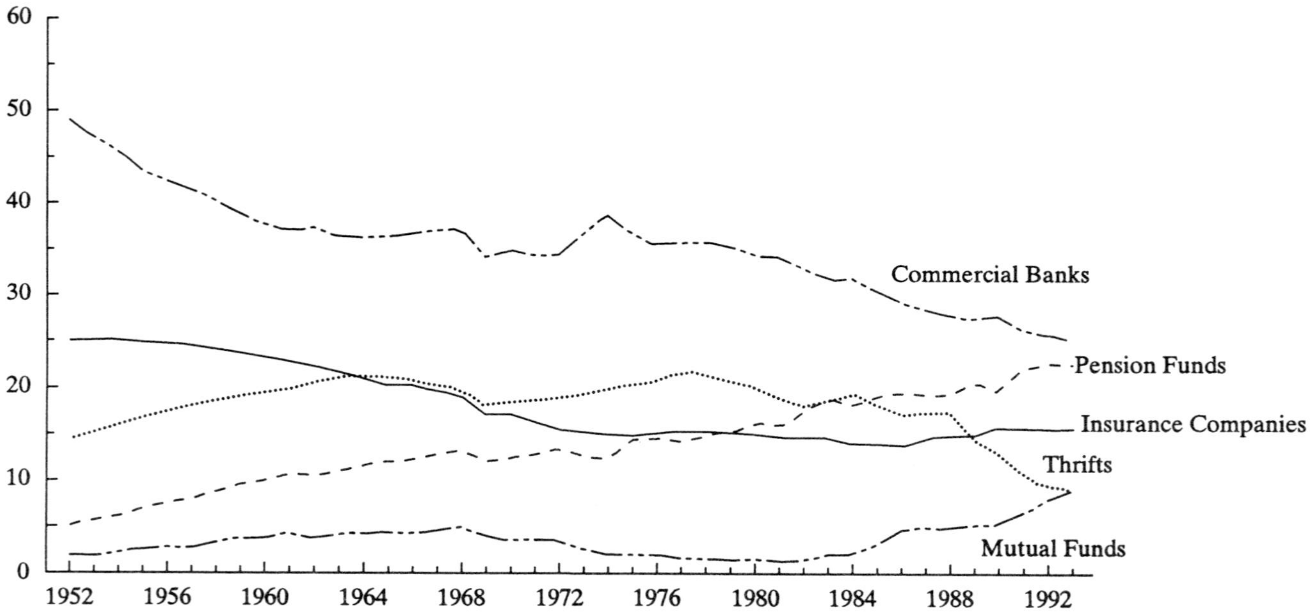

Figure 4 Assets of selected financial intermediaries (percentage of total intermediated assets).

Where Do We Go From Here?

My interpretation of Nakajima and Taguchi's chapter tells me that there is no hazard-proof system that can be devised. Furthermore, at some point the economic losses involved in attempting to implement and enforce such a system seem to be much higher than the expected benefit. Unfortunately, I even think that some of the discussions about the FDIC have occasionally focused almost solely on the fiscal aspects and not deposit insurance's systemic value.

We need to focus instead on mitigating the costs of disruption when they occur and on who bears their cost. This obviously involves the level of deposit insurance and proper capital ratios. The chapter discusses mismanagement in banks, which was a very real problem. However, there must have been a lot of mismanagement if it is the primary cause of the problems worldwide.

My own view is that much, although not all, of this mismanagement is an agency problem and an absence of adequate shareholder equity in commercial bank lending.

I do not think the Regime II System discussed in the chapter is farfetched. It seems to me another variety of the Litan narrow bank. However, I believe the problem is not with the liability but rather the asset side of the balance sheet. Specifically, in the US context there is at least a transitional concern over what the institutional source of credit would be for parts of agriculture and small- to mid-sized businesses. Ultimately, new institutions or markets would develop to meet this need, but there could be transitional problems.

Let me finish by noting that the issues raised in these chapters are not going away very soon. For example, while the US banking industry has made a dramatic recovery, it still suffers from basic franchise erosion. The factors driving this recovery are not building blocks for long-term success.

As indicated in Table 1, the improvement in US bank ROAs over the last two years is largely a result of declining provisions for loan losses and an improvement in net interest margins. The improvement in interest margins itself is in great measure the result of the decline in US banks' cost of funds.

While these developments are encouraging, they cannot go on forever. US banks continue to suffer from weak business loan demand. There has been an improvement in non-interest income, and in the future banks will have to increase their reliance on fee income. However, I am sceptical that banks' present range of products can support the current infrastructure over the long run. This problem is

Table 1 Return on average assets at US commercial banks

Components of ROAA (in basis points)	*Year*						*Change 1991–1993: H1*
	1988	*1989*	*1990*	*1991*	*1992*	*1993: H1*	
Net interest margin	350	349	345	359	386	393	34
Non-interest income	147	158	164	176	190	205	29
Non-interest expense	(331)	(337)	(346)	(367)	(379)	(394)	(27)
Loan loss provision	(56)	(96)	(96)	(101)	(76)	(50)	51
Securities gains (losses)	1	2	1	9	12	10	1
Applicable taxes	(33)	(30)	(23)	(24)	(42)	(54)	(30)
Extraordinary items (net)	3	1	2	2	1	11	9
Return on average assets	81	47	47	54	92	121	67

reflected in the increase in banks' non-interest expenses, despite the downsizing and consolidation that has already taken place.

To conclude, we have been through a very difficult episode, but the recent improvement should not delude us into thinking that troublesome issues do not still lie ahead.

5 Recent Changes in the Financial Systems of Asian and Pacific Countries

Jeffrey A. Frankel

Japan and continental Europe have recently gone into recession, joining the English-speaking world which had entered a slow-growth period in 1990. This leaves only the developing countries of East Asia still on a strong growth trajectory. They are by now important enough to constitute in themselves a significant part of global economic growth. In response to the rapid growth, and to diminished returns to investment available in the United States and Japan, international capital has been flowing into the dynamic Asian economies.

Difficulties among financial institutions, including bank failures and burst bubbles, have figured prominently in the economic downturns in Japan, the Nordic countries, and the English-speaking world. The developing East Asian countries have as yet been less affected by such failures and burst bubbles. Financial structures in this part of the world are known to be much less liberalized and financial markets to be less developed than in the industrialized world. Is it possible that these countries know something that others do not? It would be surprising if their financial systems were judged admirable, as they have generally been considered 'repressed',[1] and attempts at liberalization in the 1980s are generally considered to have been inadequate. Perhaps these countries are simply at an earlier stage of development, where advanced market-oriented financial systems are not necessary to good economic performance? The challenge is how to achieve the more liberalized system that is appropriate to a country in the process of industrializing, without incurring as many of the difficulties that the industrialized countries have incurred.

I THREE STAGES OF FINANCIAL DEVELOPMENT

One could argue that there are three natural stages of development in a country's financial system: (1) internal finance, (2) the intermediation of finance, and (3) securitization. The classification scheme is stylized. Internal finance, financial intermediaries, and securities markets in fact co-exist simultaneously in most countries. There may, however, be a natural historical progression, where the dominant emphasis in the financial system is allowed to shift over time, so that it can best serve the evolving real economy. The three-stage scheme is suggested as a hypothesis as to what might be the most natural, even the most efficient, pattern of evolution, not the one actually followed in every case.[2]

Internal Finance

An essential part of the 'takeoff' process in economic development is an increase in the saving rate and the use of these funds for investment – defined broadly, to include the accumulation of human as well as physical capital. It takes special circumstances for an individual saver to trust his money to an entrepreneur whom he does not know personally. In Stage 1, business investment is financed largely out of family savings or retained earnings. Much of the investment boom in South China is of this sort.

This mode of finance solves the problems of asymmetric information and moral hazard between saver and entrepreneur, but has obvious problems of its own. A small or innovative company at its start-up phase is likely to have few earnings to retain, despite a high expected return to capital. Furthermore, it is very risky for a family to stake all its savings and wage income on a single enterprise. In some cases, like the Korean *chaebol*, a family-run group of companies becomes large enough to transfer successfully funds from established profit-earning divisions to promising new divisions. But most countries have had trouble doing this sort of thing well.

An alternative, in a country where the government plays a more *dirigiste* role, is channeling of funds by the public authorities to sectors deemed worthy. Fry (1990) lists six major categories of selective credit instruments in use in East Asia: subsidized loan rates for priority sectors (from banks under government influence), preferential rediscount rates granted by the central bank, direct subsidies out of

Table 5.1 Selective credit instruments in sample Asian developing countries, 1990

Country	*Subsidized loan rates for priority sectors*	*Preferential rediscount rates*	*Direct budgetary subsidies*	*Credit floors*	*Credit ceilings*	*Proliferation of specialized institutions*
Indonesia	Scope reduced	Scope reduced		Yes		Yes
Korea	Scope reduced	Scope reduced		Yes	Yes	Yes
Malaysia	Yes	Yes				
Philippines	Yes	Yes	Yes	Yes	Yes	Yes
Taiwan	Scope reduced	Scope reduced				
Thailand	Yes	Scope reduced				

Source: International Monetary Fund, central bank, and government publications. As compiled by Fry (1990, p. 15).

the government budget (important until recently, e.g., in Indonesia, where revenue has been available from the oil sector), administered floors on bank credit to preferred sectors, ceilings on other bank credit, and government-owned financial institutions established to specialize in lending to particular sectors, e.g., agriculture (sometimes with cheap funds extracted from non-specialized depository institutions by means of high reserve requirements). As Table 5.1 shows, these instruments are still widely used in Asia, despite a reduction during the 1980s. Government ownership of financial institutions is particularly widespread in Indonesia and Taiwan.

An active government role in finance can work out well or badly, depending on the capability and integrity of those making the decisions. Often, when political patronage or social goals such as alleviating unemployment come to dominate, the legacy is a portfolio of non-performing assets. Simple bad judgment or bad luck can give the same outcome.[3]

Stage 1, a combination of internal finance and government-directed credit, is where Korea, for example, has been. Even though Korean banks were privatized in the early 1980s, they are generally considered bureaucratic and disinclined to take initiative without instructions from the government.[4] One should hesitate before condemning such a system as 'financial repression', given how successful the development process has been over the last thirty years.[5] Nevertheless, it may be time for countries like Korea to move on to the next stage. Korean developments are considered at greater length in Section III below.

Intermediation

In Stage 2, financial intermediation by private banks and other financial intermediaries allows effective channeling of funds from savers to businesses who do not necessarily know each other, a much more efficient way to finance investment. The Japanese post-war main bank system probably illustrates this system at its best, with the banks efficiently monitoring the activities of the firm managers to make sure they are not diverting the funds from productive investment projects toward their own purposes.[6] DeLong (1991) has argued that in the nineteenth century investment banks served this role in the United States as well. In the context of economic development, see Stiglitz (1991).

After the Great Depression in the United States, the Glass–Steagall Act weakened investment banks by requiring their separation from commercial banks, who are responsible for the payments system. Post-war Japan followed the United States in dividing banks by function, under Article 65. Japanese banks, however, remained stronger than US banks (in part because the latter were also hobbled by rules discouraging large inter-state banks, enacted in response to traditional populist American suspicion of large East Coast banks). The universal banking system of Germany constitutes a third model of banking, one that some Eastern European transition economies and other countries are now choosing to emulate.

Securitization

In Stage 3, well-established corporations find that, though intermediation is more efficient than relying on personal savings, disintermediation is more attractive still. They switch from relying on bank loans to issuing securities directly in developed financial markets, where a corporation with a good reputation and credit-rating can obtain capital cheaply. (This switch has been modeled by Diamond (1984, 1989).)

We use the term 'securitization' in a broad sense to denote increased reliance on bonds and equities, and decreased reliance on banks and other financial intermediaries. One aspect of this trend (but only one) is the practice of 'securitization' in its more narrow definition: the conversion of a bank loan into a negotiable instrument, e.g., in the United States, mortgage-backed securities or the secondary market in bank loans to developing countries.

The United States and the United Kingdom have been at Stage 3 for some time,[7] and Japan began to move there in the late 1980s. The question whether or not such a move constitutes an improvement from Japan's viewpoint is an open one. On the one hand, it seems that if Japanese corporations find it more attractive to switch from banks to securities markets, it must be because it is a more efficient way of financing investment.[8] On the other hand, it is possible that securities markets can win out over long-established banking relationships in a Darwinian sense, without necessarily being more efficient from the viewpoint of aggregate economic welfare.[9]

We should note that to describe the Anglo-American financial system as based on securities markets is not to say that a high proportion of corporate investment numerically is financed by new issues of equity, or even bonds. Mayer (1989) finds that close to 100 per cent of net sources of finance for non-financial corporations in the US and UK are accounted for by retained profits, not by new equity issues (which are often negative). Taggart (1985) also finds, from flow of funds data, that US stock issues have been a very low proportion of financing ever since 1940 (versus somewhat higher levels from 1901–39); internal funds constitute the majority of financing, although their share has been declining since the 1930s.[10] The point, however, is that the price of a firm's stock, which is determined in active and competitive markets, is a key variable determining investment and other decisions by firm managers, in a way that is not true of Japan and Germany.[11]

II THE RECENT EMERGENCE OF SECURITIES MARKETS IN THE ASIAN PACIFIC

Within the area of market-determined finance, there again appear to be several successive stages of development. Early on ('Stage 3a'), the emphasis is on determining short-term interest rates in the marketplace for the first time, rather than administratively. As part of the liberalization process, the government removes restrictions on the interest rates paid to banks and by banks (who themselves, if previously government-owned, have been privatized at Stage 2), relieves banks of the obligation to absorb government debt at artificially-low interest rates, and generally allows or encourages the development of short-term money markets.

Next the emphasis is on developing long-term securities markets

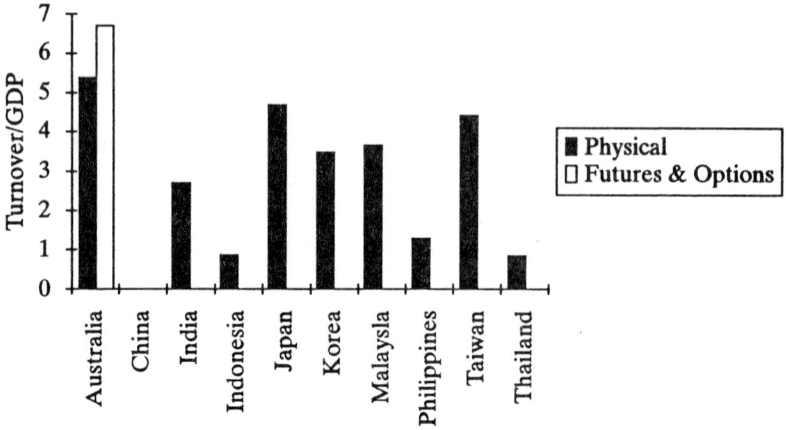

Figure 5.1 Money market turnover, 1991. *Note*: Data for Australia and Japan exclude interbank and call money.

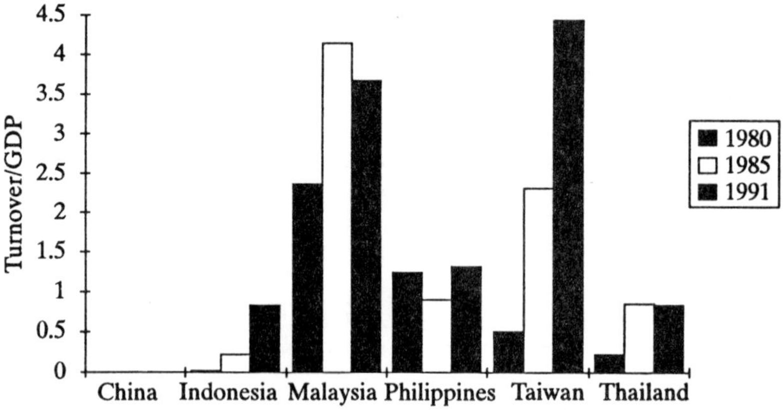

Figure 5.2 Money market turnover, 1980–91. (*Source*: Lynch and Norton (1992))

more fully ('Stage 3b'). Fry (1990, p. 28) observes that: 'Experience shows that learning-by-doing with market-determined interest rates in short-term financial markets [particularly interbank money markets] is the only viable way in which active and stable long-term securities markets can be developed.' Usually a market in government bonds is created first, followed by corporate bonds and equities.

Finally, markets in forward contracts and other derivative contracts

Table 5.2 Financial market spreads and equity commissions

	Money market (Spread basis pts)	*Government bond market (Spread basis pts)*	*Foreign exchange market (spread %)*	*Equity market (commission %)*
Australia	5	3	0.04	< 0.50
China	na	na	1.50	> 1.10
Hong Kong	25	10	0.08	> 0.25
Indonesia	150	—	1.60	1.00
Japan	5	2	0.03	> 0.08
Korea	na	—	0.04	> 0.40
Malaysia	30	2	0.08	> 1.00
New Zealand	15	4	0.06	na
Philippines	50	—	na	1.50
Singapore	12	5	0.08	> 0.50
Taiwan	25	na	0.12	0.14
Thailand	75	375	0.99	0.50

Note: Quotes are for mid-February 1993 and were provided by relevant central banks, except for Australia and Taiwan, 'na' indicates no market quotes were available and a dash the absence of sizeable market. Foreign exchange spreads are based on US$/yen quotes, except for China, Japan and Taiwan, where the US$ Renminbi, US$/DM and US$NT$ spreads are given. Equity market commissions, which cover large transactions are from *Euromoney* (April, 1993).
Source: Lynch (1993, p. 19).

are fully developed ('Stage 3c'). (Aspects of the development of securities markets in Asia are discussed by Fry, 1990, and Lynch and Norton, 1992.)

Money Markets and Bond Markets

A way to measure a country's movement from Stage 2 to Stage 3a is to look at turnover in the money market as a percent of GDP. Figures 5.1 and 5.2 (which, like those that follow, are from Lynch and Norton, 1992), show that money market turnover has been the highest in Australia and Japan, the two industrialized countries in this group. It has also reached similar levels, having risen rapidly, in Malaysia (particularly in the first half of the 1980s) and Taiwan (more recently). Next, in terms of level, comes Korea, or in terms of increase, Indonesia and Thailand. Another way to measure the development of these markets is to look at bid–offer spreads. High spreads indicate either low efficiency, low liquidity, or cartel power. Table 5.2 (from Lynch, 1993, p. 19) shows that money-market spreads are

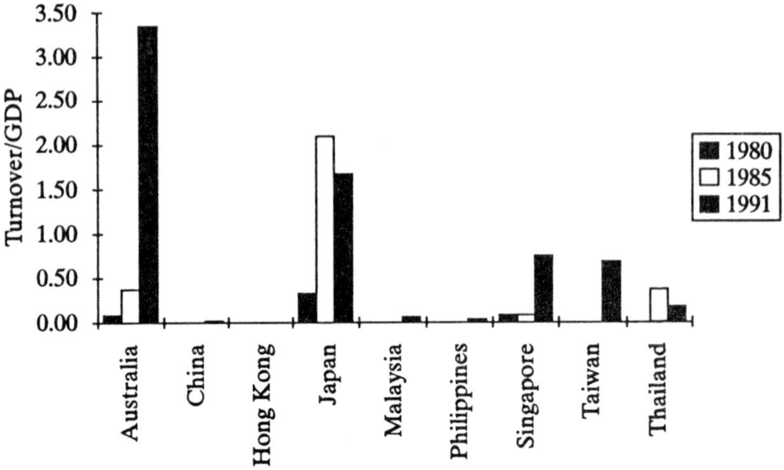

Figure 5.3 Government bond market turnover. *Note*: Data for Australia include semi-government bonds.

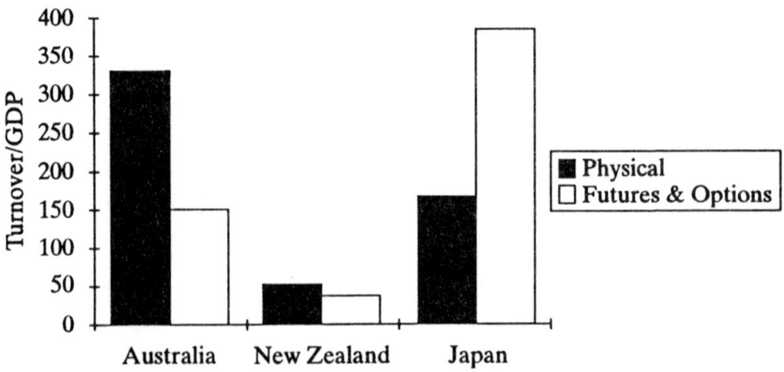

Figure 5.4 Government bonds turnover, 1991. *Note*: Futures and Options data for Japan cover 1990. Australian data include semi government bonds. (*Source*: Lynch and Norton (1992))

especially large in Indonesia, Thailand and the Philippines, and especially small in the industrialized countries.[12]

Fry (1990) and Fischer (1993, p. 119) observe that the movement towards medium-term and long-term finance in Asia has been surprisingly slow. One might say 'disappointingly slow', were it not for the very high rate of investment that most of these countries have

Table 5.3 Corporate bond markets

	Turnover				*Amount outstanding*			
	US$ billion		*Ratio to GDP (%)*		*US$ billion*		*Ratio to GDP (%)*	
	1980	*1991*	*1980*	*1991*	*1980*	*1991*	*1980*	*1991*
Australia	0	57.0	0	19.7	0	12.6	0	4.2
China	—	0.7	—	0.2	—	11.2	—	3.8
Hong Kong	1.5* (1981)	2.5*	5.1* (1981)	3.8*	0.6	3.7	2.2	4.5
Indonesia	—	—	—	—	—	1.1	—	1.0
Japan	133.0	349.5	11.2	10.6	181.5	734.4	15.3	22.4
Korea	1.1†	1.0†	1.7†	0.3†	3.4	55.0	6.0	20.2
Malaysia	—	0.4	—	0.8	—	2.6	—	3.3
Taiwan	0	0.1	0	0	0.8	6.2	1.9	3.3

Note: Data include both corporate and bank bonds and debentures.
* Data for NCDs only.
† Data exclude debentures.
Source: Lynch and Norton (1992).

produced despite this seeming handicap. Figures 5.3 and 5.4 measure the progression through Stage 3b by looking at turnover in government bond markets as a percentage of GDP. Again, Australia leads the way, followed by Japan. Only Taiwan and Singapore among the newly industrializing countries have had rapid increases in government bond market trading in recent years. According to Table 5.2, Thailand has by far the largest spread of any country where there exists a market in government bonds.

Table 5.3 reports statistics on corporate bonds. Japan, followed by Korea, makes the greatest use of corporate bonds if measured by amount outstanding, while Australia registers strongly if the yardstick is turnover. Active corporate bond markets are beginning to emerge in Hong Kong, Malaysia and China.

Equity Markets

One can think of arguments both for and against the use of equity markets in developing countries. An argument in favor, particularly as a vehicle for bringing international capital into the country, is that they have more desirable risk characteristics than bonds or other fixed-income instruments. An argument against, particularly in the context of the transitional economies of eastern Europe and the former Soviet Union, is that the current passion for them resembles a case of the 'cargo cult' disease. We briefly consider each argument.

Consider the historical difficulties attaching to capital flows from the industrialized world to developing countries. (The subject of international capital flows in East Asia is discussed at greater length in Section IV below.) The proximate cause of the LDC debt crisis that surfaced in 1982 was the unlucky combination of high world interest rates, a recession, and a fall in dollar commodity prices. The crisis had its precedents before World War II. In the nineteenth century and in the period between the wars, capital flowed from industrialized countries to colonies and developing countries more via bonds, and less via bank loans. Defaults occurred periodically, culminating in the widespread defaults of the 1930s.[13]

Capital also reached LDCs through foreign direct investment. However, when poor countries gained their political independence, most did not want foreigners owning controlling shares of their natural resources, land, or plant and equipment. To this day, even when a government proclaims its eagerness to accept foreign direct investment, investors may be concerned that a future government will nationalize it.[14]

Thus there is interest in devising some new mode of capital flow to developing countries, other than bonds, direct investment, or bank lending. The obvious candidate is equity investment. Unlike bonds or bank loans, the cost of 'servicing' equity does not stay fixed in dollar terms when the ability of the country to earn export revenue falls because of a world recession or a collapse in commodity prices. Unlike direct investment, the foreigner does not have a controlling decision-making interest in investment projects.

Another idea is the possibility of linking the repayment terms on bonds or loans to export prices, which would give them desirable risk characteristics like equities: the cost of the obligation automatically falls when the ability to pay falls. The idea makes particular sense for commodity-exporting countries like Colombia, Chile, Indonesia and Malaysia. But for some reason such commodity-indexed bonds have never caught on. There is a puzzling resistance to them, both on the supply side and the demand side.

Instead, equities are catching on in many countries.[15] Figures 5.5 and 5.6 show the growth in emerging equity markets in Asia/Pacific countries, according to turnover and capitalization, respectively. In

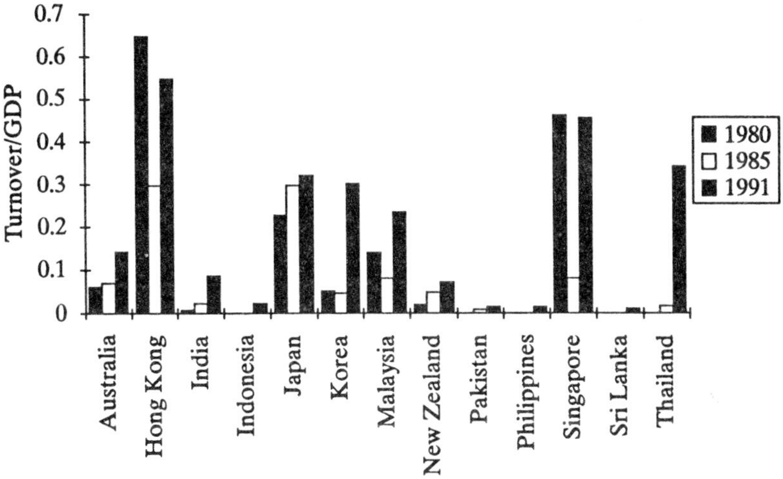

Figure 5.5 Equity market turnover.

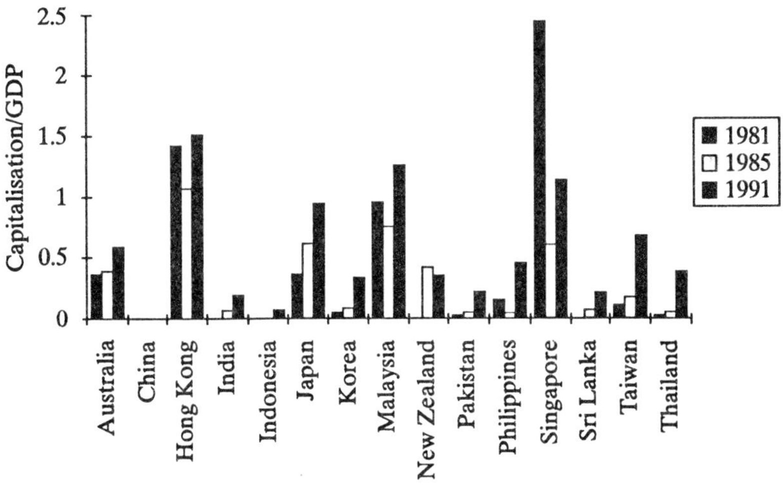

Figure 5.6 Equity market capitalisation. (*Source*: Lynch and Norton (1992))

the case of equities, the NICs, especially Hong Kong and Singapore, are ahead of Australia and Japan. Malaysia and Thailand have experienced very rapid growth. Recently Taiwan has begun to let foreigners into its stock market, and Thailand to offer American Depository Receipts to facilitate inward investment.[16]

Equity markets have also grown rapidly in other parts of the world. In the case of the transitional economies of Eastern Europe and the former Soviet Union, there is currently a particular emphasis on equity markets that may be premature. As a means of privatizing state-owned industry, the distribution of equity shares – e.g., under the voucher plan adopted in Czechoslovakia or the mutual funds discussed in Poland – has definite attractions. But the fascination in some quarters with opening up stock exchanges, like the fascination with building steel mills in many LDCs forty years ago, looks like the 'cargo cult' disease.

During World War II, natives of some Pacific islands witnessed the following sequence of events. US marines come ashore, construction crews build simple air landing strips, and cargo planes land on the strips. The planes then disgorge jeeps, men and *matériel*, and with them a spurt of Western-style material prosperity for the natives that lasts until the armed forces depart a few years later. Thereafter, cargo cults formed among the natives: they would build landing strips, in an effort to bring back the planes, consumer goods and prosperity. The confusion of causality was repeated when developing countries in the 1950s and 1960s, observing the prosperity of industrialized countries, decided that steel mills were the key. Everyone ended up with tremendous overcapacity in steel. Now some Eastern Europeans observe Wall Street and conclude that a New York Stock Exchange is what they need to bring prosperity.

The point is not that equity markets should be reserved for countries like the United States, United Kingdom and Japan. They clearly have an increasingly important role to play now in East Asia and Latin America. But it would be premature for Eastern European countries to rely heavily on them at this stage in their financial development.

Derivatives

The last stage may be the development of derivatives: forward contracts and options in the underlying securities already mentioned (bonds and equities), as well as in foreign exchange and commodities. Such markets opened in Australia in the early 1980s, followed

Table 5.4 Domestic financial futures markets turnover, 1991

		Traded since	*US $ billion*	*Ratio to GDP* (%)	*Ratio to physical market* (%)
Australia	Bank bills	1979	1 713	589	596
	Government bonds	1984	386	133	185
	Equity (SPI)	1983	43	15	101
Hong Kong	Hibor	1990	0	0	—
	Equity (Hang Seng)	1986	9	11	21
Japan	Government bonds	1985	11 271	383	148
	Equity (Nikkei & TOPIX)	1987/88	3 223	110	201
New Zealand	Bank bill	1986	108	273	na
	Government bonds	1986	14	37	74
	Equity (NZSE-40)	1987	0.2	0.4	6

Note: Turnover values are calculated as the face value of the underlying instruments multiplied by the number of contracts traded. Contracts on options are not included. Data for Japan cover 1990.

in short order by Japan, New Zealand and Hong Kong (where they were still very small, as of 1991). Table 5.4 reports some statistics. Singapore opened the SIMEX (Singapore International Monetary Exchange Ltd), offering a variety of financial futures, in 1984.[17] The aim of derivatives is to allow market participants to trade risk better, for example to hedge the exchange risk that comes when an importer or borrower is uncertain what his foreign currency obligations will be when translated into domestic currency at the uncertain future exchange rate.

Regulatory authorities in industrialized countries have expressed concern over the proliferation of derivatives in recent years. One concern is that risk created for banks or other financial institutions that deal in derivatives has in the past not appeared on their balance sheets, and thus not been covered by capital requirements (though swaps are covered by the Basle Accord). Another concern expressed is that derivatives might have exacerbated, for example, the 1987 stock market crash, in their role as a link in arbitrage and dynamic hedging (so-called 'portfolio insurance').

III THE CASE OF KOREAN FINANCIAL LIBERALIZATION

In the 1970s, Korea met the description of a financially repressed economy. The banking system was kept underdeveloped (although an informal 'curb market' became very large), securities markets were largely non-existent, and interest rates were kept negative in real terms to stimulate investment in favored sectors (especially heavy industry). The course of the debate since that time on reforming the financial system illustrates the issues facing many industrializing countries in East Asia, including the natural sequence of financial development. Here we summarize the recent historical record on Korean financial liberalization.[18]

Past Attempts at Financial Reform

By the end of the 1970s, the government recognized that financial repression was an obstacle to further growth. (An early aspect of a financial liberalization program was the establishment of two open-end trust funds.[19]) The road to banking de-regulation started in 1982 with the privatization of five national commercial banks.[20] Restrictions on bank management were reduced. The requirement that loans be made at preferential rates for policy purposes supposedly became less common in 1982. Steps toward liberalization of interest rates were taken in early 1984. But the most effective agents of liberalization were the rapidly-growing non-bank financial intermediaries.

There seems to be general agreement that the pace of liberalization slowed after 1984. 'During [the 1984–7) period no important steps were taken to further liberalize the financial sector.'[21]

In December 1988 more serious interest rate de-control was attempted by the outgoing Finance Minister, Il Sakong.[22] This process was soon frozen, however, when interest rates – rather predictably – started to rise. At the same time, 'citing unexpected economic changes, the Korean Government revised its original 1981 schedule to liberalize the securities industry.'[23] A new timetable was announced for the removal of controls on capital inflow and outflow. The measures announced in December 1988 included a schedule under which substantial liberalization was to take place in 1992.

US Pressure

In October 1988 the US Department of the Treasury, in its 'Report to the Congress on International Economic and Exchange Rate Policy' required by the Omnibus Trade and Competitiveness Act of 1988, concluded that Korea and Taiwan 'manipulated' their exchange rates, within the meaning of the legislation. The Treasury launched negotiations with Korea to induce that country to liberalize its financial markets, with improved treatment for US financial institutions specified as one major goal, and appreciation of the won presumed to be another. The Yen/Dollar talks of 1983–4 (and to some extent the Structural Impediments Initiative of 1989–90) with Japan were cited as precedents by US authorities. The Korea–US Financial Policy Talks took place in two rounds, in February and November 1990. Financial liberalization issues under contention fell into three areas: domestic liberalization, removal of international capital controls, and treatment of foreign providers of financial services.

The US Treasury evaluation of progress in the 1990 Financial Policy Talks regarding financial services was negative, even though exchange rate concerns had been satisfied. With respect to treatment of foreign banks, even though Korea had in 1984 declared national treatment for foreign-owned banks as part of a three-year deregulation plan, the report found: 'progress in resolving problems has been very slow and no timetable for dealing with them has been produced.'[24] With regard to treatment of foreign securities firms, even though Korea had (in 1988) declared that 24 foreign firms would be allowed to establish branches,[25] the report found (p. 11): 'US financial firms do not receive national treatment in Korean securities markets.'[26] With regard to overall financial liberalization, the report found: 'Until the Korean Government allows domestic banks to compete in a market environment, fully liberalizes interest rates, and eliminates credit allocation and exchange controls, there is little likelihood of major advances in equality of competitive opportunity for foreign financial service providers in the Korean market.'[27]

In 1991, foreign securities companies were for the first time allowed directly into the country as had been promised in the negotiations with the US. The Ministry of Finance in March approved four out of nine applications for branch office securities licenses, two of them American.[28]

In June 1991 restrictions were lifted on the establishment of multiple branches of foreign banks. It was also announced that application of national treatment for banks would be 'stepped up' (Oum, p. 8) and that the government of Korea was preparing a 'master plan' to liberalize interest rates and to 'rectify distortions in its term structure.'[29] (In its next report, the US Treasury appeared unimpressed, however.[30])

Since the beginning of 1992, foreign investors have been officially free to invest in individual Korean stocks on the stock market.[31] On 17 December 1991, the National Assembly approved revisions in a number of laws, including a revision to permit banks to engage in all foreign exchange business that is not specifically prohibited.[32]

The American emphasis on securities in the negotiations that began in 1990 raises the question whether it is not premature for a country to jump to Stage 3, without first having passed through Stage 2. The Japanese post-war system of relationship banking may be a good model for Korea in this respect. Weisbrod and Lee (1993, p. 33) conclude that Korea and Taiwan have been too quick to promote securities markets, at a time when banks still have an important role to play (while Japan in their view was too *slow* to move on to the market-oriented stage, with the result that the asset deflation of 1990–93 was more severe than it need have been). On the other hand, to the extent a country wants to participate actively in world financial markets, a securities market is a useful component.

KOREAN RELUCTANCE TO LIBERALIZE

Many Korean officials believe that further domestic liberalization 'could further raise the market interest rates, pushing up the firms' financing costs . . .'[33] One would think that *international* liberalization is the answer, allowing the firms to borrow much more cheaply abroad. But the government position has been the reverse: 'It is recognized that in order to minimize the negative effects on the economy as a whole, the deregulation of interest rates and domestic financial markets need[s] to precede the liberalization of foreign exchange and capital transactions.' It is not clear what are these negative effects. Perhaps the authorities wish to avoid overborrowing like that experienced by Chile in its 1970s liberalization, which caused writers on the Optimal Order of Liberalization to warn against beginning with the removal of capital controls. According to Nam (1989, p. 157), 'The fear of massive capital inflows attracted by relatively high domestic real interest rates and anticipated foreign exchange appreciation has prompted controls on capital inflows.'

One possibility is that the authorities are worried that a large capital inflow would bring about a real appreciation of the won: if the authorities intervened to resist the pressure toward nominal appreciation (which would itself require visibly abandoning the free-float spirit of the Market Average Rate system adopted in 1990), then the inflow of reserves would be inflationary. Korean exporters would lose competitiveness. One solution is to resist the nominal appreciation, but to sterilize the increase in reserves so as to prevent inflationary growth in the money supply. Indeed, the Korean monetary authorities pursued this strategy in the 1980s.

Another possibility is that the authorities are worried that Korean 'domestic financial institutions, especially banks, are not efficient and competitive enough compared to their foreign counterparts.'[34] We will consider these issues at greater length below.

The Five-year Plan of 1993

A firm commitment to the final stages of a complete 'blueprint' for financial reform[35] was delayed until after the presidential elections in December 1992. At last, in May 1993, the Ministry of Finance announced the specifics of a five-year plan of financial reform.

The measures that were laid out fell into four areas. In the area of bank deregulation, the plan promised the deregulation of interest rates beginning with those on bank loans by the end of the year, stipulations that bank management would be autonomous of the government, a reduction of policy-based loans by the Bank of Korea (with responsibility for such financing transferred to specialized banks), and steps to encourage banks to write off non-performing loans. In the area of central bank policy, the plan called for a movement toward open market operations as the principal means of monetary policy (beginning with market-determination of interest rates on government bond issues since early 1993) and a strengthening of bank supervision (with a deposit insurance system to be introduced by 1997). In the area of remodeling the structure of the banking system, the plan announced the relaxation of regulations on new entrants, the adjustment of service domains (beginning with allowing banks to lead manage the underwriting of bonds), the restructuring of specialized banks, the tightening of credit from financial institutions to their major shareholders and affiliate subsidiaries, and the fostering of an information infrastructure (including the development of credit-rating institutions, and tougher sanctions on dishonest bookkeeping and auditing). Finally, in the area of internationalization, the plan took additional steps toward liberalizing the regimes governing foreign exchange, international securities transactions, and foreign direct investment.

The new president, Kim Young-Sam, in August 1993 took a step that was as difficult and as important as the announcement of the 5-year plan itself, in that it signalled the seriousness of financial reform. This was the banning of the practice of using false names for bank accounts and other financial transactions as a means of tax evasion and corruption. Banks will now have to compete by offering depositors attractive interest rates, rather than by helping them establish fake accounts.[36]

IV THE INTERNATIONAL DIMENSION: RECENT CAPITAL INFLOWS TO LDCS

A major function of international capital markets is to allow capital to flow into countries where the expected rate of return to investment is higher than in the country of the saver, at a cost that is lower than that in the country of the borrower. Traditionally, developing countries have been thought the natural destination for such capital. In the 1980s the traditional pattern was not upheld. High real interest rates in the United States, originating from fiscal expansion not accommodated by monetary policy, drew capital to North America. Besides the role in precipitating the already-noted 1982 debt crisis, which resulted in a reversal of the previous flow of bank loans to Latin America and other developing countries, high interest rates also attracted capital to the United States from Japan and Europe.

Since 1990, the pattern has again reversed. Investors in the United States and elsewhere have increased their demand for long-term assets in developing countries in East Asia, Latin America, and even parts of the Middle East. This increase in demand has taken many forms, in microeconomic terms: loans, bonds, equities, and foreign direct investment. In macroeconomic terms, it has shown up in various countries as renewed current account deficits, increases in central bank reserve holdings, and appreciation in values of local assets and in the foreign exchange value of the local currency. The new capital flows of 1990–93 are well-documented by Calvo, Leiderman and

Reinhart (1993a, b), who attribute them to factors external to the host countries, in particular a fall in the rate of return in the United States, more than to such internal factors as monetary stabilization and economic reform in the host country. Financial liberalization in Latin America and East Asia is an important part of the story however. Less capital would be coming in if these countries had tried to retain extensive capital controls.

Do Capital Inflows Pose Difficulties?

Open capital markets have many advantages, especially in theory. In addition to long-term financing of development, international financial markets allow shorter-term consumption smoothing, and a more efficient allocation of risk through diversification. But there is also the likelihood of market failures whereby the country becomes excessively indebted and vulnerable to a sudden reversal of confidence, as happened in 1982. The problems include the absence of an enforceable international bankruptcy court, the lack of credibility of government 'no bail-out' declarations, and possible herd mentality and speculative bubbles. Such market failures could call for direct measures to discourage capital inflows.[37] If, on the other hand, the capital inflows are thought to be taking place for good reasons, e.g. in response to a commodity boom or a rapid increase in worker productivity, one should allow them to take place.

Concerns arise that monetary inflows will lead to unwanted effects of real appreciation on non-booming exports, either through nominal appreciation or inflation. They can often be addressed by the central bank intervening to prevent the currency from appreciating in nominal terms, at least in the short run, and then sterilizing the effect of the reserve accumulations on the money supply. As is well-known, the higher the degree of international capital mobility, the more difficult will it be to sterilize.

Does Financial Repression Make Sterilization Easier?

An underexplored question concerns the interaction between the extent of *domestic* financial liberalization (for a given degree of international financial openness) and the ease of sterilization. Reisen (1993a) has made the somewhat surprising claim that some Southeast Asian countries have succeeded in the theoretically impossible simultaneous achievement of exchange rate stability, open capital markets, and monetary independence. He points to the role, for example, of the Singapore Provident Fund, in absorbing government assets to offset a reserve inflow. The implication is that even when a fall in the US interest rate is transmitted to a fall in the interest rates in these countries, the capital inflow is 'sterilized' in the broad sense that it has little impact on the local money supply, aggregate demand, or inflation. Reisen apparently has in mind a domestic financial system that has so little market orientation that it is little affected by a fall in the interest rate. In classic IS–LM terms, money demand is unresponsive to the interest rate, so the LM curve is steep.[38]

On the other hand, one expects that when financial markets are not well-developed, the central bank will have difficulty sterilizing inflows, in the sense that investors will not voluntarily choose to hold government securities unless they are paid a high interest rate, with attendant future quasi-fiscal costs for the central bank. Indeed, in Korea, Colombia and many other developing countries, the absence of a market in negotiable government securities has meant that the central bank essentially must start one from scratch when it wishes to sterilize reserve inflows, selling its own 'Monetary Stabilization Bonds' to the public.[39] The resolution is as follows: to sterilize with ease, one needs not only underdeveloped financial markets, but enough financial repression in the system to be able to force supposedly-private banks or other financial institutions to absorb government securities at artificially low interest rates. The cost of such a degree of financial repression, in terms of stunting financial development, may be too high to make it desirable, for a country on the path to industrialization.

Raising reserve requirements on banks, for example, might appear a useful way to neutralize monetary expansion. It can succeed in creating a wedge that raises interest rates on bank loans (desired to cool off the economy), without necessarily raising interest rates on bank deposits (which would prolong an undesired capital inflow). The problem is that high reserve requirements, because they undermine the competitiveness of domestic banks, are not easily reconciled with opening to competition from offshore banks and from domestic non-bank institutions.

Are Foreign Investors More Bullish than Domestic Investors?

An interesting possible hypothesis regarding recent capital inflows is that foreign residents are more optimistic about domestic assets than are domestic residents. A widely-held interpretation of the massive capital flight from Latin America that took place in 1982 and the years immediately preceding it is that residents of these countries correctly perceived dangers ahead, at a time when foreign banks were foolish enough to be still lending eagerly. So far in the present episode, repatriation of past-flown capital by domestic residents seems to be as important a part of the inflows as new investments by foreign residents. Nevertheless, anyone who is concerned about a possible replay of 1982 – as are Calvo, Leiderman and Reinhart (1993a, b) – wants to be vigilant to any future signs that the locals are again losing confidence. Unfortunately, capital flight can only be estimated with a lag of a quarter or two (and, even then, very imperfectly).

Another place where it might be useful to look are the prices of country-funds that invest in the stock markets of a number of Latin American and Asian countries. Over forty of such funds have been opened on the New York Stock Exchange in recent years. They are closed-end funds, and their price in New York seldom equals the value of the constituent equities on the home-country markets. Fluctuations in the premium of the US price of the fund over the net asset value could be a measure of fluctuations in the difference in expectations of US versus local investors.

For most of these funds this premium has been higher (or the discount has been lower) during the period 1990–92 than during the preceding three years, suggesting bullish sentiment on the part of foreign investors. Hardouvelis, La Porta and Wizman (1993) argue persuasively that the existence and behavior of these premiums and discounts are inconsistent with an Efficient Markets Hypothesis, and reflect 'US investor sentiment' in imperfectly integrated markets. They note a dramatic switch in 1990 across most of the country funds, an improvement in US investor sentiment compared to the preceding three years, which they attribute to the fall of the Berlin Wall and German unification. From our viewpoint, however, the 1990 switch in the relative enthusiasm of American investors to invest in East Asia, Latin America and elsewhere, which is observable in the data on long-term capital flows, could be due to the decline in expected US returns identified by Calvo, Leiderman and Reinhart.

Figures 5.7–5.9 show the weekly discount or premium of the country funds in recent years for eight countries, two in Latin America and six in East Asia. Unfortunately, only two of the country funds in each region have been in existence long enough to allow a pre-1990 and post-1990 comparison. (Also presented is the common

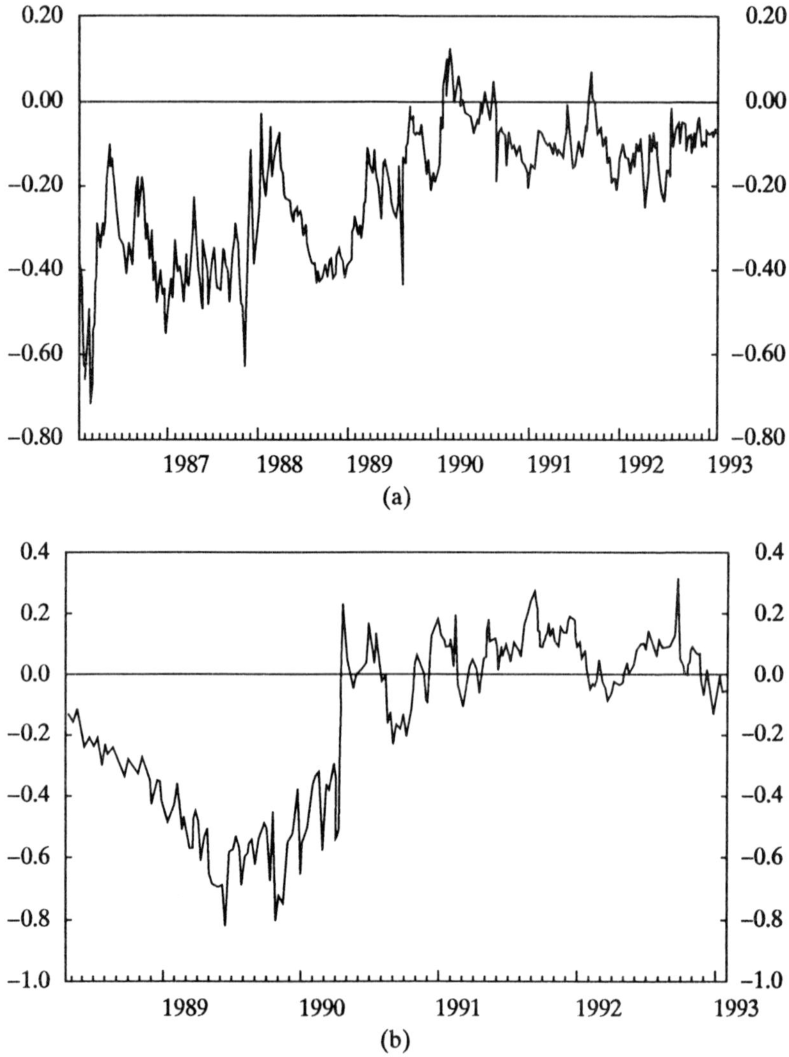

Figure 5.7 (a) Weekly percentage discount or premium of the Mexico Fund. (b) Weekly percentage discount or premium of the Brazil Fund. *Note*: The premium is computed as (PRI/NAV–1)+100, Where PRI is the price per share of the fund and NAV is the per share 1. (*Source*: Hardouvelis, La Porta and Wizman (1994))

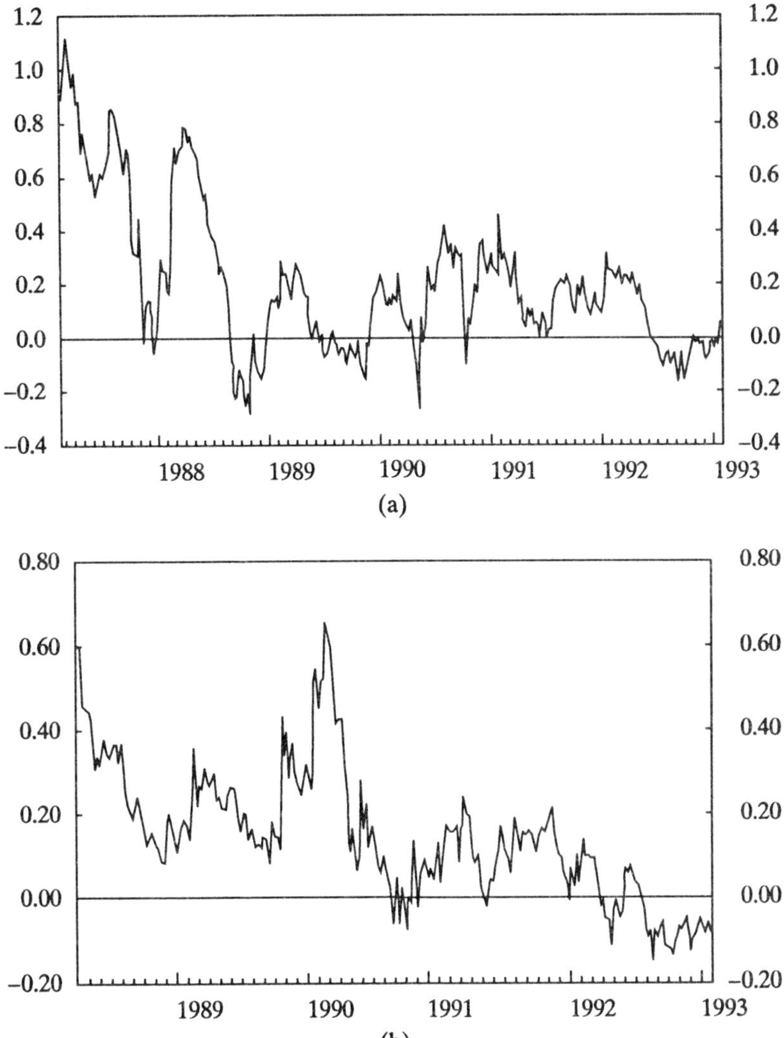

Figure 5.8(a) Weekly percentage discount or premium of the Taiwan Fund. (b) Weekly percentage discount or premium of the Thai Fund. *Note*: The premium is computed as (PRI/NAV–1)+100, where PRI is the price per share of the fund and NAV is the per share 1. (*Source*: Hardouvelis, La Porta and Wizman (1994))

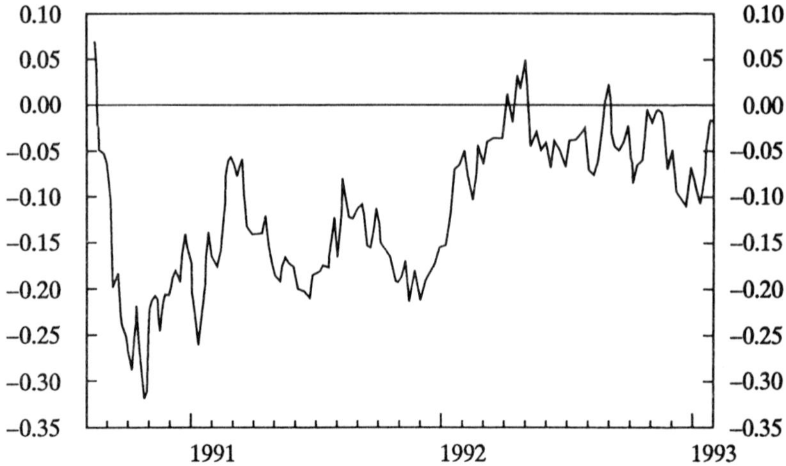

(a)

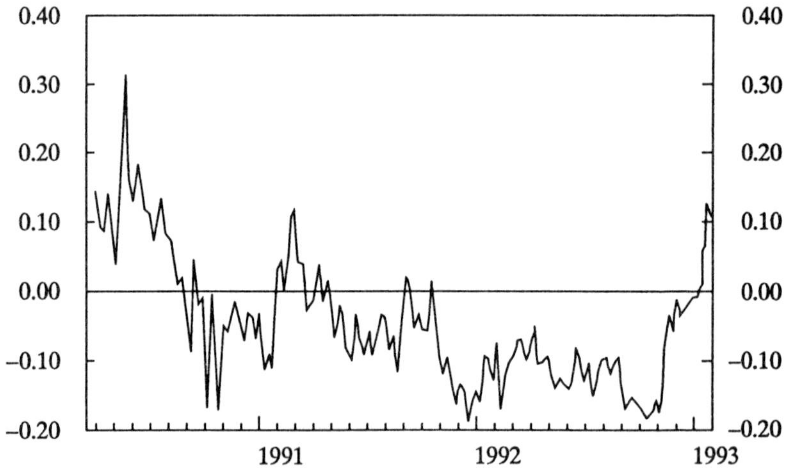

(b)

Figure 5.9 (a) Weekly percentage discount or permium of the Singapore Fund. (b) Weekly percentage discount or permium of the Malaysia Fund.

component of the nine oldest funds, as estimated by Hardouvelis, La Porta and Wizman (1994).) Mexico and Brazil (Figure 5.7) show a clearly higher level of relative US investor confidence in the three years from 1990, consistent with the trend for the Germany Fund and the common component of country funds (Figure 5.10). Taiwan and

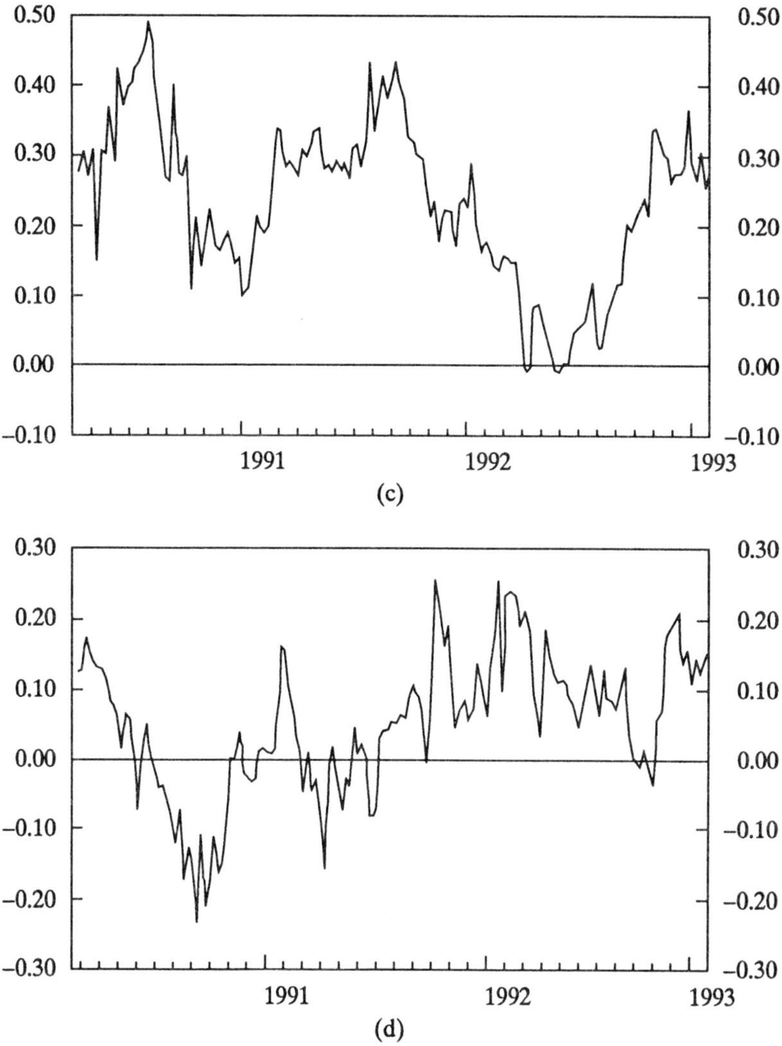

Figure 5.9 (c) Weekly percentage discount or premium of the Korea Fund. (d) Weekly percentage discount or premium of the Indonesia Fund. *Note*: The primtum is computed as (PRI/NAV–1)+100, where PRI is the price per share of the fund and NAV is the per share I. (*Source*: Hardouvelis, La Porta and Wizman (1994).

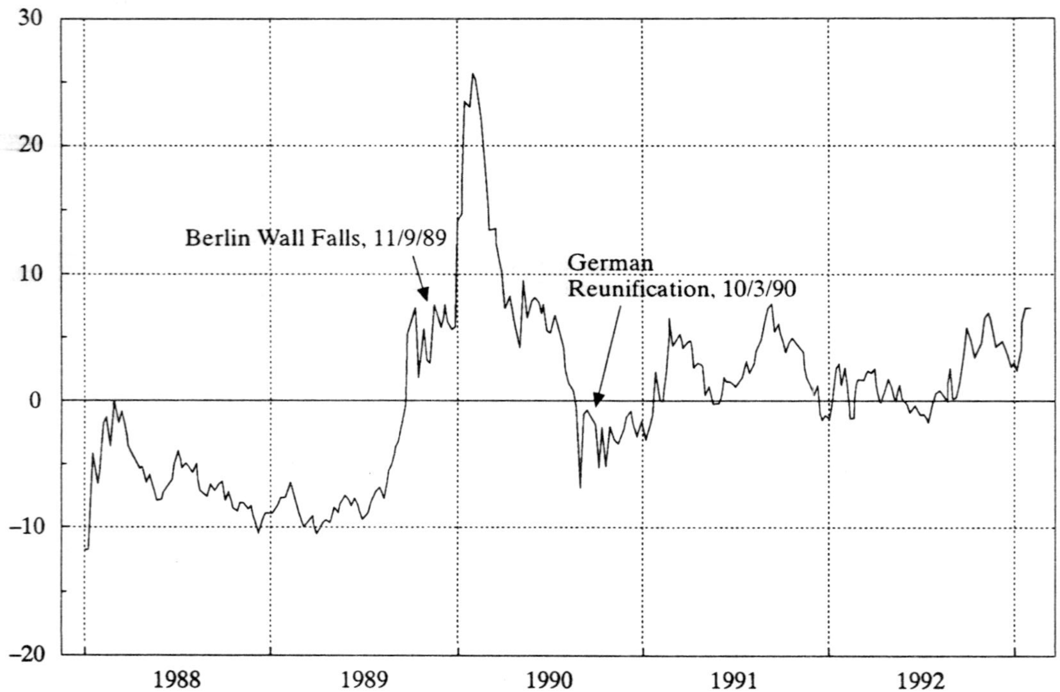

Figure 5.10 Common component in country fund discounts. (*Source*: Hardouvelis, La Porta and Wizman (1994))

Thailand (Figure 5.8) show a clearly *lower* level of US investor confidence, again as compared to the end of the 1980s. If our interpretation of the data is correct, that they represent the confidence of US investors relative to local investors, these four graphs suggest a possible replay of the period leading up to 1982: booms based relatively firmly on the ground in the case of East Asia, but based excessively on the enthusiasm of US investors in the case of Latin America. An alternative interpretation, however, is that we may merely be witnessing a general tendency for the market inefficiency of large discounts (in the Latin American case) or premiums (in the East Asian case) to be arbitraged away over time.

The Optimal Order of Financial Liberalization: International versus Domestic

The experience of Chile and other Southern Cone countries in South America with liberalization in the 1970s gave rise to a literature on the optimal sequence with which various reform measures should be adopted. Although no definitive conclusions were reached about the desirable order among such measures as trade liberalization, monetary stabilization, and domestic financial liberalization, a rough consensus did emerge on two points. First, reduction of the budget deficit should precede monetary stabilization and other measures. The reason is that a country must finance a budget deficit either by borrowing or by the inflation tax. If the inflation is eliminated before the budget deficit is reduced, the result could be excessive borrowing.[40] Second, international financial liberalization, particularly the removal of controls on capital inflow, should come last. The reason is that otherwise capital flows will be free to respond to distorted relative price signals (e.g., an excessively high relative price of non-traded goods), and the result may again be overborrowing.

East Asian countries tend to have stronger fiscal positions than Latin American countries. But many have chosen to undertake international financial liberalization more rapidly than domestic financial liberalization, with apparent success, in contradiction to the conventional wisdom regarding the optimal sequence. Japan and Indonesia are two countries often cited in this connection.[41] One possible justification for the reversed sequence concerns the already-noted problem of uncompetitive domestic financial institutions. Where domestic financial interests are able to oppose liberalization politically, or lack the know-how to compete, opening up to international financial markets may be a way to overcome this resistance, as the domestic institutions are given the example of foreign banks and securities traders to emulate, and are forced to compete.[42] The theme of providing competition for domestic banks is amplified in the following section.

V SOME MORE ISSUES FOR REGULATORY POLICY

Even for countries where banks will continue to be the dominant form of finance for the foreseeable future, a government program of financial liberalization is important. As many authors emphasize, however, liberalization does not mean an end to bank regulation.

Supervision of Banks and other Financial Institutions

Careful, professional prudential supervision of banks and other financial institutions is as important as ever. Indeed, in many countries, it needs to be strengthened as a prerequisite to full liberalization of interest rates.[43] Regulators must guard against overconcentration of loans to a single industrial group related to the bank itself.[44] (Such practices in Thailand, for example, led to large losses on the part of a particular finance company and thereby to a financial crisis in October 1983. Overconcentration of loans from banks to affiliated groups also contributed to the Chilean collapse of 1982.) It is especially important to monitor bank capital as measured by the marketplace (i.e., the value of bank shares), not just the accounting measure of capital. Given increasing market orientation, and feedbacks between bank credit and equity or land prices, supervision will require more careful attention to conditions in securities and other markets, to guard against speculative bubbles. Many countries will want to adopt the G-10's Basle capital adequacy standards for banks, as the Philippines is considering doing.[45]

Capital adequacy is also an important issue for securities firms. Supervision of banks and securities companies might be easier if conducted within a single government agency, which strategy Korea, Singapore and Taiwan seem to be following, as opposed to the US model.[46]

Information Flows

Many countries need also to improve the flow of information. This includes accounting standards, corporate disclosure, external auditing, the development of credit-rating institutions (as recently established in Malaysia), and restrictions on insider trading.[47] Those who fear that such scrutiny will inhibit the development of financial markets should consider how much tighter rules and practices are in the United States, with its well-developed financial markets, than in most Asian countries.

It should go without saying that a free and open press is also an essential part of the free flow of information. That this perhaps needs to be said is illustrated by Singapore's rocky relations with several foreign periodicals, which happen to be the ones that are the most important in the world to its development as an international financial center.

Central Bank Independence

Many countries around the world are in the process of granting increased independence to their central banks, including long terms for bank board members without easy removal by the executive branch, and a principle that professionalism should guide the bank's activities. This is a policy reform that, while helping credibly to establish non-inflationary monetary policy, can at the same time help promote financial development.[48] The Philippines, for example, adopted a law to strengthen its central bank in June 1993.[49]

The 'Bad Loan Problem'

Addressing overhangs of non-performing loans is one of the three essential areas in banking policy that Fischer (1993, pp. 127–8) lists as prerequisites for opening up to international financial markets. (The first is enhancing competition among banks, addressed below, and the second is strengthening prudential regulation and supervision, addressed above.) He recommends starting by explicitly assessing the magnitude of the problem and then either liquidating or recapitalizing. To the extent that newly entering foreign banks can participate through mergers or license takeover, they could be let in simultaneously. But Fischer suggests that if capital controls are removed before the bad loan problem is fully addressed, domestic interest rates will as in Latin American countries fail to converge to the world level.

Reserve Requirements

Domestic banks will be put at a competitive disadvantage *vis-à-vis* foreign financial institutions if international liberalization takes place while domestic reserve requirements are still high, as already noted. Indeed, this is why Indonesia sharply reduced reserve requirements when undertaking international liberalization in the 1980s.[50]

Required reserve ratios vary widely in East Asia, from high levels like 21 per cent in the Philippines, to low levels like 2 per cent in Indonesia after they were reduced. There is, however, a general move toward simplifying policy by equalizing requirements on demand deposits and time deposits within each country.[51]

High reserve requirements are one means of financial repression, and as such are in themselves bad for financial development. On the other hand, they are good for monetary control, and are often used as a means of financing a budget deficit or a means of sterilizing reserve inflows, in the sense of preventing the inflows from increasing the money supply broadly defined. They are a way for the government to get seigniorage to help finance a budget deficit, without directly leading to inflation.

Compulsory Finance May Be the Most Repressive Kind of Seigniorage

In addition to raising reserve requirements on banks, there is another way that the authorities can obtain seigniorage from the financial system, at the expense of repressing financial development. The first component is 'compulsory finance': forcing captive banks and other financial institutions to absorb government bonds at artificially low interest rates. This undermines bank profitability, and must be viewed as incompatible with the strategy of developing competition for banks via greater market-orientation domestically or greater openness internationally. Thus the second component is to continue to repress the rest of the financial system, for example through taxes on securities transactions, in order to keep the banks viable.[52]

The incompatibility comes to the fore when the budget deficit is large. Japanese banks in the 1970s absorbed ever-increasing quantities of government bonds at below-market interest rates, until their growing complaints forced the government to shift to a policy of market-determined interest rates.[53]

If the choice is between high reserve requirements on the one hand, and compulsory finance on the other, a consensus of authors seems to favor the former. The argument is that providing an environment in which banks are forced to compete is absolutely essential, and that establishing a competitive market in government bonds is the best way to begin this process. Fry (1990) and Lynch and Norton (1992) urge letting interest rates on government bonds be determined flexibly in the marketplace, as opposed to forcing captive banks to absorb them at artificially low interest rates.[54] Market-determined interest rates provide a useful indicator of the state of supply and demand of credit, which banks and corporations can use as a benchmark in their own activities, which has been a motivation for reforms in Singapore, Malaysia and Hong Kong.[55] More specifically, markets send signals to the rest of the financial system on some key magnitudes: the appropriate differential between the interest rate and inflation (positive, unlike many financially repressed countries the world over), the appropriate spread between lending rates and deposit rates (positive, unlike in some Development Finance Institutions, but just large enough to cover reasonable costs, unlike among inefficient banks), and the appropriate spread between long-term rates and short-term rates (positive most of the time).

Furthermore there are some advantages inherent in a monetary policy that is market-based, i.e., based on interest rates rather than credit ceilings. Changes in monetary policy can be transmitted rapidly and evenly throughout the economy.[56] A good summary of the position runs thus:

> Recent experience suggests that the best way of stimulating financial sector competition and efficient financial intermediation is to encourage direct financial markets. In particular, the development of auctions and secondary markets for treasury bills not only provides an efficient form of monetary control, it also . . . provides salient competition to the financial institutions. . . .
>
> (Fry, 1990, p. 32)

It has also been argued, by Cho (1986), that the development of an active equity market is a prerequisite for liberalization of the banking system. This prescription as to the optimal sequence of liberalization seems to fly in the face of the three natural stages of financial development that were proclaimed at the beginning of this chapter. Cho argues that unregulated cartelized banking systems in East Asian countries are in danger of excluding borrowers who are risky but have high expected returns, and that equity markets are needed to finance these productive firms, while the banks concentrate on the well-established safe borrowers. The logic is based on the Stiglitz and Weiss (1981) model of imperfect information, in which unregulated financial markets lead to credit rationing, and to the inefficient exclusion of risky borrowers.

Cho recommends retaining government intervention in the credit market, until equity markets can be introduced. It is far from clear, however, that equity markets are better able to solve the imperfect information problem than are banks. Indeed, the literature inspired by Japanese banking relationships argues the reverse, as noted in Section I above. Much depends on whether a country believes that its government regulators or its deregulated bankers would better be able to duplicate successfully the monitoring function of Japanese banks. Most economists would bet on the deregulated bankers.

Safeguarding the Payments Mechanism

This still leaves the issue of whether financial liberalization might not put *too much* competitive pressure on banks. Nakajima and Taguchi (1993, pp. 3–4) blame such pressure in part for the 1987–9 speculative bubbles in Japanese land and equity markets, and its costly aftermath in 1990–93. The argument is that competition from the expanding securities sector caused a sharp decline in banks' profit margins, and the banks went into risky investment projects like real estate in response.

One must say that other factors in addition to financial liberalization also played a large role in these speculative bubbles.[57] Nevertheless, there is a well-known and genuine conflict between the role of banks as players in the fast-moving world of securities markets and their role as the payments mechanism for the economy. The possibility of failure of banks where transactions accounts are kept is a sufficiently dangerous threat to the economy to justify some degree of government regulation and protection, which is politically impossible to deny anyway. This logic inclines me to support Regime II in the taxonomy of Nakajima and Taguchi (1993, pp. 24–5): public protection for the provision of payments services, but not for the service of intermediation *per se*. One possibility is for the protection to take the simple form of a regulation that banks taking liquid deposits must back them with holdings of Treasury bills, which renders the issue of government insurance almost moot.

My caveat is some skepticism as to whether 'firewalls' separating these functions within a given bank are realistic, especially in Asia. One is tempted then to conclude that universal banking might be less appropriate than separation of financial institutions into securities companies (without public protection) versus transactions banks (with protection). Arguing in favor of Regime II *without* the separation, however, is evidence that there are cost-saving complementarities between the two bank functions of taking deposits from corporations and investing in them. The goal of regulators should be to allow complementarities between the two functions to the extent possible, while making sure that only the transactions function is protected.

Acknowledgements

The author would like to thank Robert Parry, Graeme Thompson and other participants at the Bank of Japan conference for helpful comments; Eduardo Borensztein, Steven Vries and other members of the IMF Research Department for useful discussion; and Bill Norton of Macquarie University, Stephen Grenville of the Reserve Bank of Australia, and Soo Gil Lee of the Bank of Korea, for making available helpful materials. He would also like to thank Gikas Hardouvelis and Thierry Wizman for making available their data on country fund discounts, and Yutong Li for research assistance. He bears full responsibility for any views expressed.

Notes

1. The now-classic references on financial repression are McKinnon (1973) and Shaw (1973). The literature is reviewed by Fry (1993b).
2. There is some overlap between this hypothesized sequence and the patterns identified in two classic references on financial development: Gurley and Shaw (1960) and Goldsmith (1969). They described a process whereby financial interrelations, as reflected in the value of financial instruments outstanding, increase rapidly during early stages of development. Bryant (1987, pp. 10–14) gives a concise summary of the generalizations that emerged from this work.
3. Fry (1990, sections 5 and 9). (An example is the decision of the Korean government in the 1970s to channel bank funds to chemicals, steel, and other heavy industry.)
4. Studies of Taiwan, Indonesia, Thailand and the Philippines find banking sectors that are similarly inefficient, cartelized, or bureaucratized, despite privatization. Among the visible symptoms are infrequent changes in interest rates, high spreads between borrowing and lending rates, and a large number of bank branches. For example, Cheng (1986) on Taiwan (and Cole and Slade (1992) on Indonesia and Hanson and

Rocha (1986) on the Philippines). See Fry for a good overview (1990, pp. 29–31).

5. See Park (1991) on this point.
6. Main banks and their monitoring function are explored by Aoki and Sheard (1992), Hamada and Horiuchi (1987), Hodder (1991), Hoshi, Kashyap and Sharfstein (1989) and Meerschwam (1989), among others. For a survey of this and other aspects of corporate finance in Japan, see Frankel (1993a). One should note that the main bank system looks slightly tarnished now, compared with the 1980s. In cases such as the 1993 Cosmo Securities scandal, main bank monitoring does not seem to have been very effective.
7. Zysman (1983) and Bisignano (1990) are two of many references on the Anglo-American 'market-based' system versus the German–Japanese–French 'credit-based' system.
8. For example, Hoshi, Kashyap and Sharfstein (1989) suggest that there may be hidden costs to the system of bank monitoring, and a cheaper way of overcoming the information and incentive obstacles to borrowing – which is available only to older, well-established, successful firms – may be to take advantage of the firm's reputation by issuing AAA-rated bonds. It is noteworthy that agencies that rate the creditworthiness of corporations (the analogues of Moody's or Standard and Poor's) did not develop in Japan until recently.
9. Frankel (1993a), a survey of the evolving Japanese system, suggests how this might be. In terms of game theory, the co-operative equilibrium that is based on banking relationships may not be sustainable, in a world where newcomers are playing by different rules.
10. In a similar vein, Singh and Hamid (1992) find that firms in developing countries tend to use internal finance to a smaller extent than do firms in advanced countries. However, much of their external finance is borrowing from the government. Furthermore Singh and Hamid find it difficult to generalize across countries, with regard to such financial variables as gearing ratios, even within the subset of successful East Asian economies.
11. Mayer (1988) argues that, although equity markets are very well-developed in the UK and the US in the sense of volume and competition (and the Efficient Markets Hypothesis), they are not as efficient at financing investment and growth as are the financial systems of Japan, Germany and other industrialized countries.
12. The case of Australian banking deregulation in the 1980s is considered in MacFarlane (1991).
13. The parallels between the 1980s debt crisis and the experience of the 1930s are striking (Eichengreen and Portes, 1989; Fishlow, 1986).
14. This issue arose in July 1993, to take one example, in Colombia's efforts to attract British investment (into its newly discovered oil fields).
15. Many of the economists investigating equity investment in emerging markets were recently brought together by Claessens and Gooptu (1993).
16. Rhee (1992, pp. 16–17).
17. Rhee (1992, p. 48).

18. Frankel (1993b) and sources cited there give a more complete picture of the issues.
19. Kim (1990, p. 22).
20. Oum (1991) and Kim (1990, p. 11).
21. Kim (1990). Others who note the slow pace of Korean financial liberalization include Fry (1990, pp. 42–4) and Park.
22. For example, Kim (1990, p. 21).
23. US Treasury (1990b, p. 261) National Treatment Study.
24. US Treasury (1990, p. 243).
25. Eight of them American (Oum, 1991, p. 7).
26. US Treasury (1990, p. 261).
27. US Treasury (1990, p. 258).
28. Oum (1991), and *The Economist*, 'The Korea that can say no,' 23 March 1991.
29. Oum (1991, pp. 10–11). Evidently there is a need to encourage more saving in longer-term securities, instead of short term (Fry, 1990).
30. Lindner (1991, p. 18).
31. Kim (1991, p. 22) and Oum (1991, p. 9). But apparently there will be a 10 per cent limit on foreign ownership (*The Economist*, 23 March 1991).
32. *The Korea Times*, 19 Dec. 1991.
33. Oum (1991, p. 7).
34. Ibid.
35. Byrne (1992, pp. 17–20).
36. *The Economist*, 6 November 1993, p. 104.
37. Harberger (1989, p. 165) proposes dealing with 'congestion externalities' in borrowing by instituting an 'international borrowing tax'. For possible disadvantages of unrestricted borrowing, see also Diaz-Alejandro (1985) and the papers by Williamson and others in Reisen and Fischer (1993).
38. Frankel (1993d). Note Fry (1990, p. 11): 'Successful financial restriction is exemplified by . . . three effects on the demand for money: a rightward shift in the function, a higher income elasticity, and a lower interest-rate elasticity.'
39. See, e.g., Kwack (1993) and Frankel (1993d).
40. For example, McKinnon (1991), who believes that China has succeeded in limiting the fiscal deficit so as to avoid dependence on the inflation tax, as compared with Russia.
41. For example, Frankel (1984), and Marshall (1991) or Cole and Slade (1992), respectively.
42. The Philippines, for example, was in the process in 1993 of letting in foreign banks with the explicit goal of competing down domestic interest rate spreads (Manalac, 1993).
43. Asian Development Bank (1993, p. 57), Diaz-Alejandro (1985), Fischer (1993, p. 126), Fry (1990, p. 36) and Lynch and Norton (1992, p. 18).
44. Fischer (1993, pp. 126–7) and Robinson *et al.* (1991, p. 22).
45. Manalac (1993, pp. 13–15).
46. Rhee (1992, pp. 55–60, p. 52).
47. Fischer (1993, p. 127), and Lynch and Norton (1992, p. 7).

48. Fischer (1993, p. 126) remarks on the need for banking supervisors to have a strong institutional position, e.g., to be free from political interference.
49. Manalac (1993, p. 19).
50. Fry (1990, p. 32).
51. Fry (1990, pp. 16, 32).
52. Fry (1990, p. 11).
53. For example, Frankel (1984, 1993a), and the other references cited therein.
54. Fischer (1993, p. 125) concurs. But he wants reserve requirements on banks reduced as well, while the other authors see a role for keeping them up, so that the government gets needed seigniorage. Clearly a liberalizing country is better off if it does not have a large budget deficit that needs to be financed to begin with. But that is easier said than done.
55. Lynch and Norton (1992, p. 5). See also Asian Development Bank (1993, p. 40).
56. Lynch and Norton (1992, p. 18). Emery (1992) explains that the absence of an active government bond market in Korea hinders the ability to conduct open market operations. Similarly, it makes sterilization operations more difficult, as noted.
57. A major factor was expansionary monetary policy, in part motivated by a perceived need to support the dollar. One might also wonder whether major speculative bubbles have not historically been a 'rite of passage' for a new world power (Frankel, 1993c, p. 10).

References

Aoki, M., and P. Sheard (1992) 'The Role of the Main Bank in the Corporate Governance Structure in Japan', Paper presented at conference on Corporate Governance: New Problems and New Solutions, Center for Economic Policy Research, Stanford University, CA., 1–2 May.

Asian Development Bank (1993) 'Capital Markets', in *Asian Development Outlook 1993*, pp. 40–47.

Bisignano, Joseph (1990) 'Structures of Financial Intermediation, Corporate Finance, and Central Banking' (Basle: BIS).

Bryant, R. (1987) *International Financial Intermediation* (Washington, DC: Brookings Institution).

Byrne, T. (1992) 'Implications of Korea's Financial Liberalization Reforms on the National Treatment of Foreign Financial Institutions', in Chwee Huay Ow-Taylor (ed.), *Korean–U.S. Financial Issues, Joint Korea–U.S. Academic Symposium* Vol. 3 (Washington, DC: Korea Economic Institute of America).

Calvo, G., L. Leiderman and C. Reinhart (1993a) 'Capital Inflows and Real Exchange Rate Appreciation in Latin America: The Role of External Factors', *IMF Staff Papers* 40, no. 1, March: 108–150.

Calvo, G., L. Leiderman and C. Reinhart (1993b) 'The Capital Inflows Problem: Concepts and Issues', Research Department, International Monetary Fund, *Contemporary Economic Policy*, July, 1994, 54–66.

Cheng, Hang-Sheng (1986) 'Financial Policy and Reform in Taiwan, China',

in Cheng (ed.), *Financial Policy and Reform in Pacific Basin Countries* (Lexington, MA: D.C. Heath) pp. 143–59.
Cho, Yoon Je (1986) 'Inefficiencies from Financial Liberalization in the Absence of Well-Functioning Capital Markets', *Journal of Money, Credit and Banking*, vol. 18, no. 2 (May) pp. 191–9.
Claessens, S. and S. Gooptu (1993) World Bank Symposium on *Portfolio Investment in Developing Countries*, September 9–10, paper no. 228.
Cole, D. and B. Slade (1992) Indonesian Financial Development: A Different Sequencing?, in *Financial Regulation: Changing the Rules of the Game*, D. Vittas (ed.), *EDI Development Studies* (Washington, DC: World Bank) pp. 121–61.
DeLong, J. B. (1991) 'The Great American Universal Banking Experiment', from *Inside the Business Enterprise* (Chicago: University of Chicago Press).
Diamond, D. (1984) 'Financial Intermediation and Delegated Monitoring', *Review of Economic Studies*, vol. 51, pp. 393–414.
Diamond, D. (1989) *Monitoring and Reputation: the Choice Between Bank Loans and Directly Placed Debt* (University of Chicago).
Diaz-Alejandro, C. (1985) 'Good-bye Financial Repression, Hello Financial Crash', *Journal of Development Economics*, vol. 19, 1/2 (Sep.-Oct.) pp. 1–24.
Eichengreen, B. and R. Portes (1989) 'After the Deluge: Default, Renegotiation and Settlement of Foreign Loans During the Interwar Years', in B. Eichengreen and P. Lindert (eds), *The International Debt Crisis in Historical Perspective* (Cambridge: MIT Press).
Emery, R. (1992) 'Central Banks' Use in East Asia of Money Market Instruments in the Conduct of Monetary Policy', *International Finance Discussion Paper*, No. 426, Federal Reserve Board, Washington, D.C. March.
Fischer, B. (1993) 'Impediments in the Domestic Banking Sector to Financial Opening', in H. Reisen and B. Fischer (eds), *Financial Opening: Policy Issues and Experiences in Developing Countries* (Paris: OECD) pp. 119–32.
Fishlow, A. (1986) 'Lessons from the Past: Capital Markets During the 19th Century and the Interwar Period', in M. Kahler (ed.), *The Politics of International Debt* (Ithaca, NY: Cornell University Press) pp. 37–94.
Frankel, J. (1984) 'The Yen/Dollar Agreement: Liberalizing Japanese Capital Markets', *Policy Analyses In International Economics* No. 9, Institute for International Economics (Washington, DC: MIT Press) December.
Frankel, J. (1993a) 'The Evolving Japanese Financial System, and the Cost of Capital', for *International Conference on the Japanese Financial Market and Corporate Managerial Behavior*, Tokyo, May 11, 1992, sponsored by the International University of Japan. CIDER Working Paper No. C92-002. Chapter 9 in I. Walter and T. Hiraki (ed.), *Restructuring Japan's Financial Markets* (Irwin Press) pp. 235–285.
Frankel, J. (1993b) 'Foreign Exchange Policy, Monetary Policy and Capital Market Liberalization in Korea', in Chwee Huay Ow-Taylor (ed.), *Korean–U.S. Financial Issues, U.S.–Joint Korea–U.S. Academic Symposium*, vol. 3 (Washington, DC: Korea Economic Institute of America) pp. 91–107.
Frankel, J. (1993c) 'Issues in Pacific Asia: An Economist's Views', Defense Intelligence College Workshop on Asian Politics, Monterey, Ca., 18–19 March 1993; in *Memoranda to Policymakers, NBR Analysis* 4, no. 1 (June

1993), National Bureau of Asian Research, May 1993, 5–13. Reprinted in *Venture Japan*, October 1993.

Frankel, J. (1993d) 'Sterilization of Money Inflows: Difficult (Calvo) or Easy (Reisen)?' Cartagena, Colombia, 29–30 July, 1993, Latinamerican Macroeconomic Network. In R. Steiner (ed.), *Capital Inflows: Size, Nature and Policy Adaptations* (Bogota: Fedesarrollo), 1994.

Fry, M. (1990) 'Nine Financial Sector Issues in Eleven Asian Developing Countries', *International Finance Group Working Paper No.* 90–09, University of Birmingham, UK.

Fry, M. (1993a) 'Financial Opening and Monetary Control in Pacific Basin Developing Countries', in H. Reisen and B. Fischer (eds), *Financial Opening: Policy Issues and Experiences in Developing Countries* (Paris: OECD) pp. 143–65.

Fry, M. (1993b) 'Financial Repression and Economic Growth', *International Finance Group Working Paper No. 93–07*, University of Birmingham, UK.

Grenville, S. (1991) 'The Evolution of Financial Deregulation', in *The Deregulation of Financial Intermediaries* (Sydney: Reserve Bank of Australia) pp. 3–35.

Goldsmith, R. (1969) *Financial Structure and Development* (New Haven, CN: Yale University Press).

Gurley, J. and E. Shaw (1960) *Money in a Theory of Finance* (Washington, DC: Brookings Institution).

Hamada, K. and A. Horiuchi (1987) 'The Political Economy of the Financial Market', in K. Yamamura and Y. Yasuba (eds), *The Political Economy of Japan: Volume 1. The Domestic Transformation*, (Stanford, Ca.: Stanford University Press) pp. 223–60.

Hanson, J. A. and R. de Rezende Rocha (1986) *High Interest Rates, Spreads and the Costs of Intermediation: Two Studies* (Washington, DC: World Bank).

Harberger, A. (1989) 'Welfare Consequences of Capital Inflows', Chapter 6 in Ronald Findlay *et al.* (eds), *Debt, Stabilization and Development: Essays in Memory of Carlos Diaz-Alejandro* (Oxford: Basil Blackwell).

Hardouvelis, G., R. La Porta and Th. Wizman (1994) 'What Moves the Discount on Country Equity Funds?' in J. Frankel (ed.), *The Internationalization of Equity Markets* (Chicago: U. Chicago).

Hodder, J. (1991) 'Is the Cost of Capital Lower in Japan?' *Journal of the Japanese and International Economies*, vol. 5, no. 1 (March) pp. 86–100.

Hoshi, T., A. Kashyap, and D. Sharfstein (1989) 'Bank Monitoring and Investment: Evidence from the Changing Structure of Japanese Corporate Banking Relationship', NBER Working Paper No. 3079, August. In R. G. Hubbard (ed.), *Asymmetric Information, Corporate Finance, and Investment* (Chicago: University of Chicago Press, 1990).

Kim, K. (1990) 'Deregulating the Domestic Economy: Korea's Experience in the 1980s', presented at Senior Policy Seminar, Caracas; revised December.

Kwack, S. (1993) 'Sterilization of the Monetary Effects of Current Account Surpluses and Consequences: Korea, 1986–1990', Howard University, February.

Lindner, D. (1991) 'The Political Economy of the Won: US–Korean Bilateral Negotiations on Exchange Rate', presented at conference in US–Korea Economic Relations, Hoover Institution, Stanford University, December.
Lynch, D. (1993) 'Australian Financial Markets: Growth and Issues', *Australian Institute of Bankers Banking and Finance Conference*, July.
Lynch, D., and W. Norton (1992) 'Asian Financial Markets: Growth and Implications', Macquarie University, *Fifth Annual Australasian Finance and Banking Conference*, December.
MacFarlane, I. (ed.) (1991) *The Deregulation of Financial Intermediaries* Reserve Bank of Australia, Sydney.
Manalac, Ma. L. (1993) 'Recent Developments in Banking Supervision and Supervision of Interest Rate Risk and Market Risk in the Philippines', *SEANZA Forum of Banking Supervision*, 8–9 July Tokyo.
Marshall, K. (1991) *Financial Deregulation and Development in Indonesia* Ph.D. thesis, U. C. Berkeley.
Mayer, C. (1988) 'New Issues in Corporate Finance', *European Economic Review*, vol. 32 (May) pp. 1167–89.
Mayer, C. (1989) 'Myths of the West: Lessons from Developed Countries for Development Finance', Policy, Planning and Research Working Paper No. 301, November.
McKinnon, R. (1973) *Money and Capital in Economic Development* (Washington, DC: Brookings Institution).
McKinnon, R. (1991) *The Order of Economic Liberalization: Financial Control in the Transition to a Market Economy* (Baltimore).
Meerschwam, D. (1989) 'The Japanese Financial System and the Cost of Capital', in P. Krugman (ed.), *Trade with Japan: Has the Door Opened Wider*? (Chicago: University of Chicago Press, 1991).
Modigliani, F. and M. Miller (1958) 'The Cost of Capital, Corporation Finance and the Theory of Investment', *American Economic Review*, vol. 48, pp. 201–297.
Nakajima, Z. and H. Taguchi (1993) 'Toward a More Stable Financial Framework: Long-Term Alternatives – An Overview of Recent Bank Disruption Worldwide', Institute for Monetary and Economic Studies, Bank of Japan, Tokyo, July, this volume.
Nam, Sang-Woo (1989) 'Liberalization of the Korean Financial and Capital Markets', in *Korea's Macroeconomic and Financial Policies* (Seoul: Korea Development Institute), December.
Oum, B. (1991) 'Liberalization of Korea's Financial and Capital Markets', paper presented at 'New Economic Order: A U.S.–Korea Forum', 25 June, Washington, DC.
Pacific Economic Cooperation Council (1993) *Pacific Economic Outlook 1993–94*.
Park, Yung Chul (1991) 'The Role of Finance in Economic Development in South Korea and Taiwan', in *Finance and Development in Europe*, Centre for Economic Policy Research, Santiago de Compostela, 13–15 Dec.
Park, Y. C. (1993) 'Capital Movement, Real Asset Speculation, and Macroeconomic Adjustment in Korea', in Helmut Reisen and Bernhard Fischer (eds), *Financial Opening: Policy Issues and Experiences in Developing Countries* (Paris: OECD) pp. 93–118.

Reisen, H. (1993a) 'The "Impossible Trinity" in South-East Asia', *International Economic Insights* (March/April).

Reisen, H. (1993b) 'Macroeconomic Policies Towards Capital Account Convertibility', in H. Reisen and B. Fischer (eds), *Financial Opening: Policy Issues and Experiences in Developing Countries* (Paris: OECD) pp. 43–55.

Reisen, H. and B. Fischer (eds) (1993) *Financial Opening: Policy Issues and Experiences in Developing Countries* (Paris: OECD).

Rhee, S. G. (1992) *Securities Markets and Systemic Risks in Dynamic Asian Economies* (Paris: OECD).

Robinson, D., Y. Byeon and R. Teja (1991) *Thailand: Adjusting to Success – Current Policy Issues, Occasional Paper No. 85* (Washington, DC: International Monetary Fund), August.

Shaw, E. (1973) *Financial Deepening in Economic Development* (New York: Oxford University Press).

Singh, A., and J. Hamid (1992) *Corporate Financial Structures in Developing Countries, International Finance Corporation Technical Paper No. 1* (Washington, DC: World Bank).

Stiglitz, J. (1991) 'Government, Financial Markets, and Economic Development', NBER Working Paper No. 3669, April.

Stiglitz, J. and A. Weiss (1981) 'Credit Rationing in Markets with Imperfect Information', *American Economic Review*, vol. 71 (June) pp. 393–410.

Taggart, R. A. (1985) 'Secular Patterns in the Financing of U.S. Corporations', in B. Friedman (ed.), *Corporate Capital Structure in the United States* (Chicago: University of Chicago Press).

US Department of the Treasury (1989) 'Report to the Congress on International Economic and Exchange Rate Policy', October.

US Department of the Treasury (1990) *National Treatment Study: Report to Congress on Foreign Treatment of U.S. Financial Institutions* (November) pp. 242–71.

Weisbrod, S., and H. Lee (1993) 'The Role of Financial Intermediaries During Asset Deflations: Case Studies of Japan, Korea, and Taiwan', Weisbrod Group for the World Bank, July.

Zysman, John (1983) *Governments, Markets and Growth* (Ithaca, NY: Cornell University Press).

Comments

Robert T. Parry

Professor Frankel's chapter provides a very useful overview of the changing financial environment in the Pacific Basin. I would like to focus on two issues that come to mind when reading this chapter. First, as countries in the Pacific Basin continue to liberalize, must their financial systems evolve according to the 'natural' stages of financial sector development that Professor Frankel described? Second, what are the implications of financial liberalization for bank regulatory policy?

Turning to the first issue, Frankel suggests that there are 'natural' historical stages in financial development: from internal finance, to financial intermediation by commercial banks, to securitization involving the direct issuance of securities in developed financial markets. He also describes 'natural' stages of development of open markets in many countries, beginning with short-term money markets, followed by the long-term securities markets – first in government bonds, later in corporate bonds and equities – and culminating in the development of futures and derivative contracts.

I think there is some question as to the extent to which one can generalize about the stages of financial development. The historical development of financial systems that we see in most countries reflects the response of financial markets to particular government restrictions as well as the progress of technology. Financial markets are always adapting to government restrictions. There are abundant instances in which private savings have sought to move from the regulated financial sector to financial institutions and markets that lie outside these controls. In the US the growth of open securities markets is in part attributable to restrictions on deposit rates and other limits on the banking sector. In Korea and Taiwan, lending restrictions on commercial banks fostered the development of an unregulated nonbanking sector, including the 'curb' markets. In contrast, Germany, with its universal banking system, has provided relatively less incentive for the development of a corporate bond market. Thus, to the extent that countries differ in the restrictions placed on their financial markets, the natural path of their financial development may differ.

Of course, there is no doubt that technological improvements in computers and telecommunications have spurred the growth of capital markets and the development of more sophisticated securities instruments, such as futures, options and various derivatives. The interesting nature of technology is that once it is in place in one country, it is commonly transferable to another. We know that in many manufacturing industries technology can be borrowed or bought by developing countries. The same is true for financial services. Thus emerging economies can acquire the technology to assist them in developing their financial markets at an earlier stage of their evolution than many industrial countries could. Therefore, it may not be so surprising to see an emerging economy developing an equity market before it has a fully functioning corporate bond market. This suggests that not all countries necessarily have to go through the same stages of financial development.

Is it good or bad that many emerging economies are 'skipping' some stages of financial development by, say, focusing on the development of equity markets without well-functioning, efficient domestic banking sectors? Is there possibly a 'cargo cult' fascination with some aspects of financial markets in industrial countries, such as equity markets, as Frankel suggests?

Let me say that I believe that a well-functioning commercial banking system is helpful to financial development. Banks are effective institutions for pooling the resources of savers to finance large investment projects and for consolidating information-gathering and monitoring of borrowers. I nevertheless believe that it is useful to encourage the development of as many financial market alternatives to commercial banks as possible. The more financial market alternatives there are for channeling savings toward appropriate investments, the better off the overall economy will be. (This does not preclude the participation of banking institutions in these activities.) But I also agree with Frankel that countries should not merely import rules and institutions from abroad, such as equity markets, with the expectation that they will solve all problems. Ultimately any financial market, including an equity market, will operate effectively only if private participants face the proper incentives and if there is sufficient demand for the services offered by that market.

This all suggests that there may be different paths to attain the goal of an efficient financial system. Germany is perceived as having a relatively less open securities market than the US. On the other hand, with its universal banking system, Germany arguably has a more developed banking system than the US. Overall, is Germany a more or less financially developed economy than the US?

Let me turn to the second issue in Frankel's paper. What are the implications of financial liberalization for bank regulatory policy? The concern is that financial market liberalization will increase risks in banking. For example, if banks have full discretion in making lending decisions, credit risk may increase. Financial liberalization also may increase the interest rate exposure of banks. Finally, liberalization may encourage banks to increase the scope of their international transactions, exposing them to exchange rate risk.

As Nakajima and Taguchi have pointed out in their chapter, these risks are a public policy concern if bank failures have systemic effects. The usual concerns are that bank failures may threaten the payments system and credit intermediation. How have the developing countries in the area reacted to concerns about systemic risk? My reading is that most of these countries have provided a safety net to banks through implicit guarantees. In some cases large banks are asked by the authorities to buy up weaker, smaller banks that threaten to fail. In other cases, public funds are used to inject liquidity and/or buy up failing banks. In many cases these implicit guarantees are closely related to credit guidelines. If a bank follows government credit guidelines and the loan turns sour, it is natural to expect the government to cover the loss. This suggests that government credit allocation policies may be inconsistent with the goal of limiting bank risk-taking behavior. As we realize only too clearly in the US, the existence of safety nets can exacerbate the problem of risk-taking by banks through moral hazard.

The regulator's problem is how to lessen the potentially excessive risk-taking of banks. You start by muting the distortions to the incentives for risk-taking that government safety nets create. That demands explicitly laying out the goal of the safety net – to protect the payment system alone or bank intermediary services as well – and then extending the net only as far as needed to achieve that goal. This does not necessarily mean that the scope of banking has to be restricted, but it does mean that some activities of banks may have to be conducted in separate subsidiaries within a bank holding company framework. Whatever part of the financial system is supported by the safety net, strong prudential policies and effective supervision are needed to limit risk-taking behavior. Here the most important regulatory tool is capital adequacy requirements. As Frankel has pointed out, most countries have adopted the Basle risk-adjusted capital standards. These standards have forced banks to build up their capital and restrain asset growth. The Basle standards do have at least two limitations: (i) they will not work if credit allocation decisions by governments eliminate banks' incentives to make good loans; (ii) they do not fully account for exchange rate risk or interest rate risk.

One must also allow banks the tools for risk management. This requires the development of markets for managing risk. For example, as interest rates are liberalized and securities markets develop, the availability of instruments for managing interest rate risk will become increasingly important in Asian economies. The need for instruments to manage exchange rate risk has been felt for some time. I think that foreign banks could potentially play an important role in encouraging greater risk management and overcoming some of the obstacles cited above. Greater foreign bank competition gives domestic banks incentives to make proper credit decisions. Foreign banks also have the expertise to develop new risk-management instruments and to train people skilled in making credit and risk management decisions.

I would like to conclude on the issue of central bank independence. I believe that the most important contribution that a central bank can make towards financial stability is to maintain a stable monetary policy and low inflation. There are different ways that central banks can make the commitment to a low-inflation policy credible. One way is to make the central bank more independent from short-term political pressures – either through an independent structure, as in the case of the German Bundesbank, or through an explicit rule, as with the Reserve Bank of New Zealand.

But central bank independence is not the only way to gain credibility for a low-inflation policy. The other way is to *earn* it, as the Bank of Japan exemplifies. Even though the Bank of Japan has far fewer structural features of independence than the Bundesbank, the Bank of Japan has earned its credibility through a strong track record in fighting inflation.

Comments

Graeme J. Thompson

I am honoured to be able to comment on Professor Frankel's chapter on 'Changes in the Financial Systems of Asian and Pacific Countries'. I think we would all agree that Professor Frankel has given us a stimulating review of developments in the financial systems of this part of the world – a very exciting region, because growth and change is so rapid – and of some important issues with which governments and financial institutions must grapple.

Our hosts have asked that I concentrate my remarks on Section V of the chapter – which discusses a number of regulatory issues. I hope this is not because we in Australia are thought to have all the answers in this difficult area. We are, however, very familiar with the important *questions*!

It is against the background of Australian experience with financial deregulation that I offer the following comments.

Deregulation and Prudential Supervision

Professor Frankel notes that, for Asian and Pacific countries, 'the challenge is how to achieve the more liberalized (financial) system that is appropriate to a country in the process of industrializing, without incurring as many of the difficulties that the industrialized countries have incurred.' This *is* quite a challenge. But I think an important part of the resolution is in Professor Frankel's statement that 'liberalization does not mean an end to bank regulation'.

Of course, the *nature* of regulation changes as financial systems are liberalized – a system of prudential supervision must be developed.

A strong prudential regime is especially important *early* in the deregulation phase. This is when market participants are on the steepest part of the learning curve – having to acquire new skills, learning to cope with more volatility and probably most prone to mistakes and erratic behaviour.

This is a tough requirement for supervisors, because they will *also* be on a learning curve. Practical implications of the learning curve problem are:

- It is probably better to deregulate slowly, if possible. But experience in Australia and other countries is that once the deregulatory process begins, it develops a momentum which can be difficult to control.
- It is better not to deregulate when inflationary expectations are high and the economy is buoyant. Professor Frankel discusses the optimal sequence of financial liberalization. I would add that, to reduce the dangers of excessive exuberance following financial liberalization, it is preferable to have achieved monetary stabilization first.

They might not have the luxury of being able to choose the timing or control the exact pace of change in financial markets, but many Asian economies *do* have the opportunity to learn from the experience of other countries, and there are now established international benchmarks of 'good supervisory practice'.

Details will, no doubt, vary from country to country; but, on the basis of Australia's experience in the past decade, three key areas to which supervisors must pay attention are:

- *bank capital*, which is necessary to absorb losses, and is a source of confidence in the market. Professor Frankel argues that supervisors should have regard to capital as measured by the market place. There are problems, in general, with sole reliance on such measures, but it will be especially difficult in countries without well-developed, deep equities markets.
- quality of *management* and management *systems* in banks;
- quality of *information* – good accounting information about banks (supported by a sound legal framework) is critical for efficient equity markets. It is also essential if the supervisor is to be forewarned of problems developing in banks before they become full-blown and threaten loss to depositors, or to those funding insurance schemes.

In fashioning their prudential framework, supervisors need to be wary of:

- burden of '*quasi-regulation*' – supervision which intrudes in the day-to-day decision-making of banks risks damaging their efficiency and innovativeness, and can undo the main benefits of deregulation;
- *moral hazard* risks – the more intensive is the supervisors' involvement in banking business, the greater the problem of moral hazard;

- *raising expectations* too far about their capacity to keep individual banks out of trouble. Regardless of the supervisory system, banks will from time to time get into difficulty – whether because of macroeconomic fluctuations, poor management, fraud or plain old bad luck. The best efforts of supervisors – and bankers – will be brought to nothing if government does not provide a sound, stable macroeconomic environment for banks.

Serious problems in individual banks may be addressed in various ways – often determined by political considerations – but the key need is to prevent them causing damage to other banks and the fabric of the financial system. Banks have the largest direct exposures to each other in the *payments system*.

Professor Frankel's chapter touches on the payment, but only briefly, and there are ways of dealing with payments risk other than by adopting a Regime II supervision model. At a minimum, it is critical that payments systems meet high standards of:

- transparency;
- risk control;
- robust arrangements for coping with a participant's inability to meet settlement obligations. (Systems for 'real time gross settlement', being developed in some countries, do away with interbank settlement risk but have other costs which need to be weighed.)
- *Who should supervise banks*?

The chapter is rather unclear on this important point.

There are, of course, many different institutional models around the world, all of which are made to work. I would like, however, to propose some principles – in ascending order of controversy – for consideration:

- The first is that supervisors must be well-trained, knowledgable, respected in the market, capable of independent judgment, and willing to make tough decisions when a bank is in difficulty.
- The second is that bank supervision should be the responsibility of an agency which is insulated from political pressure. I think the pay-off for credibility of the supervisory process is obvious. (Wise politicians also appreciate the value of distance from supervision when a bank gets into trouble!)
- The third proposition is that there is considerable advantage in the *central bank's* being the supervisor. This is because the central bank needs a close understanding of the condition of the banking system in its monetary policy operations and because it

will be called upon, from time to time, to consider emergency liquidity support for a bank or banks. I also believe that central banks are more likely than other agencies to have the qualities I referred to earlier (although I might be biased!).

- Fourth, unlike Professor Frankel I have reservations about the wisdom of giving supervisory responsibility for all financial institutions to the one agency – a *mega-regulator*. Different financial institutions call for different regulatory skills, both because their activities vary and because the objectives of supervision will not necessarily be the same. Of course, conglomerates and universal banks pose difficult issues of overlap and co-ordination.
- *Supervisory Regimes.*

Finally, a word on Regimes I, II and III as defined in the chapter by Nakajima and Taguchi. Professor Frankel comes down in favour of Regime II, even though recognizing the difficulties of establishing firewalls and economic costs of forcing complete separation of banking services into 'transactions' and 'other'.

I suspect that, at the end of the day, political considerations determine how far the supervisory net will be cast.

Further, once that net is cast broadly it will be difficult to draw it narrower. Consequently, governments need to consider very early in the liberalization process how wide the supervisory net should be. The choice of a narrower Regime II system would need to be assessed very carefully in some countries. This is because Regime II assumes that the market is able to exercise effective 'supervision' over the *intermediation* activities of banks; this, in turn, depends on a reasonably deep and sophisticated market supported by sound accounting rules and high standards of disclosure.

6 Changing Behavior of Private Banks and Corporations and Monetary Policy in Japan

Naoyuki Yoshino

I INTRODUCTION

This chapter analyzes the impact of banking and corporate behaviour with special focus on the so-called asset bubble period of 1987–90 when banks extended huge speculative loans to real estate and non-bank financial institutions, subsequently resulting in default losses. Monetary policy at the time focused more on exchange rates than money supply since prices were stable.

Section II analyzes the behavior of private banks and businesses utilizing various data. Loans made to real estate-related concerns, non-bank financial institutions, and construction firms were substantial during the bubble period and the gap between lending and deposit rates narrowed at city and long-term credit banks. City banks and long-term credit banks expanded their overseas operations by supplying enormous funds to the Euro-market.

As for corporate business behavior, while large corporations started to rely more on stocks and bonds for financing, small businesses continued to rely more heavily on bank loans compared with large firms as seen in Section III.

Changes in the conduct of monetary policy are examined by quarterly, monthly, and daily data in Section IV. Structural changes in monetary policy can be seen in 1979 and 1985. The price level together with the exchange rate can be seen to be important in the monetary policy reaction function in the 1980s.

Section V deals empirically with the impact of monetary policy and the exchange rate on asset prices and other macroeconomic variables. A VAR estimation of the causal relationship is conducted.

Land prices were affected by changes in money supply more strongly after 1980 compared to 1970–79.

II CHANGES IN PRIVATE BANKING BEHAVIOR IN JAPAN

Assets and Liabilities of all Banks in Japan

This section overviews the behavior of banks in Japan from balance sheet data.

Table 6.1 (p. 212) gives a breakdown of the assets of all banks (city banks, long-term credit banks, trust banks and regional banks) in Japan from March 1954 to December 1992. The share of long-term government bonds has increased approximately 2 percent every year from March 1975 to March 1979 due to the high level of issues (column 4, Table 6.1). After the first oil crisis the central government was able to increase expenditures by increasing bond issues to compensate for sluggish economic growth. Private banks purchased a substantial portion of government bonds in the late 1970s (column 4, Table 6.1).

The share of corporate bonds and stocks held by all banks increased during 1988–9 and 1988–92, respectively, reflecting the high reliance on stocks and bonds for financing by large corporations (columns 9 and 10, Table 6.1). Stocks held by financial institutions (asset side) are evaluated at book value.

The share of bank loans has been on a declining trend since 1954 (column 13, Table 6.1) due to the development of various financial instruments.

Table 6.2 shows the liabilities of all banks. The share of demand deposits has been declining since the corporate sector is minimizing such deposits by investing in higher yielding financial instruments. That of time deposits, which increased until March 1981, has declined since then because of the shift to CDs. However, it increased again in March 1990 when small-denomination time deposits were deregulated. The ratio of regulated deposits to all deposits with city banks has declined since 1987, while that of deregulated deposits, such as large-denomination time deposits and CDs, increased to 78.9 percent in June 1993 (column 4, Table 6.3). Deregulation of time deposits was completed 16 June 1993. The issuance of stocks increased from 1988 until 1991 so that banks were able to attain the BIS capital adequacy ratio (column 6, Table 6.2). The share of Bank

Table 6.2 Components of liabilities of all Banks (1954–92)
(% of total assets)

End of period (1)	*Demand deposits* (2)	*Time deposits* (3)	*CDs* (4)	*Bank debentures* (5)	*Stocks* (6)	*Bank of Japan loans* (7)	*Call money* (8)	*Bills sold* (9)
3/54	35.183	38.001	0.000	6.697	1.534	15.279	0.833	0.000
3/55	33.795	42.545	0.000	7.410	1.425	7.767	1.466	0.000
3/56	36.587	45.289	0.000	7.515	1.332	0.947	2.059	0.000
3/57	34.008	44.511	0.000	6.750	1.772	5.095	2.534	0.000
3/58	28.463	45.286	0.000	6.882	1.530	9.365	2.852	0.000
3/59	28.256	48.319	0.000	7.833	1.393	5.349	3.057	0.000
3/60	27.729	48.380	0.000	8.469	1.867	4.470	2.650	0.000
3/61	27.972	47.805	0.000	8.881	1.769	5.630	1.778	0.000
3/62	25.459	46.211	0.000	8.922	1.725	10.299	2.152	0.000
3/63	28.792	44.997	0.000	8.631	1.435	8.293	2.453	0.000
3/64	28.873	44.713	0.000	8.878	1.595	6.243	3.477	0.000
3/65	28.295	44.118	0.000	9.220	1.763	4.829	5.166	0.000
3/66	28.965	44.970	0.000	9.806	1.546	4.802	3.662	0.000
3/67	27.879	46.187	0.000	10.160	1.568	4.853	3.111	0.000
3/68	26.895	46.501	0.000	10.353	1.627	3.966	3.421	0.000
3/69	26.979	47.404	0.000	10.239	1.568	3.788	3.155	0.000
3/70	27.804	47.230	0.000	9.986	1.478	4.276	3.740	0.000
3/71	28.043	46.964	0.000	9.817	1.481	4.560	3.679	0.000
3/72	29.747	47.453	0.000	9.955	1.319	0.962	2.694	0.556
3/73	29.399	46.624	0.000	9.992	1.284	2.192	2.063	1.437
3/74	29.091	45.362	0.000	10.104	1.297	2.085	1.517	4.710
3/75	27.938	44.550	0.000	10.298	1.222	1.576	2.537	5.136
3/76	28.706	45.747	0.000	10.850	1.203	1.389	2.196	3.427
3/77	27.920	46.303	0.000	11.023	1.191	1.215	2.455	3.363
3/78	26.499	46.797	0.000	11.035	1.173	1.023	2.580	2.925
3/79	27.167	47.286	0.000	10.980	1.104	1.406	2.673	2.682
3/80	25.870	47.377	0.632	10.553	1.039	0.760	3.000	2.753
3/81	22.666	49.524	0.715	10.548	1.001	0.718	3.153	1.666
3/82	22.132	48.971	0.966	10.481	0.998	0.072	4.421	0.787
3/83	21.038	47.479	1.294	10.510	0.983	0.702	4.524	1.798
3/84	19.372	46.604	2.022	10.701	0.934	0.924	4.922	1.481
3/85	18.838	45.118	2.437	10.661	0.861	0.498	5.414	1.989
3/86	16.578	44.961	2.410	10.482	0.870	0.891	6.083	3.644
3/87	15.878	43.494	2.397	10.147	0.855	1.210	5.966	4.344
3/88	14.731	44.878	2.453	9.726	1.182	1.279	6.090	3.113
3/89	14.367	44.718	3.012	9.196	1.732	1.143	6.261	3.883
3/90	14.471	48.099	3.080	8.072	2.222	0.786	6.636	2.787
3/91	14.389	50.505	2.950	8.766	2.272	0.739	5.354	2.268
3/92	14.992	49.246	2.387	9.477	2.250	0.775	6.202	2.384
12/92	14.666	48.065	2.469	9.546	2.196	1.131	8.206	2.466

Table 6.1 Assets of all banks (1954–92) (% of total assets)

End of period (1)	*Currency* (2)	*Trusts* (3)	*Securities* (4)	*Long-term govt. bonds* (5)	*Local govt. bonds* (6)	*Public corp. bonds* (7)	*Bank debentures* (8)	*Corporate bonds* (9)	*Stocks* (10)	*Investment trusts* (11)	*Call loans* (12)	*Loans* (13)
3/54	1.589	0.029	11.229	1.476	0.383	0.560	3.178	4.539	1.078	0.010	0.363	86.719
3/55	1.416	0.020	12.274	1.343	0.597	0.840	3.743	4.513	1.232	0.006	0.591	85.646
3/56	1.526	0.077	13.829	1.243	0.870	1.301	4.119	4.463	1.705	0.005	1.248	83.152
3/57	1.453	0.065	12.723	1.019	1.235	1.061	3.127	4.164	2.102	0.008	1.120	84.480
3/58	1.597	0.065	13.393	0.804	1.266	1.782	3.623	3.897	2.012	0.008	0.993	83.809
3/59	1.610	0.097	14.038	0.630	1.192	1.839	4.231	4.117	2.022	0.008	1.226	82.873
3/60	1.584	0.097	14.862	0.520	1.142	2.075	4.435	4.471	2.208	0.010	1.134	81.797
3/61	1.588	0.117	15.332	0.434	1.073	2.205	4.443	4.706	2.459	0.012	1.068	81.383
3/62	1.777	0.175	14.682	0.372	1.038	1.217	4.434	4.762	2.781	0.077	0.896	81.559
3/63	1.770	0.160	14.531	0.296	1.152	1.720	4.235	4.320	2.742	0.067	1.167	81.818
3/64	1.893	0.142	12.717	0.219	1.313	1.519	2.692	4.104	2.765	0.105	1.198	82.922
3/65	1.821	0.170	14.560	0.144	1.400	2.227	4.132	3.826	2.727	0.104	1.139	81.594
3/66	1.587	0.532	16.015	0.439	1.359	2.538	4.855	4.149	2.585	0.087	1.304	79.607
3/67	1.492	0.294	16.306	1.907	1.314	2.028	4.114	4.014	2.856	0.073	1.126	80.162
3/68	1.373	0.207	15.938	1.605	1.592	2.078	3.798	3.826	2.969	0.069	1.391	80.287
3/69	1.495	0.187	16.135	1.801	1.706	2.253	3.479	3.723	3.113	0.061	1.274	80.292
3/70	1.399	0.183	15.266	1.580	1.770	2.227	3.081	3.500	3.054	0.054	1.515	80.707
3/71	1.206	0.201	13.903	0.732	1.833	2.130	2.908	3.215	3.031	0.054	1.720	82.074

3/72	1.003	0.189	14.729	1.845	1.819	2.145	3.080	2.778	3.009	0.053	1.131	82.003
3/73	0.966	0.185	14.839	2.437	1.924	2.002	2.886	2.235	3.297	0.059	1.058	81.516
3/74	1.024	0.306	14.291	1.518	2.361	1.947	3.060	2.051	3.284	0.070	0.819	81.435
3/75	1.079	0.335	14.435	1.530	2.919	1.942	2.941	1.903	3.145	0.055	1.558	80.414
3/76	0.987	0.246	16.252	3.894	2.853	1.856	2.633	1.879	3.075	0.061	1.113	79.921
3/77	0.942	0.218	17.509	5.957	2.731	1.967	2.207	1.553	3.007	0.086	1.186	78.554
3/78	0.825	0.209	19.444	8.041	2.823	1.898	2.244	1.317	3.033	0.089	1.238	76.892
3/79	0.822	0.201	20.968	9.961	2.856	1.938	1.812	1.152	3.151	0.098	1.554	75.206
3/80	0.891	0.226	21.385	9.098	3.348	2.193	2.020	1.124	3.502	0.100	2.009	73.979
3/81	0.885	0.294	21.050	8.663	3.217	2.510	1.788	1.079	3.693	0.100	2.528	73.812
3/82	0.777	0.245	20.306	7.763	3.108	2.686	1.800	1.037	3.827	0.084	4.127	73.342
3/83	0.715	0.237	19.235	7.394	2.613	2.596	1.812	0.862	3.866	0.092	4.893	73.612
3/84	0.670	0.214	18.364	6.789	2.403	2.686	1.824	0.703	3.871	0.088	5.119	74.228
3/85	0.607	0.292	17.464	6.283	2.136	2.592	1.816	0.605	3.923	0.093	4.943	75.572
3/86	0.596	0.434	17.225	6.304	1.917	2.525	1.815	0.651	3.873	0.105	5.037	75.453
3/87	0.540	0.847	17.373	6.443	1.653	2.404	1.954	0.602	3.827	0.397	4.465	75.747
3/88	0.490	1.158	17.587	6.305	1.458	1.477	1.901	1.270	4.418	0.506	4.111	75.598
3/89	0.496	1.305	17.947	6.479	1.329	1.472	1.698	1.202	5.207	0.523	4.071	74.698
3/90	0.465	1.449	18.111	6.228	1.285	1.491	1.857	0.970	5.580	0.637	3.918	74.390
3/91	0.468	1.120	18.224	5.758	1.257	1.515	1.860	1.016	6.092	0.594	2.837	76.079
3/92	0.534	0.991	17.794	5.155	1.249	1.518	1.889	1.144	6.269	0.474	2.694	77.199
12/92	0.574	1.035	17.521	5.166	1.177	1.460	1.812	1.151	6.182	0.468	2.831	77.042

Table 6.3 Share of unregulated deposits with city banks (%)

End of period (1)	*Time deposits / Total liabilities* (2)	*Unregulated time deposits / Total liabilities* (3)	*Ratio of unregulated time deposits* (= (3)/(2)) (4)
12/50	14.235	0.000	0.000
12/55	30.259	0.000	0.000
12/60	27.987	0.000	0.000
12/65	32.590	0.000	0.000
12/70	36.266	0.000	0.000
12/75	35.851	0.000	0.000
12/79	40.815	0.000	0.000
12/80	40.989	0.000	0.000
12/81	42.199	0.000	0.000
12/82	41.760	0.000	0.000
12/83	42.262	0.000	0.000
12/84	40.574	0.000	0.000
12/85	39.926	1.719	4.306
12/86	39.860	0.468	1.173
12/87	41.693	11.516	27.622
12/88	41.609	17.204	41.348
12/89	41.593	27.257	65.531
12/90	41.680	30.942	74.238
12/91	38.817	28.927	74.521
12/92	37.502	29.346	78.250
6/93	39.648	31.272	78.873

of Japan loans has been declining since 1954, though it increased during the asset bubble period of 1987–9 (column 7, Table 6.2), reflecting lower call rates and other interest rates.

Changes in the Balance Sheets of City, Regional, Long-term Credit, and Trust Banks in Japan

Tables 6.4 to 6.7 summarize the assets and liabilities of various kinds of banks; the following characteristics can be noted:

(1) The growth rate of reserves for possible loan losses has been very high since the collapse of the asset price bubble in 1991 (column 20, Table 6.4). Such reserves became large in March 1993 due to bad loans extended to non-bank financial institutions, real estate developers, etc. as shown in column 19, Table 6.4. Large banks such as city, trust, and long-term credit banks

Table 6.4 Balance sheet of city banks (% of total assets / liabilities)

End of period (1)	*Total deposits* (2)	*Negotiable certificates of deposit* (3)	*Bank debentures* (4)	*Call money* (5)	*Bills sold* (5′)	*Borrowed money* (6)	*Foreign exchange* (7)	*Convertible bonds* (7′)	*Due to trust accounts* (7″)	*Other liabilities* (7‴)	*Reserves for possible loan losses* (8-a)
3/74	65.24	0.00	0.49	1.96	5.56	3.88	2.95	0.00	0.02	3.34	1.01
3/75	63.30	0.00	0.58	3.51	5.97	3.57	2.94	0.00	0.08	3.48	0.88
3/76	66.67	0.00	0.82	3.31	4.05	2.81	1.81	0.00	0.07	3.50	0.80
3/77	66.91	0.00	0.98	3.87	4.13	2.50	1.36	0.00	0.09	3.67	0.76
3/78	69.62	0.00	1.09	4.16	3.81	2.03	1.10	0.00	0.07	3.62	0.77
3/79	70.39	0.00	1.03	4.39	3.47	2.84	1.30	0.00	0.03	3.42	0.74
3/80	66.69	2.64	0.89	4.52	3.25	2.67	2.02	0.00	0.01	4.36	0.61
3/81	68.97	2.69	0.89	4.93	1.94	2.16	1.63	0.00	0.02	5.05	0.56
3/82	70.27	3.56	0.86	6.11	0.83	1.65	1.65	0.00	0.02	4.52	0.48
3/83	69.21	4.25	0.91	5.94	1.94	2.18	1.43	0.00	0.03	4.41	0.50
3/84	69.53	4.91	0.94	5.48	1.60	2.31	1.42	0.00	0.05	4.46	0.48
3/85	69.27	5.03	0.87	5.63	2.04	2.04	1.30	0.00	0.03	4.16	0.44
3/86	68.16	4.09	1.07	4.90	3.79	2.02	0.87	0.06	0.04	5.13	0.44
3/87	67.86	4.51	1.00	4.58	4.60	2.09	0.82	0.03	0.09	4.94	0.45
3/88	68.16	4.53	1.05	5.18	3.16	1.95	0.75	0.10	0.13	5.27	0.43
3/89	67.27	5.02	0.97	5.14	3.58	1.69	0.65	0.28	0.12	5.07	0.42
3/90	66.96	4.74	0.83	6.41	2.60	1.17	0.62	0.23	0.05	4.85	0.37
3/91	66.79	5.11	0.83	5.07	2.30	1.96	0.32	0.22	0.07	5.36	0.39
3/92	64.94	4.38	0.92	6.88	2.58	2.24	0.33	0.21	0.15	5.66	0.48
3/93	65.70	5.11	1.07	7.74	2.26	3.25	0.28	0.17	0.29	2.71	0.65

Table 6.4 (Cont'd)

Reserves for retirement allowances (8-b)	*Other reserves* (8-c)	*Reserves under special law* (8-d)	*Acceptances and guarantees* (8')	*Total liabilities* (8")	*Common stock* (9)	*New stock subscription* (9')	*Legal reserves* (9")	*Earned surplus* (9"')	*Total stockholders' equity* (9"")	*Total liabilities and stockholders' equity* (10)
0.30	0.04	0.17	12.40	97.38	0.84	0.00	0.24	1.55	2.62	100.00
0.33	0.05	0.19	12.68	97.55	0.73	0.00	0.22	1.50	2.45	100.00
0.36	0.05	0.16	13.18	97.59	0.71	0.01	0.22	1.47	2.41	100.00
0.37	0.04	0.15	12.66	97.50	0.76	0.04	0.20	1.50	2.50	100.00
0.37	0.04	0.13	10.68	97.48	0.76	0.00	0.20	1.55	2.52	100.00
0.35	0.03	0.19	9.41	97.61	0.69	0.00	0.20	1.51	2.39	100.00
0.32	0.02	0.13	9.79	97.92	0.58	0.00	0.18	1.33	2.08	100.00
0.30	0.01	0.12	8.69	97.95	0.56	0.00	0.17	1.32	2.05	100.00
0.25	0.01	0.11	7.77	98.09	0.54	0.00	0.15	1.21	1.91	100.00
0.23	0.00	0.00	7.11	98.13	0.50	0.00	0.15	1.22	1.87	100.00
0.21	0.00	0.00	6.71	98.10	0.47	0.00	0.16	1.27	1.90	100.00
0.17	0.00	0.00	7.22	98.20	0.41	0.01	0.15	1.23	1.80	100.00
0.16	0.00	0.01	7.33	98.05	0.44	0.00	0.19	1.32	1.95	100.00
0.14	0.00	0.02	6.96	98.09	0.41	0.00	0.20	1.30	1.91	100.00
0.12	0.00	0.02	6.97	97.82	0.50	0.01	0.32	1.35	2.18	100.00
0.10	0.00	0.02	7.17	97.51	0.61	0.00	0.47	1.41	2.49	100.00
0.08	0.00	0.02	8.37	97.30	0.71	0.06	0.60	1.33	2.70	100.00
0.08	0.00	0.02	8.53	97.07	0.77	0.00	0.66	1.50	2.93	100.00
0.08	0.00	0.02	8.02	96.87	0.79	0.00	0.70	1.64	3.13	100.00
0.09	0.00	0.03	7.21	96.56	0.87	0.00	0.77	1.80	3.44	100.00

Table 6.4 (Cont'd)

End of period (11)	*Cash and due from banks* (12)	*Call loans* (13)	*Bills bought* (13')	*Monetary claims bought* (13")	*Trading account securities* (13"')	*Money held in trust* (13"")	*Securities* (14)
3/74	9.87	0.28	0.00	0.00	0.00	0.00	9.85
3/75	9.64	0.92	0.00	0.00	0.00	0.00	9.57
3/76	9.22	0.60	0.00	0.00	0.00	0.00	10.38
3/77	9.38	0.58	0.00	0.00	0.00	0.00	11.27
3/78	9.89	0.62	0.00	0.00	0.00	0.00	12.61
3/79	10.52	0.92	0.00	0.00	0.00	0.00	13.51
3/80	13.70	1.77	0.00	0.00	0.00	0.00	12.05
3/81	15.89	2.52	0.00	0.00	0.00	0.00	11.48
3/82	18.90	4.22	0.00	0.00	0.00	0.00	10.25
3/83	20.85	4.54	0.00	0.00	0.00	0.00	9.99
3/84	21.20	4.43	0.00	0.00	0.00	0.00	9.82
3/85	21.83	3.71	0.00	0.01	0.16	0.00	9.57
3/86	19.14	3.31	0.04	0.00	0.59	0.00	9.92
3/87	20.38	2.92	0.01	0.00	0.54	0.00	10.27
3/88	20.04	2.56	0.00	0.07	0.32	0.00	10.54
3/89	20.98	2.48	0.10	0.17	0.17	0.00	10.50
3/90	20.58	2.58	0.09	0.29	0.26	0.55	10.77
3/91	17.46	1.51	0.00	0.04	0.30	0.45	10.66
3/92	18.83	1.13	0.00	0.03	0.24	0.39	10.58
3/93	12.76	0.92	0.00	0.07	0.47	0.39	11.31

Table 6.4 (Cont'd)

Loans and bills discounted (15)	*Foreign exchanges* (15′)	*Other assets* (16)	*Bank premises and real estate* (17)	*Customers' liabilities for acceptances and guarantees* (17′)	*Total assets* (18)	*Reserves for Loan losses (8a + 8c + 8d)* (19)	*Growth rate of (19)* (20)
57.37	7.46	1.51	1.27	12.40	100.00	1.21	NA
55.85	8.32	1.75	1.27	12.68	100.00	1.12	−7.35
55.73	7.85	1.76	1.28	13.18	100.00	1.01	−9.65
55.61	7.32	1.92	1.25	12.66	100.00	0.95	−5.97
56.78	5.98	2.17	1.26	10.68	100.00	0.93	−2.46
56.13	6.16	2.18	1.17	9.41	100.00	0.96	2.67
52.21	6.43	2.86	1.06	9.79	100.00	0.76	−20.54
51.72	5.37	3.13	1.01	8.69	100.00	0.70	−8.36
49.59	5.11	2.96	0.84	7.77	100.00	0.59	−14.84
50.09	3.81	2.93	0.68	7.11	100.00	0.50	−16.20
50.95	3.31	2.93	0.64	6.71	100.00	0.48	−3.55
51.04	3.18	2.71	0.57	7.22	100.00	0.44	−7.60
52.74	2.51	3.86	0.56	7.33	100.00	0.44	0.27
52.54	2.05	3.81	0.52	6.96	100.00	0.47	5.77
52.92	1.86	4.24	0.49	6.97	100.00	0.45	−3.05
51.26	2.20	4.54	0.46	7.17	100.00	0.44	−3.68
49.58	2.09	4.44	0.41	8.37	100.00	0.39	−11.56
54.11	1.66	4.80	0.47	8.53	100.00	0.41	6.67
57.62	1.46	5.37	0.54	8.02	100.00	0.50	20.48
62.92	1.33	1.98	0.62	0.01	100.00	0.68	35.87

Table 6.5 Balance sheet of regional banks (% of total assets / liabilities)

End of period (1)	*Total deposits* (2)	*Negotiable certificates of deposit* (3)	*Bank debentures* (4)	*Call money* (5)	*Bills sold* (5′)	*Borrowed money* (6)	*Foreign exchange* (7)	*Convertible bonds* (7′)	*Due to trust accounts* (7″)	*Other liabilities* (7‴)	*Reserves for possible loan losses* (8a)
3/74	83.63	0.00	0.00	0.14	0.00	0.26	0.07	0.00	0.01	4.81	1.09
3/75	82.95	0.00	0.00	0.21	0.00	0.20	0.15	0.00	0.02	5.61	0.99
3/76	83.55	0.00	0.00	0.26	0.00	0.28	0.11	0.00	0.03	5.37	0.87
3/77	83.90	0.00	0.00	0.23	0.00	0.31	0.11	0.00	0.04	5.38	0.79
3/78	85.03	0.00	0.00	0.21	0.00	0.39	0.07	0.00	0.03	5.13	0.74
3/79	86.04	0.00	0.00	0.23	0.00	0.36	0.09	0.00	0.02	4.61	0.68
3/80	84.97	0.33	0.00	0.40	0.00	0.30	0.15	0.00	0.02	5.44	0.59
3/81	83.91	0.45	0.00	0.39	0.02	0.28	0.12	0.00	0.01	6.38	0.55
3/82	84.54	0.48	0.00	0.59	0.05	0.24	0.17	0.00	0.02	6.07	0.50
3/83	85.03	0.70	0.00	0.56	0.04	0.24	0.14	0.00	0.04	6.06	0.48
3/84	84.26	1.33	0.00	0.68	0.07	0.30	0.16	0.00	0.05	6.38	0.47
3/85	84.59	1.61	0.00	0.95	0.19	0.30	0.09	0.00	0.06	5.57	0.45
3/86	83.03	1.48	0.00	1.44	0.53	0.26	0.04	0.00	0.07	6.70	0.44
3/87	83.27	1.12	0.00	1.90	0.53	0.27	0.02	0.03	0.07	6.50	0.43
3/88	83.23	0.56	0.00	2.62	0.73	0.25	0.02	0.25	0.06	6.23	0.40
3/89	83.33	0.80	0.00	2.53	0.94	0.23	0.02	0.30	0.06	5.72	0.36
3/90	82.95	1.21	0.00	2.92	0.90	0.34	0.02	0.20	0.03	5.15	0.31
3/91	82.59	0.92	0.00	2.62	0.59	0.93	0.01	0.17	0.02	5.67	0.32
3/92	82.81	0.58	0.00	2.17	0.52	0.94	0.01	0.13	0.05	6.25	0.34
3/93	85.67	0.58	0.00	2.27	0.54	1.17	0.01	0.11	0.10	2.55	0.41

Table 6.5 (Cont'd)

Reserves for retirement allowances (8b)	*Other reserves* (8c)	*Reserves under special law* (8d)	*Acceptances and Guarantees* (8′)	*Total liabilities* (8″)	*Common stock* (9)	*New stock subscription* (9′)	*Legal reserves* (9″)	*Earned surplus* (9‴)	*Total stockholders' equity* (9⁗)	*Total liabilities and stockholders' equity* (10)
0.36	0.01	0.16	5.08	95.63	0.87	0.05	0.63	2.82	4.37	100.00
0.39	0.01	0.15	4.91	95.59	0.87	0.00	0.64	2.89	4.41	100.00
0.39	0.00	0.14	4.70	95.70	0.88	0.03	0.58	2.81	4.30	100.00
0.39	0.01	0.13	4.54	95.82	0.85	0.03	0.56	2.74	4.18	100.00
0.40	0.01	0.07	3.82	95.89	0.84	0.01	0.57	2.69	4.11	100.00
0.39	0.00	0.17	3.43	96.03	0.82	0.02	0.55	2.58	3.97	100.00
0.37	0.00	0.10	3.60	96.27	0.77	0.01	0.54	2.42	3.73	100.00
0.37	0.00	0.08	3.77	96.33	0.72	0.03	0.54	2.39	3.67	100.00
0.35	0.00	0.08	3.38	96.48	0.70	0.01	0.51	2.30	3.52	100.00
0.34	0.00	0.02	2.89	96.54	0.67	0.00	0.51	2.28	3.46	100.00
0.33	0.00	0.03	2.54	96.60	0.63	0.02	0.49	2.25	3.40	100.00
0.31	0.00	0.03	2.51	96.67	0.61	0.01	0.47	2.23	3.33	100.00
0.29	0.00	0.04	2.40	97.71	0.60	0.01	0.47	2.21	3.29	100.00
0.27	0.00	0.05	2.28	96.75	0.58	0.02	0.47	2.18	3.25	100.00
0.25	0.00	0.05	2.12	96.76	0.57	0.05	0.49	2.13	3.24	100.00
0.22	0.00	0.06	2.09	96.65	0.64	0.08	0.59	2.04	3.35	100.00
0.19	0.00	0.05	2.17	96.42	0.83	0.04	0.81	1.89	3.58	100.00
0.19	0.00	0.05	2.22	96.29	0.86	0.00	0.87	1.98	3.71	100.00
0.18	0.00	0.04	2.23	96.24	0.84	0.00	0.90	2.02	3.76	100.00
0.19	0.00	0.05	2.31	95.98	0.87	0.01	0.96	2.17	4.02	100.00

Table 6.5 (Cont'd)

End of period (11)	*Cash and due from banks* (12)	*Call loans* (13)	*Bills bought* (13')	*Monetary claims bought* (13")	*Trading account securities* (13"')	*Money held in trust* (13"")	*Securities* (14)
3/74	7.98	1.72	0.18	0.00	0.00	0.00	12.74
3/75	7.29	2.39	0.38	0.00	0.00	0.00	13.28
3/76	7.69	2.08	0.31	0.00	0.00	0.00	14.63
3/77	7.27	2.33	0.24	0.00	0.00	0.00	15.31
3/78	6.25	2.48	0.13	0.00	0.00	0.00	17.37
3/79	6.15	2.85	0.03	0.00	0.00	0.00	18.45
3/80	6.54	2.97	0.09	0.00	0.00	0.00	19.83
3/81	6.79	2.69	0.08	0.00	0.00	0.00	19.66
3/82	5.88	3.18	0.05	0.00	0.00	0.00	20.11
3/83	5.91	3.32	0.15	0.00	0.00	0.00	19.53
3/84	6.10	4.24	0.03	0.00	0.00	0.00	18.67
3/85	5.88	4.56	0.02	0.00	0.25	0.00	17.89
3/86	5.85	4.60	0.25	0.00	0.60	0.00	17.54
3/87	6.03	4.54	0.23	0.01	0.70	0.00	18.22
3/88	6.91	4.63	0.17	0.16	0.51	0.00	17.78
3/89	7.56	4.58	0.42	0.49	0.40	0.00	17.77
3/90	8.16	4.57	0.43	0.54	0.46	1.02	17.92
3/91	6.27	3.83	0.43	0.17	0.45	0.79	18.90
3/92	6.05	4.19	0.14	0.09	0.46	0.65	17.73
3/93	6.29	4.12	0.13	0.11	0.33	0.58	17.80

Table 6.5 (Cont'd)

Loans and bills discounted (15)	*Foreign exchanges* (15′)	*Other assets* (16)	*Bank premises and real estate* (17)	*Customers' liabilities for acceptances and guarantees* (17′)	*Total assets* (18)	*Reserves for loan losses (8a + 8c + 8d)* (19)	*Growth rate of* (19) (20)
68.35	0.30	2.03	1.60	5.08	100.00	1.26	NA
67.51	0.38	2.21	1.64	4.91	100.00	1.15	−8.64
66.19	0.49	2.29	1.62	4.70	100.00	1.02	−11.35
65.69	0.53	2.48	1.60	4.54	100.00	0.92	−9.49
65.42	0.43	2.55	1.55	3.82	100.00	0.82	−11.44
64.48	0.54	2.61	1.45	3.43	100.00	0.85	3.67
61.57	0.53	3.50	1.35	3.60	100.00	0.70	−17.64
61.67	0.47	3.50	1.35	3.77	100.00	0.63	−9.34
62.19	0.49	3.38	1.28	3.38	100.00	0.58	−8.25
63.07	0.41	3.52	1.19	2.89	100.00	0.50	−13.80
63.36	0.40	3.52	1.14	2.54	100.00	0.50	−0.39
64.37	0.42	3.00	1.10	2.51	100.00	0.49	−2.15
63.04	0.35	4.31	1.05	2.40	100.00	0.48	−1.99
62.57	0.26	4.19	0.98	2.28	100.00	0.48	0.54
62.34	0.22	4.24	0.92	2.12	100.00	0.46	−5.14
61.38	0.20	4.24	0.88	2.09	100.00	0.42	−8.24
59.88	0.19	3.83	0.82	2.17	100.00	0.36	−13.49
61.79	0.19	4.06	0.90	2.22	100.00	0.37	1.29
62.76	0.17	4.53	0.99	2.23	100.00	0.38	4.79
66.49	0.15	0.59	1.09	2.31	100.00	0.46	19.98

Table 6.6 Balance sheet of long-term credit banks (% of total assets / liabilities)

End of period (1)	*Total deposits* (2)	*Negotiable certificates of deposit* (3)	*Bank debentures* (4)	*Call money* (5)	*Bills sold* (5′)	*Borrowed money* (6)	*Foreign exchange* (7)	*Convertible bonds* (7′)	*Due to trust accounts* (7″)	*Other liabilities* (7‴)	*Reserves for possible loan losses* (8a)
3/74	18.77	0.00	65.83	0.30	0.00	0.60	1.71	0.00	0.00	3.18	1.14
3/75	18.55	0.00	64.31	1.16	0.00	0.81	1.57	0.00	0.00	3.08	1.01
3/76	18.90	0.00	64.08	0.63	0.00	0.60	0.80	0.00	0.00	3.33	0.86
3/77	18.57	0.00	64.66	0.53	0.00	0.55	0.48	0.00	0.00	2.99	0.79
3/78	17.71	0.00	66.27	0.35	0.00	0.69	0.34	0.00	0.00	3.01	0.82
3/79	18.55	0.00	66.01	0.63	0.00	0.72	0.37	0.00	0.00	3.02	0.82
3/80	19.82	2.03	60.36	1.29	0.00	0.92	0.70	0.00	0.00	3.46	0.70
3/81	20.76	2.32	59.46	1.96	0.00	1.31	0.45	0.00	0.00	3.56	0.64
3/82	23.38	2.25	55.49	3.10	0.00	1.46	0.56	0.00	0.00	3.76	0.56
3/83	23.85	3.87	54.22	3.41	0.00	1.26	0.26	0.00	0.00	3.62	0.56
3/84	21.89	3.97	56.13	3.99	0.00	1.16	0.15	0.00	0.00	3.69	0.57
3/85	24.58	3.83	53.00	3.12	0.00	1.22	0.19	0.00	0.00	3.87	0.52
3/86	22.69	2.28	54.06	3.56	1.36	0.93	0.08	0.00	0.00	4.51	0.57
3/87	23.88	2.27	52.68	4.57	1.37	0.67	0.09	0.00	0.00	4.20	0.54
3/88	25.25	3.55	50.62	3.82	1.52	0.81	0.09	0.00	0.00	4.33	0.55
3/89	24.62	5.65	47.48	4.18	2.16	1.03	0.09	0.00	0.00	4.16	0.54
3/90	26.37	4.68	45.20	5.22	1.74	1.15	0.06	0.00	0.00	3.77	0.44
3/91	22.85	3.00	51.15	3.93	1.39	1.68	0.04	0.00	0.00	3.99	0.42
3/92	20.17	2.26	56.30	2.00	1.32	2.19	0.03	0.00	0.00	4.53	0.42
3/93	19.30	1.77	58.47	2.17	1.10	3.13	0.01	0.00	0.00	4.03	0.53

Table 6.6 (Cont'd)

Reserves for retirement allowances (8b)	*Other reserves* (8c)	*Reserves under special law* (8d)	*Acceptances and guarantees* (8′)	*Total liabilities* (8″)	*Common stock* (9)	*New stock subscription* (9′)	*Legal reserves* (9″)	*Earned surplus* (9‴)	*Total stockholders' equity* (9⁗)	*Total liabilities and stockholders' equity* (10)
0.13	0.02	0.06	5.49	97.26	1.02	0.00	0.20	1.52	2.74	100.00
0.12	0.03	0.11	6.63	97.38	0.98	0.00	0.19	1.45	2.62	100.00
0.14	0.04	0.11	8.00	97.47	0.98	0.00	0.17	1.38	2.53	100.00
0.14	0.03	0.07	8.70	97.52	0.93	0.00	0.16	1.39	2.48	100.00
0.14	0.03	0.04	7.93	97.34	1.04	0.00	0.16	1.45	2.66	100.00
0.13	0.03	0.09	6.99	97.38	1.00	0.00	0.15	1.47	2.62	100.00
0.14	0.02	0.06	8.09	97.59	0.87	0.00	0.15	1.39	2.41	100.00
0.13	0.02	0.03	6.95	97.59	0.85	0.00	0.15	1.41	2.41	100.00
0.12	0.02	0.03	6.99	97.72	0.78	0.00	0.14	1.36	2.28	100.00
0.11	0.00	0.00	6.67	97.84	0.69	0.00	0.14	1.34	2.16	100.00
0.11	0.00	0.00	6.21	97.87	0.64	0.00	0.14	1.35	2.13	100.00
0.10	0.00	0.01	7.65	98.09	0.54	0.00	0.13	1.23	1.91	100.00
0.09	0.00	0.02	7.94	98.11	0.51	0.00	0.13	1.25	1.89	100.00
0.09	0.00	0.04	7.79	98.18	0.45	0.00	0.13	1.24	1.82	100.00
0.08	0.00	0.04	7.06	97.71	0.64	0.00	0.37	1.27	2.29	100.00
0.07	0.00	0.05	7.16	97.20	0.85	0.00	0.62	1.33	2.80	100.00
0.07	0.00	0.05	8.40	97.16	0.89	0.00	0.69	1.26	2.84	100.00
0.07	0.00	0.05	8.43	97.01	0.89	0.00	0.71	1.39	2.99	100.00
0.07	0.00	0.02	7.57	96.88	0.89	0.00	0.72	1.50	3.12	100.00
0.08	0.00	0.03	6.11	96.72	0.93	0.00	0.77	1.57	3.28	100.00

Table 6.6 (Cont'd)

End of period (11)	*Cash and due from banks* (12)	*Call loans* (13)	*Bills bought* (13')	*Monetary claims bought* (13")	*Trading account securities* (13"')	*Securities* (14)
3/74	6.52	0.32	0.00	0.00	0.00	12.58
3/75	6.31	1.43	0.16	0.00	0.00	12.33
3/76	5.61	1.35	0.49	0.00	0.00	14.45
3/77	5.85	0.64	0.28	0.00	0.00	15.47
3/78	4.23	1.59	0.19	0.00	0.00	17.82
3/79	4.60	2.03	0.45	0.00	0.00	18.49
3/80	5.97	1.60	0.05	0.00	0.00	16.67
3/81	9.66	2.31	0.00	0.00	0.00	17.17
3/82	10.65	2.82	0.27	0.00	0.00	16.09
3/83	13.61	3.02	0.14	0.00	0.00	15.47
3/84	12.74	2.53	0.27	0.00	0.00	16.51
3/85	14.08	1.98	0.00	0.01	0.16	15.85
3/86	12.10	0.89	0.14	0.00	0.63	16.59
3/87	12.79	0.89	0.00	0.00	0.59	16.92
3/88	13.78	0.75	0.00	0.18	0.27	16.83
3/89	13.52	1.10	0.00	0.10	0.21	16.89
3/90	12.24	0.93	0.00	0.19	0.28	16.80
3/91	10.38	0.86	0.00	0.20	0.12	16.29
3/92	9.79	0.51	0.00	0.02	1.02	16.10
3/93	9.45	0.81	0.00	0.05	0.62	16.51

Table 6.6 (Cont'd)

Loans and bills discounted (15)	*Foreign exchanges* (15')	*Other assets* (16)	*Bank premises and real estate* (17)	*Customers' liabilities for acceptances and guarantees* (17')	*Total assets* (18)	*Reserves for loan losses* (8a + 8c + 8d) (19)	*Growth rate of* (19) (20)
70.62	2.13	1.71	0.63	5.49	100.00	1.22	NA
67.99	2.86	1.72	0.57	6.63	100.00	1.15	−6.14
64.96	2.78	1.86	0.51	8.00	100.00	1.00	−12.58
63.48	3.17	1.94	0.49	8.70	100.00	0.90	−10.46
63.27	2.38	2.10	0.48	7.93	100.00	0.89	−0.64
62.07	2.73	2.13	0.51	6.99	100.00	0.94	5.64
59.27	5.23	2.49	0.44	8.09	100.00	0.79	−16.53
58.00	2.72	2.56	0.41	6.95	100.00	0.70	−11.51
57.21	2.63	2.56	0.37	6.99	100.00	0.61	−12.96
56.59	1.81	2.38	0.31	6.67	100.00	0.56	−6.99
57.60	1.52	2.30	0.32	6.21	100.00	0.57	1.61
56.17	1.48	2.33	0.30	7.65	700.00	0.53	−7.32
57.52	0.92	2.98	0.29	7.94	100.00	0.60	12.36
57.31	0.53	2.92	0.26	7.79	100.00	0.58	−3.46
57.55	0.50	2.85	0.24	7.06	100.00	0.59	2.34
57.18	0.61	3.00	0.23	7.16	100.00	0.59	0.58
56.41	0.53	4.00	0.21	8.40	100.00	0.49	−17.03
59.18	0.42	2.87	0.28	8.43	100.00	0.47	−5.19
59.83	0.42	3.09	0.34	7.57	100.00	0.44	−4.85
61.15	0.43	2.15	0.42	6.11	100.00	0.56	26.06

Table 6.7 Balance sheet of trust banks (% of total assets / liabilities)

End of period (1)	*Total deposits* (2)	*Negotiable certificates of deposit* (3)	*Bank debentures* (4)	*Call money* (5)	*Bills sold* (5′)	*Borrowed money* (6)	*Foreign exchange* (7)	*Convertible bonds* (7′)	*Due to trust accounts* (7″)	*Other liabilities* (7‴)	*Reserves for possible loan losses* (8a)
3/74	60.05	0.00	0.00	1.70	0.68	0.81	6.25	0.00	6.66	3.31	0.84
3/75	57.43	0.00	0.00	2.46	0.22	1.03	6.97	0.00	7.90	3.08	0.76
3/76	57.97	0.00	0.00	1.76	0.16	0.93	6.40	0.00	7.89	2.99	0.69
3/77	55.23	0.00	0.00	1.65	0.11	1.02	4.81	0.00	14.32	2.92	0.59
3/78	54.52	0.00	0.00	0.81	0.10	1.51	2.59	0.00	20.56	2.85	0.59
3/79	51.99	0.00	0.00	1.17	0.11	1.37	2.71	0.00	25.38	2.38	0.64
3/80	45.64	3.71	0.00	3.85	0.04	0.57	4.21	0.00	24.90	3.17	0.49
3/81	48.34	4.58	0.00	5.80	0.10	0.69	3.49	0.00	21.79	3.21	0.41
3/82	49.44	2.94	0.00	10.28	0.01	0.84	3.94	0.00	20.06	2.94	0.30
3/83	51.41	2.91	0.00	12.12	0.00	0.37	2.28	0.00	20.49	2.98	0.30
3/84	46.40	3.07	0.00	11.97	0.00	0.46	2.23	0.00	25.37	2.98	0.32
3/85	47.87	2.77	0.00	13.30	0.00	0.39	1.86	0.00	22.73	3.26	0.33
3/86	41.81	2.95	0.00	16.00	0.37	0.19	1.17	0.00	23.75	4.39	0.30
3/87	44.41	4.01	0.00	14.57	0.34	0.14	0.84	0.10	21.69	4.30	0.27
3/88	47.46	3.50	0.00	11.66	0.56	0.13	0.51	0.21	20.88	5.17	0.33
3/89	46.96	3.96	0.00	11.68	0.65	0.12	0.59	0.54	20.83	4.40	0.33
3/90	49.29	4.75	0.00	10.70	0.76	0.52	0.62	0.59	18.28	3.72	0.32
3/91	47.13	3.72	0.00	9.90	0.48	0.25	0.24	0.60	21.49	4.08	0.34
3/92	41.26	2.56	0.00	8.28	0.43	1.20	0.23	0.57	28.80	3.69	0.40
3/93	34.61	1.63	0.00	7.33	0.65	1.98	0.17	0.40	40.28	1.65	0.56

Table 6.7 (Cont'd)

Reserves for retirement allowances (8b)	*Other reserves* (8c)	*Reserves under special law* (8d)	*Acceptances and guarantees* (8′)	*Total liabilities* (8″)	*Common stock* (9)	*New stock subscription* (9′)	*Legal reserves* (9″)	*Earned surplus* (9‴)	*Total stockholders' equity* (9⁗)	*Total liabilities and stockholders' equity* (10)
0.84	0.03	0.09	12.30	93.14	2.01	0.17	0.72	3.96	6.86	100.00
0.76	0.03	0.14	13.02	93.47	1.92	0.00	0.67	3.94	6.53	100.00
0.69	0.03	0.13	14.33	93.72	1.85	0.00	0.51	3.91	6.28	100.00
0.59	0.03	0.12	13.04	94.32	1.57	0.00	0.47	3.64	5.68	100.00
0.59	0.03	0.11	10.11	94.24	1.73	0.00	0.46	3.57	5.76	100.00
0.64	0.02	0.21	8.31	94.73	1.56	0.00	0.42	3.29	5.27	100.00
0.49	0.02	0.14	8.30	95.43	1.32	0.00	0.39	2.86	4.57	100.00
0.41	0.01	0.09	7.12	95.95	1.12	0.00	0.36	2.57	4.05	100.00
0.30	0.01	0.06	5.81	96.89	0.83	0.00	0.28	2.01	3.11	100.00
0.30	0.00	0.00	4.35	97.43	0.65	0.00	0.23	1.69	2.57	100.00
0.32	0.00	0.00	4.34	97.37	0.72	0.00	0.22	1.69	2.63	100.00
0.33	0.00	0.01	5.13	97.82	0.57	0.04	0.17	1.39	2.18	100.00
0.30	0.00	0.03	6.69	97.81	0.54	0.00	0.19	1.46	2.19	100.00
0.27	0.00	0.06	6.86	97.73	0.50	0.00	0.22	1.55	2.27	100.00
0.33	0.00	0.08	6.49	97.11	0.65	0.00	0.39	1.85	2.89	100.00
0.33	0.00	0.07	6.08	96.32	0.91	0.13	0.70	1.94	3.68	100.00
0.32	0.00	0.06	6.62	96.32	1.00	0.00	0.85	1.83	3.68	100.00
0.34	0.00	0.05	7.46	95.84	1.08	0.00	0.93	2.15	4.16	100.00
0.40	0.00	0.04	7.27	95.49	1.15	0.00	1.00	2.36	4.51	100.00
0.56	0.00	0.05	5.66	95.09	1.24	0.00	1.09	2.57	4.91	100.00

Table 6.7 (Cont'd)

End of period (11)	*Cash and due from banks* (12)	*Call loans* (13)	*Bills bought* (13′)	*Monetary claims bought* (13″)	*Trading account securities* (13‴)	*Money held in trust* (13⁗)	*Securities* (14)
3/74	11.37	1.18	0.00	0.00	0.00	0.00	17.70
3/75	8.73	4.33	0.07	0.00	0.00	0.00	18.11
3/76	9.00	0.97	0.62	0.00	0.00	0.00	20.44
3/77	8.26	2.59	1.07	0.00	0.00	0.00	22.26
3/78	7.50	2.93	0.45	0.00	0.00	0.00	25.88
3/79	7.41	2.17	0.16	0.00	0.00	0.00	28.14
3/80	9.56	1.75	0.05	0.00	0.00	0.00	26.85
3/81	14.69	4.68	0.00	0.00	0.00	0.00	26.82
3/82	21.17	6.87	0.08	0.00	0.00	0.00	22.32
3/83	28.84	7.82	0.09	0.00	0.00	0.00	20.12
3/84	24.42	5.93	0.01	0.00	0.00	0.00	21.81
3/85	22.73	6.40	0.22	0.00	0.20	0.00	22.87
3/86	17.60	5.58	0.59	0.00	1.21	0.00	24.14
3/87	18.66	3.87	0.24	0.00	0.99	0.00	23.32
3/88	18.19	3.00	0.03	0.02	0.37	0.00	23.56
3/89	23.28	3.08	0.28	0.22	0.22	0.00	20.73
3/90	23.77	2.77	0.01	0.49	0.25	0.95	20.76
3/91	19.40	1.78	0.02	0.57	0.51	1.18	21.90
3/92	17.10	2.06	0.03	0.52	0.33	1.19	22.36
3/93	14.98	2.42	0.03	0.23	0.43	1.26	23.02

Table 6.7 (Cont'd)

Loans and bills discounted (15)	*Foreign exchanges* (15')	*Other assets* (16)	*Bank premises and real estate* (17)	*Customers' liabilities for acceptances and guarantees* (17')	*Total assets* (18)	*Reserves for loan losses* (8a + 8c + 8d) (19)	*Growth rate of* (19) (20)
49.29	4.18	1.84	2.14	12.30	100.00	0.97	NA
45.37	6.27	1.87	2.23	13.02	100.00	0.94	−2.92
44.25	6.01	2.05	2.33	14.33	100.00	0.85	−8.92
42.03	6.20	2.23	2.32	13.04	100.00	0.74	−12.77
43.82	4.71	2.35	2.25	10.11	100.00	0.73	−2.42
44.61	4.70	2.47	2.04	8.31	100.00	0.88	20.48
40.51	7.45	2.94	1.75	8.30	100.00	0.65	−25.80
35.68	5.65	3.02	1.50	7.12	100.00	0.51	−21.36
34.18	4.34	2.99	1.13	5.81	100.00	0.37	−27.59
32.52	2.66	2.75	0.86	4.35	100.00	0.30	−18.63
38.09	1.90	2.69	0.83	4.34	100.00	0.32	7.02
37.28	1.90	2.61	0.67	5.13	100.00	0.33	3.28
38.88	1.24	3.44	0.63	6.69	100.00	0.33	−1.07
41.22	0.72	3.52	0.60	6.86	100.00	0.33	0.68
43.02	0.58	4.09	0.66	6.49	100.00	0.41	23.78
40.64	0.62	4.19	0.66	6.08	100.00	0.40	−2.34
38.94	0.61	4.22	0.63	6.62	100.00	0.38	−6.15
41.42	0.60	4.27	0.88	7.46	100.00	0.39	3.46
43.38	0.51	4.22	1.02	7.27	100.00	0.44	13.84
48.25	0.44	2.17	1.11	5.66	100.00	0.61	38.13

exhibit a relatively high growth rate of reserves for possible loan losses as they were faced with market share expansion in an even more deregulated environment during the late 1980s. This may evidence intensified competition among banks due to loosening of the regulatory environment (such as the deregulation of deposit rates) encouraging the expansionary extension of loans simply relying on the collateral value of land. Similar observations have been made by Boyd and Gertler (1993) for the United States.

(2) The share of CDs of long-term credit and trust banks was high during 1988–9 and declined 1991–2 because of the sluggish economy (column 3, Tables 6.6 and 6.7).

(3) The share of bank debentures issued by long-term credit banks was low during 1987–90 (column 4, Table 6.6) because their source of funding shifted from bank debentures to deposits (especially CDs).

(4) As for the asset side of the balance sheets of various banks, it is apparent that the share of deposits with other banks in the assets of city banks and long-term credit banks increased to around 20 percent during 1986–9. This is because city banks and long-term credit banks increased investment in the Euro-market after the change in the Foreign Exchange Control Law in 1979. The expansion of such investment in the Euro-market continued until 1989 when the BIS capital requirement rule was implemented. The BIS rule thus had a lot to do with Japanese banks shifting their focus from market share expansion to being more profit conscious. Since the Euro-market operation turned out to be not so profitable, investment declined judging from column 12, Tables 6.4, 6.6 and 6.7 (= cash and deposits with others) of city banks, long-term credit banks and trust banks.

On the other hand, regional banks do not show such an increase (column 12, Tables 6.4, 6.5 and 6.6) in the share of cash and deposits since they are mainly operating in the domestic market.

(5) The share of loans in assets fell during 1988–9 at city, regional and long-term credit banks; this was due to less reliance on bank borrowing by large firms (as mentioned in Section 6.2) reflecting the fact that they were beginning to rely on the capital market by issuing stocks and bonds. However, the share of loans extended by trust banks to non-bank financial institutions, real estate-related firms etc. increased somewhat during 1987–8

Table 6.8 Interest rate gap of city banks (%)

Year	*Average yield on loans, securities and call loans* (1)	*Average interest payments on deposits and call money* (2)	(1) – (2) (3)	*Operating costs* L + D (4)	*Operating costs* L + D + B (5)	*Personnel costs* L + D (6)	*Personnel costs* L + D + B (7)	*Personnel + equipment costs* L + D (8)	*Personnel + equipment costs* L + D + B (9)
3/75	9.40	5.26	4.15	1.09	1.01	0.66	0.61	1.03	0.95
3/76	8.54	5.32	3.22	1.17	1.08	0.70	0.65	1.09	1.01
3/77	7.83	4.80	3.03	1.17	1.08	0.69	0.63	1.08	1.00
3/78	6.86	4.24	2.62	1.14	1.04	0.68	0.62	1.06	0.97
3/79	6.08	3.76	2.32	1.07	0.97	0.64	0.58	1.00	0.90
3/80	7.05	5.01	2.04	1.01	0.92	0.61	0.55	0.95	0.86
3/81	8.80	6.76	2.04	0.98	0.89	0.57	0.52	0.91	0.83
3/82	8.94	7.84	1.11	0.90	0.83	0.52	0.47	0.83	0.76
3/83	8.09	6.63	1.47	0.84	0.78	0.47	0.44	0.76	0.70
3/84	7.30	5.66	1.64	0.80	0.74	0.44	0.41	0.72	0.66
3/85	7.45	6.39	1.06	0.74	0.69	0.40	0.37	0.67	0.62
3/86	6.59	5.13	1.46	0.69	0.64	0.37	0.34	0.63	0.58
3/87	5.74	4.32	1.42	0.67	0.62	0.35	0.32	0.59	0.54
3/88	5.43	4.22	1.21	0.65	0.60	0.30	0.28	0.55	0.50
3/89	5.62	4.61	1.02	0.61	0.56	0.27	0.25	0.51	0.47
3/90	6.52	5.96	0.56	0.50	0.46	0.25	0.22	0.47	0.43
3/91	7.52	6.73	0.78	0.49	0.45	0.24	0.22	0.47	0.43
3/92	7.02	5.89	1.14	0.53	0.48	0.25	0.23	0.50	0.46
3/93	5.23	3.92	1.31	0.56	0.51	0.26	0.24	0.52	0.48

Note: L = loans, D = deposits, B = securities investment.

compared with 1981–6 and their share of securities' holdings and call loans declined.

Interest Rate Gaps and the Operating Costs of Various Banks

Table 6.8 summarises the interest rate gap between the lending and funding of city banks. The lending rate of interest is computed from the average yield on loans, securities and call loans. The funding cost of interest consists of deposit rates and call money.

(1) The gap between the average rate of interest on loans and securities and that on deposits was 4.15 percent in 1975 (column 3 of Table 6.8). Thereafter, the gap narrowed and was down to only 0.56 percent and 0.78 percent in 1990 and 1991, respectively. It has traced an increasing trend since 1991 (column 3, Table 6.8). The gap narrowed between 1975 and 1979 because the funding rate fell faster than the lending rate when interest rates were declining. The continuing narrowing of the gap can be explained by the market share maximizing behavior of banks despite their low margins. However, the gap started to widen after 1990 because the introduction of the BIS capital adequacy rule made Japanese banks more conscious about asset quality. Furthermore, the introduction of the new short-term prime rate in 1990 induced banks to make lending rates much more flexible.

(2) Personnel costs to total business expenses (personnel plus equipment costs plus taxes) fell from 60.14 percent in 1975 to 47.11 percent in 1993 at city banks (column 2, Table 6.9). Equipment costs rose from 34.2 percent to 46.80 percent. However, the pace of reduction in personnel costs has been slower at regional banks compared with city banks: the share of personnel costs to total expenses at regional banks declined from 67.44 percent in 1975 to 55.78 percent in 1993 (Table 6.10). Regional banks are still paying more in the form of personnel costs compared to large banks (see Tables 6.11 and 6.12).

Changes in the Lending Pattern of Banks during the Bubble Period

Table 6.13 shows long-term loans as a proportion of total loans. Accordingly, the figure for all banks rose from 41.1 percent in 1981 to 56.4 percent in 1990. The maturity of loans extended by city and regional banks has expanded since 1987.

Table 6.9 Expenses of city banks (real datas, share to total and growth rate)

Year (1)	*Personnel expenses (million)* (2a)	(2a)/(5) (2b)	*Non-personnel expenses (million)* (3a)	(3a)/(5) (3b)	*Tax (million)* (4a)	(4a)/(5) (4b)	*Total* = (2a + 3a + 4a) *(million)* (5)
3/66	108 426	50.15%	82 660	38.23%	25 113	11.62%	216 199
3/67	125 163	50.59%	89 818	36.31%	32 409	13.10%	247 390
3/68	139 492	50.55%	97 877	35.47%	38 588	13.98%	275 957
3/69	177 538	54.95%	125 078	38.71%	20 492	6.34%	323 108
3/70	212 714	55.26%	149 107	38.73%	23 144	6.01%	384 965
3/71	247 114	55.22%	174 470	38.99%	25 895	5.79%	447 479
3/72	292 888	55.35%	205 333	38.80%	30 964	5.85%	529 185
3/73	352 766	56.24%	240 619	38.36%	33 811	5.39%	627 196
3/74	473 889	58.43%	292 640	36.08%	44 467	5.48%	810 996
3/75	633 525	60.14%	360 287	34.20%	59 663	5.66%	1 053 475
3/76	762 797	59.92%	419 455	32.95%	90 697	7.12%	1 272 949
3/77	831 427	58.69%	477 207	33.69%	107 960	7.62%	1 416 594
3/78	889 880	59.44%	512 644	34.24%	94 499	6.31%	1 497 023
3/79	929 048	59.67%	523 862	33.65%	104 067	6.68%	1 556 977
3/80	993 857	60.13%	557 033	33.70%	101 939	6.17%	1 652 829
3/81	1 039 436	58.58%	615 375	34.68%	119 605	6.74%	1 774 416
3/82	1 083 674	57.28%	649 852	34.35%	158 229	8.36%	1 891 755
3/83	1 135 699	56.25%	677 608	33.56%	205 729	10.19%	2 019 036
3/84	1 163 029	55.54%	712 828	34.04%	218 244	10.42%	2 094 101
3/85	1 189 897	54.15%	779 109	35.46%	228 376	10.39%	2 197 382
3/86	1 207 057	53.52%	825 935	36.62%	222 439	9.86%	2 255 431
3/87	1 251 178	51.97%	854 587	35.50%	301 662	12.53%	2 407 427
3/88	1 249 824	46.95%	988 048	37.12%	424 164	15.93%	2 662 036
3/89	1 277 271	44.72%	1 099 485	38.50%	479 187	16.78%	2 855 943
3/90	1 337 876	49.13%	1 213 065	44.54%	172 376	6.33%	2 723 317
3/91	1 407 906	47.94%	1 357 890	46.24%	170 911	5.82%	2 936 707
3/92	1 465 808	47.26%	1 460 795	47.09%	175 241	5.65%	3 101 844
3/93	1 497 063	47.11%	1 487 322	46.80%	193 516	6.09%	3 177 901

Table 6.10 Expenses of regional banks (real datas, share to total and growth rate)

Year (1)	*Personnel expenses (million)* (2a)	(2a)/(5) (2b)	*Non-personnel expenses (million)* (3a)	(3a)/(5) (3b)	*Tax (million)* (4a)	(4a)/(5) (4b)	*Total* = (2a + 3a + 4a) *(million)* (5)
3/66	74 586	59.17%	30 675	24.34%	20 792	16.49%	126 053
3/67	85 707	56.56%	44 033	29.06%	21 788	14.38%	151 528
3/68	97 702	55.95%	47 927	27.44%	29 003	16.61%	174 632
3/69	121 953	61.68%	67 891	34.34%	7 883	3.99%	197 727
3/70	132 150	62.28%	71 740	33.81%	8 290	3.91%	212 180
3/71	158 022	63.17%	82 767	33.09%	9 349	3.74%	250 138
3/72	191 518	63.63%	98 548	32.74%	10 923	3.63%	300 989
3/73	233 366	63.92%	119 313	32.68%	12 431	3.40%	365 110
3/74	309 750	64.97%	147 167	30.87%	19 817	4.16%	476 734
3/75	436 638	67.44%	189 451	29.26%	21 339	3.30%	647 428
3/76	515 548	64.22%	222 731	27.74%	64 549	8.04%	802 828
3/77	586 666	64.08%	262 048	28.63%	66 737	7.29%	915 451
3/78	668 372	63.98%	296 342	28.37%	79 910	7.65%	1 044 624
3/79	716 099	64.42%	315 756	28.41%	79 679	7.17%	1 111 534
3/80	771 798	64.80%	338 676	28.43%	80 646	6.77%	1 191 120
3/81	844 503	64.23%	380 984	28.98%	89 382	6.80%	1 314 869
3/82	897 146	64.15%	397 868	28.45%	103 445	7.40%	1 398 459
3/83	957 031	63.50%	418 812	27.79%	131 357	8.72%	1 507 200
3/84	995 318	62.74%	445 235	28.07%	145 747	9.19%	1 586 300
3/85	1 052 282	62.01%	500 501	29.50%	144 075	8.49%	1 696 858
3/86	1 096 187	61.59%	530 548	29.81%	153 113	8.60%	1 779 884
3/87	1 108 901	60.13%	562 403	30.50%	172 830	9.37%	1 844 134
3/88	1 127 658	59.32%	599 449	31.54%	173 763	9.14%	1 900 870
3/89	1 143 121	57.10%	660 817	33.01%	197 874	9.88%	2 001 812
3/90	1 180 795	58.60%	717 388	35.60%	116 758	5.79%	2 014 941
3/91	1 227 815	57.22%	803 110	37.42%	114 996	5.36%	2 145 921
3/92	1 278 295	56.27%	873 875	38.46%	119 740	5.27%	2 271 910
3/93	1 328 051	55.78%	925 183	38.86%	127 696	5.36%	2 380 930

Table 6.11 Expenses of long-trem credit banks (real datas, share to total and growth rate)

Year (1)	*Personnel expenses (million)* (2a)	(2a)/(5) (2b)	*Non-personnel expenses (million)* (3a)	(3a)/(5) (3b)	*Tax (million)* (4a)	(4a)/(5) (4b)	*Total* = (2a + 3a + 4a) *(million)* (5)
3/66	5 606	22.67%	14 505	58.65%	4 620	18.68%	24 731
3/67	6 672	24.16%	15 891	57.54%	5 056	18.31%	27 619
3/68	8 117	23.83%	20 988	61.61%	4 961	14.56%	34 066
3/69	9 439	23.08%	28 378	69.39%	3 081	7.53%	40 898
3/70	11 025	23.59%	32 382	69.17%	3 387	7.25%	46 740
3/71	12 432	23.44%	36 742	69.28%	3 857	7.27%	53 031
3/72	14 922	27.01%	35 812	64.83%	4 505	8.16%	55 239
3/73	17 632	29.27%	37 796	62.75%	4 805	7.98%	60 233
3/74	27 302	41.75%	31 712	48.49%	6 380	9.76%	65 394
3/75	31 344	37.33%	44 418	52.91%	8 194	9.76%	83 956
3/76	43 930	43.21%	44 004	43.28%	13 728	13.50%	101 662
3/77	48 158	40.90%	51 440	43.69%	18 153	15.42%	117 751
3/78	50 358	39.36%	54 683	42.74%	22 916	17.91%	127 957
3/79	52 921	42.23%	53 582	42.75%	18 826	15.02%	125 329
3/80	61 069	44.41%	58 402	42.47%	18 039	13.12%	137 510
3/81	62 710	42.94%	65 500	44.85%	17 823	12.20%	146 033
3/82	66 555	40.01%	75 930	45.64%	23 864	14.35%	166 349
3/83	73 384	39.48%	78 933	42.47%	33 539	18.05%	185 856
3/84	78 744	42.87%	75 785	41.25%	29 172	15.88%	183 701
3/85	85 070	43.23%	84 521	42.95%	27 177	13.81%	196 768
3/86	90 922	42.31%	90 441	42.09%	33 518	15.60%	214 881
3/87	94 406	40.86%	91 581	39.63%	45 085	19.51%	231 072
3/88	97 214	36.31%	101 638	37.96%	68 914	25.74%	267 766
3/89	104 425	36.52%	115 005	40.22%	66 530	23.27%	285 960
3/90	120 543	44.26%	133 671	49.09%	18 109	6.65%	272 323
3/91	128 183	45.02%	139 115	48.86%	17 442	6.13%	284 740
3/92	138 119	43.13%	165 075	51.54%	17 081	5.33%	320 275
3/93	147 497	42.39%	180 855	51.97%	19 615	5.64%	347 967

Table 6.12 Expenses of trust banks (real datas, share to total and growth rate)

Year (1)	*Personnel expenses (million)* (2a)	(2a)/(5) (2b)	*Non-personnel expenses (million)* (3a)	(3a)/(5) (3b)	*Tax (million)* (4a)	(4a)/(5) (4b)	*Total* = (2a + 3a + 4a) *(million)* (5)
3/66	16 787	40.17%	20 769	49.69%	4 239	10.14%	41 795
3/67	19 600	41.78%	22 336	47.62%	4 971	10.60%	46 907
3/68	22 622	43.90%	23 659	45.91%	5 255	10.20%	51 536
3/69	29 892	51.00%	26 205	44.71%	2 514	4.29%	58 611
3/70	34 685	51.03%	30 325	44.62%	2 960	4.35%	67 970
3/71	41 153	51.88%	34 765	43.82%	3 412	4.30%	79 330
3/72	48 741	52.35%	40 766	43.78%	3 607	3.87%	93 114
3/73	58 721	52.03%	49 805	44.13%	4 341	3.85%	112 867
3/74	80 617	54.35%	62 303	42.00%	5 411	3.65%	148 331
3/75	103 040	55.17%	75 809	40.59%	7 927	4.24%	186 776
3/76	124 683	55.11%	85 629	37.85%	15 929	7.04%	226 241
3/77	152 464	56.82%	98 753	36.80%	17 106	6.38%	268 323
3/78	161 746	57.19%	104 700	37.02%	16 376	5.79%	282 822
3/79	171 058	57.91%	106 211	35.96%	18 152	6.14%	295 394
3/80	180 044	57.71%	113 224	36.29%	18 694	5.99%	311 962
3/81	189 345	57.43%	123 849	37.56%	16 521	5.01%	329 715
3/82	200 255	56.21%	135 355	37.99%	20 671	5.80%	356 281
3/83	214 498	55.35%	146 840	37.89%	26 183	6.76%	387 521
3/84	224 024	55.92%	152 082	37.96%	24 487	6.11%	400 593
3/85	232 339	53.50%	166 622	38.37%	35 302	8.13%	434 263
3/86	241 302	50.16%	188 496	39.18%	51 267	10.66%	481 065
3/87	264 681	45.89%	216 244	37.53%	95 511	16.58%	576 136
3/88	281 925	42.35%	269 731	40.52%	114 042	17.13%	665 698
3/89	294 872	39.76%	325 745	43.93%	120 941	16.13%	741 558
3/90	319 177	44.98%	359 506	50.67%	30 860	4.35%	709 543
3/91	338 935	43.78%	405 141	52.33%	30 189	3.90%	774 265
3/92	349 225	44.67%	403 649	51.63%	28 981	3.71%	781 855
3/93	343 581	45.76%	377 280	50.25%	29 976	3.99%	750 837

Table 6.13 Share of long-term loans (% of total loans)

	1981	*1985*	*1986*	*1987*	*1988*	*1989*	*1990*
All banks	41.1	39.0	41.6	44.7	48.0	52.7	56.4
City banks	34.7	32.7	37.4	41.9	47.5	52.9	57.2
Regional banks	36.6	40.1	41.4	41.8	43.4	45.6	48.4
Long-term credit banks	81.3	70.9	67.5	70.6	69.0	77.1	79.7
Trust banks	38.3	24.4	30.5	33.8	35.5	39.1	41.4

Table 6.14 Share of loans to real estate and non-bank financial institutions (% of total loans)

	3/85	*3/86*	*3/87*	*3/88*	*3/89*	*3/90*	*12/90*	*12/91*	*12/92*
Real estate + non-bank	17.8	20.8	24.6	26.5	27.5	28.8	27.1	26.6	26.9
1 + 2 + 3	23.3	26.3	30.0	31.5	32.5	33.6	32.7	31.9	32.6
1 Real estate	7.6	8.9	11.1	11.3	11.7	12.1	11.9	12.0	12.4
2 Non-bank	10.2	11.9	13.5	15.2	15.8	16.7	15.2	14.6	14.5
3 Construction	5.5	5.5	5.4	5.1	4.9	4.7	5.1	5.3	5.7
Total	100.0	100.0	100.0	100.0	100.0	100.0	100.0	100.0	100.0

Bank loans to small businesses and individuals increased during 1985–90. Banks focused especially on real estate-related firms, non-bank financial institutions, and building contractors.

Table 6.14 shows the share of loans to real estate-related firms, non-bank financial institutions, and building contractors. The share allocated to real estate-related businesses increased from 1986 and is still high even after the collapse of the bubble economy. However, the share of lending to non-bank financial institutions, which rose to 16.7 percent in 1990, has declined as shown in Table 6.14.

Banks extended these loans mainly using land as collateral when prices were rising; however, falling land prices since 1992 have resulted in default loan losses because of the declining collateral value of land.

III BEHAVIOR OF THE CORPORATE SECTOR

Asset Side

The shares of various assets of the corporate sector are summarized in Table 6.15.

(1) The share of investment trusts jumped from 0.14 percent in March 1986 to 0.83 percent in March 1987, since rising stock prices raised yields (column 11, Table 6.15). Note that the value of stocks held by non-financial institutions (including the corporate sector) is evaluated at face value until 1982 and at sales purchase prices thereafter.

(2) The share of stocks increased during 1988–9 (column 10, Table 6.15), though it declined after reaching a peak in March 1989 because of the drop in stock prices in 1989.

(3) The share of trusts increased from March 1987 until December 1991 (column 7, Table 6.15) because the amount of loan trusts increased.

(4) The share of demand deposits (column 3, Table 6.15) continues to fall because the interest rate on demand deposits is still regulated, therefore corporations are minimizing their holdings of such deposits by shifting to other financial instruments. However, the share of CDs started to rise in 1984 and reached a peak in March 1987 (column 5, Table 6.15).

Thus, the asset side of the corporate sector recorded a shift from ordinary deposits to stock-related financial products and deregulated financial instruments during 1987–90.

Liability Side

Table 6.16 shows components of corporate sector liabilities.

(1) Borrowing from private financial institutions dropped from 72.77 percent in March 1987 to 55.58 percent in March 1988. The corporate sector continued to reduce reliance on private bank loans until March 1990 (column 9, Table 6.16).

(2) The issuance of corporate bonds started to increase in March 1986 and continued to increase until December 1991 (column 3, Table 6.16).

(3) The share of foreign bonds also started to rise in March 1986 and continued to do so until March 1992 (column 5, Table 6.16). Partly because domestic corporate bond issuance was restricted by various regulations, corporations issued bonds abroad.

Table 6.15 Asset components of the corporate sector (1954–92) (% of total assets)

End of period (1)	*Currency* (2)	*Demand deposits* (3)	*Time deposits* (4)	*CDs* (5)	*Foreign deposits* (6)	*Trusts* (7)	*Securities* (9 + 10 + 11) (8)	*Bonds* (9)	*Stocks* (10)	*Investment trusts* (11)	*CP* (12)	*Trade credits* (13)	*Others* (14)	*Total* (15)
3/54	1.51	15.11	15.55	0.00	0.00	0.90	5.38	0.75	4.47	0.16	0.00	57.92	3.65	100.00
3/55	1.39	14.79	16.96	0.00	0.00	1.13	6.17	0.85	5.16	0.16	0.00	57.22	2.34	100.00
3/56	1.32	15.73	17.43	0.00	0.00	1.55	6.72	0.98	5.63	0.11	0.00	57.25	0.00	100.00
3/57	1.28	15.48	17.43	0.00	0.00	1.84	6.87	0.83	5.92	0.12	0.00	57.10	0.00	100.00
3/58	1.19	13.34	18.66	0.00	0.00	2.11	7.30	0.89	6.33	0.08	0.00	55.30	2.11	100.00
3/59	1.04	13.35	19.20	0.00	0.00	2.06	7.01	1.06	5.84	0.11	0.00	55.00	2.35	100.00
3/60	0.90	11.70	17.29	0.00	0.00	1.93	6.26	1.19	4.94	0.13	0.00	59.16	2.77	100.00
3/61	0.89	11.62	16.93	0.00	0.00	1.92	6.36	1.36	4.85	0.16	0.00	56.94	5.33	100.00
3/62	0.77	9.76	15.96	0.00	0.00	1.92	6.99	1.56	5.20	0.23	0.00	59.74	4.86	100.00
3/63	0.78	12.58	17.24	0.00	0.00	2.02	6.88	1.83	4.89	0.16	0.00	58.25	2.25	100.00
3/64	0.79	12.04	17.95	0.00	0.00	1.95	6.17	1.69	4.29	0.20	0.00	57.67	3.43	100.00
3/65	0.63	11.85	17.66	0.00	0.00	1.86	6.88	1.62	5.10	0.15	0.00	61.11	0.00	100.00
3/66	0.55	13.04	18.66	0.00	0.00	1.73	6.49	1.65	4.74	0.10	0.00	58.56	0.98	100.00
3/67	0.49	12.10	18.21	0.00	0.00	1.58	5.68	1.57	4.05	0.06	0.00	59.95	1.97	100.00
3/68	0.50	11.23	17.23	0.00	0.00	1.49	5.26	1.53	3.70	0.04	0.00	62.01	2.29	100.00
3/69	0.52	11.16	17.68	0.00	0.00	1.51	5.11	1.56	3.53	0.02	0.00	62.38	1.63	100.00
3/70	0.52	10.93	16.81	0.00	0.00	1.45	4.56	1.38	3.16	0.02	0.00	64.56	1.17	100.00

3/71	0.54	11.82	17.73	0.00	0.00	1.52	4.64	1.47	3.14	0.02	0.00	63.35	0.39	100.00
3/72	0.55	14.29	20.27	0.00	0.00	1.79	4.76	1.55	3.19	0.02	0.00	58.35	0.00	100.00
3/73	0.58	14.30	20.34	0.00	0.00	1.97	4.68	1.44	3.23	0.01	0.00	58.12	0.00	100.00
3/74	0.53	12.64	16.92	0.00	0.00	1.61	4.20	1.13	3.06	0.01	0.00	62.95	1.16	100.00
3/75	0.60	13.36	17.04	0.00	0.00	1.76	4.38	1.24	3.13	0.02	0.00	60.48	2.37	100.00
3/76	0.58	13.55	16.79	0.00	0.00	1.54	4.39	1.43	2.94	0.01	0.00	60.37	2.79	100.00
3/77	0.58	13.60	17.09	0.00	0.00	1.57	4.47	1.56	2.89	0.03	0.00	59.61	3.08	100.00
3/78	0.61	13.86	17.79	0.00	0.00	1.79	4.60	1.59	2.97	0.04	0.00	58.74	2.60	100.00
3/79	0.63	14.03	17.97	0.00	0.00	2.01	4.79	1.87	2.88	0.04	0.00	59.27	1.30	100.00
3/80	0.59	12.30	16.49	0.46	0.00	1.95	4.95	2.29	2.62	0.04	0.00	61.21	2.07	100.00
3/81	0.55	11.18	16.79	0.48	0.00	1.97	5.17	2.62	2.52	0.03	0.00	59.91	3.96	100.00
3/82	0.54	11.44	16.89	0.75	0.00	1.88	5.62	3.04	2.54	0.03	0.00	59.07	3.82	100.00
3/83	0.56	11.48	17.50	1.04	0.00	1.99	6.08	3.46	2.57	0.04	0.00	56.89	4.46	100.00
3/84	0.53	10.81	17.47	1.54	0.00	1.93	6.00	3.49	2.43	0.09	0.00	56.32	5.39	100.00
3/85	0.53	10.97	17.16	1.90	0.00	2.26	5.92	3.50	2.30	0.12	0.00	55.30	5.96	100.00
3/86	0.54	10.79	19.07	1.97	0.00	2.82	6.36	3.91	2.31	0.14	0.00	52.18	6.27	100.00
3/87	0.55	10.31	20.09	2.21	0.00	4.77	6.36	3.34	2.19	0.83	0.00	48.63	7.08	100.00
3/88	0.43	7.25	16.96	1.59	0.70	4.96	25.41	1.71	23.11	0.59	0.03	38.26	4.41	100.00
3/89	0.45	7.17	18.57	1.61	1.04	4.98	27.21	1.39	24.91	0.91	0.40	35.05	3.54	100.00
3/90	0.47	6.17	18.90	1.65	1.41	5.66	24.99	1.48	22.69	0.81	0.54	35.21	5.01	100.00
3/91	0.47	6.63	18.56	1.49	1.82	5.79	23.45	1.85	20.87	0.73	0.56	38.12	3.11	100.00
3/92	0.50	7.65	18.52	1.24	1.93	6.54	18.66	2.02	15.88	0.76	0.67	41.00	3.30	100.00
3/93	0.50	7.96	17.43	1.39	1.52	6.91	17.81	1.89	15.15	0.77	0.40	37.10	NA	100.00

Table 6.16 Components of liabilities of the corporate sector (% of total liabilities)

End of period (1)	*Securities* (2)	*Corporate bonds* (3)	*Stocks* (4)	*Foreign bonds* (5)	*CP* (6)	*Loans* (8 + 9) (7)	*Loans made by private financial institutions* (8)	*Loans made by govt. banks* (9)	*Trade criedit* (10)	*Others* (11)	*Financial deficit* (12)	*Total* (13)
3/54	22.41	4.93	17.48	0.00	0.00	92.41	82.40	10.01	46.47	0.00	−61.29	100.00
3/55	25.81	4.94	20.87	0.00	0.00	94.65	83.63	11.02	43.23	0.00	−63.69	100.00
3/56	25.98	5.00	20.98	0.00	0.00	93.84	82.80	11.04	43.40	0.92	−64.14	100.00
3/57	27.26	5.16	22.10	0.00	0.00	92.61	82.56	10.05	45.08	0.54	−65.49	100.00
3/58	29.33	5.02	24.31	0.00	0.00	98.08	87.59	10.49	41.51	0.00	−68.92	100.00
3/59	28.40	5.15	23.26	0.00	0.00	95.15	85.08	10.07	40.73	0.00	−64.28	100.00
3/60	25.92	5.10	20.82	0.00	0.00	84.08	75.34	8.74	46.27	0.00	−56.27	100.00
3/61	27.65	6.57	21.08	0.00	0.00	82.59	74.40	8.18	44.49	0.00	−54.73	100.00
3/62	27.54	6.17	21.37	0.00	0.00	77.15	69.76	7.39	48.41	0.00	−53.11	100.00
3/63	25.64	5.48	20.16	0.00	0.00	75.85	68.95	6.90	45.90	0.00	−47.39	100.00
3/64	23.58	5.01	18.57	0.00	0.00	74.30	67.46	6.83	44.70	0.00	−42.57	100.00
3/65	22.84	4.70	18.14	0.00	0.00	73.75	66.86	6.89	46.96	0.85	−44.40	100.00
3/66	21.88	4.82	16.84	0.22	0.00	75.97	68.75	7.22	44.89	0.00	−42.73	100.00
3/67	19.69	4.51	15.01	0.17	0.00	73.25	66.05	7.20	46.81	0.00	−39.75	100.00
3/68	17.59	4.15	13.28	0.15	0.00	71.18	64.04	7.13	48.55	0.00	−37.31	100.00
3/69	17.22	4.18	12.83	0.20	0.00	73.60	66.00	7.59	48.00	0.00	−38.81	100.00
3/70	15.68	3.80	11.65	0.23	0.00	70.61	63.80	6.81	49.94	0.00	−36.23	100.00

3/71	15.57	3.86	11.51	0.21	0.00	75.15	68.09	7.06	49.66	0.00	–40.39	100.00
3/72	15.08	4.02	10.91	0.15	0.00	80.40	73.18	7.22	45.34	0.77	–41.59	100.00
3/73	13.55	3.73	9.73	0.09	0.00	81.10	74.30	6.80	47.46	1.17	–43.28	100.00
3/74	11.21	3.30	7.87	0.04	0.00	70.90	64.88	6.01	54.63	0.00	–36.74	100.00
3/75	12.01	3.66	8.25	0.11	0.00	78.36	71.29	7.06	50.67	0.00	–41.04	100.00
3/76	12.07	3.88	7.85	0.34	0.00	76.58	69.48	7.10	49.16	0.00	–37.82	100.00
3/77	11.93	3.87	7.61	0.45	0.00	77.50	70.12	7.38	47.63	0.00	–37.07	100.00
3/78	12.43	4.12	7.73	0.58	0.00	80.43	72.58	7.85	46.68	0.00	–39.54	100.00
3/79	12.09	4.04	7.41	0.64	0.00	76.78	68.95	7.83	46.69	0.00	–35.56	100.00
3/80	11.43	3.90	6.74	0.79	0.00	71.48	63.89	7.59	49.96	0.00	–32.87	100.00
3/81	10.93	3.77	6.51	0.65	0.00	71.48	63.73	7.75	48.56	0.00	–30.97	100.00
3/82	11.03	3.90	6.43	0.70	0.00	72.48	64.45	8.03	47.48	0.00	–30.98	100.00
3/83	11.49	3.89	6.55	1.05	0.00	76.53	68.07	8.46	44.65	0.00	–32.68	100.00
3/84	11.15	3.67	6.26	1.22	0.00	75.70	67.46	8.24	44.27	0.00	–31.11	100.00
3/85	11.13	3.68	6.00	1.46	0.00	76.42	68.40	8.02	43.49	0.00	–31.05	100.00
3/86	13.32	4.93	6.37	2.02	0.00	80.25	72.19	8.05	39.63	0.00	–33.19	100.00
3/87	13.54	5.07	6.21	2.26	0.00	80.29	72.77	7.52	37.15	0.00	–30.98	100.00
3/88	15.60	5.66	7.84	2.10	0.45	63.60	55.58	8.01	30.10	0.00	–9.74	100.00
3/89	16.70	5.58	8.47	2.65	1.46	65.65	57.43	8.22	27.17	0.00	–10.97	100.00
3/90	19.02	5.65	9.41	3.96	1.99	68.88	60.28	8.59	27.16	0.00	–17.06	100.00
3/91	20.51	5.94	9.71	4.86	1.68	74.62	65.09	9.53	29.40	0.00	–26.20	100.00
3/92	23.38	7.02	10.58	5.77	1.56	83.81	72.26	11.55	30.79	0.00	–39.53	100.00
3/93	23.01	7.55	10.26	5.20	1.51	84.29	71.71	12.58	27.91	NA	–41.32	100.00

(4)The share of stocks issued by the corporate sector rose continuously from March 1986 to March 1992 (column 4, Table 6.16).

(5) The financial deficit of the corporate sector was –61.29 percent in 1954 and on a declining trend until 1988. It was at a very low level during 1988–90 (column 12, Table 6.16).

In summary, the corporate sector started to rely less on bank borrowings and started to increase stock and bond issuance around 1987.

Asset Components of the Manufacturing/non-manufacturing Sectors

Figures 6.1 and 6.2 show the share of cash and deposits in the total assets of the manufacturing and non-manufacturing sectors. The corporate sector is subdivided into the following six groups according to capital size: (i) ¥2–5 million, (ii) ¥5–10 million, (iii) ¥10–50 million, (iv) ¥50–100 million, (v) ¥100 million–1 billion, and (vi) above ¥1 billion.

The following characteristics are noteworthy:

(1) Among very large firms with capital size above ¥1 billion, the share of cash and deposits rose from 1985 to 1989. However, small- and medium-sized firms saw reduced shares for cash and deposits (Figures 6.1 and 6.2).
(2) The share of stocks held by very large firms (capitalized above ¥1 billion) has risen steadily since 1985 in both the manufacturing and non-manufacturing sectors (Figures 6.3 and 6.4). However, small and medium-sized non-manufacturing firms show much more volatility in terms of stockholdings compared with their counterparts in the manufacturing sector (Figure 6.4).
(3) The share of land is relatively small for large firms capitalized above ¥1 billion (Figures 6.5 and 6.6). Nevertheless, firms of all sizes have tended ton increase their landholdings since 1985.

Liability Components of the Manufacturing/non-manufacturing Sectors

Figures 6.7 and 6.8 show the share of short-term borrowing from financial institutions.

(1) The share of short-term borrowing peaked during 1985–6 and started to fall, except at small firms (¥5–10 million) in the manufacturing

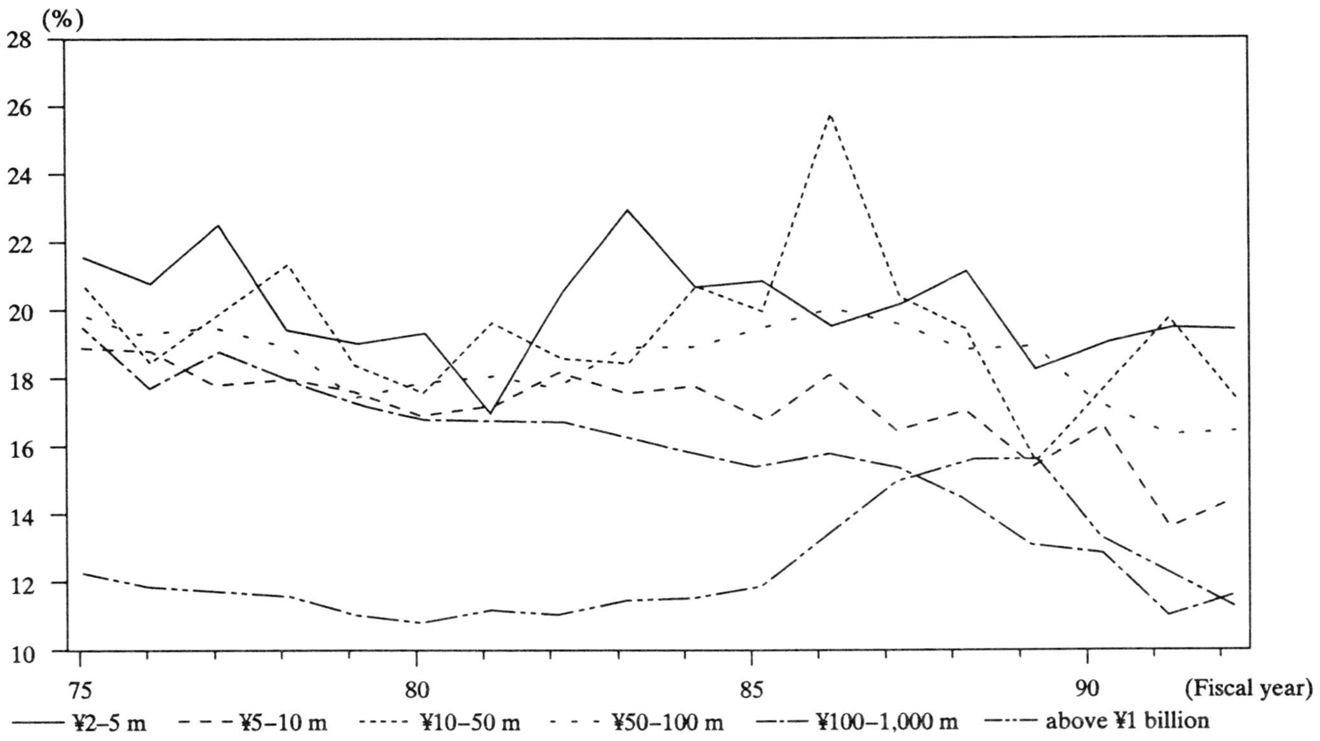

Figure 6.1 Share of cash and deposits in total assets of manufacturers by capital size (1975–92).

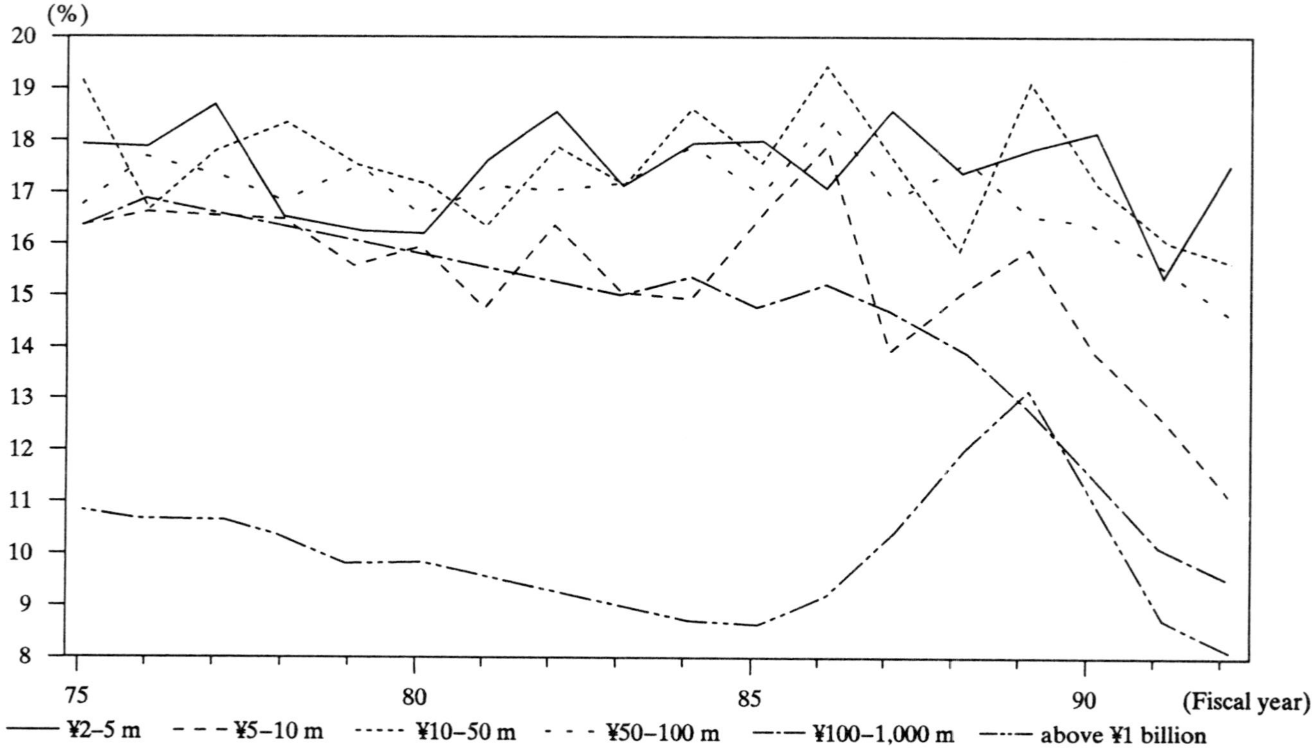

Figure 6.2 Share of cash and deposits in total assets of non-manufacturers by capital size (1975–92).

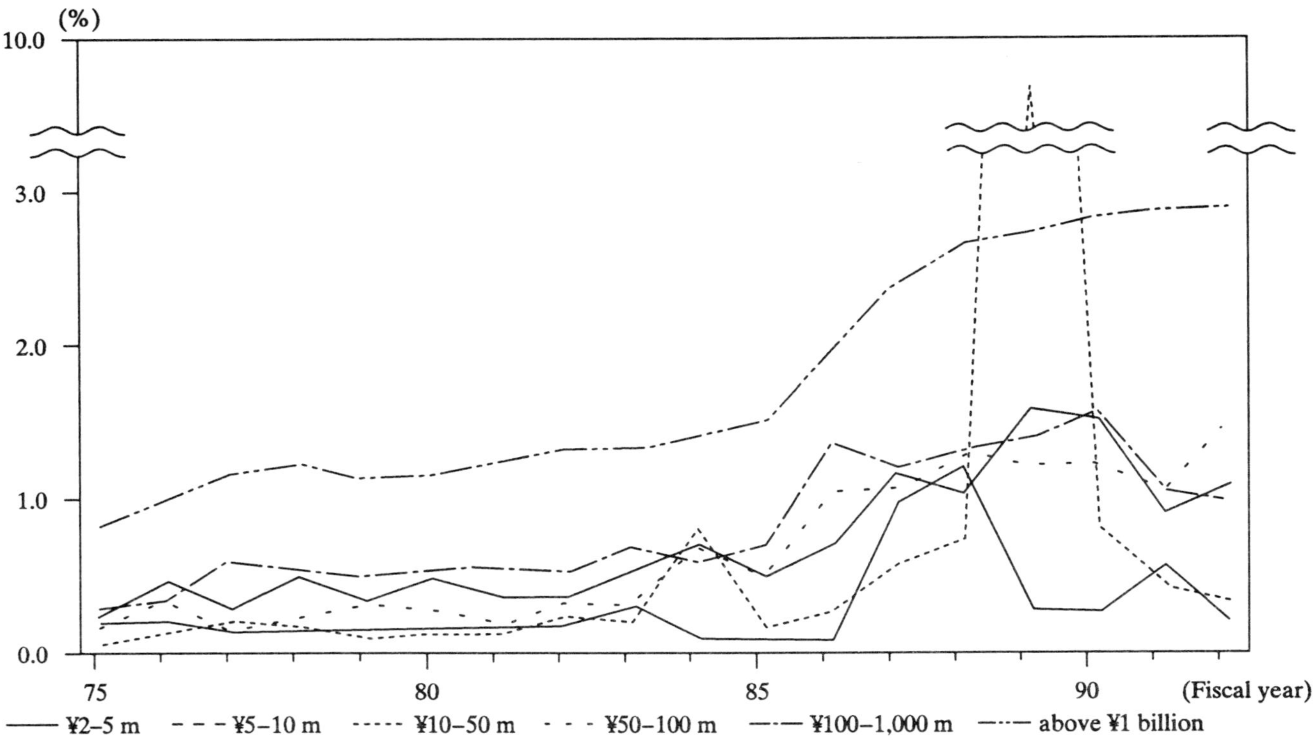

Figure 6.3 Share of stocks in total assets of manufacturers by capital size (1975–92).

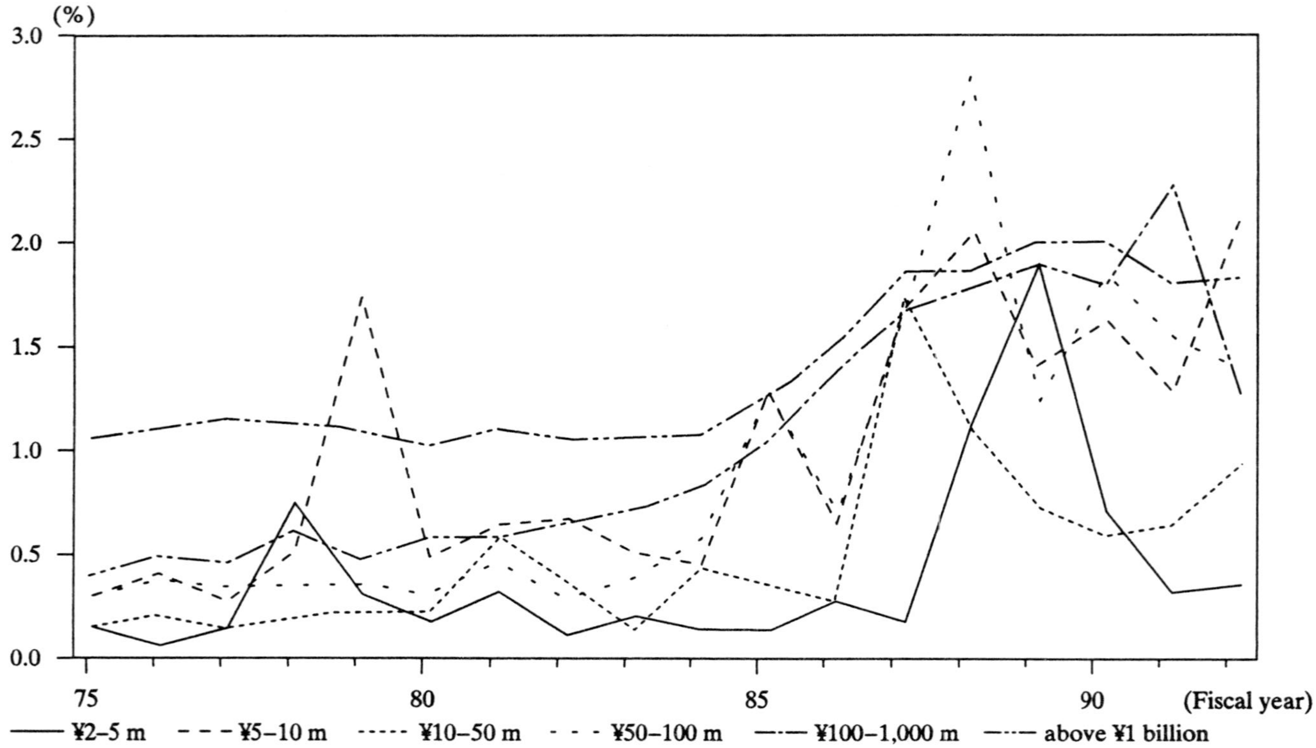

Figure 6.4 Share of stocks in total assets of non-manufacturers by capital size (1975–92).

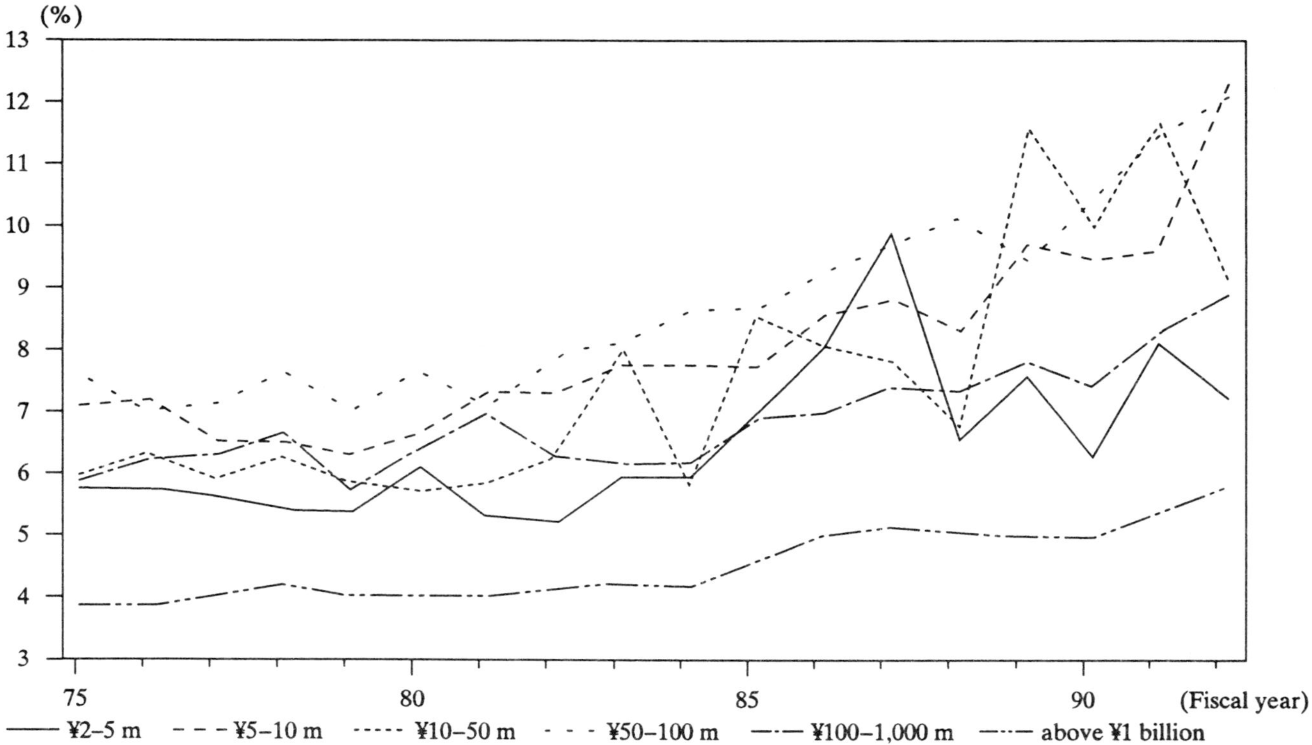

Figure 6.5 Share of land in total assets of manufacturers by capital size (1975–92).

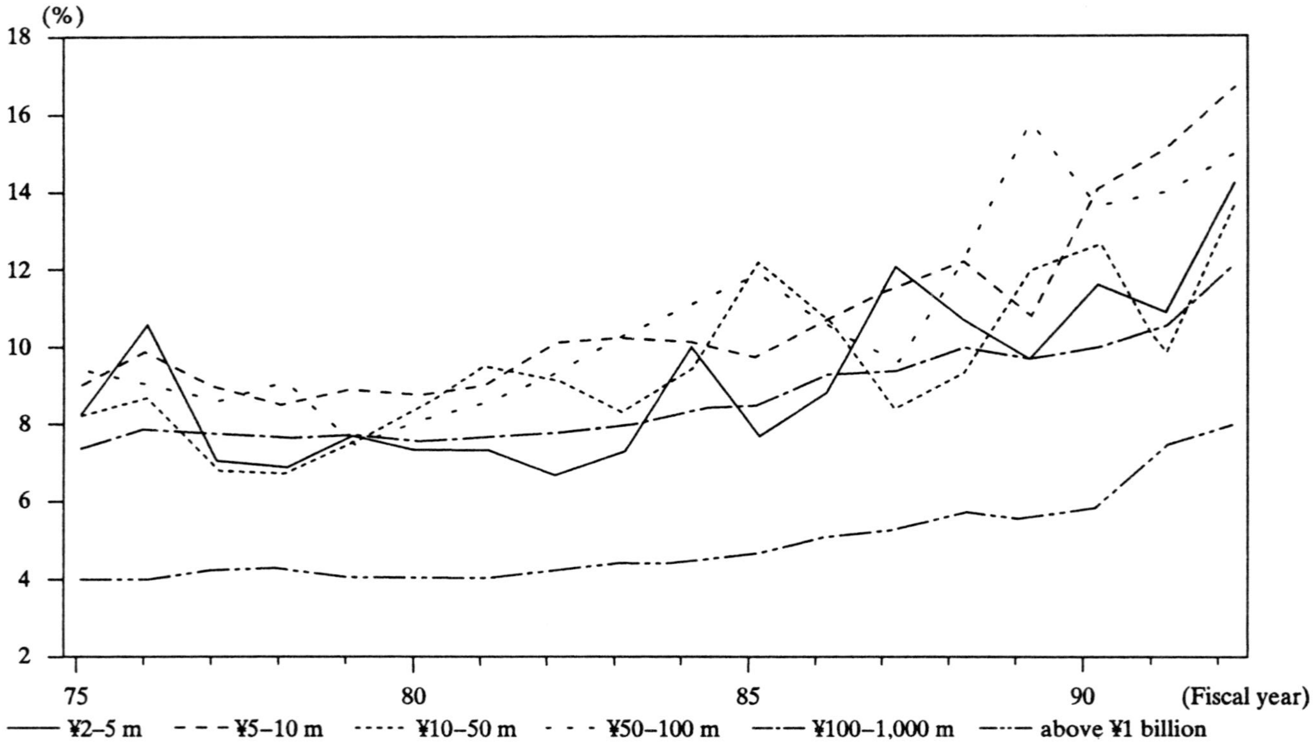

Figure 6.6 Share of land in total assets of non-manufacturers by capital size (1975–92).

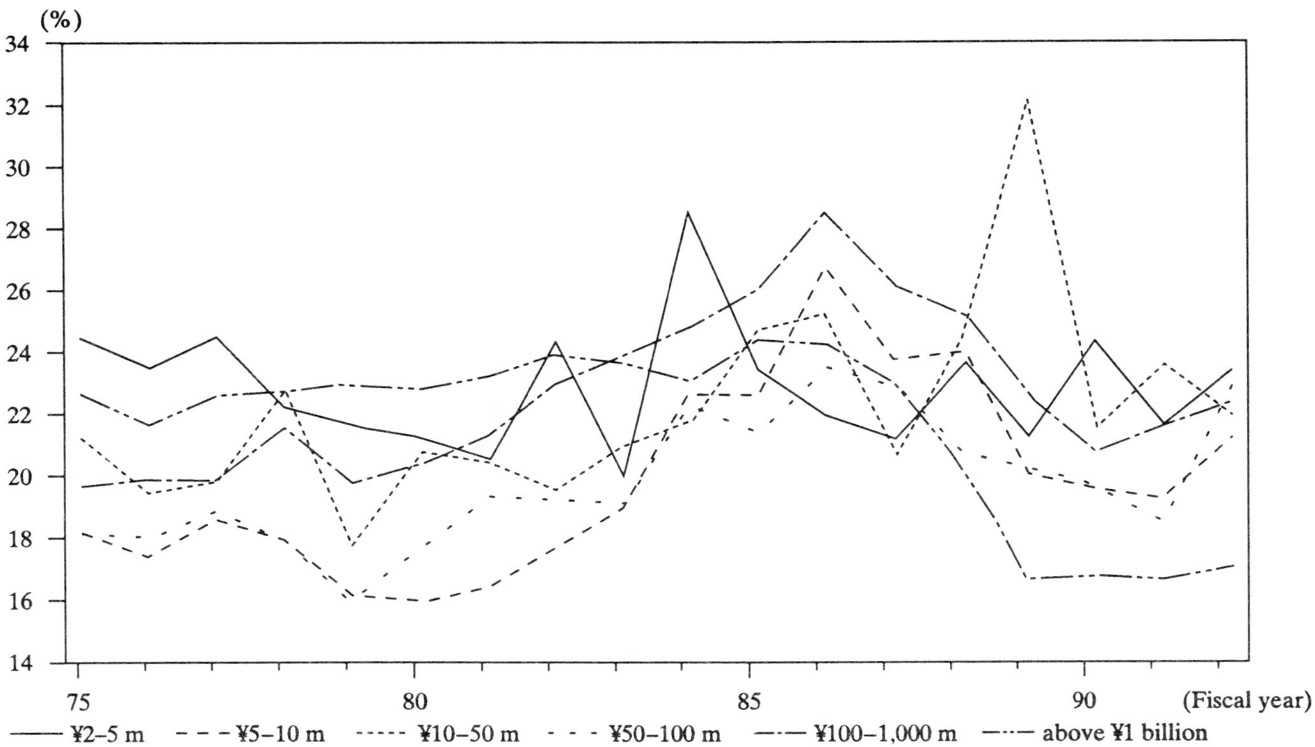

Figure 6.7 Share of short-term borrowing in total liabilities of manufacturers by capital size (1975–92).

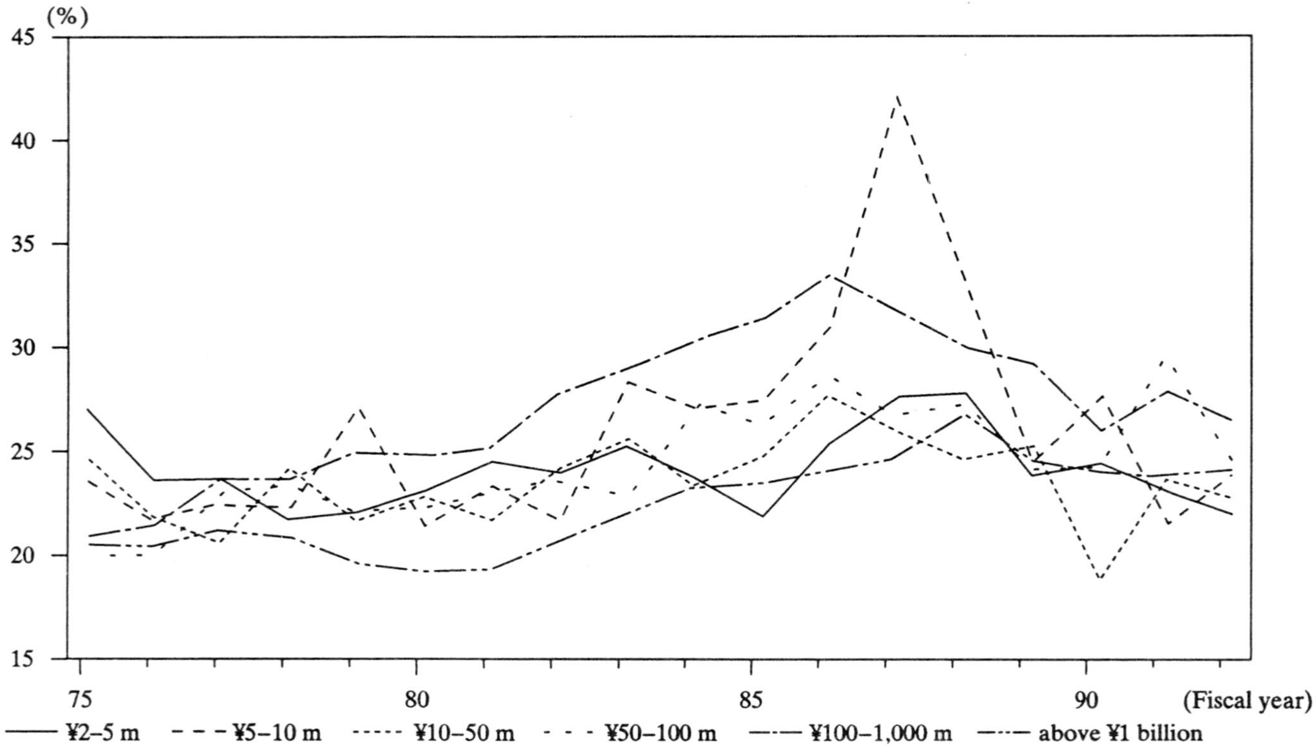

Figure 6.8 Share of stock-term borrowing in total liabilities of non-manufacturers by capital size (1975–92).

sector. The non-manufacturing sector shows an almost similar pattern.

(2) Reliance on corporate bonds by large manufacturing firms (over ¥1 billion) started to increase in 1982 and has been on an upward trend since. However, small and medium-sized firms cannot rely on corporate bonds since only large firms satisfy issuing requirements (Figure 6.9).

Dependence on corporate bonds by large non-manufacturers peaked in 1988 but is still at a high level relative to the early 1980s (Figure 6.10).

(3) Large manufacturers (over ¥1 billion) reduced reliance on long-term borrowing from financial institutions during 1975–89. However, they started to gradually increase long-term borrowing from 1990. In contrast, non-manufacturers of all sizes tend to rely increasingly on long-term borrowing (Figures 6.11 and 6.12).

(4) In very large firms in the manufacturing sector, the share of stocks among assets has been increasing since 1975. Large non-manufacturers have increased stock issuance since 1985. The capital to asset ratios of small and medium-sized firms have not changed to any considerable degree (Figures 6.13 and 6.14).

IV CHANGES IN THE CONDUCT OF MONETARY POLICY

Call Rate Control

The purpose of this section is to examine how Japan's monetary policy changed between 1965 and 1991. Did the Bank of Japan use interbank interest rates as an instrument or high-powered money as an instrument? The test of whether high-powered money or the short-term interest rate was used as a monetary policy instrument is pursued by using a weak exogeneity test developed by Revankar and Yoshino (1990). The exogeneity test using the structural form shows that the short-term interest rate (the call lending rate) was used as an instrument of monetary policy in Japan from 1980 to 1991. However, high-powered money was not used as a policy instrument judging from the estimation of the monetary policy reaction function and the

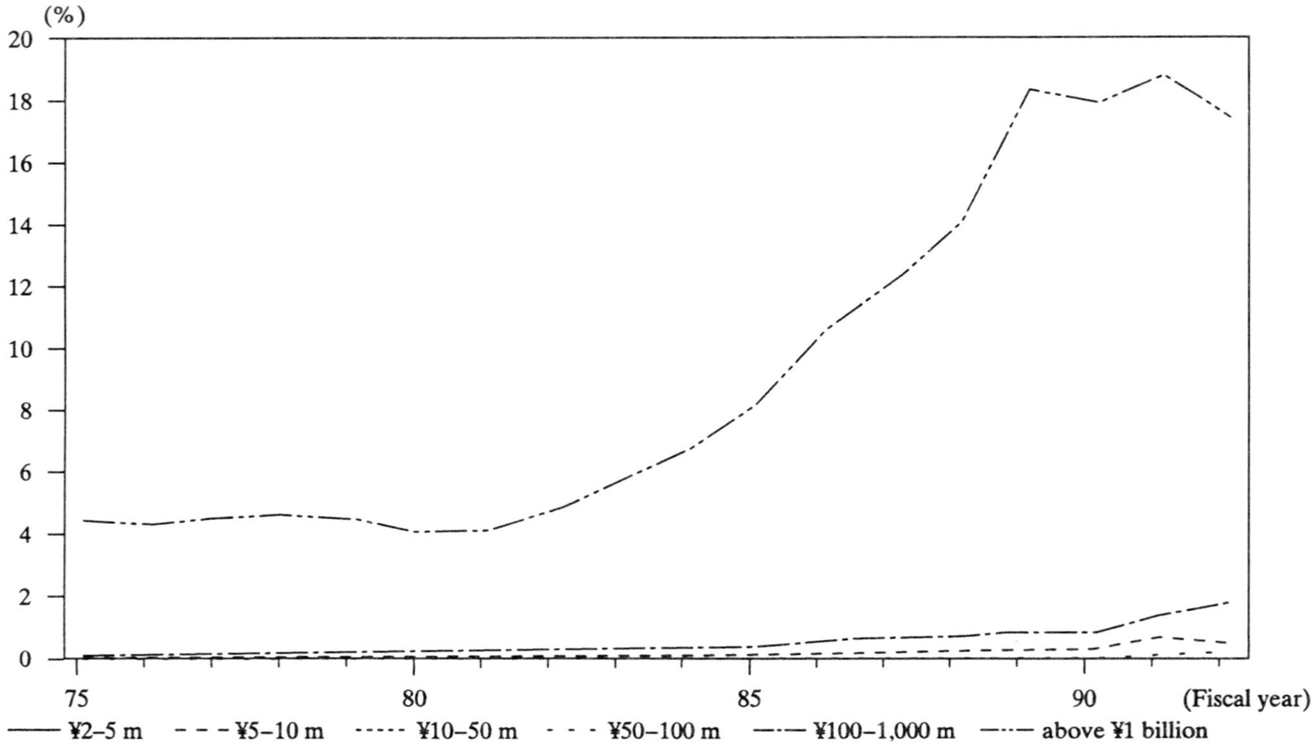

Figure 6.9 Share of corporate bonds in total liabilities of manufacturers by capital size (1957–92).

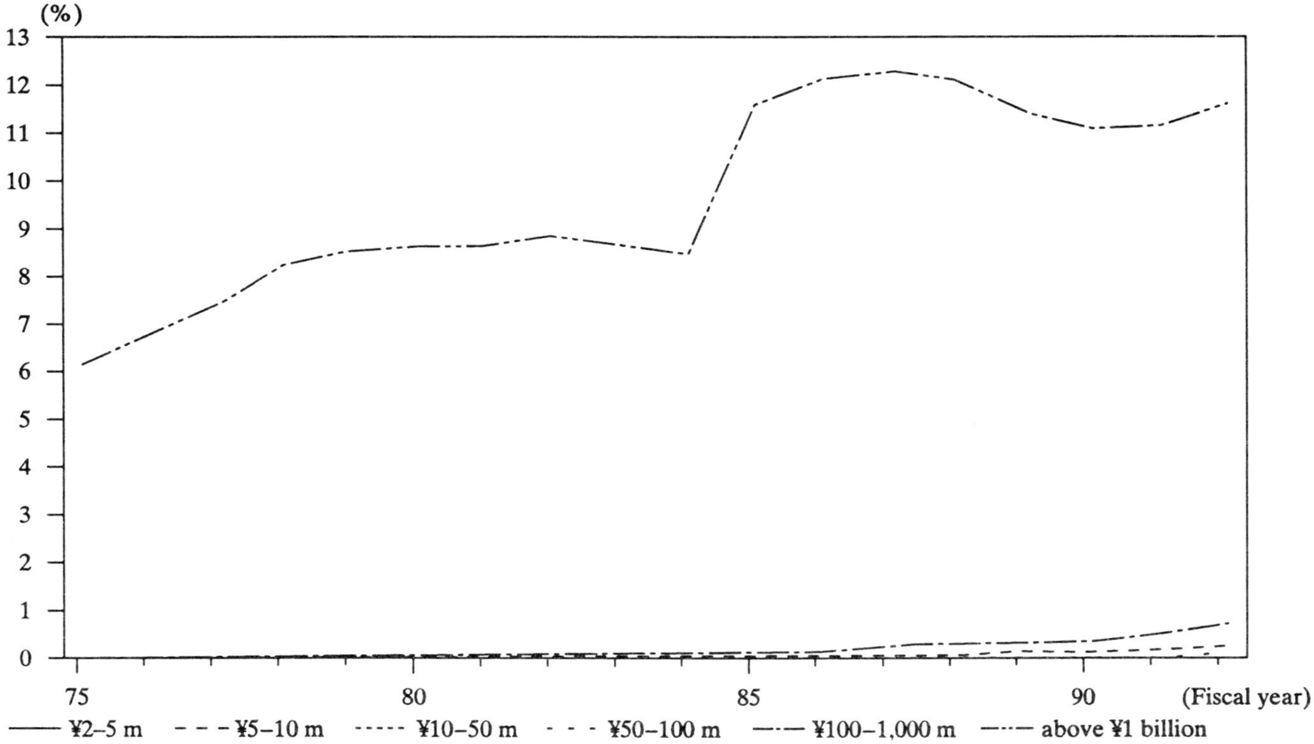

Figure 6.10 Share of corporate bonds in total liabilities of non-manufacturers by capital size (1957–92).

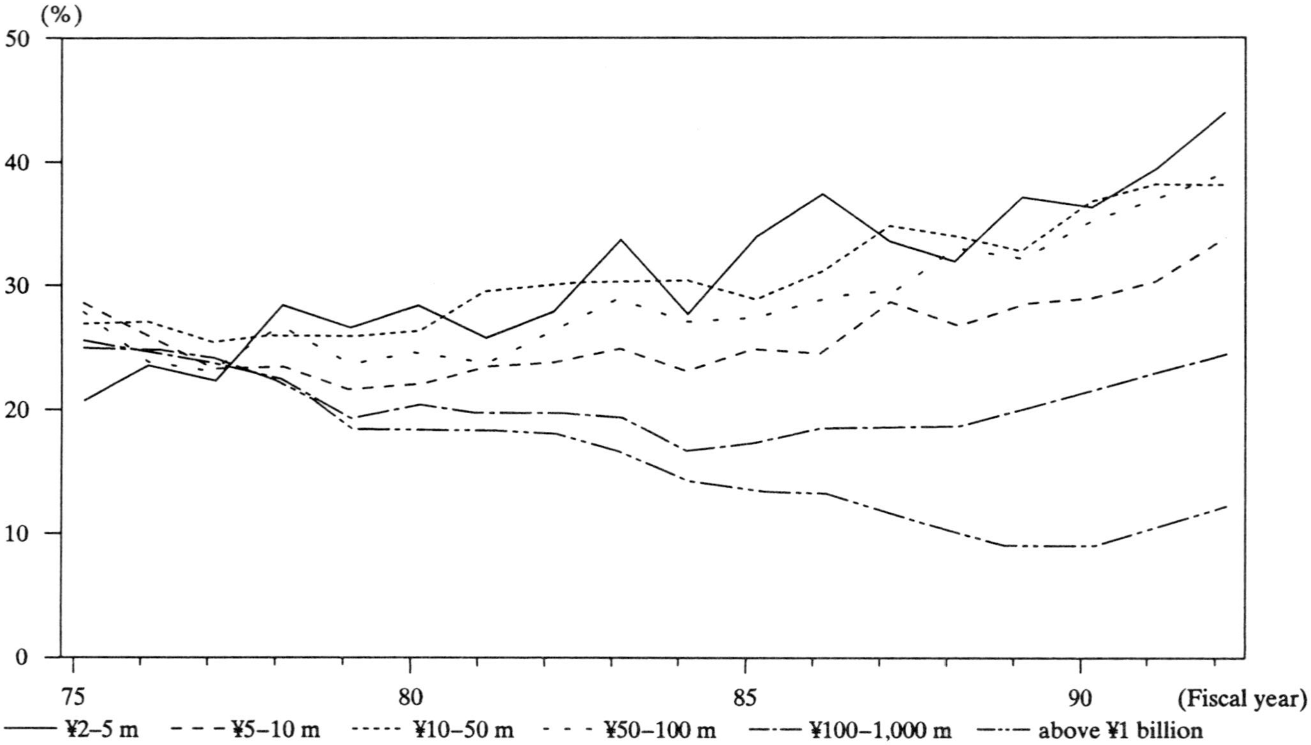

Figure 6.11 Share of long-term borrowing in total liabilities of manufacturers by capital size (1975–92).

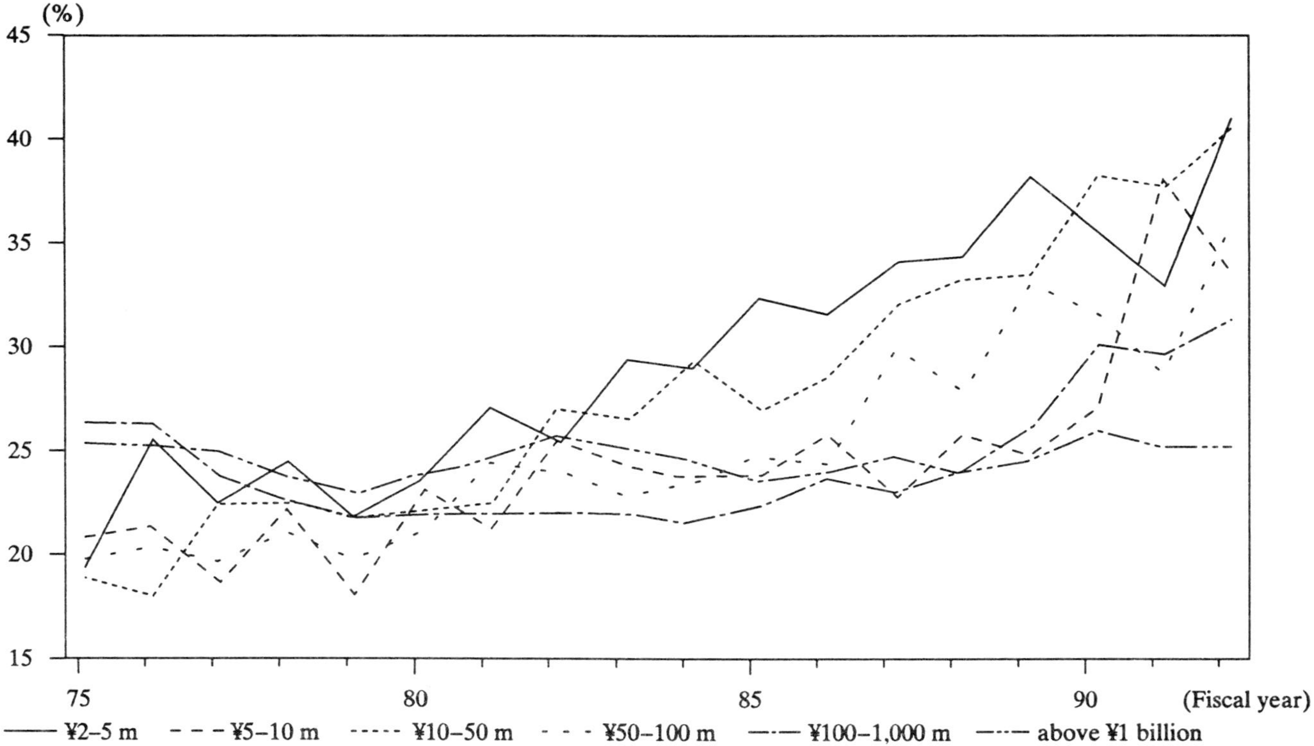

Figure 6.12 Share of long-term borrowing in total liabilities of non-manufacturers by capital size (1975–92).

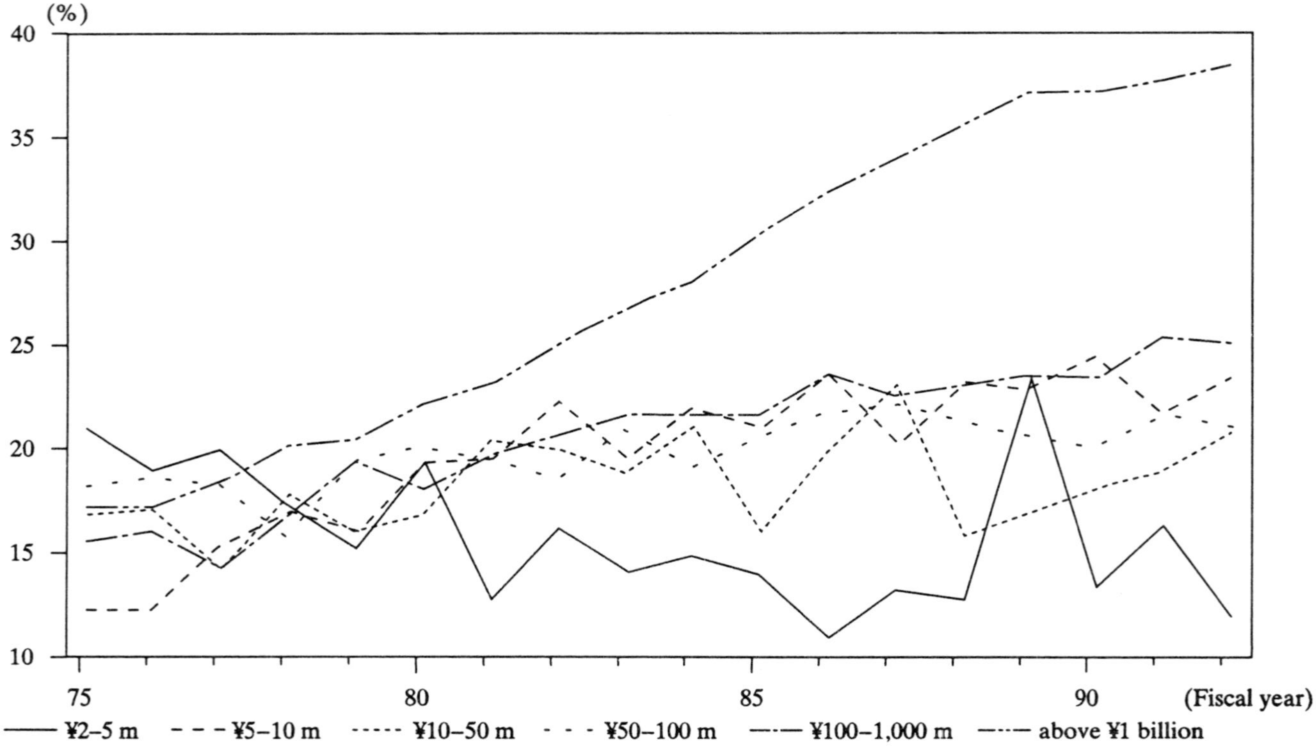

Figure 6.13 Share of capital in total liabilities of manufacturers by capital size (1975–92).

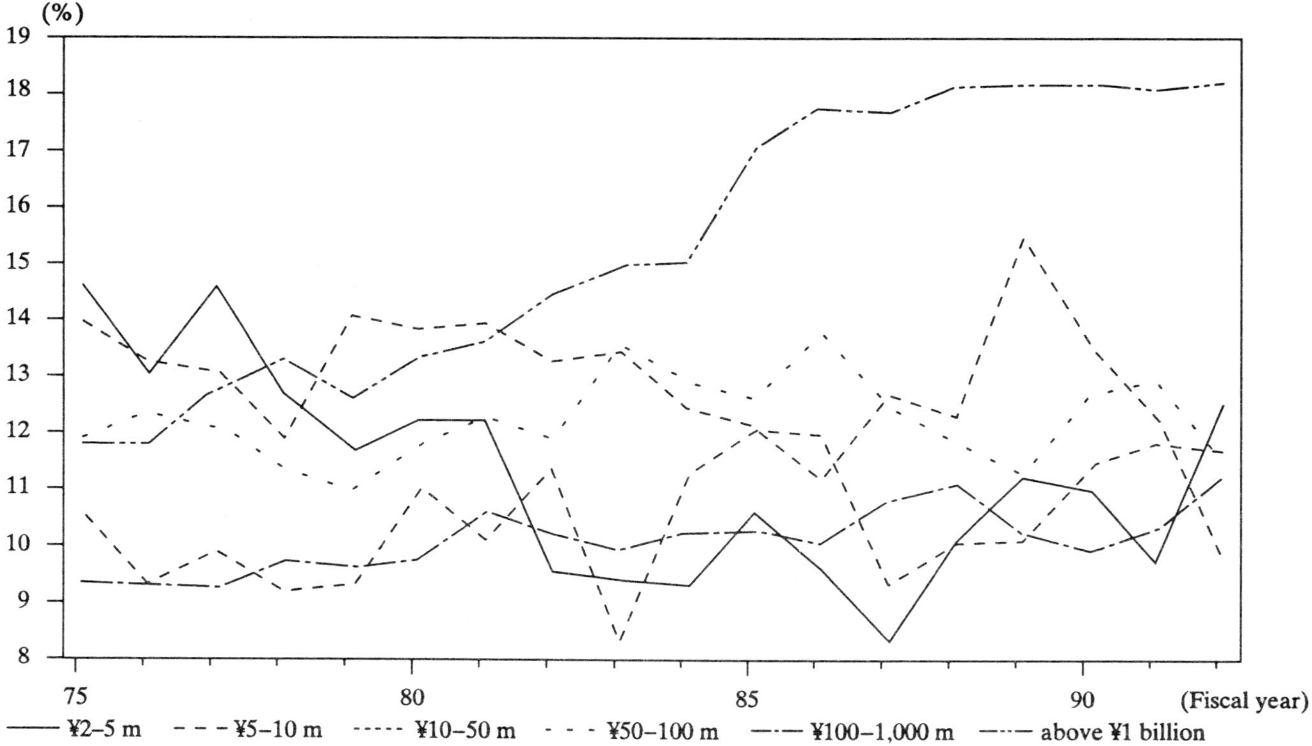

Figure 6.14 Share of capital in total liabilities of non-manufacturers by capital size (1975–92).

weak exogeneity test. Details of the estimations can be seen in Yoshino and Yoshimura (1994).

Both quarterly and monthly data show that the call rate was used as a policy instrument between 1980 and 1991. However, the call rate became endogenous; namely, it was not controlled as a policy instrument during the 1969–79 period. This is probably because of window guidance policy (the Bank of Japan regulated the growth rate of private bank loans by using administrative guidance) and the discount window policies which were used extensively during this period and which might have weakened the exogeneity of the call lending rate.

Brief History of Japanese Monetary Policy

(1) WPI was very stable during the high growth period (i.e., between 1955 and 1969). The average level of WPI was 0.5 percent during the 1960s and around 1.0 percent until the mid-1960s. CPI, however, grew more rapidly (at between 5 to 7 percent) compared to WPI during 1961–72.

(2) Monetary policy of the Bank of Japan during the 1960s was aimed at tightening the money market when the balance of payments showed a deficit. It was eased when the balance of payments came back to a normal level. However, the balance of payments posted a surplus after 1968 and WPI started to rise.

Monetary policy was tightened because of high inflation even when the balance of payments was showing a surplus.

(3) The yen appreciated from 360 to 308/$ in December 1971 for the first time since the Second World War. The Bank of Japan was expecting that this would discourage export-oriented industries. Therefore, they started to loosen monetary policy during 1972–3 in co-ordination with the expansion of fiscal policy.

(4) OPEC raised the price of oil in 1973. The import price of oil in Japan increased 77.4 percent compared to the previous year. The Japanese economy relied on foreign oil imports for 99.7 percent of its total oil requirements. WPI increased 37.2 percent and CPI 24.9 percent in 1974. Japan's real growth rate turned negative (–0.4

percent) for the first time since the end of the Second World War. Japan experienced a huge trade deficit during this period.

(5) The government started to rely on government bonds in order to stimulate the Japanese economy after the first oil crisis. More than 30 percent of total government spending was financed by issuing government bonds.

(6) Interest rates on large-denomination deposits started to be deregulated in 1979 and the Foreign Exchange Control Law was abolished in 1980. Both of these factors resulted in changes in the conduct of monetary policy and private sector behavior.

(7) Japanese monetary policy changed after the Plaza Agreement (September 1985). Japan saw high stock and bond prices from 1986 until 1990.

Summary of Estimated Results

Quarterly, monthly and daily data are used for estimating the policy reaction function since it may be different depending on the time span. There were structural changes in the policy reaction function between 1979 and 1980. A summary of the estimated results is shown in Table 6.17.

Table 6.17 summarizes the estimates of the monetary policy reaction function using quarterly, monthly and daily data. The call lending rate (i.e. the interbank money market rate) was regarded as exogenous in the money supply and money demand equations using quarterly (Q2 1980–Q4 1991) and monthly (2/1980–12/1991) data. The exogeneity test can not be conducted with respect to daily data since such data for money supply and income is unavailable. As for daily data, only the reaction function was estimated without testing the exogeneity of the call lending rate.

As is seen in Table 6.17, the structural change is observed between 1979 and 1980 in quarterly data. The structural change can also be seen after the Plaza accord (September 1985) based on monthly data. The exchange rate becomes important as one of the monetary policy indicators in the 1980s from the quarterly data and after October 1980 from the monthly data.

Monthly and daily data show lagged call rate is very significant

Table 6.17 Estimated results of monetary policy reaction function (Instrument: call rate)

	Target variables
Quarterly data	
1968/2Q–1979/4Q	Growth rate of money ($t = -2.142$)
	Rate of inflation ($t = -3.527$)
	Lagged call rate ($t = 2.041$)
1980/2Q–1991/4Q	Growth rate of money ($t = -2.158$)
	Rate of inflation ($t = -2.121$)
	Exchange rate ($t = -1.836$)
	Lagged call rate ($t = 6.137$)
Monthly data	
1980/02–1985/09	Rate of inflation ($t = -3.871$)
	Lagged call rate ($t = 8.973$)
1985/10–1991/12	Exchange rate ($t = -2.866$)
	Lagged call rate ($t = 15.464$)
Daily data	
1981/01/04–1985/09/30	
	Growth rate of money ($t = -1.986$)
	Exchange rate ($t = -2.776$)
1985/10/04–1987/10/30	Lagged call rate ($t = 50.887$)
	Rate of inflation ($t = -1.730$)
1987/11/01–1991/05/30	Lagged call rate ($t = 41.747$)
	Rate of inflation ($t = -1.581$)
1991/05/31–1991/12/31	Lagged call rate ($t = 72.852$)
	Lagged call rate ($t = 41.339$)

which suggests that the monetary authority paid attention to smooth the fluctuations of the call rate in order to avoid big fluctuations.

V SIMPLE VAR ESTIMATIONS OF THE JAPANESE ECONOMY

This section analyzes the macroeconomic behavior of the Japanese economy during the asset price bubble in comparison with the 1970s.

VAR Estimation Results

This section presents VAR estimation results of macroeconomic variables in Japan. As seen in quarterly data, the conduct of monetary policy changed between 1979 and 1980. Therefore, two sets of VAR estimations are examined, namely between 2/1971–4/1979 and 1/1980–1/1992.

The variables used for the estimation are: (i) the call lending rate (% level = *Rcall*), (ii) real output (the first difference of log of real GNP = ΔY), (iii) money supply (the first difference of log of M2 + *CD* = ΔM), (iv) price level (the first difference of log of WPI = ΔP), (v) exchange rate (the first difference of log of the ¥/$ exchange rate = Δe), (vi) share price (the first difference of log of TOPIX = ΔPs), and (vii) land price (the first difference of log of land price = ΔPL).

An augmented Dickey–Fuller test was applied to each variable by using quarterly data from 1/1971 to 1/1992. The results show that none of the variables show unit root at the significance level of 10 percent.

Rcall	ΔY	ΔM	ΔP	Δe	ΔPs	ΔPL
−4.28(**)	−4.44(**)	−3.35(*)	−4.29(**)	−4.24(**)	−3.15(+)	−3.40(+)

where (**), (*), and (+) denote the significance level of 1 percent, 5 percent and 10 percent, respectively. In each case, the four lags, constant, and time trend terms are used in the augmented Dickey–Fuller test.

The VAR estimation using quarterly data is summarized in Table 6.18 (1/1971–4/1979) and Table 6.19 (1/1980–1/1992).

(1) The call lending rate depends on lagged changes in the price, money supply, and land prices during 1/1971–4/1979. On the

Table 6.18 VAR estimation of F-values (significance value in parentheses) (1971/2Q–1979/4Q)

	Rcall	Δ*Y*	Δ*M*	Δ*P*	Δ*e*	Δ*Ps*	Δ*PL*
Rcall	349.8	0.62	3.24	3.52	0.63	0.86	13.61
	(0.00)	(0.44)	(0.084)	(0.073)	(0.44)	(0.36)	(0.001)
Δ*Y*	3.41	0.04	3.14	0.93	2.01	0.22	2.10
	(0.07)	(0.84)	(0.09)	(0.34)	(0.17)	(0.64)	(0.16)
Δ*M*	0.35	0.07	39.85	5.17	3.64	3.17	2.08
	(0.55)	(0.79)	(0.00)	(0.032)	(0.068)	(0.088)	(0.16)
Δ*P*	0.32	1.86	0.12	4.81	3.24	0.24	3.92
	(0.58)	(0.19)	(0.73)	(0.04)	(0.08)	(0.63)	(0.06)
Δ*e*	1.68	2.70	3.02	0.72	4.76	0.07	1.43
	(0.21)	(0.11)	(0.095)	(0.41)	(0.04)	(0.79)	(0.24)
Δ*Ps*	0.28	0.32	7.03	0.001	0.12	0.13	1.77
	(0.60)	(0.58)	(0.014)	(0.98)	(0.74)	(0.72)	(0.20)
Δ*PL*	4.95	2.20	6.58	5.53	0.33	0.49	59.02
	(0.04)	(0.15)	(0.017)	(0.027)	(0.57)	(0.49)	(0.00)

Table 6.19 VAR estimation of F-values (significance value in parentheses) (1980/1Q–1992/1Q)

	Rcall	Δ*Y*	Δ*M*	Δ*P*	Δ*e*	Δ*Ps*	Δ*PL*
Rcall	151.80	0.89	0.063	17.82	3.36	0.08	0.019
	(0.00)	(0.36)	(0.80)	(0.00)	(0.07)	(0.78)	(0.89)
Δ*Y*	13.65	0.65	0.77	3.20	0.05	0.51	2.57
	(0.00)	(0.42)	(0.39)	(0.08)	(0.82)	(0.48)	(0.12)
Δ*M*	1.03	0.04	15.39	0.05	1.23	4.94	0.85
	(0.32)	(0.84)	(0.00)	(0.83)	(0.27)	(0.03)	(0.36)
Δ*P*	1.18	0.25	0.39	36.16	6.03	0.90	0.68
	(0.28)	(0.62)	(0.54)	(0.00)	(0.018)	(0.35)	(0.41)
Δ*e*	0.08	0.22	0.14	0.32	7.05	0.84	1.90
	(0.78)	(0.64)	(0.71)	(0.57)	(0.01)	(0.37)	(0.18)
Δ*Ps*	0.01	0.00	0.07	0.017	0.45	1.00	3.82
	(0.93)	(0.99)	(0.79)	(0.90)	(0.51)	(0.32)	(0.06)
Δ*PL*	0.012	0.03	9.64	0.63	0.06	0.61	81.99
	(0.91)	(0.87)	(0.004)	(0.43)	(0.80)	(0.44)	(0.00)

other hand, it depends on lagged exchange rates and prices after 1980.

(2) Changes in real output depend on the call rate and money supply during 1/1971–4/1979. However, it is affected more by the call rate and price after 1980.

Causal relations of other variables are summarized in Figures 6.15 (1/1971–4/1979) and 6.16 (1/1980–1/1992).

Impulse Responses of Macrovariables

A VAR result is presented in Figures 6.17 and 6.18. The impulse responses of land price is only explained since interest lies in the response of asset price to other macroeconomic variables, such as monetary policy.

Figure 6.17 shows that land price was influenced by the call rate, money supply, and share prices during 1/1971–4/1979. The lower call lending rate and higher money supply raised the land price. On the other hand, the land price was much more influenced by money supply and less affected by the call rate during 1/1980–1/1992. This may suggest that the expansion of bank lending in the late 1980s increased money supply which led to high land prices in Japan.

Although in this final section very simple VAR estimations were presented, various other structural VAR estimations are possible. In this regard, further research is necessary.

VI CONCLUDING REMARKS

This chapter examined the changing behavior of private banks and corporations and monetary policy.

(1) The growth rate of possible loan losses has been very high since the collapse of the asset price bubble in 1991 due to bad loans extended to non-bank financial institutions, real estate developers, etc. During the late 1980s, private banks expanded loans simply relying on the collateral value of land. At the same time, city banks and long-term credit banks increased investment in the Euro-market. However, the BIS rule forced Japanese banks to shift their focus from the market share expansion to being more profit conscious.

(2) As for the behavior of the corporate sector, the share of stocks held by large firms has risen steadily since 1985 in both the manufacturing and non-manufacturing sectors. However, small and medium-sized non-manufacturers exhibit more volatility in terms of stockholdings compared with their counterparts in the manufacturing sector. Large manufacturers reduced their reliance on long-term

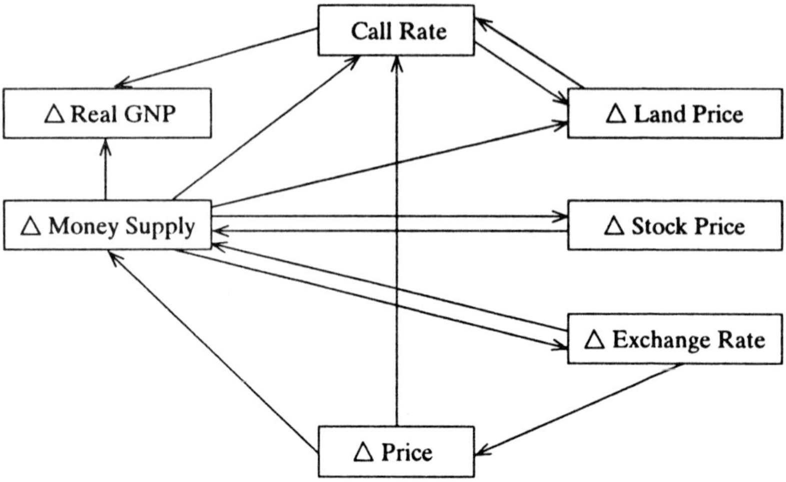

Figure 6.15 Causal relations obtained from the VAR estimation (1971:2–1979:4).

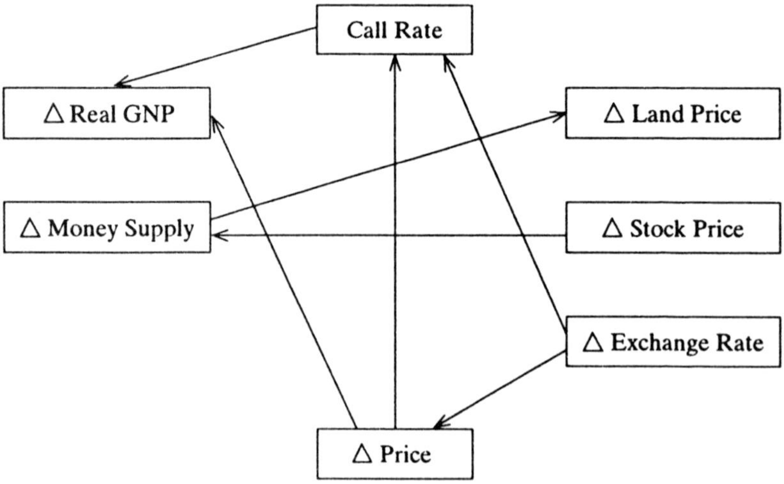

Figure 6.16 Causal relations obtained from the VAR estimation (1980:1–1992:1).

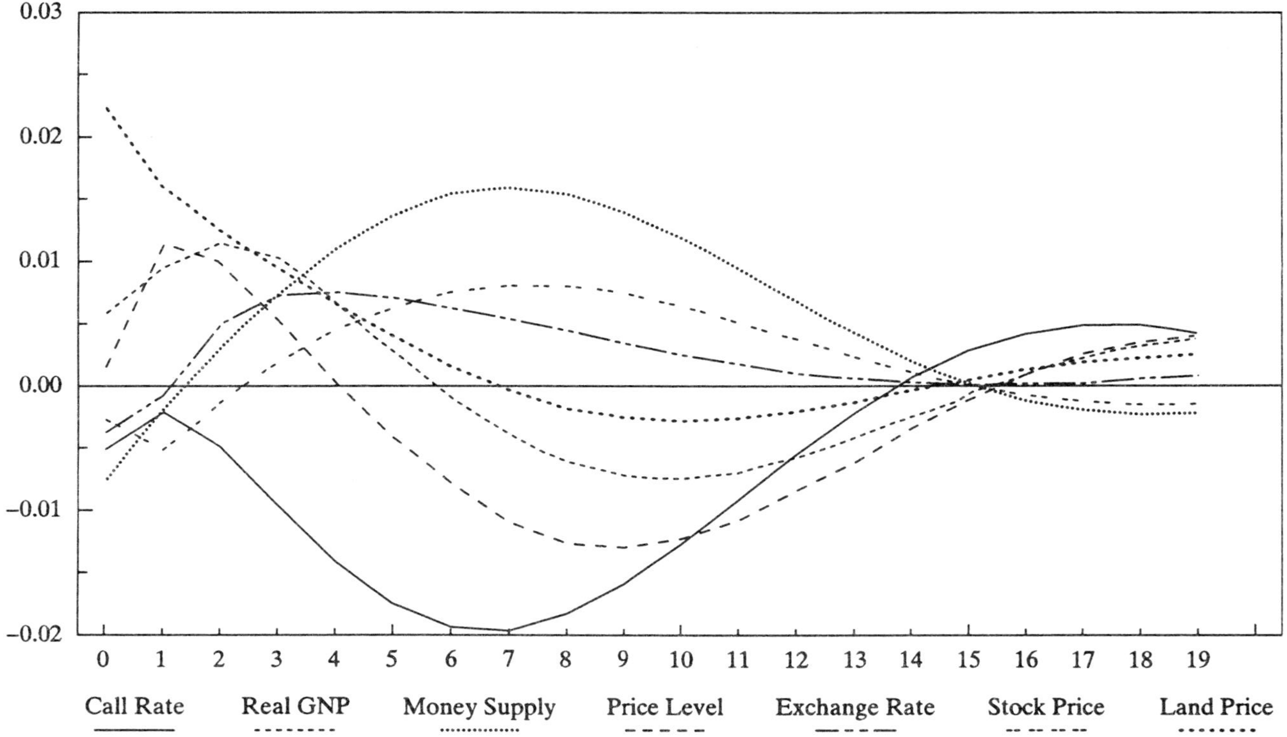

Figure 6.17 Effects on land prices – impulse response function (Estimation period: 71/2Q– 79/4Q).

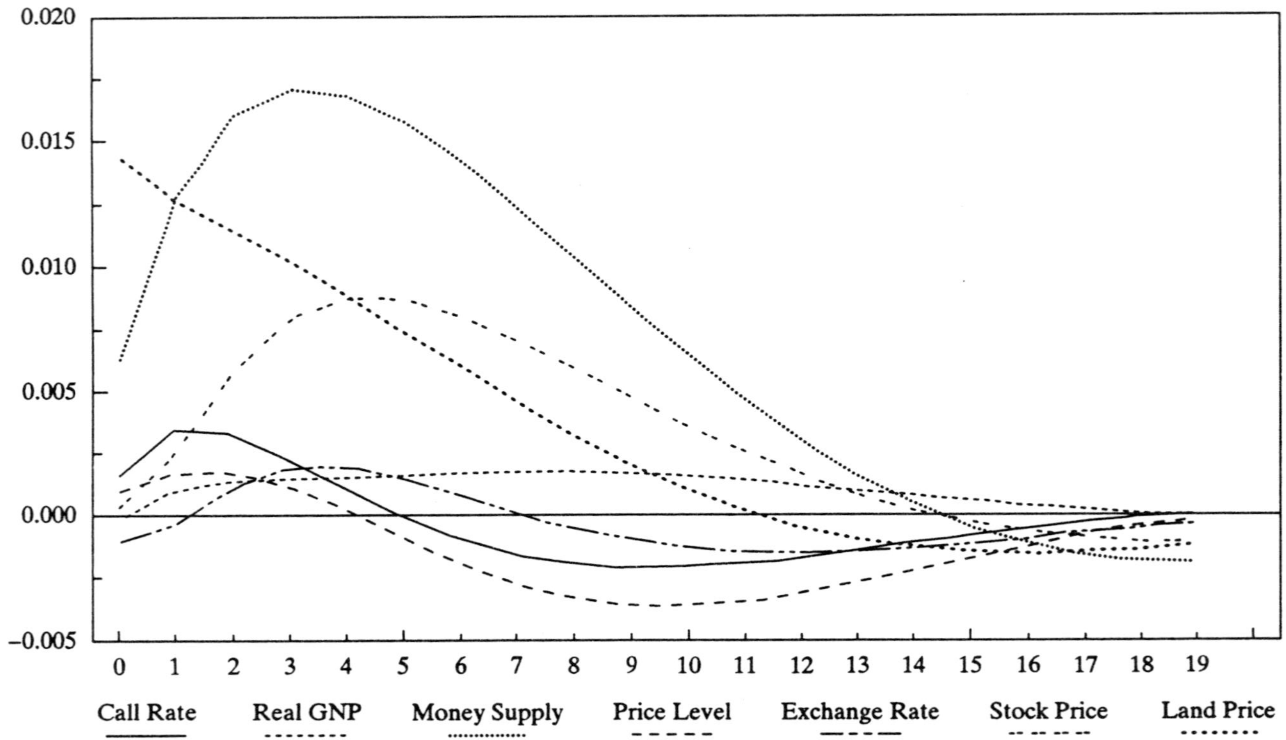

Figure 6.18 Effects on land prices – impulse response function (Estimation period: 80/1Q– 92/1Q).

borrowing from financial institutions during 1975–89 issuing more stocks and bonds; however, small and medium-sized firms increased their long-term bank borrowings during the asset bubble period.

(3) The call lending rate is used as a policy instrument in Japan, especially after 1980 judging from the weak exogeneity test. Monetary policy focused more on price level and money supply from 1965 to 1979. However, the exchange rate and price level were more focused on after 1980.

(4) Impulse responses of land price show that the call rate and money supply affected land price fluctuations between 1972 and 1979. However, money supply had a greater effect after 1980 due to the extension of loans by private banks.

Acknowledgements

I would like to thank Ulrich Baumgartner (IMF), Akiyoshi Horiuchi (University of Tokyo), Mitsuaki Okabe (Macquarie University), and conference participants for their constructive comments.

I would also like to thank Director Kuniho Sawamoto, Deputy Director Zenta Nakajima, Head of Research Division 1 Hiroo Taguchi, Makoto Ohsawa, Luke Gower, and staff of the Institute for Monetary and Economic Studies for their comments. I also acknowledge the computer assistance given by Masaharu Yoshimura and Hideo Nakano of Keio University.

References

Blanchard, O. J. and N. W. Watson (1986) 'Are Business Cycles All Alike?', in R. Gordon (ed.), *The American Business Cycle* (NBER and University of Chicago Press) pp. 123–56.

Boyd, J. H. and M. Gertler (1993) 'U.S. Commercial Banking: Trends, Cycles, and Policy'. NBER Working Paper, no. 4404, July 1993.

Corporate Financial Statistics, Annual (Ministry of Finance).

Dickey, D. A. and W. A. Fuller (1979) 'Distribution of Estimators for Autoregressive Time Series with Unit Root', *Journal of the American Statistical Association*, vol. 74, pp. 427–32.

Economic Statistics Annual (Bank of Japan, various issues).

Economic Statistics Monthly (Bank of Japan, various issues).

Engle, R. F. and C. W. T. Granger (1987) 'Co-integration and Error Correction Representation, Estimation and Testing', *Econometrica*, vol. 55, pp. 251–76.

Financial Statements of All Banks in Japan (Federation of Bankers' Associations of Japan, various issues).

Fiscal and Monetary Statistics (Ministry of Finance).
Iwata, K. (1993) 'Economics of Monetary Policy' (in Japanese, *Kinyu Seisaku no Keizaigaku*), Nihon Keizai Shinbunsha.
McNelis, P. and N. Yoshino (1992) 'Monetary Stabilization with Interest Rate Instruments in Japan', *Bank of Japan Monetary and Economic Studies*, vol. 10, no. 2, pp. 79–106.
National Income Accounts (Economic Planning Agency).
Okina, K. (1993) *Monetary Policy – From the Perspective of the Central Bank* (in Japanese, *Kinyu Seisaku – Chuo Ginko no Shiten to Sentaku*), Toyo Keizai Shinposha.
Revankar, N. and N. Yoshino (1990) 'An Expanded Equation Approach to Weak Exogeneity Tests in Structural Systems and A Monetary Application', *Review of Economics and Statistics*, vol. 22, no. 1, pp. 173–7.
Sims, C. A. (1980) 'Macroeconomics and Reality', *Econometrica*, vol. 48, pp. 1–48.
Stock, J. H. and M. W. Watson (1980) 'Testing for Common Trends', *Journal of the American Statistical Association*, vol. 83, pp. 1097–107.
Suzuki, Y. (1993) *Japan's Monetary Policy* (in Japanese, *Nihon no Kinyu Seisaku*), Iwanami Shuppan.
Tachi, R. (1993) 'Fiscal and Monetary Policy and the Japanese Economy' (in Japanese, *Nihon Keizai to Zaisei Kinyu*), Kinyu Chosa Kenkyukai Conference Paper, 27 December 1993.
Ueda, K. (1992) *Monetary Policy Under the Balance of Payments Imbalance* (in Japanese, *Kokusaishushi Fukinko ka no Kinyu Seisaku*), Toyo Keizai Shinposha.
Yoshikawa, H. (1993) 'Monetary Policy and the Japanese Economy' (in Japanese, *Kinyu Seisaku to Nihon Keizai*), *Keizai Bunseki* (Economic Planning Agency) vol. 128, March 1993.
Yoshino, N. and M. Yoshimura (1994) *Monetary Policy Reaction of the Bank of Japan and Money Supply Control* (in Japanese, *Kinyu Seisaku no Hannou Kansuu* to Manee Sapurai), Bank of Japan (Kinyu Kenkyu).

Comments

Ulrich Baumgartner

Professor Yoshino's chapter deals with banking and corporate behavior as well as monetary policy and asset price developments during the so-called bubble period of the late 1980s and early 1990s. I agree with Professor Yoshino's description of the facts in Sections II and III and also with his conclusion that the call rate, rather than high-powered money, was used as the principal monetary policy instrument during 1980–91. With regard to the estimation results reported in Section V, they are subject to the limitations implied by the simple VAR estimations. A more rigorous model would have been preferable.

To complement Professor Yoshino's chapter, I would like to summarize briefly how I see the experience from the bubble period.

The surge in Japan's asset prices in the second half of the 1980s – when stock prices tripled and land prices doubled – seems to have been caused by several factors. Although some, and perhaps most, of the increase in asset prices surely was attributable to a speculative bubble, fundamentals also played a significant role. In part, the increase in the prices of real estate and equities reflected the unusually rapid growth in the economy, which is likely to have created expectations of higher medium-term growth opportunities. Another part of the asset price inflation can be attributed to easy monetary policy which led to a decline in interest rates and to a consequent ballooning of the present values of future profits and rents. The empirical work of Professor Yoshino's chapter emphasizes the importance of this factor. A third contributing factor was excessive risk-taking associated with changes in the financial environment. Let me elaborate a little on each of these three factors.

Regarding fundamentals, expectations of growth in earnings from assets are likely to have changed after the mid-1980s. After being almost stagnant in the first half of the 1980s, corporate profits increased by 70 percent in the second half of the decade, which could have created expectations of permanently higher growth opportunities and contributed to higher stock prices. Although rents increased no faster than nominal GDP, expectations of large capital gains are likely to have fueled land price increases. The mid-to-late 1980s also witnessed deregulation and structural changes in the economy, which may have created widespread optimism about the growth prospects of the economy. Some researchers also claim that the risk premium on Japanese equities declined in the second half of the 1980s. Possible reasons for the decline in the risk premium include a change in the distribution of wealth toward less risk averse investors (such as large institutional investors).

Concerning the second factor, monetary policy, there is ample evidence of monetary ease in the late 1980s: the growth of money stock was extraordinarily rapid and interest rates were comparatively low. In addition to these indicators, it is instructive to look at a broader indicator of monetary conditions to gauge the impact on domestic demand. Such an indicator would not only consider movements in real interest rates but would also take account of exchange rate developments. A 'monetary conditions index' incorporating short-term real interest rates and the real effective exchange rate, and weighting them according to their estimated impact on future real aggregate demand, was derived by the Fund staff from the IS curve of a small macro model of the Japanese economy.[1] The model suggests that a 1 percentage point change in the short-term interest rate has about the same effect on domestic demand as a 10 percent change in the real effective exchange rate. One interesting result suggested by this indicator in that, despite low interest rates, monetary conditions in this broad sense were relatively tight during 1986–7, because of the sharp yen appreciation. This situation was reversed subsequently, partly as a result of the depreciation of the yen beginning in late 1988. In fact, fairly easy financial conditions prevailed through mid-1990, despite the increase in interest rates from mid-1989 onward. Thus, easy financial conditions continued for some time notwithstanding the tightening of monetary policy.

While monetary ease appears to have contributed to the asset price bubble, the question of causality between the rapid growth of the money stock during this period and the rise in equity prices deserves further investigation. The equity price bubble has frequently been attributed to the creation of excess liquidity, which in turn drove up asset prices. However, a closer look at the data shows that from 1985 to 1991 movements in equity prices systematically led those in monetary velocity by an average of 2–3 quarters. In fact, conditions in equity markets may well be relevant in explaining money demand through effects other than the direct impact on financial wealth (which is an explanatory variable in standard demand for money functions). For instance, a decline in equity returns may induce firms to increase liquidity by issuing a greater volume of equities and equity-linked debt. Such a phenomenon appears to have occurred in the late 1980s, when the boom in equity prices was accompanied by a surge in the issuance of equity-linked instruments by Japanese corporations. While part of the proceeds at that time were used to finance record levels of business fixed investment, the inflow of funds also contributed to the sharp increase in corporate liquidity and bank deposits. Experiments with money demand equations incorporating lagged stock prices[2] as a proxy for financing conditions in equity markets produce encouraging results. The coefficient of the equity price variable is positive and significant, and the equation tracks actual developments in money stock (M2+CDs) better than money demand specifications excluding equity prices.

This evidence, together with the fact that changes in money velocity lagged equity prices, suggests a different story from the traditional one. While the equity price bubble appears to have been, in part, associated with low interest rates, rapid money growth does not seem to have been an independent cause of asset price inflation. Rather, money growth accelerated as a result of the surge in asset prices, which in turn reflected – among other factors – low interest rates and rapid growth in economic activity and profits. Therefore, developments in money stock are not a good leading indicator of equity prices.

The third factor behind the asset price developments was the change in the financial environment in the second half of the 1980s. Japan had entered the 1980s with a tightly regulated financial system, but during the decade extensive reforms were instituted: controls on capital movements were dismantled; interest rates on deposits were deregulated; and markets were introduced for new instruments such as commercial paper, futures, and options. While the deregulation went a long way toward enhancing competition and improving the efficiency of the financial system, it also gave rise to two major developments that fueled asset price inflation in the late 1980s. First, bank and non-bank lending to the real estate sector increased sharply, reflecting changes in the behavior of both lenders and borrowers. As large manufacturing corporations had access to international capital and securities markets, their reliance on bank loans declined dramatically. This development made small- and medium-sized enterprises and households primary customers of banks and released loanable funds to non-manufacturing sectors, especially real estate. This shift led to an apparent increase in the riskiness of banks' loan portfolios, while increased competition prevented lending rates from rising sufficiently to compensate for the higher risk. By end-1989, bank loans outstanding to real estate related activities had more than doubled in value since 1985 and accounted for almost one fourth of the banks' total loan portfolio. During this period, non-banks (which are more lightly regulated than banks) were even more aggressive than banks in financing real estate transactions. Second, the liberalized financial environment, together with the easy monetary conditions, gave non-financial corporations opportunities for financial arbitrage and improved credit availability for households. As a result, financial investment increased sharply and was to a significant extent channeled into the stock market, driving equity prices up.

Notes

1. 'Discretionary Monetary Policy Versus Rules: The Japanese Experience During 1986–91', International Monetary Fund (WP/92/63).
2. Ratio of Nikkei 225 index to trend nominal GDP.

Comments

Akiyoshi Horiuchi

The purpose of Professor Yoshino's chapter is to give an overview of structural changes in the Japanese financial system during the 1980s and early 1990s from two points of view: a statistical investigation of balance sheet changes with respect to both financial and non-financial sectors and a VAR time series-based analysis of the Japanese macroeconomy.

Japan experienced rather abnormal financial expansion during the 1980s leading to some instability in the financial system in the early 1990s which we have not yet fully recovered from. Many are seriously concerned with why we experienced such financial excesses and how we can prevent a recurrence. Thus, Professor Yoshino's chapter is quite timely. But, in my opinion, his chapter is unfinished and hence I would like to make some suggestions for making it more complete.

The first part of the chapter (i.e., Sections II and III) details changes in the behavior of both the banking sector and the non-financial corporate sector from the mid-1980s, mainly relying on balance sheet statistics. The data in Professor Yoshino's chapter clearly shows that the financial system has undergone dramatic structural change. Of particular note is that corporate finance has been securitized. For example, the relative importance of bank loans has decreased considerably, whereas, in turn, the amount of funds raised by issuing corporate bonds has increased. On the other hand, the banking sector increased loans extended to real estate and non-bank financial institutions, which consequently led to the huge non-performing loan problem. Meanwhile, the gap between the average yield on loans and average interest rate on deposits decreased, exerting strong pressure on the management of banks and related financial institutions.

Although these facts are widely known, Professor Yoshino's efforts to present them in a neat format should be appreciated. However, I am a little dissatisfied with the chapter because a lot of analysis remains unfinished. In particular, the chapter needs some hypotheses to explain the structural change in the Japanese financial system.

For example, while the chapter suggests that the loosening of the regulatory environment (such as deregulation of deposit rates) encouraged banks to expand risk taking, it does not explain how and why financial liberalization expanded risk taking. In my opinion, risk taking by private banks has something to do with the existence of safety-net mechanisms as well as the decline in the franchise value of the banking industry, as emphasized in the Nakajima–Taguchi chapter. At any rate, I would like to have a more detailed explanation of structural changes than is mentioned in Professor Yoshino's chapter.

In Section IV, Professor Yoshino briefly discusses the Bank of Japan's monetary policy. Specifically, he investigates whether the Bank of Japan has used high-powered money or the interbank money market rate as an instrument of monetary control. Based on the exogeneity test introduced in another paper with Revankar, he concludes that the interbank money market rate was utilized as an instrument variable. This conclusion corresponds with what the staff of the Bank of Japan has long claimed, and I would not dispute him on the subject. The result is a noteworthy achievement. However, I cannot clearly understand why Professor Yoshino introduces the argument concerning the Bank of Japan's monetary control in this part of his chapter. He should have structured his chapter so that readers could follow the thread of his argument. Professor Yoshino found some structural changes in the policy reaction of the Bank of Japan between 1979 and 1980, which was when the Foreign Exchange Law was significantly amended with a view to liberalizing constraints on international capital movements. So, does the finding have something to do with this liberalization? Professor Yoshino should have given some explanation in this regard.

In Section V, Professor Yoshino introduced a VAR macroeconomic model consisting of seven variables such as the call rate and real output. The introduction of a VAR model seems to be somewhat abrupt to me, because this section does not have a reasonable connection with earlier sections. It is a little unfortunate that analysis in this part is practically independent from the analyses in the first half.

What story does Professor Yoshino derive from the VAR estimation? He takes up the movement of land prices. This is a good idea because we Japanese have been very concerned with volatile changes in land prices since the mid-1980s. He found that since the beginning of the 1980s, land prices have been more strongly influenced by changes in money supply. This finding is interesting, but he does not explain the implications. Needless to say, a VAR estimation is nothing more than a summary of various statistical relationships. Therefore, we need a relevant hypothesis of macroeconomic movements if the VAR estimation is to be meaningful. Frankly, I think the latter half of his chapter is also unfinished.

Part III
Prudential Policy and Financial Stability

7 Prudential Regulation for Banks

Mark J. Flannery

I INTRODUCTION

Banking firms around the world operate under extensive government supervision and regulation. In part, these regulatory structures seek to reduce the likelihood that individual banks will fail, and these are the regulatory components which I define as 'prudential' in this chapter. Prudential regulations include minimum capital requirements, liquidity or loan portfolio diversification standards, limitations on a bank's investment portfolio or lines of business, and other restrictions intended to limit the type of risks which a banking firm may undertake. This chapter's main purpose is to evaluate the role of prudential government regulation of modern banking firms in developed financial markets. This evaluation cannot be undertaken without first establishing the appropriate purpose of government bank regulation. Indeed, an argument for prudential regulation implicitly asserts that the supervision and control exerted by private market forces is somehow inappropriate. Carefully specifying and addressing this contention constitutes a large part of my analysis here.

The chapter is organized as follows. Section II lays out the appropriate way to specify the chapter's central question: what is the role of prudential bank regulation in a developed economy? The following section describes the social benefits associated with private capital market devices for monitoring, disciplining, and controlling risk-taking in unregulated firms. The argument here is that private firms (including banks) with many, complicated investment and growth options are inherently difficult to control, and that a flexible, dynamic system of market regulation can provide a serious alternative to government regulation. Section IV evaluates several prominent situations for which prior writers have contended that private markets cannot fulfill their customary supervisory role for banking firms. In particular, I address the contentions that outside investors do not adequately understand banking firms, or that bank failures entail large, external social costs.

Both theory and evidence strongly suggest that market discipline could, if left to itself, effectively identify and control bank failure risks, at least for the class of large banks with widely traded equity and debt claims. Section V considers the 'political' or 'time inconsistency' reasons for government risk-bearing in the financial sector. These powerful forces are likely to elicit important re-distributions of certain private credit losses; market expectations about these *ex post* government interventions will influence the market's *ex ante* ability to monitor and control banking firms. This analysis of private and public market failures implies an appropriate role for government regulation, which is described and evaluated in Section VI. I distinguish here between 'prudential' regulations (which are designed to reduce the probability of bank failure) and 'pricing' regulations (which are designed to make private investors confront the full social costs of their risk-taking decisions), and conclude that the role for prudential regulation is rather more limited than has been understood in the past. The final section summarizes and concludes.

II DEFINING AN ANALYTICAL FRAMEWORK

All firms with outside claimants are subjected to supervision and control by outside monitors. Indeed, many aspects of private financal contracts are designed to enhance the liquidity of corporate claims by identifying and controlling the risks to which purchasers will be exposed. Banks are unusual primarily in the extent to which this supervision is provided by government agents.

A firm's main economic problem when seeking outside financing is how to obtain the required funds without compromising the owner/manager's incentives to maximize firm (and hence) social value. Private investors not only price the risks they perceive in a firm's operations, but also take steps to control and monitor that risk via corporate governance features, restrictive covenants in debt, mandatory disclosure of relevant news, etc.[1] Outside claimants with their own welfare tied to their firms' success or failure have a strong incentive to understand, constrain, and monitor corporate decisions, without stifling the firm's incentives to undertake valuable new projects. In controlling insured banking firms, government must address the same problems the market confronts when seeking to control an unregulated firm. The goal of government supervision is to ameliorate whatever market failure has generated the need for government action, without impeding financial firms' abilities to innovate new products and provide customers with valuable financial services.[2] The alternative to government regulation is *not* a completely unsupervised banking system, but one supervised by the same market forces which presently govern unregulated firms. The recent proposals to reform government systems of financial regulation implicitly recognize the potential efficacy of market supervision. These proposals would change the relative reliance on market versus government regulation, in hope of improving the quality of oversight provided.

Market Supervision Reflects Conjectured Government Policies

Market supervisory systems intimately reflect the 'rules of the game' implicit in government supervision. Because market investors understand both the *de jure* and the likely *de facto* future actions of government agents, private institutional arrangements at any given time depend upon the pertinent government policies. Accordingly, a regulatory change will inevitably induce market responses (Kane, 1981), which we must anticipate in order to evaluate the policy change fully. For example, some observers currently claim that financial derivatives markets would be severely harmed by the failure of one large market maker. But, of course, with a conjectured government policy of protecting large banks' creditors ('too big to fail', or TBTF), market participants have no incentive to prefer a larger number of smaller OTC dealers. If government regulators were thought willing to let such a large market maker fail, traders would take steps to avoid large, undiversified credit risk exposures, and we would surely see new market makers enter. Would the augmented system of traders be more expensive? The private costs would surely rise. But current cost assessments omit the value of a conjectural TBTF guarantee, making the present system more costly than the private participants perceive.

While there is no reason to believe that the market could perfectly provide all elements of a government safety net, it can provide at least some. Considerations of regulatory reform must recognize that (actual or anticipated) changes in government actions will elicit potentially dramatic responses in private institutional arrangements. The crucial element in evaluating these changes must be a cost-benefit analysis of the entire set of changes. Such analyses are difficult because the private costs of institutional reform are generally quite apparent, while the benefits are more diffused and less obvious. It is important to emphasize that government and market supervision substitute for one another, and reducing the extent of government oversight will elicit greater oversight by the banking firms' private claimants.

Comparing Supervisory Systems

Any evaluation of regulatory reform must compare the ability of market versus government systems to induce banking firms to pursue appropriate social goals. Because neither system will be perfect in executing its responsibilities, we must make these comparisons with care. The salient question is not whether private investors *can* evaluate and control bank activities, but whether they are likely to do a *more effective* job than government. Which broad mechanism for regulating financial firms produces better results, *on average*? Empirical evidence on this important question is extremely limited, but well worth developing.[3] One difficulty encountered in trying to compare market and regulatory assessments of bank quality is that the latter are highly confidential. So long as regulators remain secretive about their assessments of individual firms' conditions, it will be impossible to determine whether market supervision is truly inferior to government supervision based on 'inside information'.

Categories of Government Regulation

In common parlance, the term 'regulation' applies to any impact of government authorities on private firms. However, the broad set of bank regulations should be divided into three distinct categories.

(1) 'Prudential regulations.' Some bank regulations prohibit or require specific actions, with the intention of limiting bank risk exposures. Examples include minimum capital and liquidity requirements, loan diversification standards, activity and ownership restrictions, deposit rate ceilings, and restrictions on the type of information banks may release to the public. These restrictions fit Stigler's definition of regulation as 'any policy which alters market outcomes by the exercise of some *coercive* government power.' (quoted in Capie and Wood (1991, p. xiii), emphasis added).

(2) 'Pricing schedules.' This set of government prescriptions does not prohibit or require specific activities, but is designed to charge

private firms a fair (i.e. non-distortionary) price for risks borne by the government. Under the Basel capital standards, for example, a bank's required capital reflects its chosen asset portfolio. Bankers are not *prohibited* from concentrating their investments in risky private loans, but if they do, the government requires additional private equity investment. Unlike prudential regulations, government pricing schedules do not seek to constrain a regulated firm's activities.

(3) 'Closure rules.' The government also influences bank operations, and bank creditors' loss exposures, by controlling the rules of closure and bankruptcy. This legal framework defines creditors' claims on troubled firms, and partially determines the type of *ex ante* contractual arrangements available to govern and control banks. The cumbersome and slow methods employed to close failed US financial institutions during the 1980s substantially raised the government's cost of absorbing financial sector risks (Pyle, 1986; Barth *et al.*, 1990). Many recent proposals to reform government safety nets include (explicitly or implicitly) a substantial element of bankruptcy policy reform for banking firms. Most prominent in this regard are the provisions of FDICIA which require regulators to close a bank that becomes 'critically undercapitalized', even when the bank's book equity value remains positive. For example, Benston and Kaufman's (1988) structured early intervention and resolution (SEIR), which was substantially incorporated into US law via FDICIA in 1991, permits regulators to close banks which remain 'critically undercapitalized', even when they show positive (book) equity value[4] (Benston in Chapter 8 describes and analyzes SEIR).

III PRIVATE RISK-BEARING AND REAL ALLOCATIVE EFFICIENCY

In many countries, a formal or informal safety net has effectively substituted public risk-bearing for private supervision in the banking sector. This substitution would be unimportant if banking firms' financial structures did not influence their investment and operating decisions so prominently. However, banks specialize in providing loan services to customers who cannot readily access public security markets because their credit characteristics are costly or difficult to ascertain. Because many bank customers are difficult to understand, outside investors cannot impose blunt prior restrictions on bank activities without reducing their economic value.[5] At the same time, however, the owners of any levered firm possess clear incentives to enrich themselves at the expense of their creditors. Consequently, appropriately controlling bank investment incentives and risk preferences is a delicate and difficult problem. This section describes how private market investors govern firm operations, in order to illustrate the type of regulatory services that government risk-bearers must reproduce.

Financing Terms Affect Real Investments and Firm Value

Although the earliest research in modern finance assumed that firms' productive activities were unaffected by their financial structure, the modern view identifies important channels through which a firm's financial structure affects its real investment choices.[6] Begin with an imaginary economy in which firms issue no debt. The actions taken to maximize shareholder value will (trivially) also maximize the value of the entire firm. In the absence of substantial external effects, firm value maximization also yields the greatest attainable social welfare. When firms have outstanding debt, however, managerial efforts to maximize shareholders' value will not necessarily maximize the firm's total value. Debt financing creates an opportunity for equity-holders to extract value from debt-holders, either by increasing leverage or by substituting riskier assets for those which had existed when the debt was first sold (Galai and Masulis, 1976). The central importance of monitoring arises because debt contracts must be structured in a way that mitigates shareholders' ability to pursue non-maximizing agendas.

If borrowing firms offered for sale only straight unsecured debt without restrictive covenants, potential investors would rationally anticipate equity-holders' future incentives to expropriate their wealth, and would accordingly lower the price they offer for new bonds.[7] This could reduce the bonds' value below the amount required to implement a new investment project, making some socially productive investments unprofitable for equity-holders to undertake. Being unable to finance worthwhile projects would reduce the value of equity-holders' stake in the firm, giving them a clear incentive to design restrictive debt covenants which will prevent detrimental asset substitutions. In other words, by agreeing to forego certain types of future activities, the equity-holders can obtain financing on terms which actually *raise* the value of their equity, as well as increasing the firm's total value added in society.

Smith and Warner (1979) report that corporate bond covenants frequently specify that:

(1) the borrower may not sell firm assets;
(2) the borrower may not hold substantial amounts of financial assets;
(3) the borrower's dividend payments are limited during the life of the debt.

It may appear that these covenants are equivalent to prudential regulations, which definitively prohibit certain firm choices. But bond covenants actually represent the outcome of a bargaining process between debtors and creditors, in which the debtor receives a lower bond rate in return for agreeing to forego certain future actions.[8] Covenants constitute an essential component of the bond pricing schedule, because they ensure that private investors bear only the risks for which they are being compensated.

Another real cost of debt financing is the levered firm's incentive to 'underinvest' in valuable projects which transfer benefits to the firms' existing debt-holders via a reduction in their default risk exposure (Myers, 1977). Once again, firm owners have the incentive to contract around this situation in order to increase the value of their equity claim. Stulz and Johnson (1985) show that a firm can profitably undertake a broader range of new investment projects if it pledges the new assets as security for the bonds issued to finance the projects. By securing new debt, but not the outstanding debt, with the new project's cash flows, the firm minimizes the wealth transferred to old bond-holders, thereby making it more profitable to implement a new, value-creating project.[9]

Finally, market supervisory forces will seek to maximize firm value by influencing the scope and corporate organization of the firm's productive activities. For example, equity-holders will vote to prevent value-destroying mergers, and takeover markets force managers to organize their firms in an optimal fashion and to spin off activities which do not add sufficiently to the firm's overall value. Within multi-divisional firms, Flannery, Houston and Venkataraman (1993) and Kahn (1993) show how the structure of subsidiaries' financing can influence the deadweight costs of leverage.

These examples clearly indicate that the private capital market does more than supply investable resources to productive firms. Market supervision selects the securities and corporate structure which best complement each firm's particular situation. Covenants are not designed to *minimize* borrower risks, but to constrain the investors' *ex post* risk to the level for which they are being compensated.[10] Market investors effectively offer borrowers a schedule of price-covenant combinations, and the borrower selects the point on that schedule which maximizes the value of his firm's attainable investment portfolio. Firms with different operating characteristics will optimally select different financial structures. Each firm employs the combination of equity, debt, and restrictive covenants which maximizes its market value. Optimal financial arrangements may change over time, both for an individual firm and for financial markets in general, as perceived risks change.

Why Prefer Private Risk-bearing?

An economist's faith in market pricing derives from the fact that investors have *voluntarily* accepted the risks associated with a particular security. Self-interested private investors gather and interpret financial information, and then design appropriate (value-maximizing) restrictive covenants for each firm seeking market finance. Indeed, because investors in developed capital markets *need not* purchase risky private securities, those who choose to do so will tend to have a comparative advantage in evaluating firms' plans and prospects.[11] Under a system of market supervision, society's best risk evaluators have their opinions impounded into security designs and prices. With many investors evaluating the potential cash flows to each firm, asset prices should reflect an informed consensus about each firm's value added in the market. Securities market prices convey these collective assessments to firm managers.

Importantly, managers need not possess extraordinary sophistication for investors' assessments to influence their real investment decisions. Suppose the manager of a widget-making firm believes that a new production process will produce her present output and quality levels at substantially lower cost. The new process requires an initial investment of, say, $1 million, which must be obtained from external sources. The project can be undertaken only if outside investors agree that the investment's expected payoffs are sufficient to compensate for the perceived risks. Put another way, the manager can sell $1 million of new securities only if she can convince many informed investors that the project is worth undertaking.[12] If numerous outside evaluators jointly make better investment decisions than a single manager would, the market valuation process generates better real investment allocations than a process which relies on fewer and/or less informed evaluators of new projects.[13]

In private financial markets, sophisticated investors provide evaluation and monitoring services which affect the riskiness and value added of the firms whose securities they hold. Because a banking firm's value depends so importantly on its incentives to make appropriate investment and asset deployment decisions, it is particularly important that its financial contracts contain appropriate constraints. Of course, private investors supply valuable monitoring services only if they perceive a sufficient benefit to themselves from controlling firm risks. If the government chooses to absorb some bank creditors' losses, it will reduce the supply of private monitoring services, *and must itself provide substitute services.* Given the prominent role of bank credit analysis in real investment allocations, therefore, government's ability to monitor and control insured banks' activities could be extremely important to social welfare.

IV DO EXTERNALITIES JUSTIFY PRUDENTIAL BANK REGULATION?

In assessing whether governments should bear risk on behalf of the banking sector, Friedman (1959, pp. 3–4) asks 'whether monetary and banking arrangements cannot be left to the market, subject only to the general rules applying to all other economic activity.'[14] One common response to this question is that private market externalities may reduce social welfare from its highest attainable level. Stiglitz (1993) states unequivocally that 'There *is* a role for the state in financial markets; it is a role motivated by *pervasive market failure*' (p. 39, second emphasis added.)

The existing literature identifies four specific market failures which (uniquely for banks?) might be corrected by government action:

(A) private investors have inappropriate incentives to obtain financial information,

(B) private investors and depositors cannot accurately evaluate the true credit condition of banking firms,

(C) private credit evaluation is inefficient or ineffective for some classes of market investors, and
(D) bank failures generate serious costs for other, unrelated agents in the economy.

I will argue that Case A is qualitatively similar for banks and non-banks, and hence cannot readily justify special treatment of banking firms. Case B is quite widely accepted, but the available (limited) empirical evidence indicates that market investors can, and do, make reasonable credit judgments about banking firms when they have the private incentive to do so. Accordingly, this possible externality provides scant support for government regulation.[15] By contrast, Case C seems to justify government intervention in banking, but only for the protection of small, unsophisticated depositors. Case D is qualitatively different from the other three potential market failures, because it could uniquely support prudential regulations if the external costs of bank failures were sufficiently large. While I know of no direct evidence measuring the external costs of bank failure, a theoretical discussion of the issues suggests that they are likely to be relatively limited.

The overall conclusion from this section is that negative banking externalities do not provide a strong basis for believing that government intervention will improve financial stability or real allocational efficiency.

Private Investors Produce Inefficient Amounts of Information

Competitive financial markets may not produce the proper ('first best') amount of financial information and analysis about individual firms' activities. When a firm is owned by many individual investors, any information gathered (or monitoring applied) by one investor will have benefits which accrue partly to the other owners of similar securities. In equilibrium, therefore, the market produces *too little* information about firm activities and credit quality. This situation limits the market's ability to impose discipline on firm managers and owners, whose private goals can conflict with social welfare maximization. Relatedly, when multiple investors must investigate and monitor a firm's investment proposals, some socially valuable projects will be unable to absorb all the (duplicate) research costs (Diamond, 1984).

However, it is by no means obvious that private markets produce too little financial information. Secondary market trading permits private gains to the acquisition of information whose cost may exceed its social value.[16] More relevant to an assessment of banking firms, multiple monitors might well produce differing assessments of a firm's true situation. When outsiders obtain noisy or heterogeneous information, no one can be certain that he has the proper ('true') view of the firm's prospects. In this situation, multiple monitors may improve real investment allocations, even net of the duplicate information costs.

All things considered, it is difficult to justify banking regulation on the basis of a broad assertion of inappropriate private monitoring. The possibility that information is not properly supplied applies to all firms with publicly traded securities, at least qualitatively. Moreover, even if bank investors *do* systematically under-produce financial information, prudential regulation would not directly address the problem.

The Market Cannot Identify or Control Bank Risks Effectively

A related contention about private investors is that they cannot evaluate bank values and strategies correctly – or, at least, they cannot do so at 'reasonable' cost. This assertion is at least plausible because banks' portfolio compositions change frequently and they specialize in financing informationally opaque assets.[17] Outside investors may find it unusually difficult to obtain timely information about their bank's credit quality. Consequently, the 'usual' devices by which outsiders control and discipline firms may function less well for banks.

The available evidence, however, fails to support this contention. In particular, three types of empirical research all indicate that market investors can and do discriminate rationally among banks: evaluations of bank default risk premia, the behavior of bank equity prices, and the behavior of small depositors during crises.[18] The Appendix provides a selective review of the empirical literature concerning bank depositors, note-holders, and equity-holders. The strong implication of these studies is that market investors can, and do, discriminate successfully among banks and identify relevant bank risk exposures *despite the fact that their incentives to do so are severely inhibited by the existence of conjectural government guarantees.*[19] This literature provides no indication that private market forces permit banks to fail too frequently, requiring government prudential regulations.

Some Bank Claimants (Depositors) Require Government Protection

Even if large, sophisticated investors *can* understand the riskiness of bank liabilities, do all depositors fit the mold of being sophisticated market investors? Garten (1986) and Merton (1990) identify an important distinction between a firm's 'investors' and its 'customers'. Investors voluntarily bear risk, and hence generate the salutary effects described in Section II. By contrast, customers wish to purchase a firm's output (e.g. a warranted automobile, a transfer of funds, or an OTC financial derivative), and must become a firm creditor in order to do so. Unlike investors, customers generally find it relatively costly to diversify their credit exposures. This constraint reduces welfare, as customers purchase less of the associated product than they would purchase if there were no credit risk attached.

Who, then, are a bank's 'customers'? One relevant group is surely individuals with relatively modest means. Their deposit balances are too small to permit effective diversification across financial service providers, and they have no comparative advantage in assessing credit risk. Accordingly, forcing these individuals to bear default risk will entail large (deadweight) costs. Such depositors will strongly prefer securities with little default or price risk (Gorton and Pennacchi, 1990). Although private market arrangements could surely cater to these individuals, they would always be subject to some residual risk.[20] In his influential paper about deposit insurance pricing, Merton (1977) asserts that government insurance is more efficient than leaving all private depositors to evaluate bank risks:

> for the small depositor particularly, there are large information and surveillance costs to be saved if the institutional structure of the bank were such that the safety of the deposits was assured without requiring these analyses.... A sensible ... choice would be to have third-party guarantees.... For the scale of the banking system, this almost certainly means that the third party would be the government or one of its agencies.
>
> (pp. 3–4)

Accordingly, it seems that both efficiency and equity arguments support government provision of deposit insurance for unsophisticated depositors.[21, 22]

Large corporations and investors also constitute 'customers' to the extent that their need for financial services forces them to accept substantial credit exposure to their banks. The analogy to small depositors is imperfect, however, for three reasons.

(1) The evidence in the Appendix indicates that these 'customers' can appropriately evaluate their banks' true risks.
(2) Physical location is less important to their banking relationships, so they can select from a greater number of financial service providers.
(3) Undiversified risk is less important to these customers, because their owners are well diversified (e.g. through traded stock, pension plan participants, etc.).

In short, large bank customers should be less sensitive to bank default risk, and better able to avoid undesired credit risk exposures.

However, changing banks is costly. As an alternative, riskier banks could develop new ways to provide large customers with financial services without credit risk exposure. Suppose a weakening bank wishes to continue providing transaction services, for which it possesses a comparative advantage. Because the bank will already understand its customers' creditworthiness, it can make payments against prearranged (overdraft) lines of credit. Alternatively, customers could invest in marketable securities (perhaps through RP agreements with their banks), and have the bank sell enough securities at day's end to cover their net debits.[23]

Another bank service which presently requires that customers bear bank default risk is derivatives trading (like swaps or foreign exchange forward contracts). For many large corporations and financial firms, the default risk on OTC derivative securities will be even more important than the risk exposures generated by payments services. During the 1980s, several large participants in the international market for swaps and forwards suffered substantial credit quality declines. As these banks weakened, their trading counterparts became less willing to deal with them, particularly for longer-dated contracts (Bank for International Settlements, 1992, p. 15). In response, some banks formed separately-capitalized subsidiaries to conduct their derivatives business. This type of structural change reflects an important type of 'market discipline', which influences not only a bank's funding costs but its ability to earn fees on brokerage transactions.

The private costs of providing payments, derivatives, foreign exchange, and other financial services are probably minimized under our current institutional arrangements. (Otherwise, why have market participants chosen the status quo?) Does this mean that alternative institutional arrangements are socially inferior? Not necessarily. Private evaluations of existing arrangements omit the social costs of the associated explicit and implicit guarantees. For example, if the central bank regulates payments system participants in order to prevent large failures, these regulations generate costs – including both the out-of-pocket costs of regulating and the potential for efficiency losses in providing financial services – which are difficult to identify and total up. Indeed, because the private costs of alternative payment or trading arrangements are obvious, while the social benefits are less tangible, it is easy to presume that the net social costs of alternative institutional arrangements are higher than the status quo's. Such presumptions are to be avoided, and cost comparisons should be based on careful cost/benefit analysis applied to all participants in the financial system.

The most efficient institutional arrangements for the financial sector will likely vary from country to country, according to the extent of the national financial infrastructure. For example, market investors can identify and control corporate risks only if they have access to a consistent accounting system with auditor-confirmed integrity. Similarly, assertions that relatively uninformed investors can obtain accurate information from private rating agencies may be appropriate in only a relatively few nations with well-developed capital markets.[24] And a collateralized system of interbank payments may be perfectly feasible for economies with deep supplies of liquid assets, but extremely expensive (or impossible) for other nations. Even while recognizing the dependence of market supervisory forces on financial infrastructure, we must reiterate that a nation's existing supply of auditors, credit raters, or liquid assets depends crucially on the private demand for these services. A shift in anticipated government actions will elicit compensating responses in private market arrangements. The need to forecast private sector changes complicates the cost-benefit analysis of institutional changes, but does not eliminate the value of such specific analyses.

Bank Failures Generate Serious External Costs

This justification for government involvement in banking is qualitatively different from the first three, in which the alleged market failures involved individuals who had *chosen* to associate with a given bank.

By contrast, if a bank's failure imposes costs on unrelated economic agents, we have a standard public goods externality. Large external costs could justify prudential regulations to reduce the number of bank failures, directly addressing the source of the inefficiency. Since governments do not generally intervene to prevent non-financial firms' failure, however, we must establish that bank failures generate larger (or qualitatively different) externalities than those associated with other firms.

Why might this be true? The existing literature contains three broad suggestions:

(1) that one bank's failure can cause other financial firms to fail, even if they are truly solvent; or
(2) that the economy's payments system could be harmed by a single bank's failure; or
(3) that numerous bank failures will interfere with efficiency in real sector investment allocations.

I consider each of these arguments in turn.

1. Financial System 'Fragility'

A substantial proportion of bank regulation derives directly from the fear that bank failures are contagious: that one bank's failure will endanger other, truly solvent, banks. If one bank's failure causes other banks' depositors to suspect their banks' solvency, they will rationally run to withdraw deposits before the bank is closed and losses are apportioned among the remaining depositors.[25] Even a solvent bank may be ruined by a depositor run, given the illiquid nature of many bank assets.

The first important thing to note about depositor runs is that not all runs are socially costly. Runs against truly insolvent banks will force them to close more promptly, which minimizes creditors' losses from the failure (Kaufman, 1993).[26] By contrast, harmful (socially costly) bank runs could occur if one bank's failure causes depositors to run against *sound* banks. The targets of these derivative runs would incur transaction or liquidity costs (at least) or bankruptcy costs (at most), in a classic case of external cost imposition. The crucial question is whether contagious runs are likely to occur often in a less regulated financial system.

Contagion requires not one, but two layers of private market error. First, depositors must be unable to reliably differentiate between solvent and insolvent banks. Evidence cited in the Appendix indicates that at least the more sophisticated bank investors and depositors can reliably identify a bank's credit condition. Nevertheless, what if sophisticated depositors mistakenly believe that their bank has become insolvent? Or what if a bank's depositors are not sophisticated enough to make a sound decision? Then other, sophisticated market lenders – such as correspondent banks or money managers – should be willing to extend sufficient liquidity to prevent a sound bank's failure. Serious costs of contagious bank failures thus require that *both* depositors and alternative suppliers of market liquidity fail to support a truly sound bank.

Surely such a joint failure is conceivable. If a large financial firm failed, rational customers would perhaps withdraw to Treasury securities in order to assess which other banks were subject to the same risks. If this reassessment takes very much time to accomplish, some solvent firms could fail in the interim. Goodhart (1988) and others conclude from this possibility that government should provide a lender of last resort facility to the financial system; the controversy is whether liquidity should be provided directly to illiquid banks, or whether open market operations should provide aggregate liquidity which can be allocated to the troubled firms via private lending mechanisms.[27]

On net, the danger of destructive, contagious bank runs seems unable to justify regulations intended to reduce banks' risk of failure. If depositors run only at banks which have been rendered insolvent by the same event(s) which caused the initial failure, runs will improve efficiency by hastening the resolution of truly insolvent institutions. No solvent bank will be threatened by a run if its depositors, other sophisticated market investors, *or* the lender of last resort is properly informed about the bank's true condition. Only if all three of these solutions seem likely to fail in practice would there be logical support for prudential regulations designed to reduce the incidence of bank failures. But in this case it seems odd to base the need for prudential government regulations on a presumption that the government lender of last resort will act inappropriately during a crisis.

2. Payments System Risk

An alternate route for financial system contagion allegedly operates through the payments system (Corrigan, 1992; Folkerts-Landau, 1990), where banks' interactions over a common network might permit one large bank's failure to impose debilitating credit losses on other banks in the system. Under standard payments system procedures, bankers deliver securities against contingent payments from other banks, and advance good funds against their customers' uncollected balances. Observers note the immense volume of daylight overdrafts generated by these payment arrangements, and worry that one bank's inability to settle will impose credit losses on other, unrelated banks. Furthermore, in the wake of a system problem firms might undertake fewer trades because of their increased awareness of payments-related credit risks, which would reduce the real sector's level of economic efficiency.

I have evaluated payments system risk in a previous paper (Flannery, 1988), concluding that payments system risk is basically a variant of credit risk. If banking firms confront appropriate incentives to control their credit risk exposures, payments system risk requires no special treatment to protect market integrity. Given the proper incentives, rational bankers would identify and control their payment system exposures in the same manner as they do for 'overnight' credit exposures.[28] The fact that these exposures are generated through the payments system elicits a further concern, that banks who are exposed to a failing institution will themselves have made intraday commitments to other institutions. If their losses to the failed institution render them insolvent, credit losses will be imposed on many other banks, even if they had no direct dealings with the initial institution.[29] The 'specialness' of payments system risk depends intrinsically on an assumption that individual banks accept – and must *continue* to accept – dangerously large daylight exposures to one another.[30]

The banks' evaluations of undiversified daylight exposures reflect their perceived risk exposure. If government is expected to provide cheap liquidity or absorb credit losses when a large bank fails, private incentives to avoid large daylight credit exposures will be blunted. Indeed, private benefits from diversifying one's intraday credit risk exposure within the current payments system seem negligible. Bankers have eschewed the opportunity to reduce their interbank exposures, despite the fact that these exposures could be substantially reduced by a small number of modest institutional changes.[31] There is no doubt that the present system of government guarantees has produced a riskless payments system. But collateralization, pricing of intraday exposures, or changes in delivery conventions for government securities could arguably provide payments stability with less government involvement. The difficult policy question is whether these institutional reforms would raise or lower social welfare.

In summary, systemic banking risks could reasonably justify

government prudential regulations, *provided* the associated costs were substantial. But the evidence that these costs might be large rests on institutional arrangements which reflect existing, conjectured government policies. Banks and their customers derive scant benefit in return for the private costs of diversification and collateralization. Accordingly, banks quite rationally operate with undiversified credit risk exposures, including exposures related to their payments system activities. If government could credibly withdraw from bearing bank default risks, it seems unlikely that the resulting levels of systemic risk would justify substantial government interventions into private market arrangements.

3. Investment Misallocations When Many Banks Fail

It has become common to hear that banks provide unique intermediation services to the economy, which enable entrepreneurs with valuable investment projects to obtain the funds required to implement their projects. For example, Bernanke (1983) observes that the decline in US economic output during the Great Depression exceeded the contemporaneous decline in monetary aggregates. He finds that real output changes during the 1930s were correlated with the number of bank failures, and suggests that bank failures tend to destroy valuable 'relationship capital' which reduces the supply of intermediation services to non-financial borrowers. Other authors have extended this notion to argue that bank failures can impose external costs on the economy's real sector, as entrepreneurs with valuable investment opportunities cannot obtain financing. Accordingly, the argument continues, the government should take steps to reduce the number of bank failures, in recognition of their external costs.

This argument can be challenged on several grounds. First, the cost of these lost relationships may not be extremely large, particularly as financial market competition becomes more intense via asset securitization and globalization. Second, it is unclear how much of the resulting costs should be counted as 'external' to the parties directly involved in the initial banking relationship.[32] Even granting that lost relationship assets would constitute a large external cost, however, provides no necessary basis for prudential bank regulation. The destruction of these valuable assets does not derive from the bank's failure, but from an inappropriate disposition of the failed bank's assets. If the existing legal structure for handling bank failures often destroys valuable relationship assets, government should seek a more appropriate mechanism for effecting financial reorganizations.

Only if this goal proves unattainable could the loss of relationship assets justify prudential regulations to prevent bank failures.[33]

To summarize this section, it seems that bank prudential regulation is difficult to justify on the basis of market externalities. Market investors are generally well informed, and would become more so if government reduced the extent of its safety net. While I would provide unsophisticated bank customers with (limited) government insurance to spare them the cost of credit analysis, the government should (and could) charge a fair premium for these risks. Thus far, therefore, we have seen no obvious role for prudential regulations in the banking system.

V GOVERNMENT BAIL-OUTS

The preceding section has evaluated the purely economic reasons why governments might reasonably regulate banking firms. This type of analysis follows directly from the familiar tenets of welfare economics. However, it suffers from two broad problems in application. First, its simple analytics provide limited 'real world' guidance: fixing one externality necessarily improves social welfare only if the economy is otherwise operating in a first-best equilibrium. Second, a broad range of potential market failures seem possible *a priori*, leaving the analyst to ponder differences of degree between similar cases, rather than the sharp-edged, qualitative differences offered by the classical microeconomic paradigm.[34]

An alternative paradigm for evaluating the need for prudential regulation might be termed the 'political' view, which holds that governments cannot avoid intervening when certain types of financial firms fail, or when certain types of voters are exposed to substantial credit losses (see, e.g., Kane (1990), Merton (1990), or Merton and Bodie (1992)). Even if all of the preceding section's arguments for government intervention in banking could be convincingly rejected on economic grounds, it would be naive to expect that banking would be left to operate in a substantially *laissez-faire* environment. Regulators would still come under irresistible *ex post* pressures to absorb or transfer some types of credit losses.[35]

Government would likely intervene in (at least) two types of financial crisis. First, if many small depositors were threatened with large losses, narrowly political factors would at least occasionally cause governments to absorb or otherwise defray those losses.[36] 'Parity' or 'equity' claims would probably enable large creditors to share in the benefits afforded their less sophisticated counterparts. Second, any situation which appeared to threaten a 'financial meltdown' would be extremely difficult for government officials to ignore. When confronting this second type of crisis, regulators' political incentives are clear: they can spend a relatively small amount of government money to bail out this (one) failing firms' creditors, or take the chance that the economy will suffer an immense loss due to government inactivity.[37]

The decision to intervene in market resolutions of a failed banking firm illustrates the time-consistency problem in government policy-making. Government would prefer to enlist the monitoring ability of private investors in their efforts to control bank risks, which makes it optimal (*ex ante*) for government to deny its willingness to absorb creditor losses. When an important banking firm fails, however, the government's cost-benefit trade-off changes. Now, the benefits of a 'non-intervention' policy have already accrued (in the form of private financial arrangements), so the potential costs of inaction tend to dominate.[38]

Discussions of time-consistent policies frequently consider the extent to which binding rules can prevent governments from revising their policies *ex post*.[39] Explicit rules make it more costly for regulators or politicians to make exceptions to *ex ante* policies, primarily because they make it easier for the public to identify such exceptions.[40] The US Congress has recently sought to replace some regulatory discretion with explicit rules for handling failed banks. (For example, FDICIA prohibits paying off uninsured depositors in full (after 1995) and requires staged interventions as a bank's capital ratio falls.) These statutory constraints are virtually unique among developed countries, yet even FDICIA does not seek to prevent all cases of *ex post* risk-bearing by governments: when the financial system is threatened, regulators can agree to implement a TBTF policy. Accordingly, it seems unrealistic to discuss regulatory policies without acknowledging the likelihood that governments will tend to bear risks *ex post*, at least in certain circumstances. Yet if the government is expected to absorb bank losses, private mechanisms for controlling and pricing risks will be compromised or eliminated, with deleterious real sector effects.[41] The risk-bearing government must replace these missing financial forces, either by charging a fair price for the risks it bears, or by otherwise negating the impact of the distorted private incentives on real investment and saving activity.

VI RISK PRICING AND PRUDENTIAL REGULATIONS

The available evidence indicates that at least some types of market discipline function appropriately, even in an environment where conjectural government guarantees severely curtail the private benefits of such behavior. If government could credibly withdraw from bearing bank risks, it seems likely that private creditors would adequately control and monitor uninsured banking firms. Realistically, however, government will never completely withdraw from bank risk-bearing. In special types of 'crisis' situations governments will decide to absorb or defray at least some private credit losses. In the best of all worlds, these cases would be rare; in reality, they are likely to be frequent enough that private institutional arrangements will prominently reflect conjectured *ex post* bail-outs. Moreover, I do not believe that small investors should be required to bear private credit risk in a market setting. Government should provide a (moderate sized) safe harbor to the sufficiently unsophisticated. While risk-free investment opportunities could be provided in the form of divisible treasury bills or a postal savings system, small savers can also be accommodated within a private banking system at relatively little net cost.[42]

Consequently, we must evaluate the need for government regulation of the financial system under the assumption that it will continue to bear some private credit risk.[43] The types of risk or the type of institution whose creditors can rationally anticipate *ex post* bail-outs must be carefully considered, but these particulars will vary from country to country. Whatever private risks the government accepts, however, will tend to distort private investment and savings decisions, causing deadweight social losses. These losses can be avoided only if the government charges for the private risks it takes on, and replaces the monitoring services that would otherwise be provided by private agents. Government 'monitoring services' take either of two forms. First, pricing schedules specify how government insurance premia vary with permissible bank activities.[44] Second, a variety of prudential regulations restrict bank risk-bearing or require specific actions to prevent private risks from spilling over into public liabilities.

Government Regulations as a Mechanism for Pricing Risk

In recent years, US (and other) regulators have been moving away from their traditional efforts to *control* insured banks' risk-taking, toward a policy of pricing the risks selected by each individual bank. For example, the Basel Accord's risk-based capital standards define a permissible tradeoff between asset risk and leverage for insured banks. Beginning in 1993, FDIC has defined nine distinct premium levels, which reflect a bank's capitalization and the regulatory assessment (CAMEL rating) of its overall condition. This insurance pricing schedule mimics market supervision via a system of explicit prices reflecting an assessment of the FDIC's default risk exposure.[45] Moreover, a bank can 'pay' for its insurance coverage by explicit fee *or* by raising its capital to reduce the insurer's risk exposure. Individual banks are free to choose their preferred combination of payments.

With symmetric information and no substantial external costs of bank failure, there is no additional role for prudential regulations which seek to limit the number of bank failures. Government should be able to define a non-distorting premium schedule for banking firms *even without* restricting their activities.[46] Banks could freely select their own risk exposures, and government would charge a compensating *ex ante* insurance premium. Serious implementation problems would accompany this type of regulatory structure. First, we would need to identify the set of 'insured' banks or creditors. Second, devising pricing rules ('covenants') for numerous types and combinations of financial activities would be a daunting task. Having addressed both these issues, however, government should passively accept all risks offered to it at the (actuarially fair) insurance premia. In other words, government should have no preference about the insured banks' probability of failure under symmetric information.

The Role of Prudential Regulations

The issues surrounding bank credit risk exposures are sufficiently complex that information is surely heterogeneous across private investors, as well as between the government and private investors. Financial firms' private risks can change quickly and the riskiness of individual activities (particularly new ones) can be subject to legitimate dispute. Finally, recall that market investors are specialists who have chosen to undertake risk evaluations, and to wager their own wealth on the proposition that they can recognize and control financial risks. Government agents are unlikely to compete effectively with private investors in assessing all types of private risk.

Under these circumstances, a government insurer must anticipate operating under a winner's curse. Insured lenders will tend to finance the activities for which market investors believe government has underpriced the risk. By contrast, if government *over*prices a risk, it will tend to be borne outside the insured financial system and hence have no distortive effect on real investment or savings. In this way, the government's prices for specific risks will unavoidably influence real resource allocations.[47] If private risk assessments are generally more accurate than government assessments, we cannot permit insured banks to operate freely in the areas for which government and private opinions differ markedly. Government can minimize real sector distortions by refusing to bear risks which are unusually difficult to value, or for which it has a large comparative disadvantage in assessments. *In other words, prudential regulations can reasonably be employed to limit the types of risks government must bear.*

I have provided a technical example of this role for prudential regulation in Flannery (1991), which evaluates the optimal means of charging for deposit insurance when the insurer measures a bank's true risk with error. Because risk measurement errors have a larger effect on fair insurance premia when the bank's leverage is higher, an insurer may rationally constrain a bank's permissible leverage when its asset portfolio appears to be highly risky. While this is not the same as a complete prohibition on some activities, the government's effort to minimize the real effects of its pricing errors will include restrictions on the bank's freedom to choose its own financial structure and portfolio composition.

Common prudential regulations include permissible investment limitations, ownership restrictions, liquidity or portfolio diversification standards, an absolute leverage constraint, and restrictions on the type of financial information banks may release to the public.[48] Rather than viewing these restrictions as government efforts to curtail the rate of bank failures, they should be viewed as necessary complements to the government's pricing efforts. If, for example, equity underwriting is too difficult for government appraisers to assess accurately, insured banks should be prohibited from underwriting. Similarly, if the potential conflicts of interest associated with an industrial firm owning a financial institution are large and impossible to control via covenants, the best response might be to prohibit such ownership.[49] Or if an insured bank's portfolio risk can be changed too quickly when it is permitted to hold equity investments, the bank should be prohibited from holding equity.

This role for prudential regulations directly implies that insured banks will appropriately be restrained from expanding into lines of business for which the regulator believes s/he has a comparative disadvantage in assessing risk.[50] Ideally, banks would be permitted to reject (explicit or implicit) insurance coverage, if regulators could not effectively supervise lines of business for which they possessed some comparative advantage. (The expanded, uninsured firm could seek a set of market supervisors who would presumably be more sympathetic toward the new activity.) Since an agreement to forego government risk-bearing would be (by assumption) time-inconsistent, however, some firms will not have the option to withdraw from the insurance system. The government's commitment to bear private risks therefore carries with it potential limitations on insured firms' activities.

As the institutional forms employed to deliver traditional financial services have evolved, many authors have advocated the principle that government should regulate the functions being performed, rather than the institutions which perform them.[51] My framework for justifying government regulation has two components. First, there are some specific firms whose failure is likely to induce government bailouts, at least under certain circumstances. Since these firms' default risk exposure must be priced accurately, pricing and prudential regulations must be directed at the institution being insured. Second, small savers' deposits will be insured at many types of banking firms. Schaefer (1992) points out that the government's risk in these cases depends on the covariation between the insured activity's payoffs and those of the rest of the firm's portfolio. Accordingly, two firms offering the same regulated product in the context of two different portfolios will properly be charged different prices for the risk they impose on taxpayers. For both these reasons, a *purely* functional basis for government regulation is inconsistent with my view of why governments should regulate banking firms.

VII SUMMARY AND CONCLUSIONS

This chapter has covered a broad range of topics, but the most important conclusions can be summarized under three specific headings: the plausibility of market supervisory systems, the need for careful assessments of alternative institutional arrangements' social costs and benefits, and the appropriate role for prudential regulation.

The broad (formal or informal) guarantee structures we presently observe in the US, Europe, much of Asia, and Japan have gone too far in absorbing private credit risks on behalf of sophisticated depositors. This overly-broad safety net has deprived banking firms of valuable oversight by talented investors who specialize in designing financial contracts which maximize firm values. Market investors who voluntarily bear financial risks appear to be well-informed; they discriminate reasonably among banks' underlying risks, even in a regulatory environment which provides little incentive for such private activities. The problems associated with monitoring and controlling risk-taking are not qualitatively different for banks and non-banks, and there seems little need for such an extensive system of bank regulation and inspection.

The challenge of undertaking regulatory reform within a framework of continued financial stability lies in comparing the social costs and benefits of the alternative institutional arrangements which can produce efficient, stable financial services. No regulatory system will be perfect; we should expect neither perfect stability nor perfect efficiency. The simple demonstration that markets (or government regulators) have made mistakes in the past does not constitute dispositive evidence that the market (government) is an inappropriate regulatory agent. Unfortunately, empirical evidence about how modern market forces behave in the absence of an extensive safety net is scarce, because this 'experiment' has never been run. Any increased reliance on market forces will therefore involve an unavoidable element of uncertainty. It seems increasingly clear, however, that continued reliance on the status quo entails deadweight efficiency losses which could be mitigated.

Regardless of the changes made in the *de jure* regulatory system, however, government is unlikely to withdraw entirely from the absorption of bank credit risks. Small investors should be provided with insured bank deposits, on equity if not on efficiency grounds. And political pressures (or time inconsistency in policy decisions) will doubtless cause governments to absorb at least some bank creditor losses under 'extreme' circumstances. The fact that government can be expected to bear certain private risks will influence investors' *ex ante* behavior in ways that weaken the allocational benefits of pure market forces. In order to avoid distorting private investment/savings decisions, government must charge an insurance premium commensurate with the risk it accepts. Generally, these risk charges should take the form of pricing *schedules*, from which an insured bank selects the combination of terms which permit it to provide the greatest volume of valuable financial services. When risks are difficult to measure, however, restrictive (prudential) regulations may be required to simplify the insurance pricing problem and avoid distorting private market prices. To the extent that government is an inefficient evaluator of new products' true risks, insured banking firms will be prohibited from innovating as extensively as their uninsured counterparts. This is a regrettable, but unavoidable, result of the government's inability to withdraw credibly from private risk-bearing in the financial sector.

Finally, this chapter has concentrated on 'what ought to be'. A separate question concerns the government's ability to regulate effectively. Whereas the naive economic view of a regulator is that she pathologically pursues the social good, less sanguine views also exist (Wolf, 1988; Kane, 1981). If government risk assessments are less accurate than the private sector's or if regulatory bodies are prone to capture by their intended charges (Stigler, 1971), unfettered market allocations might be preferable to regulated competition. I have basically ignored the possibility – some would say the likelihood – that regulations which can be justified in theory will be implemented incompetently or perversely. In doing so, I have probably overstated the case for government intervention in the financial sector.

APPENDIX: EMPIRICAL EVIDENCE ON BANK INVESTORS' ABILITIES TO DISCERN BANK CONDITION

Hard empirical evidence about the market's performance under more limited government guarantees is exceedingly scarce, primarily because that experiment has not been run under 'modern' financial conditions. Accordingly, we must seek indicative evidence where it is available. Pertinent empirical evidence exists on two dimensions of the market's ability to discern the true condition of banks with traded securities: bank debt (including subordinated notes and wholesale certificates of deposit) and bank equity values. In addition, limited evidence on the behavior of small depositors indicates that they can reliably identify weaknesses and discriminate between insolvent institutions and truly sound banks.

Bank Default Premia

If market investors perceive themselves at risk from holding certain types of bank liabilities, those liabilities should bear coupon rates related to that perceived risk. Two studies of large bank subordinated debentures (Avery, Belton and Goldberg, 1988; Gorton and Santomero, 1990) concluded that debenture rates in 1983–4 were substantially unrelated to accounting measures of bank risk. While this seems to support the contention that bank investors do not correctly perceive their credit risk exposures, there are two alternative, equally plausible, explanations. First, debenture holders in 1983 and 1984 may reasonably have conjectured that their investments were effectively guaranteed by the US government. Second, accounting measures of risk may be poor proxies for the indicators used by market participants. More recent evidence strongly suggests that bank subordinated debenture spreads incorporate substantial default risk premia: in 1990, these spreads frequently exceeded 500 basis points at the same time bank stock values were plummeting. Apparently, investors no longer perceive that strong conjectural guarantees apply to subordinated debt.

Authors studying the risk premia in large (mostly uninsured) certificates of deposit (Baer and Brewer, 1986; James, 1988, 1990; Hannan and Hanweck, 1988; Keeley, 1990; Cargill, 1989) have more frequently documented risk-related coupon rates. The most recent of these studies (Ellis and Flannery, 1992) demonstrates that large CD rates respond to the same information that moves the stock prices of six large, money-center banks. This study is particularly encouraging for proponents of market discipline, because their sample banks possess the strongest conjectural ('too big to fail') guarantees available in the market.

Bank Equity Returns

Because bank shareholders hold the residual claim on a bank's cash flows, stock prices should immediately reflect changes in perceived asset values.[1] The salient question is how market investors infer asset value changes for banking firms, and whether contagion is an important component of this revaluation process. One bank's failure might influence the market's assessment of other banks for either of two reasons (Aharoney and Swary, 1983). First, if other banks shared a risk exposure with the failed bank, their claimants would *rationally* perceive greater risk. This constitutes a normal and desirable aspect of efficient financial markets, in which investors' actions convey appropriate signals to bank managers. Second, other banks' claimants might *irrationally* infer that their own banks' quality had deteriorated.

Their irrational response – in the form of deposit withdrawals or higher required deposit rates – would impose (inappropriate) costs on other banks, perhaps to the point of forcing their failure.

However, stock market event studies can shed some light on the extent to which investors revise their assessment of one bank's value in response to information about another bank's problems. If bank shareholders react (ir)rationally to information about another bank's problems, then arguably uninsured depositors would behave similarly. Aharoney and Swary (1983) analyze bank stock reactions to three large failures from the 1970s. In two instances, they find that other banks' stock prices did not respond at all. For the third case (Franklin National Bank, in 1973), they conclude that 'the observed drop in solvent bank stock prices may be interpreted as investors' reaction to a common type of unfavorable signal, rather than a pure contagion effect' (p. 321).

Swary (1986) employs a similar methodology to evaluate market reactions to Continental Illinois' 1984 troubles. He reports that other banks experienced market value declines when Continental's problems were announced, and these negative returns were larger for poorly capitalized banks. He interprets these negative market reactions as rational conjectures about the banks' true asset values, rather than shareholders' fear of depositor runs: This finding is strongly consistent with the hypothesis that market reactions reflect a rational response under imperfect information to new evidence of regulatory policy and banks' asset quality (p. 471).

Still further evidence that bank investors rationally process new information comes from Smirlock and Kaufold (1987) or Musumeci and Sinkey (1990), who both report that negative news about LDC loans affected banks in proportion to their actual exposures.[2]

The Behavior of Small Depositors

The experience of US banks suggests that, even in crisis situations, small depositors have been able to discriminate between solvent and insolvent banks. Kane (1987) evaluates depositor withdrawals from Ohio thrift institutions during the state's insurance fund crisis of March 1985. He finds that depositors 'ran' only against state-insured thrifts, whose deposits were rendered less safe when the Ohio Deposit Guarantee Fund failed. Federally insured institutions, and even several *un*insured thrifts, in Ohio experienced no unusual withdrawals during the period.

Saunders and Wilson (1993) evaluate deposit flows at individual US banks during the last period of major bank runs, 1929–33. These authors match each failed bank with a bank headquartered in the same geographic area, which survived past 1933. They find that the banks which eventually failed enjoyed less (greater) deposit growth (withdrawals) up to three years before their demise. This finding is consistent with the hypothesis that depositors responded to perceived bank weaknesses well in advance of the bank's failure date.

Notes

1. The market value of equity will not decline dollar-for-dollar with asset values, since the bank's fixed income claimants (depositors, debenture holders, and the FDIC) share to some extent in the loss. For a previously-solvent bank, however, option pricing theory clearly indicates that the bulk of the decline in asset value should be reflected in the stock price, regardless of the extent of government protection afforded to depositors.
2. Kaufman (1993) lists a number of additional, similar studies.

Acknowledgements

George Benston, George Kaufman, Urs Birchler, Ed Ettin, Ed Frydl, Allen Meltzer, Franco Passacantando, Stanley Fischer, Charles Goodhart, Marvin Goodfriend, and William Poole provided helpful comments and suggestions on an earlier draft of this chapter. The usual disclaimer applies.

Notes

1. Broadly speaking, the need for outside control derives from two sources: the agency conflict between owners and managers (Jensen and Meckling, 1976), and the 'moral hazard' incentive of a levered firm's shareholders to increase asset risk and raise leverage (Galai and Masulis, 1976).
2. Nakajima and Taguchi in Chapter 3 provide a useful categorization of alternative regulatory 'regimes'.
3. Relevant studies include Pettway (1976), Cargill (1989) and Gilbert (1993) although none has been able to effect a direct comparison

between market and regulatory assessments of bank quality. I am presently involved in two projects designed to assess exactly this question. One study (with Allen Berger and Sally Davies of the Federal Reserve Board staff) seeks to determine whether regulatory changes in assessed bank quality are led by, or lag, institutional holders' purchases and sales of the bank's equity. The second project (Flannery and Houston, 1993) investigates whether the market obtains valuable accounting information from the federal inspection of bank holding companies.

4. Kaufman and Benston (1993) provide an 'intellectual history' of the SEIR proposals which were ultimately incorporated into FDICIA.
5. See Flannery (1994) for a more complete discussion of the effect of bank financing terms on its total value added.
6. In the interests of space, I concentrate here on potential conflicts between a firm's shareholders and bondholders, since the government becomes an effective debt-holder when it insures bank liabilities. A second potential conflict involves differences between managers' and equity-holders' preferences. Numerous studies point out that managements can become entrenched, and pursue their own agendas at the expense of maximizing shareholder (or firm) value. Market forces will not necessarily produce efficient investment choices in the presence of such agency costs. An interesting question is whether a government regulator can succeed in aligning management's interests with social value maximization to a greater extent than private bond-holders can. See, e.g., Houston and James (1993).
7. This is equivalent to raising the bond's required coupon rate.
8. When many investors each hold a small portion of a firm's outstanding bonds, monitoring and enforcing bond covenants entail a potentially severe free-rider problem. One of the services arguably provided by banking firms is the ability to design *and* enforce complex covenants (Diamond, 1984; Berlin and Loeys, 1988). Because bank managers must be provided the proper incentives to monitor borrowers, a bank's liability structure may importantly affect its ability to provide this service in the market.
9. In the United States, banks are not permitted to secure their debt, except for the pledging requirements commonly associated with government deposits (Hayes, 1987). James (1988) shows how loan sales and standby letters of credit can be interpreted as efforts by banks to avoid the underinvestment problem, within their existing statutory constraints.
10. A similar situation arises with insurance contracts, which routinely require that the insured take specific actions (such as sprinklers in a warehouse) to control the risks being insured. Insurance premia also vary inversely with the policyholder's chosen deductible amount.
11. Investors lacking a comparative advantage in identifying and bearing credit risk will tend to exit this market, perhaps via bankruptcy.
12. This example abstracts from a number of potentially important considerations, including the cost of multiple evaluations, the possibility that some investors mistakenly support a poor project or refuse to

support a good one, the impact of the firm's other assets in place of its incentive to undertake a new investment, and so forth. Nevertheless, the basic example illustrates the potential salutary effect of market security prices on real asset allocations.

13. Of course, saying that market investors tend to make correct investment choices *ex ante* does not imply that all financed projects actually succeed. A major theme in evaluating the need/role for regulation in financial markets is that neither the market nor the government will entirely avoid costly mistakes. The policy question is which system's mistakes permit higher expected social welfare.
14. An alternative way to state Friedman's question might be this: if the banking industry and its customers benefit from government oversight and regulation, why should these same benefits not be extended to other important sectors of the economy? Meltzer (1975) provides an early evaluation of some of the issues treated here.
15. Even if my assessment about Cases A and B is incorrect, there would be no obvious reason to limit their riskiness through prudential regulations. The appropriate government response to an information deficiency would be to enhance the supply of credit information, or to undertake the oversight of banking firms which could not be properly controlled by the market.
16. An extreme example is that treasury-bill traders would benefit enormously from knowing the week's money supply announcement even a few minutes early, and will spend substantial resources trying to estimate this number. The social value of these activities seems quite limited.
17. If bank assets were easy for market investors to understand, they would be financed directly in the market, where secondary market trading provides access to an immense stock of risk-bearing capacity.
18. The fact that financial firms' equity trades in active secondary markets provides further indication that investors can assign values to bank assets and liabilities.
19. Garten (1986), Macey and Garrett (1988), Mantripragada (1992) and many other writers assess the available evidence similarly. FDICIA has transferred substantial further risk to legally uninsured depositors by prohibiting payments to uninsured creditors unless there is a threat to systemic stability. Similarly, the US depositor preference law passed in August 1993 places foreign depositors and domestic non-deposit creditors at greater risk. Current levels of market discipline should therefore exceed those reflected in the referenced empirical studies.
20. For example, bankers could offer accounts in 'narrow banks', or provide deposit liabilities through subsidiaries with high levels of equity or subordinated notes. Private deposit insurance is another possibility.
21. Although this statement is both subjective and debatable, I will proceed under the assumption that government does provide limited insurance for unsophisticated investors.
22. In some developing economies, government deposit insurance may provide an additional benefit: mobilizing and concentrating the savings of many individuals to finance large new investments.

23. These arrangements essentially resemble Goodhart's (1988) proposed structure for transaction accounts, or the structure of retail relationships which link a checking account to a money market mutual fund (like Fidelity's USA Account). The important point is that risky banks could replace their traditional method of paying only against 'good', collected funds, and that these substitutions would be easier to accomplish for large depositors than for small ones.
24. For example, the Reserve Bank of New Zealand proposes to eliminate effectively all prudential regulations, and to require that banks *disclose* their large risk exposures and *publish* a privately-produced credit rating, which is renewed every six months. The efficacy of these private substitutes for prudential regulation will depend, *inter alia*, on the quality of New Zealand's accounting, auditing, and rating firms.
25. This type of collective action is socially dysfunctional, in the sense that it makes society worse off. Jackson (1986) argues that the piecemeal application of individual creditors' rights can have socially wasteful results for any type of firm. This is the traditional justification for Chapter 11 proceedings in the US
26. Barth, Bartholomew and Bradley (1990) demonstrate that the government's losses from failed thrift institutions were positively related to the length of time they remained open after first attaining zero net worth.
27. Goodfriend and King (1988) provocatively argue that the central bank should not lend directly to individual banks. Their reasoning is twofold: first, they feel that targetted lending will often result in subsidization of troubled banks; and second, they contend that private liquidity arrangements should be sufficient to protect solvent banks from runs, provided that the central bank assures the *system's* overall liquidity.
28. The primary reason why bankers largely ignored payments system risk ten years ago was that they considered daylight overdrafts an 'operations' problem rather than a credit issue. See Heldring (1986, p. 211) or Dudley (1986, pp. 127–8). The Federal Reserve System rendered a valuable service by insisting that the large banks treat overdrafts in a credit context.
29. In a rather influential paper, Humphrey (1986) evaluated the impact of a settlement failure on CHIPS for a random day in January 1983. He found that a large bank's inability to settle would, under then-current CHIPS conventions, cause an 'unwind' which finally rendered approximately half of all CHIPS participants unable to settle at the usual time of day. This situation would not occur (or at least not the same way) under present CHIPS operating procedures. More importantly, however, Humphrey's analysis concentrated on liquidity problem rather than solvency problems. With a well-functioning lender of last resort, other banks would have failed on account of the initial bank's collapse only if they were substantially exposed, in an undiversified manner.
30. The same sort of 'domino effect' could make *any* firm's failure impose losses indirectly on unrelated firms, but this is not viewed as a problem for non-financial firms.

31. Daylight overdraft caps (and pricing) on Fedwire and the Fed's insistence that CHIPS enforce bilateral and system-wide exposures exemplify the type of changes that can mitigate the credit risks associated with making and receiving payments.
32. In other words, the informed bank borrowers which would be hurt by their bank's failure should be able to pressure shaky banks into resolving their problems, in order to continue participating in the mutually profitable loan relationship.
33. This seems to be a potentially fruitful area for further research.
34. For example, information asymmetries surround many types of corporate liability. How can we be certain that the asymmetry associated with bank assets is sufficiently greater that the government should undertake a large part of the information gathering for banks, but not for industrial companies?
35. These pressures could reflect either political expediency or the time inconsistency of government forbearance policies.
36. The action might be an explicit government bail-out, nationalization of the troubled firms, or a 'voluntary' lifeboat assembled by the industry's healthy firms.
37. It is interesting to note that one famous argument for federal deposit insurance is based on the fear that government (the central bank) will *fail* to intervene in a crisis. Friedman and Schwartz (1963, pp. 441–2) support deposit insurance because it promptly and automatically replaces the deposits lost when a bank fails, thereby assuring that contractionary monetary policy will not exacerbate the effects of a financial crisis.
38. An illustrative quotation is provided by a former FDIC board member who generally preferred to regulate small and large banks similarly:

> Yet, with this admitted bias toward community banks, three times I blinked when faced with what would have been the largest bank failure in history.... Why? Simply because the information before us – the facts at hand – convinced me in each instance that the nation just could not tolerate a failure of that magnitude at that time.
>
> (Sprague, 1986, p. 244)

39. Discussions of monetary policy have frequently framed this issue in terms of 'rules versus discretion': should the monetary authority have discretion to respond to events as they occur, or should they be bound to observe a specific money supply rule regardless of economic developments? A more classical example of how a binding rule can result in better policy was provided by Odysseus, who plugged his crews' ears with wax and had himself tied to the mast in order to hear the Sirens' song.
40. However, this benefit does not come without an offsetting cost: rules also impede policymakers' ability to respond to the unique features of each situation.
41. See Flannery (1982). Penati and Protopapadakis (1988) present a

specific model in which this type of conjectural guarantee causes banks to underprice not only the guaranteed debt, but loans to small, local borrowers who would receive no direct government intervention.

42. I say this because small depositors are largely inframarginal to bank risk-taking decisions. If a private banking system is likely to supply payment services more efficiently than a postal savings system, then, this is where small customers should be accommodated.
43. This relatively imprecise description of government risk-bearing suffices to motivate my general evaluation of the various categories of existing regulatory controls, but it would not permit precise computations of 'fair' insurance premia or 'appropriate' capital standards.
44. These insurance payments could be either explicit or implicit, as explained by Buser, Chen and Kane (1981).
45. Whether the government pricing schedule *effectively* mimics market pricing is a separate question which need not be answered in order to assess the theoretically appropriate role for such a schedule.
46. See Meltzer (1975, pp. 495–9) and the recent discussion by Iwamura (1993). Rothschild and Stiglitz (1976) illustrate a competitive situation in which the market for private insurance can fail, but a monopolist insurer (like the government) should be able to break even at the appropriate price for risk.
47. Unfortunately, even if the government gets risk prices correct *on average*, its premia will still affect market prices, and hence generate real distortions. Some government financial programs (such as student loans or the Small Business Administration) are intended to change real allocations, because the associated market prices are assumed to be socially suboptimal. This is not an avowed purpose of government deposit insurance.
48. In countries where the government prevents banks from publicizing important features of their financial condition (e.g. through hidden reserves or the insistence that short-term past due loans be kept confidential), it implies to market participants that they can rely on the government to ensure bank soundness.
49. If such situations are intrinsically difficult to control, we would tend not to observe them in the private sector. *The Economist* recently reported that universal banks in Europe are splintering into legally separate subsidiaries, each of which conducts a distinct line of business. ('Pruning the Universal Bank', 21 August 1993, pp. 57–8). It is also possible that private agents can control such a structure, but government agents (with their different incentives) cannot.
50. They will also be effectively constrained from providing services for which their regulator overestimates the risks, and hence charges an insurance fee which makes the bank uncompetitive.
51. Merton and Bodie (1992) point out that fully collateralized demand deposits could be provided on the same basis by any type of firm. This assessment is true, provided that the government can monitor collateral with enough accuracy that its residual risk is zero. This is not government insurance, but government bonding, and accordingly the government bears no risk in their ideal scheme.

References

Aharoney, J. and I. Swary (1983) 'Contagion Effects of Bank Failures: Evidence from Capital Markets', *Journal of Business*, vol. 56 (3) pp. 305–322.
Avery, R. B., T. M. Belton and M. A. Goldberg (1988) 'Market Discipline in Regulating Bank Risk: New Evidence from the Capital Markets', *Journal of Money, Credit and Banking*, vol. 4, pp. 597–610.
Baer, H. and E. Brewer (1986) 'Uninsured Deposits as a Source of Market Discipline: Some New Evidence', *Federal Reserve Bank of Chicago Economic Perspectives*, Sept/Oct., pp. 23–31.
Bank for International Settlements (1992) *Recent Developments in International Interbank Relations* (Central Banks of the Group of Ten Countries) p. 15.
Barth, J. R., P. F. Bartholomew and M. G. Bradley (1990) 'Determinants of Thrift Institution Resolution Costs', *Journal of Finance*, vol. 45 (July) pp. 731–54.
Benston, G. J. (1991) 'Does Bank Regulation Produce Stability? Lessons from the United States', in F. Capie and G. E. Wood (eds), *Unregulated Banking: Order or Chaos?* (London: Macmillan) pp. 207–32.
Benston, G. J. and G. G. Kaufman (1988) 'Regulating Bank Safety and Performance', in W. S. Haraf and R. M. Kushmeider (eds), *Restructuring Banking and Financial Services in America* (Washington, DC: AEI) ch. 3.
Berlin, M. and J. Loeys (1988) 'Bond Covenants and Delegated Monitoring', *Journal of Finance*, vol. 43 (2), pp. 397–412.
Bernanke, B. (1983) 'Nonmonetary Effects of the Financial Crisis in the Propagation of the Great Depression', *American Economic Review*, June, pp. 257–76.
Bernanke, B. and M. Gertler (1990) 'Financial Fragility and Economic Performance', *Quarterly Journal of Economics*, February, pp. 87–114.
Billett, M. T., M. J. Flannery and J. A. Garfinkel (1993) 'The Effect of Lender Identity on a Borrowing Firm's Equity Return.' University of Florida Working Paper.
Buser, S. A., A. H. Chen and E. J. Kane (1981) 'Federal Deposit Insurance Regulatory Policy and Optimal Bank Capital', *Journal of Finance*, vol. 36 (1), pp. 51–60.
Capie, F. and G. E. Wood (1991) *Unregulated Banking* (New York: St. Martin's Press).
Cargill, T. F. (1989) 'CAMEL Ratings and the CD Market', *Journal of Financial Services Research*, vol. 3 (4), pp. 347–58.
Corrigan, E. G. (1992) 'Challenges Facing the International Community of Bank Supervisors', *Quarterly Review. Federal Reserve Bank of New York*, Autumn, pp. 1–9.
Diamond, D. W. (1984) 'Financial Intermediation and Delegated Monitoring', *Review of Economic Studies*, pp. 393–414.
Dudley, W. C. (1986) 'Controlling Risk on Large-Dollar Wire Transfer Systems', in A. Saunders and L. J. White (eds), *Technology and the Regulation of Financial Markets* (Lexington, MA: Lexington Books) pp. 127–8.
Ellis, D. M. and M. J. Flannery (1992) 'Does the Debt Market Assess Large

Banks' Risk?: Time Series Evidence from Money Center CDs', *Journal of Monetary Economics*, vol. 30, pp. 481–502.

Flannery, M. J. (1982) 'Deposit Insurance Creates a Need for Bank Regulation', Federal Reserve Bank of Philadelphia *Business Review*, January/February, pp. 17–27.

Flannery, M. J. (1988) 'Payments System Risk and Public Policy', in W. S. Haraf and R. M. Kushmeider (eds), *Restructuring Banking and Financial Services in America* (Washington, DC: AEI) pp. 261–87.

Flannery, M. J. (1991) 'Pricing Deposit Insurance when the Insurer Measures Bank Risk with Error', *Journal of Banking and Finance*, September, pp. 975–98.

Flannery, M. J. (1993) 'Government Risk-Bearing in the Financial Sector of a Capitalist Economy', in M. S. Sniderman (ed.), *Government Risk-Bearing: Proceedings of a Conference Held at the Federal Reserve Bank of Cleveland* (Boston: Kluwer Academic Publishers), pp. 71–100.

Flannery, M. J. (1994) 'Debt Maturity and the Deadweight Cost of Leverage: Optimally Financing Banking Firms', *American Economic Review*, March, pp. 320–31.

Flannery, M. J. and J. F. Houston (1993) 'Market Responses to Federal Examinations of Commercial Banking Firms', University of Florida working paper.

Flannery, M. J., J. F. Houston and S. Venkataraman (1993) 'Financing Multiple Investment Projects', *Financial Management*, Summer, pp. 161–72.

Folkerts-Landau, D. F. I. (1990) *Systematic Financial Risk in Payment Systems* (Washington, DC: International Monetary Fund) June.

Friedman, M. (1959) *A Program for Monetary Stability* (New York: Fordham University Press).

Friedman, M. and A. J. Schwartz (1963) *Monetary History of the United States, 1867–1960* (Princeton: Princeton University Press).

Galai, D. and R. W. Masulis (1976) 'The Option Pricing Model and the Risk Factor of Stock', *Journal of Financial Economics*, vol. 3 (1/2) pp. 53–81.

Garten, H. A. (1986) 'Banking On the Market: Relying On Depositors to Control Bank Risks', *Yale Journal on Regulation*, vol. 4, pp. 129–72.

Gilbert, R. A. (1993) 'Implications of Annual Examinations for the Bank Insurance Fund', *Federal Reserve Bank of St. Louis Review*, Jan./Feb. pp. 35–52.

Goodfriend, M. and R. G. King (1988) 'Financial Deregulation, Monetary Policy, and Central Banking', in W. S. Haraf and R. M. Kushmeider (eds), *Restructuring Banking and Financial Services in America* (Washington, DC: AEI) pp. 216–253.

Goodhart, C. A. E. (1988) *The Evolution of Central Banks* (Cambridge: The MIT Press).

Gorton, G. and G. G. Pennacchi (1990) 'Financial Intermediaries and Liquidity Creation', *Journal of Finance*, March, pp. 49–72

Gorton, G. and A. M. Santomero (1990) 'Market Discipline and Bank Subordinated Debt', *Journal of Money, Credit and Banking*, vol. 1, pp. 119–28.

Hannan, T. H. and G. A. Hanweck (1988) 'Bank Insolvency Risk and the Market for Large Certificates of Deposit', *Journal of Money, Credit and Banking*, vol. 2, pp. 203–212.

Hayes, D. C. (1987) 'Some Issues in Asset Securitization by National Banks', *Issues in Bank Regulation*, vol. 10, pp. 5–24.

Heldring, F. (1986) 'Payment Systems Risk in the United States', *Journal of Bank Research*, vol. 4, pp. 209–13.

Houston, J. and C. James (1993) 'Management and Organizational Changes in Banking: A Comparison of Regulatory Intervention with Private Creditor Actions in Nonbank Firms', *Carnegie-Rochester Conference Series on Public Policy*, vol. 38 (June) pp. 143–77.

Humphrey, D. B. (1986) 'Payments Finality and Risk of Settlement Failure', in A. Saunders and L. J. White (eds), *Technology and Regulation of Financial Markets* (Lexington, MA: Lexington Books).

Iwamura, M. (1993) 'Deposit Insurance and Moral Hazard', *Monetary and Economic Studies*, vol. 11 (1), pp. 63–85.

Jackson, T. H. (1986) *The Logic and Limits of Bankruptcy Law* (Cambridge: Harvard University Press).

James, C. M. (1988) 'The Use of Loan Sales and Standby Letters of Credit by Commercial Banks', *Journal of Monetary Economics*, vol. 22, pp. 395–422.

James, C. M. (1990) 'Heterogeneous Creditors and the Market Value of Bank LDC Loan Portfolios', *Journal of Monetary Economics*, vol. 25, pp. 325–46.

Jensen, M. C. and W. H. Meckling (1976) 'Theory of the Firm: Managerial Behavior, Agency Costs and Ownership Structure', *Journal of Financial Economics*, vol. 3 (4), pp. 305–360.

Kahn, C. (1993) 'Project Choices, Moral Hazard, and Optimal Subsidiary Structure for Intermediaries', University of Illinois Working Paper.

Kane, E. J. (1981) 'Accelerating Inflation, Technological Innovation, and the Decreasing Effectiveness of Banking Regulation', *Journal of Finance*, vol. 36 (2), pp. 355–67.

Kane, E. J. (1987) 'Who Should Learn What from the Failure and Delayed Bailout of the ODGF?', in Federal Reserve Bank of Chicago, *Proceedings from a Conference on Bank Structure and Competition*, pp. 306–326.

Kane, E. J. (1990) 'Principal Agent Problems in S&L Salvage', *Journal of Finance*, vol. 45 (3), pp. 755–64.

Kaufman, G. G. (1993) 'Bank Contagion: A Review of the Theory and Evidence', Loyola University Working Paper, April.

Kaufman, G. G. and G. J. Benston (1993) 'The Intellectual History of the Federal Deposit Insurance Corporation Improvement Act of 1991', in Kaufman and Litan (eds), *Assessing Bank Reform: FDICIA One Year Later* (Washington, DC: The Brookings Institution) pp. 19–32.

Keeley, M. C. (1990) 'Deposit Insurance, Risk and Market Power in Banking', *American Economic Review*, Dec. pp. 1183–1200.

Macey, J. R. and E. H. Garrett (1988) 'Market Discipline by Depositors: A Summary of the Theoretical and Empirical Arguments', *Yale Journal on Regulation*, vol. 5, pp. 215–39.

Mantripragada, K. G. (1992) 'Depositors as a Source of Market Discipline', *Yale Journal on Regulation*, vol. 9, pp. 543–74.

Meltzer, A. H. (1975) 'Major Issues in the Regulation of Financial Institutions', *Journal of Political Economy*, vol. 75, pp. 482–501.

Merton, R. C. (1977) 'An Analytic Derivation of the Cost of Deposit Insurance and Loan Guarantees', *Journal of Banking and Finance*, vol. 1, pp. 3–11.

Merton, R. C. (1990) *Continuous-Time Finance* (Basil Blackwell).

Merton, R. C. and Z. Bodie (1992) 'Deposit Insurance Reform: A Functional Approach', *Journal of Monetary Economics* (Proceedings of the 1992 Carnegie-Rochester Conference), June, pp. 35–40.

Musumeci, J. J. and J. F. Sinkey, Jr. (1990) 'The International Debt Crisis, Investor Contagion, and Bank Security Returns in 1987: The Brazilian Experience', *Journal of Money, Credit and Banking*, vol. 22 (2), pp. 209–20.

Myers, S. C. (1977) 'Determinants of Corporate Borrowing', *Journal of Financial Economics*, vol. 5 (2), pp. 147–75.

Myers, S. C. and N. S. Majluf (1984) 'Corporate Financing and Investment Decisions When Firms Have Information that Investors Do Not Have', *Journal of Financial Economics*, vol. 13 (2), pp. 187–221.

Penati, A. and A. A. Protopapadakis (1988) 'The Effect of Implicit Deposit Insurance on Banks' Portfolio Choice with an Application to International Overexposure', *Journal of Monetary Economics*, vol. 21 (1), pp. 107–26.

Pettway, R. H. (1976) 'The Effects of Large Bank Failures Upon Investors' Risk Cognizance in the Commercial Banking Industry', *Journal of Financial and Quantitative Analysis*, vol. 11 (3), pp. 465–77.

Pyle, D. H. (1986) 'Capital Regulation and Deposit Insurance', *Journal of Banking and Finance*, vol. 10 (2), pp. 189–201.

Rothschild, M. and J. E. Stiglitz (1976) 'Equilibrium in Competitive Insurance Markets: An Essay on the Economics of Imperfect Information', *Quarterly Journal of Economics*, vol. 90, 4, pp. 629–49.

Saunders, A. and B. Wilson (1993) 'Contagious Bank Runs: Evidence from the 1929–1933 Period', New York University Working Paper.

Schaefer, S. (1992) 'Financial Regulation: the Contribution of the Theory of Finance', Working Paper, IFA London Business School, Feb.

Smith, C. W., Jr. and J. B. Warner (1979) 'On Financial Contracting: An Analysis of Bond Covenants', *Journal of Financial Economics*, vol. 7 (2), pp. 117–62.

Smirlock, M. and H. Kaufold (1987) 'Bank Foreign Lending, Mandatory Disclosure Rules, and the Reaction of Bank Stock Prices to the Mexican Debt Crisis', *Journal of Business*, vol. 60 (3), pp. 347–64.

Sprague, I. H. (1986) *Bailout: An Insider's Account of Bank Failures and Rescue* (New York: Basic Books).

Stigler, G. (1971) 'The Theory of Economic Regulation', *Bell Journal of Economics and Management Science*, vol. 2 (Spring), pp. 3–21.

Stiglitz, J. E. (1993) 'The Role of the State in Financial Markets.' Manuscript prepared for the World Bank's Annual Conference on Development Economics, May 3 and 4.

Stulz, R. M. and H. Johnson (1985) 'An Analysis of Secured Debt', *Journal of Financial Economics*, vol. 14 (4), pp. 501–522.

Swary, I. (1986) 'Stock Market Reaction to Regulatory Action in the Continental Illinois Crisis', *Journal of Business*, vol. 59 (3), pp. 451–73.

Wolf, C. (1988) *Markets or Governments: Choosing Between Imperfect Alternatives* (Cambridge: MIT Press).

Comments

Marvin Goodfriend*

Mark Flannery's chapter is an excellent survey of a broad range of issues in bank supervision and regulation. His 'corporate governance' approach to the issues is particularly useful. While such an approach is still somewhat novel, it is fast becoming a standard framework for analyzing banking policy issues.

As the author makes clear, there is an analogy between the incentive effects of corporate debt, on one hand, and deposit insurance, on the other. Once a firm has acquired debt, wealth can be shifted from debt to equity by increasing the riskiness of the firm's assets. The reason is that bondholders are exposed to downside risk but have only a limited share in the upside potential of a firm. An equivalent possibility exists for a bank with deposit insurance. A deposit insurer is also exposed to potentially large downside losses while not participating in the upside potential. So in this case too, managers have an incentive to enrich equity interests by making riskier loans.

It is to protect bondholders from such opportunistic behavior that lenders monitor firms and bond covenants routinely restrict the asset choice of borrowers. Analogously, government supervision and regulation of banks are necessary to protect the deposit insurer from opportunistic bank managers. In fact, whenever government provides a guarantee, whether it is deposit insurance for banks, or a guarantee for home mortgages, student loans, or small business loans, etc., borrowers accept restrictions to restrain the incentive to take on excess risk once a financial guarantee is in place. For example, we have minimum bank capital requirements and portfolio restrictions for deposit insurance, collateralization and down-payment minimums for mortgage guarantees.

The corporate governance perspective naturally leads economists to apply practical and academic knowledge of private bond contracts to problems involving government financial guarantees. The chapter addresses issues in prudential bank regulation by drawing analogies with practices in private debt markets.

* The views expressed here are mine alone and do not necessarily reflect those of the Federal Reserve Bank of Richmond or the Federal Reserve System.

Since it would be hard to improve on the author's exhaustive discussion of bank regulation, I thought I would take a broader look at the issues at stake, highlighting the role that bank lending plays in the process of economic growth. I will argue that excessively intrusive regulation is particularly bad for growth, and suggest an important principle to guide the structuring of supervision and regulation. I will begin by describing the close relationship between bank lending and growth. My discussion may seem to go a bit far afield, but I hope it will seem worthwhile by the time I have finished.

Economic Growth and Bank Lending

Sustained economic growth can only take place in an environment that encourages, facilitates, and rewards technological innovation. Above all, individuals and businesses with growth prospects need the power to hire labor and capital with a minimum of interference. There must be mobile labor and capital resources, i.e., reasonably liquid factor markets. Obviously, property rights must also be secure, and the legal system must quickly resolve commercial disputes. It is also crucial that factors of production be relatively unencumbered with restrictions that limit the right to put them to private use.

Productivity improvements usually involve the 'creative destruction' of older technologies. Improved technologies ultimately make society better off, but they do so by making existing techniques economically obsolete. Growth is most easily sustained in decentralized societies that allow innovations to be implemented without social permission, in particular, without excessive concern to compensate technological losers, e.g., workers with obsolete skills or owners of out-of-date machines.

It is only by accident that firms with good ideas happen to have the resources to finance them, so, in addition to decentralized factor markets, growth requires that innovative firms get the credit that they need. Since decentralization is the key to successful growth, growth is best served by a decentralized credit market. It is not efficient, however, for innovative firms to finance themselves by issuing securities in the open market, where the details of projects to be funded would be widely publicized.

The reason is that innovators need privacy in order to appropriate the returns to new ideas. Patenting often cannot provide sufficient protection. Many business opportunities are not easily patentable. Even when they are, it takes time to develop ideas to the point where patenting is worthwhile. For example, the Wright Brothers were quietly engaged in making improvements on their Flyer five years after their initial 1903 flight. They felt that secrecy was important so that no one could steal their invention before their own rights were secure. They experimented at Kitty Hawk, North Carolina, in part, because of the privacy it provided.

We finally arrive at the critical role played by banks in financing growth. Banks certify the creditworthiness of potential growth prospects, screen out the bad risks, and finance the good ones with funds acquired on the basis of a general reputation for creditworthiness, without passing through the details of specific loans to depositors. Modern information technology may increase the securitization of bank loans over time, but confidential funding of innovative projects will remain an important banking service, one that is essential for sustaining economic growth.

Social Safety Nets and Economic Growth

Economic prosperity creates a demand for social safety nets to cushion individuals against potential losses due to bankruptcy, personal illness, the business cycle, etc. The provision of safety nets such as unemployment insurance, food stamps, health insurance, and loan and deposit guarantees, would seem to have relatively little effect on the pace of technological innovation, as long as such programs are designed to provide floors on bad economic outcomes and not to force technological winners to compensate the losers.

As discussed at the outset, however, financial guarantees must be supported by restrictions on the beneficiary's actions. Governments are often unable to levy actuarially fair premia for their social insurance programs. In order to limit potential liabilities, governments feel pressure to further restrict the freedom of action of individuals or firms covered, once safety nets are in place. For example, unemployment insurance drives governments to support failing firms, slowing the reallocation of resources to more productive industries.

Recently in the US, for example, bank regulators have been inclined, and even encouraged by Congressional legislation, to behave increasingly like debtors in possession of bankrupt firms – even with regard to solvent banks. The risk is that regulators are being drawn into micro-monitoring bank loan decisions in a way that makes banks excessively timid. This tendency is being further encouraged by the increasingly sophisticated computer and communication technology that is fast reducing the cost of monitoring banks.

The general point is this. In the name of protecting everything from deposits, to the environment, and individual rights, modern societies may be reducing the economy's ability to direct resources flexibly to their most valued uses. The extension of social safety nets creates incentives for governments to weaken the decentralized freedom of action over resources in a way that could, if carried far enough, seriously threaten economic growth.

Implications for Bank Supervision and Regulation

Micro-monitoring of bank lending by government regulators would be particularly bad for growth. As mentioned above, micro-monitoring would tend to produce excessively timid bank lending because the deposit insurer bears the downside risk with none of the upside potential. What is worse, in order to assure an equitable nationwide treatment of banks, micro-monitoring would tend to become centralized, with two additional costs. Centralization would make it more difficult to maintain the confidentiality necessary for firms to appropriate the returns to their innovations. And, centralized credit authorizations could become susceptible to pressure, making it more difficult to extend loans to innovative firms without simultaneously compensating or at least supporting firms made obsolete by creative destruction. A reliance on micro-monitoring could, thereby, gradually reduce the economy's growth potential by paralyzing the funding of innovative firms.

My argument suggests that bank supervision and regulation should avoid micro-monitoring at all costs by employing higher capital requirements together with a program for early intervention and resolution of troubled banks. This principle supports the Benston and Kaufman (1988) proposal as partially incorporated in the US Congress's FDICIA Act of 1991. Of course, some supervision and regulation would still be necessary to intervene promptly and to enforce capital standards. Micro-monitoring could be avoided, however, because bank equity interests would be exposed to greater loss due to bad loans, and so could be counted on to ensure that bank managers make efficient credit decisions themselves. Higher capital requirements are good for growth not only because they provide additional protection for taxpayers, but because they do so while strengthening the decentralization of the banking system.

References

Aghion, P. and P. Howitt (1992) 'A Model of Growth Through Creative Destruction', *Econometrica*, vol. 60, pp. 323–51.

Benston, G. and G. Kaufman (1988) 'Regulating Bank Safety and Performance', pp. 63–99, in William Haraf and Rose Kushmeider (eds), *Restructuring Banking and Financial Services in America* (Washington, DC: American Enterprise Institute).
Goodfriend, M. (19991) 'Money, Credit, Banking, and Payments System Policy', pp. 247–77, in David Humphrey, (ed.), *The U.S. Payment System: Efficiency, Risk, and the Role of the Federal Reserve* (Boston, Mass.: Kluwer Academic Publishers, 1990). Reprinted in Federal Reserve Bank of Richmond *Economic Review* (January/February) pp. 7–23.
Grossman, G. and E. Helpman (1993) 'Endogenous Innovation in the Theory of Growth', National Bureau of Economic Research Working Paper No. 4527, November.
King, R. and R. Levine (1993) 'Finance and Growth: Schumpeter Might Be Right', *The Quarterly Journal of Economics*, vol. 108 (August) pp. 717–38.
Wescott, L. and P. Degen (1983) *Wind and Sand: The Story of the Wright Brothers at Kitty Hawk* (Eastern Acorn Press).

Comments

Franco Passacantando*

1. In his chapter Professor Flannery adopts a very pragmatic approach to the issue of banks' prudential regulation since he discusses both the economic rationale and the political justification for governments' intervention in this area. In my comment, however, I will question his assertion that 'the monitoring of banks' risk taking is not qualitatively different from that of other firms' and that banks' prudential regulation cannot be justified in economic terms. In order to do this, I will first consider the features that distinguish the deposit contract from those of any other debt contract and then address the issue of the information problems associated with banks' assets.

2. Flannery acknowledges that the relationship between a bank and its depositors differs somewhat from that of non-bank firms with their debt-holders but does not consider this difference to be of a qualitative nature. He claims that a market failure may exist only for small depositors, who have no comparative advantage in assessing credit risk and whose balances are too small to permit effective diversification across financial products. For them information and surveillance costs can therefore be socially unjustifiable. The same argument does not apply to large corporate customers, which can better assess and diversify risks. Deposit insurance is therefore at most warranted for small or 'unsophisticated' depositors, for reasons that have more to do with efficiency (and possibly equity) than with the stability of the system.

My objection to this argument is that information problems and cost considerations are not related so much to the size of bank deposits or the categories of holders as to the function of bank liabilities. Perhaps deposits that are held for investment purposes, such as CDs, do not qualitatively differ from any other traded security. But bank deposits that serve transaction purposes do differ from other

* These comments were prepared while the author was visiting scholar at the Haas School of Business, University of California, at Berkeley. Discussions with David Pyle on this subject matter are gratefully acknowledged. The opinions of the author do not reflect those of the Bank of Italy.

types of securities in many respects. Even ignoring the fact that only demand deposits are redeemable at par, one can mention several other distinctive features. First, the frequency of monitoring must be greater when you hold an asset whose stock changes continuously over time than when you own a fixed amount of securities. Second, when a payment is made with bank money, for instance a check payment, the payee should assess not only his or her bank but also the risks associated with the bank of the payor, since the clearing of a check is not an instantaneous process. Finally, the holders of demand deposits must also be concerned about possible runs by other holders of deposits with the same bank.

The monitoring costs associated with the use of demand deposits as payment media can be important even for large firms. Although they can better assess risks than individuals, large firms have relationships with a much larger number of trading partners. In a totally unregulated environment the amount of real resources they would have to devote to monitoring many different banks could be significant, especially in periods of financial distress when the opportunistic behaviour of trading partners is more likely to occur. The result would be a reduction in the willingness to trade or a transfer of deposit balances to the few institutions considered risk free or 'too big to fail'.

To a certain extent the same argument also applies to banks, as the recent debate on payment system risk shows. I agree with Flannery that the exposures originated by interbank payments are not qualitatively different from overnight credit. However, the magnitudes of the exposures are not comparable to those occurring in the overnight market. Besides, they are continuously growing. As the experience of countries different from the US shows, systemic risk is present, albeit on a smaller scale even if the central bank does not provide free overdraft facilities. In a self-regulated environment, in order to economize monitoring costs, banks would most likely reduce the number of trading counterparts (Angelini and Passacantando, 1993) and restrict membership of clearing arrangements to the most creditworthy institutions (see also Goodhart, 1988).

If one does not properly stress the function of bank deposits as payment media, it is also difficult to understand why bank panics are so much feared by regulators. The real cost for economy of a chain of bank failures cannot be measured only in terms of wealth losses for deposit holders, as Friedman and Schwartz showed in their *Monetary History* (see for instance p. 351). Such losses might actually be smaller than those suffered by bond or stock-holders. The real costs are of two types. One is that associated with the cost of credit intermediation, as highlighted by Bernanke in his 1983 article and by the recent literature on the effect of bank intermediation on growth. The other, which has so far received less attention in the literature, although it is often mentioned by policy-makers, is that related to the disruption of the payment system. Even though suppliers of payment media alternative to banks are now available (and to a certain extent have always been available), it is hard to believe that they could accommodate an immediate surge in the demand for transaction services that would result from a loss of trust in bank money. This loss of trust would thus affect the velocity of circulation of money and the transaction costs of the entire economy.

3. Let me now turn to the issue of whether depositors can properly assess the quality of bank assets. It is a crucial issue because if such assets were informationally transparent, or if banks were allowed to hold only risk-free assets in their portfolios, the distinction between bank deposits and other forms of debt would be of no importance in practice.

Flannery presents the results of a number of papers which show that depositors and market investors are to a certain extent able to discriminate among banks. Since the risk of contagion cannot be attributed to 'irrational' factors, this implies that there is no need for government regulation.

Before making a few comments on this empirical literature, let me raise a very general question. If it is true that banks' depositors can assess the quality of banks' assets properly, the whole idea that financial intermediation is a response to an asymmetric information problem (Leland and Pyle, 1977) becomes questionable. Although the asymmetric information argument has probably been overemphasized in the literature of the last fifteen years, I would have some difficulty in understanding the role of banks if no information problems existed. Depositors can discriminate good banks from bad banks only if they are able to discriminate between good loans and bad loans. Why should they then put their savings into banks instead of holding the bonds issued by ultimate borrowers? And why should firms borrow from banks and not directly from the market?

Turning to the results that Flannery presents, it seems to me that they are still very mixed and do not serve to dismiss the widely held view that the risk of contagion is greater for banks than for other firms. The evidence on bank subordinated debt (p. 307) can at most be considered not inconsistent with Flannery's thesis but certainly not in its favor since it shows no relationship between debenture rates and accounting measures of bank risk. Similarly, the evidence on bank equity returns (p. 308) shows that in two cases out of four bank failures did not have any effect on other banks' stock prices. It is possible that in the two cases in which they did have an effect it was because of a rational response of asset holders, but the alternative explanation of a contagion effect cannot be ruled out. The evidence on small depositors that Kane collected does not appear to me proof that depositors are able to discriminate among banks but simply that they are able to distinguish between federally insured and state insured – which is to say weakly insured – institutions. An interesting result is that obtained by Flannery himself in a previous paper (Ellis and Flannery, 1992), which shows that CD holders respond to the same information that moves stock prices. However, this result simply says that CD holders and stockholders react to the same type of information and not that the information at their disposal is adequate, in all circumstances, to assess the value of banks' assets properly.

More generally, before reaching conclusions in terms of policy proposals from this empirical literature, one should carefully consider two aspects. The first is whether the results obtained with reference to CDs or stocks also apply to demand deposits. For the reasons mentioned earlier, the monitoring activity of demand deposit holders in very different from that of CD holders or stockholders. The second aspect to consider is whether one can draw implications about the behavior of depositors in a totally unregulated environment from the way in which they reacted to recent bank failures. Flannery claims that since these results refer to a reality with very little incentive for risk taking by private agents, they would hold *a fortiori* in an unregulated world. However, it is possible, at least in certain cases, that the absence of strong evidence of a contagion effect was due to investors' expectation of government intervention through the safety net. The paper on banks' behavior during the Great Depression that Flannery mentions shows that the banks which eventually failed had less deposit growth up to three years before their fall. This might mean that depositors were expecting the failures but might also imply that the failures themselves were caused by withdrawals.

A recent review article by Kaufman on the same subject reaches a conclusion similar to that of Flannery in many respects, except one.

It shows that depositors are able to differentiate among institutions, that contagion effects exist also for non-financial firms and that deposit holders' losses are usually smaller than those of debt holders, The article nevertheless concludes that bank contagion is faster and likely to spread to a larger proportion of the industry and involve to a larger percentage of failure than contagion in the non-banking sector (Kaufman, 1992, p. 32).

4. In conclusion, I believe that the work by Professor Flannery can help modify the opinion that banks' customers are in no case able to assess banks' behavior properly. However, it does not serve to dismiss the view that banks are 'special' because of their dual role as providers of the most widely used medium of exchange and as suppliers of credit, at a reasonable cost, to institutions that for some reason are unable to raise funds directly on the market.

References

Angelini, P. and F. Passacantando (1993) 'Central Banks' Role in the Payment System and its Relationship with Banking Supervision', Paper presented at the Conference on Prudential Regulation, Supervision and Monetary Policy, Milano, Bocconi University, 5 February.

Bernanke, B. (1983) 'Non-monetary Effects of the Financial Crisis in the Propagation of the Great Depression', *American Economic Review*, 73.

Ellis, D. M. and M. J. Flannery (1992) 'Does the Debt Market Assess Large Banks' Risk?' *Journal of Monetary Economics*, vol. 30, pp. 481–502.

Friedman, M. and A. J. Schwartz (1965) *A Monetary History of the United States 1867–1960* (Princeton: Princeton University Press).

Goodhart, C. (1988) *The Evolution of Central Banks* (Cambridge, Mass.: The MIT Press).

Kaufman, G. G. (1992) 'Bank Contagion: Theory and Evidence', Working Paper.

Leland, H. E. and D. H. Pyle (1977) 'Informational Asymmetries, Financial Structure, and Financial Intermediation', *The Journal of Finance*, vol. XXXII, p. 2.

8 Safety Nets and Moral Hazard in Banking

George J. Benston

I INTRODUCTION AND OVERVIEW

In banking, 'safety nets' refer to government guarantees provided to depositors and sometimes to all bank creditors. When some banks are considered to be 'too big to fail', and therefore are given assistance, the safety net covers all of the bank's stakeholders, including customers, employees, and (usually to a lesser extent) stockholders. 'Moral hazard' refers to the adverse incentives engendered by these safety nets. Because they do not fear losing their funds, depositors and possibly other creditors do not monitor banks as carefully as otherwise. In the absence of other constraints, bank owners and managers, therefore, have incentives to take greater risks than they would have taken, without the safety net. The essential questions considered here are how costly is the problem, and what can and should be done about this situation?

To put the issue into context, Section II describes the ways that non-government providers of insurance, which is particularly subject to moral hazard, have developed to deal with this problem. Moral hazard in financial markets is considered in Section III. This discussion leads to the conclusion that the optimal combination of the benefits from safety nets, the cost of moral hazard, and the cost of dealing with moral hazard is complex and best left to the parties affected – in general, government should not intervene.

Section IV delineates four possible reasons for government provision of financial safety nets: (1) social obligations best met by government; (2) efficiency of government-provided loans and deposit insurance; (3) reduction of negative externalities from bank runs; and (4) political expediency. (The possible negative externalities from bank runs examined include: closure of insolvent banks; the effect on other banks; disruption of the financial system generally; the effect of the failure of a giant bank; and disruption of the payments system.) The analysis leads to the conclusion that none of the first three exceptions supports government provision of deposit insurance. However, political expediency explains why depositors in most countries are protected by *de jure* or *de facto* deposit insurance.

The chapter next considers the extent to which moral hazard engendered by the politically necessary deposit-insurance safety net has been costly. Section V reviews the extent to which non-government restraints reduce deposit-insurance moral-hazard costs. These restraints include: concerns by partially insured depositors, concern of other creditors, equity-holders' concerns about their investments, and bank managers' concerns about loss of their jobs and reputations. The restraints appear to have been generally effective in reducing excessive risk taking, although this finding probably also is due to constraints imposed by the banking authorities. For this reason, and because it would be unwise for taxpayers to rely on non-government restraints to relieve them of moral hazard costs, given that they demand and get government-provided deposit insurance, constraints on banks that are or could be imposed by government are considered next.

The government-imposed constraints outlined in Section VI include: restrictions on banks' assets and activities; risk-adjusted deposit insurance premiums; risk-adjusted capital; higher capital requirements; and structured early intervention and resolution (SEIR). Restrictions are found to be ineffective, costly and counter productive, with the exception of some 'narrow bank' proposals. Risk-adjusted capital, as implemented by the Basle capital standard, suffers from some important shortcomings. The last two constraints have merit.

Section VII summarizes the conclusions. Higher required capital ratios supplemented by SEIR is suggested as the best way to deal with moral hazard problem caused by the financial safety net of government-provided deposit insurance. These requirements can and should be accompanied by greatly reduced restrictions on banks' activities to allow banks to compete with unregulated alternative suppliers of banking services.

II NON-GOVERNMENT METHODS OF DEALING WITH MORAL HAZARD IN INSURANCE

One of the earliest discussions of moral hazard in the economics literature is by Arrow (1963). In the context of medical insurance, he points out that an optimal insurance contract cannot be constructed because knowledge is incomplete. For example, an insurance company may not be able to distinguish between an illness caused by an exogenous event, such as a cancer of unknown origin, from an illness caused or exacerbated by insufficient care or harmful actions known only to the insuree, such as avoiding physical examinations and smoking. Moral hazard results from the inability of the contracting parties to state and observe all contingencies. Because all contingencies cannot be observed, one party to a contract has an incentive to take advantage of his/her private knowledge, and first-best efficiency cannot be achieved. In a comment on Arrow's article, Pauly (1968) points out that 'moral hazard' should not be viewed as equivalent to 'moral perfidy', but as rational behavior when a lower-than-market price is charged for a product. Thus, it is rational and not immoral for persons with medical insurance to use more medical services paid for by the insurer than they would have used had they paid for the services themselves.

Long before economists recognized moral hazard, insurance companies that survived were well aware of the perverse incentives resulting from safety nets their insurance provides to insurees. Generally, they deal with this problem by insisting that the insurees bear costs that tend to offset their incentives to take on more risk. For example, buyers of fire insurance usually must have substantial equity stakes in the insured property, so that they bear much of the cost of a fire. Deductibles are another way of shifting at least some of the cost of losses to insurees. Another means is charging insurance premiums that increase as the risks posed by the insurees increase. Monitoring of the insurees' actions, such as checking property for fire hazards and well-maintained sprinkler systems, can serve to reduce the risk. Finally, if the incentives for insurees to take great risks are so great that they cannot be offset by higher premiums or sufficient restraints, an insurance company would refuse to offer a policy. Thus, unless an insurance company were badly managed, the cost of moral hazard tends to be borne by the insuree or by someone other than the insurance company.

III MORAL HAZARD IN FINANCIAL MARKETS

Financial markets also are affected by moral hazard. Firms often fund their activities with both debt and equity. Debt holders determine the interest rate they will accept based on their expectations of the probability that they will be repaid as promised by the equity holders. Before the debt is sold, the equity holders have incentives to assure potential debt holders that these promises will be kept – that is, that the firm will not take greater risks than were specified and will conserve its assets to repay the debt holders. Once the debt is sold, though, unless the debt holders can force the equity holders to keep their promises, the equity holders could gain by taking greater risks or by distributing assets to themselves, given the important additional assumption of limited liability. Equity holders in corporations (and limited partners in partnerships) can limit their liability to the amount of their investments in their firms. Thus, they do not bear the full cost of risks, but can get the full benefits from them. This limited liability feature gives them an option, in that they can 'put' the firm to the creditors if losses exceed the value of the equity investments. If things turn out well, they pay the debt and keep the firm.[1]

As agency theory emphasizes (e.g. Jensen and Meckling, 1976), the ultimate cost of the limited-liability put option is borne by the equity holders. As is the practice for insurers, creditors should price their provision of debt to include the value of the option. Thus, equity holders rather than debt holders bear the cost of expected moral hazard. Equity holders can reduce the cost to them of their put option by offering credible covenants and collateral requirements that serve to assure debt holders that the promises made to them will be kept. The observation that debt holders, such as banks and other lenders, rather than borrowers, usually propose and design these credit features and instruments is not inconsistent with the conclusion that the cost of moral hazard is borne by borrowers and equity holders. Creditor control over the instruments both enhances their credibility and offers operational efficiencies through standardization and conformity with the lenders' record-keeping and monitoring systems.

In private market debtor/creditor situations, then, the causal relationship between the safety net and moral hazard is reversed. To reduce the costs of moral hazard that debt holders have reason to fear, borrowers and equity holders provide lenders and debt holders with a credible private safety net (protection against losses). The safety net may take many forms. These include: sufficient equity investments by borrowers to almost eliminate the risk of default; diversified operations and investments that reduce the impact of adverse events; covenants that restrict borrowers' opportunities to increase risk; collateral that both reduces the cost of default and borrowers' incentives to default; periodic presentation of financial statements audited by respected independent public accountants; and direct or indirect monitoring by lenders. Alternatively, borrowers can pay more to compensate the lenders for greater risk.

IV THE RATIONALE FOR GOVERNMENT PROVISION OF FINANCIAL SAFETY NETS

As just discussed, insurance companies, creditors and debtors can write contracts or make informal arrangements that tend to equate, at the margin, the structure and costs of various means of dealing with or compensating the parties for moral hazard concerns. Considering the difficulty of determining and drafting the set of formal and informal arrangements to achieve the optimal balance between the benefits from relationships that give rise to moral hazard and the costs of dealing with it, government provision of financial safety nets is likely to be dysfunctional, with four possible exceptions.

The possible exceptions are: (1) social obligations that can be fulfilled best by government, such as support for people who cannot achieve a socially specified standard; (2) efficiencies that government can achieve that could not be achieved by private parties; (3) negative externalities that can only be dealt with by government at a lower cost than the externalities would have imposed; and (4) political expediency, resulting in the transfer of resources to persons and firms with political power, at the expense of others who are unable, or unwilling, to oppose them.

Social Obligations

Financial safety nets often are provided by government in the form of loans at less-than-market rates to people or enterprises whom society deems are disadvantaged or discriminated against, presumably for reasons beyond their control, or who are viewed as particularly deserving. These entities are seen as inadequately served by private lenders. Consequently, they are offered subsidized loans by governmental units or specially chartered and subsidized banks. Some examples include loans to students, farmers, home buyers, exporters, and infant industries. (That this rationale can be effective for disguising the transfer of resources to politically powerful entities may be the operative reason for many of the loans and, hence, may be linked with the fourth, political, exception.)

The moral hazard engendered by subsidized loans is that the

borrowers may use fungible borrowed funds for purposes other than those that justified the safety net. For example, home buyers and farmers may use the proceeds of low-interest-rate mortgage loans to invest in securities and speculative real estate. Thus, resources simply are transferred to favored persons from taxpayers generally. Worse yet, the subsidized loans may induce borrowers to invest in socially costly activities. For example, property owners who expect to receive low-interest-rate flood disaster loans are more likely to build structures in flood plains. Farmers tend to grow more of the crops for which they can get low-interest-rate loans.

Efficiency of Government-provided Loans and Deposit Insurance

Government efficiency has been invoked to support the creation of government-owned banks and direct loan programs. Government agencies presumably can benefit from economies of scale and from the power of government to collect debts. For example, income tax returns might be used as a vehicle for collecting loan repayments, particularly when they are tied to the recipient's income (e.g. student loans). These possible benefits, though, might be more than offset by the tendency of government employees to be less efficient than employees of privately owned firms. It is not that government employees individually are incompetent. Rather, they often are faced with an incentive system that punishes them for visible mistakes and does not reward them for difficult-to-measure and diffuse benefits, such as the avoidance of opportunity costs. They also are subject to political pressures, such as the strong desire of some debtors not to repay their debts compared to the small benefit to taxpayers generally of the debts being repaid, which might explain why income tax returns have not been used as a means of enforcing repayment of debts to the government.

The most important application of the presumed efficiencies thesis is as a justification for government-provided deposit insurance. The argument is that the aggregate cost that would be incurred by each depositor individually in evaluating and monitoring the activities of their banks is greater than the cost to a government agency of providing deposit insurance and examining and supervising the insured banks. The saving is said to be particularly great for depositors with small balances.

The counter-argument is that banks could offer privately purchased insurance to depositors. Such insurance probably would be inexpensive if it were limited to relatively small amounts, such as deposits under US$10,000. Depositors with balances above this amount could be offered partial insurance or interest that compensated them for risk. Another possibility is cross-insurance among banks, where a group of banks guarantees the deposits of the members of the group, and possible losses to any one bank are limited through stop-loss (reinsurance) arrangements. (See Ely, 1990 and Wallison, 1990.)[2] An advantage of this procedure is that group-member banks have both the expertise to evaluate the operations of their fellow members and an incentive to control excessive risk taking, as they bear the costs of these risks. Calomiris (1990) provides evidence supporting this conclusion. He reports (p. 287) that the three successful state-chartered deposit insurance systems operated in the United States before the civil war were 'based on the principles of self-regulation and unlimited mutual liability. . . .' Most of the deposit insurance schemes established by other countries (all after 1959) are administered by the depository institutions alone or jointly with a government agency.[3] The only deposit insurance funds that have been substantially depleted or become insolvent (those in Canada and the United States) are government sponsored and administered. This situation may be due to inefficient monitoring or under funding based on an expected government bail out.

It should be noted that private guarantees of many types of financial assets are common. Interest and principal on state and local government bonds and on private mortgages are guaranteed by private insurance companies. Such companies also provide guarantees on mortgage-backed securities, and banks provide guarantees on their customers' loans, acceptances, and commercial paper. Furthermore, people purchase and hold financial obligations, including notes, bonds, and equities, that are not guaranteed. The risk of loss of funds invested in deposits, then, is no different than the risk faced by individuals and firms for investments generally. Although investors sometimes take losses, these markets work well.

With respect to government efficiency, then, I conclude that there is no valid justification for governmentally provided deposit insurance. However, there is a strong political reason for such insurance. Before considering this reason, the other major reason – externalities – is discussed.

Reduction of Negative Externalities from Depositor Runs

Fractional reserve banking and the practice of permitting depositors to withdraw their funds at par without notice gives rise to the potential of bank runs. As a result of such a rapid withdrawal of funds, a bank that is unable to quickly sell assets or borrow funds at current prices suffers a liquidity crisis and is forced to suspend withdrawals of deposits (if it can do so legally) or is closed by the banking authorities. Five effects of bank runs are distinguished: (1) closure of insolvent banks; (2) effects on solvent banks; (3) disruption of the financial system generally; (4) the failure of a giant bank; and (5) disruption of the payments system. Although deposit insurance can reduce or, if it fully covers deposits, eliminate the possibility of bank runs, the discussion presented below leads to the conclusion that runs need not result in negative externalities.

Closure of Insolvent Banks

The failure of any firm imposes costs on those who have dealings with it, including customers, employees, creditors and owners. However, some scholars argue that banks are special, in that they provide services that are vital to other enterprises. In particular, Bernanke (1983) assigns much of the cost of the 1930s US depression to disruptions in credit resulting from bank closures. Goodhart (1987, p. 86) views banks as unique because 'public information on the economic condition and prospects ... is so limited and expensive that the alternative of issuing marketable securities is either nonexistent or unattractive.' Diamond and Dybvig (1983) base their often-cited formal model on the assumption that runs should be prevented to safeguard banks' special advantage as intermediaries. Several empirical studies (e.g. James, 1987) provide evidence from stock market data indicating that bank loans have properties that enhance the value of a borrowing firm's shares. Although banks do, indeed, provide valuable services to the customers, the closure of individual banks (insolvent or solvent) is not or need not be more costly to customers, employees, and creditors than the closure of other companies of similar size or importance.

Many alternative non-banking firms provide all the products offered by banks. For example, loans may be obtained from specialized lenders, such as consumer finance companies, investment banks and securities firms, and insurance companies. Funds can be raised from public and private sales of commercial paper and other debt instruments. Individuals and companies borrow through accounts payable to companies from which they purchase goods and services. Safe deposit boxes, trust services, and other collateral banking services are offered by non-banks. Even though banks in the United States have a presumed monopoly on the transfer of funds by check, in practice securities brokers and money market mutual funds provide much the same product.

Further, bank customers can purchase similar services from other banks. Large companies can obtain loans and other banking services from banks in many cities and countries. When entry into banking is not severely restricted, people can get checking and other banking services from other banks in or near their communities. Bernanke (1983) found evidence of a significant disruption in credit facilities because the United States of the 1930s was characterized by unit banking, and almost all of the banks that failed were unit banks located in small communities (White, 1983). In the United States and most other countries today, with greatly improved communication and transportation, the closure of one or several banks does not leave people without other banking alternatives. This is not to say that the closure of a bank would not disadvantage its customers, particularly borrowers who obtain funds only from that bank. However, the disruption is likely only to be temporary, as the borrower can seek out or be sought out by many alternative suppliers.

The situation for employees in banks that fail usually is better than that faced by employees of other failed firms. Bank employees' skills are almost the same as those used in other banks and similar to those used in many commercial companies. Consequently, unlike the situation for workers with firm-specific skills, employees of banks that close due to runs can more readily find similar jobs.

As Kaufman (1988) points out, in the absence of deposit insurance, bank runs reduce the cost to depositors who cannot withdraw their funds in time, because the runs cause the prompt closing of a bank that otherwise might take greater risks, as the moral hazard hypothesis predicts. Consistent with this expectation, he finds that losses to US depositors in the pre-deposit insurance years were considerably less than losses to creditors of other companies and much less than losses largely absorbed by the federal deposit insurance funds (FDIC and FSLIC) in the post-deposit insurance years. Not only is the closure of a bank not more costly than the closure of many (perhaps most) other companies, but runs that close insolvent banks are desirable. When there is less than 100 percent deposit insurance, runs by uninsured depositors play a beneficial role in forcing the banking authorities to close insolvent or close-to-insolvent banks rather than delay for political reasons. Thus, runs on insolvent banks reduce the negative externality of moral-hazard costs imposed on solvent banks or taxpayers, because insolvent banks that are allowed to remain open might gamble for resurrection, and lose.

Furthermore, consumers and workers lose when government seeks to reduce the incidence of bank failures by restricting entry into banking, thereby increasing the value of bank charters and bank owners' capital. Although fewer banks are likely to fail, consumers and workers will be faced with less competition for their trade and services. The cost to the economy may very well be higher than if more banks failed.

Effect on Other Banks

An externality might result from depositors' inability to distinguish among banks with respect to their solvency. Solvent (as well as insolvent) banks are particularly prone to liquidity crises because, unlike the liabilities of most other firms, many deposits are repayable on demand at par. Furthermore, because banking necessarily (and desirably) involves the use of private information by bankers, loans and similar bank assets are difficult for depositors and other creditors to value (Diamond, 1984). Hence, depositors, unlike the creditors of other firms, can and might remove their funds rapidly (run) based on poor and possibly incorrect information, following the dictates of 'better safe than sorry'.

A run on a solvent bank can be costly if the bank must sell assets at 'fire sale' prices or borrow funds at high rates of interest. The costs resulting from these transactions can render the bank insolvent if its capital is not sufficient to absorb the losses. An additional limited externality might result if the bank suffering the run has to reduce its lending and other services to customers.

However, there are good reasons to believe that the possibility of runs provides strong banks with benefits that could exceed the expected costs of mistaken runs. Some scholars (e.g. Calomiris and Kahn, 1991 and Flannery, 1993) have noted that the demand-liability form has the desirable property of reducing banks' agency costs. By offering depositors the right to withdraw their funds on demand, bankers give them assurance that their banks will not be operated in a manner that would cause them to run. This safety net of immediate withdrawal at par is an important means for prudently run banks to avoid the cost of moral hazard that (in the absence of deposit insurance) depositors might impose on them.

In addition, solvent banks can take steps to reduce the probability that depositors will run because they are misinformed or insecure.

These banks can hold higher ratios of net worth to assets, hold diversified portfolios of assets, and offer depositors time-dated deposits. Indeed, strong solvent banks can benefit from runs on weak and insolvent banks. In the absence of full-coverage deposit insurance, concerns about a bank's safety would lead depositors to bank at or transfer their funds to strong banks. Thus, bank runs reward well-capitalized, prudently managed banks.

Furthermore, banks can structure co-operative arrangements that serve to mitigate the effects of financial stress. Dwyer and Gilbert (1989) review the evidence on bank runs in the United States before enactment of deposit insurance and the methods adopted by banks to cope with them. After analyzing a considerable amount of data on banking panics between 1857 and 1933, they conclude (ibid., p. 60):

> While several runs on the banking system took place before the formation of the Federal Reserve System in 1914, banks took actions that limited their effects. By issuing clearinghouse loan certificates that other banks accepted to clear checks, banks operated temporarily with relatively low reserve ratios. In the more severe runs, bankers jointly restricted payments but continued operating. Moreover, even prior to the creation of the federal safety net in the United States, runs on the banking system were infrequent. The banking system can operate for many years without runs on the banking system, even in recessions.

Finally, it should be noted that if there were no deposit insurance, many depositors (or information services, such as Standard and Poor's) would assess the risk of a bank's failing, much as creditors of non-banks now assess the risk of their debt. At the same time, prudently run banks would provide depositors with the requisite information. Bank assets, while not transparent, are not that difficult to value. Losses from loan defaults often are limited by collateral and covenants. Information can be obtained as to which banks hold undiversified portfolios, and how changes in interest rates and economic conditions affect banks' net worths. (Contrast this situation with that faced by creditors of companies with investments in specialized plant and equipment, advertising, and research and development.) Furthermore, because (absent deposit insurance) banks' capital would be higher (as it was prior to the enactment of credible federal deposit insurance), in most instances depositors could limit their assessment to the cash flow required to repay their deposits, as promised, rather than to the valuation of banks' assets.

Hence, despite their holding demand debt, depositors generally did not and do not readily remove their funds precipitously, and runs on solvent banks by uninsured depositors (and depositors generally before the creation of federal deposit insurance) are (and were) rare.[4] Furthermore, it is not necessary that all or even that most depositors evaluate banks; all that is required is that a sufficient marginal number move their funds according to the safety and returns offered by alternative depositories and investments.

In conclusion, although depositors may mistakenly believe that solvent banks are insolvent and impose a liquidity crisis on solvent banks, it seems just as or more likely that the possibility as well as the consequence of runs benefit solvent banks. Consequently, avoidance of negative externalities from runs on solvent banks as a justification for deposit insurance does not seem warranted.

Disruption of the Financial System Generally

Runs on banks could result in a systemic failure under two conditions, neither of which should occur in the modern world. First, depositors might withdraw their funds in the form of currency which they do not re-deposit in other banks (termed a 'currency run'). Second, if there is a run to currency, the central bank might not take adequate offsetting actions.

Prior to the availability of credible deposit insurance, runs to currency occurred when people used specie (usually gold or silver) as their money. The specie could be exported or hoarded, thereby resulting in a reduction of base money and a multiple contraction of the money supply. For example, in 1890 Baring Brothers, an important London banking firm, failed and its European creditors insisted that the firm's US customers repay their debt in gold. This reduction in US base money caused a small panic in 1891, which was fueled further by gold hoarding due to fears that the US government would abandon the gold standard, thereby devaluing the purchasing power of currency and increasing the value of gold. As a result, over 600 banks and thirteen of every 1000 businesses failed. The only other time in United States history that a run to currency was accompanied by a large number of bank failures was in 1930–33.[5] A run to currency is not likely to occur today in most developed countries (even absent deposit insurance), because it is preferable for fearful depositors to transfer their funds to other banks. Holding funds in currency would not only subject the former depositors to the risk of theft, but would deny them the benefits of transferring funds by check. It should be noted that, while transfers of deposits among banks may harm the sending bank, the money supply and total bank credit will be altered only to the extent that banks hold different ratios of reserves to deposits and have different lending patterns. Furthermore, transfers from domestic to foreign banks do not affect the domestic money supply, as long as currency is not physically exported.

Even if there were a run to currency, the multiple contraction of the money supply that would result could be offset by central bank open market operations or by direct (discount window) lending. For example, if people hoarded or exported currency, the central bank could buy securities, thereby increasing banks' reserves and offsetting the decline in base money. Or it could lend funds directly to the affected banks. Thus, the provision of government-supplied deposit insurance is not required to prevent or ameliorate bank runs. Such crises can be prevented by central bank actions.[6] In fact, as Schwartz (1988) demonstrates, most countries' central banks have learned to supply reserves when the public ran to currency. In a review of data from seventeen countries, she finds that after 1915, banking panics were experienced only by Italy (1921), Japan (1927), Austria (1931), Germany (1931) and the United States (1930–33).

The Failure of a Giant Bank[7]

The greatest fear of the banking authorities in most countries appears to be the failure of a giant bank. They are concerned that depositors in other giant banks will lose confidence in the entire banking system and withdraw their deposits. Just why presumably financially sophisticated corporate treasurers would be unable to distinguish among banks and how they expect to pay their companies' bills without checking accounts or where they would keep the withdrawn funds are questions the authorities seem not to ask. The authorities also are concerned that their countries' giant banks should have the reputation of being prudently managed.

There is no empirical support for the authorities' apparent belief that the failure of a giant bank would result in contagious runs on other giant banks or on banks generally (nor is there reason to expect a systemic failure, as is discussed at p. 340). Kaufman (1994) reviews studies of the effect on other banks of the failures of six large banks in the United States between 1973 and 1988, three bank failures in Hong Kong between 1982 and 1985, two bank failures in Canada in 1985, and the unexpected announcement of suspended debt repayments by Mexico, Brazil and other Latin American countries in 1982,

1983 and 1987. These studies found no failures of similar banks and little evidence of deposit outflows. Most of the studies examined the stock prices of other banks to determine whether the failure or lesser problems of a large bank affected the economic value of similar banks. Kaufman (1994, p. 129) reports that

> [w]ith only rare exceptions, these studies report strong evidence that [share] return contagion occurred only for banks in the same market or product area as the initially affected bank. The stock market (investors) successfully differentiated among banks on almost all occasions. Strong shocks at one bank or small group of banks did not spill over to other banks randomly or to all banks.

Regardless of this evidence, many (perhaps most) countries follow a 'too big to fail – TBTF' policy (Kaufman, 1990). In the United States, the banking authorities' concern resulted in the guarantee of all the liabilities of the Continental Illinois Corporation when its subsidiary, the Continental Illinois Bank, failed in 1984, despite a previously announced and applied policy of not bailing out uninsured depositors (called 'modified payoffs'). The Bank of England provided substantial aid in 1979 to several banks with international obligations (Slater Walker Ltd and Edward Bates & Sons Ltd), and in 1984 it arranged for and supported a guarantee of the liabilities of Johnson Matthey Bankers, one of five officially recognized London gold dealers. In 1965 the Bank of Japan made large, unsecured loans to Yamaichi Securities to forestall its failure.[8] It seems likely that other countries would act similarly should one of their giant banks be in danger of failing.

Disruption of the Payments System

A bank participating in the payments system that failed could disrupt the system, if other banks held its uncleared funds and did not honor them. This possibility, though, can be diminished considerably by several actions. First, banks could limit their exposure with bilateral credit limits and net debit caps. They also could be required to hold capital or collateral sufficient to cover net uncleared funds. Or, participants could protect themselves much as they do when dealing with their other customers and correspondents or respondents, by refusing to deal with banks that are undercapitalized. Second, the legal obligations of all participants in the payments system can be clearly specified to reduce the cost of controversies. Third, participants in the system could agree to guarantee the obligations of a defaulting institution, with each assuming a pro rata share of its settlement obligation. These procedures are employed by the multilateral payment netting and settlement system operated by the New York Clearing House Association (CHIPS).

Government-run payments systems can charge for overdrafts, which would give participants incentives to reduce the amount of uncleared funds outstanding, thereby reducing the risk assumed by the government agency. Or, the system could permit only transfers against funds known to be in place.

The domestic check collection system faces little danger of major disruption from the failure of a participating bank. At worst, a bank that presents checks for payments would incur losses only to the extent that it could not charge the account of its customer who deposited checks drawn on the failed bank. (The customer, then, would absorb the loss.) Nor would correspondent banks lose much if their respondent failed, as long as they limited their deposits in such banks much as they limit loans to a single borrower. In fact, the losses are likely to be smaller than when a customer fails, in part because banks ought to be able to evaluate and monitor other banks better than other kinds of enterprises.

Considering the availability of methods for reducing the cost and risk of settlement defaults, deposit insurance that might prevent runs on solvent banks is not justified as a means of preventing disruption to the payments system.[9]

Conclusion – Externalities from Bank Runs

Theory and evidence do not support justifying government-provided deposit insurance as a means of mitigating the cost of negative externalities related to depositor runs. The threat of runs has the salutary effect of encouraging solvent banks to avoid risks and hold sufficient capital so that depositors have no reason to withdraw their funds precipitously. Runs, when they occur, have the desirable property of closing insolvent banks promptly.[10] In the unlikely event that depositors run to currency, the central bank can prevent a multiple contraction of the money supply with open market operations or direct loans to banks.

Political Expediency as a Justification of Government-provided Deposit Insurance

It is generally accepted in almost all commercially developed countries that depositors, alone among investors generally, have a right to government-provided guarantees. The Department of the Treasury (1991, Chapter XXI, Table 2) lists thirty countries as having formal deposit insurance systems. Bartholomew (1989) analyzes eighteen of these systems. He reports that membership is strictly voluntary in seven countries.[11] Seven systems are officially sponsored and administered.[12] Five countries' systems are administered by an industry association,[13] and six jointly by the industry and government.[14] Following adoption of the Second Banking Directive in 1992 by the European Union, deposit insurance will be required in all member countries.

Kane (1988b and 1992) has put forth a persuasive model that explains the incentives for government officials to provide explicit or implicit insurance of deposits. He points out that these officials benefit from assuring depositors that their funds are safe when a bank appears to be failing, since the officials suffer damage to their careers by not offering such assurance. Hence, even when deposit insurance only partially protects depositors or when there is no explicit obligation of government to protect depositors, government officials extend the financial safety net either by paying them off with taxpayers' funds or arranging for the merger with financial assistance of the failed institutions and assumption of depositors' liabilities.

Kane's model is supported by the experience of the United States and other countries. Although deposit insurance in the United States has been limited to a maximum amount per account (presently US$100,000, increased from US$40,000 in 1980, and originally US$2500 in 1933), in practice almost all deposit balances have been covered. Prior to the early 1980s, almost all insured depository failures were resolved by the purchase of the assets and assumption of the liabilities of the failed bank or thrift (P&As) by other depository institutions, with the Federal Deposit Insurance Corporation (FDIC) or Federal Savings and Loan Insurance Corporation (FSLIC) making up the difference, when there was one. Prior to the failure of the Penn Square Bank (Oklahoma City) in 1982, depositors had lost only US$3 million of US$19,959 million in deposits at failed banks (FDIC, 1982). Uninsured depositors in Penn Square Bank were not covered because this bank failed under conditions in which many of its depositors with large balances were considered to have been complicit, and the bank had outstanding very large amounts of contingent liabilities (letters of credit) that legally would have had to have been treated equally with deposits had uninsured deposits been protected. In addition, the bank's location in a unit banking state made finding a purchaser difficult for the FDIC. Following the Penn Square failure, a few banks were liquidated with losses to uninsured depositors, but this practice was ended in 1984 when all creditors of Continental Illinois were bailed out by the FDIC. The situation for thrifts was similar. Furthermore, although the US federal government did not have a legal obligation to bail out the insolvent FSLIC, the insurer of savings and loan association deposits, President Bush announced that no depositor would lose a penny, and Congress later provided a Treasury bail-out of the bankrupt fund.

Few politicians in the United States have suggested that government-backed deposit insurance might be replaced with private insurance, although the Federal Deposit Insurance Improvement Act of 1991 (FDICIA) requires the FDIC to operate a pilot program in which it would share risk with private insurance companies. However, the United States's experience with private deposit insurance systems has not been good. English (1993) reviews the 30 such systems that were in existence in 1982, of which only eight survived into the 1990s. Of these eight, only five provide primary deposit insurance (the other three supplement FDIC insurance). English finds that the private systems failed or were dissolved for two major reasons. 'First, the systems' designs were flawed' (ibid., p. 61). The funds were too small, strong institutions could leave the system, and consequently the funds could not be augmented after a major failure had depleted them.

> The second problem was that the regulation of the insured institutions – and particularly that of the largest institutions – was weak. Members were allowed to make risky investments, violate state regulations on the sizes of loans, and engage in self-dealing and other fradulent [*sic*] activities. It is clear that state regulators and deposit insurance officials knew about many of the improper activities far in advance of the crises they caused. It appears that they failed to act to avoid the crises because of the economic and political power of the insured institutions (ibid.).

In the three largest such failures (Ohio, Maryland and Rhode Island), state legislators acted to bail out depositors.[15]

The experience of the United States has been mirrored in many other countries, including those with and without formal deposit insurance. Examples include the effective bail out of all depositors when several Ontario Canada trust companies and two banks in western Canada banks failed. Even though Canadian deposit insurance is limited to CAN$60,000 per account, the banking officials delayed closing the affected institutions until depositors with greater deposit balances had time to remove or draw them down. When the banks finally were closed, the government compensated depositors not covered by deposit insurance.[16] In Israel, despite the absence of deposit insurance, depositors in a failed bank were repaid with taxpayer funds when the banking authorities admitted that they had failed to uncover a fraud by the bank's principal owner. A few years later, an Israeli bank failed as a consequence of having made risky investments. Although its depositors benefited from having received above-market interest rates, they successfully argued that they, too, should be bailed out. (Some other examples are described above at p. 341.)

The consequence of the 1990 failure of the Farrow Group of building societies in Victoria, Australia is instructive, in part because it is well described by Kane and Kaufman (1993), on which this narrative is based, and in part because its depositors knew they were not protected by insurance. The Farrow Group had grown tenfold in the six years beginning in June 1981, and doubled in size in its last year and one-half. It paid deposit interest rates of some two to four percentage points above equivalent rates offered by more conservative institutions. The funds were invested largely in commercial mortgages. When it failed, Farrow had A$2.9 billion in assets (55 percent of the Victoria building society sector) and negative net worth of more than A$500 million. Although the deposits were not insured, to forestall a run, government officials announced that 'all relevant authorities [would] ensure that depositors' funds are secure' (Kane and Kaufman, 1993, p. 23). 'Although', as Kane and Kaufman (p. 18) report, 'the Victoria premier initially voiced his opposition to a taxpayer bailout of depositors', legislation was enacted that repaid depositors at par over a five year period. Thus, although depositors absorbed some of the losses (measured by the present value of the payouts), they were essentially bailed out by their fellow taxpayers.

Perhaps the only exceptions to this pattern is the experience of depositors in the British Commonwealth Merchant Bank (BCMB) and the Bank of Credit and Commerce International (BCCI). Following the failure and closing of these banks, the UK banking authorities did not give the depositors more than the amounts covered by deposit insurance – 75 percent of deposits with a ceiling of £20,000. (BCCI depositors in African and Asian countries also appear to have taken losses.)[17] However, when some 26 'secondary' banks took large real-estate and consumer loan losses and were in danger of failing, the Bank of England and the London clearing banks arranged a 'lifeboat' of financial support that rescued the secondary banks' depositors. (The Bank of England also guaranteed the liabilities of Slater Walker Ltd, Edward Bates & Sons Ltd, and Johnson Matthey Bankers – see p. 342.)

Thus, with a few exceptions, theory and experience leads to the expectation that depositors will be provided a safety net by governments. The question considered next is the extent to which moral hazard really is a problem for which government-imposed constraints on banks are required.

V NON-GOVERNMENT RESTRAINTS ON DEPOSIT-INSURANCE MORAL HAZARD

Among the non-government restraints that keep bankers from taking full advantage of government-insured deposits are: (1) concerns by depositors whose funds may be only partially insured; (2) concerns by other creditors whose obligations may not be insured; (3) equity holders' concerns about loss of their investments; and (4) bank managers' concerns about loss of their jobs and reputations. There is reason to believe that these restraints have been important in reducing the adverse effects of moral hazard engendered by government-provided deposit insurance.

Partially Uninsured Depositors[18]

Most deposit insurance systems limit the amount that is insured (e.g. US$100,000 per account in the United States and ¥10,000,000 in Japan) or insure a portion of depositors' balances (e.g. 75 percent in the United Kingdom and Colombia, up to a maximum amount). Consequently, depositors with large balances are at risk of loss should their bank fail before they can remove their funds. Depositors with time-dated deposits (e.g. certificates of deposits and time accounts) cannot withdraw their funds without penalty until the dates specified in their contracts. Hence, they are at risk. However, until 1992, in practice 100 percent of deposits in the United States and other countries generally have been covered, as the banking authorities have tended to arrange for the merger of a failed bank with the acquiring bank assuming all deposit liabilities. Alternatively, the authorities provide the failing bank with resources and delay its closing, which gives uncovered depositors time to remove their funds. The Federal Deposit Insurance Corporation Improvement Act of 1991 (FDICIA) should alter this situation, as it requires the authorities to resolve a failed bank in the manner which results in the least cost to the FDIC, including liquidating the bank with losses imposed on uninsured depositors.

Uninsured depositors' uncertainty about what the authorities might do gives them an incentive to monitor the risks taken by their banks. Even during the periods when it was likely that failed banks would be resolved at no loss to uninsured depositors, empirical studies have found that riskier banks and bank holding companies paid higher market rates of interest on partially insured bank or uninsured bank-holding-company certificates of deposit (CDs).[19] The uncertainty also has led to the banking authorities' concerns (e.g. Randall, 1989) that uninsured depositors (particularly those with accounts at very large banks) might 'run', thereby possibly disrupting the financial system. Although there is good reason to believe that the authorities' fears are not well founded, they appear to be disinclined to permit such runs to occur.

Non-deposit Creditors

Non-deposit creditors ought not rely on deposit insurance to protect them from loss should a bank fail. Prior to passage of the Financial Institutions Reform, Recovery, and Enforcement Act of 1989 (FIRREA), though, US courts held that the FDIC had to treat all creditors alike; if all deposits were *de facto* insured, so were all liabilities unless they were explicitly subordinated to deposits. FIRREA authorized the FDIC to discriminate among classes of creditors with equal standing. Depositor preference was enacted in the tax act of 1993. Thus, data on risk-premiums charged by many non-deposit creditors in the United States prior to 1993 is of limited value.[20]

It seems clear, though, that debt that is not explicitly or implicitly insured against loss would yield interest at a rate that reflects its risk. Furthermore, such debt has many desirable qualities from the standpoint of reducing the cost of moral hazard. Uninsured debt holders, unlike equity holders, do not get the benefits of risks that turn out well, but do bear the cost of risks that turn out badly and that more than deplete equity. Hence, these debt holders have considerable incentives to monitor banks' activities, and banks have incentives to operate and hold levels of equity that reduce the interest charge to an optimal level (as is discussed above). In effect, then, the interest rate on uninsured debt is like a risk-adjusted deposit insurance premium. (Uninsured debt has additional beneficial properties that are outlined in Section VI, pp. 356–7 and 358–62.)

Equity Holders

Equity holders have incentives to reduce the cost of uninsured debt, as discussed in Section III. If government deposit insurance is provided to depositors and the government does not protect its interests as would private debtholders, the equity holders can benefit by taking greater risks, as is also discussed in Section III. However, if the amount of equity investment is sufficiently large, the incentives for equity holders to take high risks are very small. With deposit insurance provided by the government, most depositors no longer need be concerned about the amount of capital available to absorb losses. Hence, it is not surprising that equity as a percentage of assets at US insured commercial banks dropped from about 14 percent in 1933 to less than 9 percent in the period following the Second World War. In addition, the provision of double liability for shareholders in national banks was eliminated in 1936.

However, the book value of equity does not include the value of intangible assets. Before the late 1970s, entry into banking markets in the United States was constrained and a bank charter had considerable value. Thus, the owners of banks stood to lose considerally more than the book values of their equity from taking high risks. The inflation of the late 1970s and interest ceilings on bank deposits that were considerably lower than market rates of interest induced alternative suppliers of banking services to enter banks' markets. This increased entry and competition reduced the value of banks' charters, thereby reducing the amount of their equity. As discussed in Section III, the value of the deposit-insurance (limited liability) put option increases as equity decreases, *ceteris paribus*. The reduction of banks' capital is responsible for many of the failures in the 1980s, as banks that incurred losses on real-estate and other loans had insufficient capital to absorb those losses.

Bank Managers' Concerns About Their Jobs and Reputations

Banks that are managed by executives who do not have substantial equity investments in their institutions are faced with an agency problem. Although bank owners might benefit from their bank's being operating at a high level of risk, bank managers stand to lose their jobs and reputations should the risks turn out badly.[21] In this event, both present and future employers probably would find it difficult to distinguish between *ex ante* desirable risk-taking and bad management. Hence, unless managers' wealth is invested largely in the stock of their banks or they are directly paid for risk taking with high salaries and perquisites and unless they place a relatively low value on their reputations, it is likely that they will not involve their banks in high risk investments and activities. Furthermore, in some countries (notably, the United States, particularly since passage of FDICIA in 1991), bank managers and directors are subject to civil monetary fines and criminal prosecution for operating their banks in an unsafe and possibly fraudulent manner, which further restrains their undertaking high-risk ventures.

Conclusions – Non-government Restraints on Deposit-Insurance Moral Hazard

Even in the presence of government-provided deposit insurance that is underpriced with respect to risk, banks generally have not taken risks that would serve to optimize the value of their put option. There have been very few commercial bank failures in countries other than the United States, which is characterized by a large number of unit banks and restrictions on banks' portfolios and activities that restrain them from diversifying effectively. Despite these restrictions, there were very few bank failures in the United States before the 1980s, when bank equity levels were higher and when depositors were more at risk than in the subsequent years.

A study of savings and loan failures also provides evidence that is inconsistent with the hypothesis that moral-hazard-driven risk taking was largely responsible for the large losses imposed by insolvent thrifts on US taxpayers. Benston and Carhill (1994) revalued the net worth of all thrifts operating at year-end 1984 (over 3000) to current values, and examined the growth in investments, losses of the thrifts to year-end 1988, and their closure to mid-year 1990. They found that, on average, the economically insolvent and close-to-insolvent thrifts grew at lower rates and invested less in risky assets compared to the stronger thrifts. These data are inconsistent with the hypothesis that most of the US$150 billion in losses incurred by US thrifts during the 1980s were due largely to credit-risk-taking that was engendered by the moral hazard related to federal deposit insurance. Most of the thrifts' losses resulted from reductions in the value of long-term fixed-interest mortgages when interest rates increased sharply in 1979–81. Moral hazard considerations probably played an important role in these losses. Without deposit insurance, it seems doubtful that short-term savers would have placed their funds in institutions predominantly holding such duration-unbalanced portfolios and having capital-to-asset ratios as low as 6 percent.

Somewhat similar findings are reported for a study of undercapitalized (less than 5.5 percent of assets) commercial banks between 1985 and 1989. Gilbert (1991) examined the 531 such banks, 87 percent of which had total assets of less than $100 million. He reports that '[m]ost reduced their assets substantially while undercapitalized, consistent with the desires of bank supervisors. A sizable number, however, actually experienced rapid asset growth' [44 banks (8 percent) grew by more than 25 percent] (ibid., p. 24). He also finds that only 15 percent of the banks paid dividends and 24 percent reported their highest level of insider loans while undercapitalized. Those that violated these constraints, though, had the same recovery rates as those that did not.

Gilbert (1992) also compared the losses imposed on the FDIC's Bank Insurance Fund (BIF) to the pre-failure behavior of 552 commercial banks that failed in 1985 to 1990. He divides the banks into three groups: those with capital/asset ratios below 5 percent for five or more quarters before failure, those with such ratios in the last two quarters before failure, and the balance. He reports an average shrinkage in assets by the first two groups and some (2.5 percent) asset growth by the better capitalized balance. Of greatest importance, Gilbert (1992) finds no statistically significant relationship between the losses/total assets of the failures borne by the BIF and dividends-paid/total assets or capital/assets (variously defined) four quarters before failure. However, he finds that BIF losses/assets are significantly and inversely related to asset growth.

The fact that losses due to moral-hazard-induced behavior have not been greater or do not appear to have occurred may be due to constraints imposed by government banking authorities (which is Gilbert's explanation), rather than to self-imposed constraints by bank managers. Some evidence to this effect is provided by Calomiris's (1990) study of pre-FDIC state deposit systems in the United States. He finds that the systems that went bankrupt were characterized by fraud and unsound banking practices. These banks apparently were owner-operated, and poorly regulated. Hence, they were relatively unconstrained.

Considering that depositors generally in most countries believe that they are protected from loss or expect to be bailed out by government (that is to say, taxpayers), it would be unwise to expect that non-government constraints would be adequate to reduce moral hazard costs sufficiently. I turn now to methods that government could adopt that might serve this purpose.

VI GOVERNMENT-IMPOSED CONSTRAINTS ON DEPOSIT-INSURANCE MORAL HAZARD

Among the constraints that banking authorities have imposed or could impose on banks with insured deposits to control moral hazard costs are: (1) restrictions on banks' assets and activities, including limiting investments to short-term marketable securities; (2) risk-adjusted deposit insurance premiums; (3) risk-adjusted capital; (4) higher capital requirements; and (5) structured early intervention and resolution (SEIR). Other possible actions that are not considered herein include mixed government-private deposit insurance and very low levels of coverage (e.g. US$5,000 per account). These alternatives are excluded because the analysis presented in Section IV (p. 343) leads to the conclusion that governments will bail out all or almost all depositors, regardless of legal requirements. Hence, government should face up to the moral hazard risk that accompanies this safety net. Because I believe that SEIR (together with a high required capital/asset ratio) is the best solution, I describe its benefits and shortcomings rather fully.

Restrictions on Banks' Assets and Activities

Legislators and the banking authorities have attempted to reduce the risks that banks might undertake by prohibiting them from offering some products and services. The most important of these, restrictions on securities and insurance sales and underwriting, are analyzed below (p. 353). An extreme form of restriction would require banks to invest or collateralize insured deposits only in or with short-term marketable securities. This 'narrow bank' proposal is analyzed below (p. 354).

Restrictions on Securities and Insurance Sales and Underwriting
Banks in the United States and Japan (on which US banking laws were imposed) have been legally restricted from offering products and services that banks in most other countries can offer. These include full-service securities brokerage and underwriting, investments in equities, insurance sales and underwriting, and travel services. Some of these constraints clearly are due to the political power of banks' competitors (insurance agents, travel agencies and securities brokerage). Other constraints have been justified on the grounds that the safety net of deposit insurance should not cover securities and life insurance underwriting. This argument, though, is both logically and empirically incorrect.

The claim is illogical because the safety net relates only to deposits, not to assets or sales of products, and banks can take the optimal level of risk whether or not they are permitted to offer securities and life insurance products. Assuming that risk-adjusted deposit insurance premiums or capital, or SEIR and higher capital requirements, were not sufficient to eliminate the deposit-insurance subsidy, the issue is whether the amount of the subsidy is affected by the assets in which banks invest or the activities that they can undertake. Such a relationship might exist if these restrictions prevented banks from taking additional risks that might serve to maximize the value of the deposit-insurance put option. However, without the restrictions, banks are not limited in the amount of risk they can assume. For example, banks can make loans that are very risky, including equity participation loans. They can buy and sell financial futures, options and other derivatives and hold duration-unbalanced portfolios. Thus, the addition of securities and insurance sales and underwriting adds little or nothing to the risks banks otherwise can choose to take.

Nor is there any logic supporting the claim that banks might use the deposit insurance subsidy to cross-subsidize securities or insurance products. Why should banks want to subsidize purchasers of these products rather than transfer the resources to their shareholders or managers? Alternatively, whether or not banks get a subsidy, they could use shareholders' funds to subsidize whatever they wish. There is no necessary relationship, therefore, between the deposit insurance subsidy and the assets in which banks might invest.

Rather, constraints on banks' investments and activities might increase the risk of their failure, for two reasons. One is that banks might be prevented from producing and offering an optimal combination of products and services, which reduces their profitability. The other is that banks might be prevented from reducing risk optimally. Although the banned products and services may present net cash flows that have higher variances than those from the bank's other operations, their covariances with these other cash flows would be imperfect and could be negative. Hence, removal of asset and activity restraints could reduce banks' risk by lowering the variance of their total net cash flows.

Empirically, a number of simulation studies find that commercial banks in the United States could increase their net profits with either little change or a decrease in the variance of returns by combining securities and insurance operations with commercial banking operations.[22] These studies necessarily do not include savings from economies of scope. However, a study of the pre-Glass–Steagall Act period found that commercial banks with securities activities and holdings failed at much lower rates than other, roughly similar banks (White, 1986). Additional analyses of allegations that banks engaged in securities activities were more prone to failure than other banks are examined by Benston (1990, Ch. 3), and found to be unsupported.[23] This evidence, plus the observation that very few universal banks have failed, indicates that restrictions on banks' assets and activities tends to increase rather than decrease the likelihood that costs will be imposed on government-provided deposit insurance funds or taxpayers.

'Narrow Bank' Proposals

If all deposits were invested in or collateralized by assets that could be liquidated immediately at prices sufficient to cover the deposit obligations, there would be no need for deposit insurance, with two exceptions: fraud and/or a substantial unexpected decline in the value of the assets that was not covered by the bank's capital.[24] The assets would include government obligations and highly rated commercial paper and might include other assets traded on well-organized secondary markets. The durations of the assets would have to be matched with the durations of the deposits; hence, interest-bearing assets probably would be limited to those that are repriced within 90 days. Thus, most loans would not be included among the permissible assets.

One problem with the narrow-bank proposal is that, by limiting banks to deposits and short-term marketable assets, economies of scope derived from relationship banking and common production of financial products and services cannot be obtained. However, some of these benefits could be kept if the narrow bank were operated within a holding company, subsidiaries of which engage in other activities (such as direct lending, securities and insurance sales and underwriting). The alternative of collateralizing deposits with short-term marketable assets would permit banks to function as they now do, although some additional operations costs would be incurred.[25]

An important remaining problem, though, is the cost of the system to depositors. Short-term marketable securities usually have relatively low yields.[26] Consequently, depositors probably would be charged for fund-transfer services. Other suppliers of fund-transfers services and short-term investments probably would develop and successfully compete with products that are similar to checks and savings accounts, much as negotiable orders of withdrawal (NOW) from savings accounts and brokers' drafts are indistinguishable from demand deposit checks. These firms could pay 'depositors' interest on their balances, because they could invest the funds in illiquid assets. Should one or more of these firms fail, the theory and evidence presented in Section IV (p. 343) indicate that government will bail out the 'depositors'. Hence, the problem will only be delayed, not solved.

Risk-adjusted Deposit Insurance Premiums

It seems obvious that deposit-insurance premiums should be adjusted for the risk imposed on the government, much as insurance companies charge premiums that reflect the risks they assume. If the premiums accurately reflected risk, the moral hazard problem would be solved. Unfortunately, despite many calls for such premiums by academics and legislators in the United States, not much has been done to implement the concept. Before 1992, the US federal deposit insurance agencies charged all insured institutions the same percentage of total domestic deposits.[27] Following a requirement of the FDICIA, in 1992 the FDIC instituted a small differential in premiums based on banks' capital-to-asset ratios. No other country imposes a premium based on a bank's risk. For example, a flat rate is imposed by Germany and Japan. France and Italy also used flat rates, but these are based on the losses to the insurance funds during the year.[28]

In an important sense, most countries impose a form of risk-adjusted deposit insurance premiums in the form of increasingly severe and costly (to banks) supervision of banks that are believed to be imprudently managed.[29] Explicit risk-adjusted premiums, however, require an acceptable procedure to calculate the rates, and such a procedure has not been developed as yet. Among the methods that have been considered and rejected are premiums based on banks' investments in groups of assets (estimates are imprecise, not based on evidence, not reflective of covariances among asset returns, and may be used by government agents to direct credit toward or away from some borrowers), option-pricing formula (which are sensitive to small changes in assumptions, usually based on stock market data that are not available for many – in the United States, most – banks), and rates charged by private reinsurers that provide partial deposit coverage (a tactic that has been proposed but, to my knowledge, never tried). *Ex post* settling up also has been suggested, where banks establish escrow accounts with the deposit insurance agency that are charged for the losses they impose (Benston *et al.*, 1986). This method would give banks incentives to constrain risk taking.

Aside from computational difficulties, risk-adjusted premiums suffer from five important, additional problems. One is the concern that the additional premiums could not be sufficiently great to dissuade some bankers from taking risks that the deposit insurance agency considers to be excessive. The second is the moral hazard that bank owners with low levels of capital would benefit from paying high premiums for the right to take great risks, because they cannot lose more than their bank capital investments.[30] Third, risk assessment almost always is based on *ex post* experience, which for many bank risks is a notoriously bad predictor. For example, although US thrifts held portfolios that were very much subject to interest-rate risk (long-term, fixed-interest mortgages financed with short-term savings), particularly after the Second World War, it was not until the interest rates increased sharply in 1979 that the industry was destroyed. Real estate collapses have happened before, but it seems clear that many bankers did not predict the present collapse. Risk-seeking bankers, therefore, could and would have incentives to invest in problematic assets and activities that had not been identified as especially risky. Fourth, a closure rule still is required, particularly as banks that have reason to believe they will soon be closed have much to gain and would lose little in the form of higher premium rates by taking great risks. Indeed, if banks were closed before they become insolvent, required insurance premiums could be very small. Fifth, the premiums might be assessed primarily as a means of allocating assets to ends preferred by government agencies.

It should be noted once more that interest on time-dated debt that is explicitly not insured (subordinated debentures) offers an effective form of risk-adjusted deposit insurance premiums. Furthermore, if such debt were publicly traded, the banking authority could view the interest rate on the debt as measuring the market's assessment of a bank's risk taking behavior, which is likely to predate the authority's assessment. If the debt had staggered maturities, problems faced by a bank in refinancing its debt would serve as a useful signal, whether or not the debt was publicly traded.[31]

Risk-adjusted Capital[32]

The risk-adjusted capital requirements established by the Basle Committee on Banking Regulations and Supervisory Practices in 1988 have been accepted by most developed countries. This standard specifies two tiers of capital and four risk classes. It is applied to banks on a consolidated basis that includes subsidiaries undertaking banking and financial business, and also includes off-balance sheet items. Half of the capital must be in the first tier, 'core capital'. It includes common stock, non-cumulative perpetual preferred stock and post-tax retained earnings, less goodwill and investments in unconsolidated financial subsidiaries. At most subordinated debt can comprise half of the second tier, 'supplementary capital'. No capital is required against the first risk class, primarily cash and claims against specified governments and domestic public-sector entities and central banks. Capital is required against 20 percent of the second risk class, which includes claims on multilateral development banks and on banks in some countries and on loans guaranteed by them, short-term (less than one year maturity) loans guaranteed by other banks, cash items in the process of collection, and government-guaranteed mortgage-backed securities. Capital is required against 50 percent of mortgage loans on borrower-owned or rented residential property, the third risk class. All other assets require the full capital ratio of 8 percent. Off balance-sheet exposures must be added to the amounts in the four risk classes to which they relate, after weighting by 'credit conversion factors'.

There is some reason to believe that the risk categories specified in the Basle capital standard represent an improvement over counting all assets as equally risky. Avery and Berger (1991) find that the statistical correlation between measures of bank risk (e.g., level and variability of earnings, nonperforming loans, loan charge-off rates, and failures) is higher for risk-adjusted capital than for unadjusted capital. Bradley, Wambeke and Whidbee (1991) report that the risk-based capital is more effective than unweighted capital in identifying prospective failures and in predicting the cost of failure resolution. Cordell and King (1995) estimate the market-determined capital/asset ratio from stock market data and correlate this measure with the four risk categories and off-balance sheet items. They find that the weights of the 100 percent category for banks and 50 percent category for thrifts is reasonably closely related to the market measure, but find little distinction among the weights of the other categories. In addition, they find that some off-balance sheet items for banks may reduce risk, which implies that a portfolio approach should be taken for measuring risk. In a related paper Cordell and King (1992) dissagregate the 100 percent risk category, and find significant variation in risk within that category. Construction and development loans and installment consumer debt have market risk ratings that are more than one-and-a-half to twice the Basle weights. They also find that bank size is inversely related to risk, that asset concentration is positively related to risk, and that risk varies considerably among regions.

Although risk-weighted capital appears to be somewhat superior to unweighted capital, the Basle capital standard suffers from some serious shortcomings. Interest-rate risk, which is responsible for most of the costs of the US$150 billion thrift disaster (Benston and Carhill, 1994), is not yet included (although the standard is supposed to be amended to include this risk). Nor is foreign-exchange risk accounted for. The fourth (100 percent) risk category is very broad – e.g., all commercial loans, whether to speculative enterprises that pay high interest rates or to stable enterprises that pay low interest rates, are weighted equally. The 50 percent risk rate on residential mortgages overstates credit risk and understates interest rate risk when banks hold duration-unbalanced portfolios. From past experience, it seems likely that the weights imposed are likely to reflect politically motivated hoped-for asset allocation. Most importantly, the standard fails to recognize the effect of diversification on risk. Nor is the agency problem of regulatory forbearance dealt with by the standard.

Higher Capital Requirements

Capital is the key to reducing the cost of moral hazard. Its role in this regard is considered first. Objections to high required ratios of capital to assets are then delineated and evaluated. The conclusion, given at the end of the section, is that it is both socially desirable and administratively feasible for the supervisory authorities to require much higher levels of capital at banks with insured deposits.

The Purpose of Capital[33]

Capital plays two important roles in reducing moral hazard costs. First, capital owners resist excessive risk because, as is discussed in

Section III, the value of the deposit-insurance put option decreases as equity holders' investments increase. Debt included in capital (subordinated debentures) further reduces equity holders' incentives to take risk, as the interest rate required on this debt must be sufficiently high to compensate debt holders for down-side risk.

Second, capital reduces the exogenous probability and cost of failures. Capital acts as a 'buffer' that absorbs losses before they are imposed on the deposit insurance fund or taxpayers. Whether or not moral-hazard drives banks to take risks, unexpected exogenous events can result in banks incurring considerable losses. Capital can be sufficient to absorb almost all losses, particularly when a bank is reasonably well diversified, except those resulting from massive fraud.

Were it not for the safety net of government-provided deposit insurance, market forces would move banks towards an optimal level and mix of debt and equity. But, as is discussed above, when the deposit insurance is underpriced, banks have incentives to hold lower levels of capital. As discussed on pp. 355–6, it is doubtful that an adequate risk-adjusted insurance premium can be devised and implemented. In any event, as Flannery (1989) and Iwamura (1993) show, when portfolio risk is imperfectly observed, higher levels of capital serve to reduce the effect of errors in estimating the value of the limited-liability put option.

It should be noted that capital should be measured in terms of market or current (present) values, rather than at historical accounting cost. Traditional accounting numbers tend to misstate economic values when prices have changed (particularly interest rates when banks hold duration-unbalanced portfolios). The expected present value of loans often is not recorded unless the loans are sold. Intangible assets (such as the core-deposit intangible) are not recorded and the value of off-balance sheet assets and liabilities may not be well measured. As is discussed elsewhere, market- or current-value accounting is not as difficult to implement as has been alleged.[34]

Objections to a High Required Ratio of Capital to Assets

Banks may object to having to have a high ratio of capital to assets, because they would lose most of the subsidy from previously underpriced deposit insurance. Since this objection is so blatantly self serving, it rarely is put forth. Rather, those who object to high capital requirements allege that capital is so costly that banks would not be able to compete successfully with unregulated suppliers of financial products and services. The further claim is made that higher capital requirements might cause banks to take more, rather than less, risk to compensate for the higher costs of capital.

Equity capital generally is said to be costly for two reasons. First, in the United States and many other countries with corporate income taxes, factor payments to shareholders are not deductible, unlike interest on debt.[35] This problem can be solved if the authorities would permit banks to hold subordinated (uninsured) debentures that count fully in meeting banks' capital requirements. As long as banks were not allowed to redeem debentures included in capital before the authorities could act to close a bank, subordinated debentures would protect the deposit insurance fund from loss at least as much as does equity. Indeed, because debenture holders do not gain the benefits from risk taking, the moral hazard problem is not present. (However, when a bank's equity is sufficiently depleted or eliminated, subordinated debt holders take on the moral-hazard attributes of equity holders.)

Second, empirical studies have found that issuance of equity capital tends to decrease share prices (e.g. Asquith and Mullins, 1986), apparently because of the tax effect just discussed and because risk is shifted from debt to equity holders. However, two studies report that equity issues by bank holding companies suffer a smaller decline in stock values than is reported for other firms (Wall and Peterson, 1990, and Wansley and Dhillon, 1989). Furthermore, if banks also issued subordinated debt, the higher costs of equity would be offset in large part by lower debt interest cost. In any event, agency cost and the transactions cost of issuing equity (or debt) is incurred by banks' non-regulated competitors as well.[36] Thus, other than loss of the deposit-insurance put option and absent regulatory constraints on subordinated debentures, and holding risk constant, the cost of capital is not higher for banks than for other firms.

The claim that greater amounts of more costly equity capital might drive bankers to assume greater risks also is without foundation. This assertion is contrary to the common-sense expectation that people with more of their own funds at risk would tend to take on less rather than more risk. However, some scholars point to a paper by Koehn and Santomero (1988) which seems to show that higher capital requirements would cause a utility-maximizing bank owner-manager to increase asset risk. However, Keeley and Furlong (1991) show that this result is due to two inappropriate assumptions. One is Koehn and Santomero's use of the capital-asset pricing model, which posits a positive relationship between risk and return. The other is their assumption that the bank's borrowing rates are constant; hence its costs are independent of portfolio (default) risk. Keeley and Furlong (1991) demonstrate that these assumptions may be appropriate only when the probability of failure is zero. Using a state-preference model, they show that, even with deposit insurance and constant deposit interest, the net marginal cost of deposits increases as leverage decreases, because the value of the put option is less with lower leverage. Furthermore, because lower leverage increases the probability of bankruptcy, the cost of uninsured deposits also increases. These higher costs make the assumption of greater risk unprofitable for a bank. They also demonstrate in an earlier paper (Furlong and Keeley, 1989, p. 891) that 'higher capital requirements reduce the incentives for a bank to increase asset risk'. They continue: '[o]ur results also indicate that a value-maximizing bank prefers to meet higher required capital ratios by raising additional capital, rather than merely by selling assets and retiring deposits'.

Finally, note that capital ratios are higher for institutions offering bank-like products that do not hold government-insured deposits (e.g. sales and consumer finance companies and commercial lenders.) Furthermore, capital ratios maintained by US banks were over 10 percent in the years before federal deposit insurance was enacted.

Conclusions – Higher Capital Requirements

Higher required capital need not be costly to banks (other than by depriving them of a subsidy) if they are not constrained from counting subordinated debentures as part of capital. Nor should such requirements have the perverse effect of driving banks to take greater risks, if the requirements are enforced and banks are promptly closed before their capital is depleted.

Indeed, it would be operationally very easy for most banks to implement higher capital requirements. Banks that have outstanding a sufficient amount of time deposits or CDs with maturities of at least a year need only replace them, as they mature, with obligations that are explicitly not covered by deposit insurance and not redeemable by the issuing bank. These debentures could be replaced, however, by other subordinated debentures; in fact, when the debentures had remaining maturities of about two years, they would have to be rolled over into debentures with longer maturities. These subordinated debentures should have a face value that would make it clear that they were not insured deposits (perhaps no less than US$10,000).

A bank's inability to meet the capital requirement would provide strong evidence that it is viewed by the market as insolvent.

It has been argued, though, that small banks could not sell subordinated debentures, as the size of the issue would be insufficient to repay investors' information costs at an interest cost these banks could pay. It seems likely, though, that some investors in a small bank's market area would have personal knowledge of the bank's owners, managers, and situation. Funds that specialize in analyzing and monitoring small banks and that offer investors a diversified portfolio of small-bank subordinated debentures might develop, much as venture-capital funds and corporate bond funds have evolved. In any event, if small (or any) banks cannot pay the interest rates that uninsured investors demand or alternatively cannot issue equity, they have not met the market test for existence that other firms must pass, and they should not continue operations (assuming that banks are not burdened with excessive regulatory costs).

The final issue to be considered is how the capital standard can be enforced, considering the agency problem posed by reluctant banking authorities and politically powerful or persuasive banks.

Structured Early Intervention and Resolution (SEIR)

The Basic Concept

Structured early intervention and resolution calls for explicit rules that govern when and how the bank supervisory authority first may and then must impose sanctions should a bank's capital decline below prespecified percentages of total assets. Benston and Kaufman proposed this system in 1988.[37] Since then, it has been endorsed and improved by a panel of economists sponsored by the Brookings Institution,[38] and by the Shadow Financial Regulatory Committee (1989). A modified version is included in the Federal Deposit Insurance Corporation Improvement Act of 1991 (FDICIA). In particular, FDICIA imposes lower capital/asset ratios and harsher penalties against bank officers for operating banks in an unsafe manner.[39]

SEIR is based on the belief that banks would voluntarily maintain their non-burdensome capital or go out of business before their capital was depleted, if faced with prespecified sanctions. Should capital-short banks not take advantage of these options, the deposit insurance fund would incur but small losses if they were closed before their capital declined to the point where losses to the fund would exceed the banks' remaining capital. However, this point rarely should be reached, as structured early intervention mimics the actions that would be taken by market participants in the absence of deposit insurance, with one exception. Bank examinations would continue to be made (although less often for adequately capitalized banks, which should reduce losses from fraud and gross mismanagement). With SEIR in place and capital measured at current values, banks can and should be permitted to provide any product or service, because bank owners would have sufficient capital to absorb almost all of the losses that might result.

The Benston–Kaufman Proposal[40]

Bank capital should include equity and all debt that is explicitly not guaranteed by the deposit insurance agency or government and that cannot be redeemed by the bank before the supervisory agencies can act. Subordinated debentures with present maturities of at least one year fit this requirement. Capital should be measured in terms of the economic market values of a bank's assets and liabilities. However, the proposed scheme also can be effective when capital is measured according to traditional accounting values.[41]

Four explicit, predetermined ranges or tranches of capital-to-asset ratios are specified.[42] Assets include off-balance sheet accounts. Assets are not classified according to risk because of the difficulties in measuring *ex-ante* risk accurately (as discussed above, p. 357).

(1) Banks are considered to have adequate capital when capital is, say, 10 percent or more of their total assets, measured in terms of market or current values.[43] Banks falling into this first tranche would be subject to minimum regulation and supervision.

(2) Banks with capital-to-asset ratios of, say, 6 to 9.9 percent are at the first level of supervisory concern. A bank in this second tranche is subject to increased regulatory supervision and more frequent monitoring of its activities. It is required to submit a business plan to raise more capital. At its discretion, the bank supervisory authority could require the bank to suspend dividend payments and obtain approval before transferring funds within a holding company system and could restrict the bank's asset growth.

(3) The third tranche is the second level of supervisory concern; it is reached when a bank's capital ratio falls below 6 percent and is at least 3 percent. Banks in this range are subject to intense regulatory supervision and monitoring. The supervisory authority

is required to suspend dividends, interest payments on subordinated debt, and unapproved outflows of funds to the bank's parent or affiliates. The institution must submit an emergency plan for its immediate recapitalization to the tranche one level.

(4) When a bank's capital falls below 3 percent of its assets, it is in tranche four – mandatory recapitalization and reorganization. The supervisory authority is required to quickly recapitalize the bank, merge it, or liquidate it in an orderly fashion by the sale of individual assets. The present owners and subordinated debt holders (who might, by then, be the owners) have two options; they may implement quickly the plan submitted when the institution moved into tranche three, or they could elect not to inject additional funds into the bank. If the owners and debt holders chose not to recapitalize the bank, any residual value from its sale or liquidation of its assets would be returned to them, after allowing for costs incurred.

The Advantages of SEIR

SEIR offers several advantages, in addition to the substitution of market forces for supervisory judgment and actions that accompanies a higher capital requirement including subordinated debentures. These advantages include: (1) low cost to the deposit insurance fund and, consequently, low premiums; (2) greater efficiency in the production of banking services; (3) greater efficiency in bank regulation and supervision; and (4) operational and political feasibility, since radical changes are not made to the banking structure and deposit insurance can be maintained.

Low Cost to the Deposit Insurance Fund. When banks are taken over and restructured or dissolved before their capital declines to some point above zero (Benston and Kaufman proposed 3 percent and the FDICIA specifies 2 percent of assets), the deposit insurance fund would suffer little in the way of losses. However, losses could result when (1) conditions deteriorate before the banking authority could act, (2) capital is overstated, and (3) government agents manage taken-over banks' assets incompetently.

The first situation can be reduced, if not completely eliminated, by the structured early intervention process and relatively high capital levels. The second can be reduced if market-value (or current-value) accounting were used to measure capital rather than historical-cost (traditional) accounting, which often yields significant mismeasurements of capital. The third cost is best avoided, as government employees' incentives tend to make them poor managers of private assets. SEIR works to avoid this cost, because it makes government take-over of banks unlikely. Shareholders would get the first priority to recapitalize, sell, or liquidate their banks. Considering the losses they would incur should their banks be taken over, shareholders should take one of these options, as long as their banks have positive economic net worth. Hence, with SEIR, deposit insurance premiums would be required only to pay administrative and monitoring costs and to compensate depositors in banks that failed because of fraud, gross mismanagement, or particularly adverse endogenous conditions. The premiums, therefore, should be very low.

Greater Bank Efficiency. Banks' efficiency would increase if they did not have to follow the dictates of regulators and if they were free from constraints, such as restrictions on where their offices may be located and which products and services they may offer. The present constraints are justified as necessary to protect the deposit insurance fund from excessive risk taking by insured depositories. Because SEIR provides adequate protection, the constraints generally would be superfluous. Consequently, banks would be free to change their products and operations to meet changing market conditions and operations costs. The result should be a more efficient allocation of resources and greater consumer welfare.

In fact, continued constraints on banks would be based principally on only two factors. First, politically determined restrictions on competition might be imposed, despite the fact that they are economically undesirable for consumers, because those who benefit have sufficient political power to maintain their rents. Second, if capital were measured according to current-value accounting and bank supervisors were unable to assess the value of certain assets or the risk inherent in certain activities, they would tend to undervalue the assets, which has the effect of increasing a bank's capital requirement.

Greater Regulatory Efficiency. SEIR reduces the need for regulatory control and supervision of banks that are well capitalized. Instead, supervisors can concentrate on banks with lesser levels of capital. These banks would be closely monitored, and their activities would be constrained, as is outlined above. Regulations would be restricted to those dealing with less-than-adequately capitalized banks. Hence, for most banks, regulators would not have to pass on applications for branches, mergers, product offerings, and the like. Furthermore, as noted above, the banking authority could get early warnings of problems with individual banks if banks' capital included subordinated debentures.

Operational and Political Feasibility. Unlike schemes such as the 'narrow' fail-safe bank, almost no operational change would be required to implement SEIR. As noted in Section VII (p. 361), all that would be required is for banks to convert some of their presently partially insured large certificates of deposit with maturities of at least one year for similar but completely and explicitly uninsured debentures. Small banks, particularly those controlled by a few shareholders, probably would find floating debentures more desirable than increasing equities. Increasing equity would be costly, because they might not have the personal resources, might be loath to give up control to new investors, or might find that new investors expect a relatively large discount to accept a minority position.

SEIR should be politically feasible because well-run, strong banks would benefit from the weaker banks' demise. As noted, the strong banks would not have to change their operations, except to take advantage of their new powers. These bankers, then, would have incentives to operate their banks effectively. Maximization of shareholder wealth would not include increasing the value of the deposit-insurance put option. Hence, strong banks should support the change.

Regulators who want to protect the deposit insurance fund and reduce other costs imposed on the economy should welcome SEIR, as it is compatible with these related goals. Banks that meet the first capital tranche would require little supervision. Regulators could exercise discretion in dealing with banks in the second tranche. The mandatory actions that must be imposed when banks decline into the third tranche would free regulators from political pressures. As noted, few banks would fall into the last tranche and have to be taken over.

Weak banks and regulators who enjoy discretionary power, though, would tend to lose, as is discussed below. Hence, they would tend to oppose SEIR.

Possible Shortcomings of SEIR

Conceptually, three objections might be brought to the SEIR proposal: (1) a rule requiring the taking over of banks with positive capital could be seen as an illegal taking of private property; (2) early intervention might result in banks taking even greater risks prior to intervention; and (3) SEIR does not take account of differences in risk among banks, or even measure the potential cost of risk. The following analysis leads to the conclusion that the concerns are not valid, with the partial exception of the third objection.

Government Take-over of Solvent Banks May Be an Expropriation of Private Capital. A government take-over of a book-value solvent bank should not be considered to be an illegal or improper taking of private capital, since the current shareholders could avoid this situation by recapitalizing the bank to bring it into conformance with the capital requirements, merging it with another institution, or selling the assets and paying off the liabilities. By allowing the government to exercise its option to take over the bank, the shareholders are indicating that they believe the bank is economically insolvent. In any event, the shareholders would be paid the net value received for the institution from a sale, merger, or liquidation. Moreover, to the extent that SEIR was effective, few banks would deteriorate through all the tranches, so there would be few failures and take overs.

Early Intervention Would Result in Banks Taking Greater Risks. Several theoretical studies show that moral hazard behavior would not be reduced by 'early' resolution of banks at positive levels of capital, essentially because banks' incentives to increase risk get greater as their capital decreases (Levonian, 1991, 1992; Davies and McManus, 1991). That is why SEIR supplements prompt resolution before a bank's capital is fully depleted with a series of capital tranches that impose prespecified progressively increasing and more mandatory penalties on banks as their performance declines. This procedure serves to reduce the incentive for risk taking and increase the incentive for corrective action. Such a structure proxies for the operation of the market in dealing with troubled firms in unregulated industries. SEIR also serves to slow the deterioration of banks, thus providing time for the authority to take effective corrective action as well as to develop a paper trail of regulatory initiatives in case banks later challenge the actions on the basis of arbitrariness or insufficient warning.

SEIR Does Not Account for Risk Differences. SEIR does not explicitly include adjusting capital to account for differences in risk among banks. Consequently, banks with poorly diversified portfolios and banks investing in assets subject to widely varying cash flows would have the same capital requirement as banks investing in, say, short-term government securities. SEIR, as originally conceived by Benston and Kaufman (1988), could be modified to include additional capital requirements for various levels of interest rate risk, much as the US Office of Thrift Supervision now requires. Diversification rules might be constructed to reduce the cost of adverse endogenous or exogenous events. However, these rules might penalize banks that can achieve economies of specialization and those of a size that can only serve limited markets. Structuring capital requirements that differ according to the assumed risk of various groupings of assets, such as is specified in the Basle risk-based capital requirements, is of limited value (as discussed in Section VI, p. 367).

Rather, risk considerations can best be dealt with in four ways. First, banks should be required to hold higher levels of capital. Second, capital should be measured in terms of current values. Third, subordinated debt should be included fully as part of bank capital. Indeed, if subordinated debt were required to be part of capital, the interest rate charged by debt holders would serve as a market-determined risk-adjusted deposit insurance premium. Furthermore, as the debt matures, banks' ease or difficulty in rolling it over or floating new debt would give the authorities valuable information about the market's assessment of bank-related risk. Fourth, banks could hold sufficiently collateralized insured deposits as an alternative to these other requirements.

VII CONCLUSIONS

Government-provided loans and guarantees to depositors are safety nets that result in moral hazard costs. To put the issue in perspective, the ways that this situation is dealt with in insurance and financial markets are described in Sections II and III. The conclusion drawn is that optimal arrangements for trading off the benefits of safety nets and costs of moral hazard are complex and best left to private parties.

Four possible exceptions that might justify or explain government provision of financial safety nets are delineated in Section IV. The safety net of subsidized-interest loans may be used to fulfil social obligations to disadvantaged or deserving people and enterprises; however, the moral hazard costs may more than offset the presumed benefits. Achievement of government efficiencies has been suggested as a justification for government-provided deposit insurance. The most important justification for deposit insurance is reduction in negative externalities that are assumed to result from bank runs. The analysis of the efficiency and externalities reasons for deposit insurance leads to their rejection. The conclusion of this section is that financial safety nets generally exist because it is politically expedient for legislators and government officials to provide them to the public.

Although, as discussed in Section V, costly moral-hazard behavior appears to have been largely restrained by non-government factors (such as partially insured depositors' concerns, owners' equity, and agency conflicts between bank managers and owners), government-imposed constraints also have been operative. Because it would not be wise to ignore even incompletely checked moral hazard-behavior resulting from government-provided deposit insurance, government should impose constraints on banks.

Among the several 'solutions' to the problem identified in Section VI that have or might be used, constraints on banks' assets are judged to be unnecessarily costly and probably ineffective. Risk-adjusted deposit insurance premiums and risk-based capital requirements suffer from important measurement and implementation difficulties. However, banks could choose to over-collateralize deposits with short-term, marketable, almost credit-risk-free instruments (such as government obligations). If this alternative were adopted, or if 'narrow' banks that invested only in the short-term marketable instruments were established, other liabilities offered by those banks or by companies associated with them should be clearly identified as not insured.

For most banks, I suggest that the best solution is higher capital requirements (including subordinated debt), supplemented with a system of structured early intervention and resolution (SEIR). Higher capital requirements need not be costly to banks (except in that they eliminate the subsidy of underpriced deposit insurance) if irredeemable subordinated debentures with remaining maturities of one or two years count fully as capital (which removes the tax disadvantage of equity capital when payments to equity holders are not deductible). SEIR gives banks strong incentives to maintain required capital/asset ratios and deals effectively with the agency conflict between the banking authorities and taxpayers. It also permits the authorities to almost totally deregulate banking (except for the level and monitoring of capital requirements) and would reduce the deposit insurance premium almost to zero, thereby giving banks the ability to compete effectively with alternative suppliers of financial goods and services.

Acknowledgements

The author gratefully acknowledges useful comments and suggestions from Randall C. Benston (President, Gateway American Bank, Ft. Lauderdale, FL.) and George G. Kaufman. R. Alton Gilbert pointed out several problems that, I hope, were dealt with satisfactorily.

Notes

1. See Black and Scholes (1973) for the classic formulation of the pricing of options. Merton (1977) is the first to apply this model to deposit insurance. Also see Kareken and Wallace (1978) and Dothan and William (1980).
2. See Department of the Treasury (1991, Chapter VII, pp. 1–19) for a good description and critique of this proposal. The major objection given therein to the proposal is uncertainty about how the private insurance consortia actually would work, especially with respect to closing insolvent banks.
3. Barthomew (1989) describes the deposit insurance systems in seventeen countries outside the United States. Those administered by the industry include Austria, Finland, France, Germany, and Switzerland. Jointly administered systems include Belgium, Japan, Lebanon, Netherlands, Norway and Spain.
4. See Kaufman (1994) for evidence.
5. See Kaufman (1994) for data and an extensive discussion.
6. This is not to say that deposit insurance would not be helpful in preventing runs to currency.
7. See Randall (1990) for well-presented concerns about multiple failures of large banks, and Benston (1993) for responses to those concerns.
8. See Department of the Treasury (1991, Chapter XXI, pp. 6–16) for descriptions of the actions taken by the authorities in Canada, France, Germany, Italy, the United Kingdom and Japan.
9. See Department of the Treasury's study (1991, Chapter III, pp. 31–35 for a more extensive discussion.
10. The Department of the Treasury study (1991), which devotes much space to a review of the theory and evidence on deposit insurance, reaches (but does not state clearly) this conclusion in one chapter, but a different conclusion in another chapter. Chapter I reviews the history of deposit insurance and the rationale for its continued existence. The benefits and purpose of deposit insurance are discussed in a 6 page section (C) of the 51 page chapter. Despite the authors' describing only a weak positive case for deposit insurance, they conclude that '[d]eposit insurance provides important economic benefits which the

market could not achieve on its own . . .' (p. I–11). Chapter III devotes its 56 pages to the 'scope of deposit insurance'. In that chapter, after much more extensive discussions and references to research and theory, I believe the authors essentially refute the case for government-provided deposit insurance. Chapter VII's 37 pages consider 'alternatives to federal deposit insurance'. As I read the chapter, the authors seem to favor privately provided deposit insurance, but shrink from this conclusion because '[i]t is not certain . . . that a private insurance system would work as envisioned by its advocates' (p. VII–18). Consequently, the authors suggest an experiment with private insurance supplementing federal insurance.

11. Argentina, Belgium, France, Germany (except for savings banks and credit cooperatives), India, Spain and Switzerland.
12. Argentina, Canada, India, Philippines, Turkey, United Kingdom and United States.
13. Austria, Finland, France, Germany and Switzerland.
14. Belgium, Japan, Lebanon, Netherlands, Norway and Spain.
15. See Kane (1992) for detailed analyses of the Ohio and Maryland situations.
16. See Dowd (1989); banks that advanced funds to the banks were not compensated for their losses.
17. See Herring (1993) for a description of rise and fall of BCCI. Herring reports that 'sophisticated market participants had disengaged from BCCI long before the crisis occurred. . . . International banks and institutional investors are notably absent from the list [of depositors who lost money]' (ibid., p. 84).
18. See Benston (1993) for a more extensive analysis, including references to the relevant literature.
19. See Department of the Treasury (1991), pp. III-3–5, for a review of and citations to these studies, and Benston (1993, pp. 73–74) for a review of additional studies and citations thereto.
20. Gorton and Santomero (1990) find a weak positive relationship between bank holding companies' risk and the interest rates they paid on their subordinated debt.
21. See Houston and James (1993) for evidence to this effect.
22. See Benston (1989a) for a review of and citations to these articles. Also, see Wall, Reichert, and Mohanty (1993) for a comprehensive simulation study of the effects of merging commercial banks with investment, insurance, real estate, and other financial companies. They find that some pairwise mergers would temporarily increase risk, and that multiple mergers would decrease risk; returns, in most cases, would increase. Multiple mergers, generally, would both decrease risk and increase returns.
23. Charges that banks offering securities transactions and underwriting were guilty of conflicts of interest are examined in great detail in Benston (1990, Ch. 4). Almost none of the allegations are found to be valid.
24. Perhaps the most prominent of the proposal's recent advocates is Robert Litan. See Benston and Kaufman (1988, Appendix A) for

citations to Litan and other authors and for a critique of the proposal. Also see Brookings Task Force (1989) and Department of the Treasury (1991, pp. VII-24–VII-30) for descriptions and critiques of the proposal.

25. See Brookings Task Force (1989) for a description of these variants of the narrow-bank proposal.
26. Gilbert (1988) shows that a bank restricted to holding only US Treasury securities would be unprofitable without an addition source of revenue.
27. This charge was biased not only against prudently run and well-capitalized banks, but against banks with high levels of uninsured domestic deposits (generally, large money center banks). Mitigating this latter feature was the FDIC's practice of not imposing costs on uninsured depositors, particularly when their banks were very large. Not charging deposit premiums on deposits held at foreign branches also benefited international banks, as it is unlikely that the FDIC would not or could not pay off or protect depositors at US banks' foreign branches.
28. See Department of the Treasury (1991, Ch. XXI, Table 2) for a summary of the premium pricing schemes in thirty countries.
29. See Benston *et al.* (1986, Ch. 9), for a description and evaluation of the effectiveness of banking supervision in the United States.
30. See Benston and Kaufman (1988, pp. 34–8), and Department of the Treasury (1991, Chapter VIII) for more extensive analyses.
31. Wall (1989) has suggested that banks be required to float puttable subordinated debt. Debt holders would have the right to request redemption of the debt at any time. The bank would have ninety days to honor the requests, which would force it to obtain replacement debt from the market. If it could not do so, it would be considered to be insolvent.
32. See Benston (1992b) for a full description and critique.
33. Also see Benston (1992a) and Department of the Treasury (1991, Chapter II).
34. See Benston (1989b) for a description and analysis. Also see Department of the Treasury (1991 Ch. XI) for a somewhat different view.
35. Indeed, Berkovec and Liang (1990) find that the decrease in the stock prices of bank holding companies that issue additional stock decrease stock prices almost exactly by the amount of the tax.
36. These firms benefit from not having to incur regulatory costs. However, these costs could be substantially reduced, perhaps almost eliminated, if higher capital requirements and SEIR were adopted, as is discussed on p. 362.
37. Benston and Kaufman (1988).
38. Brookings Institution Task Force (1989).
39. See Benston and Kaufman (1993) for a comparison of the proposal and the provisions of FDICIA.
40. This description and much of the material that follows is taken largely from Benston and Kaufman (1993).
41. See Benston (1989b) for an analysis of the difference between traditional and current value accounting.

42. The material that follows is taken largely from the Shadow Financial Regulatory Committee (1989).
43. The capital/asset ratios are not based on research findings; hence, they are arbitrary. If traditional accounting values rather than current values are used to measure capital, the required ratios should be higher to compensate for overstated capital.

References

Arrow, K. (1963) 'Uncertainty and the Welfare Economics of Medical Care', *American Economic Review*, vol. 53, pp. 941–73.

Asquith, P. and D. W. Mullins, Jr. (1986) 'Equity Issues and Offering Dilution', *Journal of Financial Economics*, vol. 56, pp. 61–89.

Avery, R. B. and A. N. Berger (1991) 'Risk-Based Capital and Deposit Insurance Reform', *Journal of Banking and Finance*, vol. 15, pp. 847–74.

Bartholomew, P. F. (1989) 'Foreign Deposit Insurance Systems', *Special Report*, Federal Home Loan Bank Board, Office of Policy and Economic Research (March).

Benston, G. J. (1989a) 'The Federal "Safety Net" and the Repeal of the Glass-Steagall Act's Separation of Commercial and Investment Banking', *Journal of Financial Services Research*, vol. 2, pp. 287–305.

Benston, G. J. (1989b) 'Market-Value Accounting: Benefits, Costs and Incentives', *Proceedings of a Conference on Bank Structure and Competition* (Chicago: Federal Reserve Bank of Chicago) pp. 547–69.

Benston, G. J. (1990) *The Separation of Commercial and Investment Banking: The Glass–Steagall Act Revisited and Reconsidered* (New York, NY: Oxford University Press, and London: Macmillan).

Benston, G. J. (1992a) 'The Purpose of Capital for Institutions with Government-Insured Deposits', *Journal of Financial Services Research*, vol. 5, pp. 369–84.

Benston, G. J. (1992b) 'International Bank Capital Standards', in James R. Barth and Philip F. Bartholomew (eds), *Research in International Business and Finance: Emerging Challenges for the International Financial Services Industry*, 9 (Greenwich, CN: JAI Press) pp. 51–73.

Benston, G. J. (1993) 'Market Discipline: The Role of Uninsured Depositors and Other Market Participants', in *Safeguarding the Banking System in an Environment of Recurring Financial Cycles*, R. E. Randall (ed.). Federal Reserve Bank of Boston Conference Series No. 37, pp. 65–95.

Benston, G. J. and M. Carhill (1994) 'The Causes and Consequences of the Thrift Disaster: Tests of Hypotheses', *Research in Financial Services*, G. G. Kaufman (ed.) (Greenwich, CN: JAI Press) pp. 103–69.

Benston, G. J., R. A. Eisenbeis, P. M. Horvitz, E. J. Kane, and G. G. Kaufman (1986) *Perspectives on Safe and Sound Banking* (Cambridge, MA: MIT Press).

Benston, G. J. and G. G. Kaufman (1988) *Risk and Solvency Regulation of Depository Institutions: Past Policies and Current Options*, Monograph Series in Finance and Economics, Salomon Brothers Center for the Study of Financial Institutions, Graduate School of Business Administration, New York University, Monograph 1988–1. A shorter version appears in *Restructuring Banking & Financial Services in America*, W. S. Haraf and R.

M. Kushmeider (eds) (Washington, DC: American Enterprise Institute for Public Policy Research) pp. 63–99.
Benston, G. J. and G. G. Kaufman (1993) 'Improving the FDIC Improvement Act: What Was Done and What Still Needs To Be Done to Fix the Deposit Insurance Problem', in G. G. Kaufman (ed.) *Reforming American Financial Institutions and Markets* (Boston: Kluwer Academic Publishers) pp. 99–121.
Berkovec, J. and N. Liang (1990) 'Changes in the Cost of Equity Capital for BHCs and Their Effects on Raising Capital', Financial Structure Section, Federal Reserve Board, July.
Bernanke, B. S. (1983) 'Nonmonetary Effects of the Financial Crisis in the Propagation of the Great Depression', *American Economic Review*, vol. 73, pp. 257–76.
Black, F. and M. Scholes (1973) 'The Pricing of Options and Corporate Liabilities', *Journal of Political Economy*, vol. 81, pp. 632–59.
Bradley, M. G., C. A. Wambeke and D. A. Whidbee (1990) 'Risk Weights, Risk-Based Capital, and Deposit Insurance', *Journal of Banking and Finance*, vol. 14, pp. 875–93.
Brookings Task Force (G. J. Benston, R. D. Brumbaugh, Jr., J. M. Guttentag, R. J. Herring, G. G. Kaufman, R. E. Litan and K. E. Scott) (1989) *Restructuring American's Financial Institutions* (Washington, DC: The Brookings Institution).
Calomiris, C. W. (1990) 'Is Deposit Insurance Necessary? A Historical Perspective', *The Journal of Economic History*, vol. L (June), pp. 283–95.
Calomiris, C. W. and C. M. Kahn (1991) 'The Role of Demandable Debt in Structuring Banking Arrangements', *American Economic Review* (June).
Cordell, L. R. and K. K. King (1992) 'A Market Evaluation of the Importance of Considering Non-Credit Risk in Setting Risk-Based Capital Standards', *Proceedings of a Conference on Bank Structure and Competition* (Chicago: Federal Reserve Bank of Chicago) pp. 151–77.
Cordell, L. R. and K. K. King (1995) 'A Market Evaluation of the Risk-based Standards for the U.S. Financial System', *Journal of Banking and Finance*, vol. 18, forthcoming.
Davies, S. M. and D. A. McManus (1991) 'The Effects of Closure Policies on Bank Risk-Taking', *Journal of Banking and Finance*, vol. 15, pp. 917–938.
Department of the Treasury (1991) *Modernizing the Financial System: Recommendations for Safer, More Competitive Banks* (Washington, DC: The Department of the Treasury) (February).
Diamond, D. W. (1984) 'Financial Intermediation and Delegated Monitoring', *Review of Economic Studies*, vol. LI, pp. 393–414.
Diamond, D. W. and P. H. Dybvig (1983) 'Bank Runs, Deposit Insurance, and Liquidity', *Journal of Political Economy*, vol. 91 (June), pp. 401–419.
Dothan, U. and J. Williams (1980) 'Banks, Bankruptcy and Public Relations', *Journal of Banking and Finance*, vol. 4, pp. 65–88.
Dowd, K. (1989) 'Some Lessons from the Recent Canadian Bank Failures', *Research in Financial Services*, vol. 1, pp. 113–128.
Dwyer, G. P. Jr. and R. Alton Gilbert (1989) 'Bank Runs and Private Remedies', *Review* (Federal Reserve Bank of St. Louis), vol. 71 (May/June) pp. 43–61.

Ely, B. (1990) *Making Deposit Insurance Safe Through 100% Cross-Guarantees* (Washington, DC: National Chamber Foundation).

English, W. B. (1993) 'The Decline of Private Deposit Insurance in the United States', Deposit Insurance Reform: A Functional Approach', *Carnegie-Rochester Series on Public Policy*, vol. 38, pp. 57–128.

Federal Deposit Insurance Corporation (1982) *Annual Report*, Table 128.

Flannery, M. J. (1989) 'Pricing Deposit Insurance When the Insurer Measures Risk With Error', *Proceedings of a Conference on Bank Structure and Competition* (Chicago: Federal Reserve Bank of Chicago) pp. 70–100.

Flannery, M. J. (1994) 'Debt Maturity and the Deadweight Cost of Leverage: Optimally Financing Banking Firms', *American Economic Review*, vol. 84, pp. 320–31.

Furlong, F. T. and M. C. Keeley (1989) 'Capital Regulation and Risk-Taking: A Note', *Journal of Banking and Finance*, vol. 13, pp. 83–9. Reprinted in *Economic Review*, Federal Reserve Bank of San Francisco (Summer 1991) pp. 34–9.

Gilbert, R. A. (1988) 'A Comparison of Proposals to Restructure the U.S. Financial System', *Economic Review*, Federal Reserve Bank of St. Louis, 70 (January/February) pp. 3–18.

Gilbert, R. A. (1991) 'Supervision of Under-capitalized Banks: Is There a Case for Change?', *Review* (Federal Reserve Bank of St. Louis), vol. 73 (May/June) pp. 16–30.

Gilbert, R. A. (1992) 'The Effects of Legislating Prompt Corrective Action on the Bank Insurance Fund', *Review* (Federal Reserve Bank of St. Louis), vol. 74 (July/August) pp. 3–22.

Goodhart, C. A. E. (1987) 'Why Do Banks Need a Central Bank?', *Oxford Economic Papers*, vol. 39, pp. 75–89.

Gorton, G. and A. M. Santomero (1990) 'Market Discipline and Bank Subordinated Debt', *Journal of Money, Credit and Banking*, vol. 22, pp. 119–128.

Herring, R. J. (1993) 'BCCI: Lessons for International Bank Supervision', *Contemporary Policy Issues*, vol. XI, pp. 76–86.

Houston, J. and C. James (1993) 'Management and Organizational Changes: A Comparison of Regulatory Intervention with Private Interractions in Non-bank Firms', *Carnegie-Rochester Series on Public Policy*, vol. 38, pp. 143–77.

Jaffe, D. M. (1975) 'Housing Finance and Mortgage Market Policy', in Karl Brunner (ed.), *Government Credit Allocation* (San Francisco: Institute for Contemporary Studies) pp. 93–122.

James, C. (1987) 'Some Evidence on the Uniqueness of Bank Loans', *Journal of Financial Economics*, vol. 14, pp. 217–235.

Jensen, M. C. and W. H. Meckling (1976) 'Theory of the Firm: Managerial Behavior, Agency Costs and Ownership Structure', *Journal of Financial Economics*, vol. 3, pp. 305–360.

Kane, E. J. (1988a) *The S&L Mess: How Did it Happen?* (Washington, DC: The Urban Institute Press).

Kane, E. J. (1988b) 'How Market Forces Influence the Structure of Financial Regulation', in W. S. Haraf and R. M. Kushmeider (eds), *Restructuring Banking & Financial Services in America* (Washington, DC: American Enterprise Institute for Public Policy Research) pp. 343–82.

Kane, E. J. (1992) 'How Incentives-Incompatible Deposit-Insurance Funds Fail', in G. G. Kaufman (ed.), *Research in Financial Services: Private and Public Policy*, vol. 4, (Greenwich, CT: JAI Press) pp. 51–91.

Kane, E. J. and G. G. Kaufman (1993) 'Incentive Conflict in Deposit-institution Regulation: Evidence from Australia', *Pacific-Basin Finance Journal*, vol. 1, pp. 13–29.

Kareken, J. H. and N. Wallace (1978) 'Deposit Insurance and Bank Regulation: A Partial Equilibrium Exposition', *Journal of Business*, vol. 51, pp. 413–438.

Kaufman, G. G. (1988) 'Bank Runs: Causes, Benefits, and Costs', *The Cato Journal*, vol. 7 (Winter), pp. 559–87.

Kaufman, G. G. (1990) 'Are Some Banks Too Large To Fail? Myth and Reality', *Contemporary Policy Issues*, vol. VIII, pp. 1–14.

Kaufman, G. G. (1994) 'Bank Contagion: A Review of the Theory and Evidence', *Journal of Financial Services Research*, vol. 8, pp. 123–50.

Keeley, M. C. and F. T. Furlong (1990) 'A Reexamination of the Mean-Variance Analysis of Bank Capital Regulation', *Journal of Banking and Finance*, vol. 14, pp. 79–84. Reprinted in *Economic Review*, Federal Reserve Bank of San Francisco, Summer 1991, pp. 40–48.

Koehn, M. and A. M. Santomero (1988) 'Risk in Banking and Capital Regulation', *Journal of Finance*, vol. 43, pp. 1219–33.

Levonian, M. E. (1991) 'A Note of Caution on Early Bank Closure', *FRBSF Weekly Newsletter*, Federal Reserve Bank of San Francisco, November 20.

Levonian, M. E. (1992) 'What Happens If Banks Are Closed Early?', *Rebuilding Banking* (Chicago: Federal Reserve Bank of Chicago) pp. 273–95.

Merton, R. C. (1977) 'An Analytic Derivation of the Cost of Deposit Insurance and Loan Guarantees', *Journal of Banking and Finance*, vol. 1, pp. 3–11.

Merton, R. C. and Z. Bodie (1993) 'Deposit Insurance Reform: A Functional Approach', *Carnegie-Rochester Series on Public Policy*, vol. 38, pp. 1–34.

Meltzer, A. H. (1975) 'Credit Availability and Economic Decisions: Some Evidence from the Mortgage and Housing Markets', in K. Brunner (ed.), *Government Credit Allocation* (San Francisco: Institute for Contemporary Studies) pp. 123–50.

Pauly, M. V. (1968) 'The Economics of Moral Hazard: Comment', *American Economic Review*, vol. 58, pp. 531–39.

Randall, R. E. (1989) 'Can the Market Evaluate Asset Quality Exposure in Banks?', *New England Economic Review* (July/August), pp. 3–24.

Randall, R. E. (1990) 'The Need to Protect Depositors of Large Banks, and the Implications for Bank Powers and Ownership', *New England Economic Review*, September/October, pp. 63–75.

Schwartz, A. (1988) 'Financial Stability and the Federal Safety Net', in W. S. Haraf and R. M. Kushmeider (eds), *Restructuring Banking and Financial Services in America* (Washington, DC: American Enterprise Institute) pp. 34–62.

Shadow Financial Regulatory Committee (1989) 'An Outline of a Program for Deposit Insurance and Regulatory Reform' (Statement No. 41, February

13). Reprinted in *Journal of Financial Services Research*, vol. 6 (1992) S-78–S-82.

Wall, L. D. (1989) 'A Plan for Reducing Future Deposit Insurance Losses: Puttable Subordinated Debt', *Economic Review*, Federal Reserve Bank of Atlanta, July/August, pp. 2–17.

Wall, L. D. A. K. Reichert, and S. Mohanty (1993) 'Deregulation and the Opportunities for Commercial Bank Diversification', *Economic Review*, Federal Reserve Bank of Atlanta, September/October, pp. 1–25.

Wall, L. D. and P. P. Peterson (1988) 'Valuation Effects of New Capital Issues by Large Bank Holding Companies', Federal Reserve Bank of Atlanta, working paper, December.

Wallison, P. J. (1990) *Back from the Brink: A Practical Plan for Privatizing Deposit Insurance and Strengthening Our Banks and Thrifts* (Washington, DC: The AEI Press).

Wansley, J. W. and U. S. Dhillon (1989) 'Determinants of Valuation Effects for Security Offerings of Commercial Bank Holding Companies', *Journal of Financial Research*, pp. 217–233.

White, E. N. (1983) *The Regulation and Reform of the American Banking System* (Princeton, NJ: Princeton Univ. Press).

White, E. N. (1986) 'Before the Glass–Steagall Act: An Analysis of the Investment Banking Activities of National Banks', *Journal of Economic History*, vol. 47, pp. 739–55.

Comments

Pierre Duguay*

Professor Benston presents a comprehensive and pragmatic review of the public provision of safety nets for financial institutions. While he sees no need for government protection, he argues that governments will find it politically expedient to offer it and looks for ways to contain the moral hazard resulting from such protection, whether implicit or explicit. He concludes that restrictions on bank activities, risk-based insurance premiums, risk-adjusted capital requirements are all sources of economic inefficiency. He favours higher capital requirements combined with structured early intervention and resolution (SEIR) as a means of limiting risk to the government or to the deposit insurance fund. In his proposal, institutions would be closed while there was still capital (or subordinated debt) left to provide a buffer to the deposit insurer. Professor Benston has a powerful answer to the charge that this proposal amounts to expropriation of private capital: in electing not to recapitalize the bank 'shareholders are indicating that they believe the bank is economically insolvent'.

Professor Benston's case is tightly argued and, on the whole, quite convincing. The fact that the United States has moved towards a variation of Professor Benston's proposal bears testimony to the power of his arguments. One practical question I would like to put to Professor Benston is how long would he allow or expect institutions to remain in various tranches.

What I will do in my comments is to raise some points that were left unexplored by Professor Benston: (1) the provision of deposit insurance as a means to lower barriers to entry into banking, (2) the need to clarify the mandate and accountability of the supervisor, (3) the importance of disclosure and (4) the issue of transition. I will then present a list of points that I feel may have been somewhat overstated.

* The views expressed in these comments are those of the author; no responsibility for them should be attributed to the Bank of Canada.

Deposit Insurance as a Means to Lower Barriers to Entry

Deposit insurance lowers the barrier to entry represented by the need for newcomers (or smaller institutions) to offset a lack of reputation (and diversification) by posting a larger equity stake or some performance bond. It also provides an offset to the distortions created by investors' expectations (warranted or not) that larger institutions benefit from an implicit guarantee from government.

This may help explain why deposit insurance tends to be sponsored by government. Large institutions would generally find that they have little need for deposit insurance. In Canada, for example, large banks tend to regard the levy of flat premiums as a subsidy to smaller deposit-taking institutions. A private regime of cross-insurance among banks would raise major public policy issues regarding access and control over closure. (A private fund would not necessarily have the power to close institutions, but could in practice precipitate closure through denial of insurance.)

Mandate and Accountability of the Supervisory Authorities

One aspect which is overlooked in Professor Benston's SEIR proposal is the importance of an appropriate mandate for the supervisor and the extent to which the absence of a clear mandate or an inappropriate mandate would affect supervisory behaviour.

One problem with government supervision is its implication that as long as an institution stays open its financial condition is acceptable. This means that a supervisor that has exercised forbearance in an attempt to restore the financial health of an institution will feel reluctant to close the institution in a timely manner, especially if he sees his mandate to be the prevention of financial institution failures. The effectiveness of SEIR could be strengthened with an appropriate mandate which made it the supervisor's responsibility, for example, to minimize losses to depositors and other creditors of financial institutions.

While the deposit insurer may not face the same dilemma as the supervisor, again the question of mandate is important. With a wrong or vague mandate, there is always a risk that inappropriate, politically driven solutions will be imposed, with the costs being borne by future depositors and borrowers.

Clarification of the supervisor's mandate would not necessarily preclude the government from issuing instructions to the supervisor, but in the absence of explicit instructions, the supervisor would be fully accountable for the achievement of clear goals. The government's exercise of discretion could be limited by the requirement that instructions to the supervisor be made public and put to the scrutiny of Parliament or Congress. Of course, a transparent and predictable regime for dealing with troubled institutions would also have to be in place.

Disclosure

Professor Benston says little on disclosure in this chapter, though he has written extensively on the topic. I think that it is worth stressing that disclosure is essential to ensure informed market discipline. It can help prevent unwarranted contagion and it would condition the exercise of judgment by the managers of financial institutions and by the supervisory authorities.

SEIR relies heavily on those judgments, particularly when it comes to setting up provisions for loan losses. The responsibility of managers, directors and auditors of financial institutions for prompt recognition and reporting is thus critical and needs to be emphasized.

Transition Problems

Changes in the provision of a safety net – changes to capital requirements, changes to deposit insurance, removal of implicit subsidies, introduction of new rules, etc. – if they are at all meaningful are bound to cause transition problems. I raise this not as an argument for inaction, but as an argument for the need to manage the transition carefully. For while SEIR would reduce the risk of failure in steady state, it may well increase that risk during the transition.

One important aspect of the transition to a new regime is the prior need to strengthen (or risk-proof) settlement systems. I think it is too easy to dismiss settlement risk on the ground that procedures can be implemented to reduce it, when currently many institutions face daily exposures that can run many times their capital. Professor Benston's remark to the effect that losses to correspondent banks resulting from the failure of their respondent are likely to be smaller than those resulting from the failure of any other customer is particularly sanguine in view of the large sums that may be involved. Of course, an important obstacle to the adoption of more prudent settlement conventions and procedures – the belief that some institutions are too large to fail – will be eroded by a credible transition to a new safety net regime. However, another important obstacle – the ambiguity of the legal status of multilateral netting in the case of default – is not so easily overcome, and it can not merely be assumed away, as Professor Benston seems inclined to do.

I would now like to turn to minor points in Professor Benston's argument that I feel may have been overstated or that particularly intrigued me. My comments will be presented in the same order as the statements to which they refer.

- Professor Benston contends that 'The only deposit insurance funds that have been substantially depleted or become insolvent (those in Canada and the United States) are government sponsored and administered'. Given the large losses that have been experienced elsewhere, notably in Scandinavian countries and possibly still in Japan, I would not say that Canada and the United States distinguish themselves in terms of poor monitoring or underfunding of the insurance fund.
- When citing loans from finance companies and issues of commercial paper as alternatives to bank loans Professor Benston should note that bank loans are an important source of financing for finance companies and that issues of commercial paper are often backed by a bank line of credit.
- I do not find the evidence on the absence of contagion from bank failures to be very convincing. On the one hand, we are told that 'studies found no failures of similar banks and little evidence of deposit outflows' but, on the other, we are informed that 'contagion of share returns occurred . . . for banks in the same market or product area'. Regarding the Canadian evidence reported in this section, I would stress that the two banks that failed in 1985 were in fact small regional banks accounting together for only 1 percent of total assets of the Canadian banking system (where the six largest banks represent over 85 percent of the total). None the less, these failures did cause sufficient difficulties for a larger and more diversified mid-sized bank that it ended up merging with a stronger one.
- I was intrigued by the finding that moral hazard risk taking was not responsible for the large losses of the US thrift industry, and

I look forward to reading the details of the forthcoming study by Benston and Carhill on that issue.

- Professor Benston dismisses the justification for restricting bank activities in terms of preventing the extension of the safety net with: 'The safety net relates only to deposits, not to assets'. But surely, the ultimate beneficiary of the deposit insurance subsidy is not exclusively the depositor. Borrowers and shareholders also benefit. It is not very difficult to imagine circumstances under which banks may attempt to cross-subsidize securities or insurance products.
- The evidence that 'very few universal banks have failed' does not allow any strong inference, since presumably very few universal banks have been allowed to fail.
- Professor Benston refers to a paper by Cordell and King which includes instalment consumer debt among the assets that have a high 'market risk rating'. Given that consumer loan portfolios typically consist of a large number of small loans, I would have thought that the pricing of these loans could be managed to absorb even large average losses from consumer defaults and leave minimal portfolio risk. How plausible is the measurement of market risk rating?
- Finally, I feel that Professor Benston overstates the substitutability of subordinated debentures and equity. While both provide a 'buffer that absorbs losses before they are imposed on the deposit insurance fund or taxpayer', they do not provide equity holders or bank managers with the same incentive to manage risk. Subordinated debt provides its incentive *ex-ante*, or when it has to be refinanced. Once it is locked-in, the incentive may no longer be there. (Would this be an argument for preferring shorter term debentures?) So, while it is true that 'debenture holders do not gain the benefits from risk taking', it is also the case that their influence in reducing moral hazard is primarily limited to the type of covenants that they may impose on equity holders. As for the development of funds that specialize in offering a diversified portfolio of small bank subordinated debentures, would not that weaken the influence of debenture holders on equity holders? On balance, I feel that the preference for true equity merits being stated more explicitly. In the Basle capital accord, for example, subordinated debentures included in tier 2 capital are limited to a fraction of tier 1 capital.

To summarize, although I expressed a number of quibbles, I basically like the argumentation presented in the chapter and the regulatory framework proposed by Professor Benston. If it were adhered to in a time consistent manner, we could expect fewer failures and less costly ones from the point of view of the deposit insurance fund or the taxpayer. The main points that I want to stress are that this framework still requires the exercise of discretion, that discretion can be conditioned with appropriate disclosure requirements and with a clarification of the mandate and accountability of the supervisor and deposit insurer, and that transition issues must be carefully addressed.

Comments

Kazuhito Ikeo

I firmly believe that most academic researchers who major in bank regulatory policy, myself included, will agree with Professor Benston's chapter. If the government provision of safety nets cannot be removed because of mainly political reasons, then the policy mix of requiring relatively high capital ratios and prompt corrective action is the second best solution. This conclusion of Professor Benston's chapter is absolutely right. At the same time, however, the second best solution is distinctly unsatisfactory in that it would mean significant social cost stemming from regulation failure, if it were accepted.

To what extent can we require banks to increase capital ratios? There must be a social cost. If there were no social cost, 100 percent ratios would be desirable. However, we could not call them 'banks' if they were not financed by deposits.

First, higher capital/asset ratios mean lower deposit/asset ratios so that higher capital requirements result in restricting banks' provision of maturity transformation through deposit taking. If maturity transformation services provided by the banks are socially beneficial, requiring higher ratios is costly.

Second, provided a bank seeks value-maximization, higher capital requirements reduce the incentives for it to increase asset risk. Although I think this is logically true, does every bank always seek value maximization? In other words, we have to take into account the existence of conflicts of interest between bank managers and bank shareholders. Higher debt ratios have a role in disciplining managers (see Grossman and Hart, 1982). With lower debt ratios and less possibility of default, bank managers tend more to seek their own interests instead of maximizing a bank's value. Higher capital requirements may increase this sort of agency cost.

In short, requiring higher capital ratios surely contributes to protecting taxpayers. However, we have to evaluate any policy according to its effect on social welfare. The current policy of protecting depositors exclusively at the sacrifice of taxpayers is wrong. Similarly, the protection of taxpayers at any social cost cannot be the ultimate goal of public policy.

Professor Benston asserts that government officials incline to provide depositors with a full guarantee to avoid damaging their careers so that it is politically impossible to reduce the coverage of the safety net. Similarly, I think that government officials tend to resist closing insolvent banks promptly. They prefer a policy of forbearance. Since introducing a system of structured early intervention and resolution (SEIR) results in cutting down subsidies from the government provision of safety nets, even strong banks may oppose SEIR.

Why is it politically impossible to reduce the coverage of safety nets in spite of the fact that it is politically possible to introduce SEIR? The Federal Deposit Insurance Corporation Improvement Act of 1991 (FDICIA) introduced a modified version of SEIR. This fact undoubtedly shows the political feasibility of SEIR. At the same time, FDICIA prohibited a 'too-big-to-fail' policy. The Federal Deposit Insurance Corporation (FDIC) was prevented from guaranteeing uninsured deposits. Does this prove that the reduction of safety nets is politically feasible, at least in the United States?

Are bank regulators successively able to monitor whether each bank satisfies capital requirements? Banks with low capital ratios can pretend they have sufficient capital. Bank regulators may not detect this sort of window dressing. The monitoring ability of bank regulators is inferior to that of market participants as a whole. In addition, although SEIR significantly reduces moral hazard costs, it does not completely eliminate them. It is because of this that a very lucky bank which wins a gamble is not punished under SEIR, no matter how risky the gamble is.

In my opinion, it is indispensable to dramatically reduce the coverage of safety nets although I admit that it is a very politically tough task to do so. In order to cut down the social costs of regulation failure, market discipline has to be enhanced by removing the government provision of safety nets.

Reference

Grossman, S. J. and O. D. Hart (1982) 'Corporate Financial Structure and Managerial Incentives', in E. Lippman and J. McCall (eds), *The Economics of Information and Uncertainty* (University of Chicago Press).

Part IV
Role of Central Banks in Maintaining Financial Stability

9 Monetary Policy Rules and Financial Stability

Bennett T. McCallum

I INTRODUCTION

The subject matter of this chapter is the relationship between the two ultimate goals recognized by most central banks, namely, macroeconomic stability and financial-system stability.[1] This is an extremely broad topic and one that could be approached by various distinct methods of analysis – evolutionary/historical, welfare theoretic, institutional, etc. But given my own experience relative to others on the program, it seems most appropriate to narrow the scope of the chapter by focusing primarily on one limited but extremely important set of issues.

These issues, which are closely interrelated, concern macro-oriented rules for monetary policy and the central bank's role as a lender of last resort. Are macro-oriented rules – such as those advocated by McCallum (1988, 1993), Meltzer (1987), or Taylor (1988, 1993) – inappropriate because of their neglect of financial market conditions? If so, might these rules be modified so as to overcome that neglect? What are the implications concerning lender-of-last-resort responsibilities? Does acceptance of these responsibilities require the operation of a discount window? Or could they be satisfied, as suggested by Goodfriend and King (1988), by means of open market operations that involve smoothing of interest rates?

As here formulated, the answers to these questions depend to a large extent upon the accuracy with which it is possible for the central bank to hit intermediate quarterly targets for the monetary base by means of an interest rate instrument while practicing smoothing – i.e., while avoiding large week-to-week changes in the interest rate. Consequently, a substantial portion of the chapter is devoted to an attempt to measure this accuracy empirically. As the econometric methods utilized are rather rudimentary, our results must be regarded as exploratory, rather than definitive, in nature. But estimation of a fully structural model is inhibited by data limitations and identification problems, so our first-pass analysis may be difficult to improve upon substantially. In any event, it will provide a starting point for further consideration of the issue.

Organizationally, the analysis begins in Section II with an overview discussion of the broad topic of Part IV, a discussion which serves to justify our attention on the narrower set of issues described above. Section III is then devoted to a background review of some results relating to monetary policy rules, formulated at the quarterly frequency, in which the monetary base is treated as a policy instrument. Section IV develops a framework for the study of a system in which quarterly-average base values are viewed as targets to be achieved by manipulation at the weekly frequency of an interest rate instrument. Basic simulation results pertaining to this system are given in Section V while Section VI takes up some alternative formulations. Finally, Section VII contains a brief recapitulation.

II MONETARY POLICY RULES FOR THE LENDER OF LAST RESORT?

Before focusing our attention as described above it will be useful to justify that strategy by reference to the broader topic assigned for Part IV: the relationship between the goals of macroeconomic and financial stability. The tension between these goals has recently been expressed by Folkerts-Landau and Garber (1992), writing about the design of the European Central Bank, in terms of the aphorism, 'A bank or a monetary policy rule?' More generally, many economists have expressed doubts as to the compatibility of a strict monetary policy rule – or in any case one featuring a monetary base instrument – with central bank acceptance of lender-of-last-resort (LLR) responsibilities.[2] The achievement of a base path as dictated by the rule would conflict, according to this position, with the need to supply liquidity at times of crisis in accordance with the central bank's role as a LLR.

Recent discussions of alternative viewpoints pertaining to the LLR role – see e.g., Bordo (1990), Humphrey (1992), and Summers (1991) – have identified four main positions. These are (i) the classical Thornton–Bagehot doctrine, (ii) a 'modern-pragmatic' position that calls for more lenient management of the discount window, (iii) the so-called 'free banking' contention that no public LLR is needed, and (iv) a 'monetarist' scheme, developed primarily by Goodfriend and King (1988), that calls for LLR actions via open-market operations rather than the discount window.[3]

As most readers will know, the classical doctrine developed by Thornton (1802) and Bagehot (1873) calls for the LLR to lend aggressively at times of crisis,[4] to any solvent institution providing good collateral, but at a penalty rate (a concept discussed below). This policy should, moreover, be publicly known to prevail. A major objective is to support illiquid but solvent institutions, thereby providing protection for the banking system rather than for individual banks.[5] Actual practice of the Federal Reserve in recent years has deviated from the Thornton–Bagehot prescription in a number of ways (Garcia and Plautz, 1988). Thus the Fed lends only to depository institutions, rather than to any sound institution, and at rates that represent subsidies to the borrowers. It has not spelled out its policies publicly and has apparently been willing occasionally to lend to insolvent banks. Summers (1991) expresses support for this more lenient mode of behavior, expressing the opinion that LLR policy 'is probably an area where James Tobin's insight that "it takes a heap of Harberger triangles to fill an Okun gap" is relevant. . . . This at least is the modern pragmatic view that has worked so far' (p. 153). To the present author, it is surprising that a prominent writer would take such a sanguine view of US policy in this area.[6] Perhaps Summers's argument rests on a presumption that the massive late-1980s expenditures by the FDIC represented only transfers, not lost output. I would suggest, by contrast, that the construction of a useless and unoccupied shopping center does not constitute output. In any event, the desirability of the modern pragmatic view has implicitly been the topic of an enormous volume of analysis.[7] It should be more useful for this chapter's attention to be addressed to other viewpoints.

Proposals of the 'free banking' type have, despite the efforts of White (1984), Selgin (1987), Glasner (1989), and Dowd (1989), received little support among monetary economists in general. Different writers on the subject have expressed different criticisms of the proposals. Laidler (1992, p. 192), for example, has suggested that 'the very nature of banking precludes its being simultaneously unregulated and competitive [because of economies of scale in reserve holding], and that arguments against the regulation of banking based on the assumption of competition are therefore inconsistent'. Summers (1991, p. 147) follows Goodhart (1987), in emphasizing that the true asset value of the bank's (non-marketed) loans is always subject to uncertainty though their nominal value is fixed [the latter occurring because of the informational advantage of borrowers over even the lending bank] and that 'under these conditions, it will benefit both bank and depositor to denominate deposit liabilities also in fixed nominal terms' (Goodhart, 1987, pp. 86–7). But 'the combination ... of the nominal convertibility guarantee, together with the uncertainty about the true value of bank assets, leads to the possibility of runs on individual banks and systemic crises' (1987, p. 87) thereby requiring the assistance of a LLR. Humphrey, finally, argues that 'occasional shocks such as the threat of war or the failure of a large firm may trigger moneyholders' desire to switch from inside to outside money' (1992, p. 573) which can only be supplied under a fiat-money system by a central bank or LLR. These criticisms have been disputed by the proponents of free banking but, as stated above, most analysts remain unconvinced.

My own view is that there is an especially glaring weakness in the case for free banking that has not been emphasized by its critics. That weakness involves the basic argument of free-banking proponents that competition will induce profit-seeking bank firms to issue liabilities (banknotes and deposits) that maintain their purchasing power over time because they are redeemable in commodities or bundles that are designed to have reasonably constant value, relative to a comprehensive consumption bundle. But it seems highly uncertain that individual banking firms would in fact choose to offer that type of liability under today's conditions. The free banking literature is largely written in a manner that appears to suggest that historical evidence supports the questionable proposition under discussion, but that suggestion is (I believe) unwarranted. For the principal historical examples occurred during the era of commodity money standards, during which banks were legally required to keep their banknotes redeemable in the standard commodity (e.g. gold or silver coin).[8] But the situation is, of course, crucially different in today's era of fiat money.

The fourth position mentioned above, that of Goodfriend and King (1988), would retain central banks and their role as a LLR, but would have LLR activities conducted by means of open market actions. In particular, discount window lending would be eliminated and with it the need for most – if not all – of the central bank's regulatory and supervisory activities. The main point of the Goodfriend–King argument is that the job of the LLR is to prevent systemic breakdown, not to protect individual banks. But systemic crises involve sharply increased demands for high-powered money, which can be satisfied by open-market purchases without discount window loans.[9] Indeed, such purchases will be triggered automatically in a regime with interest rate smoothing, since sharply increased demands for high-powered money would result in sharply higher interest rates if no central bank response were forthcoming.

A number of objections to the Goodfriend–King analysis have been put forth. Meltzer (1988), for example, has suggested that it would be preferable to retain the discount window but for lending to take place only at a penalty rate. 'Even a small penalty . . . would ensure that the lender of last resort would do no lending except in a severe banking crisis when (or if) markets do not function' (1988, p. 445). Furthermore, Meltzer believes that regulation and supervision would not be required for such loans. And his 'reason for insisting on retaining the lender-of-last-resort function is to avoid catastrophes like that of 1931–1933 when the [Fed] refused to lend. Having penalty-rate loans [available] as an option means that banks have access to base money even if the central bank repeats its major error of the 1930s' (1988, p. 446).

In evaluating this suggestion, it is important to consider what is meant by a 'penalty rate'. It must presumably not be a rate in excess of the current market rate because the latter is the rate at which borrowers can obtain funds. What Meltzer has in mind, I believe, is a rate that is somewhat above recent market rates. An example for the United States might be the previous week's average for the Federal Funds rate plus 2 percentage points (annualized).

Under this interpretation it becomes clear that the Meltzer and Goodfriend–King position are, though different, highly compatible. For interest rate smoothing, as prescribed by the latter, would presumably never permit the Funds rate to rise to a level as much as 2 percentage points (for example) above the previous week's average. At some lower value – its exact position depending on the precise smoothing rule adopted – the Fed would begin to supply base money in virtually unlimited quantities. So the penalty rate would never materialize. Alternatively, Meltzer's proposal would keep the discount window open, with a penalty rate, and eliminate the practice of interest rate smoothing. But market rate changes from week to week would then be limited by the penalty margin.

Cagan's (1988, p. 256) main objection to the Goodfriend–King proposal is that interest rate pegging leads to dynamic instability.[10]

His argument does not adequately distinguish between interest rate pegging and the use of an interest rate instrument, however, the latter being the relevant practice. And the analysis in McCallum (1981, 1986) suggests that there is in fact no instability or indeterminacy problem in this case if expectations are formed rationally, provided that the central bank's policy rule for setting the interest rate instrument reflects some concern for some nominal magnitude – i.e., possesses a 'nominal anchor'.[11]

Summers (1991) objects to the Goodfriend–King position rather strongly, presenting three arguments. One of these involves a 'reasonably clear lesson from the [October 1987] crash period. It would not have been sufficient for the Fed to keep the money stock growing steadily.... Their successful action involved rapid money growth' (1991, p. 149). But this point is irrelevant, since the Goodfriend–King prescription does not call for the Fed to keep money growth steady. A more relevant claim of Summers's goes as follows: 'The crucial point here is that driving down the federal funds rate is not likely to be sufficient to stop prophesies that predict the failure of banks or securities firms from proving to be self-fulfilling. A more ambitious set of lender-of-last resort policies would seem to be necessary' (1991, p. 150). But Summers's 'demonstration' in this case is based neither on experience nor theoretical reasoning, but on a totally imaginary 'scenario' that he created out of thin air and used in several places in this paper. There is very little reason, consequently, to give any weight to this second claim.

The only substantial argument put forth by Summers, then, is that 'because of the relationship-specific capital each has accumulated, reserves at one bank are an imperfect substitute for reserves at another. Maintaining a given aggregate level of lending is not sufficient to avoid the losses associated with a financial disturbance' (1991, p. 149). But this argument again seems to miss its target. The object of LLR policy is not to 'avoid losses' but to prevent systemic failure. And 'maintaining an aggregate level of lending' is an inaccurate characterization of the policy under discussion.

My conclusion from this review is that convincing refutations of the Goodfriend–King position have not yet been presented. Accordingly, that position warrants further consideration, since it offers a possible way for a central bank to provide LLR insurance against financial system breakdown while generating little moral hazard and avoiding the need for an extensive regulatory and supervisory role.[12]

There is, however, an important gap in the argument of Goodfriend and King that remains to be filled. In particular, their analysis relies upon the existence of interest rate smoothing but does not provide any evidence that such smoothing can be practiced without undermining longer-run attention to nominal macroeconomic goals such as the avoidance of inflation. The analysis in McCallum (1981) provides theoretical support for the notion that an appropriate behavioural rule might be feasible. But there remains a need for a constructive example, with some empirical foundation, of a policy rule for manipulation of an interest rate instrument that combines smoothing behavior – and its automatic LLR services – with a longer term trajectory that achieves the objective of macroeconomic stability. An attempt to provide such a rule will be presented in Section IV, but first some matters concerning macro-oriented rules require discussion.

III POLICY RULES FOR MACROECONOMIC STABILITY

In previous studies I have explored the properties in terms of macroeconomic stabilization – the avoidance of inflation and sharp cyclical fluctuations – of a specific, concrete, and operational rule for the conduct of monetary policy. (See McCallum, 1988, 1990a, 1990b, 1993.) The objective of the rule is to generate a time path for nominal aggregate spending that grows smoothly at a non-inflationary rate, with nominal GNP being the spending measure used in existing studies. The indication of these studies, implemented for the economies of the United States and Japan, is that the rule would perform quite well from a macroeconomic perspective. It would, that is, result in a nominal GNP growth paths that are less inflationary and smoother than those that have prevailed historically.

An objection that has been raised by some critics of the rule is that it relies upon the monetary base as an instrument variable. Actual central banks strongly prefer, of course, to focus their day-to-day operations on short-term interest rates, such as the Federal Funds rate in the United States or the overnight call rate in Japan. This preference arises from a belief that day-to-day and week-to-week interest rate volatility would be greatly increased if attempts were made to keep the monetary base (or any other reserve aggregate) in strict conformity with the values specified by the policy rule in question.

But since the rule pertains to quarterly-average values of the base, there exists the conceptual possibility of achieving these values to a fairly high degree of accuracy while using an interest rate variable as the control instrument on a daily or weekly basis. And obviously this possibility is closely related to the Goodfriend–King method for providing LLR services, which we discussed in the previous section. It is conceivable, in other words, that an interest rate rule could be devised that would provide smoothing behavior and yet also achieve monetary base targets – now intermediate targets – dictated by a macroeconomic policy rule such as the one investigated in my previous studies. If the design of such a rule could be achieved, it would then serve the double purpose of (i) completing the case for the Goodfriend–King scheme for the LLR function and also (ii) modifying the case for the macroeconomic policy rule given in McCallum (1993) so as to rely upon operating procedures more like those employed by the Fed, the Bank of Japan, and other actual central banks.

In Sections IV–VI, accordingly, a rule for weekly adjustments of the Federal Funds rate will be proposed and investigated using US data. That rule will be designed to hit weekly targets for the monetary base that will yield quarter-average values for the base that are dictated by the quarterly macroeconomic rule used in McCallum (1993). The remainder of this section will be devoted to an explanation of that rule, some results concerning its performance in simulations of the US economy, and the generation of intermediate target values for the monetary base that will be used to generate weekly targets for the exercise in Sections IV–VI.[13]

The rule used in my previous US studies may be written as in equation (9.1), where x_t and b_t denote quarter-average values of the log of nominal GNP and the log of the monetary base:

$$\Delta b_t = 0.00739 - (1/16)(x_{t-1} - b_{t-1} - x_{t-17} + b_{t-17}) + \lambda(x^*_{t-1} - x_{t-1}) \quad (9.1)$$

Here λ is a positive policy parameter and x^*_t the target value of x_t. In my earlier studies for the United States the x^*_t values were taken to increase each quarter by 0.00739, i.e., to reflect constant growth of nominal GNP at a rate of 3 percent per year. This value was chosen to give a time path of realized x_t values that would grow at approximately the rate of long-term annual growth of *real* GNP, since that would yield an average inflation rate of approximately zero. The purpose of the three terms on the rule's right-hand side are as follows. First, the 0.00739 constant term is a 3 percent growth rate expressed in quarterly logarithmic units. Next, the second term subtracts a magnitude equal to the average growth rate of base velocity over the previous four years. The purpose of that term is to provide a correction for long-lasting changes in velocity stemming from regulatory and technological change. A four-year average is used to avoid incorporation of cyclical movements in velocity. Cyclical influences, finally, are accounted for by the third term, which calls for a stimulative increase in the base growth rate Δb_t when the previous quarter's value of nominal GNP was below its target value.

To determine whether the macroeconomic policy rule (9.1) could in fact keep nominal GNP close to a steady target growth path, given the existence of random shocks of various types, the researcher needs to conduct simulations that include such shocks in a system consisting of the rule and an econometric model that depicts the response of x_t to the rule-generated values of b_t.[14] The fundamental difficulty is that there is no agreed-upon model – in part because the macroeconomics profession has not developed a satisfactory model of the short-run dynamic behavior of aggregate supply that governs the response of real variables to monetary policy actions.[15] Because of that problem, my preferred method of investigation has been to determine whether policy rule (9.1) will perform reasonably well in a variety of different models. Thus my 1988 study of the US economy included simulations with two single-equation atheoretic specifications, several vector autoregression (VAR) systems, and three models that were intended to be structural (i.e. policy invariant). These latter models are quite small in scale but are designed to represent three leading theories of business cycle dynamics – the 'real business cycle' (RBC) theory of Kydland and Prescott, the 'monetary misperceptions' theory of Lucas and Barro, and a more Keynesian theory (PC) patterned on the Phillips curve and price-adjustment specifications of the Fed's quarterly MPS model.

Principal results for the US economy, in counterfactual simulations pertaining to the period 1954.1–1985.4, are summarized in Table 9.1. The entries in this table are root-mean-square errors (RMSE) – i.e., deviations from the target path – in simulations with systems including rule (9.1) and the five models indicated.[16] In each case the simulation begins with initial conditions prevailing at the start of 1954 and continues with shocks fed into the system each quarter, these shocks being estimated as residuals from the equations estimated in the various models. It will be seen that for λ values in the range of 0.1 to above 0.25, the RMSE values are about 0.02 (that is, 2 percent) with all five models.[17] Thus performance is satisfactory in all of these

Table 9.1 Basic results for US economy, 1954–85. RMSE values with five models

Model	*Value of λ in Rule* (9.1) 0.00	0.10	0.25	0.50
Single equation	0.0488	0.0249	0.0197	0.0162
4-Variable VAR	0.0479	0.0216	0.0220	0.1656
Real business cycle	0.0281	0.0200	0.0160	0.0132
Monetary misperceptions	0.0238	0.0194	0.0161	0.0137
Phillips curve	0.0311	0.0236	0.0191	0.0174

cases, and distinctly superior to that with $\lambda = 0$. Higher values of λ give rise to the possibility of dynamic instrument instability, which occurs with $\lambda = 0.5$ in the VAR system (and with $\lambda = 1.0$ in the other four systems). But with moderate values of λ, the rule succeeds in generating paths of x_t that are non-inflationary and, in addition, somewhat smoother than those that have obtained historically. A plot of x_t and the constant rising target path of x_t^* for the PC model and $\lambda = 0.25$ is shown in Figure 9.1.[18]

Recently I have come to believe that a strong case can be made for expressing the GNP target in terms of growth rates, rather than levels corresponding to a single predetermined growth path. The main reason is that, since real shocks that affect the economy's natural-rate output level are highly persistent, it may be undesirable to quickly drive x_t back to the predetermined x_t^* path after shocks have arrived. Instead, it would seem preferable to treat past shocks as bygones, which could be accomplished by adopting $x_t^{**} = x_{t-1} + 0.00739$, rather than $x_t^* = x_{t-1}^* + 0.00739$, as the target value for period t. This sort of rebased growth-rate target has been favoured by several economists, including Feldstein and Stock (1993).[19] And the suggestion of using rebased growth rate targets merits serious consideration for two additional reasons. These are that instrument variability should be reduced for any given value of λ and that it should accordingly be possible to use larger λ values, implying stronger feedback, without inducing instrument instability.

Consequently, in my study of the Japanese economy (McCallum, 1993), I conducted several simulations using a modified version of rule (9.1) that substitutes x_t^{**} for x_t^*. These simulations produced encouraging results. They suggest, however, that an even more attractive rule would be one that uses a weighted average of x_t^* for x_t^{**} as

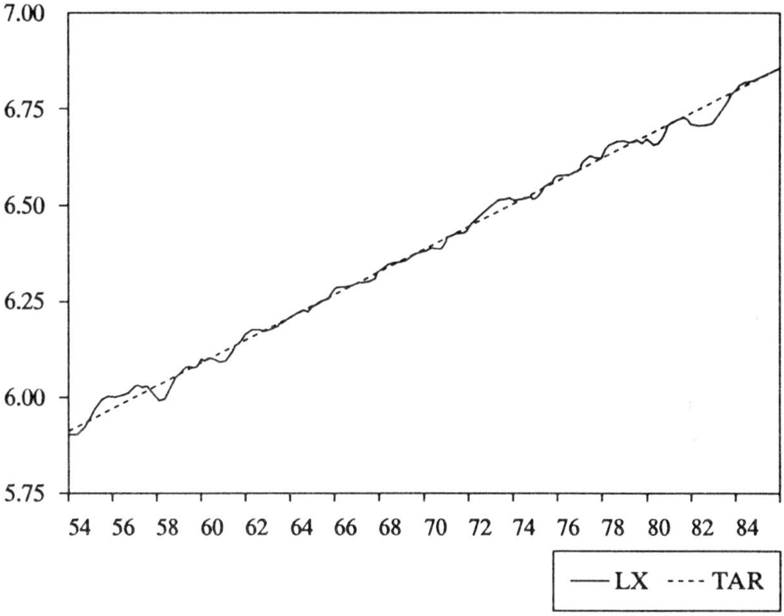

Figure 9.1 Simulation with policy rule (9.1), Philips curve model, and λ = 0.25: 1954–85. LX, log of nominal GNP, simulated; TAR, target path x_t^*.

the target variable. Such a target would seem to provide most of the benefits of x_t^{**} without eliminating entirely the tendency to drive x_t back to a fixed path. A large portion of the Japanese study was, therefore, conducted with a target of this type. The weights chosen were 0.2 and 0.8 for x_t^* and x_t^{**} so the target variable utilized was x_t^{*a} = 0.2 x_t^* + 0.8 x_t^{**}. The resulting simulations indicated that RMSE values relative to the x_t^{**} path suffered very little deterioration while performance relative to the x_t^* path was substantially enhanced, relative to the case with x_t^{**} targets.

Let us then consider performance with our five models of the US economy when x_t^{*a} is used as the target variable. Summary results for the simulation period 1954–85 and λ = 0.25 are reported in Table 9.2. There it will be seen that RMSE values relative to the x_t^{*a} target are only about 0.01 and that RMSE values relative to the x_t^* path are not too far from those in Table 9.1. Furthermore, the variability of the Δb_t instrument is reduced considerably relative to its magnitude in the simulations of Table 9.1, in which x_t^* is the target.

Table 9.2 Additional results for US economy, 1954–85. Results with x_t^{*a} target value and $\lambda = 0.25$

Model	*RMSE relative to* x_t^{*a}	*RMSE relative to* x_t^{**}	*RMSE relative to* x_t^{*}	*Standard deviation of* Δb_t	*Standard deviation of* Δb_t *using* x_t^{*} *target*
Single equation	0.0102	0.0104	0.0244	0.0041	0.0063
4-Variable VAR	0.0104	0.0105	0.0218	0.0039	0.0069
Real business cycle	0.0105	0.0109	0.0197	0.0043	0.0054
Monetary misperception	0.0110	0.0116	0.0184	0.0039	0.0051
Phillips curve	0.0104	0.0103	0.0234	0.0048	0.0066

Table 9.3 Updated results for US economy, 1954–91, x_t^{*a} Target values

Model	$\lambda = 0.25$ *RMSE relative to*			$\lambda = 0.50$ *RMSE relative to*		
	x_t^{*a}	x_t^{**}	x_t^{*}	x_t^{*a}	x_t^{**}	x_t^{*}
Single equation	0.0125	0.0099	0.0413	0.0109	0.0099	0.0305
4-Variable VAR	0.0111	0.0100	0.0306	0.0107	0.0104	0.0239
Phillips curve	0.0110	0.0099	0.0343	0.0103	0.0100	0.0260

In addition, for three of the models RMSE values have been obtained for an updated estimation and simulation period that extends through 1991.4. This updating is of interest and importance because of recent shifts in base demand and because the evidence of Hess, Small and Brayton (1993) suggests that the performance of rule (9.1) with the x_t^* target has deteriorated in recent years. The models utilized are the basic single-equation version (because of its simplicity), the VAR system (which because of lags is perhaps the most difficult to stabilize), and the Phillips curve model (which is empirically the most satisfactory of the structural specifications). Summary results with λ values of 0.25 and 0.50 are reported in Table 9.3, with a plot of the Phillips curve case ($\lambda = 0.5$) shown in Figure 9.2. As can readily be seen, performance relative to the steady x_t^* path deteriorates noticeably, relative to Table 9.2, with $\lambda = 0.25$. The higher value of λ yields smaller RMSE values, however, as conjectured above. Most importantly, we see that performance relative to the utilized target, x_t^{*a}, is almost as good as with the shorter sample period. And since the argument above suggests that the x_t^{*a} targets are the

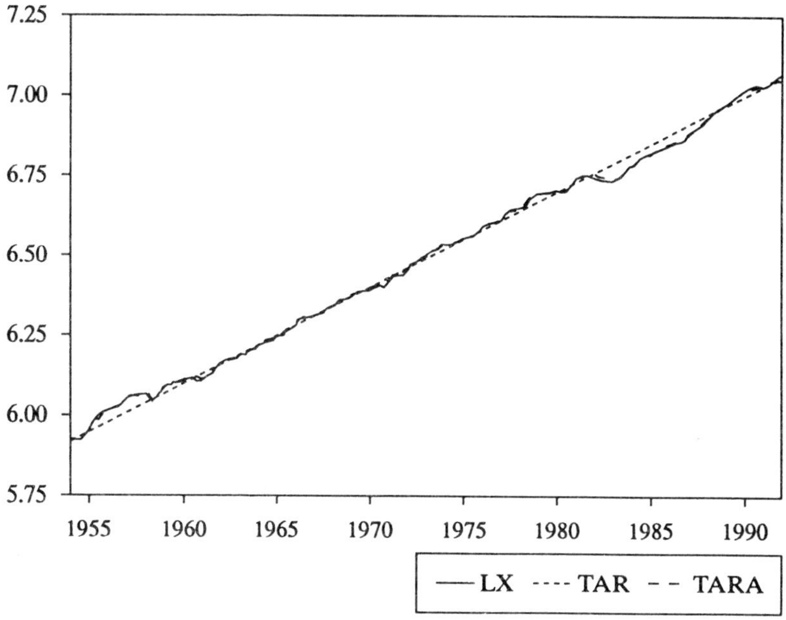

Figure 9.2 Simulation with target x_t^{*a}, Phillips curve model, and $\lambda = 0.5$: 1954–91. TARA, target path x_t^{*a}.

most appropriate of those considered, the Table 9.3 results are quite encouraging.

We are now finally in a position to proceed with the main business of this section from the perspective of the present chapter. That business is to generate quarterly time paths for the monetary base that conform to the macroeconomic policy rule (9.1), in order to determine whether a funds rate instrument can be used at the weekly frequency to achieve these base values at the quarterly frequency. For that purpose, let us adopt the time path of Δb_t implied by the 1954.1–1991.4 simulation with $\lambda = 0.50$ in the Phillips curve model. This model has been chosen as the one that is perhaps the most similar to models used by policy makers while the higher λ value has been chosen since it is the more demanding from the perspective of our upcoming examination. Values of b_t for this simulation, which are reported in Table 9.4, imply corresponding Δb_t growth rates that will be used in the next section as the basis of intermediate targets specified at the weekly level, with the federal funds rate treated as the instrument variable.

Table 9.4 Quarterly values of monetary base implied by simulation with Rule (9.1), Target x_t^{*a}, and $\lambda = 0.5$

obs	*LB*			
1954	3.699 626	3.699 201	3.701 861	3.700 723
1955	3.695 663	3.685 769	3.678 821	3.670 292
1956	3.663 447	3.660 838	3.653 607	3.646 640
1957	3.635 705	3.622 726	3.617 845	3.607 567
1958	3.610 314	3.617 946	3.615 145	3.602 111
1959	3.587 843	3.577 400	3.565 968	3.567 536
1960	3.566 199	3.553 598	3.555 266	3.555 225
1961	3.565 991	3.571 272	3.569 220	3.566 943
1962	3.562 037	3.554 727	3.551 242	3.550 338
1963	3.554 655	3.556 308	3.559 981	3.559 844
1964	3.562 261	3.561 246	3.564 794	3.567 481
1965	3.574 026	3.566 553	3.565 190	3.563 168
1966	3.557 531	3.550 862	3.552 993	3.553 147
1967	3.551 403	3.552 872	3.557 957	3.557 715
1968	3.559 741	3.555 497	3.550 994	3.550 638
1969	3.552 911	3.550 609	3.552 800	3.552 005
1970	3.558 019	3.565 338	3.571 514	3.576 477
1971	3.591 054	3.586 729	3.592 183	3.599 308
1972	3.609 258	3.607 779	3.609 905	3.614 645
1973	3.613 902	3.609 248	3.610 332	3.613 725
1974	3.609 658	3.616 153	3.617 774	3.620 023
1975	3.622 591	3.633 976	3.636 605	3.629 527
1976	3.624 797	3.619 938	3.622 463	3.625 583
1977	3.624 269	3.621 913	3.615 692	3.610 757
1978	3.615 292	3.616 438	3.599 481	3.594 176
1979	3.585 975	3.581 275	3.576 563	3.570 283
1980	3.571 408	3.566 808	3.577 621	3.579 534
1981	3.571 942	3.559 871	3.563 561	3.562 610
1982	3.570 922	3.584 987	3.595 935	3.613 094
1983	3.631 518	3.649 563	3.661 737	3.677 940
1984	3.690 174	3.697 853	3.710 630	3.726 509
1985	3.744 710	3.761 105	3.781 000	3.800 733
1986	3.821 689	3.839 503	3.864 610	3.886 189
1987	3.909 599	3.927 389	3.946 029	3.963 543
1988	3.978 593	3.995 090	4.010 744	4.026 279
1989	4.039 557	4.051 177	4.062 631	4.073 216
1990	4.084 578	4.093 219	4.103 212	4.112 802
1991	4.128 195	4.144 728	4.159 743	4.172 677

Note: LB is the log of the St. Louis Fed's adjusted monetary base, measured in $ billions.

IV HITTING BASE TARGETS WITH AN INTEREST RATE INSTRUMENT

The purpose of this section and the next two is to determine whether it would be possible to exert sufficiently accurate base control, as suggested above, with an operating procedure that uses an interest rate instrument and involves rate smoothing as a means of providing LLR protection to the financial system. Our approach will be to conduct simulations with a system that pertains to weekly data for the United States. The system will consist of a policy rule that sets weekly values of the federal funds rate, together with a weekly model of monetary base determination that is intended to reflect the effects of federal funds rate behavior on realized magnitudes of the base. The model will be extremely simple, but should give some indication of the accuracy with which quarterly base targets can be achieved while holding down funds-rates movements, i.e., engaging in funds-rate smoothing.

The form of policy rule involved will be as follows, with time periods referring to weeks:

$$R_\tau - R_{\tau-1} = -\theta[b^*_{\tau-1} - b_{\tau-1}] \tag{9.2}$$

Here R_τ denotes the funds rate (in annual percentage points) and b_τ denotes the log of the monetary base, both averaged over the week. The value b^*_τ is the target value of b_τ for week τ. The idea is that values of b^*_τ would be derived in practice from quarterly magnitudes specified by a higher-level policy rule such as those generated by equation (9.1) of Section III. For the purposes of the present exercise, b^*_τ values will be treated as exogenous and one objective will be to determine how closely realized b_τ values track those for b^*_τ. The magnitude of θ determines the tradeoff between feedback response and smoothing; small values imply a high degree of R_τ smoothing with relatively little response to b_τ target misses. The possibility under consideration is that, for a range of θ values, feedback responses will be strong enough to keep b_τ close to b^*_τ while weekly ΔR_τ values are nevertheless small (say, always less than 2 percent and typically much less).

The second ingredient of our system, then, is a model at the weekly frequency of the response of b_τ to fluctuations in R_τ. In principle, one would like to utilize a carefully specified and estimated structural model pertaining to banks' demand for reserves and the public's demand for currency. Data non-availability and time constraints have,

Table 9.5 Weekly ARMA models for Δb_τ

Coefficient	*Jan. 1969– Dec. 1978*	*Jan. 1974– Sept. 1979*	*Oct. 1979– Sept. 1982*	*Jan. 1983– Dec. 1991*†	*Jan. 1988– Dec. 1991*†
Const.	0.0022	0.0026	0.0027	0.0034	0.0028
	(0.0002)	(0.0002)	(0.0004)	(0.0003)	(0.0003)
AR (1)	−0.4270	−0.4383	−0.6082	−0.7091	−0.6225
	(0.044)	(0.055)	(0.075)	(0.044)	(0.061)
AR (2)	−0.0925	−0.0264	−0.2593	−0.4633	−0.3819
	(0.047)	(0.060)	(0.087)	(0.050)	(0.068)
AR (3)	−0.1208	−0.1920	−0.3893	−0.1977	−0.2384
	(0.043)	(0.055)	(0.075)	(0.043)	(0.057)
MA (26)	0.1480	0.3237		0.1737	0.4977
	(0.045)	(0.056)		(0.046)	(0.064)
R^2	0.193	0.328	0.439	0.449	0.574
SE	0.0029	0.0024	0.0042	0.0043	0.0037
DW	1.99	1.92	1.97	2.03	2.12
Q(36)	39.6	47.6	97.7	38.1	43.9

† Dummy variables also included for first week of 1991.

however, made that infeasible. What I have done instead is to estimate a weekly univariate ARMA model for Δb_τ, which should serve to depict with fair accuracy the autocorrelation structure and variability of movements in the base. A term reflecting current-week responses to changes in the funds rate R_τ is then added to this relation, with the response coefficient being based partly on values taken from Federal Reserve literature and partly on empirical estimates. These estimates are generated from weekly movements in the funds rates and non-borrowed reserves, by means of a procedure that will be explained below. First let us consider the univariate dynamic behavior of b_τ, the log of the base.

Weekly ARMA models for Δb_τ have been estimated for five time periods, including Jan. 1969–Dec. 1978, Jan. 1974–Sept. 1979, Oct. 1979–Sept. 1982, Jan. 1983–Dec. 1991, and Jan. 1988–Dec. 1991. The estimates are presented in Table 9.5. In all five periods an AR(3) specification was found to be reasonably appropriate, but with point estimates that are fairly different for samples before, during, and after the 1979–82 experience with 'non-borrowed reserves targeting'. In addition to the three AR terms, it was found that a moving-average term at lag 26 was significant in all five cases.[20] My interpretation is that this reflects some type of seasonal aberration that is present in the data but not in the market relationships that our ARMA model is intended to represent. This component will, accordingly, be suppressed in the simulations reported in Section V. The same is true for a dummy variable pertaining to one observation at the start of 1991, which will be discussed below.

Examination of the results in Table 9.5 suggests that the three later periods differ markedly from the first two, with negative coefficient estimates summing to absolute values greater than 1.0 in all post-1979 samples. Our first experiment, accordingly, will be based on one of the earlier periods. For the sake of sample-period homogeneity, the second sample – with exactly 300 observations – will be utilized.

To complete our model, that equation is augmented with the term $-0.0025\Delta R_\tau$, designed to reflect the immediate impact on the base of the open-market purchase or sale needed to bring about any programmed change in the funds rate. The magnitude of the slope coefficient was chosen on the basis of three different sources of information. The first of these is the rule-of-thumb relationship between borrowing levels and the funds rate-discount rate spread that, according to Cook (1989, p. 9) 'the Fed has long used'. That rule of thumb is described as $400 million per percentage point, but I would expect the *ratio* of borrowed to total reserves to be related to the interest spread with greater stability. A $400 million change in borrowed reserves would then amount to approximately a fraction of 0.02 of total reserves with the latter being about $20 billion at the date (May 1981) referred to by Cook. But a change in borrowed reserves brought about by an open market action would have an effect on the base of about the same magnitude in terms of *dollars*, so the percentage change in the base would be much smaller (and of the opposite sign). Taking 8 as the ratio of base to reserves, the 0.02 fraction in terms of reserves translates into about 0.0025 in terms of the base.[21]

Our second source of information is a slope coefficient in a 'daily reaction function' for the open market desk as estimated by Feinman (1993). The third column of Feinman's Table 1 suggests that a one percentage point excess of the funds rate, over its expected value, would induce the open-market desk to supply $1461 million in additional reserves. Presuming that the desk's action is designed to restore the funds rate to its expected level, this estimate appears at first to be considerably larger than that of the previous paragraph. But Feinman's quantity variable refers to the magnitude of effect on the average value of reserves over a two-week reserve maintenance period. So his value of $1461 million implies that this would be the magnitude of an action taken on the first day of the reserve maintenance period, with the implied figure being only half as large for an action taken in the middle of the two-week period. Taking this to be a 'typical' day, we get a magnitude of $730 million per percentage point to be comparable to the $400 million of the previous paragraph. But Feinman's value pertains to a sample period of Jan. 1988–Dec. 1990, during which time the average level of reserves was about $39 billion rather than $20 billion. So the fractional effect would be 0.730/39 = 0.0187 $billion/percentage point, which agrees very closely with the 0.02 figure (pertaining to reserves) of the previous paragraph.[22]

The third source of information is based on direct estimation of an equation similar to the one being considered, but in terms of non-borrowed reserves rather than the base. The reason that we have not attempted to estimate this relation with base data, by simply adding a ΔR_τ term to the ARMA models of Table 9.5, is that weekly movements in the base are dominated by changes in currency or reserve demand rather than actions taken by the open market desk. But an increase in reserve demand would tend to produce an increase in the funds rate, so the estimated slope coefficient would tend to be positive rather than negative. With demand changes providing most of the movement, the response of concern is not identified in the data. There is more reason to believe, however, that the relevant response will be identified if non-borrowed reserves are used instead of the base.[23] And, indeed, least-squares estimation over the period Jan. 1974–Sept. 1979 yields the following values (with n_τ denoting the log of non-borrowed reserves):

$$\begin{aligned}\Delta n_\tau &= \underset{(0.0012)}{0.0012} - \underset{(0.0557)}{0.5471}\Delta n_{\tau-1} - \underset{(0.0605)}{0.2312}\Delta n_{\tau-2} - \underset{(0.0547)}{0.2783}\Delta n_{\tau-3} - \underset{(0.0054)}{0.0190}\Delta R_\tau \\ R^2 &= 0.292 \qquad SE = 0.0212 \qquad DW = 1.97 \qquad Q(36) = 92.2 \qquad (9.3)\end{aligned}$$

Thus the estimated slope coefficient is almost exactly equal to the rule-of-thumb value cited by Cook (1989), in terms of reserve movements. So division by 8 will give almost the same slope coefficient as mentioned above for the base. The three sources of information agree quite closely in suggesting a response coefficient of about −0.0025.

In sum, the second equation in our simulation system is

$$\begin{aligned}\Delta b_\tau = \text{const.} &-0.4383\Delta b_{\tau-1} - 0.0264\Delta b_{\tau-2} \\ &- 0.1920\Delta b_{\tau-3} - 0.0025\Delta R_\tau + e_{4\tau}.\end{aligned} \qquad (9.4)$$

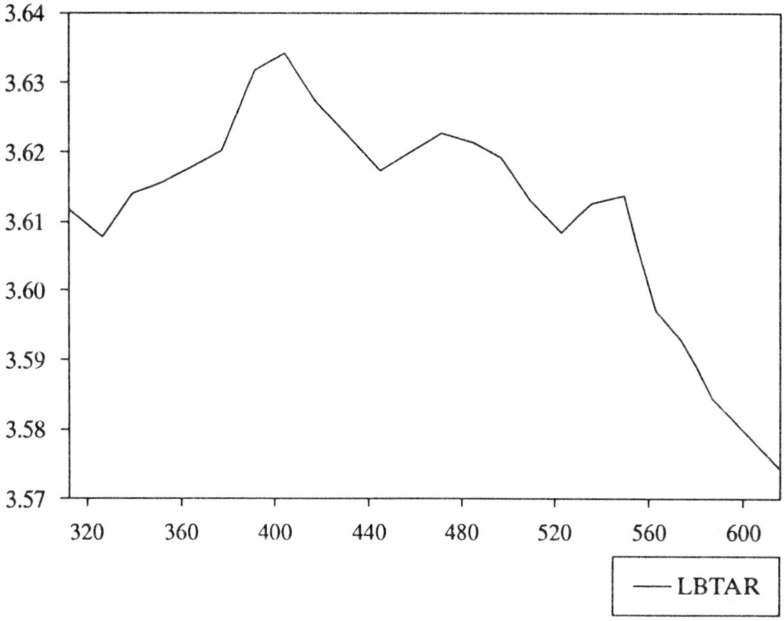

Figure 9.3 Weekly target path for the monetary base, Jan. 1974–Sept. 1979.

Here $e_{4\tau}$ is the residual from the estimated equation in the second column of Table 9.5, so our simulation will feature shocks each period that reflect estimates of the shocks that actually occurred over the sample period of Jan. 1974–Sept. 1979.[24]

The other ingredient needed for simulation of the system (9.2) (9.4) is a set of values for the weekly targets b^*_τ. These are derived from the quarterly targets b^*_t, generated by policy rule (9.1), reported in Table 9.4. The quarterly values of b^*_t imply quarter-to-quarter growth rates Δb^*_t. These values have been divided by 13 to yield weekly growth rates Δb^*_τ that are constant within each quarter but change at each quarter's end.[25] Those Δb^*_τ rates then imply weekly values of b^*_τ. The target path so generated for Jan. 1974–Sept. 1979 is plotted in Figure 9.3.

Finally, an adjustment needs to be applied to the ARMA equation's constant term.[26] The reason is as follows. As a glance at Figure 9.3 will reveal, the base target values b^*_τ are decreasing, rather than growing, on average over the years 1974–9. But the constant term in the estimated Δb_τ model in Table 9.5 is positive, since the base was actually growing over the sample period. In a complete model the

Table 9.6 Simulation results, system (9.2) (9.4), Jan. 1974–Sept. 1979

For $b^*_\tau - b_\tau$	$\theta = 50$	$\theta = 100$	$\theta = 150$	$\theta = 200$
RMS	0.00534	0.00370	0.00317	0.0030
MAV†	0.0145	0.0120	0.0108	0.0100
For ΔR_τ				
RMS	0.265	0.369	0.474	0.600
MAV†	0.73	1.20	1.62	1.99

† MAV denotes 'maximum absolute value'.

average growth rate of the base would be determined endogenously, but our simplified weekly system does not include any component that would accomplish such an endogenization. That is, the system includes no mechanism that would generate a positive relationship between R_τ and Δb_τ values at low frequencies – i.e., on average over long spans of time. Only the short-term negative relationship is included. But the average value of Δb_τ generated in the simulation needs to match that of the Δb_τ targets; otherwise the weekly variations cannot possibly be matched. Consequently, the constant term in the ARMA model is altered to provide this match. In particular, the 0.0026 value reported in Table 9.5 for the Jan. 1974–Sept. 1979 sample is replaced with the value −0.000208 in the simulation runs.

V BASIC SIMULATION RESULTS

Let us now consider the outcome of the experiment described in the previous section. Some statistical results for four different values of θ, the policy parameter in rule (9.2), are given in Table 9.6. Before examining them, however, it may be useful to consult Figure 9.4, which plots the target path b^*_τ (denoted LBTAR) and the simulated path b_τ (denoted LB) in the case with $\theta = 100$. Visual inspection will show that the rule is rather successful in this simulation in keeping b_τ close to b^*_τ, especially when the unusually erratic nature of the target path is recognized.

In Table 9.6, summary statistics are reported for the following values of θ: 50, 100, 150, and 200. In the first row we have root-mean-square (RMS) values of the target miss, $b^*_\tau - b_\tau$, over the 300 weeks of the simulation period. Since b^*_τ and b_τ are natural logarithms, the RMS value is a measure of the typical error in fractional relative form. The second-column value 0.00370, for example, can be thought

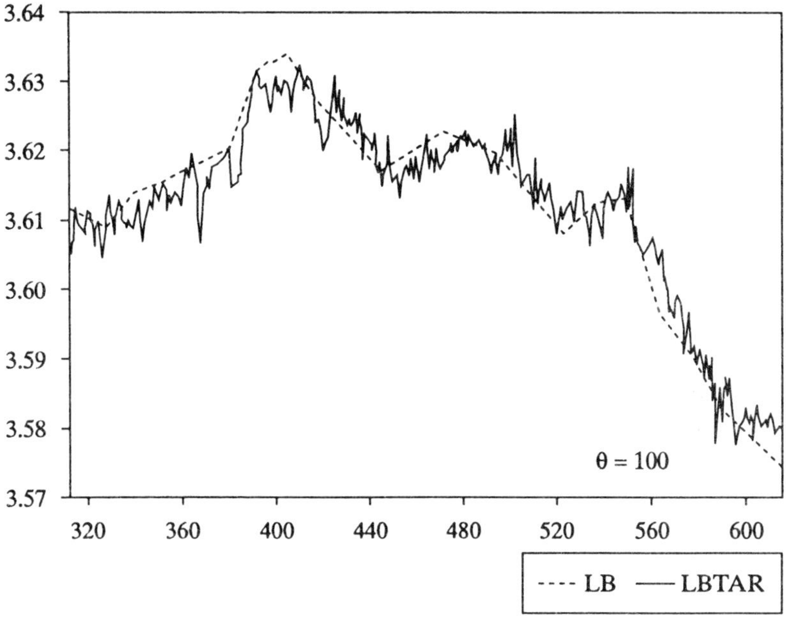

Figure 9.4 Simulation with system (9.2) (9.4), Jan. 1974–Sept. 1979. LB, log of monetary base, simulated; LBTAR, target path, b^*_τ.

of as slightly above one-third of 1 percent. The second row indicates in the same fashion that the *maximum* deviation of outcome from target was just over 1 percent with $\theta = 100$, or nearly $1\frac{1}{2}$ percent with $\theta = 50$.

But how much interest rate variability is entailed? The last two rows give statistics pertaining to ΔR_τ, i.e., simulated weekly changes in the funds rate. Since R_τ is measured in (annualized) percentage points, these statistics also have those units. Thus in column two, we see that with $\theta = 100$ the RMS change is about 37 basis points while the largest week-to-week change in the 300 week sample is 120 basis points. These figures do not compare too badly with the actual historical record of Jan. 1974–Sept. 1979, the actual RMS value being 0.21 and the largest absolute change being 158 basis points (which occurred between 26 June and 3 July of 1974).

The foregoing results are, I would contend, predominantly favorable to the suggestion under study, namely, that it would be possible to exert accurate base control with a procedure that involves smoothing – with its associated LLR properties – of an interest rate instrument. In the simulation with $\theta = 100$, for example, the implied degree of base control is highly accurate and funds rate variability is not excessive. In particular, there are no instances in which the required change in R_τ from the previous week would exceed 2 percent, the magnitude mentioned in Section II as a plausible limit reflecting Meltzer's penalty rate or the Goodfriend–King bound under a regime with LLR smoothing.[27]

In this context it may be of interest to determine how much R_τ variability would be entailed, in the model at hand, by *exact* base control. An answer can be obtained by replacing equation (9.2) in our simulation system with the condition $b_\tau = b^*_\tau$ and using (9.4) to determine a time-path for R_τ. That exercise indicates that the RMS value for ΔR_τ, the one-week change in the funds rate, would be 0.998 percent, almost three times as large as in column 2 of Table 9.6. The maximum weekly change furthermore would be 3.64 percent – again about three times as large as with rule (9.2) and $\theta = 100$.

Now let us turn to our second selected time period for estimation and simulation results, namely, Jan. 1988–Dec. 1991.[28] The simulation system is similar conceptually to the one used above and indeed includes policy rule (9.2) as before. The target path for b^*_τ is, however, quite different: it rises continually (though at varying rates) in contrast to the up-and-down path of Figure 9.3. The relation to be used in place of (9.4), based on the final column of Table 9.5, is as follows:

$$\begin{aligned}\Delta b_\tau = {} & \text{const.} - 0.6225\Delta b_{\tau-1} - 0.3819\Delta b_{\tau-2} \\ & - 0.2384\Delta b_{\tau-3} - 0.0025\Delta R_\tau + e_{5\tau}\end{aligned} \tag{9.5}$$

Here the utilized constant term is 0.0024, designed to match the sample trend as explained above for equation (9.4), and the MA(26) term has again been dropped for the simulation. In addition, the dummy variable mentioned in Table 9.5 has been suppressed. This dummy was included in the estimation stage because the St. Louis Fed's base statistics show a $10 billion increase in the week of 2 Jan. 1991, which is then reversed in the week of 9 Jan. 1991. This spike would appear to reflect a year-end or some other type of aberrational effect that our model is not intended to reflect.

The same slope coefficient for the effect of ΔR_τ on base growth is used in (9.5) as in (9.4). That specification has been retained to be conservative despite the suggestion of a steeper slope provided by a regression estimate comparable to (9.3) but for the sample period 1988–91.[29] There are two features of equation (9.5) that need to be mentioned. First, the values of the AR coefficients sum to −1.257, a

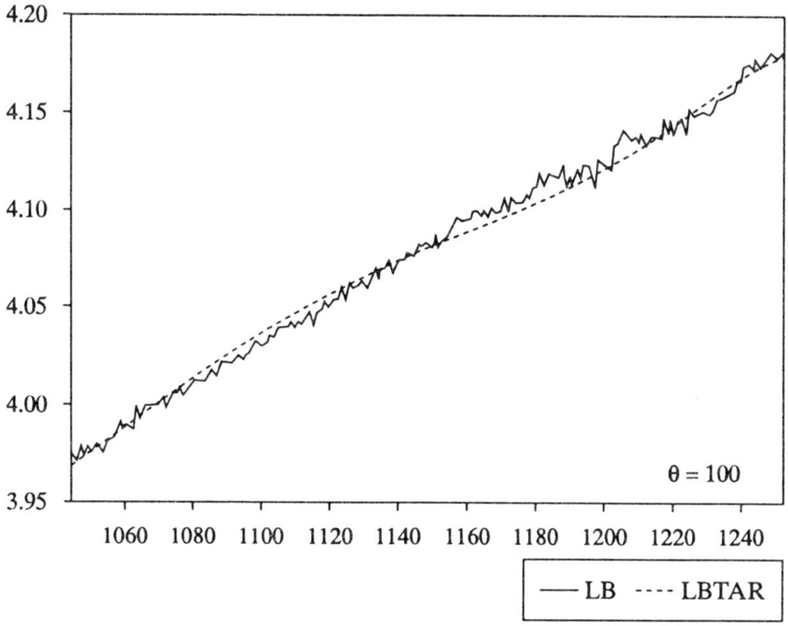

Figure 9.5 Simulation with system (9.2) (9.5), Jan. 1988–Dec. 1991.

Table 9.7 Simulation results, system (9.2) (9.5), Jan. 1988–Dec. 1991

For $b_\tau^* - b_\tau$	$\theta = 50$	$\theta = 100$	$\theta = 150$	$\theta = 200$
RMS	0.00739	0.00529	0.00461	0.00447
MAV	0.0213	0.0161	0.0146	0.0148
For ΔR_τ				
RMS	0.369	0.529	0.692	0.893
MAV	1.06	1.61	2.20	2.96

somewhat larger negative number than in (9.4). Second, the variability of $e_{5\tau}$ is – as shown in Table 9.5 – considerably greater than for $e_{4\tau}$, making accurate base control somewhat more difficult.

Results of the simulations are presented in Figure 9.5 and Table 9.7. The target path in the former is so different from that in Figure 9.4 that comparison is difficult. The statistic values reported in Table 9.7 verify, however, that base control is somewhat less accurate than in the 1974–9 regime for a given level of ΔR_τ variability. Thus, a value of $\theta = 50$ yields about the same RMS value for ΔR_τ as with $\theta = 100$ in Table 9.6, but the RMS control error for b_τ is 0.0074

Table 9.8 Additional simulation results

		Period 1974–9		*Period 1988–91*	
		$\theta = 100$	$\theta = 150$	$\theta = 100$	$\theta = 150$
System A					
$b^*_\tau - b_\tau$	RMS	0.0037	0.0032	0.0053	0.0045
	MAV	0.0127	0.0120	0.0159	0.0153
ΔR_τ	RMS	0.343	0.418	0.469	0.559
	MAV	1.00	1.44	1.41	1.77
System B					
$b^*_\tau - b_\tau$	RMS	0.0030	0.0039	0.0045	0.0053
	MAV	0.0100	0.0107	0.0147	0.0180
ΔR_τ	RMS	0.300	0.581	0.446	0.795
	MAV	1.00	1.62	1.48	2.70
System C					
$b^*_\tau - b_\tau$	RMS	0.0029	0.0027	0.0041	0.0039
	MAV	0.0114	0.0103	0.0155	0.0153
ΔR_τ	RMS	0.245	0.316	0.323	0.416
	MAV	0.93	1.31	1.03	1.43

Note: Systems A and C use the average $b^*_\tau - b_\tau$ discrepancy for τ–1 and τ–2 in rule (2); systems B and C use 0.005 as the ΔR_τ slope coefficient in models (9.4) and (9.5).

instead of 0.0037. Nevertheless, the results are still reasonably supportive of the Goodfriend–King proposal. With $\theta = 50$ or $\theta = 100$, the maximum value of ΔR_τ in the simulations stays below 2.0 and fairly tight base control is achieved. The actual sample values of RMS and MAV for ΔR_τ, incidentally, are 0.18 and 1.14.[30]

VI ADDITIONAL RESULTS

In addition to the basic results reported in the previous section, a few more have been obtained using variants of the equations of the simulation system. The first variant alters the policy rule (9.2) so as to use the average value of $b^*_\tau - b_\tau$ over the previous two weeks, rather than one week, as the discrepancy to which the Fed responds. Because of the large negative value attached to $\Delta b_{\tau-1}$ in the ARMA models (9.4) and (9.5), it seems possible that such a change could reduce R_τ variability without substantially impairing the extent of base control. Results relevant to that possibility are presented in the top panel

(System A) of Table 9.8, where it can be seen that there is not much difference for the 1974–9 period, but that a noticeable reduction in variability of R_τ occurs in the later (1988–91) period. With $\theta = 100$, for example, the RMS value for ΔR_τ is reduced from 0.529 to 0.469 and the maximum absolute value from 1.61 to 1.41.

A second variant to the system involves a change in the slope coefficient attached to ΔR_τ in our model of base determination – equation (9.4) or (9.5). It was mentioned above that our estimation of a relation like (9.3) for 1988–91 yielded a larger estimate of the slope than those in the three basic sources of information. Furthermore, the rule-of-thumb cited by Cook (1989) pertains only to the slope of the borrowing function and thus does not include any effect working through money demand – e.g., any tendency for an open-market purchase and reduction in R_τ to increase the quantity of money demanded. That neglect is perhaps appropriate for a one-week response coefficient, but it might be argued that it tends to understate the magnitude of the response. In any event our experiment in the middle panel of Table 9.8 presumes that the slope is –0.005, twice the value used above.

With $\theta = 100$, the rule's performance is somewhat better than previously, especially for the 1988–91 sample period. But with $\theta = 150$, performance is actually worsened. That outcome is somewhat surprising, since a larger slope would seem to imply that Δb_τ would be more controllable via manipulation of R_τ. But apparently the system becomes uncomfortably close to suffering from instrument instability with the larger feedback coefficient θ.

That problem is mitigated, however, when the averaged discrepancy in the policy rule of System A is combined with the stronger response coefficient of System B. In the resulting System C, the performance measures (given in panel three of Table 9.8) are almost uniformly better than those in Tables 9.6 and 9.7. Indeed, with $\theta = 100$ they are quite favorable. This finding suggests that other specifications of the policy rule could be substantially superior to our equation (9.2), but a systematic investigation of that possibility will have to be reserved for future study. The object of the present chapter is to explore the feasibility of a Goodfriend–King type of rule, not to attempt an optimization analysis.

The two sample periods utilized in our study were chosen for reasons – concerning possible regime changes and conformity with previous studies – that have considerable merit. Several commentators on the chapter have suggested, however, that the study's value would

Table 9.9 Simulation results, system (9.2) (9.6), July 1987–December 1991

	Basic system		*System B*	
For $b^*_\tau - b_\tau$	$\theta = 100$	$\theta = 150$	$\theta = 100$	$\theta = 150$
RMS	0.00512	0.00451	0.0044	0.0051
MAV	0.0153	0.0148	0.0149	0.0183
For ΔR_τ				
RMS	0.512	0.677	0.438	0.760
MAV	1.53	2.23	1.49	2.75
	System A		*System C*	
For $b^*_\tau - b_\tau$	$\theta = 100$	$\theta = 150$	$\theta = 100$	$\theta = 150$
RMS	0.0051	0.0044	0.0040	0.0039
MAV	0.0153	0.0155	0.0156	0.0154
For ΔR_τ				
RMS	0.449	0.541	0.316	0.412
MAV	1.35	1.71	1.00	1.43

be greater if the stock market crash of September 1987 were included in the second sample and simulation period. Accordingly, additional results have been obtained with that period extended so as to include July 1987–Dec. 1991, rather than Jan. 1988–Dec. 1991.

With that extension, the estimated weekly ARMA model corresponding to those in Table 9.5 differs only slightly from the results in the final column. In particular, the SE value rises only to 0.0038 (from 0.0037) and the Q(36) statistic actually falls somewhat, to 38.4. With the MA(26) coefficient and the 2 Jan. 1991 dummy variable again suppressed, and the constant term obtained as before, the implied base growth model is as follows:

$$\Delta b_\tau = 0.0035 - 0.6436\Delta b_{\tau-1} - 0.4038\Delta b_{\tau-2} - 0.2156\Delta b_{\tau-3} - 0.0025\Delta R_\tau + e_{6\tau}. \quad (9.6)$$

Results using the basic policy rule (9.2) with θ values of 100 and 150, and also the three variants introduced in this section, are reported in Table 9.9. There it will be seen that inclusion of the October 1987 stock market crash in the sample and simulation periods does not significantly alter the outcome of our exercise. In fact, the results are slightly *better* than those reported for 1988–91 in Tables 9.7 and 9.8. That finding, which is somewhat surprising, stems from the fact that residuals from the estimated ARMA model for Δb_τ are not so large at the time of the crash as to outweigh their relatively small size during the remainder of the second half of 1987.

VII CONCLUSION

It may be useful to conclude with a summary of the foregoing analysis and results. The argument begins by noting that a central bank's dual objectives of macroeconomic and financial stability imply a tension that may be expressed in terms of the following question: is the adherence to a macro-oriented rule for monetary policy compatible with satisfaction of a central bank's lender-of-last-resort (LLR) responsibilities? In Section II, a brief review of alternative views on the LLR role indicates that a proposal by Goodfriend and King (1988) might provide a way of reconciling the two objectives. For the proposal is to have LLR assistance supplied entirely by open-market operations, with no discount window lending but with high-frequency smoothing of movements of a money market interest rate. The point is that smoothing of day-to-day or week-to-week movements in this interest rate would automatically trigger open-market purchases whenever a sharp increase in the demand for high-powered money happened to occur. But such week-to-week smoothing could perhaps be compatible with use of this interest rate as an instrument for hitting slightly lower-frequency (e.g. quarterly average) intermediate targets conforming to a monetary policy rule designed to yield desirable macroeconomic performance.

The bulk of the present chapter constitutes an attempt to explore this possibility quantitatively. Previous results pertaining to one macro-oriented quarterly policy rule for the United States are reviewed and used to generate weekly intermediate targets for the monetary base. Then (in Sections IV–VI) an empirically based weekly model of monetary base determination is developed and simulated together with a federal funds rate rule that entails weekly smoothing. The base growth model consists of an estimated ARMA equation with an additional term reflecting the response of the base to weekly changes in the federal funds rate, with the response coefficient based on three (compatible!) sources of information. Counterfactual weekly simulations, in which the funds rate is adjusted so as to hit base targets while practicing smoothing, are conducted for two sample periods; Jan. 1974–Sept. 1979 and Jan. 1988–Dec. 1991. Residuals from the ARMA model are fed into the simulation runs as estimates of shocks hitting the system.

The results of these simulations are predominantly supportive of the idea that the scheme under investigation would be successful. In particular, they suggest that quarterly base targets could be achieved rather accurately – with weekly root-mean-square (RMS) errors of about 0.5 percent – while holding weekly interest rate changes to less than 2 percentage points in all weeks and with a RMS average of about 0.5 percentage points. This last figure naturally reflects somewhat more interest rate variability than has been experienced in the United States, but the increase is not dramatic – actual RMS values for our two sample periods were about 0.2 percentage points with a maximum of almost 1.6.

It would admittedly be desirable in principle to conduct this type of exercise with a more elaborate and more nearly structural model of base determination. But data limitations and identification problems make the feasibility of such a study questionable. In any event, the results developed here should be useful as an initial quantitative indication of the workings of a macroeconomic policy rule for the lender of last resort.

Acknowledgements

I am indebted to Tim Cook, Bob Hetzel, Hiroo Taguchi, Michael Bordo, Tom Humphrey, Allan Meltzer, and especially Marvin Goodfriend for extremely helpful discussions and suggestions. Thoughtful comments were provided by Mervyn King, Thomas Melzer, and Jean–Pierre Patat. Thanks are also due to Sandra Baker for help with the data.

Notes

1. Here I have described the first goal as 'macroeconomic stability' rather than 'price level stability' since most central banks are evidently concerned with the mitigation of cyclical fluctuations in economic activity as well as the avoidance of inflation. Issues involving the relative weight to be attached to these two aspects of macroeconomic stability will not be explicitly considered in this chapter.
2. See, for example, Summers (1991) and Solow (1982).
3. Friedman (1960) argued much earlier for elimination of the discount window. His proposal is significantly different from that of Goodfriend and King, however, since it calls for a system with 100 percent reserves and does not promote interest rate smoothing. Other recent arguments for closing the discount window have been put forth by Kaufman (1991) and Schwartz (1992).
4. Since Bagehot's proposal involves a penalty rate, it would appear that

one could replace 'at times of crisis' with 'at all times'. This implication was not mentioned by Bagehot, however, and has also been ignored by most writers on the subject.

5. For a more complete discussion of Bagehot's position, see Humphrey (1989, 1992).
6. More typical, I believe, is the view taken by Nakajima and Taguchi (1993).
7. Although their main purpose is to present their own analysis and proposal, Merton and Bodie (1993) provide a large number of references. A synopsis of bank failures is provided by Goodhart and Schoenmaker (1993).
8. As I have not provided evidence on this point, my statement is actually a conjecture. To develop such evidence adequately would itself consitute a major study.
9. Regarding this claim, Humphrey (1992, p. 572) asserts that 'Bagehot undoubtedly would have concurred'!
10. Cagan also puts forth the argument that the incremental social costs of maintaining the discount window (and reserve requirements) are low, given that elimination of deposit insurance and its associated regulatory apparatus is politically out of the question.
11. It might be thought that a counterargument involving learning behavior, rather than rational expectations, has recently been put forth by Howitt (1992). It is my impression, however, that this argument pertains to pegging rather than use of the interest rate as an instrument.
12. That the central bank's role in providing daylight overdraft credit to the payments system does not fundamentally conflict with the Goodfriend–King proposal is implied by the analysis of Nakajima and Taguchi (1993, p. 32) who conclude that 'if the role of the central bank . . . is limited to settlement risk, . . . [then] hardly any conflict of interest would arise between its regulatory responsibility and its monetary objective.'
13. Some readers may ask why we do not simply design an interest rate rule at the quarterly frequency to hit the macroeconomic targets, i.e., nominal GNP values. The answer is that the evidence in McCallum (1990a) and (1993) suggests that it is much more difficult to design an interest rate rule at the quarterly frequency with good macroeconomic properties. Indeed, attempts to date have been rather unsuccessful.
14. The next few pages draw on the discussion in McCallum (1993).
15. For additional discussion of this point, see McCallum (1988).
16. Only one of the VAR systems considered in McCallum (1988) is included.
17. It might be noted for comparative purposes that the RMSE value for the actual historical path is 0.771, over 30 times as large as the cases with the rule and a moderate λ. A more relevant comparison is the RMSE for the actual historical path relative to a fitted trend line; that value is 0.0854.
18. These results were developed in my 1988 paper. In McCallum (1990a) it was found that substitution of an explicit price level target, rather than nominal GNP, is somewhat less satisfactory since it leads to an

increased likelihood of instrument instability. Also, a few experiments with an interest rate instrument were attempted. In McCallum (1990b) the purpose was to determine whether adherence to rule (1) would have prevented the Great Depression of the 1930s. Counterfactual historical simulations for 1923–41 were conducted with a small model of GNP determination, estimated with quarterly data for 1922–41. The simulation results suggest that nominal GNP would have been kept reasonably close to a steady 3 percent growth path over 1923–41 if the rule had been in effect, in which case it seems extremely unlikely that real output and employment would have collapsed, as they did in fact.

19. Such a target would result in a nominal GNP path that has a unit-root component – indeed, that is close to a random walk with drift. But if the drift magnitude were 0.00739, or whatever is the average rate of output growth, then expected inflation over any horizon would be zero. Furthermore, price level variability over practical planning horizons would not be excessive if the variability of $x_\tau - x^{**}_\tau$ were small.

20. This term is not included in the third column results of Table 9.5, which pertain to the Oct. 1979–Sept. 1982 period. The reason is that it enters much too strongly when included, suggesting a parameter redundancy situation.

21. The argument of this paragraph can be spelled out more explicitly as follows. Let $\theta = (1/TR)dBR/drs$ be the parameter that is estimated as 0.02 on the basis of the quoted rule of thumb, with *BR*, *TR*, *NBR*, and *rs* denoting borrowed reserves, total reserves, non-borrowed reserves, and the funds rate-discount rate spread. But we presume that the relevant experiment is an open-market purchase (sale) that increases (decreases) non-borrowed reserves leaving borrowed reserves unaffected. The estimate of θ is then interpreted as $(-1/TR)dNBR/drs$ = $(-1/TR)dNBR/drs$ and therefore as $-d\log TR/drs$. But with currency assumed not to respond within the week, we have $dB/dTR = 1$ (where *B* denotes the base) so $d\log B/d\log TR = (TR/B)dB/dTR = TR/B$. Thus we finally obtain $d\log B/drs = (d\log B/d\log TR)d\log TR/drs = -\theta(TR/B) = -0.02/8 = -0.0025$.

22. Feinman (1993) reports a smaller estimated value for the sample period Feb. 1984–Oct. 1987. But policy behavior during the 1988–90 period should be more like that of 1974–9, since both of these featured tighter control of the funds rate. During 1984–7 the operating procedure was one of the 'borrowed reserves targeting' type.

23. This suggestion is related to a major theme of a recent paper by Christiano and Eichenbaum (1992).

24. A weakness of our procedure that pertaims to this sample period is as follows. Since our simulation exercise presumes that total reserves (not currency) is the component of the base that responds during the week to open market actions, we are implicitly assuming that the regime is not one with lagged reserve requirements (which makes the demand for reserves almost entirely predetermined). That is of course counterfactual for 1974–9.

25. There is a slight timing inconsistency in my procedure, since quarter-to-quarter growth rates based on quarterly *averages* have been used

for each week *within* a quarter. But that is of virtually no consequence, given the purpose of the present study – to see if the b^*_τ path can be matched by simulated b_τ values.

26. This adjustment provides the reason why the constant term is designated 'const.,' with no numerical value listed, in equation (9.4).
27. One unattractive feature of the results is that ΔR_τ values are predominantly negative over one long portion of the simulation period, and thus lead to large negative values for the *level* of R_τ. But that is arguably an artifact of the functional form used in (9.4): if a log-log function had been used instead, it would not have been possible to drive R_τ negative. I have kept the semi-log form nevertheless to avoid departing even further from the Fed's 'rule of thumb' relationship between borrowing and the funds-discount rate spread.
28. In this case the initial date was chosen to coincide with that promoted by Feinman (1993). A few readers have suggested that the period of 'non-borrowed reserves targeting', Oct. 1979–1982, would be appropriate for the study. My belief is just the opposite; the combination of a reserves instrument plus a regime with lagged reserve requirements is extremely poorly suited to monetary control and so would suggest much greater volatility than would be experienced under a more sensible regime.
29. For this period, weekly-average statistics on non-borrowed reserves include observations only for every other week. With ΔR_τ denoting the two-week change in R_τ, the estimated relation is $\Delta n_\tau = 0.0017 - 0.4812\Delta n_{\tau-2} - 0.1665\Delta n_{\tau-4} - 0.033\Delta R_\tau$, with $R^2 = 0.314$, $SE = 0.017$, and no evidence of autocorrelation in the residuals.
30. Again we can find how much R_τ variability would be required for exact base control, according to our model. The RMS and MAV figures are 1.50 and 5.50 for the 1988–91 internal, considerably larger – as one would expect – than for 1974–9.

References

Bagehot, W. (1873) *Lombard Street: A Description of the Money Market* (London: H. S. King).

Bordo, M. D. (1990) 'The Lender of Last Resort: Alternative Views and Historical Experience.' Federal Reserve Bank of Richmond *Economic Review*, vol. 76 (January–February) pp. 18–29.

Cagan, P. (1988) 'Commentary', in W. S. Haraf and R. M. Kushmeider (eds), *Restructuring Banking and Financial Services in America* (Washington: American Enterprise Institute).

Christiano, L. J. and M. Eichenbaum (1992) 'Identification and the Liquidity Effect of a Monetary Policy Shock', in A. Cukierman, Z. Hercowitz and L. Leiderman (eds), *Political Economy, Growth, and Business Cycles* (Cambridge MA: MIT Press).

Cook, T. (1989) 'Determinants of the Federal Funds Rate: 1979–1982', Federal Reserve Bank of Richmond *Economic Review*, vol. 75 (January–February) pp. 3–19.

Dowd, K. (1989) *The State and the Monetary System* (Oxford: Philip Allan).

Feinman, J. (1993) 'Estimating the Open Market Desk's Daily Reaction Function', *Journal of Money, Credit, and Banking*, vol. 25 (May) pp. 231–47.

Feldstein, M. and J. H. Stock (1993) 'The Use of a Monetary Aggregate to Target Nominal GDP', in N. G. Mankiw (ed.), *Monetary Policy* (Chicago: Univ. of Chicago Press), forthcoming.

Folkerts-Landau, D. and P. M. Garber (1992) 'The ECB: A Bank or a Monetary Policy Rule?', in M. B. Canzoneri, V. Grilli and P. R. Masson (eds), *Establishing a Central Bank: Issues in Europe and Lessons from the U.S.* (Cambridge: Cambridge Univ. Press).

Friedman, M. (1960) *A Program for Monetary Stability* (New York: Fordham Univ. Press).

Garcia, G. and E. Plautz (1988) *The Federal Reserve: Lender of Last Resort* (Cambridge MA: Ballinger).

Glasner, D. (1989) *Free Banking and Monetary Reform* (Cambridge: Cambridge Univ. Press).

Goodfriend, M. (1991) 'Money, Credit, Banking, and Payments System Policy', Federal Reserve Bank of Richmond *Economic Review*, vol. 77 (January–February) pp. 7–24.

Goodfriend, M. and R. G. King (1988) 'Financial Deregulation, Monetary Policy, and Central Banking.' Federal Reserve Bank of Richmond *Economic Review*, vol. 74 (May–June) pp. 3–22.

Goodhart, C. (1985) *The Evolution of Central Banks* (London: London School of Economics and Political Science).

Goodhart, C. (1987) 'Why Do Banks Need a Central Bank?' *Oxford Economic Papers*, 39, pp. 75–89.

Goodhart, C. and D. Schoenmaker (1993) 'Institutional Separation Between Supervisory and Monetary Agencies', Working Paper, London School of Economics.

Hess, G. D., D. H. Small and F. Brayton (1993) 'Nominal Income Targeting with the Monetary Base as an Instrument: An Evaluation of McCallum's Rule', in M. Goodfriend and D. H. Small (eds), *Operating Procedures and the Conduct of Monetary Policy: Conference Proceedings* Finance and Economics Discussion Series, Federal Reserve Board.

Howitt, P. (1992) 'Interest Rate Control and Nonconvergence to Rational Expectations', *Journal of Political Economy*, vol. 100 (August) pp. 776–800.

Humphrey, T. M. (1989) 'Lender of Last Resort: The Concept in History', Federal Reserve Bank of Richmond *Economic Review*, vol. 75 (March–April) pp. 8–16.

Humphrey, T. M. (1992) 'Lender of Last Resort', in P. Newman, M. Milgate and J. Eatwell (eds), *The New Palgrave Dictionary of Money and Finance* (London: Macmillan).

Kaufman, G. G. (1991) 'Lender of Last Resort: A Contemporary Perspective', *Journal of Financial Service Research*, vol. 5 (October) pp. 95–100.

Laidler, D. (1992) 'Free Banking: Theory', in P. Newman, M. Milgate, and J. Eatwell (eds), *The New Palgrave Dictionary of Money and Finance* (London: Macmillan).

McCallum, B. T. (1981) 'Price Level Determinancy with an Interest Rate

Policy Rule and Rational Expectations', *Journal Of Monetary Economics*, vol. 8 (November) pp. 319–29.
McCallum, B. T. (1986) 'Some Issues Concerning Interest Rate Pegging, Price Level Determinacy, and the Real Bills Doctrine', *Journal of Monetary Economics*, vol. 17 (January) pp. 135–60.
McCallum, B. T. (1988) 'Robustness Properties of a Rule for Monetary Policy', *Carnegie-Rochester Conference Series on Public Policy*, vol. 29 (Autumn) pp. 173–203.
McCallum, B. T. (1990a) 'Targets, Indicators, and Instruments of Monetary Policy', in W. S. Haraf and P. Cagan (eds), *Monetary Policy for a Changing Financial Environment* (Washington: American Enterprise Institute).
McCallum, B. T. (1990b) 'Could a Monetary Base Rule Have Prevented the Great Depression?', *Journal of Monetary Economics*, vol. 26 (August) pp. 13–26.
McCallum, B. T. (1993) 'Specification and Analysis of a Monetary Policy Rule for Japan', Bank of Japan *Monetary and Economic Studies*, vol. 11 (November), pp. 1–45.
Meltzer, A. H. (1987) 'Limits of Short-Run Stabilization Policy', *Economic Inquiry*, vol. 25 (February) pp. 1–14.
Meltzer, A. H. (1988) 'The Policy Proposals in the AEI Studies', in W. S. Haraf and R. M. Kushmeider (eds), *Restructuring Banking and Fiancial Services in America* (Washington: American Enterprise Institute).
Merton, R. C. and Z. Bodie (1993) 'Deposit Insurance Reform: A Functional Approach', *Carnegie-Rochester Conference Series on Public Policy*, vol. 38 (Spring) pp. 1–34.
Nakajima, Z. and H. Taguchi (1993) 'Toward a More Stable Framework: Long Term Alternatives', Working Paper, Bank of Japan.
Schwartz, A. J. (1992) 'The Misuse of the Fed's Discount Window', Federal Reserve Bank of St. Louis *Review*, vol. 74 (September–October) pp. 58–69.
Selgin, G. (1987) *The Theory of Free Banking* (Totowa, NJ: Rowman and Littlefield).
Solow, R. M. (1982) 'On the Lender of Last Resort', in C. P. Kindleberger and J. P. Laffargue (eds), *Financial Crisis: Theory, History, and Policy* (Cambridge: Cambridge Univ. Press).
Summers, L. H. (1991) 'Planning for the Next Financial Crisis', in M. Feldstein (ed.), *The Risk of Economic Crisis* (Chicago: Univ. of Chicago Press).
Taylor, J. B. (1988) 'Japanese Monetary Policy and the Current Account Under Alternative International Monetary Regimes', Bank of Japan *Monetary and Economic Studies*, vol. 6 (May) pp. 1–36.
Taylor, J. B. (1993) 'Discretion vs. Policy Rules in Practice', *Carnegie Rochester Conference Series on Public Policy*, vol. 39 (Autumn) pp. 195–214.
Thornton, H. (1802) *An Enquiry Into the Nature and Effects of the Paper Credit of Great Britain* (Fairfield NJ: Augustus M. Kelley).
White, L. H. (1984) *Free Banking in Britain: Theory, Experience, and Debate, 1800–1845* (Cambridge: Cambridge Univ. Press).

Comments

Jean-Pierre Patat

Professor McCallum's chapter makes a valuable contribution to the discussion of two important topics: the role of the Central Bank in preserving the stability of the financial system and the debate about rules-versus-discretion in monetary policy matters.

The originality of his contribution lies in using the same approach for both topics, which are all too often considered separately. This common approach should help make the central bank's responsibility towards the financial system, which is usually considered to be a discretionary activity by virtue of the 'constructive ambiguity' principle, compatible with adherence to a strict macroeconomic stability rule. The unity of this approach is not its only attraction. It is also realistic in that it recognizes the close link between macroeconomic stability and that of the financial system. It further acknowledges that one of the central banks' main tasks is to help preserve both types of stability. Therefore, Professor McCallum's proposals can provide a sounder basis for central bank action.

I shall make some comments about his proposals, then I shall explain the spirit in which the Banque de France fulfils its dual macroeconomic and macrofinancial roles.

COMMENTS ON PROFESSOR MCCALLUM'S PROPOSALS[1]

I would like to start by commenting on the choice Professor McCallum made in the light of his critical review of the literature on the topic.

Critical Review of the Relevant Literature

One of the questions raised when the very first central banks were set up was how to make sure that their intervention, when needed to preserve the stability of the financial system, was compatible with the rules of financial orthodoxy. In this matter, Professor McCallum harks back to the thinking of nineteenth-century economists like Thornton or Bagehot.

The most detailed discussion is devoted to Goodfriend and King's proposal[2] that central banks respond to a systemic crisis by providing liquidity via open market operations. Replacing bilateral relationships with market relationships would make it possible to eliminate the discount window and do away with the central bank's regulatory and supervisory activities, without hindering the smoothing of very-short-term interest rates. McCallum reviews the objections that have been raised to Goodfriend and King's position. He maintains that there are no really fundamental differences between Meltzer's suggestion[3] that discount window lending should be retained, but at a penalty rate, along with the regulatory and supervisory activities, and Goodfriend and King's proposal, as long as the penalty rate is not much higher than the Fed funds rate. McCallum suggests a premium of two percentage points. He should be acknowledged for making this remark, which raises two additional points:

- Meltzer's rule seems to be well suited to procedures for supplying liquidity that make it possible to define a 'corridor' for interest rates, as is the case in France and Germany, while Goodfriend and King's rule seems better suited to central banks using an operational interest-rate target, as is the case in the United States and Great Britain;
- Meltzer's rule, which retains bilateral relationships, may make central bank intervention more effective: the supply of liquidity under the terms of Goodfriend and King's rule may only reach the most illiquid banks at interest rates carrying a high risk premium. In fact, it may not reach them at all, if the risk is considered too great, and the most illiquid banks will eventually become insolvent. On the other hand, the higher rates will have to be paid by all banks, but this drawback must be seen in the light of several considerations. First of all, it would be short-lived. It could be seen as a premium charged by the central bank for protecting the banks against systemic failure. This premium would also be justified to reduce 'moral hazard'. The economies of scale made possible by the combination of the central bank's lender-of-last-resort functions with its regulatory and supervisory functions mean that it would be a small premium to pay.

McCallum cites Summers's objection[4] to Goodfriend and King's proposal, which is that it does not necessarily produce the most effective distribution of reserves. Summers states that, 'reserves at one bank are an imperfect substitute for reserves at another. Maintaining a given aggregate level of lending is not sufficient to avoid the losses associated with a financial disturbance'. But McCallum does not subscribe to this argument because, for him, 'the object of LLR policy is not to "avoid losses" but to prevent systemic failure', and maintaining an aggregate level of lending is an inaccurate characterization of Goodfriend and King's proposal.

Professor McCallum's Proposals

Professor McCallum undertakes to incorporate adherence to Goodfriend and King's rule in a rule that ensures macroeconomic stability. His proposal is in line with his monetarist leanings, which he has never taken pains to conceal.[5] He had already suggested in 1984[6] that the American monetary authorities control the growth rate of the monetary base by automatically adjusting it to the actual growth of nominal income in the previous quarter. This procedure is somewhat 'activist', but is clearly incompatible with discretionary policy. Today, Professor McCallum completes it by suggesting a rule for governing the 'Fed funds' rate. This is to be done to achieve a monetary base target that is consistent with a nominal GDP target ensuring price stability in the medium term.

For all its attractions, Professor McCallum's method is not above criticism. The main objections to it are practical ones having to do with the conditions for implementing the rule he proposes and theoretical ones relating to the way the rule is worked out.

The practical objections include:

- The usual objection to discretionary policies is that there is a time lag before they become effective. The rule proposed does not eliminate the problem entirely. For one thing, the nominal GDP figure for the previous quarter is not known until some time after the quarter has ended.
- Professor McCallum's results may not be as promising as he says. After a simulation of the period from January 1988 to December 1991, with $\theta = 100$, the standard deviation implied for variations in the 'Fed funds' rate (root-mean-square-errors) works out to 53 basis points, and the maximum week-to-week change in the rate is 161 basis points, as opposed to 18 and 141 basis points respectively for the actual sample values. In any case, this volatility is much greater than that which the Fed seemed willing to accept over the period. In addition, it could be thought that the use of call-money rates to control variations in the monetary base would make it necessary to accept even greater rate volatility in a coun-

try like France, where the reserves held by banks are infinitesimal in absolute terms, as well as in relation to the monetary base. This would lead to exchange rate volatility, which is a further reason for favouring Meltzer's rule in the case of a country like France.

- The results are drawn up for specific sub-periods and this raises two sorts of problems. The first is how the monetary authorities can spot a switch in regimes so as to adjust the λ and θ parameters governing their stance accordingly. This raises the problem of time lags. The second sort of problem has to do with Professor McCallum's choice of sub-periods, i.e. 1974–9 and 1988–91. These were not periods of great financial instability. On the other hand, he did not choose the period in which the Fed's behavior was most in line with what he recommends, i.e. 1979–82, and which may have some bearing on the problems that American banks ran into afterwards.

The theoretical objections centre on:

- The fact that the model is incomplete, as Professor McCallum himself recognizes. A function for the banks' demand for reserves should have been included. This function should have taken into account a large number of factors such as interest-rate expectations, the profit function of commercial banks, non-financial agents' choices in terms of debt and portfolios, etc. The model is not integrated either. There is no feedback effect from interest rates to the economy. And finally, like some of the other small-scale monetarist models, such as the St Louis model, it gives the impression that one is dealing with a 'black box'.
- Furthermore, there is the problem of 'Goodhart's Law'.[7] In other words, if the monetary authorities were to adopt Professor McCallum's rule, would this move in itself not create a change in agents' behaviour that could lead to instability, at least initially?

RECONCILING MONETARY STABILITY WITH THE STABILITY OF THE FINANCIAL SYSTEM

What Type of Financial Environment is Best Suited to Reducing Systemic Risk?

France's experience suggests that there are three eminently suitable operating principles.

Universal Banking
In a financial system undergoing constant change, banks are better equipped fro survival if they are allowed to diversify their business. This is why disintermediation and the surge in market financing have not done any real harm to the French banks, which have managed to keep a large share of the business of underwriting and raising financing for business, by managing mutual funds, helping to raise funds on markets and securitizing loans. This diversification may increase costs, particularly when banks raise resources through mutual funds, but it has meant that banks have not seen their business contract sharply and they have not been tempted to undertake high-risk-high-return activities to make up for such a contraction.

A strong role for central banks in maintaining the stability of the financial system
Central banks play a key role in two areas.

The payment system. Central banks play a leading role in payment systems, and this role must include action to prevent risks.

The Banque de France is setting up a comprehensive programme in which gross and net settlement procedures are used according to the type of transaction. The programme is based on:

- finality of settlement,
- monitoring and control of daylight overdrafts on central bank accounts, with limits and collateral requirements,
- the creation of a specialized gross-settlement large-value fund transfer system called Transferts Banque de France (TBF),
- constant monitoring of transactions for rapid detection of critical situations.

Financial intermediaries. A central bank must be very closely involved. It does not matter how liable it is legally for the supervision and regulation of the banking system, nor whether it carries out these tasks directly or through a specialized agency. Its close contacts with the banks and the constant flow of statistical and accounting information that the banks are required to provide for the implementation of monetary policy give the central bank a unique capacity to:

- design and implement regulations to suit changing conditions. Real-time monitoring of market positions is a complement to prudential ratios;
- enforce compliance;

- detect the symptoms of a crisis, diagnose the source of the problem and provide the remedy.

The central bank's involvement reinforces crisis management, both when individual remedies are applied and when a bank's shareholders or the banking community as a whole are called on to help an institution in difficulty in accordance with the first and second paragraphs of Article 52 of the 1984 Banking Act. These solutions are not necessarily easy to apply, but it can be argued that the central bank, which is the institution at the heart of the payment and settlement system having thorough and up-to-the-minute knowledge of every aspect of the credit institutions' business, is in the best position to do so.

There is, however, one reservation about central bank involvement, namely that it should not be concerned with any deposit protection schemes, where such schemes exist.

Unified Banking Supervision in Collaboration with the Market Supervision Authorities

It is important that the banking supervision authority, be it the central bank or an offshoot thereof, has an overview of all of the problems relating to credit institutions. This is part and parcel of the universal banking principle.

It is also essential that banking supervision not be isolated from market supervision in a financial system featuring despecialization and a blurring of the boundaries between different types of business. However, market supervision must be the responsibility of another authority than the central bank and, in many countries, this task falls to the Finance Ministry. In France, the confidentiality obligation has been lifted on exchanges between the banking supervision authority and the market supervision authority. There is also a liaison committee for the supervisors of financial markets and institutions.

Can Monetary Policy Help Reconcile Monetary Stability and the Stability of the Financial System?

Steadfast adhesion to the goal of price stability is a guarantee of stability for the financial system.

The best way for monetary policy to contribute to the stability of the financial system is for it to stick to the basic and achievable goal of price stability.

Attempts to trade off higher inflation for higher growth, or to use monetary policy to achieve the ideal combination of growth, low inflation, balanced trade and full employment always lead to disappointment. They can also destabilize the financial system. If the central bank allows credit to mushroom in periods of high growth, the liquidity created may be used in the financial sphere, as well as in the real economy, thus leading to unconsidered exposures to risk. And when the central bank moves to curb the resulting inflation, it can spell trouble for the banking system.

French and German monetary policy experience since the mid 1980s shows that the persistent high real interest rates, resulting from an unwavering monetary stance, actually helped to contain the growth of credit. This prevented the formation of a financial bubble and, in the end, protected French and German financial institutions from the critical problems encountered in other countries.

Monetary Policy and Financial Asset Price Stability

Some observers feel that price inflation, which is the instability of prices in the real economy, is now a secondary matter and that the real problem now is asset volatility.

Central banks can curb exchange rate volatility by co-ordinating their monetary policies, thus helping to prevent destabilizing expectations in the markets. The crash of October 1987 stemmed from exchange rate instability, which in turn stemmed from a lack of co-ordination in monetary policy.

While monetary policy has an undisputed influence on the price of financial assets, such as bonds, shares and derivatives, it is not equipped to ensure market stability. To that end, the central bank would have to intervene in long-term securities on such a large scale that it could run into losses, without even being sure of achieving results commensurate with its action.

Such a move would be a disaster for everyone. Sooner or later it would be bound to harm the reputation of the central bank, whose very image helps to ensure the stability of the financial system.

The Importance of Monetary Policy Procedures

Lender-of-last-resort services can be provided in many ways, including conventional openmarket operations. But in addition to providing this type of assistance, which is never institutionalized nor automatic, it seems important that the central bank's monetary policy actions on the money market not be concentrated on a single transmission mechanism.

Monetary policy should use several tools, whether for offsetting the excess liquidity caused by intervention, or else for preventing specific illiquid institutions from being overly penalized by a restrictive monetary stance, for example when market rates are increased to preserve the exchange rate. Such tools include:

- reserve requirements, where the principle of meeting a monthly average helps to attenuate the impact of temporary cash shortages and helps to smooth day-to-day changes in interbank interest rates.
- a two-window system, with an ordinary refinancing window and a second window that could provide unlimited refinancing, but at a penalty rate, or else on a discretionary basis. This makes it possible either to help illiquid institutions, as long as they have enough good collateral, or else to prevent the banking system as a whole from being penalized by money market intervention that does not stem from domestic monetary policy concerns.

Notes

1. This section of the paper is largely due to Christion Pfistor, Head of the Studies on Monetary Policy Unit of the Banque de France.
2. M. Goodfriend and R. G. King, 'Financial Deregulation, Monetary Policy and Central Banking', *Federal Reserve Bank of Richmond Economic Review*, May–June 1988.
3. A. H. Meltzer, 'The Policy Propoeale in the AEI Studies'. In W. S. Haraf and R. M. Kushmeider (eds). *Restructuring Banking and Financial Services in America*, 1988.
4. L. H. Summers, 'Planning for the Next Financial Crisis', in M. Feldstein (ed.), *The Risk of Economic Crisis* (Chicago: University of Chicago Press, 1991).
5. See B. T. McCallum, 'Monetarist Rules in the Light of Recent Experience', *American Economic Review, Paper and Proceedings*. May 1984.
6. See B. T. McCallum, 'Credibility and Monetary Policy', NBER Working Paper, No. 1490, November 1984.
7. This is also called the 'Lucas Critique', see R. Lucas, 'Econometric Policy Evaluation: A Critique', in K. Brunner and A. Meltzer (eds), *the Phillips Curve and Labor Markets*, Carnegle-Rochester Conference Series, 1976.

Comments

Mervyn King

The chapter is in two distinct parts. The first deals with the potential clash between the two main core objectives of a central bank – price stability and stability of the financial system. The second discusses a monetary rule which sets interest rates week by week so as to produce a predetermined state-contingent growth rate of the monetary base. In order to link the two issues, McCallum argues that policies to achieve financial stability should take the form of open market operations and not lending via the discount window. The latter would permit the central bank to discriminate among recipients of lender of last resort (LLR) assistance and impose institution-specific terms for assistance. McCallum takes the view that to avoid a systemic failure it is sufficient to provide assistance via open market operations, and follows the work of Goodfriend and King in thinking that the discount window is unnecessary for the purpose of LLR support. I am inclined to think, for reasons set out below, that there is more to LLR policy than can be achieved by open market operations alone. But this does not detract from the value of McCallum's monetary rule which provides a practical way for central banks to use the main instrument at their disposal – short-term interest rates – to achieve the growth of a chosen monetary aggregate and yet accommodate high frequency fluctuations in the demand for money of the kind which might accompany a financial crisis.

In my discussion I shall focus on three aspects of LLR policy:

(1) The potential conflict between monetary policy and the LLR function;
(2) The choice between open market operations and lending via the discount window;
(3) Principles of LLR support.

It is helpful to distinguish five possible types of conflict between monetary policy, on the one hand, and supervisory and LLR policies, on the other. Only the first relates strictly to LLR support; the final four relate to conflicts between supervision of banks and monetary policy. But supervision and regulation are part of the regime within which more general support of the financial system takes place, and it is important to see the relationship between LLR and supervisory issues in context.

(1) The provision of LLR support might clash with the appropriate money supply rule to achieve price stability. For high-frequency shocks the monetary rule proposed by McCallum deals with this issue but it is possible that financial disturbances have repercussions on the demand for money beyond one quarter. Such disturbances amount to a shift in the demand for money function and can, in principle, be accommodated by changes in the monetary target. The regime for LLR policy proposed by Bagehot would achieve this. The point to note here is that the monetary rule proposed by McCallum might have to take into account the need to adjust the quarterly monetary target as a result of disturbances which created the need for LLR support.

(2) The existence of a supervisory role for the central bank creates policy instruments which it might be tempted to use to reinforce its monetary policy. For example, in the debate on the 1946 Bank of England Act it was suggested that the Bank be given powers over banks to enable it to enforce credit controls. More recently, it has been suggested that capital requirements be adjusted in a counter-cyclical manner. There are clearly dangers in going down this road, and no group is more aware of them than the supervisors themselves.

(3) Information gained in a supervisory capacity might be used in money market operations. For example, knowledge of the balance sheets of a central bank's counterparties might be useful to those involved in daily operations, but to prevent exploitation of this position Chinese walls between operators and supervisors are erected.

(4) Difficulties in supervisory performance may lead to 'reputational infection' of the central bank's credibility in monetary policy.

(5) The complex nature of both monetary policy and supervisory issues can place enormous strains on the demands of top management time.

Although, in principle, there are potential conflicts between monetary policy and the LLR function, these can easily be overstated. There remains much truth in the observation by Bagehot that there is no adverse consequence for monetary policy of LLR support which accommodates high-frequency fluctuations in the demand for money.

The second issue concerns the choice between open market operations and lending via the discount window as the method of providing LLR support. McCallum claims that the former is adequate to achieve the objectives of LLR support. In contrast, most central banks believe that LLR and supervisory functions go together. There are, I think, two reasons for this. First, most central banks are involved in some way or another with supervision of banks. A threat to financial stability can usually be traced to a particular individual or group of institutions. Given that central banks have a good deal of information about the position of these institutions, it seems natural to tackle the problem at source. This is particularly true when the central bank is likely to be in a better position than the market to judge whether an institution is illiquid or insolvent. Bagehot's rule for providing LLR support – lend to all institutions against marketable collateral – is difficult to implement when most of the assets of banks do not have observable market values. Second, the objectives of the central bank in the area of 'financial stability' are more complicated and diverse than those which can be described as the provision of LLR support. Central banks are clearly concerned to avoid systemic failure. But they are also concerned – in some cases legally charged – with the responsibility for the protection of depositors, and they may also take into account the losses which would result from the failure of specific financial institutions. In this respect, the potential loss of relationship-specific capital when one financial institution closes and transfers its loan book to another is relevant. Following the closure of BCCI in the UK in 1991, it became clear that not only did depositors lose but also some borrowers from the failed bank. These borrowers who had entered into a banking relationship with BCCI found it difficult to open a new relationship with another bank because of the difficulty of escaping the clutches of the liquidator. Within the existing system, it is not easy for central banks to avoid such issues. The appropriate long-term solution relates to the institutional structure of the banking system, as discussed by Allan Meltzer.

The principles of LLR support are usually either lost in the mists of time or shrouded in the clouds of 'constructive ambiguity'. One of the key features of Bagehot's principles for LLR support was that the nature of the regime be made publicly known. In his recent LSE lecture, the Governor of the Bank of England (*Bank of England Quarterly Bulletin*, November 1993) has set out the principles according to which the Bank of England engages in LLR support. As a matter of practice, LLR support is provided via lending to individual institutions. The principles governing this are:

(1) No institution is too big to fail; a systemic threat means that some institutions may be too important to fail;
(2) Lending is made against collateral;
(3) There is a clear exit plan for the central bank which may involve a run down of a bank if necessary to realise the best value for the collateral;
(4) Any losses must fall first on the shareholders and managers of the bank – this reduces moral hazard;
(5) Secrecy in the provision of support may be necessary to prevent a systemic run but *ex post* reporting of the activity and of losses is made in order that the bank is accountable to Parliament.

In conclusion, the potential conflicts between LLR support and the operation of monetary policy may be less acute than suggested by McCallum in his chapter. Nevertheless, the ability to smooth interest rates within a period of, say, a quarter and still hit the desired path for the chosen monetary aggregate is a valuable contribution of the McCallum monetary policy rule. It would be interesting to see further empirical applications of this idea to countries other than the United States.

Comments

Thomas C. Melzer

Professor Bennett McCallum presents simulation results from a model in which the monetary authority endeavors to smooth interest rates in the short run, while simultaneously fixing its sights on its long-run price stability objective. Achievement of these goals is a consequence of following the McCallum rule to keep the monetary base on a path consistent with stabilizing nominal GDP growth.

In most respects, I like the author's approach. It is similar in spirit to a proposal I made to the FOMC a few years ago. Both of us recognize the problem of focusing monetary policy too narrowly on interest rates rather than monetary aggregates and price stability. The danger is that the long-run growth in the monetary base or some narrow monetary aggregate will be determined by a series of short-run actions to stabilize interest rates. I proposed that the Fed constrain itself to achieve its long-run objectives by keeping the quarterly growth rate of the monetary base within some specified range. Policymakers would be free to pursue other short-run policy objectives, such as smoothing the federal funds rate, so long as they did not violate the quarterly growth rate bands. As with McCallum's approach, under my proposal reserves injected within the quarter to stabilize interest rates in the face of financial market disturbances would be withdrawn if they compromised the Fed's longer-run objectives.

My personal sympathy with McCallum's approach notwithstanding, several questions occurred to me as I read the chapter. First, I noticed that his measure of weekly variation in the federal funds rate was two and one-half times as large in his simulations as in actual experience. This increased level of volatility is nearly identical to the increase in the variability of the federal funds rate that was observed during the period when the Fed was targeting non-borrowed reserves in the early 1980s compared with the period since. A frequent criticism of non-borrowed reserve targeting was that it resulted in too much interest rate volatility. Consequently, I am not sure McCallum's simulations would be generally accepted as interest rate smoothing.

I also cannot help but wonder whether the relationships among interest rates, the monetary based and total spending, upon which McCallum's simulation results depend, would have been different had the federal Reserve implemented monetary policy in a manner consistent with both McCallum's and my views.

Finally, I wonder whether the relationships would change during financial crises. For example, if some event suddenly changed the public's perception of the soundness of the banking system, the risk premiums that one bank would charge another on loans would rise. Such changes would likely alter the relationships among interest rates, the monetary based and nominal GDP precisely when one would like to rely on them the most.

Having stated my general sympathy with the approach that McCallum has taken and having raised a few concerns, I would like to address the remainder of my remarks to the somewhat broader question that his chapter raises: can a central bank fulfil its role as lender of last resort without the option of lending directly to individual banks? McCallum answers yes to this question, arguing that the remaining gap in the argument for eliminating the discount window is whether interest rate smoothing can be practiced without undermining the Fed's longer-run policy objectives.

I doubt that the Fed can deal adequately with all disturbances to the banking system through open market operation alone. It could if information were costless. But that is just not the case. The distinction between insolvency and illiquidity is often judgmental, and judgments can be clouded – especially during financial crises. As a policymaker, I am uncomfortable relying on the assumption that market participants will always make a correct, instant diagnosis of insolvency versus illiquidity. Consequently, I am not certain that the market should be relied upon to always supply reserves to illiquid but solvent institutions.

Having an open discount window with a penalty discount rate seems like a relatively efficient way to ensure that liquidity will be allocated to such institutions. A penalty discount rate would give banks incentive to repay their loans from the central bank as soon as they had dealt with their liquidity problems. I might also point out that there is nothing inconsistent with interest rate smoothing through open market operations and maintaining the discount window to lend directly to illiquid but solvent banks at a penalty discount rate.

Besides this information problem, I think there are incentive problems in co-ordinating the allocation of reserves in a financial crisis. The history of banking in the United States indicates the need for some central authority to carry out this function. Prior to the establishment of the Federal Reserve, banks acted co-operatively in allocating reserves through clearing-houses. These clearing-houses were especially useful in supplying individual banks with liquidity during financial crises.

Banks recognized a conflict between their interests as individual banks and the interests of the banks as a group. In a financial crisis, the incentive of an individual bank would be to hold on to its reserves and to increase its reserve ratio. If it loaned reserves to an illiquid bank, it would risk becoming illiquid itself. Nevertheless, the group recognized that the failure of a banks in its community might trigger runs on all banks in the area. The bank in various communities attempted to deal with these conflicting incentives by allocating reserves through their clearing-houses. This history illustrates the necessity for a central authority to allocate reserves in a financial crisis. The Federal Reserve was formed to do this job of the clearing-houses, but more effectively.

The operation of organizations that settle transactions among financial institutions creates special reasons for central banks to keep the option to lend to individual banks. These settlement organizations, some of which have been created by exchanges for the trading of securities, have been designed to minimize transactions costs and, to some extent, risk. A primary example in the United States is CHIPS, which is important for settlement of the dollar side of foreign exchange transactions.

It is in the interest of each member of a settlement organization that others have the reserves necessary at the end of the day to settle their positions with the settlement organizations. If one member cannot meet its settlement obligations, unwinding the transactions involving the defaulting member can make other members short of the necessary reserves. An 'unwind' of all transactions for the day would disrupt the business of their customers and possibly increase solvency risk of some members of the settlement organization.

Although CHIPS members have incentive for CHIPS to settle each day, they may be reluctant to lend reserves to the member that defaults, depending on the reasons for the default. As in the historical example of clearing-houses prior to the formation of the Federal Reserve System, some central authority is necessary to reconcile this difference in incentives of individual members of a settlement organization and its membership as a group.

In the United States, banks have looked to the Federal Reserve as that central authority for allocating reserves to illiquid banks. It is important that settlement organizations settle the transactions among their members to avoid disruptions of financial systems. In a financial crisis, it should be a high priority of a central bank to facilitate the settlement of transactions through the major settlement organizations. Response of the Federal Reserve to the sharp decline of stock prices in 1987 illustrates this priority. In dealing with this potential financial crisis, the Federal Reserve sought to ensure that the organizations that clear transactions in stocks and derivatives continued functioning in their roles of settling transactions.

I believe that access to the discount window facilitates the operation of such settlement organizations. For example, suppose the settlement of CHIPS were threatened because a bank did not have enough reserves to cover its transactions. Suppose further that there were rumors that the bank was insolvent. Injecting additional reserves into the banking system through open market operations would not alter the reluctance of other banks to lend to this bank. Consequently, it would not necessarily increase the chances for settlement of CHIPS without at least a partial unwinding of transactions. If the Fed does not provide credit through the discount window to illiquid banks to avoid such problems, the settlement organizations would have to design other mechanisms to deal with such liquidity crises.

Of course, if a central bank makes credit available to facilitate the settlement of transactions, collectively banks will not assume this responsibility. Moreover, if banks know that the central bank is committed to providing individual banks with the reserves necessary to facilitate settlement, then members of settlement organizations will assume that there is no risk of default by other members. In recent years, central banks have set standards for the operations of settlement organizations designed to deal with this moral hazard problem. The following are the major types of standards:

- Mechanisms for limiting the risk exposures between members, such as bilateral credit limits between each pair of members.
- Collateral requirements, such as a pledge of enough collateral with the settlement organization to cover default by any one member.
- Loss sharing arrangements in the event of default by a member.

Such standards expose members of settlement organization to risk of losses if a member defaults on its payments, even if the central bank provides the reserves to facilitate settlement. This arrangement gives members of settlement organizations an incentive to extent credit lines only to those counterparts they consider to be in sound condition. Moreover, central banks of major developed nations have been working to develop and enforce standards for the operation of international settlement organizations. Setting and enforcing standards for settlement organizations is, in my opinion, one of the important forms of co-operation among central banks, a topic that Charles Goodhart discusses.

In conclusion, I largely share McCallum's view that limiting variation in the monetary base and nominal spending would make a contribution to the goal of long-term price stability. In such an environment there might be more financial stability than what we have observed historically. None the less, I remain unconvinced that there is not a significant role for central bank lending to individual institutions for liquidity reasons, particularly in those unpredicted crisis circumstances when, without such lending, the payments system is threatened.

10 Price Stability and Financial Fragility*

Charles A. E. Goodhart

I INTRODUCTION

If asked to provide a practical, quantitative definition of price stability, most people would offer something like a rate of increase in the RPI, or the GDP deflator, of 0–2 percent. This is the kind of numerical objective which those Central Banks with a direct inflation target, e.g. New Zealand and Canada, are aiming to achieve. While I have great sympathy for such an approach, I want to start by arguing that the standard measures of inflation used in such targets may be incorrect, at least in principle. Such measures concentrate on current service flow prices, and ignore future service flow prices, changes in which are indicated by changing interest rates and asset prices. This thesis was cogently argued by Alchian and Klein in a paper in 1973; they put the case so well then, that I felt that I could do no better than repeat it. So, much of Section II consists of selections from their earlier work.

Asset prices do move differently from current service flow prices. In recent years they have had a much more violent cycle of boom and bust. The focus on current service flow prices as the sole index of inflation has been one of the main reasons why monetary policy has been systematically mishandled in several countries, too lax 1988–1990, too restrictive thereafter.

This asset price cycle has been closely related, with strong causal links operating in both directions, with a cycle in bank credit expansion, in broad money, bank profits and in banking (and financial) fragility. In Section III I argue that one would normally expect to find a link between banking fragility and asset price deflation, though which sets of asset prices are most important for the banking system may vary over time. Consequently, occasions when the banking system needs support are likely to be periods of general (asset price) deflation, when the achievement of price stability might anyhow indicate a more expansionary monetary policy. On this view there is no normal, or necessary, conflict between the two objectives. As noted in Section IV, however, there *is* a conflict between the prudential regulations imposed by the authorities, e.g. the Basle capital adequacy ratios, and the macro-economic objectives of monetary policy, since the former will usually only bind during period of deflation.

Be that as it may, the recent period of asset price deflation has been accompanied by an upsurge in actual, or potential, bank failures over a wide range of countries. Central Banks, in these circumstances, have pursued their traditional policies of lender of last resort and arranging rescues. I note in Section IV that most classical monetary economists oppose such activities; they would limit LOLR lending strictly to cases of illiquidity, and would instead use general market measure to sustain a steady expansion of certain monetary aggregates. But in my view it is both safer and more efficient to nip contagious panics in the bud by such Central Bank rescues.

I end this section with a brief glance at the use of 'narrow' banks and deposit insurance as a way of preventing systemic panics. I am doubtful about both, as a remedy against contagious failure. However, the allocation of responsibility for (limited) deposit insurance to 'home' monetary authorities, as contrasted with 'host' banking supervisors, might help to prevent multinational banks flying under flags of convenience. In Appendix A we discuss international co-operation and co-ordination among Central Banks in dealing with cases of distress in multinational banks. Most large banks now have branches or subsidiaries in several countries outside their domestic base. Section V concludes.

II 'ON A CORRECT MEASURE OF INFLATION'

It is remarkable that, at a juncture when so much of macro and monetary economics has been recast in terms of dynamic *inter-temporal* utility maximisation (e.g. Sargent, 1987), that the same has rarely been done for the analysis of price inflation.[1] This is so despite a cogently argued plea for this to be done in an excellent, but rarely referenced, article, by Alchian and Klein, whose title I have taken above as the heading for this section, written some twenty years ago (JMCB, Feb. 1973). They note that the price indices that 'dominate popular and professional literature and analyses', e.g. the Bureau of Labour Statistics' Consumer Price Index and the Commerce Department's GNP deflator only measure 'current consumer service flow price inflation'. Such indices are 'inappropriate' for a broader assessment of inflation and 'result in significant errors in monetary research, theory, and policy' (quotes from pp. 173, 174 and 186).

They start by noting that, 'For many situations we are interested in measuring the *money* cost of a fixed welfare or constant utility vector of goods as money prices change. . . . However, as early as 1906, Irving Fisher (and others earlier, we conjecture) pointed out that an iso-utility vector included claims to future consumption.' They further refer to Fisher's (1911) comment that 'To base our index number [of purchasing power] for time contracts solely on services and immediately consumable goods would therefore be illogical' (p. 174).

They continue,

> Assume, initially, that markets exist for every consumption service flow to be delivered at every moment of time. At any moment an individual is assumed to be constrained by a scalar W(wealth), which he allocates over claims to present and future consumption flows at present prices quoted on these markets. If at each (current and future) moment there are n consumption services, then
>
> $$W_A \equiv \int_0^{\infty}\left[\sum_{i=1}^{n} q_A(i, t)\,P_A(i, t)\right]\mathrm{d}t$$
>
> where W_A is the individual's current nominal wealth, p_A (i, t) is the current rental price of the ith consumption service for moment t (i.e., present prices include prices of present claims to future consumption) and q_A (i, t) is the magnitude of the ith consumption service flow at moment t which at the current price vector and wealth level maximizes the individual's intertemporal utility. All of these values are described as given under condition A.
>
> Let present flow prices, including present prices of future consumption services, change and describe this new state as condition B. The question we are asking is whether prices, measured by a constant-utility index, have risen or fallen. We can, in principle, compute at the new set of present prices, $[p_B$ $(i, t)]$, the cost of an iso-utility consumption service vector, $[q_B$ $(i, t)]$. If, for example, the new cost under price condition B, W_B, is greater than under the initial price condition A, we can say that the money cost of an iso-utility vector of goods has risen. The iso-utility price index implicit in this can be represented by

$$P_{AB} \equiv \frac{W_B}{W_A} \equiv \frac{\int_0^\infty \left[\sum_{i=1}^{n} q_B(i, t) P_B(i, t) \right] dt}{\int_0^\infty \left[\sum_{i=1}^{n} q_A(i, t) P_A(i, t) \right] dt}$$

where q_B (i, t) represents the (i, t) element in the minimum cost consumption vector that yields the same condition A utility at the new condition B price vector. If P_{AB} is greater than one, the nominal money cost of condition A utility has increased; an inflation has occurred.

To emphasise the intertemporal nature of this price index and the fact that it does not refer solely to the cost of the current moment's consumption it could less misleadingly be called the current 'cost of life' index. Current instantaneous prices of current consumption flows enter this index, but insignificantly.

* * *

The major difficulty in making our index operational is that separate futures markets or contracts do not exist for all future consumption services. As a result, some futures prices required for a complete iso-utility price index will not be directly observable in explicit market prices. But since assets are sources of future services, asset prices provide clues to prices of present claims on future consumption. Current wealth can be represented by the sum of all asset values, or, equivalently, interpreted as the sum of all present valued claims to all consumption service flows over time. Symbolically, if there are m assets, wealth is denotable by:

$$W_A \equiv \sum_{j=1}^{M} P_A(j) Q_A(j) \equiv \int_0^\infty \left[\sum_{i=1}^{n} q_A(i, t) P_A(i, t) \right] dt$$

where W_A is the individual's current nominal wealth and $[Q_A\ (j)]$ is the current vector of asset quantities that would yield his intertemporal utility maximizing consumption service stream, $[q_A$ $(i, t)]$. If assets are standardized in terms of their present and future service flows, the current vector of asset prices, $[P_A\ (j)]$, can therefore be used as a proxy for current futures prices, p_A (i, t).

When relative prices change, one can, in principle, determine the vector of assets, $[Q_B(j)]$, which will yield the minimum cost iso-utility consumption service stream $[q_B(i, t)]$ at the new set of asset prices $[P_B(j)]$ and implicit futures prices $p_B(i, t)$. Current asset prices can therefore be ussed to construct our constant welfare price index

$$P_{AB} \equiv \frac{W_B}{W_A} \equiv \frac{\sum_{j=1}^{m} P_B(j)\, Q_B(j)}{\sum_{j-1}^{m} P_B(j)\, Q_A(j)}$$

where W_B is the nominal cost of the vector of assets that will yield a flow of present and future consumption services equal in utility to the initial condition A consumption service stream.

It is crucial to emphasize that the vectors $[Q_A(j)]$ and $[Q_B(j)]$ must include all assets – consumer and producer, durable and non-durable, tangible and intangible, financial and non-financial, human and non-human. All sources of present and future consumption services must be considered. The vectors do not represent the actual assets held by the representative individual, but the asset combination that would yield the individual's desired consumption service flows. An individual may hold some assets that yield the exact pattern of consumption service flows that he demands over time, e.g., a house that yields his present and future desired housing service flow. But, more generally, due to transaction costs individuals will hold some assets not because they yield services that coincide with their consumption plans, but because they are an efficient form in which to hold wealth. The services from these assets or the assets themselves are later sold and exchanged for desired consumption services. Human capital is the most obvious example.

Since our asset price index is not constructed on the basis of assets actually owned by an individual we are therefore not measuring whether the individual is better or worse off after a change in prices, only whether he requires more or less money to reach the same utility level.

A money prices index based on considerations we have outlined is fundamentally different from the CPI, which is constructed on the basis of prices of *current* consumption services. The CPI considers the prices of only a part of the utility function and is therefore inadequate in principle as a constant utility money price

> measure. The CPI attempts to measure changes in the cost of only the iso-utility current consumption flows and therefore supplies an answer to a question distinct from whether the present money cost of consumer utility has changed.
>
> Current service flow prices are related to asset prices by implicit real rates of interest and therefore our iso-utility price index is logically equivalent to an index based on current service flow prices and a broadly defined interest rate vector. If our representative individual moved to a new society where current service flow prices are identical but where real interest rates are higher, our iso-utility price index would fall. The individual would substitute future consumption for present consumption and his money cost of life would decrease (pp. 174–8).

Here we get to the crux of the matter. The first point is that, in a correctly defined price index, a higher real interest rate implies a *lower* price level, *ceteris paribus*. Although the treatment of housing in price indices still varies considerably from country to country, it remains the case that in some countries a higher (nominal) interest rate feeds through positively into measured current housing costs, and hence is associated with a *higher* calculated price level. Second, this analysis provides an academic basis for the view that asset price movements *should* be taken into account in any proper, overall assessment of price stability. If current consumer flow prices are steady, but equity, land and housing asset prices are plummeting, then price stability has *not* been achieved. I follow Alchian and Klein in believing that, *conceptually*, asset prices and real interest rates should enter into assessments of inflation.

One major problem is that there are massive *practical* difficulties in combining asset prices and current flow prices to construct an acceptable 'cost of life' index. We cannot observe their 'broadly defined interest rate vector'. Asset markets are notoriously incomplete. Even where asset markets operate,

> surprisingly little reliable information exists on current prices of assets and given the assumed importance of these prices in the transmission of monetary impulses, some effort in this direction would seem to be clearly economic. Collection of transaction price data on land, commercial and residential property, producer and consumer durables, and other tangible and financial assets and the

> construction of a crude quarterly wealth price index would probably be worthwhile (p. 187)

and they applaud proposals by Stigler and Snyder to move in that direction (n. 27).

Besides the considerable problems in obtaining the basic data, there are far greater difficulties in adjusting for *quality* changes than when a current flow price index is used. If an equity price rises, is this because of

> (i) a change in the price of an unchanged future service flow from the asset, (ii) a shift in preferences for this asset's service relative to other assets, (iii) a shift in preferences for present consumption relative to future consumption, or (iv) a change in the anticipated magnitude of service flow from the asset. Any or all of these changes are likely to be occurring simultaneously and therefore the cause of a change in a particular asset price is difficult to determine. Changes (ii) and (iii) represent a shift in tastes while (iv) represents a change in asset quality; however, they are not conceptually different from the problems encountered in constructing the presently used indices (p. 188).
>
> * * *
>
> The empirical problems involved are enormous. But whatever efforts may be made in this direction and whatever the results, we believe it is an error to assign all of the change in common stock and other asset prices to changes in anticipated future service flows with no change in present prices of such future flows . . . which is what is implicitly done now in commonly used price indices that ignore asset prices (p. 189).

Next, there is a problem of perception. Inflation is treated not only as a measure of the change of the real current value of the monetary unit, but more generally as an index of the loss of welfare and purchasing power of someone with a given nominal income. This latter view may be associated with the fact that normally the expected flow of nominal income over a year is much larger than the initial inventory value of current consumer goods. Only if one is a producer does the rise in the price of one's product, relative to other products, become positively desirable. All this alters when we turn to asset prices. Many of us, especially the cohort aged 50–65 who usually dominate policy decisions, are relatively long on owned assets, equities, bonds, houses, land. An increase in housing prices, when I already own two, quite large houses, improves my own welfare. So I do *not* assess a change in housing prices in the same, uniformly hostile, light as I do current inflation.

Alchian and Klein ask

> But why, then, isn't there a demand for a price index that includes asset prices and why do movements in the CPI appear to be politically important? Within the context of our model it is difficult to find a rationale for the fact that rising consumer service flow prices are generally unpopular while falling asset prices are generally unpopular. The relevance of our intertemporal iso-utility index appears to be seriously questioned by common attitudes. One possible explanation may be that individuals fail to recognize that price changes of assets they do not own may significantly affect their money costs of life and their welfare. While individuals that, for example, own houses are aware of the decrease in their wealth when prices of houses fall, individuals that do not own houses do not appear to recognize that such a price change also affects them by lowering future housing service prices. Individuals are more fully aware of changes in their nominal wealth than of changes in the nominal cost of future consumption, possibly because an intertemporal consumption index is not now published (p. 186).

Such perceptions are economically important. It is arguable that a fall in the price of (financial) assets arising from an increase in the interest rate at which future, assumed unchanged, dividends are discounted should have a positive wealth effect. Those already holding such assets can look forward to an unchanged future service flow; those short of such assets can now obtain them more cheaply. In practice, however, we believe that the wealth effect of lower asset prices will be negative, whereas that of lower goods prices will be positive. King, in his Presidential address to the European Economic Association, (1993), emphasises the asymmetric distributional effects of shifts of wealth between creditor and debtor households. Indeed, one of the curiosities of the 1987 stock market crash was why the anticipated negative wealth effect did not appear. Besides the fact that this was an occasion in which monetary policy was adjusted appropriately in the face of asset price movements, one reason that is often given for the resilience of consumer expenditures was the shift of equity holdings from individual investors to financial intermediaries, e.g. pension funds and insurance companies. When an asset is owned on my behalf by such an intermediary, or by the State, and the change in the present value of my future claims, consequent on the current asset price change, is uncertain and perhaps hard to calculate, my response is, perhaps, likely to be much more muted than when I am the immediate beneficial owner.

There are, therefore, many problems involved in constructing, or interpreting, an *inter-temporal* price index. But the existence of such problems is not, of itself, a justification for concentrating solely on an objective which is expressed solely in terms of current consumer flow prices, ignoring asset prices. The failure to take into account asset price changes will lead to mis-specification and errors, both theoretically and in policy operation.

Thus Alchian and Klein note that

> the use of the GNP deflator as the relevant price variable in the demand for money function remains theoretically unjustified. Money is used to purchase assets of varying durability and age. The demand for money therefore cannot be dependent solely on the prices of current output flows which represent only a part of what money can buy. Hence, within the context of a transactions demand framework or a wealth portfolio choice framework, the GNP deflator is incomplete and the purchasing power of money could be more meaningfully measured in terms of our more inclusive price of wealth index (p. 182).

But their greater concern was with resulting policy errors. In my view, this same syndrome has been repeated in recent years, *mutatis mutandis*; so I shall restate their conclusions incorporating my current amendments in square brackets.

> Reliance on these biased numbers as an indicator or target of monetary policy makes it difficult for the monetary authorities to know what they are doing, let alone what they should be doing. And action on the basis of these numbers can lead to inappropriate decisions; policy changes will often come too late and move too far. Recent monetary policy provides an instructive example. The authorities' preoccupation with the movement of inappropriate flow prices indices to the almost complete exclusion of asset prices was partially responsible for a monetary policy that was too easy for

too long a period (1967–68) [1988–89] and then a policy that was too tight for too long a period (1968–69) [1991–92] followed by a policy that was once again too easy (1969–early 1971) [1994?]. A crude modification of the CPI, with, say, an index of stock prices [housing and property] would have provided a much more useful indicator and target for price level stability (p. 185).

[Most of the comments and discussion at the two Conferences at which I presented this paper concentrated on this part of my presentation, the Alchian/Klein definition of inflation. Some argued that this was theoretically incorrect, though I was not convinced by their points. Others proposed that 'price stability' should imply certain constraints on the *expected future* time path for current consumer flow prices, e.g. that this should not be a trended I1 series. While they agreed that movements in current consumer flow prices today might give an unsatisfactory impression of the expected future time path of such prices, they felt that movements in asset prices were far too noisy, and affected by quality changes, etc., to be used in any *formal* assessment of the expected future time path of current consumer flow prices. The practical difficulties of incorporating asset prices into a price index (e.g. their noisiness, the impossibility of adjusting for quality changes, the problems of providing associated inter-temporal quantity indices), were widely stressed. *None* of those present, who spoke, would have been happy to have an Alchian/Klein/Shibuya index used as the *main* measure of inflation. Some would be interested to see such an index regularly calculated to see if it would have any significant (lead) relationship with more conventional price indices; others felt that such an index could be dangerously misleading.

By contrast, however, almost all the participants did agree that movements in asset prices often could contain valuable leading information on potential future goods price changes, since asset prices were comparatively flexible whereas prices of current goods and services exhibited inertia. In the longer run, asset and goods prices should be cointegrated, so a marked deviation in asset prices could be expected to be followed *either* by a resultant shift in goods prices (as in the early 1970s), *or* a reversal of asset prices (as in the boom and bust cycle of 1988–92). Either result, following an asset price explosion, could cause problems to the monetary authorities. It was generally agreed that there was no mechanical method for taking account of asset price inflation, but that attention and care should be given to it, perhaps more so than in recent years, but that this would still have to be done in a broadly subjective and discretionary fashion.]

Another of the problems of taking asset prices into account for policy purposes is that the identity of the key asset market(s) that link monetary policy to the real economy appears to shift over time. Alchian and Klein give the equity market pre-eminence in their account of the 1969–71 cycle that they study. In a number of countries, Scandinavia, UK, Australia, USA, the swings in housing and property prices were more important in the last cycle, 1988–93. In Japan, equity and land prices moved quite closely together (see Nakajima and Taguchi, 1993 and Shimizu, 1992). In the UK in 1979–85, the link between monetary developments and the exchange rate was probably the main transmission mechanism.

Such shifts in the importance (for monetary policy) of differing asset markets may, in part, reflect changing patterns of asset ownership (e.g. the rise in the importance of owner-occupation, the switch from personal to institutional ownership of equities). It will also reflect shifts in the importance of differing asset markets for bank (lending) business. The switch of bank loan portfolios away from lending to large corporations, whose credit rating and direct access to (wholesale) funds, e.g. via the commercial paper market, has become relatively stronger than that of the banks themselves in recent years, has been much remarked (e.g. Boyd and Gertler, 1993, also see Chapter 6, this volume, for Japan). In their place banks have tended to substitute mortgage lending and loans to persons and small businesses, often collateralised by, or related to, housing, construction and property, see Nakajima and Taguchi (1993). Black, de Meza and Jeffreys (1992) have noted that the main influence on the rate of start-up of new businesses in the UK has been the level of housing prices, in some large part presumably because this represents the main source of equity available as collateral for outside (bank) funding.

Thus it is possible that housing/property prices have become relatively more important, and equity prices less so, in relation to bank loan business, both as an influence on the demand for loans, as collateral for such loans, and as a factor determining the rate of bad debts. It would be nice to have some direct measure of the proportion of loans which is housing/property related, or equity connected, but given the difficulty of obtaining data on what is used as collateral, *inter alia*, that would be difficult, and time consuming for me, to do satisfactorily. See this volume, Chapter 6, and Shimizu (1992) for data on this for Japan.

Instead, what I have attempted is to explore whether the data can give us any indication of the relative, changing influence of housing/ property and equity prices on bank lending to the private sector, in both the US and the UK. The data for the USA are annual, from 1919 to 1991, and for the UK annual from 1939 to 1991. The data set consists of a measure of bank lending to the private sector, and indices of prices (CPI), real output, stock market prices and the price of houses, and interest rates on Treasury Bills.[2] The most problematic series is the housing price index. Not only is this complicated by the heterogeneous characteristic of housing, and questions of quality changes, but also we failed to obtain a single consecutive index for the USA. Instead we spliced together data for prices of existing houses, (1919–47) and of new houses (1947–91); we were only partially comforted by finding that, in the period 1970–89 when these two series overlapped, the correlation between them in levels was 0.985, and in first differences 0.467.

We were forced to use a shorter data period for the UK, since 'In the inter-war there is as yet no detailed record of house prices, though the material with which to construct it may still exist in building societies' records' (Holmans, 1990, p. 112). The index used here, from 1939 till 1991, is taken from the same source, (ibid., pp. 113–114). In practice, however, owing to direct controls over both prices and bank lending, we generally omitted the years 1939–45, starting in 1946.[3]

All these series, with the exception of interest rates in the UK, which are also on the borderline in the USA, are trended, I1, series. Taking the US exercise first, we began by examining whether bank lending was cointegrated with prices (CPI) and real output.

The ADF value of the residuals was –4.60, compared with a 95 percent critical value of –3.86. Next we ran the same regression in first difference form, with the result:

$$\underset{}{\mathrm{d}BLP} = \underset{(0.009)}{0.027} + \underset{(0.133)}{0.222}\ \mathrm{d}OUT + \underset{(0.162)}{1.077}\,\mathrm{d}PRI$$

With the coefficient on the percentage change in the price index being insignificantly different from unity, we took as our dependent variable, the real change in bank lending to the private sector, d*RBLP*. This was then regressed against the percentage changes in real output, stock prices and housing prices, plus current levels of interest rates (trying this both in nominal and in real terms, i.e. after subtracting the current rate of CPI inflation), the residuals from the cointegrating equation, with, and without, a lagged dependent variable.

The main problem, from an econometric point of view, with this equation, is that neither housing prices, nor the stock price index, nor some of the other variables, can be considered independent of the current annual change in bank lending. Our concern, however, was *not* to examine the determinants of bank lending, but to explore for indications of changing *two-way* relationships between bank lending and equity and housing prices.

Our basic equation, over the period, 1920–91, was as follows:

$$\underset{}{\mathrm{d}RBLP} = \underset{(0.011)}{0.008} + \underset{(0.137)}{0.095}\ \mathrm{d}OUT + \underset{(0.131)}{0.330}\ \mathrm{d}PHS + \underset{(0.044)}{0.122}\ \mathrm{d}PEQ$$

$$+ \underset{(0.002)}{0.002}\ \mathrm{RInt} \quad \underset{(-0.000)}{-0.000}\ \mathrm{ECM}$$

$$R^2 = 0.22 \quad DW\ 1.27$$

The coefficients on the percentage change in the housing and equity indices were significant. However, there were clear signs of autocorrelation in the error term, with a low DW ratio for an equation in first differences. When a lagged dependent variable was introduced, the coefficient on d*PHS* fell sharply, and became insignificant, as follows:

$$\mathrm{d}RBLP = \underset{(0.010)}{-0.001} + \underset{(0.123)}{0.140}\ \mathrm{d}OUT + \underset{(0.119)}{0.112}\ \mathrm{d}PHS + \underset{(0.038)}{0.136}\ \mathrm{d}PEQ$$

$$+ \underset{(0.002)}{0.002}\ Int \ \underset{(-0.000)}{-0.000}\ ECM + \underset{(0.097)}{0.496}\ \mathrm{d}RBLP_{t-1}$$

$$R^2 = 0.440 \text{ Lagrange multiplier test } 1.07$$

Our main interest, however, is whether this relationship has exhibited changes over time. For this purpose we reran both regressions over separate sub-periods, and did a rolling regression, starting with 1919–39, and extending the period by one year at a time. We chart the coefficients for d*PHS* and d*PEQ* from the second equation, i.e. with a lagged dependent variable, with their associated one standard deviation bands in Figure 10.1 (a–b). The coefficients, and associated standard errors, from four selected different sub-periods are shown in Table 10.1 below.

These results suggest, somewhat tentatively, that the relationship between equity price movements and bank lending remained relatively important and stable over the early years of this period, but

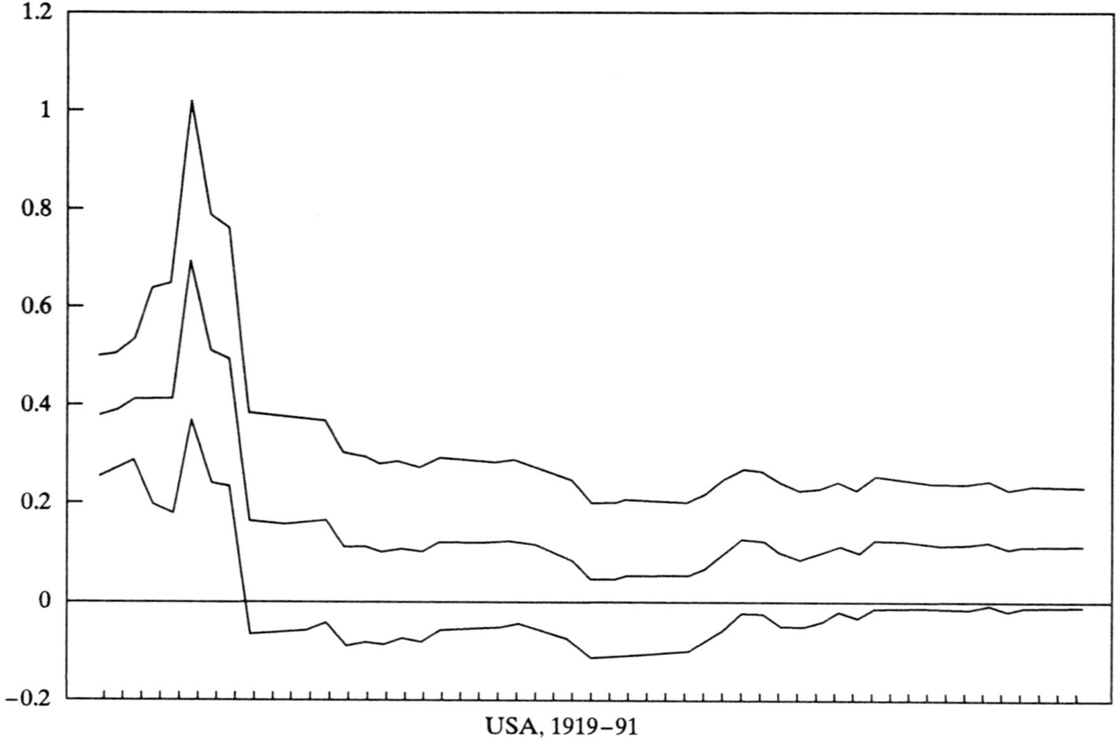

Figure 10.1 (a) Coefficients of d*PHS* from a regression of d*RBLP* on d*CONSTY*, d*PHS*, d*PEQ*, *REALINT*, *ECM*, d*RBLP*(−1).

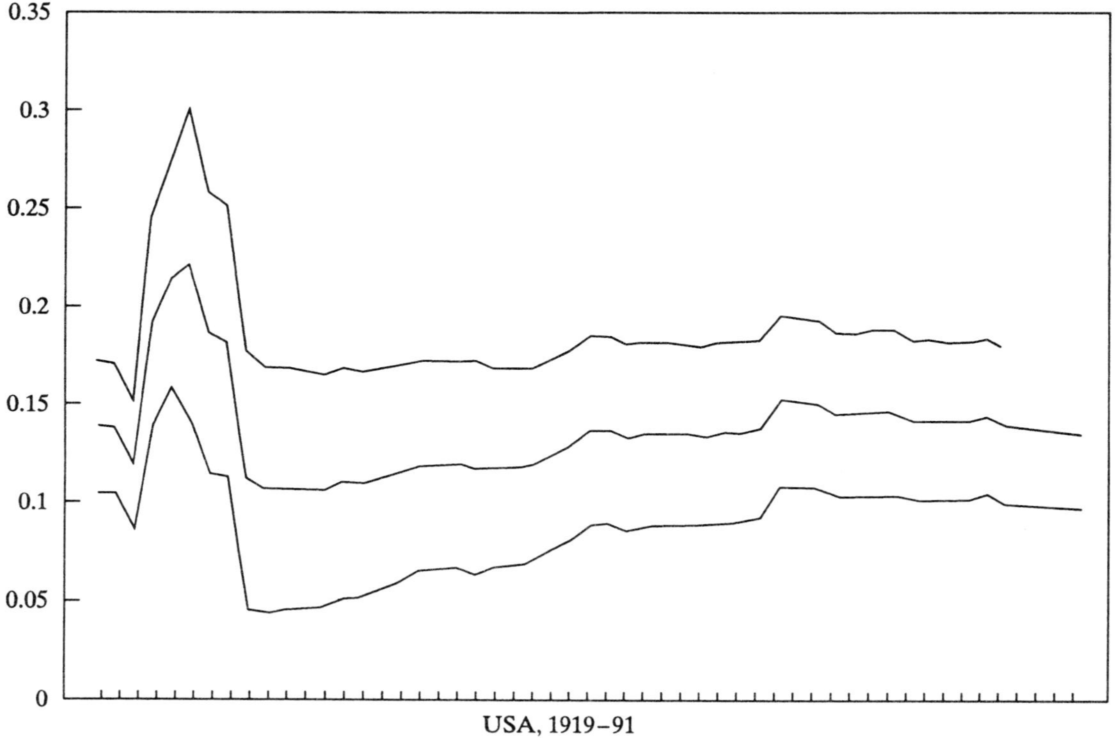

Figure 10.1 (b) Coefficients of d*PEQ* from a regression of d*RBLP* on d*CONSTY*, d*PHS*, d*PEQ*, *REALINT*, *ECM*, d*RBLP*(–1).

Table 10.1

United States, 1919–91
Regression of d*RBLP* on d*CONSTY*, d*PHS*, d*PEQ*, *REALINT*, *ECM*

	d*PHS*		d*PEQ*	
Period	*Coefficient*	*t ratio*	*Coefficient*	*t ratio*
1919–91	0.330	2.526	0.122	2.788
1919–39	0.331	1.340	0.131	1.990
1939–55	–0.096	–0.237	0.061	0.333
1955–79	–0.181	–0.756	0.129	1.674
1979–91	0.645	2.081	–0.087	–0.977

Regression of d*RBLP* on d*CONSTY*, d*PHS*, d*PEQ*, *REALINT*, *ECM*, d*RBLP* (–1)

	d*PHS*		d*PEQ*	
Period	*Coefficient*	*t ratio*	*Coefficient*	*t ratio*
1919–91	0.122	0.940	0.136	3.634
1919–39	0.378	3.046	0.139	4.086
1939–55	–0.180	–0.355	1.003	0.432
1955–79	–0.241	–1.040	0.143	1.935
1979–91	0.552	1.707	–0.068	–0.739

United Kingdom, 1946–91
Regression of d*BLP* on d*CONSTY* d*CPI*, *INTEREST*, d*PHS*, d*PEQ*, *ECM*, *DBLP* (–1)

	d*PHS*		d*PEQ*	
Period	*Coefficient*	*t ratio*	*Coefficient*	*t ratio*
1946–91	0.966	5.016	–0.001	–0.012
1946–63	0.550	2.144	0.116	0.685
1963–79	1.200	4.423	–0.151	–2.370
1979–91	1.428	1.544	–0.113	–0.220

may have diminished in strength recently. By contrast the relationship between conditions in the housing market and in bank lending was comparatively strong in the inter-war period and in recent years, since 1979, but was weak in the intervening years, 1940–79. In any case there does seem some evidence, especially in the bank lending–housing nexus, of changing relationships over this, quite lengthy, data period.

When we turn next to the UK data, the strength of the relationships between bank lending and housing prices, over our shorter data period, appears generally stronger and more stable than in the USA. We found it, however, hard to obtain a cointegrating equation between bank lending in the UK and real output and CPI inflation. When housing prices were added as an additional regressor, it was clear that this was the dominant variable, with a t value of over 30. Indeed, with housing prices included, the coefficients on output and CPI inflation became negative. Even so, their inclusion 'improved' the cointegrating equation, though it remained rather unsatisfactory and marginal; over the period 1939–91 the ADF was −4.36 (−4.32 being the 95 percent critical value), over the period 1946–91 the ADF fell to −4.13 (compared with −4.36 at the 95 percent critical value).

Unlike the USA, there was no evidence in the UK of an X percent rise in the CPI being matched by a similar X percent rise in bank lending to the private sector. Hence in our equations the percentage change in nominal bank lending is the dependent variable, and both the percentage change in the CPI and in nominal interest rates are entered separately as regressors. Otherwise the form of the equations (including lagged dependent variable) are the same as tested for the USA.

The results are shown below:

$$\underset{}{\mathrm{d}BLP} = \underset{(0.037)}{0.058} - \underset{(0.693)}{0.872}\ \mathrm{d}OUT - \underset{(0.409)}{0.329}\ \mathrm{d}CPI$$

$$- \underset{(0.004)}{0.002}\ INT + \underset{(0.193)}{0.966}\ \mathrm{d}PHS - \underset{(0.058)}{0.001}\ \mathrm{d}PEQ - \underset{(0.000)}{0.000}\ ECM$$

$$+ \underset{(0.141)}{0.205}\ \mathrm{d}BlP_{t-1}$$

The coefficient on the percentage change in housing prices is highly significant, more so than in the US case, but the coefficient on the percentage change in the equity price is insignificant, and even negative.

Again we wanted to examine the stability over time of the relationships between asset prices and bank lending. Data for subperiods are shown in Table 10.1, and the rolling regression, from the second equation, in Figures 10.1 (c and d). These results suggest that housing prices have developed a stronger association with bank lending, since the immediate post-war period, whereas the relationship between movements in the equity index and bank lending has been weakening.

The tentative conclusion of this, broad-brush and rough, preliminary statistical exercise is that the nexus between housing prices and bank lending has been strengthening in recent decades, and forms the major link between asset prices and bank lending in the UK. By contrast, earlier stronger relationships between equity prices and bank

Figure 10.1 (c) Coefficients of d*PHS* from a regression of d*BLP* on d*CONSTY*, d*CPI*, *INTEREST*, d*PHS*, d*PEEQ*, *ECM*, d*BLP*(–1).

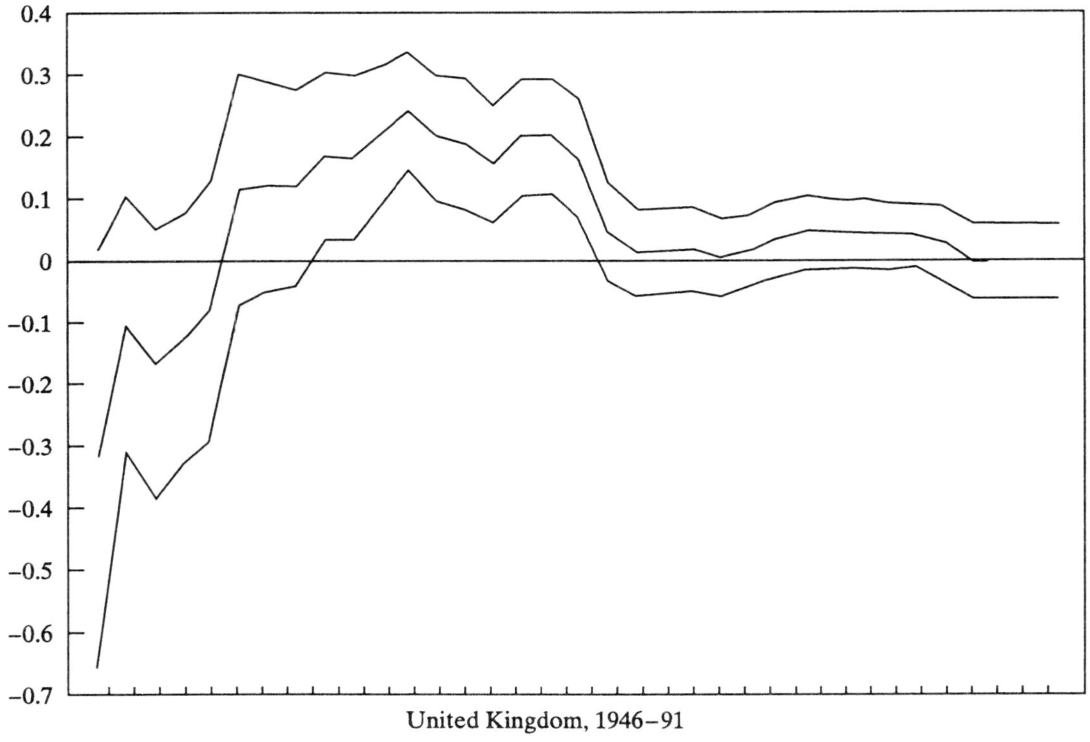

Figure 10.1 (d) Coefficients of d*PEQ* from a regression of d*BLP* on d*CONSTY*, d*CPI*, *INTEREST*, d*PHS*, d*PEEQ*, *ECM*, d*BLP*(−1).

lending, especially strong in the USA, appear to have weakened recently.

III FINANCIAL FRAGILITY AND ASSET PRICE INSTABILITY

The relationship, in both directions, between the banking system and the real economy is primarily via asset prices. In Keynesian analysis the transmission mechanism from a monetary impulse to the real economy runs primarily through a specified, and limited, set of financial assets, short rates on Treasury bills, long rates on bonds, equity yields (Tobin's q) on to investment. Whereas monetarists deny the validity of such tight restrictions (Friedman and Meiselman, 1964, e.g. p. 217), in their formulation also monetary impulses pass through to the real economy via a shift in the relativity of generalised asset prices *vis-à-vis* current flow prices (see Friedman and Schwartz, 1963, pp. 229–31, and Alchian and Klein, 1973, p. 179).

In turn, movements in asset prices, as noted in the previous section, affect the demand for, and bad debts on, bank loans. In particular, bank crises and financial fragility are generally connected with the collapse of certain asset prices, rather than a fall of current consumer flow prices (though, as will be discussed further, the two sets of prices are usually positively correlated). This is not invariably so. The LDC crisis in 1982, and the following years, was in some large part related to the fall in commodity export prices from those countries rather than any specific LDC asset prices.

Nevertheless we could look back to the gold standard period of the nineteenth century as a time when the general current price level was fairly firmly anchored by the exchange rate regime. This did not avert banking crises, and these were mainly related to, and triggered by, some asset price decline. Some documentation of this claim is given in Appendix B.

Asset price instability is generally associated with bank instability, with the causation running strongly and simultaneously in both directions. A bubble economy will normally be accompanied by a surge in bank lending, and perhaps to a lesser extent in broad money, on the upswing, and the collapse of the bubble will equally result in a welter of bad debts and a drastic slowing of credit and monetary expansion. We can all think of recent occasions. This general type of analysis has been put forward by Fisher (1932), Kindleberger, Minsky, etc.

Wherein, however, lies the conflict, if any, between the pursuit of

Table 10.2

	USA					
	Levels			*1st Difference*		
	CPI	*HSN*	*EQ*	*CPI*	*HSN*	*EQ*
CPI						
HSN	0.993			0.436		
EQ	0.950	0.963		0.223	0.259	
	UK					
	Levels			*1st Difference*		
	CPI	*HSN*	*EQ*	*CPI*	*HSN*	*EQ*
CPI						
HSN	0.958			0.103		
EQ	0.951	0.984		–0.006	0.132	

price stability and financial stability? One aspect of the recent property/financial cycle was that the authorities did not react quickly, or strongly, enough to the housing/property price surge in the latter years of the 1980s, because they did not factor it into their assessment of inflation, incorrectly as we have already argued. If asset prices had been taken into account in assessing potential inflation, monetary policy would have been less accommodative prior to 1990, and more expansionary recently. Such action would have helped not only to stabilize the banking system, but also to achieve greater price stability on an Alchian–Klein 'life cost' index basis.

If movements in asset prices, and in current consumer flow prices, were uncorrelated, or negatively correlated, then a recommendation to give some weight to the former, in interpreting the objective of 'price stability' would, perhaps, be more controversial. In practice, however, current consumer flow prices and asset prices have been positively correlated, though not strongly so, over the years.

In Table 10.2 the correlations between the levels and the percentage changes in the indices of current consumer flow prices (CPI in both the US and the UK), housing prices and equity prices, are reported for the USA and UK.

Next we examined the temporal, 'causal', structure of relationships between these three sets of asset prices by regressing the percentage

Table 10.3

US			
Dependent variable	d*CPI*	d*PHS*	d*EQ*
t value on constant	0.57	2.20	1.08
d*CPI* –1	8.12	1.44	–0.55
d*CPI* –2	–3.15	–0.27	0.80
d*PHS* –1	2.65	2.71	–1.37
d*PHS* –2	2.61	1.30	1.96
d*EQ* –1	0.19	1.08	1.46
d*EQ* –2	–2.93	–1.59	–1.88

UK			
Dependent variable	d*CPI*	d*PHS*	d*EQ*
t value on constant	1.99	1.71	2.16
d*CPI* –1	4.26	–1.83	–0.53
d*CPI* –2	2.26	2.14	1.74
d*PHS* –1	4.75	5.82	–1.74
d*PHS* –2	–3.70	–1.87	–0.37
d*EQ* –1	–5.04	1.03	–1.69
d*EQ* –2	–2.45	–1.25	–1.55

changes of each price series on its own lags, and the lagged changes in the other two series; two lags were taken in each case. The results for the US, in Table 10.3, indicated that CPI inflation was strongly autocorrelated, and Granger caused by housing inflation, and, with a negative sign, by changes in equity prices lagged two years; this latter, however, was largely due to outliers in the early 1930s. Housing inflation was rather more mildly autocorrelated, and equity prices not significantly different from random walk (n.b., housing price changes are autocorrelated, when d*Eq* is regressed in the same equation with $dPHS_{t-1}$ removed, the *t* value of the coefficient on $dPHS_{t-2}$ falls to 1.54).

The results for the UK, over the shorter period 1946–91, are broadly similar. CPI inflation has been strongly autocorrelated, and Granger caused by housing price inflation. Again, as in the USA, there is a significant negative relationship between CPI inflation and prior changes in equity prices, and, once more, this is due to a couple of outliers, though in this case to high inflation rates in 1974 and 1975 following sharp reductions in equity prices in 1973 and 1974 respectively (see Figure 10.1e). Housing inflation is also strongly

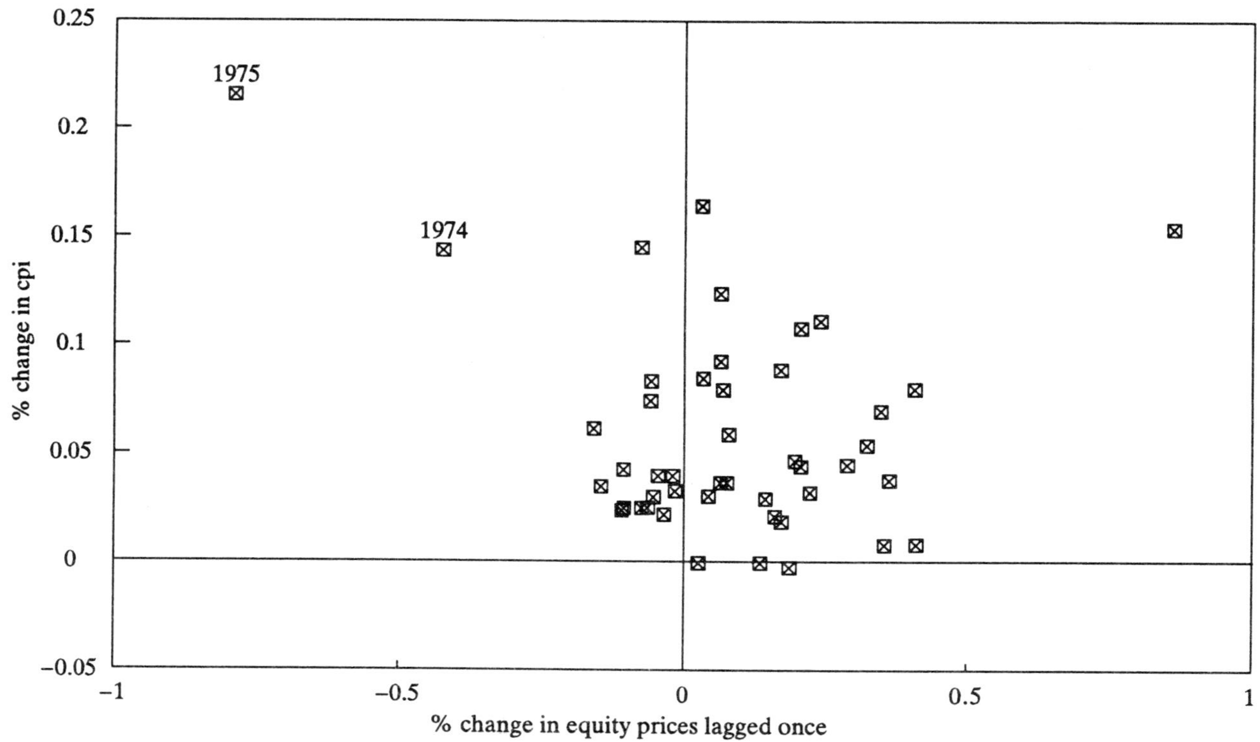

Figure 10.1 (e)   United Kingdom, 1946–91.

autocorrelated, with some slight signs of Granger causality from CPI inflation; finally, equity prices show no indications either of autocorrelation, or of Granger causality from these other variables.

Overall, therefore, one would expect that bank failures, and prolonged periods of financial fragility, would take place during periods of disinflation, when the rate of change of asset prices was (sharply) declining, and with asset price levels perhaps even falling; and that the same would be true, though to a less marked extent, for current flow prices. This is difficult to test in the UK since, within the oligopolistic British system, bank failures have been so sporadic. It does, however, fit the case of the most serious post-war example of financial fragility in the UK rather well, to wit the secondary banking crisis in 1973/74. This occurred at a time when a surge in asset prices in equities, housing and property peaked and then sharply reversed, whereas the rate of inflation in current flow prices showed more inertia. This is shown in Figure 10.2 for 1971–76.

It is easier to examine the relationship between bank failures and inflation in the USA, where any tendency to oligopoly has been limited by branching restrictions.

Figure 10.3 shows the relationship between the percentage change in the rate of inflation, i.e. the second difference of prices, in the USA and the number of bank failures, as a percentage of the total number of banks. This indicates that bank failures tend to be more frequent when the rate of inflation is subsiding. This chart excludes the outlying years of 1930, 1931, 1932 and 1933. They are off the scale. In two of these years the second difference of prices was positive, so if all years, including these outliers, were taken into account, the negative relationship shown in Figure 10.3 would disappear.

Figure 10.4 shows the relationship between bank failures and the percentage change, i.e. first difference, in housing prices. This has a somewhat less marked negative correlation of –0.30310. In this case, however, the relationship with the outlying four years was also negative. A regression of bank failures on the change in house prices, with and without the outliers, gave the following result, (A without outliers, B with outliers)

$$\text{A \% Failures} = \underset{(0.14)}{0.78} - \underset{(0.017)}{0.043}\, d\mathit{PHS}$$

$R^2 = 0.078$

$$\text{B \% Failures} = \underset{(0.49)}{2.69} - \underset{(0.060)}{0.275}\, d\mathit{PHS}$$

$R^2 = 0.22$

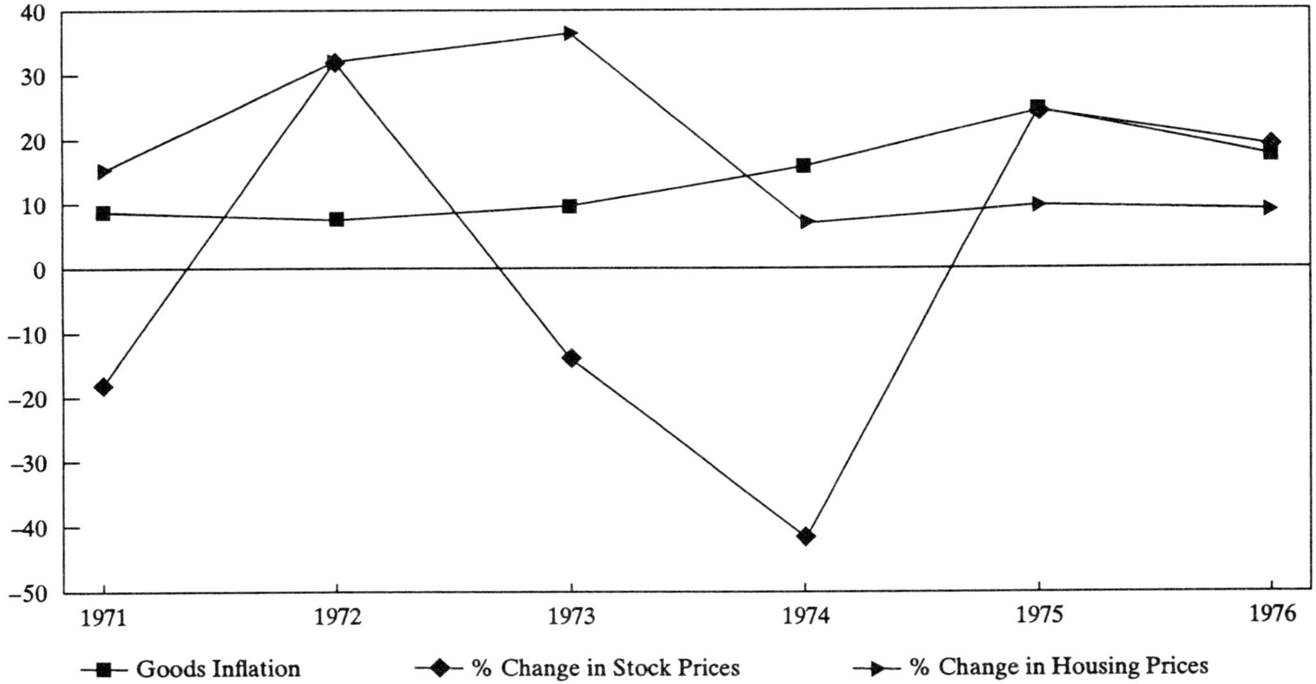

Figure 10.2 United Kingdom, 1971–76. (*Source*: *CSO Economic Trends*)

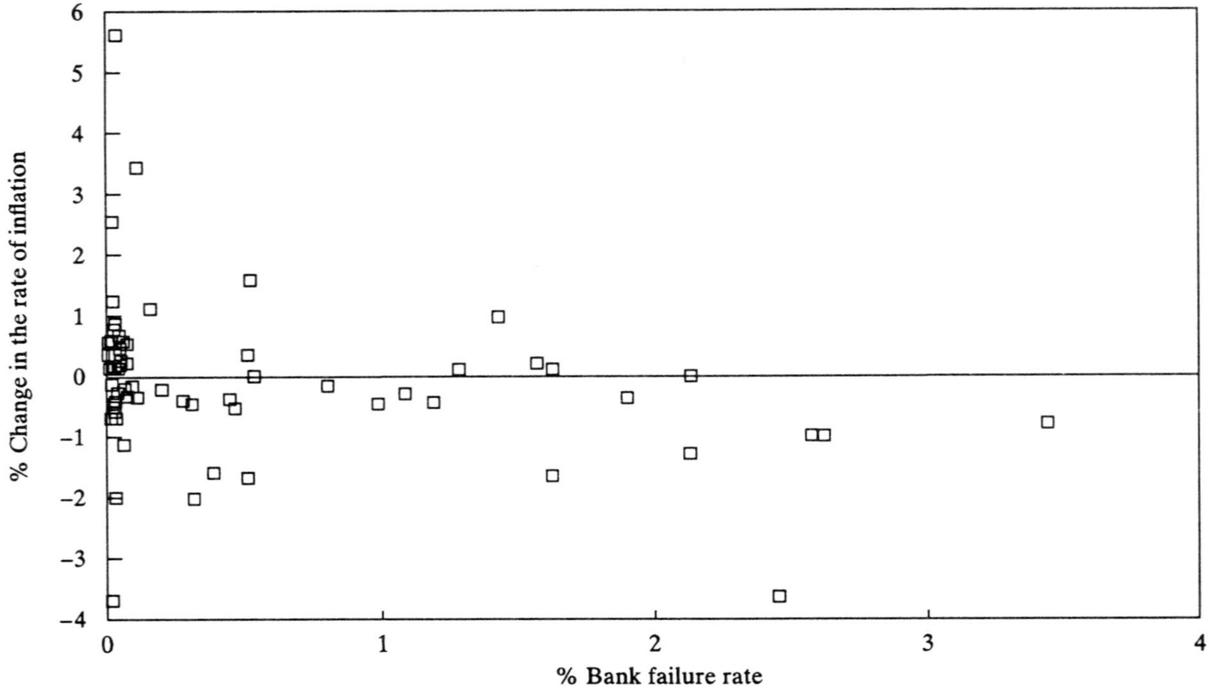

Figure 10.3 United States, 1919–91. (*Source*: Bureau of the Census: *Statistical Abstract of the United States*. Not including observations on 1930, 1931, 1932, 1933)

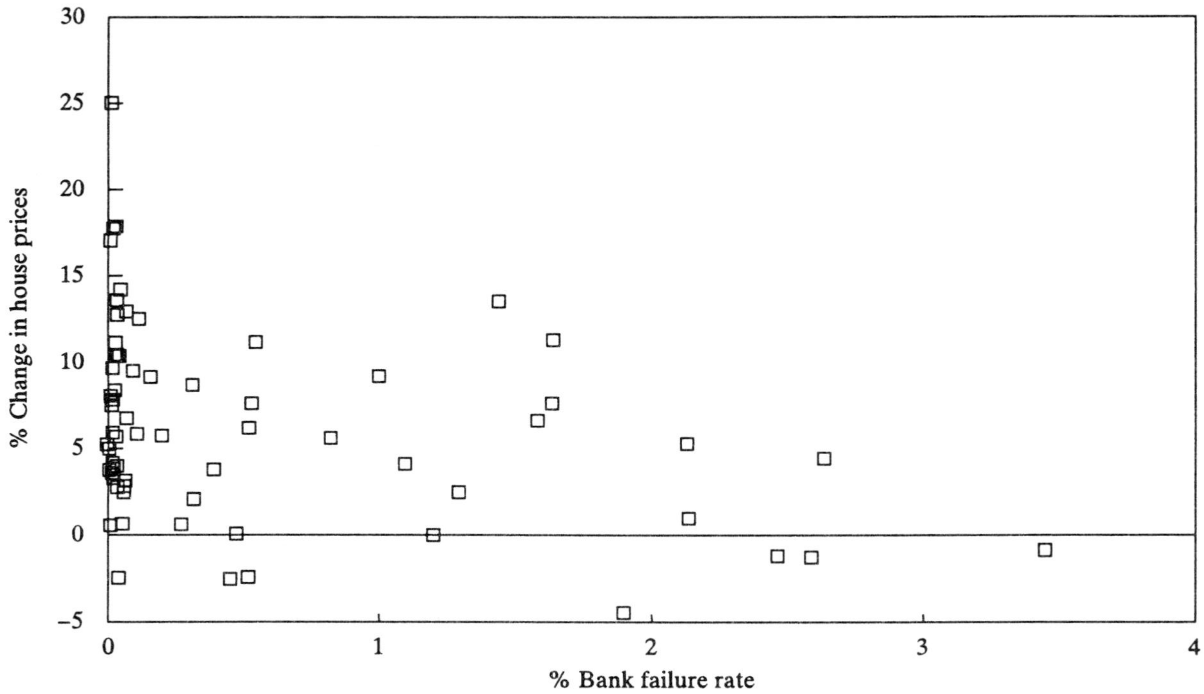

Figure 10.4 United States, 1919–91. (*Source*: Bureau of the Census: *Historical Statistics Colonial Times to 1957*; *Statistical Abstract of the United States*. Not including observations on 1930, 1931, 1932, 1933)

Figure 10.5 shows the relationship between bank failures and the percentage change, first difference, in equity prices. The relationship, both with and without the four outlying years is far less close; indeed in similar equations to those above the coefficient on d*PEQ* is insignificant without outliers, and just significant with these years (Case B).

$$\text{A \% Failures} = \underset{(0.11)}{0.46} + \underset{(0.006)}{0.006}\, \mathrm{d}PEQ$$

$R^2 = 0.004$

$$\text{B \% Failures} = \underset{(0.043)}{1.52} \quad \underset{(0.021)}{-0.049}\, \mathrm{d}PEQ$$

$R_2 = 0.055$

In general, though not invariably, bank failures will be high when asset (especially housing and property) prices have peaked, and have started to decline, and when the rate of inflation of current flow prices is starting to decline. Wherein, therefore, lies any conflict between the achievement of price stability and the preservation of financial stability? Resisting the asset price boom in the upswing, and supporting the banking system in the downswing are both likely to assist price stability.

There are, perhaps, two main junctures at which such conflict *may* arise. The first is that the increase(s) in interest rates necessary to puncture the inflationary surge (in current service flow and/or asset prices), or to achieve other macro-economic objectives (e.g. adherence to an Exchange Rate Mechanism), may imperil the solvency of financial and banking firms, both directly and indirectly via the effect on asset prices more generally. If the monetary authorities were able to raise interest rates sufficiently *quickly* and vigorously, to avert the asset price bubble, in a perfect world such a potential conflict should rarely occur, since the bubbles would not be allowed to expand to dangerous dimensions in the first place. When it does, however, a Central Bank can not let itself be constrained by the threat of potential future financial fragility from taking appropriate action to achieve its macro-economic objectives. Otherwise it could be blackmailed into immobility by the threat of systemic financial dangers ahead. The eventual cyclical outcome, the boom and bust, would most likely be *worsened* by any such constraints on the freedom of Central Bank action.

A recent study of Central Banking in a game theoretic context,

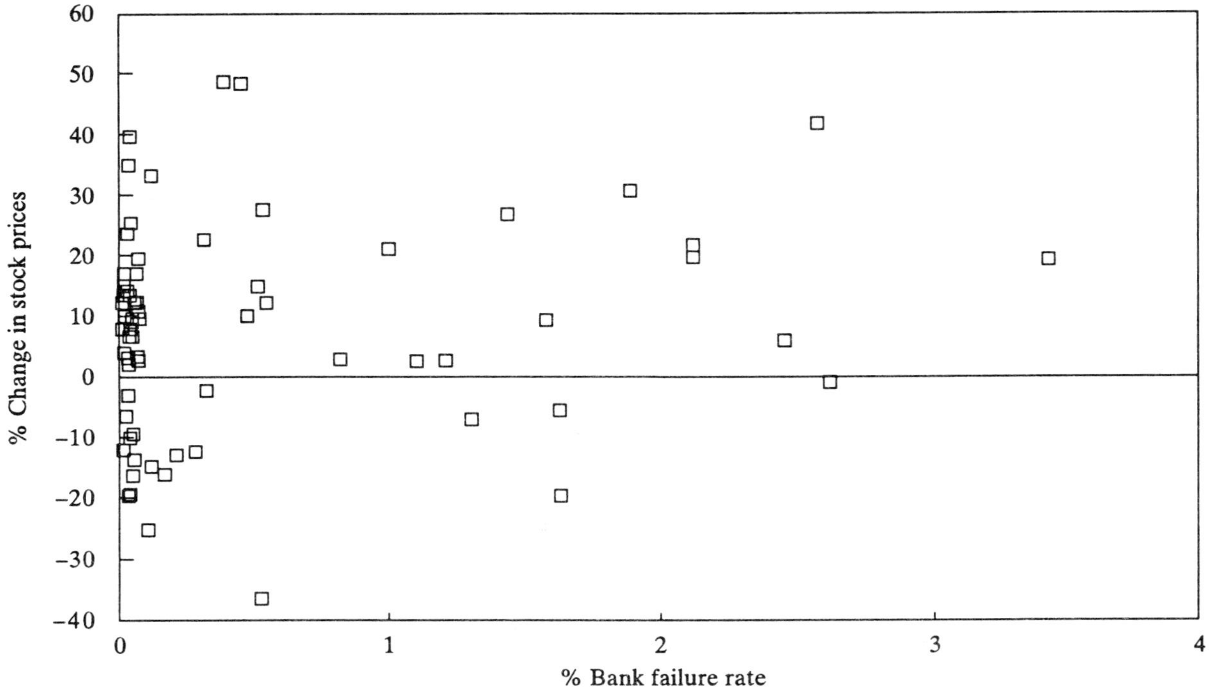

Figure 10.5 United States, 1919–91. (*Source*: R.J. Shiller: *Market Volatility* (MIT Press, Cambridge, MA. 1989); *Statistical Abstract of the United States*. Not including observations on 1930, 1931, 1932, 1933)

Cukierman (1992) has suggested (Chapter 7) that Central Banks are more likely to smooth interest rates, relative to the appropriate level for the achievement of price stability, when they are most concerned with the fragility of the banking system, i.e. when bank profits are low. When low profits herald problems with systemic stability, so he conjectures, Central Banks may refrain from raising interest rates sufficiently to offset inflationary shocks, and hence may have to restrain interest rate decreases more during downturns in order to regain counter-inflationary credibility. I sought to give a first-pass test of this hypothesis by examining the correlation between average bank profitability and the variance of inflation.

The data for the USA are taken from the *Statistical Abstract*, and cover the period 1919–91. The data from the UK, from the BBA, *Annual Abstract of Banking Statistics*, cover a shorter period, 1969–91; prior to 1969 both profits and capital were reported after undisclosed transfers to hidden reserves, and are generally regarded as potentially seriously biased. In both cases, we compared the average ratio of bank profits to bank capital against the calculated standard deviation of inflation in non-overlapping windows of 5, 7 and 9 years for the USA, and five years for the shorter UK data period. The results for the UK, with only four data points, were indecipherable, but the results for the USA appear to be the reverse of that hypothesized by Cukierman. See Figures 10.6–10.9. Of course, all that this indicates is that the level of bank profits has not *by itself* been negatively correlated with the variance of inflation. If the variance of inflation was conditioned on a more complete set of variables, then the partial effect of bank profitability on the variance of inflation *might* be perceived to be negative.

An associated problem is that structural changes, e.g. deregulation, which may be desirable in themselves, may disturb the extent of competition, profit margins and risk assessment, and hence lead to financial fragility. Davis (1992), p. 216, notes that

> periods of financial instability, which may culminate in crises, are often preceded by changes in conditions for entry to financial markets. Such developments lead to heightened competition in the market concerned, whether due to actual new entry (tending to perfect competition), effects of potential new entry on the behaviour of incumbents (heightened contestability), competitive responses of incumbents to the threat of entry (strategic competition), or indeed 'managerial' growth maximisation. Such heightened

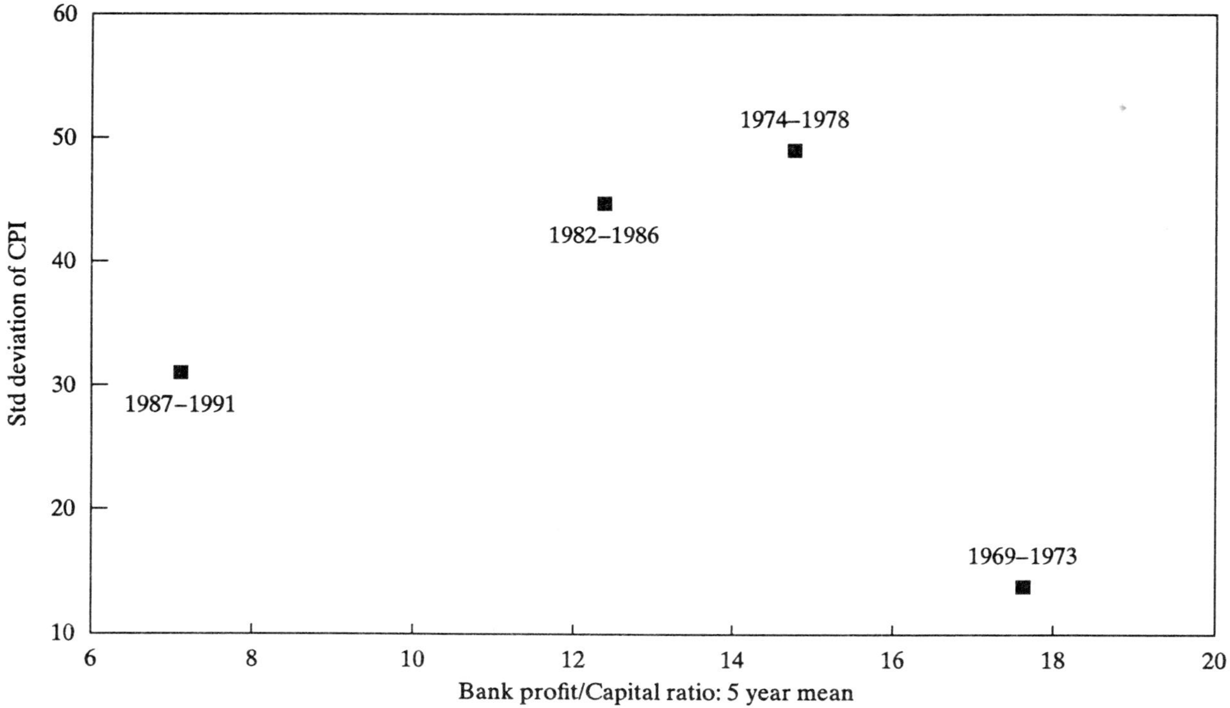

Figure 10.6 United Kingdom, 1969–91. (*Source*: British Bankers' Association, *Annual Abstract of Banking Statistics*; CSO: *Economic Trends*)

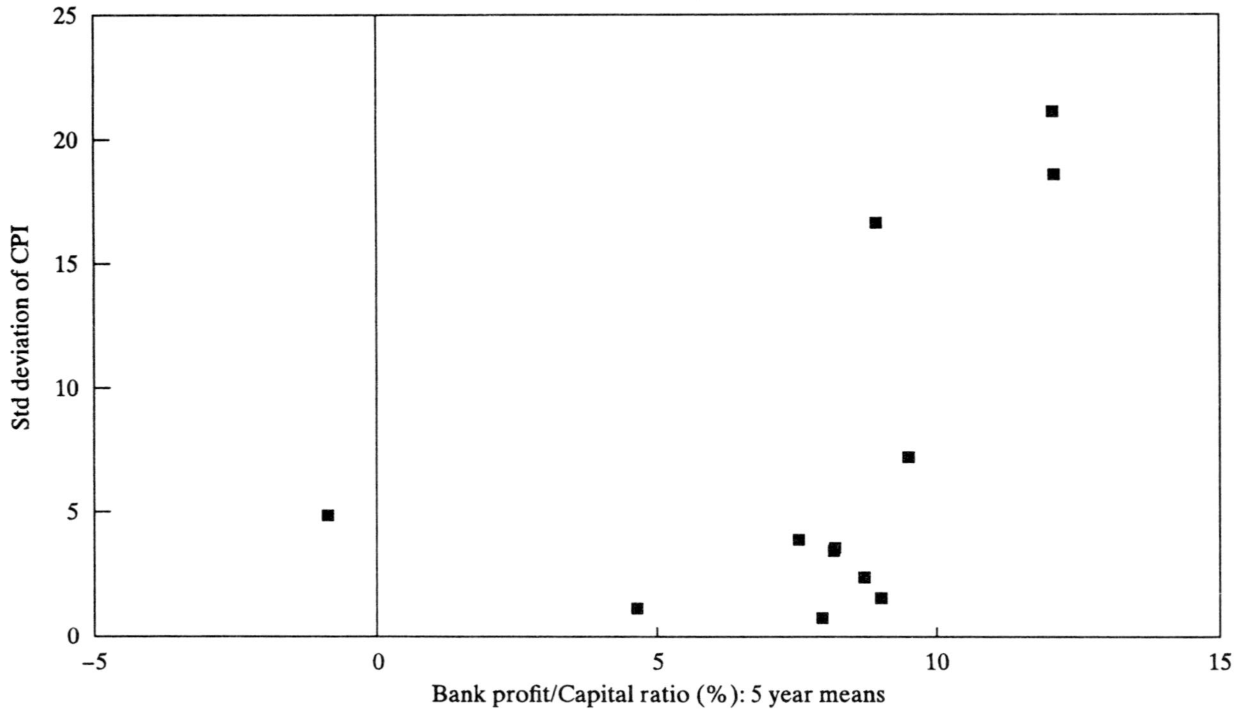

Figure 10.7 United States, 1919–91. (*Source*: Bureau of the Census: *Historical Statistics Colonial Times to 1957; Statistical Abstract*)

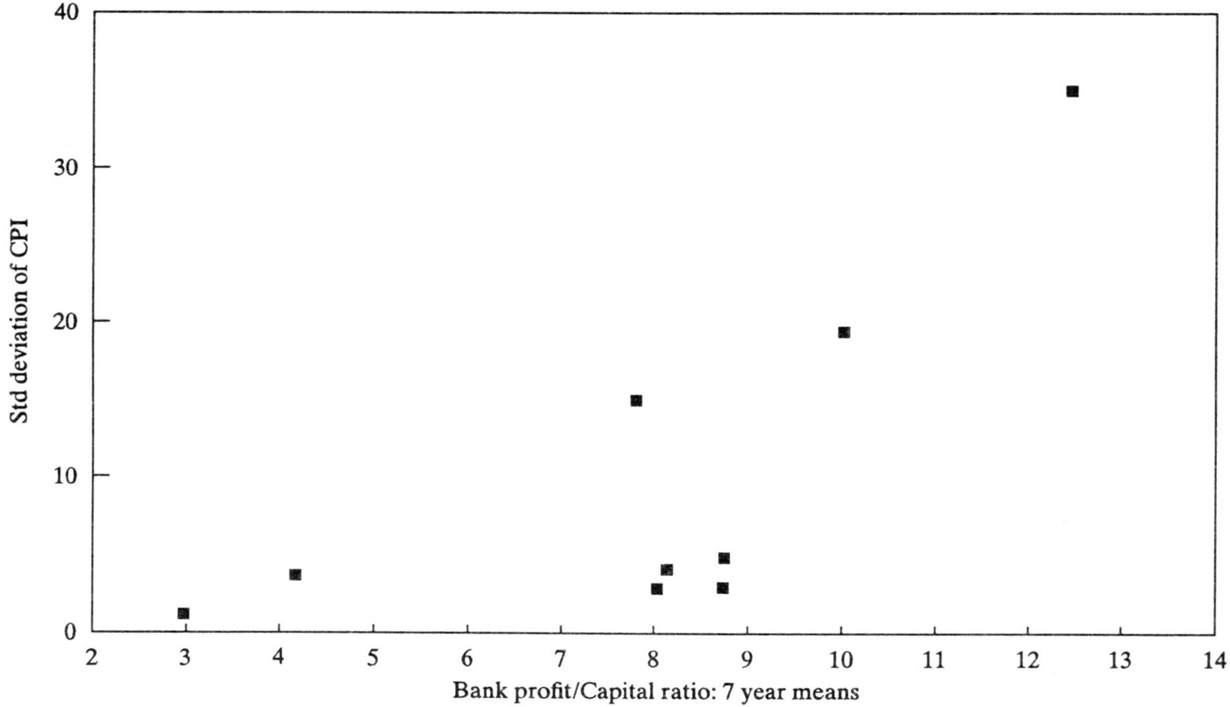

Figure 10.8 United States, 1919–91. (*Source*: Bureau of the Census: *Historical Statistics Colonial Times to 1957; Statistical Abstract*)

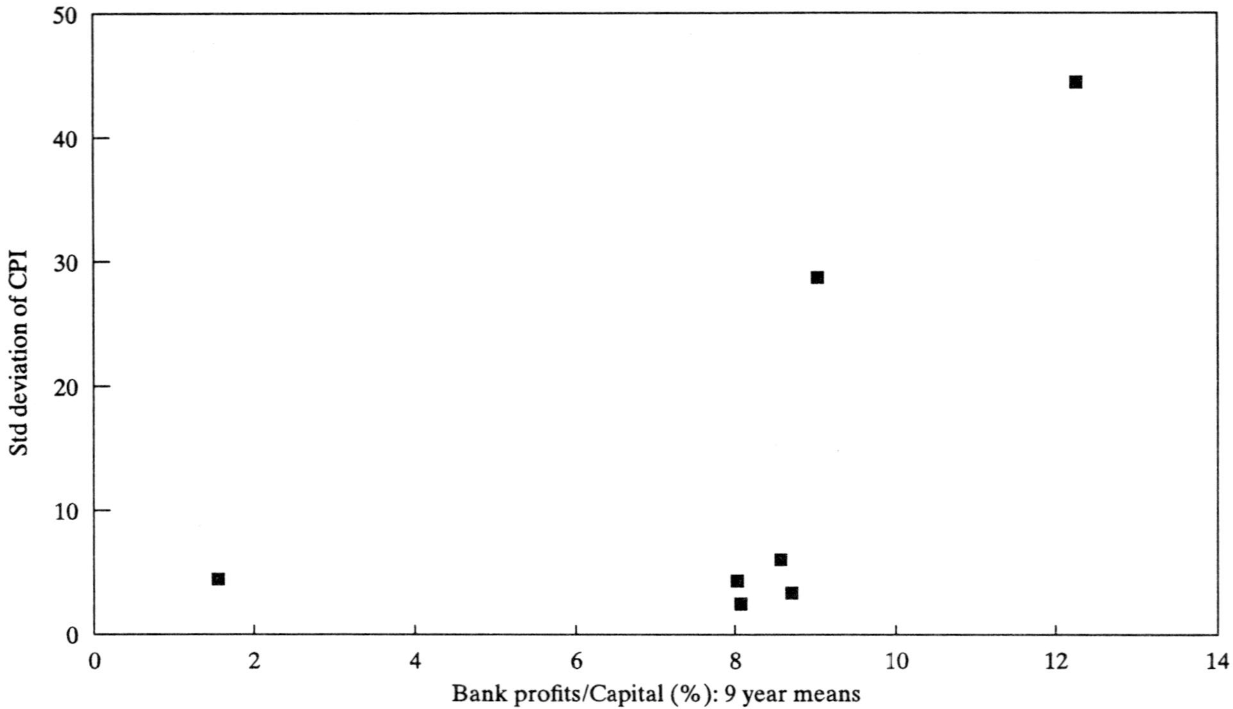

Figure 10.9 United States, 1919–91. (*Source*: Bureau of the Census: *Historical Statistics Colonial Times to 1957; Statistical Abstract*)

> competition may provoke reductions in prudential standards (which may be manifested in lower prices and higher quantities in credit markets, as well as declining capital ratios), especially in the absence of appropriate prudential supervision. This in turn can lead on to financial instability. In effect, the market may overshoot the level of competition which is sustainable in long-run competitive equilibrium, and various market imperfections and distortions (many of which are discussed in the existing literature on financial crisis) can be adduced to explain this.

The analysis of the causes of recent instability in banking systems around the world in Nakajima and Taguchi in this volume is closely similar.

Be that as it may, I have argued that bank failures will generally occur *after* the asset price cycle has peaked and started to retreat. Hence once bank failures actually appear, restrictive monetary policy will usually have done the major part of its job. Hence, there should rarely be a serious macroeconomic problem about the provision of support for a banking system in which serious, potentially systemic, bank failures are occurring. It is difficult to make a strong case that Central Bank rescues of failing banks, e.g. in the recent crises in Scandinavia, New England, etc., in the secondary banking crisis in the UK in 1973/74, etc., have had any significantly adverse effect on macroeconomic, or price, stability. The more obvious cases of macroeconomic instability occurred when banks were *not* rescued, as in the case of the USA, 1907 (Goodhart, 1969), 1929–33, especially the Bank of United States (Friedman and Schwartz, 1963, Ch. 7), or the Credit Anstalt (1931). Academic disputation has not focused so much on the need for *overall* support in such cases, but rather on how that support should be delivered. We turn to that next.

IV HOW TO SUPPORT A FRAGILE BANKING SYSTEM

There are two common nostrums among more classically-oriented monetary economists about bank rescues. The first is that Central Bank assistance ought only be given to commercial banks which are illiquid, but not insolvent. This has a heritage going back to Thornton and Bagehot, see Humphrey (1975) and Humphrey and Keleher (1984). The second is that systemic support should be provided by open market operations to the banking system as a whole, and not channelled via discount window, or other special lending facilities, to individual weak banks (Goodfriend and King, 1988). On this view, the objective should be to keep the rate of growth of certain key quantitative monetary aggregates steady, and not the incidence and frequency of bank failures as such.

Neither nostrum is valid. The first is invalid, because (except in exceptional cases of technical difficulty, e.g. the Bank of New York computer failure), an illiquid bank will, almost always, be able to borrow additional liquid funds to meet a short-term liquidity problem from wholesale (often inter-bank) money markets – at a rate cheaper than (unless such lending is specifically subsidized), and without the adverse reputational effects of, last resort lending – unless the market already suspects its solvency. A bank which cannot borrow from the money market to meet its liquidity needs is, almost by definition, a bank whose solvency is suspect in that market. Those suspicions may, of course, be more, or less, well-founded. Nevertheless many, perhaps most, rescues which start out, and will usually be presented as, temporary liquidity problems by the commercial bank in distress, will turn out to involve longer-term solvency concerns. The two conditions are, given the present structure of (money) markets, closely intertwined. A Central Bank will sometimes find itself faced with an ultimatum that bank X will close on the next working day, unless supported, and with next to no time to sort out the 'true' valuation and solvency position of the bank involved. Often it takes weeks, rather than days, to obtain a clear view of a distressed commercial bank's balance sheet, and time is not on the side of Central Bankers in such cases.

At this point the second nostrum comes to the fore. On this view, if Central Banks have *any* doubts about the solvency of the applicant bank, they should refuse assistance. If failures then take place, they should be offset by open market operations aimed at maintaining aggregate, macro-level stability by achieving a continuing, steady-state rate of growth of the monetary aggregates. While I understand the theoretical grounds for such an argument, I believe that it fails in practice. The reason is the Lucas critique. Any major failure, with adverse effects on depositors' wealth (we shall discuss deposit insurance later), which is widely publicized, is likely to change prior behaviour patterns. Normal ratios, of reserves, or currency, to deposits, of differing kinds of liquid asset to income (or wealth), normal risk premia, etc., are all likely to shift if a contagious panic takes hold.

Recall how Kaldor (1983) criticized Friedman on the grounds that the rate of growth of base money *accelerated* during 1929–33. Although ex post there may, perhaps, turn out to be surviving stable relationships between certain monetary aggregates (and/or interest rates) and the economy during a severe panic, *ex ante* one must suspect that crises and panics will disturb and disrupt the prior pattern of statistical (econometric) relationships. Amidst a flurry of failing banks, screaming headlines in news stories, can anyone be confident that the monetary guideposts (weak as they have been) may not shift some considerable way further? How much easier then, how much less disruptive, how much more *efficient* to nip the panic in the bud, to prevent the contagion before it gets hold, by organising a rescue. And that is exactly what Central Bankers have traditionally done. The probability, and exact form, of the rescue, therefore, depends mainly on two factors, first the potential solvency gap to be filled as a consequence of the mismanagement or fraud of the previous bank management, and second the splash that would be made if that bank were to be allowed to fail. Bigger bank failures make larger waves; hence 'too big to fail'.

Such a typical Central Bank approach is widely condemned by the classical monetary economist as short-term, myopic and conducive to moral hazard. The high probability of depositor rescue means that depositors will not monitor bank safety (though the ability of ordinary depositors to do so has always been doubtful), so that high risk banks will continue to be able to attract depositor funding (e.g. by offering slightly higher interest rates, as BCCI did). In such circumstances bank managers will be tempted to adopt higher-risk strategies, especially where their capital is already impaired. The analysis is well known and valid. In addition, the too-big-to-fail syndrome is either inequitable, in that it gives a competitive edge to larger banks, especially when, and if, small banks are perceived to fail: or alternatively, if competitive equity is to be retained, leads to the complete rescue of all banks.

A partial solution to both problems has been provided by the American proposal enacted in the FDICIA (1991), which came into effect in 1993, for a graduated response to an erosion of capital ratios. Benston (1993) describes these as, 'capital requirements with structured early intervention and resolution (SEIR) rules', also see Benston and Kaufman (1988) and Shadow Financial Regulatory Committee Statement 41 (1992). Outside the USA, such SEIRs are in the process of being adopted by New Zealand (Dale and RBNZ,

Financial Regulation Report, June 1993). One of the main problems with any ratio procedure, whether it is a reserve ratio or capital ratio, à la Basle, is what to do if a bank fails to meet its ratio. An on/off trigger ratio, whereby a bank is allowed to do as it likes if it meets the ratio requirement, but is closed if it drops an iota below, involves a non-credible threat.

The precise definition of appropriate ratio levels, and the associated measurement of such ratios, is always going to be somewhat arbitrary. It is, in my view, much more important to work out a credible *sequence* of responses to progressive capital erosion than to worry whether the appropriate level is 8 percent, or 10 percent. The Basle capital adequacy requirements totally failed to do this, whereas the American proposals incorporate such a graduated sequence as their main new idea. If adopted, such measures should check the danger that managers would be tempted to undertake higher risk policies, as their capital became eroded, by placing increasing limitations on their freedom of action as their capital position weakens. Even so, this will not check the consciously fraudulent, a continuing source of failure.

Whether the proposal to make bank asset values more accurate, and balance sheets more transparent, by valuing on a mark-to-market basis, as best as possible, would help to check fraud, is not clear to me. It is certainly difficult to be opposed to greater accuracy, or transparency. If asset price movements were normally distributed, I would have no qualms in this respect. Unfortunately kurtosis, very large price jumps, is a phenomenon of such markets. If a system of progressive responses to capital ratio erosion, combined with mark-to-market asset pricing was to be established, I would advocate giving the Central Bank the right to 'override' the otherwise automatic stages of the graduated capital ratio, preferably for an identifiable group of banks, but possibly even, *in extremis*, for a single named bank.

When one thinks of sudden major shocks, such as the LDC crisis in August 1982, the Stock Market collapse in October 1987, the ERM crisis in 1992/93, would one really want large segments of one's banking system suddenly shifted into immobility, restrained from further lending? The counter-argument, presented by participants at the Conferences at which this chapter was presented, is that the existence of such a potential 'override' would weaken the credibility of the existing ratio requirements, and leave the Central Banks open to political pressures to use, or misuse, this facility.

Dewatripont and Tirole (1993, p. 73) note that

> Unlike historical cost accounting, market value accounting makes the solvency measure very volatile and generates inappropriate transfers of control rights. We argued in favor of an intermediate method of accounting, in which, as under historical cost accounting, market specific fluctuations are not reflected in the solvency measure, but in which, unlike historical cost accounting, an automatic adjustment of the net worth offsets the change in the shareholders' incentives.

If the flexibility to respond to such shocks by accounting procedures is to be removed, should not the responsible authorities be provided with an alternative source of flexibility? If the Central Bank should invoke such an override, it would have to do so openly and be prepared to justify it publicly. It could be obliged to obtain legislative support for any extension of the initial override beyond, say, six months.

Much of the opposition to the flexible use of accounting procedures, as a means of adjusting to shocks, is their partially covert nature. A Central Bank might be excessively *reluctant* to use a transparent override for fear of the public criticism that might ensue. I doubt whether there is any analytical way of deciding whether any such override would be over, or under-utilised, in advance of experience.

Dewatripont and Tirole (1993, pp. 72–3), take somewhat the same line.

> Because [bank] managers (by definition) do not control macroeconomic shocks, their welfare, and therefore their compensation and the interference they face from outsiders, should be insensitive to such shocks. Because interference by shareholders depends on the bank's capitalization, the macroeconomic shock should be perfectly offset by an equal distribution of dividends if the bank's performance exceeds the minimum solvency ratio.
>
> Conversely, if the macroeconomic shock puts the bank's solvency below the minimum ratio, managers are unduly punished if control shifts to debtholders, or (in the context of voluntary recapitalization as in the Basle agreement) if shareholders refuse to recapitalize and leave control with the regulator. On the other hand, a mere adjustment in the minimum solvency ratio to the average solvency of banks is too lax a policy, as shareholders are more prone to take risk [*sic*] when the bank is poorly capitalized.

> This reasoning thus calls for a recapitalization requirement softened by some contribution of the regulatory agency in bad times, for example through pro-cyclical deposit insurance.

The problem with this is that an objective measurement of the effect of an 'exogenous' macroeconomic shock is hardly possible, while the introduction of 'some contribution' from the regulatory agency in 'bad times' would be politically contentious. In my view a discretionary 'override' of limited duration would be more practicable.

Most measures aimed at encouraging more prudent bank behaviour are liable to be procyclical in the short run, whereas, as argued earlier, Central Bank actions to support banks through crises are likely to be anti-cyclical. During periods of falling asset prices, bank profits are down, and bad debts are up. Capital ratios are under pressure, and new equity issues unpopular and difficult. Regulatory measures, e.g. capital ratios, whether graduated or not, tend to bite during (asset price) depressions, and are more commonly non-binding during (bubble) booms.

This has been so with (the introduction of) the Basle capital adequacy requirements recently. Falling asset prices, bad debts and low bank profits have meant that such requirements have become more binding on the size of bank books than had been expected. There is a sizeable literature on the putative responsibility of such supply-side constraints for the sharp falls in bank credit expansion that have been experienced (e.g. Wojnilower, 1980; OECD, 1991; Bank of England, 1991; Bernanke and Lown, 1991; Federal Reserve Bank of New York, 1993). It is extremely hard to distinguish, and identify, the relative effects of demand and supply factors. I do not have the time or the facilities to add to this literature, but it would in my view be hard to deny that these prudential requirements had *some* additional restrictive effect.

There is, therefore, an inherent conflict between attempts at countercyclical monetary policy and the pro-cyclical effect of prudential/regulatory controls. For an account of a similar earlier (1938) conflict, see Simonson and Hempel (1993). My answer to that is threefold, (1) only relax the automatic operation of graduated capital ratios by an override in cases of severe asset price shocks, (2) continue, whenever banks still seek rescues, with present Central Bank policies, and (3) pay much more attention in the tactical design of monetary policy to the course of asset prices, as well as current service flow prices.

The pro-cyclical nature of most mechanisms for regulating bank risk would be exacerbated by narrow-bank schemes, whereby only those banks investing in a restricted set of liquid, safe assets would be (100 percent) insured. Narrow banks would, therefore, be compelled to offer much lower rates of interest than risky banks. During cyclical upturns, and periods of high confidence, there would be large transfers of funds, on relative interest rate grounds, from narrow to risky banks, and vice versa during periods of asset price declines, on relative risk grounds. As I have warned elsewhere (Goodhart, 1993) the narrow bank proposal would make cyclical fluctuations more, rather than less, extreme.

Let me turn finally, and briefly, to deposit insurance. If such insurance is 100 percent, the adverse moral hazard effect has been made clear by the S & L débâcle. Even so, a much more limited scheme, with partial pay-back, e.g. 80 percent, or in other words co-insurance, can prove helpful in allowing the authorities to *countenance bank failures*, in conditions where the political outcry, about the losses to widows, orphans and other innocent depositors, might otherwise impel a full rescue. It is at least arguable that the limited deposit insurance scheme adopted in the UK helped to strengthen both the Bank of England's and the UK government's resolve to let BCCI fail. It is surprising that so much effort has been put into trying to devise risk-weighted premia, which is notoriously difficult to do, and so little into assessing the optimal amount of co-insurance, which can easily be put into operation.

But this brings us to the final subject of this session, the optimal design of international co-operation, since the allocation of deposit insurance to the host, or home, country is one of the current issues in this field. This discussion has been put into Appendix A, since the material is somewhat tangential to the main themes of the chapter.

V CONCLUSIONS

During the last few years many nations in the industrialised world have experienced a dramatic boom and bust in certain asset markets, notably housing and property, associated with a milder cycle in the goods markets. Current service flow prices exhibited more inertia, with their rate of inflation being slower to rise than asset prices, and dropped back in the last year, or so, to low positive levels rather than becoming negative.

The asset price cycle was both driven by, and drove, an accompanying cycle in bank credit expansion, and to a somewhat lesser extent in broad money. The collapse of these asset markets after 1990 was associated with a widespread rise in bad debts, in the need for bank provisions and in a fall in bank profits. In many countries banks either failed, or exhibited considerable distress. Prudential regulations, e.g. the Basle capital adequacy ratios, bit more tightly, and will, to some largely unquantifiable extent, have aggravated the constriction of bank credit. Central banks in these circumstances held to their last, and sought to support their banking systems by organising rescues, lender of last resort action, and various other stratagems. They did not, however, seek to abrogate the introduction of the Basle prudential requirements. Although banks failed in several countries, in the sense that their debts were greater than their asset values (negative equity), the banks were, in most cases, e.g. in the Nordic countries, kept open for business, and contagious panics were prevented.

How does one score this recent record of monetary policy and Central Bank activity? In my view macro-policy has been systematically mishandled. The monetary authorities were far too lax in the late 1980s, 1988–1990, and too restrictive thereafter. This was partly because they were concentrating on a limited index of inflation, current service flow prices, and ignoring the message about inflation given by asset prices. This misjudgment was exacerbated, in some countries, by a disinclination to give much weight in policy judgments to the rate of growth of bank credit and broad money, whose drastic decline in the early 1990s was not taken seriously enough.

The monetary authorities, therefore, share responsibility, along with the commercial banks, for the recent asset price/banking cycle. Having helped to bring about the fragility in the banking system, they then at least helped to pick up the pieces by behaving in their traditional way to prevent contagious panics by providing much needed support to their banking systems. There was no conflict between price stability and the provision of support to an ailing banking system.

There is an inbuilt conflict, however, between the imposition of generalised prudential regulations and macro-monetary stability, since the former, almost by definition, must bite harder at times of (asset price) deflation, and hence must, to some extent, aggravate the accompanying credit contraction. But it would make a mockery of such regulations, and negate their impact, if they were to be regularly relaxed at such times; though I would advocate that Central Banks should have a, carefully restricted, right of override of these regulations at times of severe, unforeseen shocks. Faced with this conflict, the correct response for the Central Banks is to take more aggressive expansionary action during such deflations, while still using their traditional rescue policies, to prevent systemic panics, in the time-honoured fashion.

APPENDIX A INTERNATIONAL COOPERATION AMONG CENTRAL BANKS

C. Goodhart and D. Schoenmaker

As with other financial services, commercial banking has become multinational (Benston, 1990; Gardener, 1991; Fingleton and Schoenmaker, 1992). Most of the largest commercial banks have branches, or subsidiaries, in a variety of financial centres outside their home country. The main response of Central Banks and bank supervisors has been to try to identify a single lead supervisory body, who takes overall responsibility for the health and solvency of each banking entity; the intended effect is to focus the responsibility for dealing with financial fragility on a single, identifiable 'home' authority, thereby reducing the need for international co-ordination and co-operation. As noted below, this does not remove the need for such co-ordination in dealing with liquidity and solvency problems that arise between parent bank and foreign-based subsidiary and/or branch, or from the operation of payment systems (see Folkerts-Landau, 1990, and below), but otherwise it is not clear that there should be any particularly serious problems in this context arising out of concerns with financial fragility.

Whereas bank supervisors have focused, to some extent, on how far it is either necessary, or desirable, to impose common prudential standards, e.g. a level playing-field (the Basle Accord on Common Capital Requirements, agreed in 1988, is a prime example of this), methods to deal with fragile banks or banking sectors differ widely across countries both in their composition and use (Goodhart and Schoenmaker, 1993). Such measures to deal with bank failures include deposit insurance schemes, lender of last resort actions, and assisted bank mergers or take-overs. International co-operation among lenders of last resort has, therefore, to be analysed in conjunction with other parts of the safety net. Rather than harmonising these different domestic practices, the key issue is, in our opinion, whether the costs of bank failures can be internalised at the 'home' authorising and supervisory authorities, e.g. to make them responsible for the payment of deposit insurance in the event of failure. Home supervisory authorities (and Central Banks) of international banks may then have an additional incentive to supervise conscientiously, i.e. to prevent bank failures, and may be better situated, if such failures happen, to make informed decisions on the proper course of action, ie rescue versus closure.

Most banks will be registered and head-quartered in the country where their main domestic operations are undertaken. The banking supervisor of that country, whether Central Bank or specialist institution (for a discussion of whether supervision is, and should be, undertaken by the CB or a specialist, see Goodhart and Schoenmaker, 1993), is then, under the Basle Concordat of 1975, revised in 1983 (see Table A.1), designated as the lead supervisor, responsible for examining, and satisfying itself, about the solvency and the adherence to prudential standards, of the *bank as a whole.* So long as each bank has an *effective* lead supervisor, responsible for its consolidated supervision, there would seem to be little call for any international body to undertake lender of last resort functions: for discussions on possible roles for an international lender of last resort, see Humphrey and Keleher (1984) and Guttentag and Herring (1983).

Where the bank has branches abroad, the host country will be responsible for operational controls, e.g. maintenance of liquidity ratios and codes of conduct, e.g. on money laundering, etc., but the home country will retain responsibility for solvency and overall capital ratios (see Table A.1). Within the EC, authorisation will be for the home country; more normally authorisation is for the host country in discussion with the home country. Branch closure may be by the host country, e.g. for transgressing the legal code. If the bank as a whole is closed, the branch will automatically follow.[4]

The situation is somewhat more complicated when the bank has separately established subsidiaries abroad. The host country of that subsidiary (i.e. the country of incorporation, which can be regarded as its 'home' country) will authorise it, monitor its capital adequacy and adherence to prudential standards, and clearly has the legal locus to close it down. But the reputation and the credit rating of the parent bank and its subsidiaries are so closely interlinked, that the Central Banks, and separate bank supervisors if such exist, of *both* the subsidiaries and the parent bank must coordinate before any

Table A.1 The assignment of supervisory responsibilities in the two Basle Concordats

Type of bank	*Supervisory issues*	
	Solvency	*Liquidity*
1975 Concordat		
Branches	Parent	Host
Subsidiaries	Host	Host
Joint ventures	Host	Host
1983 Concordat		
Branches	Parent	Host/parent
Subsidiaries	Host/parent	Host
Joint ventures	Host	Host

* When one bank is a dominant shareholder, then possibly host/parent.
Source: Gardener (1991), p. 112.

closure/bankruptcy is imposed. Moreover, the parent bank can shift assets from foreign subsidiaries to other subsidiaries or to the parent in ways that are difficult to detect for host supervisors (Benston, 1993). This problem can be met by reliance on the parent supervisors, which stresses the need for co-operation between host and parent supervisors of subsidiaries (e.g. in the form of exchange of information or joint examinations), as introduced in the 1983 Concordat (see Table A.1). There may also be concerns among the supervisors of improper electronic fund transfers between the parent and subsidiaries for nefarious purposes (Scott, 1992).

In particular, both the parent bank, and its Central Bank/supervisor, must be given an adequate opportunity to avert a potential failure in a subsidiary, initiated by its local Central Bank/supervisor. Otherwise, a major international commercial bank could suffer a serious weakening in its reputation from the aggressive action of a small country supervisory authority. More rarely, perhaps, but still a practical possibility, subsidiaries, and their local Central Bank/supervisor, need to be given a chance to preserve their legally separate status and continue trading after the collapse of the parent bank. For example, an attempt was made to salvage BCCI, Hong Kong, even after BCCI had ceased trading elsewhere. On these legal aspects, see Key and Scott (1991).

The position, however, becomes much more complicated when

there is no obvious single lead Central Bank/supervisor, and/or when the lead bank supervisor is unable to undertake full, co-ordinated unified surveillance over the bank as a whole. Both of these conditions appertained to BCCI. It was formally registered in Luxembourg, but its main business, and *de facto* Head Office, were in London. It carefully constructed its business, and organised its own audits, in order to prevent any single outside body getting proper unified surveillance over the condition of the bank as a whole. It is a normal phenomenon for business entities to register in states, where the regulatory costs are least, and the protective benefits greatest, e.g. Panama and Liberia for shipping, Delaware in the USA for company charters, etc.

In the aftermath of the BCCI collapse, banking supervisors have undertaken action on two lines to close these regulatory loopholes. The first such action is aimed at identifying, beyond doubt, the lead supervisor responsible for consolidated supervision and ensuring a *transparent* group structure. To this purpose the Basle Supervisory Committee reformulated and extended some of the principles of the earlier Concordats (which have the status of recommended guidelines) as minimum standards in June 1992. The basic requirement is that host countries should not permit foreign branches unless the parent bank is capably supervised on a consolidated basis by the home country. If the bank is structured in such a complex way that unified supervision is difficult to conduct, host authorities have to satisfy themselves both by communication with the home authority and, if felt necessary, also directly, that proper unified surveillance of the commercial bank as a whole is possible, and is being so conducted by the home authority. Furthermore, the creation of cross-border banking establishments would need the prior consent of both the host and home country, and supervisory authorities should establish bilateral arrangements for the exchange of information. However, the standards do not provide any safeguard against the possibility of inadequate supervision by host supervisors, as Dale (1992) argues. The EC Commission (1993) has recently made similar proposals, amending the Second Banking Directive, to reinforce prudential supervision.

The second line of action is to make the lead supervisor liable for the costs of bank failures in order to provide this supervisor with an incentive to supervise adequately. This proposed approach is not without problems and is, therefore, still very much under discussion. A major problem is that, for example, deposit insurance payouts, organised on a home country basis, will give rise to different levels of deposit protection. To date deposit insurance schemes are organised on a national basis (i.e. the host country principle) which guarantees equal treatment of depositors. Another problem is that, in a regime of self-contained national banking systems, bank rescues, organised by the Central Bank and financed by the domestic banking industry, may still be viable, but it is less likely to succeed if it involves the bailing out of foreign establishments. But it can be argued that such CB led rescues, financed by the domestic banks, have anyhow become more difficult to organise because of the breakdown of strong bank cartels, owing to international competition and deregulation (Goodhart and Schoenmaker, 1993).

What follows from all this for international cooperation among lenders of last resort, the theme of this appendix? Although classical monetary analysis views the lender of last resort function as connected with liquidity supervision, largely the domain of the host supervisor (see Section IV above, and Table A.1), we argue, as Guttentag and Herring (1987) do, that it is more connected with solvency supervision, mainly the domain of the parent (i.e. home) supervisor.

Foreign branches are an indistinguishable part of the main, or parent bank and, hence, they can borrow, if they experience liquidity problems, under the parent brand name and credit rating or, alternatively, parent banks can borrow (in their markets) and swap it to their foreign branches. As the solvency (and liquidity) of a branch is thus basically as good as that of its parent and the parent country is responsible for supervision, it follows naturally that lender of last resort responsibility, for a foreign branch (and its parent), will be assigned to the parent Central Bank. Although the parent Central Bank will then have prime responsibility for lender of last resort actions, if any, co-operation among parent and host Central Banks may be required in the form of providing information to the parent Central Bank or helping the parent country to perfect their legal claim to the bank's assets in order to arrange a collateralised loan (Guttentag and Herring, 1987). Moreover, the host Central Bank may provide emergency liquidity assistance on behalf, and at the risk, of the parent Central Bank, when the parent bank or Central Bank cannot provide timely assistance, e.g. because their market is closed, and liquidity problems at the foreign branch are so pressing that the host Central Bank would feel compelled to support this branch, e.g. when the branch faces settlement problems at the close of the payment system, as discussed below.

Foreign subsidiaries are separately capitalised and incorporated in the host country. As they are mainly subject to host country supervision, host Central Banks could be assigned as lenders of last resort to these subsidiaries. However, as argued above, foreign subsidiaries and their parents are closely interlinked, and the revised Basle Concordat considered the supervision of solvency as a joint responsibility of both host and parent authorities (see Table A. 1). As a result co-operation among the supervisors and lenders of last resort is required. The US authorities, for example, apply the source-of-strength doctrine which requires foreign banks seeking to establish banking operations in the US to serve as a source of strength to their banking operations in the US (Key and Scott, 1991, p. 31). Another example is the Bank of England requiring 'comfort letters', written acknowledgements from overseas parent banks that they accept a moral responsibility for their banking subsidiaries in London that goes beyond the narrow limits laid down by laws of limited liability (Guttentag and Herring, 1983, p. 15).

This all means a gradual shift of lender of last resort responsibility towards the parent Central Bank. The question is whether Central Banks would (and could) be prepared to back the worldwide operations of their international banks.[5] Although powers to provide temporary liquidity are set out in Central Bank statutes or laws, the modalities and rules for activating such powers are usually not specified and publicised on the grounds that the existence of an explicit commitment for implementing them could result in undue reliance on such facilities (Pecchioli, 1987). A formal statement regarding the international division of lender of last resort reponsibilities is thus not to be expected.[6]

Turning again to deposit insurance, the EC (Commission, 1992) put forward a proposal to make deposit insurance the responsibility of the authorising home country.[7] All bank branches should then publicly be required to exhibit on their bank counters the details both of their depositor insurance arrangements, which would hence differ from bank to bank depending on country of residence, and which country and Central Bank/agency was responsible for meeting such insurance claims. Whether depositors would find the insurance guarantees of supervisory authorities of convenience credible, and whether the Central Banks of large countries would avoid the time inconsistency temptation to step in in place of a failing supervisory authority of convenience, would have to emerge from experience.

The widely differing levels of deposit protection within the EC at present appears to be the main obstacle for adopting the Directive. The Commission chose to solve this problem by requiring a minimum level of deposit protection of 15,000 ECU (which was subsequently increased to 20,000 ECU by the European Parliament) without setting a maximum level. However, if host countries had a higher insurance pay-out than home countries, home country branches could be at a competitive disadvantage in host countries. It would be for discussion whether a top-up to host country levels would then be allowed, and, if so, which authority/scheme would be responsible for the extra slice. In the original proposed EC directive home country deposit insurance could *voluntarily* be topped up by the host country scheme if the latter is higher. A fundamental objection to host country topping-up is that the principle of no deposit insurance without supervision, established implicitly by the introduction of the home country principle, would be partially abrogated, since the host country would not get any supervisory powers. Furthermore, difficulties could arise when a bank branch is a member of two schemes, e.g. one scheme might prefer to reorganise the bank, while the other might prefer to close it and make the payments under its part of the guarantee. Disputes about the problem of which national scheme should be permitted to apply for the topping-up and the degree, if any, of co-responsibility in the insurance have stalled the progress on the EC directive (Stanhope, 1993).

The question of deposit insurance for home country bank *subsidiaries* in host countries is quite tricky. If the home country is to be responsible, as with branches, for deposit insurance, whereas the host country takes closure decisions, then the home country's supervisory authority/insurance scheme can be put at risk by an action of the host's supervisory authority which it disputed. And what would happen then if the home country refused to pay out of its scheme. *Per contra*, if the host country was responsible for insuring depositors in subsidiaries, then the likelihood of failure would be enhanced if the home regulator allowed that parent bank to flout proper prudential standards and subsequently to go bankrupt. All these, and other conundrums, relating to the home/host deposit insurance decision are rehearsed in Schoenmaker (1993) and Key (1992).

The purpose of recent regulatory efforts in this field is to try to ensure both that it is transparently clear who has the lead responsibility for decisions concerning prudential oversight, rescues and closure of every banking entity, irrespective of location, *and* that each regulating authority has an incentive, through the requirement to make deposit insurance a home country obligation, to do the job to proper international standards. Even so, there will be many occasions when international communication and co-operation is essential, particularly where banking subsidiaries are involved.

A problem that may yet arise, which is not dealt with by the above formulation, is where an entity established in country A, which is a non-bank in that country, wishes to set up a banking business, presumably as a separately established subsidiary in country B, and possibly also further such subsidiaries in countries C and D as well. Presumably, the host country in each case would have to take responsibility for deposit insurance, if any, and whether to authorise the bank in the first place. Under the EC regulations, however, a non-bank registered in say, the C. . . . n Islands, might obtain authorisation to establish a bank subsidiary in Luxembourg or Greece. Once that was done that subsidiary could branch, or set up secondary subsidiaries, in all other EC countries. That might prove a loophole. The point is not trivial, since investment banks prevented from doing commercial banking in the USA under Glass–Steagall, may wish to do a wider range of banking business under the more relaxed universal banking regulations in Europe.

[Comment: Luxembourg or Greece would be the home supervisor according to the Second Bank Directive and would be responsible for deposit insurance of its branches according to the proposed Deposit Insurance Directive. They would thus have an incentive to supervise properly, or to refuse authorisation. Does that then solve the problem?]

At the moment, however, the exercise is primarily one of allocating primary responsibility clearly to a single national monetary authority in each case, and for organising *ad hoc* 'colleges' of supervisors when problems between parent bank and foreign subsidiaries/branches make such communication and co-ordination desirable.

There are, however, two further, interconnected, areas where there will be debate about the allocation of international responsibility for supervision/regulation. The first concerns surveillance and potential lender of last resort responsibility in (inter)national payment and settlements systems. The second involves the division of responsibility between the European Central Bank and the national Central Banks, should EMU and the ESCB come into operation. The second issue is of particular European concern, and may, perhaps, be ducked for the purpose of this Conference; useful references are Folkerts-Landau and Garber (1992), Giovannini (1992) and Monticelli and Vinals (1993).

A problem, as discussed above, can arise when a foreign branch participates in the payment system of the host country. If such a branch faces liquidity problems and neither the parent bank nor the parent Central Bank can provide timely liquidity assistance, because, for example, the home money market is closed, the host Central Bank may have to advance liquidity to avoid disruptions in its payment system. A possible solution is to deny foreign branches direct access to the payment system, as the Banque de France, for example, does. Alternatively the host country can impose special limits on the settlement positions of foreign branches or require that these positions be fully collateralised (Scott, 1992). The problem can be stated more generally by asking whether foreign banks should be required to be incorporated (as a subsidiary) before they can start banking operations in the host country. The USA is moving in this direction and the FDIC Improvement Act of 1991 has authorised a study by the US supervisory authorities into this question (Scott, 1992).

One of the risks in payment systems used for the settlement of foreign exchange deals is Herstatt risk, i.e. that the two legs of the transaction are settled at different times in different localities. There is, therefore, a risk that a bank will close between the times of the two transactions, and delivery versus payment (DVP) cannot be exactly achieved. One proposal is to transform such international payments, at least for all payments bilateral with the US$, on to a 24-hour real time, gross settlement basis, and to establish links between these payment systems to ensure that settlement of one leg cannot be made without settlement of the other. If so, it would effectively end the fiction of banks being closed outside formal market hours. Central Bank officials would have to be prepared to take rescue and lender of last resort decisions on a 24-hour a day basis, with true market breaks occurring only at the week-end. While this would not exactly enhance the present pleasures of the life of Central Bank officials, and could on occasions force them to make even more instantaneous decisions, than now, it does not seem at first glance to us to cause any enormous difficulties of principle.

Concluding Remarks

Whereas international co-ordination among supervisory authorities started with establishing the home country principle, recent efforts are aimed at reinforcing *effective* consolidated supervision to close regulatory gaps, which were highlighted by the BCCI collapse. We have argued that the responsibility for, and costs of, dealing with banking fragility should also be based on the home country principle (to link it with supervision) and, consequently, be assigned to the lead supervisor of international banks. Each regulatory authority would then have an incentive to do the job properly or, alternatively, to refuse authorisation. This approach would also require co-operation among Central Banks/supervisors, as at present. The main problem would be that organising the safety net (i.e. lender of last resort actions, deposit insurance, and assisted bank mergers) on a home country basis would give rise to different levels of deposit protection within a country (mainly reflecting differing national philosophies about the appropriate level of Central Bank/government intervention in banking). However, these differences have to be accepted, if the costs are to be internalised at the home supervisor.

APPENDIX B

In the USA, Sprague (1910) quotes (pp. 36–7) the *Commercial and Financial Chronicle* about the events leading up to the crisis of 1873,

> This suspension [of Kenyon, Cox & Co., a stock broking house], although important in stock circles, was of far less general influence than that of Messrs Jay Cooke & Co., which occurred on Thursday [September 18], and of Fisk & Hatch, which was announced on Friday morning, and followed by the failures of a number of smaller stock-brokerage firms during the day. . . . The excitement and general distrust which followed this [Jay Cooke & Co] suspension caused a general and rapid calling in of loans, . . . , and with the great fall in stocks produced the other disasters. . . . The excitement in Wall Street and vicinity was intense, and was heightened by a run on the Fourth National Bank and the Union Trust Co.

Again in 1884, the panic followed 'breaks in prices on the stock exchange' (p. 109), followed by brokerage firm failures, and 'a considerable further decline in the stock market' (p. 110). In contrast to the crises of 1873 and 1884, the 1890 stringency in New York was caused primarily by events in London, and gold outflows causing pressure on bank reserves. While stock prices fell, in response to rising interest rates, 'The disturbance . . . was of short duration and did not at any time get beyond control' (p. 142). This contrasts with the longer-lasting 1893 crisis. The first stage in May was marked by 'a severe stock panic' connected with the failure of the National Cordage Company and the Philadelphia and Reading railroad, and the third stage by the failure of the Erie railroad, while 'the stock exchange suffered the worst decline of the year' (p. 176). In 1907 confidence had been weakened by the 'rich men's panic' in March. 'Never before or since have such severe declines taken place on the New York stock exchange'. The banking system weathered that, and the actual collapse was triggered by losses by supposedly bank-related copper company speculators (ibid., pp. 247–51).

Matthews (1954) addresses trade cycles in the UK between 1833 and 1842. Referring to the collapse of the boom of 1837 in the USA, he writes (ibid., p. 59), 'Despite the easing of credit conditions after the suspension, the year 1837 in the United States was one of violent recession in the financial sphere. Security prices and commodity prices fell catastrophically. The speculative real-estate boom came to an end, . . . The volume of domestic trade fell a good deal less severely, but it too was affected. The prostration of banks was widespread, especially in the South. The speculative nature of the boom determined largely the character of the crash. So long as funds are ample and confidence is not impaired, there exists no inherent force tending to bring to an end real-estate or commodity speculation based on expectation of ever rising prices. The analogy is rather to a stock-exchange boom than to a boom based, for instance, on industrial investment'. Meanwhile in the UK there was 'a railway mania' in 1836, 'a promotion boom, not a construction boom'; 'share speculation was rife', and the consequence was that confidence first 'passed, and had turned first into recession and then, in the early summer of 1837, into something near panic' (pp. 111–12). This boom was further intensified by the rapid growth of joint stock banks in 1836. 'There is plenty of evidence that the joint-stock banks actually intensified the boom by relaxing security requirements and pressing loans on their customers in an attempt to increase their business. In this way the supply of credit, so far from imposing a brake on the growth of activity, actually acted as a destabiliser' (p. 198). This was partly because the Bank of England, responding to the condition of its gold reserves, rather than to asset prices, allowed discount rates to soften in 1835 and the first half of 1836 (ibid., Chapter XI). 'It could of course be argued – as it was argued by Tooke and others – that the Bank *should* have brought about financial tightness in 1835 and early 1836 . . . , but . . . for the Bank to have deliberately brought about a rise in interest rates at a time when the exchanges were actually favourable, merely on the grounds that they might subsequently become unfavourable, would have been to go well beyond its avowed policy' (p. 172). Plus ça change, . . .

Acknowledgements

My thanks are due to Horst Bockelmann, Franco Bruni, Stan Fischer, Jerry Jordan, Mervyn King, Ian Macfarlane and Hiroo Taguchi for helpful comments; to Niral Maru for research assistance; and to the participants of the Bank of Japan Conference on 'Financial Stability in a Changing Environment', 28/29 October 1993 and of the Conference on 'Financial Stability', at the H. C. Coombs Center for Financial Studies, Sydney, 31 October and 1 November, 1993, for their many views and suggestions. I have not, however, always followed these in my revision, and responsibility for all remaining errors remains, as always, with me.

Notes

1. Perhaps not surprisingly, the main recent exception is to be found in an article by a Japanese economist, H. Shibuya (*Bank of Japan Monetary and Economic Studies*, 1992), who also references Pollak (1975) Carlson (1989) and Shigehara (1990). I am grateful to Hiroo Taguchi for drawing my attention to this paper.
2. The data from the USA were taken from the Bureau of the Census, *Historical Statistics: Colonial Times to 1957*, subsequent *Statistical Abstracts of the United States*, and the Federal Reserve Board, *All Bank Statistics*. The series used for bank lending to the private sector was column 22 in Table X20–41 on page 623 in *Historical Statistics*, and conformable data from subsequent Abstracts. The indices for prices and real output were taken from B. R. Mitchell, *International Historical Statistics: Americas and Australia*. The index of stock market prices was constructed by Shiller in *Market Volatility*. The series for interest rates was found in X 311 in the *Historical Statistics*, suitably extended.
3. The housing price data are from Alan Holmans, 'House Prices: Changes through time at National and Sub-National Level', UK Government Economic Service Working Paper, no. 110 (1990). Data on the CPI are taken from B. R. Mitchell, *International Historical Statistics: Europe 1750–1988* (Macmillan, Basingstoke, 1992). The equity price index is the Barclays de Zoete Wedd Equity Index. Data on bank lending are from B. R. Mitchell and P. Deane, *Abstract of British Historical Statistics* (Cambridge University Press, 1962), and from IMF, *International*

Financial Statistics (IMF Publication Service, Washington DC). Output data are from F. Capie and A. Webber, *A Monetary History of the United Kingdom, 1870–1982*, (George Allen & Unwin, London, 1985); suitably extended. Interest rate data are from CSO, *Annual Abstract of Statistics* (HMSO, London).

4. One murky legal area is what are the respective rights of home and host countries to control over bank assets situated in their country on the advent of failure. For example, if the BCCI branch in Tokyo transfers funds to a BCCI branch in USA to invest in US Treasury bills, what are the proper legal rights to such assets, after closure, of the creditors (prior depositors) of BCCI in USA, Japan, UK, Luxembourg, elsewhere. Scott (1992), p. 507, argues that the bankruptcy procedures need to be aligned with those for deposit insurance, i.e. either (1) host-country deposit insurance and host-country bankruptcy jurisdiction over the assets of insured branches, or (2) home-country deposit insurance and home-country bankruptcy jurisdiction over the worldwide assets of failed foreign banks.
5. In a national context Bisignano (1992) discusses the problem of a widening of central banks' responsibilities due to a shift of banking business to non-bank financial institutions and other markets, such as the commercial paper market. He notes the reluctance of Central Banks to assume wider responsibilities, and their response with demands for greater bank capital.
6. The revised Basle Concordat of 1983 states this explicitly:

> The report deals exclusively with the responsibilities of banking supervisory authorities for monitoring the prudential conduct and soundness of the business of banks' foreign establishments. It does not address itself to lender-of-last-resort aspects of the role of central banks.

7. In the USA the problem is tackled in a somewhat different way (Scott, 1992). The FDIC Improvement Act of 1991 requires that in future foreign banks that 'accept or maintain' deposits of less than $100,000 (so-called retail deposits) do so through insured subsidiaries rather than through insured branches.

References

Alchian, A. A. and B. Klein (1973) 'On a Correct Measure of Inflation', *Journal of Money, Credit and Banking*, vol. 5, no. 1, Pt. 1 (February), pp. 183–91.

Bank of England (1991) 'Is there a "Credit Crunch?",' *Bank of England Quarterly Bulletin*, vol. & fol. 31, no. 2 (May), pp. 256–9.

Benston, G. J. (1990) 'U.S. Banking in an Increasingly Integrated and Competitive World Economy', *Journal of Financial Services Research*, vol. 4 (December), pp. 311–339.

Benston, G. J. (1993) 'International Harmonization of Banking Regulations and Cooperation Among National Regulators: An Assessment', in J.

Fingleton and D. Schoenmaker (eds), *The Internationalisation of Capital Markets and the Regulatory Response* (London: Graham and Trotman, 1992), revised version, June 1993.

Benston, G. J. and G. G. Kaufman (1988) *Risk and Solvency Regulation of Depositary Institutions: Past Policies and Current Options* (New York: New York University Graduate School of Business Administration, Salomon Center Monograph Series in Finance and Economics, Monograph 1988–1).

Bernanke, B. S. and C. S. Lown (1991) 'The Credit Crunch', *Brookings Papers on Economic Activity*, vol. 2, pp. 205–248.

Bisignano, J. (1992) 'Banking Competition Regulation and the Philosophy of Financial Development: A Search for First Principles', in J. Fingleton and D. Schoenmaker (eds), *The Internationalisation of Capital Markets and the Regulatory Response* (London: Graham and Trotman), pp. 69–102.

Black, J., D. de Meza and D. Jeffreys (1992) 'House Prices, the Supply of Collateral and the Enterprise Economy', University of Exeter Department of Economics, Working Paper.

Boyd, J. H. and M. Gertler (1993) 'U.S. Commercial Banking: Trends, Cycles, and Policy', Paper presented at CEPR/ESF Conference on 'Financial Regulation', Toulouse, June 1993; also intended for *NBER Macroeconomics Annual*, 1993.

Carlson, K. (1989) 'Do Price Indexes Tell Us About Inflation? A Review of the Issues', *Federal Reserve Bank of St. Louis Review*, November/December.

Commission of the European Communities (1992) 'Proposal for a Council Directive on Deposit Guarantee Schemes', COM(92) 188 final – SYN 415, Brussels (June 1992).

Commission of the European Communities (1993) 'Proposal for a Council Directive to Reinforce Prudential Supervision', COM(93) 363 final – SYN 468, Brussels (July 1993).

Cukierman, A. (1992) *Central Bank Strategy, Credibility and Independence: Theory and Evidence* (Cambridge, Mass; MIT Press).

Dale, R. (1992) 'Basle after BCCI', in *Financial Regulation Report* (Financial Times Business Information: London, June), p. 1.

Dale, R. (1993) 'Do We Need Supervisors', in *Financial Regulation Report* (Financial Times Business Information: London, June), pp. 1–2.

Davis, E. P. (1992) *Debt, Financial Fragility and Systematic Risk* (Oxford University Press).

Dewatripont, M. and J. Tirole (1993) 'The Prudential Regulation of Banks'. Paper presented at the CEPR/ESF Conference on 'Financial Regulation', Toulouse, June 1993.

Federal Reserve Bank of New York (1993) Colloquium on 'The Role of the Credit Crunch in the Recent Recession', 12 February 1993.

Fingleton, J. and D. Schoenmaker (eds) (1992) *The Internationalisation of Capital Markets and the Regulatory Response* (London: Graham and Trotman).

Fisher, I. (1906) *Nature of Capital and Income* (New York: The Macmillan Company).

Fisher, I. (1911) *The Purchasing Power of Money* (New York: The Macmillan Company).

Fisher, I. (1932) *Booms and Depressions* (New York: Adelphi).

Folkerts-Landau, D. F. I. (1990) *Systemic Financial Risk in Payment Systems* (Washington, DC: International Monetary Fund).

Folkerts-Landau, D. and P. M. Garber (1992) 'The ECB: A Bank or A Monetary Policy Rule', in M. B. Canzoneri, V. Grilli and P. R. Masson (eds), *Establishing a Central Bank: Issues in Europe and Lessons from the US*, (Cambridge: Cambridge University Press), pp. 86–110.

Friedman, M. and A. J. Schwartz (1963) *A Monetary History of the United States 1867–1960* (Princeton University Press).

Friedman, M. and D. I. Meiselman (1964) 'The Relative Stability of Monetary Velocity and the Investment Multiplier in the United States, 1897–1958', Research Study no. 2 in *Stabilization Policies: Commission on Money and Credit* (Englewood Cliffs, NJ: Prentice-Hall).

Gardener, E. P. M. (1991) 'International Bank Regulation and Capital Adequacy: Perspectives, Developments and Issues', in: J. J. Norton (ed.), *Banking Regulation and Supervision in the 1990s* (London: Lloyd's of London Press), pp. 97–120.

Giovannini, A. (1992) 'Central Banking in a Monetary Union: Reflections on the Proposed Statute of the European Central Bank', *CEPR Occasional Papers*, no. 9.

Goodfriend, M. and R. G. King (1988) 'Financial Deregulation, Monetary Policy, and Central Banking', *Federal Reserve Bank of Richmond Economic Review*, vol. 74, no. 3 (May/June), pp. 3–22.

Goodhart, C. (1969) *The New York Money Market and the Finance of Trade, 1900–1913* (Cambridge, Mass: Harvard University Press).

Goodhart, C. (1993) 'Can We Improve the Structure of Financial Systems?' *European Economic Review*, vol. 37, nos 2/3 (April), pp. 269–91.

Goodhart, C. and D. Schoenmaker (1993) 'Institutional Separation between Supervisory and Monetary Agencies', Financial Markets Group, LSE, Special Paper no. 52, April 1993.

Guttentag, J. M. and R. Herring (1983) 'The Lender-of-Last-Resort Function in an International Context', *Princeton Studies in International Finance,* no. 151.

Guttentag, J. and R. Herring (1987) 'Emergency Liquidity Assistance for International Banks', in R. Portes and A. K. Swoboda (eds), *Threats to International Financial Stability* (Cambridge: Cambridge University Press), pp. 150–86.

Holmans, A. (1990) 'House Prices: Changes through time at the National and Sub-National Level', UK Government Economic Service Working Paper, no. 110.

Humphrey, T. M. (1975) 'The Classical Concept of the Lender of Last Resort', *Economic Review*, Federal Reserve Bank of Richmond, vol. 61 (January/February) pp. 2–9.

Humphrey, T. M. and R. E. Keleher (1984) 'The Lender of Last Resort: A Historical Perspective', *Cato Journal*, vol. 4, no. 1 (Spring/Summer), pp. 275–317.

Kaldor, N. (1983) 'Keynesian Economics after Fifty Years', Paper delivered at the Keynes Centenary Conference in Cambridge, June 1983, and printed in J. Trevithick and G. N. D. Worswick (eds), *Keynes and the Modern World*

(Cambridge University Press, 1983); also Chapter 2 in *Further Essays on Economic Theory and Policy* by Kaldor, eds F. Targetti and A. P. Thirlwall (London: Gerald Duckworth & Co Ltd., 1989).

Key, S. J. (1992) 'Deposit-Protection Schemes: Issues for an E. C. Directive', CEPS Research Report, no. 11, Brussels, December.

Key, S. J. and H. S. Scott (1991) 'International Trade in Banking Services. A Conceptual Framework', Group of Thirty Occasional Papers, no. 35, Washington DC.

Kindleberger, C. P. (1984) *A Financial History of Western Europe* (London: Allen & Unwin).

Kindleberger, C. P. (1989) *Manias, Panics and Crashes*, 2nd edn (London: Macmillan).

King, M. A. (1993) 'Debt Deflation: Theory and Evidence', Presidential address to the European Economic Association, Helsinki, August 1993.

Matthews, R. C. O. (1954) *A Study in Trade Cycle History* (Cambridge University Press).

Minsky, H. P. (1977) 'A Theory of Systematic Fragility', in E. I. Altman and A.W. Sametz (eds), *Financial Crisis: Institution and Markets in a Fragile Environment*, (New York: Wiley).

Minsky, H. P. (1982) 'The Financial Instability Hypothesis: Capitalistic Processes and the Behaviour of the Economy', in C. P. Kindleberger and J. P. Laffargue (eds), *Financial Crises: Theory, History and Policy* (Cambridge University Press), pp. 13–29.

Monticelli, C. and J. Vinals (1993) 'European Monetary Policy in Stage Three: What are the Issues?', *CEPR Occasional Papers*, no. 12.

OECD (1991) Ad Hoc Group of Monetary Experts, 'A "Credit Crunch"? The Recent Slowdown in Bank Lending and its Implications for Monetary Policy', Economics and Statistics Department draft, 9 December 1991.

Pecchioli, R. M. (1987) *Prudential Supervision in Banking* (Paris: OECD).

Pollak, R. (1975) 'The Intertemporal Cost-of-Living Index', *Annals of Economic and Social Measurement*, vol. 4, no. 1.

Reserve Bank of New Zealand (1993) 'Proposed Revisions to Banking Supervision Arrangements', in *Financial Regulation Report* (London: Financial Times Business Information, June 1993), pp. 2–10.

Sargent, T. J. (1987) *Dynamic Macroeconomic Theory* (Cambridge, Mass: Harvard University Press).

Schoenmaker, D. (1993) 'Home Country Deposit Insurance?,' in P. Arestis (ed.), *Money and Banking* (London: Macmillan Press).

Scott, H. S. (1992) 'Supervision of International Banking Post-BCCI', *Georgia State University Law Review*, vol. 8, no. 3 (June), pp. 487–510.

Shadow Financial Regulatory Committee, Statement 41 (1992) 'An Outline of a Program for Deposit Insurance and Regulatory Reform', issued 13 February 1989, *Journal of Financial Services Research*, vol. 6, Supplement, S78–S82.

Shibuya, H. (1992) 'Dynamic Equilibrium Price Index: Asset Price and Inflation,' *Bank of Japan Monetary and Economic Studies*, vol. 10, no. 1 (February), pp. 95–109.

Shigehara, K. (1990) 'Shisankakaku No Hendo To Infureshon' (Asset Price Movement and Inflation)', *Kinyu Kenkyu*, vol. 9, no. 2 (July).

Shimizu, Y. (1992) 'Problems in the Japanese Financial System in the Early 1990s', *Hitotsubashi Journal of Commerce and Management*, vol. 27 (November), pp. 29–49.

Simonson, D. G. and G. H. Hempel (1993) 'Banking Lessons from the Past: The 1938 Regulatory Agreement Interpreted', *Journal of Financial Services Research*, vol. 7, no. 3, (September), pp. 249–68.

Snyder, C. (1928) 'The Measure of the General Price Level', *Review of Economic Statistics*, (February), pp. 46–52.

Sprague, O. M. W. (1910) *History of Crisis under the National Banking System*, National Monetary Commission, 61st Congress, 2nd Session, Senate Document, no. 538 (Washington DC: Government Printing Office, 1910).

Stanhope, N. (1993) 'Proposed Directive for Co-ordination of Deposit Guarantee Schemes', in *Financial Regulation Report* (London: Financial Times Business Information, June 1993), p. 14.

Stigler, G. J. (1981) in U.S. Congress Joint Economic Committee, *Government Price Statistics*, 2 Parts (Washington DC).

Wojnilower, A. (1980) 'The Central Role of Credit Crunches in Recent Financial History', *Brookings Papers on Economic Activity*, vol. 2, pp. 277–339.

Comments

Horst Bockelmann

Past discussions on how monetary policy should react to sharp rises in asset prices, at a time when consumer price rises were slow and slowing down further, were largely inconclusive. Not enough was known about the theoretical and empirical properties of asset prices as leading indicators of inflation to prompt central banks into action. One-time adjustments to financial deregulation seemed to play a part in the rise. When asset prices started to fall it was generally concluded that monetary policy had been quite right not to react as bubbles were taking care of themselves: they were bound to burst, and all the sooner the faster they were inflating. This, I believe, is a fair description of attitudes in most countries. For Japan, the story may be rather different, but I leave comments on that to others who are more competent on this score.

Charles Goodhart devotes a surprisingly large part of his chapter to a study by Alchian and Klein of 1973, which argued on the one hand that a theoretically satisfactory index of inflation would include asset prices as well as current service flow prices, but had to admit on the other that the necessary data were unavailable and that it would be extremely difficult to determine the asset quantity vectors to be used. Assets and current service flows, it seems to me, while both meeting human needs, have characteristics sufficiently different to make it inappropriate to combine them in one price index. Lumping goods prices and asset prices in the same index would blur an important distinction: that between prices which are determined by the current state of excess demand and those which are largely determined by expectations of future events, such as profits growth or expected real economic performance.

I may mention in passing that work has recently been undertaken at the BIS using an aggregate asset price index comprising real estate and equity prices. There have been precedents for this approach at the Reserve Bank of Australia. We hope that this index will prove to be useful. But let me come to the substance of the issue.

There may indeed have been serious mistakes in recent years in the conduct of monetary policy in some countries. But to attribute these to the lack of a common price indicator for consumer goods and real assets looks to me like a *non sequitur*. This might perhaps become a serious issue if, at some time in the future, monetary policy in some countries were to be tied closely to a current price index. That has not been the case so far. Consumer price movements are known to be lagging indicators, which is one of the main reasons why central banks have been looking for suitable intermediate targets. Financial innovation and structural changes have recently raised doubts about the usefulness of such indicators in some countries, but, with the prevailing more eclectic approach, there was nothing, and certainly not a lack of information or of attention, to stop central banks from taking asset price movements into account in setting their policy, had they had a clear view on how this should be done.

The 1987 equity price fall had surprisingly little impact on aggregate demand. Policy was eased following the crash in some countries. We are not certain of the wealth effects of sharp changes in asset prices. Responding to them in the manner that we respond to inflation in current goods prices might indeed lead to even greater undesired volatility in asset prices. We know that inflation distorts relative prices and that it causes inequitable redistributions of wealth between borrowers and lenders. But we might compound the problem if policy-makers were to respond to an index which included a volatile asset price component and whose impact on the real economy was, moreover, uncertain and might even change overtime. In addition, in a deregulated global financial environment asset prices might behave quite differently from the real economy in a particular country. If the stock market is booming while the real economy is weak, a policy reaction might worsen real economic prospects.

Later in his chapter Goodhart links asset prices to the issue of financial instability, arguing that greater stability in asset prices would induce greater stability in the financial sector. I am afraid I did not find his analysis of the issue very enlightening. It may be true at times that a policy to prevent asset bubbles from occurring may be consistent with other macroeconomic objectives. But, I can only repeat, to directly focus monetary policy on asset prices (in a general price index or on the basis of the separate information at present available) could in my opinion easily lead monetary policy astray. Financial stability should be the specific concern of prudential policy. Monetary policy may at times generate difficulties for financial institutions, as it does for non-financial institutions. Enterprises have the responsibility to steer themselves through good and bad times and not feel that monetary policy may be designed to prevent certain market occurrences, such as a sharp rise or even a bubble in equity prices. To have monetary policy place more emphasis on asset prices could, in my opinion, only aggravate the moral hazard problem facing the central bank.

Goodhart then stresses the conflict between pro-cyclical capital requirements and counter-cyclical monetary policy (see also Goodhart and Schoenmaker, 1993). Two points can be made in this connection. In general, the pro-cyclicality of capital standards arises only to the extent that banks adhere to what the authorities regard as the bare *minimum* consistent with an appropriate cushion against losses. No pro-cyclical effect would occur if banks were wise enough to provide in good times against bad times, as sound banking practice would imply. True, monetary policy may be less effective when the constraint on bank expansion is capital rather than access to, or the cost of, borrowed funds. However, it seems inappropriate to sacrifice prudential concerns on the monetary policy altar in cases of severe asset price shocks. This would relax supervisory standards precisely when they are most needed. Announcing such a general rule in advance would only compound the problem. I think I can stop here.

Reference

Goodhart, C. and D. Schoenmaker (1993) 'Institutional Separation between Supervisory and Monetary Agencies', Financial Markets Group, LSE, Special Paper No. 52, April 1993.

Comments

Franco Bruni

Professor Goodhart's chapter discusses two questions: (i) should asset prices enter the price index that guides monetary policy?; (ii) if the answer to the first question is yes: what are the consequences for prudential policies?

The first question is very important, given the current emphasis on price stabilisation as a statutory objective of central banks. The second question is related to another currently much debated issue, i.e. the involvement and responsibilities of central banks in prudential matters, on which Goodhart and Schoenmaker (1993) recently contributed a precious essay.

My comments will be mainly on the first question. For lack of space I will only briefly touch upon the second.

I will start by saying that we must be grateful to Professor Goodhart for having proposed us to re-read the interesting article by Alchian and Klein (1973), twenty years later. However, Goodhart does not report a passage of the article that I find crucial for understanding what is the main reason for considering asset prices in evaluating inflation pressures.

What 'makes a current service flow price index an especially poor short-run indicator and target of monetary policy' is, according to Alchian and Klein, 'a major systematic discrepancy in the transitory movement of that index and a current asset price index .... Differential adjustment speeds among prices of consumption and capital goods (or of service flows and durable assets) are [the cause of that discrepancy and] a cornerstone of Keynes's theory of the trade cycle' (pp. 178–9).

The essential question is therefore, I think, one of different speeds of adjustment. To the extent that asset prices react in a more prompt and flexible way to changes in the money supply, they have to be carefully monitored to understand the stance of monetary policy. In this I fully agree with Charles Goodhart. But my agreement heavily depends on the fact that asset prices can be considered anticipatory variables of current service flow prices, where the discrepancy between the behaviour of the two sets of prices is due to a different degree of stickiness. After all, it is precisely the stickiness in goods prices that renders the interest rate such an important variable in the transmission of monetary policy.

Even if asset prices perform as anticipatory variables, one must be careful when they are reacting to *expectations of future* monetary policy, as opposed to current effective policy. In that case, price stabilization becomes a difficult credibility game, and the best policy is probably much more complicated than stabilizing the current value of a composite index of assets and goods prices.

Let me now consider the case where the issue is *not* one of different speeds of adjustment and asset prices are not looked at as indicators of future goods' prices. In this case I am much more doubtful about the way monetary policy should take into account the price of assets. I think it can even be dangerous for the authorities to pursue the stability of a composite index, including prices of both goods and assets.

Suppose a change in the relative price of assets with respect to the current flow of goods can be thought as cased by a change in the equilibrium real rate of interest. The latter could be due to an exogenous change in time preferences, or in expected productivity, or in risk premia. In this case monetary policy should not interfere with intertemporal relative price adjustments if allocative distortions have to be avoided.

Theoretically, the issue is straightforward. Consider first the case of two consumption goods. If there is a long-run negative supply shock in the production of apples, the relative price of apples in terms of pears will increase. This will in general cause a change also in the CPI, that will be overstated if we use fixed weights, but that will be present also if we compensate along the indifference curve for the substitution in consumption. Therefore, *in principle*, a price-stabilizing monetary policy should react to this relative price change.

By the same principle, a permanent change in the real rate of interest, causing a change in the relative price of assets with respect to the current service-flow-price index, changes the amount of utility that can be bought with a given amount of money, and should therefore be relevant for monetary policy. But is the calculation of the correct reaction of monetary policy possible and worthwhile? I do not think so. The optimal reaction is probably smaller than the probable mistakes that will be done in reacting. Moreover, the reaction could be badly influenced by *political pressures from asset holders*. For them asset prices have a special meaning and their changes have a special microeconomic wealth effect that must not be confused with inflation issues.

As an example, suppose asset holders start considering more risky the expected output of their capital. The real interest rate will then increase by a risk premium and, *ceteris paribus*, the price of capital assets will decrease. Some substitution will take place with currently produced goods, that will probably increase in price, but at the end a decrease in the money price of one unit of utility will result. In principle this could be compensated by increasing the money supply, in the same way as we can compensate the effect on the CPI of the relative price of apples and pears. But in this case the calculation problem is even worse. One risk is that the whole decrease in asset prices is considered as a contribution to deflation. Asset holders will lobby for this interpretation. But this would be incorrect because, after the change in the assessment of risk, the price of an asset corresponds to a smaller amount of *risk adjusted* utility, and it *must* therefore be lower. An excessive support of the asset prices would be *in*flationary and it will also interfere with the reallocation of the now more risky assets towards the portfolios of those who have less risk aversion.

By resisting a non-transitory change in the real interest rate, well justified by a shift in time preferences, one ends up with inflation and misallocations. A similar example could be made dealing with a change in expected productivity: in this case asset price stabilization could be justified only by the authorities on the grounds that they have superior information and they know the expectation is wrong.

In conclusion, I think inflation targeting must carefully consider those temporary changes in asset prices, relative to CPI or GNP deflators, that anticipate and bring about overtime changes in flow price indices. When the abundance (or the scarcity) of money and credit does not show up in the CPI or in current production, it is often signalling its presence somewhere else in the system, like in asset price inflation (or deflation).

But asset price indices must not guide monetary policy to the point of risking a damaging resistance to rational and non-transitory changes in expectations, risk evaluations, risk aversion, time preferences, technical productivity and the like.

Let me now turn to the second question of Professor Goodhart's chapter: what are the consequences for financial stability of a monetary policy that stabilizes price indices accounting also for asset prices?

Table 1

	Instability in asset prices due to		
	Monetary policy	*Private credit behaviour*	*Change in the real rate of interest*
Monetary stabilization	Yes	Yes	No
Rescues and easing of capital ratios	Some*	No	Yes†

* To deal with post-stabilization bank crises.
† If the change, and the financial crisis that follows, have been truly unexpected and exogenous.

Consider first those fluctuations in asset prices which are symptoms and anticipatory indicators of general monetary inflation and deflation. These fluctuations can be associated with an unstable and non-credible behaviour of the supply of money. In this case the authorities should correct monetary policy and help the banking system to bear the cost of stabilization.

Asset price fluctuations can also be caused by a destabilizing behavior of bank credit, or private credit in general. In this case I agree with Charles Goodhart that capital ratios are not the solution, because they act procyclically tending to be non-binding during bubble booms. Remunerated reserve requirements would work better. But I also think that the problem becomes worse if, as he suggests, the authorities nourish the expectations that, after the required restrictions in monetary policy have been set in place, capital ratio regulations will be suspended and banks will be rescued.

I understand his argument that bail-out expenditures would not be inflationary, as they would just be following a monetary restriction. But the problem is the substantial moral hazard that would result for bankers and private lenders whose behaviour is supposed to be at the roots of the asset price inflation. By expecting to be rescued, lenders would be ready to build and finance new price bubbles. I would therefore minimize rescues of banks that have contributed to the bubble in asset prices.

On the contrary, a less strict prudential policy could serve to cope with a crisis in asset prices due (as illustrated in the previous discussion) to an *unexpected, exogenous* change in the real rate of interest, caused by changes in expected productivity, time preferences, risk assessments or risk aversion. In this case, some generosity in rescuing banks and in overriding capital ratio regulations could be optimal for the long-run stability of the financial system.

Table 1 contains a highly simplified synthesis of what I have been saying here on how monetary and prudential policies should react to asset price instability.

References

Alchian, A. A. and B. Klein (1973) 'On a Correct Measure of Inflation,' *Journal of Money, Credit and Banking*, February.

Goodhart, C. and D. Schoenmaker (1993) 'Institutional Separation Between Supervisory and Monetary Agencies', *Giornale degli Economisti e Annali di Economia*, forthcoming.

Comments

Jerry L. Jordan

Charles Goodhart's chapter is very interesting and timely, and I am sure it will generate lively discussion well into the future. The topic is timely because many people have become concerned about a possible 'asset bubble' in the United States. If the recent run-up in equity market prices is indeed a bubble, then does it contain any information about future inflation?

The dramatic increase in equity and commercial real estate prices in Japan in the second half of the 1980s (when consumer prices rose very slowly) is taken by Goodhart to mean that monetary policies were 'too lax' at the time and 'too restrictive' since then. He focuses on US and British real estate prices in the early 1990s and concludes that monetary policies were 'too restrictive'.

I was pleased that Goodhart resurrected the Alchian/Klein paper of 1973, in part because I was a student of Alchian's and I like to see his work get more attention. The Alchian/Klein paper is best understood if grounded in another, and more fundamental, essay of Alchian's entitled '*Why Money*',[1] or in a more thorough treatment of the topic by Brunner and Meltzer.[2]

The role of monetary policy has to be related to one's view of the role of money. Paraphrasing Alchian and Brunner and Meltzer, a society will use as money that entity that economizes best on the use of other real resources in gathering information about relative prices and conducting transactions. Alchian (1977) said that 'low recognition cost' is the key attribute of the entity that comes to serve as money.

But recognize what? Recognize the true value of the good. Currency evolved because it has an easily recognized value. If most exchange were in current consumables (in an agrarian, near-barter economy), the intertemporal value would not be so important. As transactions in claims to future consumption increase, the intertemporal dimension becomes of interest. What is difficult to recognize is the future purchasing power of a currency.

The equation of exchange, $MV = PT$, is a useful way to organize our thoughts about money and prices. For issues involving intertemporal decisions, the right-hand side, PT, should be a measure of permanent income. Alchian/Klein and Goodhart are essentially asking, 'What is the appropriate deflator for permanent income?' They argue that it should include a complete set of asset prices – the present price of future consumption rights as well as of current consumption.

Alchian, and more explicitly Brunner and Meltzer, argues that an entity must first become a commonly used 'medium of exchange' in transactions involving current consumables before it takes on the characteristics of a 'unit of account' or 'standard of value' for contracts involving intertemporal exchanges. A problem may exist because price indexes measure the price of current consumption, but the ideal price index would also include the current price of future consumption.

Goodhart says that he 'follows Alchian/Klein in believing that, conceptually, asset prices and real interest rates should enter into the assessment of inflation'. But Alchian/Klein do *not* say that real interest rates should enter into the assessment of inflation.[3]

I would restate the quotation of Alchian/Klein as follows: 'If our representative individual moved to a new society where current service flow prices are identical, but where real interest rates are higher, our iso-utility index would *be lower* (Alchian/Klein say *fall*). The individual would substitute future consumption for present consumption, and *the purchasing power of money would be higher*', (Alchian/Klein say, 'his money cost of life would decrease').

This is a static analysis. It is not the same thing as saying that the *rate of change* of the purchasing power of money will be lower in the future. This is where I think Alchian/Klein's exposition misled Goodhart. Goodhart writes, '. . . in a correctly defined price index, a rise in real interest rates reduces the price level, and brings down the rate of inflation'. I would say 'In a correctly defined price index, higher real interest rates are associated with a lower price level.' Goodhart goes wrong when he says that higher real interest rates bring down the rate of inflation. That is not necessarily so. A higher real rate of return on real productive capital does not imply a lower price level, and it tells us nothing about future rates of change of output prices or asset prices.

The basic question is, 'Does an increase in the real interest rate increase or decrease welfare?' The answer is, unambiguously, yes.

Which it is – an increase or a decrease in welfare – depends on the cause of the changes in real interest rates.

All references to changes in real interest rates can be translated into changes in relative prices of short-lived versus long-lived assets. Since monetary policy actions cannot produce a *permanent* change in the *ex ante* real rate, Goodhart is essentially asking whether an apparent transitory decline in the real rate during the expansion phase of an asset price bubble (followed by on apparent rise in the real rate when the bubble bursts) can be taken as an indicator of first, 'too lax' monetary policy actions and, second, 'too restrictive' monetary policy actions.

As Goodhart quotes Alchian/Klein, there are four causes of a change in relative long-lived asset prices, only one of which is related to the future purchasing power of money.

What we are left with is that an index of only current output prices can *potentially* be a biased measure of the purchasing power of money. We just cannot be sure in which direction it is biased. We want all *relative* prices to be free to change – asset prices as well as current prices of goods and services.

A change in expectations about the future purchasing power of money has opposite implications for prices of real assets versus financial instruments (such as conventional bonds), and ambiguous implications for a firm's equity price, depending on its net monetary debtor or net monetary creditor status. The effects of changing inflation expectations are explained in an earlier article by Alchian and Kessel.[4] This brings us to Goodhart's discussion of bank lending and asset prices, including references to bubbles and financial fragility.

It is often said in banking circles that 'the purpose of inflation is to convert bad loans into good loans'. But that ignores how they came to be 'bad loans' in the first place. Presumably there was a set of assumptions about the future – including the future purchasing power of money and associated earning streams – that pegged them as 'good loans' when they were first originated.

That was George Benston's point in Chapter 8 when he referred to the *ex ante* versus *ex post* view of the assets underlying lending. A one-time permanent increase in the expected rate of inflation involves redistribution from net creditors to net debtors. The net worth of holders of real assets rises, which the net worth of financial asset holders falls.

If the higher real asset values are then used as collateral for debt issuance in an attempt to convert the apparent wealth gain into current consumption or some other type of asset (such as a better store value), and then there is a reversal in the expected rate of inflation (net debtors lose while net creditors gain), we have a 'bad loan'.

None of this would happen if the purchasing power of money were *expected* to be stable. In my view, the objective of monetary policy is to create an environment in which people make decisions with the expectation that the future purchasing power of the currency will be the same as it is today. That in turn will allow an economy to obtain the highest production possibility boundary consistent with the endowment of resources (including human capital).

In his conclusion, Goodhart says, 'This misjudgement was exacerbated, in some countries, by a disinclination to give much weight in policy judgements to the rate of growth of bank credit and broad money, whose drastic decline in the early 1990s was not taken seriously enough.'

However, we need to avoid confusing a 'dollar' with 'a dollar's-worth-of-something' – meaning assets denominated in dollars. In the same context, it means that we should not confuse a yen with a yen's-worth-of-something, or assets denominated in yen.

We want to stabilize the expected purchasing power of currency over time. We do not want to stabilize the prices of assets denominated in that currency any more than we would want to stabilize the prices of individual goods. Goodhart has appropriately raised the question, 'How do we know when we have price stability?'

We are still in search of an answer.

Notes

1. Armen Alchian, 'Why Money', *Journal of Money, Credit and Banking*, vol. 9, no. 1, part 2 (February 1977), pp. 133–40.
2. Karl Brunner and Allan H. Meltzer, 'The Uses of Money: Money in the Theory of an Exchange Economy', *American Economic Review*, vol. 61 (December 1971), pp. 784–805.
3. This discussion and the quotes refer to Goodhart's original draft as presented at the Conference. Goodhart's current version has been revised in response to the discussion at the Conference.
4. Reuben A. Kessel and Armen A. Alchian, 'Effects of Inflation', *Journal of Political Economy*, vol. 70, no. 6 (December 1962), pp. 521–37.

Part V
Concluding Summary

11 Conference Summary

Edward J. Kane

On behalf of all participants, I want to express the deep appreciation and admiration we have for the hospitality and organizational acumen of the Institute for Monetary and Economic Studies of the Bank of Japan. We salute the Institute for its gracious welcome and congratulate the Bank's leaders for their willingness to bring together academics and regulators from around the world to debate in freewheeling fashion a series of politically treacherous, bureaucratically painful, and economically tough issues. Each and every one of us is honored to have been invited to participate in this important program.

Most conferences focus on a few big questions, but explore a multitude of smaller questions that lurk inside the large ones. Precisely because the big questions tend to be conceptually intractable, conference time tends to flow toward smaller issues. I plan to focus on what conferees had to say about the major points, without trying to characterize the extravagantly rich dialogue that bounced back and forth among the realms of political science, macroeconomics, corporate finance, econometric modelling, and industrial organization.

Financial institution activities and central bank policy strategies are time and place specific. Governor Yasushi Mieno identified the conference's overarching issue as how to reconcile a conflict between the primary and secondary missions society has traditionally assigned to central-bank monetary policy. The primary mission is to pursue an effective program of macroeconomic stabilization. The secondary mission is microfinancial: to minimize adverse effects this stabilization program might have on the fabric of regulated financial institutions. This secondary goal may be characterized as maintaining in safe and sound condition the network of financial institutions through which in each given time and place monetary policy acts.

The Governor posed the reconciliation he sought as an analytical challenge. He urged conferees to find a 'solid framework' for institutional supervision. A solid framework of prudential supervision is one that would be simultaneously compatible with effective strategies of monetary control and responsive over time to evolving technologies of information and communication. He rightly emphasized that conferees must approach this problem in an explicitly global context. Domestically supervised firms interact in world and domestic markets with institutions supervised by other central banks and with international co-ordinating institutions as well.

To provide an experiential basis for designing an improved supervisory framework, the Governor subdivided his challenge into two parts. He first asked conferees to identify and to make allowances for differentiating features of regulatory, supervisory, and macroeconomic priorities in different countries. Using this knowledge as a backdrop, he hoped we could go on to derive general lessons from similarities in the policy problems, policy decisions, and economic consequences many countries have experienced during the last decade.

With this task in mind, several conferees closely reviewed the experience of individual countries and groups of countries. Naoyuki Yoshino, Ulrich Baumgartner, and Akiyoshi Horiuchi analyzed Japanese experience. Jeff Frankel examined Korean experience in a broad East Asian context. This experience led him to offer some hypotheses about the optimal sequencing of financial regulatory structures. William Poole explored commonalities in policy behavior and macroeconomic events in the United States and major European countries.

Poole saw the common lowering of inflation rates in these Western countries as a triumph of discretionary monetary policy and an argument against constraining individual central banks to adhere slavishly to a money growth targeting scheme. He stressed that monetary and exchange-rate policy choices in these countries had been more appropriately constrained by disciplinary pressures generated by increasingly integrated capital markets.

Poole's discussants emphasized that discretion about how to resolve the losses an individual country's banking system experiences from disinflation supported some divergences in individual country policy experiences. In the most distressed countries and regions, banks had disproportionately engaged in high-risk lending. Questionable loans and investments were often secured implicitly or explicitly by assets whose values proved highly inflation-sensitive. As disinflation set in, aggressive institutions rapidly began to sink under the weight of problem loans. Göran Lind clarified important ways in which bank losses in Sweden were unique. Richard Syron similarly discussed how the real and financial economies of one subregion of the United States (New England) diverged from patterns experienced in the US economy as a whole.

In one of the conference's keynote presentations, Stanley Fischer stressed that the ongoing integration of capital markets helped to account for the broad commonality of individual country experiences. International capital flows rapidly spread the consequences of domestic debt defaults to banks in other countries. At the same time, international institutions such as the International Monetary Fund and World Bank served as forums in which to hammer out a cross-country supervisory consensus about how to handle asset write-downs at troubled banking institutions and when and how to allow exit from a nation's banking market structure.

The good news common to all countries reviewed is that domestic payments and banking systems survived not only massive initial shocks (e.g. in real estate prices), but in many cases a series of aggravating supervisory policy mistakes. The bad news is not just that discretionary policymakers repeatedly made mistakes, but they typically had no strategy for minimizing the opportunity cost of staving off banking disaster.

Allan Meltzer's keynote address developed this last point. He reframed the macroeconomic task of an individual central bank as that of providing a background of stable non-inflationary policies that are conducive to sectoral asset-price stability. This more circumscribed formulation of a central bank's macroeconomic responsibility dramatically lessens opportunities for conflict with its supervisory responsibilities. Meltzer emphasized the need to view the central bank's supervisory mission in a specifically dynamic context. He asked authorities to seek dramatically more efficient ways of supervising safety and soundness, and interpreted efficiency as minimizing the net burden of financial regulation across society through time.

Meltzer's focus on the time profile of unfolding benefits and burdens from central bank policies embodies implicitly a corporate-finance perspective on the central bank as a government enterprise. From a microfinancial point of view, a central bank is a public corporation. The implicit and explicit cash flows it generates by its monetary and supervisory policies accrue properly to the bank's taxpayer owners. The managers of private and public corporations alike face incentive conflicts between the duties of loyalty and care they owe their corporation's owners and strongly felt pressures to develop net benefits for contending narrower interests. That such conflicts will usually be resolved fairly and efficiently is by no means assured.

The central paper of the conference was presented by Zenta Nakajima and Hiroo Taguchi. This chapter constructed an overview of individual country events and policy experiences. The chapter documents the approximately simultaneous occurrence of similar patterns of deposit-institution risk-taking and resulting financial distress in many countries. These authors also note a qualitative similarity in the sequence of policy choices made in different countries on the macroeconomic and supervisory fronts. Similar decisions were made in many countries about inflation and disinflation and about extending *implicit* and sometimes explicit government support to troubled deposit institutions. Nakajima and Taguchi conclude that supporting weak institutions combined with changing information technology to undermine regulatory discipline. The net effect was to eliminate longstanding deterrents to risk-taking that had in times past kept bank moral hazard in check.

The authors went on to construct a model for safety-net reform that served as a lightning rod for agreement and disagreement. Nakajima and Taguchi reframed Governor Mieno's request for a solid framework for evolutionary supervision as making an informed choice between three prototype supervisory regimes:

(1) One with no public safety net to protect the institutions that transmit monetary policy;
(2) One that puts a public safety net *only* under 'transactions balances' at policy-transmitting deposit institutions so as to eliminate interbank settlement risk;
(3) One that guarantees not just transactions balances, but also to some extent balances held for investment at deposit institutions.

The authors argue that society would be best served by deciding to adopt some variant of Regime 2. However, Edward Frydl, William Witherell, and other regulators such as Graeme Thompson and Robert Parry took issue with this. They saw more hope in exploring regimes adapted from Regime 3. Their plan is to make comprehensive depositor guarantees economically more efficient by focusing financial supervision more precisely on avoiding market-value insolvency than in the past. All schools of thought expressed interest in introducing a collateralization of selected deposits.

Macroeconomic perspectives on central bank policies were emphasized by many participants (especially William Poole) and the tension between the macroeconomic and microfinancial missions was explored in different ways in the conference's final session. Bennett McCallum focused on the benefits and costs of following explicit policy rules designed to internalize possible tensions between fighting inflation with tight money and accommodating the liquidity needs of a nation's banks at the central bank discount window. Charles Goodhart analyzed the usefulness of tying monetary policy actions specifically to their effects on asset prices. These authors' respective discussants, Jean-Pierre Patat, Mervyn King, Thomas Melzer, Horst Bockelmann, Franco Bruni and Jerry Jordan questioned whether either type of policy restraint offered much promise of correcting the defects in the incentives under which government prudential supervision of bank risk-taking patterns prototypically operates.

Explaining how a global 'deprivatization' of bank supervision and risk taking has occurred was the primary focus of the conference's middle session. Establishing a corporate-finance perspective on supervision, Mark Flannery and George Benston explained that it was fully feasible to rely on *private* supervisory services to monitor banks and stressed that government guarantee programs inevitably displace such services. Flannery noted that outside private parties understand information about bank risk-taking well enough to price bank stock shares in global trading and to assign credible credit ratings to bank certificates of deposit. Both authors conclude that officials in many countries have gone too far in absorbing privately insurable risks and that government prudential supervision of bank risks has been deformed by defective incentives. The result has been unduly to lessen private monitoring activity and to distort risk premiums in private markets.

Marvin Goodfriend emphasized the unfortunate real effects of extensively nationalizing the economic activities of risk absorption and monitoring. Intrusive government supervision can restrict the flow of productive investment by blocking the exit of insolvent financial firms and sustaining inappropriately the inefficient 'losing' businesses that these insolvent firms have financed. He called for at least a partial privatization of the deposit insurance system. However, Franco Passacantando offered a contrary and hotly contested qualification that settlement risk was special and ought in any scheme to be assigned to the central bank.

Conferees energetically disputed the question of how (if at all) bank failures might cause deadweight social losses that could not be classified as privately insurable. Several conferees noted that private insurability could be greatly enhanced by straightforward adjustments in the terms of the equity and debt contracts that banks issue. For example, there is no reason not to allow: the liability of stockholders to be extended; the redemption value of deposit balances to be calculated in mutual-fund fashion as a pro-rata share of a clearly defined portfolio of assets; or private bonding companies to coinsure or reinsure specific layers of an accountholder's deposit insurance coverage.

George Benston praised the benefits of a rational bank run as a private disciplinary device. Theoretically, Benston formulated the problem of bank supervision as seeking to 'equate, at the margin, the structure and costs of various means of dealing with or compensating the [affected] parties for moral hazard concerns'. Practically, he felt that this balance of multifold loss control efforts could be established through capital requirements that were backed up by rules that forced government supervisors to undertake a 'structured' series of early interventions when and as an institution's financial condition worsened.

Kazuhito Ikeo cautioned that high capital requirements backed up by structured early supervisory intervention might reduce the efficiency with which banks produced financial services. Pierre Duguay promoted the alternative of preserving supervisory discretion by clarifying regulators' mandate and establishing accountability for minimizing the present value of losses suffered by the deposit-insurance funds. Enhanced accountability for government officials was said to have worked in England (by Mervyn King) and in Switzerland (by Urs Birchler).

More transparency in government policymaking and greater privatization of financial monitoring and risk-bearing activities promise to yield more efficient patterns of financial-institution supervision. For me, the touchstone of conference presentations and discussions lies in how squarely and how extensively each does or does not confront the issue of establishing accountability for ordinary and emergency supervisory actions. Divergent attitudes towards the necessity of explicitly analyzing policymakers' incentive conflicts symbolizes a balkanization that has occurred in the once-unified academic discipline of money and banking. Money has evolved into a subfield of *macroeconomics*, while banking has become a subfield of *corporate finance*. Monetary policy specialists and central bankers seemed at home with macroeconomic tools and logic, but uncomfortable with corporate finance perspectives on bureaucratic decisionmaking. Only a precious few macroeconomists, such as Allan Meltzer and Marvin Goodfriend, were able to bridge the two camps. These bridge-builders stress the microfinancial implications of looking at central banks as taxpayer-owned enterprises whose managers should be contractually accountable for not wasting stockholder value.

One advantage of this corporate-finance point of view is that it can set to rest a longstanding macroeconomic controversy over whether a so-called 'penalty' interest rate should be set on bank borrowing from the discount window. A 'penalty' risk premium over the risk-free rate is needed precisely because taxpayer funds are at risk in discount-window lending. This risk comes from the probability that the funds being supplied through the discount window to an individual bank are in fact a badly structured form of *equity* financing that sustains the ownership claims of bank stakeholders whose stakes should more appropriately be wiped out. Discount-window lending becomes equity funding when it serves to finance the safe departure of uninsured depositors from an insolvent institution even though these parties had voluntarily and contractually exposed themselves to the risk of bank insolvency. The safe departure of these private risk bearers from an insolvent institution and the collateralization of central bank loans reduce the deposit insurer's ability to *recover* value for taxpayers from liquidating or recapitalizing the private ownership stake in an economically insolvent institution.

Central bankers must equip themselves to make more openly the financial assessments by which they reconcile the corporate-finance, political, and macroeconomic dimensions of monetary stabilization. Central bank efforts to stabilize first growth or employment and then inflation tend to whipsaw cyclically the very institutions society has traditionally assigned it to safeguard. Stop-and-go monetary policies damage secularly the deposit-institution industry through which monetary policy is typically channeled. Efforts to patch this damage by stabilizing year by year the *market structure* and *profitability* of existing deposit institutions serve to destabilize industry structure and profitability over longer periods. In most of the leading nations of the world, industry stabilization efforts have simultaneously retarded the exit of insolvent and inefficient deposit institutions and restrained the expansion of efficient deposit institutions. This restraint has made it easier for foreign and competing types of domestic financial institutions and market-makers to invade banking markets in backhanded ways. In country after country, non-traditional competitors in the securities, sales-finance, and insurance industries have been able to use emerging information technology to fashion substitute products with which to take corporate financing opportunities and household savings intermediation away from the domestic deposit institution industry.

The worth of a banking franchise includes its depositor relationships and other 'going-concern values' designed to recognize that embodying a collection of tangible assets and liabilities in a particular enterprise may substantially enhance that portfolio's earning capacity. Intangible assets record the capitalized value of higher returns that can be projected on tangible positions beyond the returns that the same positions could realize if all tangible positions were each held alone.

Many conferees commented on the secular decline of the intangible value of banking franchises around the world. Some observers supposed it would be possible to restore intangible capital to the banking systems of individual nations by rigorously restricting future entry into the banking business. However, in a world in which bank products face a legion of creatively adapted substitute instruments, a nation's banks have an unlimited number of actual and potential competitors. The high deposit institution profit margins and draconian restrictions on the entry of new banks that a franchise-enhancing strategy seeks to establish are impossible to enforce over long periods. High profit margins retard the exit of inefficient deposit institutions and attract the entry of other types of institutions that find creative ways of performing for customers the functions filled by a deposit institution's traditional activities.

The corporate finance perspective likens the technologically driven loss of intangible capital in banking to Humpty Dumpty's fall. Not even All the King's Horses and All the King's Men can put Humpty together again. This insight underscores that it is exit policy and not entry policy that financial supervisors need to revise. George Benston's chapter makes it clear that taxpayer loss exposure in deposit institutions can be measured and controlled by an exit policy that is codified in well-calibrated and well-enforced requirements for tangible capital. In most respects, intangible and tangible sources of deposit-institution capital have completely parallel effects in financing risk-taking. The major difference between tangible and intangible capital is that, in market-value or opportunity-cost methods of accounting for value, intangible going-concern value cannot be conveyed separately from the enterprise as a whole. Few forms of intangibles can be sold off to other parties or distributed to stockholders without transferring title to the enterprise itself.

Let me finish by renewing my thanks and congratulations to the Institute and to the entire Bank of Japan. This has been an ambitious conference. Conference papers pose and wrestle with a series of profound riddles and paradoxes. The deepest riddle is how monetary and financial policymakers can forge *stability* in the face of deeply disruptive and largely uncontrollable changes in the real economic environment. Stabilization policies seek to hold a nation's economy and deposit-institution sector to stationary time-paths, at the same time that technological developments and geopolitical upheavals call for vast and discontinuous changes in the character and sectoral distribution of capital, labor, and financial activity around the world. From a first-best, welfare economics point of view, this is an insolubly paradoxical assignment.

Although the efficiency of the safety net can be improved importantly in straightforward ways, hazard-proof safety nets do not and cannot exist. The best hope is to set up policy rules and managerial and institutional contracts that realistically promote improved supervisory performance. For these rules and contracts to be enforceable, conflicts among alternative policymaking goals must be made plainly visible and meaningful evidence must be produced on how efficiently government and private supervisors are making tradeoffs among conflicting policy goals.

Program of the Conference

THURSDAY, OCTOBER 28

Morning

Opening statement: Yasushi Mieno (*Governor, Bank of Japan*)

Keynote speeches:
Allan H. Meltzer (*Carnegie Mellon University*) 'Regulatory Arrangements, Financial Stability, and Regulatory Reform'
Stanley Fischer (*Massachusetts Institute of Technology*) 'International Capital Flows, the International Agencies, and Financial Stability'

Session I: Recent Changes in the Financial System – Background and Consequences

Chairman: Silas Keehn (*Federal Reserve Bank of Chicago*)

Papers by: Zenta Nakajima and Hiroo Taguchi (*Bank of Japan*), 'Toward a More Stable Financial Framework: Long-term Alternatives – An Overview of Recent Bank Disruption Worldwide'; William Poole (*Brown University*), 'Monetary Policy Implications of Recent Changes in the Financial Systems in the United States and Europe'

Leading discussants: Edward Frydl (*Federal Reserve Bank of New York*); William Witherell (*Organisation for Economic Cooperation and Development*); Göran Lind (*Sveriges Riksbank*), Richard F. Syron (*Federal Reserve Bank of Boston*)

General Discussion

Afternoon

Session I (continued)

Chairman: Keimei Kaizuka (*University of Tokyo*)

Papers by: Jeffrey A. Frankel (*University of California at Berkeley*), 'Recent Changes in the Financial Systems of Asian and Pacific Countries'; Naoyuki Yoshino (*Keio University*), 'Changing Behavior of Private Banks and Corporations and Monetary Policy in Japan'

Leading discussants: Robert T. Parry (*Federal Reserve Bank of San Francisco*); Graeme J. Thompson (*Reserve Bank of Australia*); Ulrich Baumgartner (*International Monetary Fund*); Akiyoshi Horiuchi (*University of Tokyo*)

General Discussion

FRIDAY, OCTOBER 29

Morning

Session II: Prudential Policy and Financial Stability

Chairman: Arnout H. E. M. Wellink (*De Nederlandsche Bank*)

Papers by: Mark J. Flannery (*University of Florida*), 'Prudential Regulation for Banks'; George J. Benston (*Emory University*), 'Safety Nets and Moral Hazard in Banking'

Leading Discussants: Marvin Goodfriend (*Federal Reserve Bank of Richmond*); Franco Passacantando (*Banca d'Italia*), Pierre Duguay (*Bank of Canada*); Kazuhito Ikeo (*Kyoto University*)

Afternoon

Session III: Role of Central Banks in Maintaining Financial Stability

Chairman: David W. Mullins, Jr. (*Board of Governors of the Federal Reserve System*)

Papers by: Bennett T. McCallum (*Carnegie Mellon University*), 'Monetary Policy Rules and Financial Stability'; Charles A. E. Goodhart (*London School of Economics*), 'Price Stability and Financial Fragility'

Leading Discussants: Jean-Pierre Patat (*Banque de France*); Mervyn King (*Bank of England*), Thomas C. Melzer (*Federal Reserve Bank of St. Louis*); Horst Bockelmann (*Bank for International Settlements*); Franco Bruni (*Bocconi University*); Jerry L. Jordan (*Federal Reserve Bank of Cleveland*)

General Discussion

Concluding Summary: Edward J. Kane (*Boston College*)

Participants

Ulrich Baumgartner *Assistant Director, Central Asia Department, International Monetary Fund*

George J. Benston *Professor, Emory University*

Urs W. Birchler *Director and Head, Banking Studies, Banque Nationale Suisse*

Horst Bockelmann *Economic Adviser and Head, Monetary and Economic Department, Bank for International Settlements*

Franco Bruni *Professor, Bocconi University*

Ralph C. Bryant *Senior Fellow, Economic Studies Program, Brookings Institution*

Thomas F. Cargill *Professor, University of Nevada, Reno*

Thanasak Chantarovas *Deputy Director, Department of Financial Institution Supervision and Examination, Bank of Thailand*

Pierre Duguay *Adviser, Bank of Canada*

Stanley Fischer *Professor, Massachusetts Institute of Technology*

Mark J. Flannery *Professor, University of Florida*

Jeffrey A. Frankel *Professor, University of California at Berkeley*

Edward Frydl *Vice President and Assistant Director of Research, Research Administration Division, Federal Reserve Bank of New York*

Toshihiko Fukui *Executive Director, Bank of Japan*

Marvin Goodfriend *Senior Vice President and Director of Research, Research Department, Federal Reserve Bank of Richmond*

Charles A. E. Goodhart *Professor, London School of Economics and Political Science*

Tadayo Homma *Director, Financial and Payment System Department, Bank of Japan*

Akiyoshi Horiuchi *Professor, University of Tokyo*

Awang Adek Hussin *Manager, Economics Department, Bank Negara Malaysia*

Kazuhito Ikeo *Associate Professor, Kyoto University*

Jerry L. Jordan *President and Chief Executive Officer, Federal Reserve Bank of Cleveland*

Keimei Kaizuka *Professor, University of Tokyo*

Edward J. Kane *Professor, Boston College*

Silas Keehn *President, Federal Reserve Bank of Chicago*

Mervyn King *Chief Economist and Executive Director, Bank of England*

Kunio Kojima *Executive Director, Bank of Japan*

Reiner König *Head of the Economics Department, Deutsche Bundesbank*

Soo Gil Lee *Director, Institute for Monetary and Economic Research, Bank of Korea*

Göran Lind *Senior Manager of Supervisory and Structural Issues, Sveriges Riksbank*

Bennett T. McCallum *Professor, Carnegie-Mellon University*

Allan H. Meltzer *Professor, Carnegie-Mellon University*

Thomas C. Melzer *President, Federal Reserve Bank of St. Louis*

Yasushi Mieno *Governor, Bank of Japan*

David W. Mullins, Jr. *Vice Chairman, Board of Governors of the Federal Reserve System*

Zenta Nakajima *Deputy Director, Institute for Monetary and Economic Studies, Bank of Japan*

Peter Nicholl *Deputy Governor, Reserve Bank of New Zealand*

Robert T. Parry *President and Chief Executive Officer, Federal Reserve Bank of San Francisco*

Franco Passacantando *Director, Monetary and Financial Sector, Research Department, Banca d'Italia*

William Poole *Professor, Brown University*

Guy Quaden *Executive Director, Banque Nationale de Belgique*

Hartadi A. Sarwono *Manager of General Economics Division, Economics and Statistics Department, Bank Indonesia*

Kuniho Sawamoto *Director, Institute for Monetary and Economic Studies, Bank of Japan*

Anita Sison *Acting Associate Director, Department of Economic Statistics, Central Bank of the Philippines*

Richard F. Syron *President and Chief Executive Officer, Federal Reserve Bank of Boston*

Hiroo Taguchi *Chief Manager of Research Division I, Institute for Monetary and Economic Studies, Bank of Japan*

Graeme J. Thompson *Deputy Governor, Reserve Bank of Australia*

Arnout H. E. M. Wellink *Executive Director, De Nederlandsche Bank*

William Witherell *Director, Financial, Fiscal and Enterprise Affairs, Organisation for Economic Cooperation and Development*

Fot Chyi Wong *Senior Economist, Special Studies Division, Economics Department, Monetary Authority of Singapore*

Yutaka Yamaguchi *Director, Policy Planning Department, Bank of Japan*

Naoyuki Yoshino *Professor, Keio University*

Index

Notes: contributions to this volume are shown in **bold** type; page numbers in *italics* indicate references in figures or tables only and not in text.